Pennsylvania Dutch

YOUNG CENTER BOOKS IN ANABAPTIST & PIETIST STUDIES

Donald B. Kraybill, *Series Editor*

Pennsylvania Dutch

The Story of
an American Language

Mark L. Louden

JOHNS HOPKINS UNIVERSITY PRESS
Baltimore

© 2016 Johns Hopkins University Press
All rights reserved. Published 2016
Printed in the United States of America on acid-free paper
2 4 6 8 9 7 5 3

Johns Hopkins University Press
2715 North Charles Street
Baltimore, Maryland 21218-4363
www.press.jhu.edu

Library of Congress Cataloging-in-Publication Data

Louden, Mark Laurence.
Pennsylvania Dutch : the story of an American language / Mark L. Louden.
pages cm. — (Young Center books in Anabaptist and Pietist studies)
Includes bibliographical references and index.
ISBN 978-1-4214-1828-5 (hardcover) — ISBN 978-1-4214-1829-2 (electronic) —
ISBN 1-4214-1828-2 (hardcover) — ISBN 1-4214-1829-0 (electronic) 1. Pennsylvania
Dutch—Languages. 2. Pennsylvania Dutch—History. 3. Pennsylvania Dutch—
Religion. 4. Pennsylvania Dutch—Social life and customs. 5. German Americans—
Pennsylvania—Language. 6. Languages in contact—Pennsylvania. 7. Berks County
(Pa.)—Languages. 8. Berks County (Pa.)—Social life and customs. I. Title.
PE3102.P45L68 2016
427'.9748—dc23   2015006256

A catalog record for this book is available from the British Library.

*Special discounts are available for bulk purchases of this book. For more information,
please contact Special Sales at 410-516-6936 or specialsales@press.jhu.edu.*

Johns Hopkins University Press uses environmentally friendly book materials,
including recycled text paper that is composed of at least 30 percent post-consumer
waste, whenever possible.

For Don Yoder (1921–2015),
with deep respect and abiding affection

Contents

Preface   ix
Acknowledgments   xix

CHAPTER 1. What Is Pennsylvania Dutch?   1

CHAPTER 2. Early History of Pennsylvania Dutch   63

CHAPTER 3. Pennsylvania Dutch, 1800–1860   119

CHAPTER 4. Profiles in Pennsylvania Dutch Literature   179

CHAPTER 5. Pennsylvania Dutch in the Public Eye   237

CHAPTER 6. Pennsylvania Dutch and the Amish
and Mennonites   298

CHAPTER 7. An American Story   355

Notes   373
Bibliography   437
Index   457

Preface

It's just before five o'clock on a Saturday evening in a small community in western Berks County, Pennsylvania. Harry and Ida, married for more than sixty years and now in their eighties, are walking into the fellowship hall of the local UCC church to attend a *fersommling*, a banquet and program devoted to the celebration of the Pennsylvania Dutch language and culture. Harry and Ida are Berks County natives, and both grew up speaking Pennsylvania Dutch with their family and friends. Over the years, though, English became the main language of their community and in their own family. Harry and Ida still enjoy speaking their *Mudderschprooch* (mother tongue) with each other and an ever-smaller circle of relatives and friends, but with their children, grandchildren, and now great-grandchildren they use just English, albeit with a slightly "Dutchy" accent.

This evening they'll be speaking and hearing a lot of Pennsylvania Dutch. They'll sing "America" in Pennsylvania Dutch, recite the Pledge of Allegiance in Pennsylvania Dutch, bow their heads while a prayer is read in Pennsylvania Dutch, and then enjoy a delicious banquet starting off with *Obscht-hahneschwanz* (fruit cocktail) and a number of sides, decide between the *Gebackne Schunkefleesch* (baked ham) and the *Hinkel-Schenkel* (chicken legs), then wrap up with a piece of *Kuche* (cake) topped off with *Eis Raahm* (ice cream). While sipping a cup of *Kaffi*, they'll sit back and enjoy a program of singing and skits, all in Pennsylvania Dutch. This fersommling is one of the few opportunities Harry and Ida have nowadays to use the language their ancestors had spoken since the eighteenth century, and they'll leave tonight looking forward to coming back next year.

Some 1,200 miles southwest of Berks County, in eastern Oklahoma, Harvey and Ada Mae, a young Amish couple, have just been dropped off at home by their van driver after an afternoon of hitting garage sales and shopping at the Walmart Supercenter. In their late twenties, Harvey and Ada Mae have been married for about five years now and have two children. The oldest, Marlin, is four, and he spent the afternoon playing at the home of his grandparents, which is just across the road from Harvey and Ada Mae's place. Ellen, the baby, went along with Mom and Dad. Like Harry and Ida, Harvey and Ada Mae speak Pennsylvania Dutch, as did their Amish ancestors in this country going back almost as far as Harry's and Ida's.

Unlike Harry and Ida, Harvey and Ada Mae use Pennsylvania Dutch all the time. It is the main language they speak at home and with their fellow Amish, unless they're around someone who doesn't understand their *Mudderschprooch*. At that point they'll switch quickly to English, which they speak just as fluently as any of their monolingual friends and neighbors. English is also the language of pretty much everything Harvey and Ada Mae read and write, from the list they brought with them to Walmart to the family circle letter they want to get finished this evening yet. Tonight, before reading a Bible story in English to Marlin and Ellen and putting them to bed, Harvey and Ada Mae will remind themselves of the Scripture passages to be covered in church tomorrow and then read them in their bilingual Luther German–King James English Bible. Harvey is also a pretty good singer, so chances are good he'll get tapped tomorrow to lead one of the three German hymns from the *Ausbund* to be sung. He'll probably take a few moments after leading the family's evening devotions in German to have a look at the text of the hymns and practice singing the tunes.

Harry and Ida and Harvey and Ada Mae are all native-born Americans whose ancestors have been in this country for more than two centuries, and they share a common language, Pennsylvania Dutch. Yet in many ways these two couples live in different worlds. Harry and Ida, like any American who reads a newspaper and watches television, know who the Amish are, and, since they also happen to live in southeastern Pennsylvania, they have probably crossed paths at some point with Amish people. But it's quite possible they have never actually spoken Pennsylvania Dutch with Amish, or with members of another group, the Old Order Mennonites, who also speak the *Mudderschprooch*.

Back in Oklahoma, Harvey and Ada Mae probably have no idea that there are people like Harry and Ida, in Pennsylvania or anywhere else in the country, who can speak Pennsylvania Dutch and are not of Amish or Mennonite background. In fact, they're sometimes puzzled when outsiders refer to their language as *Pennsylvania Dutch*, since as far back as they know their family history, their ancestors all lived in the Midwest. When an outsider asks Harvey or Ada Mae what they speak at home, they'll probably say "German" but then qualify that by saying that the way they speak is pretty different from the way that folks from Germany talk.

This book will explore the past and present of the worlds of people like Harry and Ida and Harvey and Ada Mae, speakers of a language that is as old as the United States. Pennsylvania Dutch, though used by only a minuscule portion of the American population, is a sociolinguistic wonder. It has been spoken continuously since the late eighteenth century even though it has not been "refreshed" by later waves of immigration from abroad. It has never enjoyed any official recognition or legal protection, nor has it has been taught in schools. Most speakers of the language never read or write in Pennsylvania Dutch, and, in any case, there is very little available for them to read in the language. On top of all this, those outsiders, and not a few insiders, who have formed any opinions about Pennsylvania Dutch do not hold the language in particularly high esteem. They compare it to German and English, and it falls short on both scores.

The health of Pennsylvania Dutch is mixed. On the one hand, among people like Harry and Ida, the descendants of mostly Lutheran and German Reformed immigrants from German-speaking Europe to colonial Pennsylvania, who are known collectively as *church people* or *nonsectarians*, Pennsylvania Dutch is now nearly gone. There are few fluent speakers under the age of seventy anymore; within the next few decades, it is likely that there will be no more people like Harry and Ida living, that is, nonsectarian Pennsylvania Dutch speakers who can communicate well in the *Mudderschprooch*. On the other hand, the outlook for Pennsylvania Dutch is very bright among people like Harvey, Ada Mae, and tens of thousands of other Old Order Amish and Old Order Mennonite *sectarians*, whose ancestors came to colonial Pennsylvania at the same time the church people did, albeit in much smaller numbers. Pennsylvania Dutch has become a vital part of the socioreligious identity of the Old Order groups, and since their numbers are doubling every twenty years due to a combination of high birth rates and low attrition, there is little likelihood that Pennsylvania Dutch will be disappearing among their people any time soon.

The chapters that follow will explore the language of Harry, Ida, Harvey, and Ada Mae, what it is, what it is not, and how it has developed. Chapter 1 establishes some basic facts about Pennsylvania Dutch, beginning with what it is called. In line with the preference of most native speakers themselves, in this book the language is referred to as *Pennsylvania Dutch* rather than the somewhat less misleading *Pennsylvania German*. Along the way I also address the question whether Pennsylvania Dutch is more properly referred to as a *language* or a *dialect*. (The book's subtitle suggests what my response will be to that question.) I go on in this first chapter to clarify the common misunderstanding that the *Dutch* in *Pennsylvania Dutch* is due to a faulty translation of *Deutsch* (or *Deitsch*). This chapter also gives an overview of the basic structures of the language and considers how they compare to those of dialects of German spoken in Europe. And since English has always played some kind of role in the development of Pennsylvania Dutch, I devote a section of this chapter to the contact situation between the two languages. Chapter 1 concludes with information on various subgroups of Pennsylvania Dutch speakers, including, of course, the two major ones, nonsectarians and sectarians.

Chapters 2–6 move largely chronologically, beginning in chapter 2 with a discussion of the immigration and early history of the Pennsylvania Dutch founder population both before and right after the American Revolution. This chapter also explores some basic facts about the cultural setting of early Pennsylvania Dutch speakers. Chapter 3 deals with what is known about Pennsylvania Dutch during the first half of the nineteenth century, when the social conditions experienced by Pennsylvania Dutch–speaking farmers and craftspeople were largely stable. It was during this time that the first writings in Pennsylvania Dutch began to emerge, mainly in German-language newspapers published for a

Pennsylvania Dutch–speaking readership. Although only a minority of Pennsylvania Dutch have ever been able to read and write their mother tongue, a sizable body of folk literature in the language was produced, especially in the late nineteenth and early twentieth centuries. These prose and poetic texts, which number in the thousands, were written by and for native speakers of Pennsylvania Dutch; very few have ever been translated into English. An important goal of this book is to bring just a few of these precious materials to light to go back in time and listen in on the conversations Pennsylvania Dutch people long ago had with one another. The focus of chapter 4 is on four major figures in the development of Pennsylvania Dutch literature, though there were many, many more whose lives and writings also merit our attention.

Chapters 5 and 6 center mainly on Pennsylvania Dutch in the twentieth century, which marked an important turning point in the history of the language. Since the earliest days of its existence, Pennsylvania Dutch was always endangered to some degree. The people who successfully maintained it into adulthood and passed it on to their children were rural dwellers of modest social and geographic mobility who lived in relatively homogeneous ethnic Pennsylvania Dutch communities and married other Pennsylvania Dutch speakers. Those speakers who moved "up and away," that is, pursued higher education, entered the professions, and married non–Pennsylvania Dutch speakers typically stopped using the language regularly, and their children almost always became English monolinguals. The twin forces of industrialization and urbanization conspired to break the protective sociolinguistic barrier surrounding the Pennsylvania Dutch, promoting the shift to English.

The first half of the twentieth century marked the beginning of the end for Pennsylvania Dutch, but only among nonsectarians. The Old Order Amish and Old Order Mennonites have successfully charted a course of limited accommodation with the larger society that has enabled them to preserve many aspects of the way they live out their Christian faith, including their maintenance of Pennsylvania Dutch and German. The looming demise of Pennsylvania Dutch among nonsectarians did not, however, go unaddressed, and chapter 5 explores some of the efforts to promote the language, including the establishment of the fersommlinge and Grundsow Lodges, which are still active today.

Chapter 6 addresses the present and future situation of Pennsylvania Dutch in Old Order sectarian communities. Their members actually have knowledge of three languages—Pennsylvania Dutch, German, and English—each of which occupies an important position in their verbal ecology. This chapter therefore devotes an entire section to the sociolinguistic situation of each of these languages.

The book wraps up by considering some of the ways that the story of Pennsylvania Dutch is woven into the fabric of American history, with a special emphasis on the role of faith in the maintenance of Pennsylvania Dutch. This leads into a comparison of Pennsylvania Dutch–speaking Amish and Mennonites to three other faith communities in North and South America that have also successfully maintained heritage languages: the Old Colony Mennonites, the Hutterites, and the Haredi Jews.

There is an inherent challenge in writing a book about a language that most of its readers do not speak. Even though Pennsylvania Dutch shares much in common with German, those who are familiar with that language will still have considerable difficulty making sense of Pennsylvania Dutch. At the same time, it is difficult to write about a language and not share any of the details of how it actually looks or sounds, so this book includes a number of samples of original writings in Pennsylvania Dutch as well as the forms of German that Pennsylvania Dutch speakers have employed. These texts will always be accompanied by English translations. And those interested in becoming more familiar with the texts and excerpts featured in this book are directed to the book's companion website, padutch.net, which features lengthier texts in their original, transliterated, and translated forms, as well as audio recordings of Pennsylvania Dutch so that visitors to the site can actually hear the language in addition to reading it.

A few words about Pennsylvania Dutch orthography are in order. If a language has a writing system, which about half of the world's seven thousand known languages do not, it is always an imperfect representation of how that language is actually pronounced. English is of course notorious for its imperfect matchings of sounds and letters. The situation with German is somewhat better yet still far from perfect. Whenever native speakers of Pennsylvania Dutch have put the words of their language to paper—an exceptional exercise since historically their literacy needs have been met by German, English, or both—they have done so in the absence of prescribed norms. Not surprisingly, most Pennsylvania Dutch writers have ended up following German or English rules of spelling—often a mixture of the two—which can be confounding for readers who do not speak the language.

In the twentieth century, two native Pennsylvania Dutch–speaking linguists, Albert F. Buffington and Preston A. Barba, developed a system for writing Pennsylvania Dutch that was based largely on German orthography, and this system was modified by a former student of Buffington's, C. Richard Beam. Although it might have been easier for readers of this book to see all texts written following the Buffington-Barba-Beam system, I decided to reproduce Pennsylvania Dutch texts exactly as they were set down by their writers so as to avoid any inadvertent distortions of the original material. However, on the book's companion website, all texts that were written in a way substantially different from the norms of the Buffington-Barba-Beam system are given in both original and transliterated versions.

By way of ending this preface and preparing the reader to engage with the Pennsylvania Dutch language as a vibrant medium of expression, I reproduce the following poem by John Birmelin (1873–1950) on the question of how to write Pennsylvania Dutch.

WIE SOLL MER SCHPELLE?	***HOW SHOULD YOU SPELL?***
Saagt mer mol, wie soll mer schpelle.	*So tell me, how should you spell?*
Sel macht immer bissel Schtreit;	*That always makes a bit of an argument.*
Was ner nau net hawwe welle,	*What you don't want to deal with,*
Schiebt mer graad mol uf die Seit.	*You just push off to the side.*
Saagt, wie soll mer buchschtawiere	*Tell me, how should you orthographize*
In de scheene deitsche Schproch!	*In the beautiful Pennsylvania Dutch language!*
Brauch mer noh ke Zeit verliere,	*No point in wasting any time,*
Macht mer's ewwe yuscht so nooch.	*You just follow whatever model you please.*

Soll mer Deitsch wie Englisch schreiwe?	*Should you write Dutch like English?*
Deel, die meene sel waer recht.	*Some think that would be correct.*
Soll des Deitsch beim Deitsche bleiwe?	*Should Dutch stay with German?*
Nau—sel guckt emol net schlecht!	*Now, that doesn't look that bad!*
Harbaugh, Fischer, Grumbine, Brunner,	*Harbaugh, Fisher, Grumbine, Brunner,*
Waare vun de gude Alde;	*Were among the good old ones;*
Un, des iss aa gaar ken Wunner,	*And, this is no surprise,*
Hen sich ganz beim Deitsche g'halde.	*Kept totally with German.*
"Solly Hulsbuck"—"Boonestiel,"	*"Solly Hulsbuck"—"Boonestiel,"*
Die hen's Deitsch wie Englisch g'schriwwe;	*They wrote Dutch like English;*
Waar des yuscht fer Ewweviel?	*Was that just out of indifference?*
Waar'n verleicht dezu gedriwwe.	*Maybe they were forced to do that.*
'm "Bumpernickel Bill" sei Sache	*Pumpernickel Bill's writings*
Sin im Land rumhaer bekannt;	*Are famous far and wide;*
Bringe 'n mancher noch zum Lache,	*They bring many to laughter*
Lest 's en mancher mit Verschtand.	*Many can read and understand them.*
Deel, die hen en annrer Glaawe,	*Some have a different view,*
Denke viel vum Parre Stoudt;	*And think much of Reverend Stoudt;*
Kenne's Deitsch noch gut verdraage,	*They can still tolerate German well,*
Glaawe noch an Sauergraut.	*And still believe in sauerkraut.*
Lambert schreibt mit "e-e-e,"	*Lambert writes with German "e's"*
Alsemol mit "j un j" (yott un yott)	*And sometimes with German "j's"*
Saagt er daed aa druf beschteh;	*He says he insists on it;*
Ei, ya well! 's iss wie mer's hot!	*Oh, well! It is what it is!*

Un der Fogel, so politisch,	*And Fogel, so political,*
Bringt en annri Aart Geles.	*Brings a different way of reading,*
Mit Gegritzel diakritisch,	*With diacritic scribbling,*
Universitaetsgemaess.	*Like you'd find in a university.*
Reichard, Brendle, Moll un Barba,	*Reichard, Brendle, Moll, and Barba,*
Yeder nooch seim Abbedit;	*To each his own;*
Doch des Schreiwe hot sei Naube,	*But this writing has its tricks,*
Kenner macht debei Brofit.	*Nobody is benefitting from it.*
Iss es Schpelle?—Buchschtawiere?	*Should it be spell? Orthographize?*
Frogt mer weiter net dernooch:	*Don't ask me any more about it.*
Un fer was dann dischbediere?	*And what's the point of arguing?*
's iss yo doch die Mutterschproch!	*After all, it's our mother tongue!*[1]

Acknowledgments

Some thirty years ago, in February 1985, I attended an Old Order Amish church service for the first time. Thus began my personal odyssey through diverse Amish and Mennonite communities, which set me on my ongoing faith journey and simultaneously sparked my interest in Pennsylvania Dutch. I am deeply grateful to all my Amish and Mennonite brothers and sisters, including the members of my immediate faith family at Milwaukee Mennonite Church, especially Steven Hartman Keiser, for their gifts of friendship and hospitality. I would not be who I am, nor would this book be what it is, without them.

My gratitude extends to numerous friends and colleagues in the Department of German and at the Max Kade Institute for German-American Studies and the Center for the Study of Upper Midwestern Cultures here at the University of Wisconsin–Madison for their shared interest in Pennsylvania Dutch, including Monika Chavez, Rob Howell, Cora Lee Kluge, Kevin Kurdylo, Jim Leary, Ruth Olson, Antje Petty, and Mark Wagler. Early in my career, while still at the University of Texas at Austin, I had the privilege of getting to know the late professor Lester W. J. "Smoky" Seifert, who was one of my predecessors here in Madison. I gained very much from Smoky's expertise in German American linguistics, and Pennsylvania Dutch in particular, and I will always recall his gentle kindness, faith, and wisdom with affection. Hearty thanks also to my friend Joshua R. Brown (UW–Eau Claire) for all the good work he does for Pennsylvania Dutch studies and for the many good discussions we have about our shared interests. I have benefitted considerably from feedback on earlier drafts of this book by one former and one current doctoral student, Shannon Dubenion-Smith (Western Washington University) and Joel Stark (UW–Madison). Joel's research for his own dissertation on the *Reading Adler* has yielded numerous important resources from that newspaper that I have incorporated into multiple chapters.

My friend and colleague Karen Johnson-Weiner (SUNY Potsdam) has been of immense assistance in the production of this book. Her expertise in both linguistics and Amish studies is invaluable. Feedback from my old and dear friend Ivan W. Martin of Penn Yan, NY, a native speaker of Pennsylvania Dutch and one of the most erudite people I know, was of immense help to me in conceptualizing this book, especially the parts dealing with sectarian speakers of Pennsylvania Dutch. I also acknowledge with gratitude two other sectarian friends who have assisted me in my research over the years: David Luthy of the Heritage Historical Library (Aylmer, ON) and Amos B. Hoover of the Muddy Creek Farm Library (Ephrata, PA).

Since early in my career, I have benefitted considerably from the friendly guidance of colleagues in Pennsylvania, including C. Richard Beam (Millersville University) and Marion Lois Huffines (Bucknell University), as well as B. Richard Page and Michael Putnam (Penn State University). William W. Donner and Patrick Donmoyer, both of Kutztown University, have been of great help to me in many respects; I am especially grateful to Bill for providing me with crucial materials related to Abraham Reeser Horne and the Grundsow Lodges. Diane Skorina, of the Myrin Library at Ursinus College, and Christopher Raab, of Franklin and Marshall College, gave me access to early Pennsylvania Dutch documents that were exceptionally important for the book. Jennifer Groff, archives assistant at the Evangelical and Reformed Historical Society, helped with invaluable resources related to Henry Harbaugh. Chrissy Bellizzi, librarian at the German Society of Pennsylvania, provided me with a copy of a rare and fascinating text that proved to be a useful addition to the book. I also want to thank Lisa Minardi, assistant curator at the Winterthur Museum, for generously sharing a copy of a portrait of Simon Snyder from her private collection.

A very special thank-you to Donald Kraybill of the Young Center for Anabaptist & Pietist Studies at Elizabethtown College for his long-standing support of this project and encouragement at every step in the process. I also gratefully acknowledge the assistance and friendship of the late Stephen Scott, who was also on the staff at the Young Center. Especially warm words of thanks are due to Don Yoder, who taught for decades at the University of Pennsylvania, and who, quite simply, is my role model as a scholar. This book is dedicated to Don, who passed away in August 2015.

Colleagues in Germany, especially at the Universities of Marburg and Freiburg, deserve special thanks for their invaluable feedback on my research in so many ways: Jürg Fleischer, Joachim Herrgen, Roland Kehrein, Alfred Lameli, Oliver Schallert, Jürgen Erich Schmidt, and Richard Wiese (Marburg); and Peter Auer, Göz Kaufmann, Friedel Scheer-Nahor, and Tobias Streck (Freiburg). I have had the privilege of knowing and working with Göz for most of my career, going back to the early 1990s when he, as a student of another dear colleague from Germany, Klaus Mattheier (University of Heidelberg), conducted fieldwork on Plautdietsch-speaking Mennonites in northern Mexico and Texas. My respect for Göz as a scholar and teacher is profound. Special thanks also to Werner Enninger and Joachim Raith (both from the University of Essen), Ludwig Eichinger (Insitut für Deutsche Sprache–Mannheim), Jan Wirrer (University of Bielefeld), Guido Seiler (University of Munich, formerly of Freiburg), and Alexandra Lenz (University of Vienna, formerly of Marburg) for many hours of stimulating discussions about Pennsylvania Dutch over the years. Stateside, I owe thanks to Neil Jacobs (Ohio State University), Achim Kopp (Mercer University), and Steven Nolt (Goshen College) for their kind assistance and feedback over many years. My friend Jack Thiessen from north of the border (University of Winnipeg) is an ongoing source of wisdom and encouragement to me, both professionally and personally.

I want to thank Walter Sauer (University of Heidelberg), whose help in deciphering early Pennsylvania Dutch texts for this book was very welcome. Likewise, I owe a huge debt of gratitude to Rudolf Post (University of Freiburg), whose scholarly expertise in Palatine German is unmatched. I have always valued Rudolf's kind support. And I would be remiss in not recognizing the important work of my friends Michael Werner, Frank Kessler, Helmut Schmahl, and the members of the German-Pennsylvanian Association devoted to the advancement of Pennsylvania Dutch language and culture, both in Europe and America.

As this book made its way into production, I had the good fortune of working with Cynthia Nolt, of the Young Center, as well as Greg Britton, Catherine Goldstead, Hilary Jacqmin, Juliana McCarthy, and Courtney Bond, all of Johns Hopkins University Press. My sincere thanks to each one of them for their expertise and good cheer. Cartographer Bill Nelson (Bill Nelson Maps) did an outstanding job producing the maps of Pennsylvania and of German-speaking Europe, and Carrie Watterson's copyediting and preparation of the final manuscript were superb.

I owe my greatest debt of thanks to Jeanne and Clara for their gift of unconditional love.

Pennsylvania Dutch

CHAPTER 1

What Is Pennsylvania Dutch?

*The language used by our German-speaking countrymen [in
Pennsylvania] is a pitifully broken mishmash of English and German
with regard to words as well as their combination.*
—JOHANN DAVID SCHÖPF, 1788

Pennsylvania Dutch or Pennsylvania German?
Language or Dialect?

Over the entire history of what I refer to in this book as the *Pennsylvania Dutch language*, there has been a remarkable lack of consensus as to what to call this linguistic variety (to adopt a neutral term) in English. While most people say *Pennsylvania Dutch*, others prefer *Pennsylvania German*. And is it a *language* or a *dialect*? Here again, that depends on whom one asks. Starting with the first question, the majority of speakers themselves, especially those living in the Commonwealth of Pennsylvania, call their mother tongue *Pennsylvania Dutch*, in most cases fully aware that its linguistic roots lie in German-speaking Central Europe and not the Low Countries. Pennsylvania German, by contrast, is the term generally preferred by scholars as well as by some language advocates keen on stressing the language's European German heritage.

Outside of Pennsylvania, where most speakers of the language actually live today, the modifier *Pennsylvania* is sometimes problematic, since there are differences between Pennsylvania Dutch in Pennsylvania and varieties spoken in other areas. Many midwestern speakers, for example, understand Pennsylvania Dutch to refer to only the varieties that are spoken in Pennsylvania and therefore often say *German* when referring to their language in English, even though they are aware of the significant differences between what they speak and European German. In Pennsylvania Dutch itself, the language is called *Deitsch*, which means either 'Pennsylvania Dutch / German' or 'German'. There is no native term for the language spoken in the Netherlands and parts of Belgium; Pennsylvania Dutch speakers call that language *Holland Dutch* in both Pennsylvania Dutch and English.[1] In earlier times, some speakers used the terms *Pennsilfaanisch Deitsch* or *Pennsilfaanisch*, but those are archaic today. To add to the mix, some Old Order Amish speakers of Pennsylvania Dutch, who account for the great majority of today's active users of the language, refer to it as *Amisch*, but such usage is generally limited to children.

The name *Pennsylvania Dutch* is a source of confusion for some people, since the language is descended from varieties of speech brought to eighteenth-century Pennsylvania by immigrants who spoke forms of German and not Dutch (Netherlandic).[2] Contrary to a widespread belief among both nonscholars and scholars, though, the *Dutch* in Pennsylvania Dutch is not a historical mistranslation of the native word *Deitsch*, as originally pointed out by Don Yoder.[3] Although the words *Deitsch* and *Dutch* do share a common Germanic etymology, both *German* and *Dutch* were used in earlier American English to mean 'German'. The two synonyms differed in terms of formality. The word *German*, which was borrowed from Latin, traditionally had a neutral or formal connotation, while *Dutch* was used in more familiar and informal ("folksier") contexts. Since most active Pennsylvania Dutch speakers have historically been farmers, craftspeople, and laborers, it is understandable that *Dutch* has been their label of choice.

An additional factor in the preference by Pennsylvania Dutch people for *Dutch* over *German*, at least in Pennsylvania, has to do with their identity distinct from that of other Americans of German descent. Most ancestors of the Pennsylvania Dutch came to America during the first half of the eighteenth century, before the European Enlightenment and the emergence of an elite German-language culture of *Deutschtum* (Germanness) grounded in a body of secular literature and music. Between approximately 1760 and 1830, German immigration to America was almost nonexistent. When German speakers started coming in great numbers again in the nineteenth century, many brought with them a strong sense of identification with the works of such cultural icons as Johann Wolfgang von Goethe (1749–1832), Friedrich Schiller (1759–1805), Wolfgang Amadeus Mozart (1756–1791), and Ludwig van Beethoven (1770–1827), all of whom made their mark on German culture long after the ancestors of the Pennsylvania Dutch had left Europe. The cultural distance between the Pennsylvania Dutch and German Americans is reflected in how the former group referred to the latter: they were not typically called *Deitsche* but *Deitschlenner*, 'Germany people'.[4] For their part, most *Deitschlenner* likewise felt little kinship with the Pennsylvania Dutch. Thus, the moniker *Dutch*, distinct as it is from *German*, evokes the difference, both perceived and real, between the Pennsylvania Dutch and other Americans of German heritage.

The historical and sociocultural divide between the Pennsylvania Dutch and immigrants from German-speaking Europe and their descendants is important in understanding how Pennsylvania Dutch language and culture developed. Historian Richard H. Shryock's observations on this question are apt here:

The latter immigrants from the Fatherland were frequently of middle-class origin, became widely distributed throughout the country, and were rapidly Americanized. All this meant that they soon became an English-literate group, and displayed a decided interest in their place in American society. Moreover, they represented—even though many were political refugees—a new Germany. Their intellectual leaders reflected the current romantic idealism, and their *Weltanschauung* had little in common with that of Pennsylvania Germans whose traditions were rooted in the pietism of post-Reformation days. Such differences tended to make each group keep its distance. The newcomers apparently thought the "Dutch" provincial and backward; while the latter—thoroughly American despite their language—seem to have looked down on the " '48ers" as foreigners.[5]

The Pennsylvania Dutch and the *Deitschlenner* thus differed in a number of important ways. The former were primarily farmers and craftspeople whose Pietist-leaning Christian faith was central to their identity, while the latter, many of whom settled in towns and cities, were more secular and cosmopolitan in their outlook.

The social, cultural, and linguistic differences between Pennsylvania Dutch and *Deitschlenner* are the theme of a short poem written in Pennsylvania Dutch by the Reformed pastor Eli Keller (1828–1919).[6] Titled "En Tremp" (A tramp), the poem tells the story of a European-born, standard German–speaking hobo who comes knocking at the door of a Pennsylvania Dutch farmhouse. The farmer's wife, who is alone at the time, allows the hungry, bedraggled stranger in and gives him a hearty meal. To her disappointment, however, the man lingers and picks up a book written in Pennsylvania Dutch. After the German turns his high nose up at the "gibberish" (*Keuterwelsch*; standard German *Kauderwelsch*) in which the book is written, his sturdy Dutch hostess loses her patience and sends the arrogant guest packing. The message conveyed in the poem is that, despite their humble social status and language, the Pennsylvania Dutch merit more respect than they are accorded by *Deitschlenner*, even by those individuals who may happen to be at the bottom of the socioeconomic ladder.

> Die Mutter hot em Vater was zu klage—
> (Un seufts derbei—wie aus em diefste Mage)
> Denk just mol hie—en Deutscher kummt,
> Un kloppt mer an der Küche Deer—
> Ich sag dann: "Rei"—un er—er brummt:
> "Ich moechte Epess—bin ganz leer!"
>
> Ich sag: Du kannst dert uf der Bank hiesitze—
> (Er wor bedreckt, war grauslich ah am Schwitze.)
> Ich schneid dann Fleesch, un schneid ah Brot,
> Un streich noch schöner Butter druf—
> Un geb eem Kaffi—der dut not—
> Un drag em schö, un sauwer uf!
>
> Du hetst den Mann just sehne solle esse—
> Den hot mer gar net nötig kat zu heese,
> Grad so—wie ah ken anri Sau!

So frog ich dann: "Un wars genunk?"
"Ach ja!—vortrefflich—gute Frau:
   Das Essen—un der gute Trunk!"

Dann bleibt er noch (ken Wunner) länger hocke,
   Un endlich sag ich: "Mach dich uf die Socke!"
Er frogt: "Was is das für ein Buch,
   Das Sie da hatten in der Hand?"
"Des is der Wart, den ich drin such;
   Vun Pennsylvani—Leut un Landt!"

Dann biet ich em dei Buch, un sag: "Wid leese?"
   Un richtig, loszt er sich ken zwee mol heese!
Eer setzt sich uf sei hochi Naas,
   En merkenswärtig groszi Brill—
Dann sagt er: "Na! was ist dann das?
   Ein Keuterwelsch, das ich nicht will!"

Hei ja! sag ich: Mei Esse stärkt dei Mage—
   Wann du des Buch net wid—hots Nix zu sage!
Doch, mach dich gschwind un sauwer fort—
   Un jo noch eb der Vater kummt—
Gewisz, er is vun anner Art,
   Un deer gets schlecht, wan er deer brummt!
     Adje!

Mother has something to complain to Father about—
   (And sighs—as from deep in her stomach);
Just imagine—a German comes
   And knocks on my kitchen door—
I say, then, "Come in"—and he—he grumbles:
   "I would like something—I'm quite empty!"

I say: You can sit on the bench over there—
   (He was filthy, and also sweating terribly.)
I cut some meat, then, and cut also bread,
   And spread some good butter on it—

And give him coffee—he is in need—
   And serve him nice and proper!

You should have just seen the man eat—
   It wasn't necessary to invite him to do so,
Just like that—like no other pig!
   So then I ask: "And was it enough?"
"Ah yes!—outstanding—good woman:
   The food—and the good drink!"

Then he still stays (no surprise) sitting there longer,
   And finally I say: "Go on your way!"
He asks: "What book is that
   That you had in your hand?"
"It is worthwhile for me to look through it;
   Of Pennsylvania—People and Land!"

Then I offer him your book and say "Do you want to read it?"
   And of course, he doesn't need to be asked a second time!
He sets onto his high nose
   A remarkably large pair of glasses—
Then he says: "So! What is this?
   A gibberish that I don't want!"

Well! I say: My food fills your stomach—
   If you don't want this book, it has nothing to say!
So get out of here fast—
   And especially before Father comes—
To be sure, he is of a different temperament,
   And you will be in bad shape when he growls at you!
   Good bye![7]

The view of Pennsylvania Dutch as something less than a real language, some kind of odd gibberish, was widespread among *Deitschlenner*, especially in the nineteenth century, when German immigration to America reached a high point. Immigrants who knew European standard German well, especially those with above-average levels of formal education, tended to scorn Pennsylvania Dutch since it was derived from nonstandard forms of German (regional dialects) and contained vocabulary borrowed from English. Although neither Pennsylvania Dutch nor European German dialects are historically descended from standard German, critics nonetheless viewed Pennsylvania Dutch as a degenerate form of speech that represented a linguistic fall from the grace of a mythic "pure" German language.

An example of how many *Deitschlenner* perceived Pennsylvania Dutch is a lengthy poem that appeared in the *Reading (PA) Adler* on January 22, 1878. Titled "The Desecration of the German Language" (*Die Schändung der deutschen Sprache*), the unnamed poet devotes nineteen verses to the elaboration of how "his" language has fared among illiterate American speakers of German descent. It begins, in English translation, as follows:

> It is well known that in this country
> There are many who call themselves German
> Yet who—what a disgrace!—
> Cannot read a word of German.
>
> And too awful is the language
> That many Germans use.
> "Buhtschäck" [bootjack] is what they call a *Stiefelknecht*,
> And "spellen" [to spell] is *Buchstabi[e]ren*.
>
> How the horse "hat gekickt" [kicked]
> And the "Hinkel" [chickens] "gekrischen" [squawked];
> The "Butscher" [butcher] shipped the "Bief" [beef];
> My "Freddy" is "gehn fischen" [gone fishing].
>
> "Vell" [Well], call in "Däd" [Dad] "nau" [now],
> I have "Bräckfäst" [breakfast] "reddy" [ready];
> Say hello to "Tschäck" [Jack] and "Emmelein" [little Emma];
> The "Horses" are pulling "shteddy" [steady].[8]

The *Deitschlenner* poet, despite his viscerally negative assessment of Pennsylvania Dutch, is nonetheless largely accurate in the words he attributes to the language: most of the English loan vocabulary and trans-lated expressions he lists are indeed part of Pennsylvania Dutch, as are all the examples of words derived from European German dialects. As I will establish below, however, the general picture he paints of Pennsyl-vania Dutch as a degenerate language in which nearly every other word is from English is a highly distorted one. He concludes his poem with an admonition to the users of this degraded American tongue who have lost their German linguistic anchor:

> Now is it not a disgrace and a dishonor
> How in so many places
> The precious, beautiful German language
> Has been debased in its words?

> Say "ja" and "nein" for "yes" and "no",
> Instead of "kicken" say "schlagen",
> And instead of that silly "Window"
> You can certainly say "Fenster".

> Change your "Hinkel" right now
> Into "Hühner" or "Hennen";
> You can call your "Bräckfäst" in German
> Your "Morgenessen".

> In Germany many people would
> Not understand your German at all;
> They would think, "In America
> It must look sorry."

> You were born a German;
> You should remain a German;
> Therefore learn cheerily and incessantly
> To speak, read, and write German.[9]

Interestingly, both Pennsylvania Dutch and *Deitschlenner* identified strongly with American ideals. For most *Deitschlenner* after the first generation, that meant assimilating linguistically and eventually abandoning German, the attitudes of those such as the anonymous author of the poem above notwithstanding. The Pennsylvania Dutch, however, invoked the classically American notion of liberty to justify their right to maintain a language with roots extending into the colonial period that had become uniquely their own. Pennsylvania Dutch was just similar enough to German for the *Deitschlenner* to scorn it as a degraded form of their ancestral language yet sufficiently different to render a label for it other than *German* more appropriate. For their part, the Pennsylvania Dutch were quite content to identify themselves and their language in a way that reflected the very real divide between them and their distant European and German American cousins. The motivation, therefore, for using *Pennsylvania Dutch* rather than *Pennsylvania German* in this book, despite its apparent historical inaccuracy, is grounded in the usage of the majority of the speakers themselves, especially those residing in Pennsylvania.

Turning now to the second question posed at the beginning of this section, is Pennsylvania Dutch a *language* or a *dialect*? Here again, opinions, both popular and scholarly, are divided. From a scientific-linguistic point of view, the differences between languages and dialects have more to do with their social status than with any real structural characteristics. Linguistic systems that are dubbed languages typically enjoy a measure of political or geographic autonomy relative to other languages. Languages "stand on their own," while dialects are viewed as subordinate to some larger language in that their communicative range is limited to certain geographic regions or they are spoken by cultural or ethnic minorities. For many people, including linguists, the term *dialect* is synonymous with *regional variety*. For example, European German dialects such as Bavarian, Swabian, and Berlinish are geographically defined constructs. The situation in North America is similar, with examples of dialects such as Canadian English, Brooklynese, and Texan.

Another important difference between the popular uses of *dialect* and *language* has to do with writing. Many linguistic varieties that are recognized as languages serve as vehicles of written communication, while dialects are primarily oral media. Nonlinguists frequently assume that "written down" languages are somehow more "correct" than less visually tangible forms of speech, including dialects. The scientific reality here is that writing is a secondary linguistic phenomenon: human languages are fundamentally oral in nature, and the writing systems developed to represent (some of) them are inevitably imperfect. The gap between "proper" English spelling and how words are actually pronounced in the spoken language is an apt example of the inherent gap between speech and writing.

There are no objective criteria that may be used to determine whether a linguistic system should be recognized as a language or a dialect. Although lack of mutual intelligibility would be a plausible standard according to which languages could be distinguished from one another, this is not linguistic practice. Examples from the Germanic language family, to which Pennsylvania Dutch, German, and English all belong, are instructive in this regard. Norwegian and Swedish, whose standard varieties are highly mutually intelligible, are treated as distinct languages, mainly because they are associated with two separate nation-states, Norway and Sweden. In contrast, the regional varieties of German spoken (and sometimes also written) in Switzerland, which are largely unintelligible to standard German speakers from elsewhere, are considered dialects of German. In yet another situation, the Germanic variety indigenous to the Grand Duchy of Luxembourg, which is as difficult for German speakers to understand as Swiss German dialects, was legally recognized as the national language by a constitutional revision only in 1984. Luxembourgish, as it is officially known, went from being a dialect of German to a language in its own right without undergoing any linguistic evolution; its change of status was effected by the stroke of a pen.[10]

Whether a linguistic variety is called a language or a dialect is therefore decided by nonlinguists for reasons that have more to do with the social and political status of its speakers than with the internal structure of the variety itself. In this context, a stigma is frequently attached to the term *dialect*. Dialect speakers are often viewed as employing structures that are at best "rustic" or "quaint" but more commonly "illogical," "uneducated," or simply "incorrect." In the United States, for example, dialects associated with regions such as the South, New York City, Southern California, and elsewhere are often held up to ridicule. Adding to the stigma is the application of *dialect* to ethnically defined varieties of speech, one of the most well known being "black dialect" (more properly, African American Vernacular English). *Ethnolects* in the United States are almost universally viewed as inferior to the ways in which stereotypical upper-middle-class Anglo-Americans are thought to speak. Therefore, dialects, synonyms for which include *jargon, slang,* and *lingo,* have often been applied to groups of people who fall short of an implicit social, cultural, or ethnic norm, which in the United States is the traditional stereotype of an affluent, urban, well-educated "white Anglo-Saxon Protestant."

For a variety of reasons, then, most people, especially outsiders, have been inclined to view Pennsylvania Dutch as "just" a dialect. It is a primarily oral language that is related to German but different enough from German as to be considered inferior or at least subordinate to it. Its active speakers are American "ethnics" who live mainly in rural areas and are of modest social status. Also, unlike other immigrant heritage languages spoken in the United States, Pennsylvania Dutch lacks a perceived historical connection with a cultural homeland abroad. Many German Americans (*Deitschlenner*) were different in this respect. Though they, like the Pennsylvania Dutch, viewed themselves as completely American, German Americans, especially in the nineteenth century, often took a certain pride in being associated with German-speaking Europe and a transnational *Deutschtum.* By contrast, most Pennsylvania Dutch have felt little connection with post-Enlightenment European German culture. However, many active speakers of Pennsylvania Dutch have also had reading knowledge of a form of written standard German, albeit one that differs from European standard German. Known as *Pennsylvania High German,* this is a variety that was used in many nineteenth-century publications produced by and for Pennsylvania Dutch, especially local newspapers and other texts produced in America.

Today, the primary speakers of Pennsylvania Dutch, the Old Order Amish and horse and buggy–driving Old Order Mennonites, no longer read periodicals in Pennsylvania High German, but they do use German as a liturgical language, calling it *Hochdeitsch* (High German).[11] The relationship between vernacular Pennsylvania Dutch and the more formal (Pennsylvania) High German is an example of what linguists call *diglossia.*[12] A classic example of diglossia that parallels the Pennsylvania Dutch situation is German-speaking Switzerland, in which regional dialects coexist with Swiss Standard German. Other diglossic communities are found throughout the Arabic-speaking world, in which informal oral communication is conducted in a regional dialect (Egyptian Arabic, Lebanese Arabic, etc.), while Modern Standard (Literary) Arabic is used for many formal purposes.[13]

The diglossic relationship between Pennsylvania Dutch and High German accounts for the fact that most Pennsylvania Dutch speakers use the label *dialect* when describing their mother tongue in English. Some will even express the view that as a "dialect," Pennsylvania Dutch is somewhat inferior to High German. That does not imply, however, that speakers feel negatively about the language. On the contrary, Pennsylvania Dutch enjoys what the sociolinguist William Labov calls *covert prestige*.[14] Covertly prestigious (that is, overtly stigmatized) varieties are associated with a positive sense of belonging to a well-defined in-group. For those Pennsylvania Dutch who have historically been content to live in a traditional Pennsylvania Dutch community, speaking "the dialect" connotes positive associations of warmth, comfort, familiarity, and a connection to one's heritage. Conversely, people who grow up in a Pennsylvania Dutch–speaking environment but for whatever reasons choose to move away (or "up" socially) into an English-monolingual environment often adopt the view that, since it is "just a dialect," Pennsylvania Dutch has little value.

In the discussion above of the terms *Pennsylvania Dutch* and *Pennsylvania German*, I noted that in the language itself there is just one word, *Deitsch*. So it is also for the equivalent of the English terms *language* and *dialect*. In Pennsylvania Dutch, *Schprooch* means both, which in some ways renders the language/dialect label question moot.[15] The terms *Deitsch* and *unser Schprooch*, 'our language/dialect', are synonymous.

To sum up, I have decided to follow popular usage in referring to the subject of this book as *Pennsylvania Dutch*, rather than *Pennsylvania German*, but I prefer to refer to it as a language rather than as a dialect. Both choices are intended to underscore the autonomy of Pennsylvania Dutch from European German, despite the relatively close historical and to some extent sociolinguistic connections between the two languages. In the following section I make clear just what those connections are.

The German Roots of Pennsylvania Dutch

Despite its misleading name, Pennsylvania Dutch is derived from the German dialects spoken by immigrants from southwestern Germany and Switzerland to colonial Pennsylvania. The historian Marianne Wokeck estimates that between 1683 and 1774 nearly 81,000 German speakers arrived in Pennsylvania via the port of Philadelphia, most of whom immigrated in the first half of the eighteenth century, especially during the years 1749–1755.[16] At that point in history, essentially all the inhabitants of the territories that correspond today to the countries of Germany, Switzerland, and Austria spoke regional, mainly oral dialects. There was already a more or less unified standard variety of German in which books, newspapers, and other print media were written, but most German dialect speakers' knowledge of this variety, known as High German (*Hochdeutsch*), was limited to mainly reading and, to a lesser extent, writing. Owing to the low mobility of Central Europeans in the eighteenth century, it was not necessary for most of them to actually speak standard German in their daily lives. Oral production of standard German, especially among the Protestant, Anabaptist, and Pietist groups that comprised the majority of the ancestors of the Pennsylvania Dutch, was limited to use in worship, for example, as the language of prepared sermons and prayers.

German-speaking immigrants to colonial Pennsylvania came from a number of regions in Central Europe, but by far most came from the territories on either side of the Rhine, extending from Switzerland northward to the region known as the Palatinate (*Pfalz*, in German).[17] A critical mass of speakers, likely arriving during the peak of immigration at midcentury, could well have come from the eastern Palatinate (*Vorderpfalz*), more specifically from a region west-southwest of the city of Mannheim in the southeastern Palatinate, since Pennsylvania Dutch most closely resembles the dialects from that relatively compact area.[18] These varieties belong to the West Central group of the so-called High German dialects.[19] However, there is not one particular German dialect, even in the Mannheim area, that is identical to Pennsylvania Dutch in its core features. Pennsylvania Dutch was affected by contact among mul-

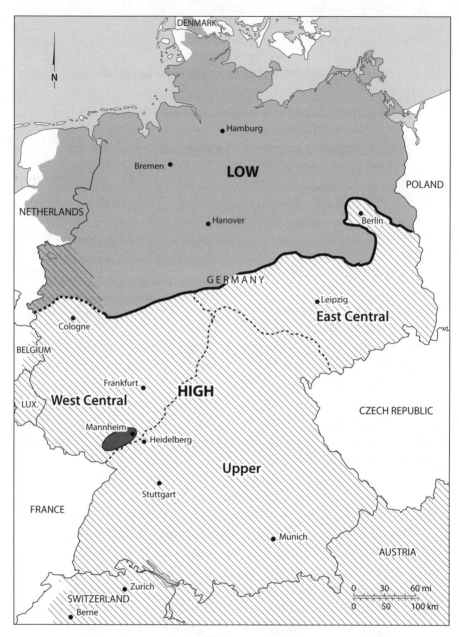

German dialect territory. Dark ellipse indicates the area within the Palatinate region where the dialects spoken most closely resemble Pennsylvania Dutch.
Source: Map by Bill Nelson.

tiple dialects, as well as independent development, after it coalesced into a relatively uniform variety by the end of the eighteenth century.[20]

One consequence of the process of dialect contact was the formation of regional subvarieties across the original Pennsylvania Dutch language area of southeastern Pennsylvania in which most points of variation are lexical, rather than based on sound patterns, word formation, or syntax.[21] Time and the migration of Pennsylvania Dutch speakers outside of southeastern Pennsylvania to other US states and Canada have not, however, yielded varieties of Pennsylvania Dutch that are mutually unintelligible. While there are clear regional differences, as well as differences across Pennsylvania Dutch–speaking subgroups, especially religious communities, all Pennsylvania Dutch speakers are easily able to communicate with one another.[22]

The basic grammar of any language consists of four major components: a phonology, specifying how individual sounds are produced and combined with one another; a morphology, which determines how words are formed and modified; a syntax, the system according to which words are linked to form phrases and clauses; and an inventory of words, its vocabulary or lexicon. In all four structural components, modern Pennsylvania Dutch demonstrates a decidedly southeastern Palatine German character. Over the more than two centuries of its existence, Pennsylvania Dutch has changed, though mainly in its vocabulary. Phonologically, there has been some alteration in its inventory of vowels, but its consonants are the same today as they were in the eighteenth century. Also, the rules determining how Pennsylvania Dutch sounds are combined with one another are likewise largely unchanged since the eighteenth century. Pennsylvania Dutch morphology and syntax are also quite conservative, though there are some notable changes in the latter area of structure, discussed later in this book. To demonstrate the fundamental similarity between Pennsylvania Dutch and modern Palatine German, especially the Mannheim dialect, consider the table below focusing on vowels, where one would expect the most divergence over time, compared to other areas of structure.

The relatively greater susceptibility of words and vowels to change over time as compared with consonants and phonological, morphological, and syntactic rules is consistent with what is observed in the histories of many languages, including American English. What table 1.1

Table 1.1 Comparison of selected vowels between Pennsylvania Dutch and Mannheim (Palatine) German

Pennsylvania Dutch		Mannheim German		Standard German		English
[ɔ:] as in dog	Daag, Fraa	[ɔ:] as in dog	Daag, Fraa	[a:] as in Tom; [aʊ] as in brow	Tag, Frau	day, woman
[a] as in pot	mache, Schpatz	[a] as in pot	mache, Schpatz	[a] as in pot	machen, Spatze	to make, sparrow
[a] as in pot; [æ] as in cat	blarre (blærre), Gscha (Gschæa), Watt, Dascht, Hatz, da:fe (dæafe), Vaddel (Væddel)	[a] as in pot; [æ:] as in bad; [ɔ:] as in caught	blære, Gschæa, Woat, Doascht, Ha:tz, dæfe, Væddel	[æ] as in cat; [ɪ] as in fit; [ɔ:] as in caught; [ʊ] as in put; [ɛ] as in bet; [ʏ] as in déja vu; [i:] as in fear	plärren, Geschirr, Wort, Durst, Herz, dürfen, Viertel	to whine, dishes, word, thirst, heart, to have permission, quarter
[e:] as in bay	Gees, schee	[e:] as in bay; [æ:] as in bad	Gees, schää	[aɪ] as in ice; [ø:] as in Goethe	Geis, schön	goat, beautiful
[ɛ] as in bet	geschder, nemme	[ɛ] as in bet	geschdert, nemme	[ɛ] as in bet; [e:] as bay	gestern, nehmen	yesterday, to take
[i:] as in feast	schiesse, siess	[i:] as in feast	schiesse, siess	[i:] as in feast; [y:] as in déja vu (long)	schießen, süß	to shoot, sweet
[ɪ] as in fit	siwwe, widder	[ɪ] as in fit	siwwe, widder	[i:] as in feast	sieben, wieder	seven, again
[o:] as in low	gross, blose	[o:] as in low	gross, blose	[o:] as in low; [a:] as in Tom	groß, blasen	large, to blow
[ɔ/ʌ] as in buggy	Voggel, gloffe	[ɔ/ʌ] as in buggy	Voggel, geloffe	[o:] as in low; [aʊ] as in brow	Vogel, gelaufen	bird, walked
[u:] as in two; [o:] as in low	Blut, wu (wo)	[u:] as in two	Blut, wu	[u:] as in two; [o:] as in low	Blut, wo	blood, where

Table 1.1 *continued*

Pennsylvania Dutch	Mannheim German	Standard German	English
[ʊ] as in put	*dunkel, un*	[ʊ] as in put	*dunkel, un*	[ʊ] as in *put*	*dunkel, und*	dark, and
[a:] as in Tom	*Ha:s, bra:che*	[aʊ] as in brow	*Haus, brauche*	[aʊ] as in brow	*Haus, brauchen*	house, to need
[aɪ] as in ice	*greische, nei*	[aɪ] as in ice	*greische, nei*	[aɪ] as in *ice*; [ɔɪ] as in toy	*kreischen, neu*	to scream, new
[ɔɪ] as in toy	*Oi, Hoi*	[ɔɪ] as in toy; [aɪ] as in *ice*	*Oi, Hei*	[aɪ] as in *ice*; [ɔɪ] as in toy	*Ei, Heu*	egg, hay

Data from Bräutigam 1934, Haag 1956, and Post 1992.

shows is that even in the most malleable area of language structure after vocabulary, namely vowels, modern Pennsylvania Dutch has not diverged all that much from its Palatine German origins.

To get a more precise sense of the extent to which Pennsylvania Dutch resembles Palatine German, it is instructive to compare it to a sample of speech produced by a male Palatine German speaker from the village of Gimmeldingen west of Mannheim.[23]

Rural Palatine German
(speaker born in 1893 or 1894, interviewed in 1956)

Also, wie mer aus der Schul waarn, wie ich aus der Schul waar, do waar's Allererschte, da hot mer mol Vadder e neii Sens kaaft. Da hot mer laerne maehe. Un wie's so waar, net, maehe, do hot mer als in der Bodem neighackt, un do hot mer herumstudiert, bis mer's faerdich gebrocht hot. Am Heumache, do is noh schlecht gange. Wie emol des Omet mache kumme is schpeeder, na, do hot mer schun besser maehe kenne. Do hot mer nimmi so viel in der Bodem ghackt, do hot mer der Boge schun besser haus ghadd.

Pennsylvania Dutch translation[24]

Well, wie mir aus der Schul waare, wie ich aus der Schul waar, noh s'erscht Ding, noh hot mol der Daed mer en neii Sens (ge)kaaft. Do hot mer glannt maehe. Un wie's waar, gel, fer maehe, noh hot mer als in der

Bodde neighackt, un noh hot mer als widder browiert, bis mer's recht
grigt hot. An Hoimache-Zeit, noh is's schlecht gange. Wie mol die Zeit
kumme is fer's Omet mache schpeeder, noh hot mer schunt besser maehe
kenne. Mer hot nimmi so viel in der Bodde ghackt, mer hot's noh besser
duhe kenne.

*Well, when we got out of school, when I got out of school, the first thing,
Father bought me a new scythe. Then you learned to mow. And as it was
with mowing [for the first time], you would chop into the ground, and then
you would try over and over again until you got it right. At hay making
time, it went poorly. When it was time to make the second cutting later,
then you could mow better. You didn't chop so much into the ground anymore, you could do it better.*

Overall, there are numerous similarities in every respect, phonologically, morphologically, syntactically, and lexically, yet no two clauses are
identical. In other words, Pennsylvania Dutch is not a Palatine German
dialect that has been transplanted to America with some English loanwords added. Rather, it is a language that, structurally and lexically, resembles several dialects from a relatively compact region of Germany
without being identical to any one of them. Pennsylvania Dutch and
Palatine German are at least as different from one another as, say, Norwegian is from Swedish.

We have documentary evidence of Pennsylvania Dutch going back to
around 1800, which is quite early in the history of the language. Relatively speaking, two to two and a half centuries is not that long a span of
time in the history of human languages, so it is unremarkable that the
differences between older and contemporary varieties of Pennsylvania
Dutch are not so great as to prevent a modern speaker from understanding earlier forms of the language. Like all living languages, Pennsylvania Dutch has evolved, especially in its vocabulary, but no more or less
quickly than languages of other speech communities.[25]

Before comparing an early nineteenth-century sample of Pennsylvania Dutch to its equivalent in today's language, it would be useful for
modern English–speaking readers to consider a representation of colloquial Pennsylvania English from the same period. This text is drawn
from an 1808 English-language textbook for German Pennsylvanians

authored by Christian Becker, a schoolmaster in the rural Dutch Country.[26] Becker's book contains a chapter titled "Familiar Dialogues" presented in English and translated into standard German (more precisely, Pennsylvania High German). Below is the text of "The 5th Dialogue: Of Eating and Drinking in a Cook-shop, (an Ordinary)."[27] Only the capitalization of nouns and punctuation have been altered to follow modern orthographic norms; the rest of the dialog is unchanged.

"Good morning."

"Welcome, sir."

"Can I have some good victuals here?"

"Yes, sir, as any where in the United States. There is good beef, good mutton, good veal and pork, boiled and roasted."

"Let me have some veal."

"How much?"

"A quarter dollar's worth / (half a crown's worth)."

"Boy, show the gentleman a room."

"Pray, sir, walk up, I will send it you immediately."

"Bring me a napkin, a knife and fork, sallat, and some cheese."

"Presently, sir."

"Drawer, bring a tankard of good drink, and a half pint of wine."

"Yes, sir, will you have it warmed?"

"Yes, warm it a little."

"What is to pay? / (What am I to pay?)"

"Half a dollar."

"How can that be?"

"Yes, sir, there is so much indeed: dinner a quarter of a dollar, wine eighteen cents and a half, and beer six cents."

"It is very right, there is your money."

"Sir, I thank you."[28]

Elsewhere in his textbook Becker gives extensive information on how to pronounce English, which shows that the differences between the speech of his time and present-day American English involve mainly vowels. This suggests that the accent of speakers of early nineteenth-century Pennsylvania English would strike contemporary American ears as somewhat different but probably no more dramatically so than if the speaker were from, say, somewhere in Britain. Lexically, there are several words that are either no longer used or are used differently, such as *victuals, drawer, pray, walk up,* and *tankard.* And certain expressions are also archaic today, for example, *I will send it you* and *What is to pay?* Overall, though, the conversation, in its context, is completely comprehensible to modern American English speakers. Such is the impression that hearing Pennsylvania Dutch from two centuries ago would likely have on contemporary speakers of the language.[29]

The earliest extant examples of written Pennsylvania Dutch date to about the same time that Christian Becker was active as a teacher and textbook author in rural Pennsylvania, the beginning of the nineteenth century. Comparing them with their equivalents in modern varieties of the language, some lexical differences appear but very few phonological, morphological, or syntactic ones, much as is the case when comparing the Becker dialog to modern American English. Below are the first two lines from a humorous item written by a Pennsylvania Dutch man claiming to have lost a horse. It appeared in the German-language *Nordwestliche Post* (Northwestern Post) from Sunbury, PA, on January 1, 1819.[30] Below it is a modern rendering of the same excerpt, along with standard German and English translations. Differences between the older and contemporary Pennsylvania Dutch versions are underlined in the latter. The spelling of the original text is exactly as it appeared in 1819. The contemporary version follows the modern Buffington-Barba-Beam orthographic system.[31]

Earlier Pennsylvania Dutch (1819)
"Wu is mai schwarzer Gaul?"
Weggeloffa oder gestohla oder durchganga, mai großer schwarzer Gaul, ungefähr 14 oder 15 Hand und 6 oder 7 Zoll hoch. Er hot führ schwarza Beh, zwee hinna un zwee vorna, un is ganz über schwarz, hot aber Paar weißa Blacka uf'm Buckel g'hat wie die Haut weggeriebe war, aber ich hab sie geschmiert, nau sin sie wieder all schwarz.

Modern Pennsylvania Dutch
"Wu is mei schwatzer Gaul?"
Weckgloffe oder gschtohle oder <u>fattgschprunge</u>, mei grosser schwatzer Gaul, <u>ebaut</u> 14 oder 15 Hand und 6 oder 7 Zoll hoch. Er hot vier schwatz<u>i</u>

Bee, zwee hinne un zwee vanne, un is gans iwwer schwatz, hot awwer [en] paar weissi Blacke uff em Buckel g'hatt wu die Haut weckgriwwe war, awer ich hab sie gschmiert, nau sin sie widder all schwatz.

Standard German
"Wo ist mein schwarzes Pferd?"

Weggelaufen oder gestohlen oder durchgegangen, mein großes schwarzes Pferd, ungefähr 14 oder 15 Handbreit und 6 oder 7 Zoll hoch. Er hat vier schwarze Beine, zwei hinten und zwei vorne, und ist überall schwarz, hat aber ein paar weiße Flecken auf dem Rücken gehabt, wo die Haut weggerieben war, aber ich habe sie geschmiert, nun sind sie wieder alle schwarz.

"Where is my black horse?"

Walked off, stolen, or run away, my large black horse, about 14 or 15 hands and 6 or 7 inches high. He has four black legs, two in the back and two in the front, and is black all over, but had a few white spots on his back where the skin was rubbed off, but I smeared them again and now they are all black again.

Some details of earlier Pennsylvania Dutch in texts are difficult to interpret because writers were often inconsistent in their spelling practices, following either German or English or both. This is especially tricky with phonology, since Pennsylvania Dutch speakers who were literate in standard German often wrote the German equivalents of Pennsylvania Dutch words that would have been pronounced differently from German. Such is the case, for example, with the words *Gaul*, 'horse' and *Haut*, 'skin'. In the contemporary language, what used to be a diphthong (rhyming with English *ow*) is now pronounced with a long vowel that rhymes with English *ah*. When writing these words, however, many speakers will still write *Gaul* and *Haut*. In the text above there is no way to determine which vowel the writer would have used in speech. There are, however, two other possible phonological differences: (a) the loss of he vowel in most verb participle prefixes, for example, *gestohla > gschtohle*, 'stolen'; and (b) the lowering of all short vowels preceding an [r] to a short [a] and the dropping of the [r], as in *vorna > vanne*, 'in front'. Since these words already contain non-German spellings (*gelaufen* and *vorne*

Early Pennsylvania Dutch text,
Nordwestliche Post, January 1, 1819.

Wu is mai schwarzer Gaul?

[Uf Ersuchen eingerückt.]

Weggeloffa oder gestohla oder durchganga,
mai großer schwarzer Gaul, ungefähr 14 oder
15 Hand und 6 oder 7 Zoll hoch — er hot führ
schwarza Beh, zwee hinna un zwee vorna, un
is ganz über schwarz, hot aber Paar weißa
Blacka uf'm Buckel g'hat wie die Haut weggeriebe war, aber ich hab sie geschmiert, nau sin
sie wieder all schwarz — er geht den Trott, un
den Kander, un den Paß, un manchmol aach
den Schritt, un wann er den Schritt geht, so
thut er den ena Fuß noch'm annera ufheba—er
hot zwee Ohra uf'm Kopp, die ennanner gleich
sin; ehns is aber schwärzer wie's anner; er
hot zwee Aaga, ehns ist aber rausgeschlaga un
das anner is uf der ehna Seit vom Kopp, un
wann du uf die anner Seit gehst, so kann er
dich nit sehna; er hot'n langa Schwanz, der
hinna nimmer hankt, ich hab ihn aber vor paar
Taga abg'schnitta un nau is er nimmi so lang
wie er war; er is ringerum beschlaga, aber
seine Hinnereisa sin abganga un hot nau nim-
ma noch Eisa vorna; er is nit gar alt, un
wann er laaft oder springt, dann geht sei Kopp
vorna naus un sei Schwanz kommt hinna noch,
aber wann er sich umdreht und bos is, dann
kommt sei Schwanz des erst. Wer den Gaul
zurück bringt soll. 5 Thaler bezahla, und wer
den Dieb mitbringt soll noch beseids 20 Thaler
bezahla mi noch nit froga.

Stauuken Fonderländer, Esq.

are the cognate words in standard German), it is quite possible that the
graphic representations reflect phonetic reality.

Morphologically, there is just one small difference between the original text excerpt and its modern equivalent: the ending on plural adjectives such as *schwarza*, 'black (pl.)', and *weißa*, 'white (pl.)', is now [i]
rather than a schwa. In terms of syntax, there are no differences between
earlier and contemporary Pennsylvania Dutch with respect to this short
text. The remaining three differences are, not surprisingly, lexical. Two
words, *durchganga*, 'ran off', and *wie*, 'how, like, as', have been replaced
with two native (Palatine German–derived) synonyms: *fattgschprunge*,

'ran away', and *wu*, 'where'. Both older words, however, still exist in modern Pennsylvania Dutch, albeit with different meanings or usages.[32] The third word, *ungefähr*, 'about, approximately; by chance', has been replaced with the English-derived loanword *ebaut*, though again here, *ungfaehr* still exists. In the modern language, its meaning is now limited to 'by chance'.

The impression that both the original text of nearly two hundred years ago and its modern equivalent leave is that of a language that is very close to its Palatine German origins, which is consistent with the comparison of Pennsylvania Dutch and the German dialects from Mannheim and Gimmeldingen above. Also, Pennsylvania Dutch is as distinct from standard written German as the dialects of the Palatinate are, phonologically, morphologically, and especially lexically. However, syntactically, there are no major differences between this brief text and its standard German equivalent, which is what is found across the European German dialectal landscape. To be sure, there are a number of ways in which the syntax of German dialects operates differently than the standard written variety, but most dialect-standard variation is at the levels of sounds and words.

Many standard German speakers, however, perceive the differences between dialects and the standard to be more extensive. More specifically, oral varieties overall, including dialects and Pennsylvania Dutch, are believed to be structurally "simpler" than the written standard German language, a view that is consistent with the widespread negative stereotypes of dialects when compared to written standard languages. While that is true in some instances, it is not in others; that is, certain dialectal structures are often just as complex as their standard counterparts, in some cases even more so. Even where the loss of certain structures in dialects has occurred, that loss is typically compensated by the development of new structures that take on the communicative functions that used to be performed by older structures. In general, language change does not lead to communicative impoverishment; that is, it does not hinder speakers from being able to communicate their ideas effectively.

One area where Pennsylvania Dutch is superficially simpler than German has to do with case, a tool used to mark the grammatical and semantic functions of nouns. Standard German has four cases with full nouns: Nominative for grammatical subjects, Accusative for direct objects, Dative for indirect objects, and Genitive to express possession.[33] The oldest varieties of Pennsylvania Dutch had three cases for nouns, Nominative, Accusative, and Dative; the Genitive had already been lost in Palatine German prior to the eighteenth century, its functions being taken over by the Dative. In the nineteenth century the Accusative in Pennsylvania Dutch was largely merged with the Nominative to form a Common case,[34] and then, in the twentieth century, the Dative case was also lost, though only in certain varieties spoken by Old Order Amish and Old Order Mennonite sectarians. Below are examples reflecting the three stages of case loss in Pennsylvania Dutch based on a sample sentence meaning 'The woman gave the children this rake', with its equivalent in German for comparison.

earliest PD:	Die Fraa$_{NOM}$	hot de Kinner$_{DAT}$	den Reche$_{ACC}$ gewwe
19th-c. PD:	Die Fraa$_{COM}$	hot de Kinner$_{DAT}$	daer (do) Reche$_{COM}$ gewwe
20th-c. PD:	Die Fraa$_{COM}$	hot die Kinner$_{COM}$	daer (do) Reche$_{COM}$ gewwe
German:	Die Frau$_{NOM}$	hat den Kindern$_{DAT}$	diesen Rechen$_{ACC}$ gegeben
	the woman	*has the children*	*this rake given*

Although the case system for full nouns in modern Pennsylvania Dutch is simpler than in its antecedents, and also in comparison to standard German, the language has not lost any of its expressive power. That is, Pennsylvania Dutch has been able to "afford" the loss of case markings on full nouns because speakers are still able to distinguish among subjects and direct and indirect objects. This is achieved partly through word order (the typical order of nouns in a Pennsylvania Dutch sentence is subject > indirect object > direct object), through verb inflections (subjects agree with conjugated verbs), and through real-world knowledge of the situation to which a sentence refers. Pennsylvania Dutch, like German, allows for nouns other than subjects to be placed in the first position of a sentence, for purposes of emphasis, without creating ambiguity.

20th-c. PD:	Die Kinner$_{COM}$	hot die Fraa$_{COM}$	daer (do) Reche$_{COM}$ gewwe
	the children	*has the woman*	*this (here) rake given*
20th-c. PD:	Daer (do) Reche$_{COM}$	hot die Fraa$_{COM}$	die Kinner$_{COM}$ gewwe
	this (here) rake	*has the woman*	*the children given*

The first modified sentence above means 'It was the children that the woman gave that rake to'; the second means 'That rake is what the woman gave to the children'. Even though objects (indirect in the first and direct in the second) occupy the first position of the sentence, where subjects often reside, there is no risk of misunderstanding who gave what to whom, even with the complete loss of case markings on the definite articles, since agreement between the subject (*die Fraa*) and the third-person singular verb (*hot*, 'has') rules out *die Kinner* from being interpreted as the subject in the first sentence. And in the second sentence, the real-world knowledge that a rake may not give a woman to children assures comprehensibility. Thus a superficial impoverishment on the part of Pennsylvania Dutch (and many European German dialects) relative to standard German with regard to the case of nouns in no way adversely affects the ability of speakers to get their meanings across.[35]

In other respects, Pennsylvania Dutch grammar is actually more complex than standard German. Modern Pennsylvania Dutch, like English, regularly distinguishes between simple and progressive tense forms, for example *Ich schwetz Deitsch*, 'I speak Pennsylvania Dutch', versus *Ich bin an Deitsch schwetze*, 'I am speaking Pennsylvania Dutch'. The tense system of German makes no such regular grammatical distinction between simple and progressive forms, meaning that German speakers do not automatically distinguish between actions that are not ongoing or continuous versus those that are, so the German equivalent for both these sentences is *Ich spreche Deutsch*. The simple/progressive distinction carries through all Pennsylvania Dutch verb forms, as shown below.

Ich schwetz Deitsch	*I speak PA Dutch*
Ich bin an Deitsch schwetze	*I am speaking PA Dutch*
Ich hab (als) Deitsch gschwetzt	*I spoke (used to speak) PA Dutch*
Ich waar an Deitsch schwetze	*I was speaking PA Dutch*
Ich zeel / figger Deitsch schwetze	*I will speak PA Dutch*
Ich zeel / figger an Deitsch schwetze sei	*I will be speaking PA Dutch*

These progressive tense forms in Pennsylvania Dutch derive from a Palatine German construction *am*, 'at the', + verb infinitive, which is still widespread in many German dialects, but no European German dialect has expanded the progressive tense to apply automatically to all verbal expressions in the way that Pennsylvania Dutch has. This development in Pennsylvania Dutch is therefore an example of complexification of its grammar that is not found in European German varieties. Further, the likely explanation for why this change has occurred, which is most observable in modern sectarian varieties of Pennsylvania Dutch, is the semantic influence of English, whose verbal system is, in this respect, more complex than that of German. Thus, contact with English, rather than "weakening" Pennsylvania Dutch by making it more different from German, as is sometimes assumed, has actually enriched its expressive capacity.

One final point of contrast between Pennsylvania Dutch and German that illustrates the inherent grammatical complexity of the former language has to do with word order. Pennsylvania Dutch, like its European German relatives, both the standard and regional varieties, and unlike English, places the conjugated verb in different positions in main and subordinate clauses. In main clauses, the verb occupies the second clause slot, while in subordinate clauses it is placed at or near the end.

PD:	Ich will gehe	*I want to go*
G:	Ich will gehen	
PD:	Ich hab gehe welle	*I wanted to go*
G:	Ich wollte gehen[36]	
PD:	Ich will gehe schwimme	*I want to go swimming*
G:	Ich will schwimmen gehen	
PD:	Du weescht, . . .	*You know . . .*
G:	Du weißt, . . .	
PD:	. . . as ich gehe will	*. . . that I want to go*
G:	. . . dass ich gehen will	
PD:	. . . as ich gehe will schwimme	*. . . that I want to go swimming*
G:	. . . dass ich schimmen gehen will	
PD:	. . . as ich gehe hab welle schwimme	*. . . that I wanted to go swimming*
G:	. . . dass ich schwimmen gehen wollte	
	/ . . . dass ich habe schwimmen gehen wollen	

The multiple verbs that can build up at the end of clauses in German and Pennsylvania Dutch, especially in subordinate clauses, form what are known as *verb clusters*. The rules underlying verb cluster formation in Pennsylvania Dutch are at least as complex as those in European German, if not more so, and are utterly impervious to influence from English, again underscoring both the inherent richness of Pennsylvania Dutch grammar relative to German and English as well as its overall autonomy from those two languages.[37]

The fundamentally complex, well-ordered, and in many respects German (dialectal) character of Pennsylvania Dutch is at odds with appraisals of the language made by speakers of standard German going back to the very birth of the language in the eighteenth century. The earliest fairly extensive description of Pennsylvania Dutch and its speakers is from a two-volume work by a European German physician, botanist, and zoologist named Johann David Schöpf (1752–1800). Schöpf came to America in 1777 to serve as the chief surgeon for a regiment of Hessian troops. After the Revolution, in 1783 and 1784 he undertook a journey from the Mid-Atlantic states south to Spanish Florida and from there to the Bahamas, making extensive notes on the flora, fauna, landscape, and people he encountered. After returning to Europe in 1784, he produced in 1788 *Reisen durch einige der mittleren und südlichen vereinigten nordamerikanischen Staaten nach Ostflorida und den Bahamainseln*, parts of which appeared in English translation in 1911 under the (more succinct) title *Travels in the Confederation (1783–1784)*.

In the first volume of his book, Schöpf dedicates five pages to the language situation of his "German countrymen" (*deutsche Landesleute*) in Pennsylvania, beginning, "The language used by our German countrymen [in Pennsylvania] is a pitifully broken mishmash of English and German with regard to words as well as their combination. Adults who come over from Germany partially forget their mother tongue as they attempt, unsuccessfully, to learn a new one. Those born here almost never learn their mother tongue properly and purely."[38] In addition to characterizing the German spoken in Pennsylvania as a "broken mishmash of English and German," Schöpf, later in his account, uses the expression "bastard gibberish" (*Bastard-Kauderwelsch*) to describe what he heard.[39] This is a stereotype of Pennsylvania Dutch that has endured right down to the present.

Essentially all early descriptions of Pennsylvania Dutch, from the popular to the scholarly, make mention of the influence of English on it, usually in negative terms that suggest an unnatural linguistic pairing. To cite one example, in an 1869 reprint of what is reputed to be the earliest poem written in Pennsylvania Dutch, the scholar who introduces the poem describes the language in which it was written as a "mongrel dialect."[40] Somewhat more soberly, the first scholarly treatise on Pennsylvania Dutch, which was written by Samuel Stehman Haldeman in 1872, is titled *Pennsylvania Dutch: A Dialect of South German with an Infusion of English*. Most treatments of Pennsylvania Dutch overstate the role English has played on the development of the language. In the following section I clarify just what the "infusion of English" in the language consists of and consider also the implications of contact between Pennsylvania Dutch and English in the other direction.

Pennsylvania Dutch in Contact with English

In the same way that all living languages change, all languages also show the effects of contact with other languages. Every human society is inevitably influenced to some degree, directly or indirectly, by groups of people who live, think, and speak differently than they do. The effects of human contact are everywhere, in the spread of tangible items such as foods and technology, as well as in the exchange of ideas and values, including those that are imported and exported with religions and political systems. It stands to reason, then, that the influence of different groups on one another should be reflected in what (and how) they speak. To be sure, a greater degree of "language mixing" is expected among people who come into direct contact with outsiders, such as immigrants, than in societies that are more sedentary and isolated. Taking the example of the United States, the world's largest country of immigration, all varieties of languages spoken by non-English-speaking arrivals from abroad, and in many cases their US-born descendants, show some influence from the majority language, English. In his classic work on language in the United States, for example, H. L. Mencken discusses how English has affected the immigrant varieties of no less than twenty-eight languages spoken in this country, from Arabic to Yiddish.[41]

The influence of English on immigrant languages, as on Pennsylvania

Dutch, is usually viewed negatively, especially by speakers in the countries of origin. In contemporary America, for example, heritage varieties of Spanish, when compared to what is spoken in Spain and Latin American countries, are often derided as "Spanglish." Hybridity disturbs people more when it comes to language with other cultural products. Like hybrid flowers or automobiles, "fusion" music and cuisine are often highly valued, but "fused" languages are disdained as the products of "linguistic miscegenation."[42] Language contact, unlike culinary, musical, or technological contact, often suggests intimate contact across ethnic or racial lines, a troubling notion for many people.

The effects of language contact can be found in all areas of structure—phonology, morphology, syntax, and vocabulary—but by far the most susceptible of these to change is vocabulary. Most people's speech habits, for psycho-developmental reasons, are largely in place by the onset of puberty, but there are no limitations on the ability to acquire new words or to alter the meaning or use of older ones. Given the inherent malleability of vocabulary, *lexical borrowing*, the incorporation of words from one language into another, is the most common form of language contact. English, a member of the Germanic family, is an excellent example of a language that has been strongly affected by the borrowing of words from non-Germanic languages, especially Latin and French. To illustrate this, the previous sentence is repeated below, with elements of non-Germanic stock underlined.

English, a <u>member</u> of the <u>Germanic family</u>, is an <u>excellent example</u> of a <u>language</u> that has been strongly <u>affect</u>ed by the borrowing of words from <u>non</u>-<u>Germanic sources</u>, <u>especially</u> <u>Latin</u> and <u>French</u>.

Compare the modern Pennsylvania Dutch version of the short text, "Where is my black horse?" discussed above. All English-derived elements are underlined.

"Wu is mei schwatzer Gaul?"
Weckgloffe oder gschtohle oder fattgschprunge, mei grosser schwatzer Gaul, <u>ebaut</u> 14 oder 15 <u>Hand</u> und 6 oder 7 Zoll hoch. Er hot vier schwatzi Bee, zwee hinne un zwee vanne, un is <u>gans iwwer</u> schwatz, hot awwer [en] paar weissi Blacke uff em Buckel g'hatt wu die Haut weckgriwwe war, awer ich hab sie gschmiert, nau sin sie widder all schwatz.

This text contains just three instances in which influence from English is identifiable, only one of which is an outright borrowing, namely *ebaut*, 'about'. The other two are examples of a *loan shift* and a *calque* (or *loan translation*), individual words or idioms that are patterned on the meaning of parallel words or phrases from English but using only native vocabulary.[43] *Hand*, 'hand', in this instance represents an expansion or "shift" of the original meaning of the word to match the English sense of *hand* as a unit of measurement of the height of horses. *Gans iwwer* is a calque, or word-for-word translation, of the English adverbial expression *all over* (*gans*, 'all, completely', + *iwwer*, 'over, above').[44]

Few language purists would dispute the appropriateness of borrowing words for new or imported objects or ideas. It would be difficult in English, for example, to find native Germanic equivalents for words like *bamboo*, *banana*, or *bar mitzvah*. Likewise, the motivation is clear for Pennsylvania Dutch speakers to draw on English for words like *Beesballe*, 'baseball', *Boggi*, 'buggy', and *Boi*, 'pie' (in addition to *Bamboo*, *Banana*, and *Bar Mitzvah*). Rather, critics' hackles are raised when borrowed words appear to displace older, native equivalents. Recall here the comments of Johann David Schöpf, who chastised German immigrants to Pennsylvania for "partially forget[ting] their mother tongue as they attempt, unsuccessfully, to learn a new one." A closer look at the effects of lexical borrowing reveals the opposite to be true. When speakers incorporate new words into their vocabulary, be they neologisms in their native language or foreign borrowings, older vocabulary items are typically not displaced.

Again, consider the examples of English influence in the contemporary Pennsylvania Dutch text above. As I noted in the previous section, the modern Pennsylvania Dutch word *ebaut* has indeed supplanted the older *ungfaehr*, which originally meant not only 'about' or 'approximately', but also 'by chance'. Today, *ungfaehr* means only 'by chance'. Instead of displacing an older, native lexical item, borrowing *ebaut* from English has enriched the vocabulary of Pennsylvania Dutch by increasing its size (by one word) and by simultaneously narrowing the semantics of the older word, that is, rendering that word less polysemous. The loan translation *gans iwwer* is yet another example of this kind of lexical efficiency or economy. In earliest Pennsylvania Dutch, 'all over' was likely expressed by either *iwwerall* or *iwweraalich* (cf. Ger. *überall*), which also meant 'everywhere, every which way'. This is the sense of *iwwerall/iwweraalich* in modern Pennsylvania Dutch.

The efficiency of lexical borrowing as a process of linguistic enrichment is illustrated by another example from Pennsylvania Dutch. The image below is of a coaster advertising Old Reading Beer, which was produced in the heart of the Dutch Country for a sizeable Pennsylvania Dutch–speaking customer base. The quote at the top of the coaster, *Die Fraa waert die Hosse* (adapted to follow modern Pennsylvania Dutch orthography), is a loan translation of the American English idiom *The wife wears the pants*. The verb *waert*, 'wears', is itself a borrowing from English: *waere* is the infinitive verbal form meaning 'to wear'. Critics of language mixing such as Schöpf would deride such borrowings, arguing that since there was an older, Palatine German–derived word in Pennsylvania Dutch that meant 'to wear', *draage*, borrowing the English verb is unnecessary and can only be interpreted as a symptom of language decay. In fact, no lexical loss has occurred. Pennsylvania Dutch *draage*, as its standard German equivalent *tragen*, originally meant both 'to wear' and 'to carry'. *Draage* is still used in Pennsylvania Dutch, but only with the latter meaning. Thus, where the Pennsylvania Dutch lexicon in earlier times had one word with two meanings, it now has two words with one meaning each. Here again, language contact, properly viewed, is an enriching process. And the structural integrity of Pennsylvania Dutch remains unaffected by lexical borrowing from English: the new verb *waere* is adapted to the native phonology and morphology of the language, that is, it is pronounced and conjugated according to Palatine German–inherited patterns.

In a discussion of the English influence on Pennsylvania Dutch vocabulary, it is fair to ask just how many Pennsylvania Dutch words are of English origin. Precise numbers are impossible to come by, since it is not possible to calculate the total number of words in any language, not just Pennsylvania Dutch. But analyzing the proportion of native to borrowed words in samples of some reasonable length gives a general sense. Below are simple percentages of loan vocabulary in four modern samples of Pennsylvania Dutch, two written and two oral. The two written texts were produced by speakers of Amish background and were selected in part because the genres and topics differ considerably. The first deals with religion, so fewer English loans would be expected, while

Coaster advertising Old Reading Beer.

the second is a story narrating silly mishaps in a largely non-Amish context. The religious text is from a collection of short Bible stories written for Amish children, from which eight stories were selected to get a sample of some length.[45] The second, humorous story was written by an anonymous Amish person ("Bruder Henner," 'Brother Hank') about an unfortunate excursion to Walmart.[46]

The two oral samples similarly deal with different content. The first, produced by a nonsectarian Pennsylvania Dutch woman, focuses on community traditions, including healing arts. In the second oral sample, the speaker, a young Amish man, discusses a practice that is indigenously American, the production of maple syrup.[47] Since it happens that mainly nouns, verbs, and adjectives (*content words*) are borrowed from one language into another, only words in these categories are tallied. Adverbs, prepositions, conjunctions, numbers, articles, possessives, and pronouns, which are overwhelmingly native (i.e., of Palatine German origin), are all omitted. The results are in the table below.

Overall, in each sample, nouns are borrowed more frequently than verbs, and adjectives are borrowed the least frequently. The number of loanwords in the Bible stories is the lowest of all four samples, with the total of English-derived nouns, verbs, and adjectives adding up to 11%. In the Walmart story and the free conversation about community traditions, borrowed vocabulary accounts for 18% of nouns, verbs, and adjectives. Not surprisingly, the description of the production of maple syrup has the highest percentage of loan vocabulary: more than half the nouns, for example, are English derived. But most of these borrowed nouns are themselves non-Germanic words in English, for example, *evaporator*, *filters*, *impurities*, *season*, *syrup*, and *thermometer*. The same is true for their counterparts in standard German; of these six nouns, for example, only one has a native equivalent in German: the word for 'impurities', *Unreinheiten*. The remaining German nouns are all of Romance origin

Table 1.2 Raw numbers and percentages of nouns, verbs, and adjectives borrowed from English in four samples of modern Pennsylvania Dutch, two written (W) and two oral (O)

	Nouns	Verbs	Adjectives	Totals
Bible stories (W)	17/114 = 15%	6/98 = 6%	4/45 = 9%	27/257 = 11%
Walmart story (W)	18/74 = 24%	13/89 = 15%	7/43 = 16%	38/206 = 18%
Traditions (O)	46/181 = 25%	11/108 = 10%	2/46 = 4%	59/335 = 18%*
Making syrup (O)	49/86 = 57%	21/64 = 33%	10/41 = 24%	80/191 = 42%

* Speaker MOE 092, born in 1897, uses eight nouns that are no longer common in sectarian Pennsylvania Dutch: *Achding*, 'care, attention', *Braut*, 'bride', *Breidicham*, 'bridegroom', *Geig*, 'violin', *Hallichkeit*, 'happiness', *Schleier*, 'veil', *Volkfescht*, 'folk festival', and *Walse*, 'waltzes'. Four of these nouns refer to entities that do not figure in Amish or Old Order Mennonite life. Musical instruments and dancing are avoided (hence no violins or waltzes), many sectarians do not attend fairs or festivals, and Amish and Mennonite brides do not wear special veils. However, speaker MOE 092 also uses one English loan, *wire*, that has a productive native equivalent in sectarian Pennsylvania Dutch, *Droht*. All native and borrowed verbs and adjectives in the sample from MOE 092 are consistent with modern sectarian norms. Adjusting the percentages of loan vocabulary in this sample to match sectarian usage yields 29% borrowed nouns and 19% borrowed nouns, verbs, and adjectives overall.

and in fact cognate with their Pennsylvania Dutch equivalents: *Evaporator*, *Filter*, *Saison*, and *Sirup*.

This suggests that the tendency for Pennsylvania Dutch to borrow vocabulary, especially nouns, is not substantially different than it is for European German. Even after two and a half centuries, the Pennsylvania Dutch lexicon is still strongly Palatine German. Keeping in mind that the statistics above are based on only a subset of Pennsylvania Dutch vocabulary, namely nouns, verbs, and adjectives, the total percentage of non-German words in speech samples that deal with subject matter that is not heavily English based, including words from other classes, such as adverbs, prepositions, etc., is between 10% and 15%.[48] If this estimate is compared with the situation in English, where about two-thirds to three-quarters of its vocabulary is of non-Germanic stock, the "foreign element" in Pennsylvania Dutch is rather modest.

Looking at the core vocabulary of Pennsylvania Dutch, the Palatine German character of the language is even clearer. Historical linguists often use lists of basic concepts called *Swadesh lists* to determine whether or how closely languages are related to one another.[49] Examples of words from a 207-item Swadesh list include pronouns (*I, you, he,* etc.), human and animal features (*hair, eye, bone,* etc.), actions and events (*eat, drink, flow,* etc.), and other terms that deal with fundamental aspects of human experience. Since such core vocabulary items are of high frequency in any language, they are less likely to be borrowed. Not surprisingly, very few of the Pennsylvania Dutch words for the 207 concepts on the Swadesh list used for Germanic languages are English derived, only five (2.4%), in fact: *Rewwer*, 'river', *Leek*, 'lake', *Schmook*, 'smoke', *floode*, 'to float', and *flowe*, 'to flow'. Interestingly, the first two words, *Rewwer* and *Leek*, which in English itself are loanwords from French, have also been borrowed into many other German-American varieties. Although the progenitors of the Pennsylvania Dutch would surely have had words for these bodies of water in their native German dialects, since the rivers and lakes they would have encountered in the New World would already have been named and designated as such in English, it is not surprising that in Pennsylvania Dutch the English words came to displace the older native ones.

More puzzling are the remaining three loanwords *Schmook*, *floode*, and *flowe*, for which an obvious motivation for borrowing is lacking. For an additional ten concepts on the Swadesh list, Palatine German– and

English-derived words coexist, and in every case there is a clear reason the English terms have been borrowed, including for the purpose of disambiguation, as the *draage/waere* example above showed. For example, the native Palatine German word for 'sky' was *Himmel*, which also meant 'heaven'. Out of a concern to make clear the difference between these two very distinct realms, Pennsylvania Dutch speakers reserve *Himmel* exclusively for 'heaven', while referring to the sky as either *Luft*, 'air', or the English-derived *Skei*.

Another example of a borrowing into Pennsylvania Dutch from English with a clear motivation is the word *bikahs*, 'because'. Pennsylvania Dutch, like European German varieties, employs multiple words or phrases to express causation, depending on the context. For example, when the reason something has occurred is familiar to both interlocutors in a conversation or is simply expressed in a neutral way, Pennsylvania Dutch speakers use *weil* (*as*). In such clauses, the conjugated verb appears at the end. If the content of the *because*-clause contains newer or more emphatically expressed information, then speakers prefer *bikahs*. The verb in such clauses is then in the second position, rather than at the end. Examples are below.

Mir sin net datt niwwer gange, <u>weil as</u> sie uns gheese ghadde hen$_{verb}$, mir sin gange, <u>bikahs</u> mir hen$_{verb}$ sie surprise welle.

We didn't go over there because they invited us, we went because we wanted to surprise them.

Since *bikahs* introduces Pennsylvania Dutch clauses in which the verb appears early, as in English, some observers have been tempted to assume that borrowing *bikahs* is altering the basic word order patterns of Pennsylvania Dutch. This is not the case. Going back several centuries, all varieties of European German have had two different clause types, one with the verb at the end (dependent clauses) and the other with the verb in the second position (main clauses). Dependent clause word order is used for expressions made with a neutral tone, while main clauses contain newer, more foregrounded information. In earlier Pennsylvania Dutch, *weil* introduced both main and dependent clauses, as it still does in colloquial spoken German in Europe today. The borrowing of *bikahs*—which did not displace the older, Palatine-derived *weil*—thus represents another instance of the economy of lexical borrowing into Pennsylvania Dutch whereby the overall size of the Pennsylvania Dutch vocabulary has increased (both *weil* and *bikahs* are now part of Pennsylvania Dutch) as the range of meaning or usage of an older word (*weil*) has been narrowed.[50]

Aside from vocabulary, has the basic Palatine German structure of Pennsylvania Dutch been in any way altered by contact with English? The answer is, very little. In each of the three main areas of core linguistic structure, dealing with sounds and their combination (phonology), word formation and modification (morphology), and phrases and sentences (syntax), influence from English is minimal.

Looking first at Pennsylvania Dutch phonology, there is only one example of a sound that has been borrowed from English, namely the "American" retroflex /r/.[51] In the Pennsylvania Dutch varieties spoken by people in and from Lancaster County, PA, the American English /r/ has replaced the native Palatine German /r/, which was produced by a single tap of the tip of the tongue. This older /r/ is still used in other varieties of Pennsylvania Dutch, especially in the Midwest, where most Pennsylvania Dutch speakers currently live.[52] But even in the Lancaster County variety, the *distribution* of /r/ in different places in a word remains the same as it always was, which is different from when /r/'s are pronounced in the English spoken in Pennsylvania and most of the rest of the United States. Pennsylvania Dutch, like most European German varieties, as well as many British and a few American English dialects, is "r-less," that is, an /r/ is pronounced as an *uh*-like vowel ("dropped") unless it occurs at the beginning of a word or syllable. For example, the Pennsylvania Dutch adjective *besser*, 'better', is pronounced "bessa". But if an ending is added to this word, as in the phrase *besseri Eppel*, 'better apples', the /r/ is pronounced. The influence of English phonology in the matter of /r/ is therefore limited: a single sound is borrowed, but its distribution across Pennsylvania Dutch words still follows native Palatine German patterns. In general, most loanwords from English obey the rules of Pennsylvania Dutch phonology, as the r-less pronunciation of borrowed words such as *Lawyer* ("law-yuh") and *schuur*, 'sure' ("shoo-uh"), shows.

The autonomy of Pennsylvania Dutch phonology relative to English is further underscored by the existence of certain sounds and sound combinations that are not found in the latter language. For example, Pennsylvania Dutch has two sounds that are lacking in English, namely the front and back consonant sounds in *Buch*, 'book' (as in the German family name *Bach*), and *Bicher* (which resembles the first sound in the word *human*). Another phonological difference is that Pennsylvania Dutch allows for the pronunciation of /t/ and /s/ together at the beginning of words, as in *Zeit*, 'time', and *zu*, 'to'. This combination is not native to English, hence the tendency for English speakers to pronounce words such as *tsetse fly* and *tsunami* as "teetsee" (or "seetsee") and "sunami".

Pennsylvania Dutch morphology and syntax show essentially no influence from English. Nouns and verbs, for example, including borrowed vocabulary, are formed and inflected according to native patterns. Looking at nouns first, the integrity of Pennsylvania Dutch word-formation patterns inherited from Palatine German is nicely illustrated in the process of compounding, that is, the formation of complex nouns and adjectives out of shorter words. Unlike in English, when two nouns or a noun and an adjective are put together in Pennsylvania Dutch to form a compound, the first noun often appears in a plural form. In English, by contrast, the first noun must be singular, even when a plural would make more sense, as with *bookstore* and *toothbrush* (i.e., not *books-store* or *teeth-brush*). Examples of Pennsylvania Dutch compound nouns with plural first elements are given below. These examples were selected because they are actually calques from English. The compounds' meanings are patterned after English equivalents, but their actual formation follows a native Palatine German / Pennsylvania Dutch rule.

Bicherschdoor
bookstore (lit. 'books-store')

Redderschduhl
wheelchair (lit. 'wheels-chair')

Eppelsaes
apple sauce (lit. 'apples sauce')

This rule allowing plural nouns as first elements in compounds extends to adjectives, too, as in the following example:

meednarrisch
girl-crazy (lit. 'girls-crazy')

The independence of Pennsylvania Dutch morphology from English can be observed with verbs also, including those derived from English. Take, for instance, the verb *tietsche*, 'to teach (secular subject matter)'.[53] In the present tense, this verb is conjugated like native verbs: *ich* (I) *tietsch*, *du* (you) *tietschst*, *er/sie* (he/she) *tietscht*, *mir* (we) *tietsche*, *dir* (you pl.) *tietschet*, *sie* (they) *tietsche*. And the past participle is *getietscht*, not **taught* or **getaught*, which obeys a rule inherited from German according to which borrowed verbs may not be inflected irregularly (as *teach* is in English).[54]

Turning to syntax, fundamentally German-like (and un-English-like) structures are preserved in Pennsylvania Dutch. For example, as mentioned above in the discussion about *weil* (*as*) and *bikahs*, in main and dependent clauses in Pennsylvania Dutch, as in German, the placement of the conjugated verb differs. In main clauses, it is the second sentence element, but in dependent clauses it appears at the end. Further, unlike English, uninflected verb forms in Pennsylvania Dutch, namely infinitives and participles, appear after a direct object, rather than before it.[55] Examples are below, with word-for-word glosses immediately underneath the Pennsylvania Dutch sentences.

Ich hab sie gekennt.
I have them known
I knew them.

Hoscht du gwisst, as ich sie gekennt hab?
have you known that I them known have
Did you know that I knew (was acquainted with) them?

Another difference between Pennsylvania Dutch and English with respect to word order has to do specifically with main clauses. Pennsylvania Dutch, like German but unlike English, requires that no word or phrase may intervene between the first element in the clause, such as a subject, object, or adverbial expression, and the conjugated verb in the second position. This is known as the *verb-second rule*. For example, the English sentence *I hardly knew them* would be rendered as *Ich hab sie haerdly gekennt* and not **Ich haerdly hab sie gekennt*.

Apart from basic word order, there is some influence from English discernible in two areas of modern Pennsylvania Dutch grammar: future tense (e.g., *I will go*) and progressive aspect (e.g., *I am going*). Earlier Pennsylvania Dutch, as Palatine German, had two basic tenses: one for expressions of past time and one that covered both present and future time. This is different from English, which has a distinct future tense separate from the present, expressed by the auxiliaries *be going to* and *will* (and *shall* in British English). Modern Pennsylvania Dutch has "promoted" two verbs of counting / calculation, *zeele* and *figgere*, to the status of future auxiliaries. Verb forms are underlined.

Ich ess en Schtick Kuche alli Daag.
I eat a piece of cake every day.

Ich zeel / figger noch en Schtick Kuche esse, wann du nix drum gebscht.
I will eat another piece of cake, if you don't mind.

A second instance of possibly contact-induced change in Pennsylvania Dutch syntax has to do with the Palatine German–derived construction, *am* (lit. 'at the') + infinitive, which corresponds to the English progressive, as in *We are reading* (versus *We read*). The use of the *am* + infinitive construction was originally more restricted than it is in English. In contemporary Pennsylvania Dutch, the frequency of this construction has now expanded to essentially match its distribution in English, yielding expressions that are not documented in older forms of the language. Examples are given below with the relevant verb forms underlined.

Er grigt sei Septic Tank ausgebutzt ee Mol 's Yaahr.
He gets his septic tank cleaned out once a year.

Er is sei Septic Tank am (an) ausgebutzt griege heit.
He is getting his septic tank cleaned out today.

In both these changes affecting the verbal system of Pennsylvania Dutch, the development of a new future auxiliary verb and the expansion of the progressive aspect, the catalyst for change is semantic (meaning based). That is, these changes do not involve the importation of novel grammatical structures into the language from English, rather they facilitate the intertranslatability of the two languages. Especially to-day, when many Pennsylvania Dutch speakers use both languages inten-sively (e.g., in work settings in which Pennsylvania Dutch and English speakers mingle), the need to switch back and forth quickly and easily between both languages is increased.

The semantic influence of English on Pennsylvania Dutch, as ex-emplified especially by the loan shifts and calques discussed earlier as well as the changes to the verbal system, comports nicely with the folk linguistic intuition of many Pennsylvania Dutch speakers themselves. When asked to reflect on how their language differs from German, many will say, *Du musscht Englisch denke un Deitsch schwetze*, 'You have to think [in] English and speak Dutch/German'. But as I have shown above, Pennsylvania Dutch, contrary to the opinions of observers such as Jo-hann David Schöpf, is anything but a "mishmash of English and Ger-man." Such stereotypes are ironic coming from European Germans since standard German itself has long been enriched by contact with other languages, especially French, Latin, and Greek, just as English and all other European languages have.

In more recent times, especially in the Federal Republic of Germany, English borrowings into German, with the advance of American-led globalization, have been a source of concern for many observers. Pur-ists decry the "invasion" of English lexical items such as *shoppen* and *downloaden* into their language via business, technology, and popular culture. The battle cries heard in contemporary Germany against "Den-glish" (Ger. *Denglisch*, from *Deutsch + Englisch*)[56] echo complaints about Pennsylvania Dutch two and a half centuries ago. In both cases, though, puristic fears are misplaced. Both Pennsylvania Dutch and German, whose speakers have extensive commercial and cultural ties to outsiders, show the effects of language contact, but only in very limited ways. The core phonological, morphological, and syntactic structures of both lan-guages preserve an overwhelmingly Germanic character. And although the vocabulary of each language does indeed include "foreign elements," the actual number of such words is quite modest, and these borrowings rarely displace older, native words. Language contact, in Pennsylvania Dutch and all other languages, is a process of linguistic enrichment.

Having explored the influence of English on Pennsylvania Dutch, I will consider what impact Pennsylvania Dutch has had on the English spoken in Pennsylvania. One the most salient stereotypes outsiders have had of the verbal behavior of Pennsylvania Dutch people has related not to their heritage language itself but to their English. As early as 1868 there is evidence of the stereotyping of Pennsylvania Dutch people as speaking English in a distinctive way. Consider the following poem from that year, which appeared in the *Guardian*, a Reformed Church periodical for Pennsylvania youth founded by the Rev. Henry Harbaugh (1817–1867), whose significance for the history of Pennsylvania Dutch chapter 4 will explore in depth. The poem is titled "The Pensilwan'yah Inglish"; its author is listed only as "Templeton."

> I don't want to go no furder,
>> Fur to hear *Erratums* sung,
> Then to my most sweetest Mother
>> Pensilwan'yah Inglish Tung.
>
> It's a fashun kep a-goin',
>> Fur to call them Dutchmens fools;
> And to say, jist their Talk's owin',
>> 'Cause it's never larned in schools.
>
> Sure this is a poorty story,
>> When we know that good Queen Bess,
> Gettin' from her grave up hoary,
>> Wouldn't know our Inglish mess.
>
> Some, who are well edekated,
>> Ever say "Noo-ral-i-gy;"
> Others, right smart kultevated,
>> Speak of Roy-al-*i*-ty!
>
> "Readin'" "'Macqua" and "Phildelfy;"
>> Wildern*iss* and "Jimson-Weed;"
> Valentine is turn'd to "Felty,"
>> And "pertaturs" run to seed.
>
> Flowers now stand in our "win*ders*,"
>> While our heads on "pil*lars*" lie;
> Nor is there a thing that hinders,
>> To build our "*pe*titions" high.

Larn'd men write "Feb-*u*-ary;"
  Jist as many—"Wed-*ens*-day;"
"Breth*ern*," say the wise and wary—
  "Gosp*ill*," tidy preachers say.

Mary now is always "Mollie"—
  All will wear their baby-names:
"Livie," "Sally," "Mattie," "Pollie"—
  Have we now for shaded dames!

Very few prepare to pucker
  Up their lips for double U;
What a mixtur' when they utter
  Them words—"Vine" and "Waterloo!"

"May" and "Might" fare little better:
  "Shall" and "Will," "Have," "Had," and "Should;"
And by missing but one letter,
  "Would" becomes the same as "Could!"

People now do their own "*settin'*"—
  They don't need no *clucks* for that—
And are constantly forgetting,
  That a man don't crouch down flat.

Hear them callin': "Fath-*ah!*" "Moth-*ah!*"
  *Ah*in' every word, of course:—
Sweetest "Sis-*tah!*" Sweetest "Broth-*ah!*"
  Oh*ah* "Mist*ah!*"—And so forth.

Has the Yankee, Hoosier, Buckeye—
  E'en the Chivalry—so much
Room to pipe his quackin' duck-cry,
  O'er the "*Pensilwan'yah Dutch?*"[57]

  "The Pensilwan'yah Inglish" is a very early example of what has come
to be known as *Dutchified* or *Ferhoodled English* (< PD *verhuddelt*, 'con-

fused'), more technically as *Pennsylvania Dutch English*. Since the early twentieth century, with the advent of Pennsylvania Dutch–themed tourism, examples of what is purported to be Dutchified English, as in this 1868 poem, have found their way onto countless items marketed to visitors to the Dutch Country, including the postcard below. It is questionable whether many of the supposed examples of Dutchified English were ever actually produced by native speakers under natural circumstances or whether they were merely the inventions of imaginative marketers looking to exoticize the Pennsylvania Dutch, but, as with most stereotypes, there is some basis in reality for Dutchified English.[58]

While some of the examples of "Pensilwan'yah Inglish" above could be due to interference from a speaker's native Pennsylvania Dutch in her English, most are simply features of nonstandard regional American English that were or are still common in the speech of rural southeastern Pennsylvania. For example, the difficulty distinguishing between [v] and [w] in English, as in the words *Pensilwan'yah*, *vine*, and *Waterloo*, has been a real one for native speakers of Pennsylvania Dutch. The substitution of [d] for the <th> sound [θ] in *furder* is another possible example of phonetic interference from Pennsylvania Dutch. But forms such as *jist* (just), *larned* (learned), *poorty* (pretty), *gettin'* (getting), *edekated* (educated), *pertaturs* (potatoes), and the like, even though they may well have been produced by native speakers of Pennsylvania Dutch, are or once were widespread among rural Pennsylvania English speakers across ethnic lines. Some examples are even part of standard American English, such as the pronunciation of *February* as "Feb-u-ary".

In addition, Templeton, to enhance the comic effect of his poem, employed an orthographic phenomenon known as *eye dialect*, which is the use of nonstandard spellings of words that often follow pronunciations more closely than their standard counterparts—though they need not do so—and generally flag written speech as especially colloquial. Examples of eye dialectal spellings from the poem that likely do reflect real nonstandard pronunciations include *fur* (for), *kep* (kept), *owin'* (owing), and *'cause* (because). By contrast, eye dialectal spellings such as *Inglish* (English), *tung* (tongue), *fashun* (fashion), and *kultevated* (cultivated), serve only to exoticize the text without indicating any actual divergence in pronunciation from what would be considered prescriptively correct.

The first scholarly treatment of the English spoken by Pennsylvania

Vintage "Pennsylvania Dutch
Talk" postcard.

Dutch people appeared in 1935.[59] Its author, George G. Struble, was a
professor of German at Lebanon Valley College, which is located in a
traditionally heavily Pennsylvania Dutch–speaking area. Struble identified two major sources for dialectally distinctive elements in the speech
of ethnic Pennsylvania Dutch: Pennsylvania Dutch itself and colonial
speech, especially varieties of English brought to eighteenth-century
Pennsylvania by immigrants from the British Isles. Struble's research
was complemented by two other important publications from the
same era, the first being a short article by Eugene R. Page, a professor
of English at Central College (today, Central Penn College), also situated in close proximity to many Pennsylvania Dutch speakers.[60] Page

built on Struble's work by describing a social stratification in the use of Dutchified English, observing that its frequency appeared to correlate inversely with a speaker's level of formal education. Finally, J. William Frey, a Pennsylvania Dutch speaker from York County who wrote his doctoral dissertation on the language of his native community, added to the descriptions of Struble and Page, who had based their work on the speech in counties east of the Susquehanna River, by providing data on the English spoken in York County, located on the western periphery of the Dutch Country heartland.[61] In what follows I begin by considering only examples of English spoken by Pennsylvania Dutch people (and many of their neighbors) that may be traced directly or indirectly to Pennsylvania Dutch, in other words, truly "Dutchified" English.

Among the most salient examples provided by Struble, Page, and Frey of Dutchified English involve the direct transfer of features of pronunciation from Pennsylvania Dutch. The following six sound substitutions were among the most common features of a "Dutchy" accent in English:

- [v] ≈ [w]: In most varieties of Pennsylvania Dutch, these two English sounds correspond to a single sound that is intermediate to [v] and [w], namely [β]. This results in a confusion between [v] and [w] in Dutchified English. Examples: *veal*, *vinegar*, and *vines* would be pronounced like "weal", "winegar", and "wines"; likewise, the name *Howard* would be pronounced as "Hahverd".
- [tʃ] instead of [dʒ]: The "j" sound does not exist in Pennsylvania Dutch; thus *Jane* and *chain* would both be pronounced like "chain" in Dutchified English.
- [a] instead of [ʌ]: Pennsylvania Dutch lacks the open-midback unrounded vowel [ʌ] in words like *nothing*, *comfortable*, and *country*, which sound like "nahthing", "cahmfertable", and "cahntry" in Dutchified English.
- [n] instead of [ŋg]: The <ng> in words such as *finger*, *hungry*, and *English* is pronounced in Dutchified English as the <ng> in *singer*. The [ŋg] cluster does not exist in Pennsylvania Dutch.
- [s] instead of [z]: The Dutchified pronunciations of *zipper*, *Lizzie*, and *fuzz* would be "sipper", "Lissie," and "fuss". Pennsylvania Dutch lacks a [z] sound.

- [p, t, k] instead of [b, d, g] at the ends of words or syllables:
  English *rib*, *hid*, and *bag* would be pronounced like "rip", "hit",
  and "back". Pennsylvania Dutch and German share a rule of
  terminal devoicing (Ger. *Auslautverhärtung*) whereby voiced
  consonants, (sounds that are produced by the vibration of the
  vocal cords [vocal folds]), are rendered voiceless (whispered) at
  the ends of words or syllables.

In a later study of the languages of a Pennsylvania Dutch revivalist
sect based in Lebanon County known as the *Hoffmansleit* (Hoffmanites,
United Christians), Mary C. Kreider observed additional features of a
"Dutchy" accent in the English of her consultants:[62]

- [a] instead of [aʊ]; [o] instead of [ow]: English *power* and *lower*
  would be pronounced like "par" and "lore".
- [æ] instead of [aɪ]: The main vowel in the words *fire*, *desire*,
  inspired, *fight*, and *quite* would sound less like "eye" and more like
  the vowel in "badge".[63]
- [u] instead of [ju]: English *endure* would rhyme with "poor".
- [i] instead of [ɪ]: The short vowel in words like *given*, *women*,
  Timothy, and *bit* would be lengthened to more of an "ee" sound.
- [r] would be vocalized ("dropped") before consonants or at the
  end of a word or inserted in place of a final [a] sound: English
  morning would sound like "mahning" and *Hallelujah* would be
  pronounced "Hallelujar". (Compare the examples *Fathah*,
  Mothah, *Sistah*, and *Brothah* in the Templeton poem above, as
  well as *winders*, *pillars*, and also *pertaturs*.)

Another feature of pronunciation transferred from Pennsylvania
Dutch into Dutchified English has to do with what is called *falling
question intonation*.[64] It occurs with simple yes-no questions and what
J. William Frey calls "backward questions," questions that express as-
tonishment or disbelief. The pitch of the voice is raised on the capitalized syllables in the Dutchified questions below. The first two examples,
from Struble's article, are simple yes-no questions, while the latter two
are "backward question" reactions to the statement, *John has finally decided to leave his wife.*

Is your MOTHer home?
Haven't you FOUND it yet?

IS he gonna leave his wife?
IS he though?

In his 1937 article, Eugene Page adds that speakers with a "Berks County Accent" produced not only yes-no questions with the distinctive "rise-fall" intonation pattern but also simple declaratives. His example is of how a Dutchified speaker would spell the name *Smith* out loud differently from other English speakers. In non-Dutchified English, one would say "s-m-i-t-h", with each letter being uttered at the same rate and using an intonational curve that falls only when saying "h"; a Berks County Dutchman would say "s-m-I-t-h", making a rise on the letter "i" and inserting audible pauses both before and after the letter.[65]

Other examples of the direct influence of Pennsylvania Dutch on Dutchified English include a number of lexical borrowings, including the following: *blotz*, 'to bounce around' (< *blotze*); *dopp*, 'to walk clumsily' (< *dappe*); *elbedritsch*, 'imaginary creature'; *ferhoodle*, 'to jumble, botch' (< *verhuddle*); *gowl*, 'horse' (< *Gaul*); *hex*, 'witch' (< *Hex*); *hommie*, 'calf' (< *Hammi*); *hutzel*, 'dried-up fruit' (< *Hutzel*); *rutch*, 'to wriggle, squirm' (< *rutsche*); *schussel*, 'hasty, clumsy person' (< *Schussel*); *speck*, 'fat meat' (< *Schpeck*); *spritz*, 'to spray, sprinkle' (< *schpritze*); *strubbly*, 'unkempt' (< *schtruwwelich*); *toot*, 'small paper bag' (< *Tutt*); *wamus*, 'man's work jacket' (< *Wammes*); *wutz(ie)*, 'little pig' or call to pigs (< *Wutz[i]*). To these words one can add calqued words, that is, words translated but not directly borrowed from Pennsylvania Dutch into English: the question tag *ain't (not)?* (< *gell [net]?*); *all*, 'all gone' (< *all*); *dare*, 'be permitted to' (< *darrefe*); *jellybread*, 'bread with jelly spread on it' (< *Tschellibrot*); *make down*, 'to rain hard' (< *nunnermache*); the adverb *once*, connoting 'vague emphatic or limiting force' (< *mol*); *what for*, 'what kind of' (< *was fer*); *(it) wonder(s me)*, 'to be amazed at' (< *wunnere*); *wonderful*, 'very, awfully' (< *wunnerbaar*).[66]

Mary Kreider also notes the use of *for to* meaning '(in order) to' in the speech of her Lebanon County consultants, as in *He has a desire for to hear the Gospel* and *It is in his power for to take us*. This could well be an example of a syntactic transfer from Pennsylvania Dutch, which in earlier varieties used a *fer . . . zu* construction for what are known as infinitival complements.[67] Kreider quotes the following as the Pennsylvania Dutch equivalents for these two expressions: *Es luschdert ihn, fer es Evangelum zu heere*; *Es iss in seinre Macht, fer uns zu nemme.*[68] Two examples of this phenomenon occur in the "Pensilwan'yah Inglish" poem above: *fur to hear Erratums sung* and *fur to call them Dutchmens fools.* To be sure, the *for to* construction is amply documented in British and American dialect syntax, so it could be that *for to* in Dutchified English was derived from non-Dutchified Pennsylvania English and reinforced by the native Pennsylvania Dutch structure.

The tourist literature on "Ferhoodled English" abounds with examples of what is claimed to be common in the English of native speakers of Pennsylvania Dutch, some of which are more plausible than others. For example, those expressions that have direct parallels in Pennsylvania Dutch could well have been (or still be) produced by speakers under natural circumstances. However, one should be skeptical of allegedly Dutchified statements that cannot be translated back directly into Pennsylvania Dutch. The first quotation in the postcard shown above includes both more and less likely examples of real Dutchified English. *The pie is all* lines up directly with Pennsylvania Dutch *Der Boi is all*, but *the cake is yet* does not: in Pennsylvania Dutch one would say *s'is noch Kuche*, 'there's still cake', but not **der Kuche is noch*. The first three examples of supposedly Dutchified English below closely match their equivalent expressions in Pennsylvania Dutch, while the latter three do not:[69]

This is the first time since I'm here = Des is's erscht Mol zidder as ich do bin
It wouldn't suit just now = Es deet net suite graad nau
Don't let me keep you up = Loss mich dich net uffhalde

He climbed the fence over ≠ Er is iwwer die Fens gegraddelt (over the fence)
Today is my off ≠ Heit hawwich ab (I have off)
He will surely be here this after ≠ Er zellt ferschuur do sei denomiddaag (this afternoon)

A number of nonstandard or otherwise attention-getting words and phrases that are reliably documented in the English spoken by Pennsylvania Dutch people are not due to interference from their native language but are derived historically from the speech of their ancestors' English-monolingual neighbors. One particularly notable example is the verb *outen* in the expression *outen the light*. In Pennsylvania Dutch, the equivalent expression is *mach's Licht aus* (lit. 'make the light out', which itself is also attested in descriptions of Dutchified English). The verb *outen* is not found in British English dialects but was apparently an American innovation patterned after other verbs formed by adding the suffix *-en* to adjectives, such as *broaden, darken, harden, lighten, moisten,* and *widen*. Whether it was originally Pennsylvania Dutch speakers who coined *outen* or English-monolingual Pennsylvanians, the word is not modeled on anything in Pennsylvania Dutch.

One of the most popular publications dealing with the "quaintly amusing expressions [supposedly] heard among the Pennsylvania Dutch folks" is a pamphlet titled *Ferhoodled English,* which first appeared in 1964. In it are numerous examples of allegedly Dutchified English that are merely nonstandard English and not calques from Pennsylvania Dutch, including *et* (*ate*); *is* (*are*, as in *the beans is all*); *vittals*; *ain't*; *lay* (for *lie*, as in *lay on the ground*); *a body* (*somebody*); *went* (*gone*); *don't* (*doesn't*); *got to* (*have to*), *boughten* (*bought*); *bodderation*; *critter*; numerous gerund verb forms that end in *-in'* rather than *-ing* (e.g., *talkin', restin', eatin'*; also *somethin'*); the adjectival suffix *-like* (as in *ugly-like*); *befuddled*; *quick* (*quickly*); *where at* (*where*); *school-teach*; *them* (*they*, as in *them that works*).[70]

Today, Dutchified English is largely a thing of the past, mainly because the nonsectarian Pennsylvania Dutch–speaking population has declined so dramatically. Among Amish and Mennonite sectarians, Dutchified English has also receded—but for a different reason. Many contemporary Old Order speakers of Pennsylvania Dutch place a premium on speaking English "properly," that is, in accordance with prescriptive norms, and their parochial schools, which are conducted entirely in English, play a major role in rooting out Dutchisms that might serve to stigmatize their speech.[71] However, the survival of some features of Dutchified English that have spread into general usage among Pennsylvanians of diverse ethnic backgrounds (e.g., *spritz the flowers, the cake is all,* etc.) points up the fact that Pennsylvania Dutch has left an indelible imprint on regional American English . . . yet.

Who Speaks Pennsylvania Dutch?

For many people, the terms *Pennsylvania Dutch* and *Amish* are synonymous and for good reason: most of today's speakers of Pennsylvania Dutch are members of Old Order Amish churches and their children, who together currently number nearly three hundred thousand across North America.[72] The only other sizable group of active speakers are the closely related horse and buggy–driving Old Order Mennonites (ca. thirty thousand in the United States and Canada). Among the Old Orders, who are the most numerous and visible among several conservative Anabaptist sects in North America, Pennsylvania Dutch is the main language for oral communication within their communities, but all speakers are bilingual in English as well.[73] Because of the high growth rate and geographic mobility among Old Order sectarians, Pennsylvania Dutch is now spoken by more people outside of Pennsylvania than within it.[74] Old Order communities (i.e., concentrations of Pennsylvania Dutch speakers) are to be found today in thirty-one US states and in the Canadian province of Ontario.[75]

Given the high visibility of Old Order Amish and Mennonite speakers of Pennsylvania Dutch today (the "Plain people"), it is surprising for many to learn that for most of the history of the language, Anabaptist sectarians constituted just a very small percentage of the total Pennsylvania Dutch–speaking population. Of the nearly 81,000 German-speaking immigrants to colonial Pennsylvania, only about 5% were members of Anabaptist and Pietist sects (*sect people,* Ger. *Sektenleute*). The historian Aaron Spencer Fogleman estimates that between 3,077 and 5,550 sectarians were among the 80,969 immigrants documented by Marianne Wokeck, or between 3.8% and 6.9% of the total number of arrivals.[76] What were the religious affiliations of the remaining approximately 95% of the Pennsylvania Dutch founding population? The great majority were members of Lutheran and German Reformed congregations. Into the twentieth century, these nonsectarians (also known as the *church people* [Ger. *Kirchenleute*] and later the *Fancy* or *Gay Dutch*) still made up the bulk of Pennsylvania Dutch speakers. The Old Order Amish, for example, numbered only about 5,300 in 1900.[77]

Over the course of the twentieth century, Pennsylvania Dutch receded rapidly among the nonsectarians, while the Old Order population has doubled nearly every twenty years. Today, there are virtually no nonsectarian native speakers of Pennsylvania Dutch younger than seventy years of age, and many of these speakers do not use Pennsylvania Dutch actively with their spouses, children, or grandchildren. Nearly all Fancy Dutch live in rural southeastern and south-central Pennsylvania, that is, in or near the heart of the traditional Dutch Country, with especially large concentrations in Lehigh, Berks, Lebanon, and Lancaster Counties.[78] Among the sectarians, in contrast, most of whom live outside of Pennsylvania in communities as far flung as Idaho, Maine, and Florida, maintenance of Pennsylvania Dutch, along with distinctive dress and selective use of technology, has become a tangible symbol of their group identity. Old Order sectarians are likely to become the sole speakers of Pennsylvania Dutch by the middle of the twenty-first century.

Why is it, then, that nonsectarian ethnic Pennsylvania Dutch born after 1930 or 1940 no longer maintained their heritage language nearly two hundred years (about six generations) after their ancestors immigrated from Europe? And why did the Old Order sectarians not also become English monolinguals at the same time? Since the eighteenth century, the social and demographic factors that correlate with maintenance of Pennsylvania Dutch have been largely the same for both nonsectarians and sectarians. The typical active speaker of Pennsylvania Dutch is a person who lives in a rural area with a high concentration of other Pennsylvania Dutch speakers and who is engaged in occupations such as farming, carpentry, or other trades connected to rural life. Endogamy, that is, marrying within the Pennsylvania Dutch–speaking community, is another crucial factor in determining whether the language is actively maintained in the home and community. Maintenance of Pennsylvania Dutch is thus closely linked to the limited geographic and social mobility of its speakers.

Whenever ethnic Pennsylvania Dutch men and women who acquired the language in childhood go on to pursue careers that take them out of the country, or when they marry non–Pennsylvania Dutch speakers, the shift from Pennsylvania Dutch to the exclusive use of English is typically swift. This is the situation of virtually all nonsectarian speakers living today, with the added fact that the areas of rural Pennsylvania where they live are now more connected—physically, economically, and culturally—to nearby towns and cities where use of English is the norm. Further, more people of non–Pennsylvania Dutch background have moved into the traditional Dutch heartland as part of a larger trend of exurbanization. The Old Order sectarians, by contrast, as a result of their rurally based, endogamous socioreligious lifestyle, have naturally maintained Pennsylvania Dutch (alongside English, it should be pointed out) without any special effort, in effect "by inertia."[79] Conversely, the relatively few people (approximately 15%) who are born into Old Order families but as adults choose not to join or remain in Old Order churches frequently, though not always, shift to using English predominantly or exclusively after leaving. So strong is the bond between actively speaking Pennsylvania Dutch and being affiliated with an Old Order community.

The loss of Pennsylvania Dutch among nonsectarians is mirrored in other minority language communities across the United States, which suggests that common external factors are at play here. Nearly all heritage languages in America that are not supported by fresh immigration from abroad can be considered endangered, that is, likely to disappear within the next generation or two. For example, varieties of French spoken in Louisiana and parts of New England, Spanish in northern New Mexico, and German in many areas of the Midwest, whose roots in these regions often go back a century or more, are essentially as moribund today as Pennsylvania Dutch is among nonsectarians. And among indigenous heritage languages, that is, Native American languages, the situation is nearly as grim: all are recognized to be endangered, and fully half of the approximately 150 still spoken today are estimated to lose their native speakers by the middle of this century.[80] This dramatic loss of linguistic diversity in the United States is part of a larger trend globally. Languages spoken by small, rural, minority populations, indigenous and immigrant, in Africa, the Americas, Asia, and Europe are threatened with extinction through the shift of younger community members to the languages spoken by larger populations, such as Spanish and Portuguese in South America, and Russian and Mandarin Chinese in Asia. When the rural isolation of smaller human populations becomes less common, as it has in the United States through urbanization, industrialization, and increased mobility, then minority languages disappear.[81]

Thus, the loss of Pennsylvania Dutch among nonsectarians is not a unique phenomenon, either across America or around the world. But how exceptional are the Old Order communities among whom Pennsylvania Dutch continues to thrive? Interestingly, there are parallels between these groups and other, similar populations in the United States. That is, there is a small number of minority languages whose speakers are not threatened by external pressures to assimilate to the majority language, English. Aside from Pennsylvania Dutch, there are six such languages, three of which are spoken by members of other conservative, socially isolated religious groups. Coincidentally, all three of these languages are, like Pennsylvania Dutch, part of the Germanic language family: Hutterite German, spoken by Hutterites, a communal Anabaptist group; Mennonite Low German, spoken by the most conservative descendants of Mennonites of northern European background who settled in the Russian Empire in the eighteenth century; and Yiddish, used among the Haredim, ultraorthodox Ashkenazic Jews, most of whom lived in Eastern Europe until the Shoah (Holocaust). The remaining three relatively healthy US minority languages are American Sign Language, used by members of the Deaf community in the United States and English-speaking Canada; Romani, the Indic language spoken by many Romani people ("Gypsies"); and Shelta, a language with roots in Hiberno-English, Irish, and Gaelic that is spoken by people known as the Irish Travelers. Although these last three languages are not associated with a religious identity, they do serve as important symbols of in-group identity, reinforced by a heritage of occasional stigmatization and even discrimination. While rurality is a supporting factor only among the Anabaptist languages (Pennsylvania Dutch, Hutterite German, and Mennonite Low German), endogamy strongly promotes the maintenance of all of these languages.

It is safe to say that the majority of people who identify themselves as ethnically Pennsylvania Dutch, including nonspeakers of the language, can trace most of their ancestors to German-speaking lands in Central Europe. Yet, apart from the most conservative Anabaptist sects (and even among them there was some exogamy), Pennsylvania Dutch–speaking society was never ethnically closed or entirely endogamous, meaning that there was intermarriage between Pennsylvania Dutch speakers of German and Swiss stock and members of other ethnic groups, many of whom assimilated to Pennsylvania Dutch. Further, there is historical evidence of nonethnic Pennsylvania Dutch learning the language through close contacts with native speakers short of intermarriage. Writing in

1950, Frederic Klees had this to say about ethnic diversity across Pennsylvania Dutch–speaking society.

> Dutch is spoken not only by the descendants of the original Germans but also by their fellow citizens and neighbors of English, Scotch-Irish, Welsh, and French Huguenot descent. An Italian immigrant in Reading apologized for his poor English with this explanation: "When I come to America I think I learn speak English. I get job digging ditch. I listen to what man working on one side of me say to man working on other side. Every little while I learn a word. 'Dunnerwetter,' he says; 'dunnerwetter,' I say. Ha, I thought, now I learn English; I real American. But no, I no learn English. I learn Pennsylvania Dutch!" Strangest of all is to hear the dialect from the lips of a Negro or gypsy. A few of the old Negro families who settled in the Dutch country shortly before or after the Civil War adopted the speech and customs of their Dutch neighbors a long time ago; while to the gypsies, many of whom came from the Rhineland, Dutch is as much their mother tongue as Romany.[82]

Klees's reference to "gypsies" is particularly interesting, since these people, more properly called Romani people or Romanies, were a part of Pennsylvania Dutch–speaking society from the very start, yet that fact has received very little recognition. Just as important is his mention of African-American speakers of Pennsylvania Dutch.

A review of Pennsylvania newspapers from the second half of the nineteenth century yields multiple accounts of blacks who knew Pennsylvania Dutch. After the Civil War, a number of African Americans migrated north into the Pennsylvania Dutch country. In the rural area where Berks and Lebanon Counties meet, blacks came into such close proximity with Pennsylvania Dutch speakers that many of them even adopted the language as their mother tongue. The following item, titled "German Colored Folk, a Commercial Traveler's Experience in Pennsylvania," appeared in the Washington, DC, *Morning Times* on October 10, 1898. It was reprinted from the *New York Sun*.

> Reading, Pa., Oct. 8—"One of the most unusual experiences I have ever had," said a commercial traveler, "occurred two days ago in Lebanon County. I met a number of colored men, women, and children who

spoke nothing but German. Before the day was around I met at least fifty colored people who spoke German. And when it came to speaking English they were not at all at their ease. I asked how this came about and was told that the colored people came, twenty, thirty and forty years ago, up from the South and settled among the quiet Pennsylvania German farmers of the Blue Mountain districts. The colored children grew up on the farms, where they worked and heard nothing but German spoken. They soon forgot nearly all the English they knew and now rarely speak anything but German. Their children go to English country schools in Winter, but as quickly as they are out of sight of their teacher they begin to talk the German dialect, and nothing else. I have been told that in recent years in Germany colored people speaking the language can be found in numbers, but they also speak English. These Pennsylvania German negroes of whom I speak use absolutely nothing but the German in their ordinary affairs of life. They are good farmers, live on Pennsylvania German cooking and have all the habits and customs of the Germans."

A second account of Pennsylvania Dutch–speaking blacks appeared a few years later, in 1901, under the title "German Negroes, a Curious Community in a Remote Region Revealed by a Murder." This story also appeared first in the *New York Sun*; it was reprinted in the July 30, 1901, issue of the *Topeka (KS) Daily Capital*:

The arrest of William F. Jones, a negro, in connection with the murder of John Edwards, a white man, in the western part of [Berks] county, developed the fact that the colored residents of Berks and Lebanon counties freely speak the Pennsylvania German language.

Jones speaks German fluently because he says he has been raised among the farmers who speak only the Pennsylvania German. He says that all his relatives and colored friends, who are quite black, use only German among themselves, but when they are away from home they can speak enough broken English to get along. Whites and blacks mingle freely. . . .

The German colored people can neither read nor write, as a general thing, and their vocabulary hardly embraces more than 300 words. Some cannot speak any English at all. This is particularly true among the black children. These people generally live in the wilds or in the woods and come in contact with few people. Strangers who are white and well-dressed are a curiosity. These blacks know very little of church or Sunday school. They work on farms and in the quarries, and are squatters, owning nothing. To hear a bunch of them in animated conversation, using only Pennsylvania Dutch, is an oddity.—Reading, Pa., telegram to the *New York Sun*.

A lack of documentation of black speakers of Pennsylvania Dutch after this report, aside from personal anecdotes, points to the fact that the descendants of these people assimilated to the English-speaking social majority in the twentieth century.

A second group of historical Pennsylvania Dutch speakers who were not of Germanic ethnicity were Romani people. Thanks to folklorist Henry W. Shoemaker (1880–1958), some information on the history of the Pennsylvania Dutch Romanies and their language is available.[83] In 1926 Shoemaker published a three-page article titled "The Language of Pennsylvania German Gypsies," which, despite its brevity, offers valuable insight into this important Pennsylvania Dutch–speaking subgroup.[84] Among one of the world's most misunderstood peoples, Romanies, who trace their ancestry to northwestern India, had lived in German-speaking Central Europe for centuries before large numbers of immigrants from the Rhineland and Switzerland came to Pennsylvania in the eighteenth century. The Romanies were part of this movement and settled in what was to become the Dutch Country of southeastern Pennsylvania. The Pennsylvania Dutch Romanies spoke both Pennsylvania Dutch and Romani, and they became known among other Pennsylvania Dutch speakers as *She-kener*, which is likely related to Pennsylvania Dutch word for 'Gypsy', *Zigeiner* (Ger. *Zigeuner*). By the 1920s, when Shoemaker wrote his article on the language of the She-kener, their number in Pennsylvania had dwindled to approximately three hundred. According to Shoemaker, the She-kener enjoyed good relations with other Pennsylvania Dutch, with whom they shared a common language.

Shoemaker concludes his article with a list of forty-four She-kener words he collected, most of which appear to be Pennsylvania Dutch, though some differ from known words and others are not attested at all in other Pennsylvania Dutch varieties. This suggests the existence at one time of a distinct She-kener subvariety of Pennsylvania Dutch. A sampling of Shoemaker's She-kener vocabulary is given below, preserving his orthography and giving the contemporary Pennsylvania Dutch equivalents. The eight examples are divided into two groups. The first four words are identical or nearly identical between She-kener and attested Pennsylvania Dutch; the remaining four are Pennsylvania Dutch–related but apparently unique to She-kener.

She-kener	Pennsylvania Dutch	English
Flend	Flint	'gun'
Haws	Haas	'rabbit'
Sal	Seel	'soul'
Shiflwoga	Schiffwaage	'Conestoga wagon'
Wekawdler	Aadler	'vulture'
< Weeg, 'road', + Aadler, 'vulture'		
Letterorsh	Schannschteebutzer	'chimney sweep'
< Ledder, 'leather', + Aarsch, 'rear end'		
Shekener-Bawm	Buche	'beech tree'
< She-kener, 'Gypsy', + Baam, 'tree'		
Hausleita	Graemer	'peddler(s?)'
< Haus, 'Haus', + Leit, 'people' (= fig. 'lice' in Palatine German)		

Henry W. Shoemaker's interest in little-known groups of people in Pennsylvania extended beyond Pennsylvania Dutch Romanies to include multiethnic "mountain people," whose speech he documented in a small book titled *Thirteen Hundred Old Time Words of British, Continental or Aboriginal Origins, Still or Recently in Use among the Pennsylvania Mountain People.*[85] Several dozen of the 1,300 words Shoemaker collected are of Pennsylvania Dutch origin, which suggests that some of the mountain people, although English speaking, were of Pennsylvania Dutch background. Examples of Pennsylvania Dutch–derived words used by Pennsylvania mountain people include the following:

PA Mountain English	Pennsylvania Dutch	English
baachie	batschich	'nasty tasting'
bush-nipple	Buschgnippel	'woodsman, hermit'
dudelsok	Dudelsack	'bagpipes'

harsh	Hasch	'deer'
lotta warrick	Lattwarrick	'apple butter'
nochtigal	Nachtigaal	'whippoorwill'
strubbly	schtruwwelich	'unkempt'

As was the case with the Pennsylvania Dutch spoken by Romani people, there are words in the speech of the mountain people that are clearly derived from Pennsylvania Dutch but attested nowhere else:

PA Mountain English	Pennsylvania Dutch	English
arsle	rutsche	'to sit unquietly'
< Aarsch, 'rear end'		
donsie	leichtkeppich	'light-headed'
< danse, 'to dance'		
stump-harsh	—	'moose'
< Schtamm, 'trunk, stem', + Harsh, 'deer'		
wassa-bull	—	'bittern'
< Wasser, 'water', + Bull, 'bull'		

A number of the mountain words deal with superstitions and pow-wowing associated with some Pennsylvania Dutch groups, including the following:

PA Mountain English	English
Black Book	'reputed seventh book of Moses'
bonnarings	'cabalistic stars and circles painted on barns'
< barn rings (?)	(i.e., hex signs)
disturber	'state of uneasiness and distress put on a person by a hechs' [PD *Hex*, 'witch']
good-man	'charm' (sold by Gypsies, usually the face of Christ cut out of paper; cf. PD *Schattebild*, 'shadow picture')
Heaven's letter	PD *Himmelsbrief*
hechs	'witch' (PD *Hex*)
hechsenhammer	cf. Black Book
overlooked	'bewitched, hexed'
< iwwergucke, 'to inspect'	

pow-wow	'muttering of cabbalistic words' (by a hex or would-be spell-binder)
spook	'ghost, apparition'

In Shoemaker's word list are also compounds containing the word *Dutch*, including:

PA Mountain English	English
Black Dutch	'dark Pennsylvania mountain people'
to talk like a Dutch uncle	'to express positive opinions'
Dutch fox	'grey fox'
Dutch splash dam	'splash dam opened by knocking out the key log'
≠ Yankee splash dam	'splash dam opened with gates'
Dutch crow	'fish crow'

What is interesting about the phrase *to talk like a Dutch uncle* is that the meaning is overall positive. In other varieties of English, a Dutch uncle is a negative concept, defined by *Merriam-Webster* as someone who "admonishes sternly and bluntly," which suggests that the mountain people had a generally good impression of the Pennsylvania Dutch. By contrast, three words in the list make reference to German (as distinct from Pennsylvania Dutch) ethnicity, two of which are clearly negative: *Hessian*, 'loud-mouthed overbearing person' (cf. PD *du dummer Hess*, 'you dumb Hessian'); and *Hog-Dutch*, 'High German' (cf. PD *Hoch-Deitsch*). As mentioned earlier, the relations between the Pennsylvania Dutch and other Americans of German background were often strained. The cultural gap between the Pennsylvania Dutch and the *Deitschlenner* was thus reflected in the speech of Pennsylvania's mountain people.[86]

THIS CHAPTER CONSIDERED some basic facts about Pennsylvania Dutch and its history. Although it is closely related to German, specifically the dialects of the Palatinate region, it is an autonomous language—structurally, lexically, and sociolinguistically—that arguably deserves its own branch on the family tree of Germanic languages. Owing mainly to the demographic situation of its speakers, however, most of whom have traditionally been rural dwellers of modest socioeconomic status—

including people from historically stigmatized ethnic groups, African Americans and Romanies—Pennsylvania Dutch has had something of an "image problem." Worldwide, languages whose speakers are not socially dominant typically do not enjoy popular esteem. Further, the relationship of Pennsylvania Dutch to German, both structurally and sociolinguistically (in diglossia), almost inevitably leads the former to be compared negatively to the latter. Added to this conundrum is the common stigmatization of "language mixing" generally, especially among people with knowledge of standard German. Even though the degree to which English has affected Pennsylvania Dutch is limited, including in the area of vocabulary, purists nevertheless regard the language as a peculiar and unnatural "mishmash."

Reacting to such criticisms, a lawyer by profession and Pennsylvania Dutch poet by avocation, Henry Lee Fisher (1822–1909), offered an early defense of his beloved native language in verse:

> Edhel Leut mache juscht'n G'schpass
> Fon Pennsylfanisch-Deutsch;
> Ich dhet's net meinde; "Ei warum?"
> Ei juscht for das, sie sin zu dumm—
> 'S isch juscht ihr Lappigkeit;
> Sie sage, 's isch f'rmixt, un lache;
> Ei so sin all die gute Sache.

> Es muss doch, g'wiss, 'n dummer Ochs sei,
> En grosser odder'n Kleener—
> Net so fiel wees—d'r Rahm fon zwee,
> So fon de allerbeschte Küh,
> Isch besser as fon eener;
> Gel, g'lernter Buch-wurm, du, do hinne,
> Kanscht nix'eso in Bücher fünne.

> Es isch ken Schprooch in dere Welt,
> Wie Pennsylfanisch-Deutsch;
> For alle Wort kummt fon'm Herz,
> Un's hot me'h Peffer, Salz un Querz'—
> F'r loss dich druf, es schneid;

Wan's Mädel em net will, f'rschtee,
Dan sagt's es *awful* Wörtli, NE.

Un's geht em besser fon d'r Zung
  As *English, don't you see?*
In *English* sage sie, *O! yes,*
Un ebmohl's sage sie, *I guess,*
  Un ebmohls *Yes sir-ree;*
Doch isch ken Wort das schteht in *Law,*
Wie's Pennsylfanisch-Deutsch Wort, Jah.

Some people just make fun
  Of Pennsylvania Dutch.
It doesn't bother me; "Why not?"
Why, just because they're so dumb,
  It's just their carelessness.
They say it's all mixed up, and laugh;
Why, that's how all good things are.

It would definitely have to be a dumb blockhead,
  Big or small,
Who doesn't know that the cream from two
Of the very best cows
  Is better than from one.
Hey, you educated bookworm back there,
You can't find anything like that in books.

There's no language in this world
  Like Pennsylvania Dutch.
For every word comes from the heart,
And it has more pepper, salt, and spices.
  You can count on it, it'll cut.
If a girl doesn't want you, you see,
Then she'll say that awful *little word, "Nee."*

And it rolls off the tongue better
  Than English, *don't you see?*

In English *they say,* "Oh, yes!"
And sometimes they say, "I guess,"
And sometimes "Yessiree."
But there's no word in the law
Like the Pennsylvania Dutch word, "Ja."[87]

In Fisher's view, Pennsylvania Dutch, like a blend of premium creams, is enriched by contact with English. And yet the two languages are distinct. Pennsylvania Dutch simply has a more honest "ring" to it than English; which is to say that the people who speak Pennsylvania Dutch use their mother tongue in a straight-talking manner different from the more roundabout (and perhaps less sincere) speech style of English speakers. Pennsylvania Dutch is a language that can cut to the chase, a language in which *ja* means 'yes' and *nee* means 'no', and it can also serve as the vehicle for an eloquent expression of a poet's sincere affection for his *Mudderschprooch*.

As the rest of this book will demonstrate, despite the enduring stigma attached to Pennsylvania Dutch by outsiders, the speakers of the language are having the last laugh (or quiet chuckle). Unlike nearly all other minority languages in the United States that are not supported by immigration from abroad, Pennsylvania Dutch, at least among the Old Order sectarians, is thriving. Amish and Mennonite speakers are doing an end run around the jokes about their mother tongue and its lack of official recognition, and they are preserving a vital part of the American cultural and linguistic mosaic. A closer look at the history of Pennsylvania Dutch begins in the next chapter, as I consider the genesis of the language in the eighteenth and early nineteenth centuries.

CHAPTER 2

Early History of Pennsylvania Dutch

May our children seek not only to acquire the German language,
but also the German spirit of years ago, a spirit of simplicity
and faithfulness, surrounded by industry and wealth.
—NEWSPAPER EDITORIAL, 1819

Where and When Did Pennsylvania Dutch Come to Be?

The year 1683 marks the symbolic beginning of the German presence in America with the establishment of the first German settlement in Pennsylvania, Germantown, now a part of Philadelphia. The settlers consisted of thirteen Quaker and Mennonite families from the city of Krefeld, which is located in central-western Germany, close to the border with the Netherlands. However, the cultural orientation of Germantown was very much directed toward the city of Philadelphia and not to the rural areas to the north and west of Philadelphia that are known today as the Pennsylvania Dutch Country. The geographic "cradle" of Pennsylvania Dutch was not in Germantown, Philadelphia, or any other town or city, but in the hinterlands of southeastern Pennsylvania.[1]

The next group of Germanic immigrants to Pennsylvania were ethnic Swiss Mennonites from the Palatinate who settled in 1710 between the Pequea Creek and the Conestoga River in what is today Lancaster County. Among the first settlers in this area was the family of Hans Herr, whose son Christian's house, built in 1719, is the oldest extant Germanic building in North America and also the oldest Mennonite meetinghouse on the continent.[2] Not long after the Swiss and Palatine Mennonites arrived in the Pequea/Conestoga area, in 1723 another group of Palatine Germans from Schoharie, NY, under the leadership of Conrad Weiser (1696–1760) founded a settlement along the Tulpehocken Creek in what is today the township of Heidelberg and the borough of Womelsdorf in western Berks County at the border with Lebanon County, north of Lancaster County.[3] Weiser and his fellow settlers were soon joined by many more German-speaking immigrants, again mainly Palatines, who arrived through the port of Philadelphia. These arrivals comprised approximately 90% of the early settlers of Berks County, which was formally created out of parts of Philadelphia, Chester, and Lancaster Counties in 1752.[4] Also noteworthy is that the first Amish community in America was established by 1740 in western Berks County along the Northkill Creek, which feeds into the Tulpehocken. The Northkill Amish community, which was the largest until the 1780s, played an important role in both the history of Amish settlement in America and the spread of Pennsylvania Dutch outside of Pennsylvania.

Overall, the historian Marianne Wokeck estimates that just under 81,000 German-speakers entered the port of Philadelphia between 1683 and 1775. Approximately 58,000 (two-thirds) immigrated before 1755, of whom the majority (ca. 35,000) arrived in just a five-year period, 1749–1754.[5] After 1755 German immigration to Pennsylvania declined dramatically up to the American Revolution, at which point immigration all but ceased, not to resume again until the nineteenth century. The period between 1750 and 1780 corresponds to roughly one generation, which was likely the critical era for the genesis of Pennsylvania Dutch. The children of German immigrants who were born in rural southeastern Pennsylvania in the mid-eighteenth century and who reached adulthood around the time of the Revolution were almost certainly the first speakers of nascent Pennsylvania Dutch. It is thus probable that by 1780 or so Pennsylvania Dutch, a language bearing a strong resemblance to dialects of the German Palatinate but not identical to any one of them, had come to be in something close to its modern form. Although there is no direct proof of this, there is strong indirect evidence, discussed later in this chapter, that supports the long-standing consensus among linguists that the Pennsylvania Dutch language existed at the latest by 1800.[6]

Returning to the question of where Pennsylvania Dutch emerged, on the basis of data from the first federal census in 1790, ethnic Germans comprised 38% of the population of Pennsylvania, or approximately 165,000 people. Of these 165,000, over one-half resided in the counties of Berks, Lancaster, Northampton, and York, where they accounted for 85.4%, 71.9%, 62.9%, and 48.7% of the total populations, respectively, most of the rest of whom were of English, Welsh, Scotch-Irish, Scottish, or Irish stock.[7] In 1812, the southwestern and heavily German portion of Northampton County became Lehigh County, and in 1813 the county of Lebanon was formed out of areas formerly belonging to Lancaster and Dauphin Counties. Today, six counties, Berks, Dauphin, Lancaster, Lebanon, Lehigh, and York, make up the Dutch Country in which the Pennsylvania Dutch language developed.

Who were the German settlers in the Dutch Country? The previous chapter established that Pennsylvania Dutch society has traditionally included two major subgroups, the *church people* or *nonsectarians*, mainly Lutherans and members of German Reformed churches, and the *sect people*, including Mennonites and Amish. Of the approximately 81,000 German-speaking immigrants to eighteenth-century Pennsylvania, the overwhelming majority consisted of nonsectarians. As mentioned in the previous chapter, Aaron Spencer Fogleman estimates that between 3,077 and 5,550 German-speaking sectarians, mostly Mennonites, came to the American colonies, or 3.8% and 6.9% of the total Pennsylvania Dutch founder population.[8] Fogleman's table breaking down the sectarian ("radical pietist") arrivals according to group is reproduced below.

The low number of sectarians among the earliest Pennsylvania Dutch, especially Amish, is striking in light of the modern situation of the language. Recall that the majority of active speakers of Pennsylvania Dutch today are members of Old Order Amish churches. It is surprising for observers to learn that the ancestors of the Amish comprised less than 0.5% of the Pennsylvania Dutch founder population.

Many accounts of the relations between the nonsectarian German-speaking majority and the sectarian minority in eighteenth-century Pennsylvania have presumed, according to historian Richard MacMas-

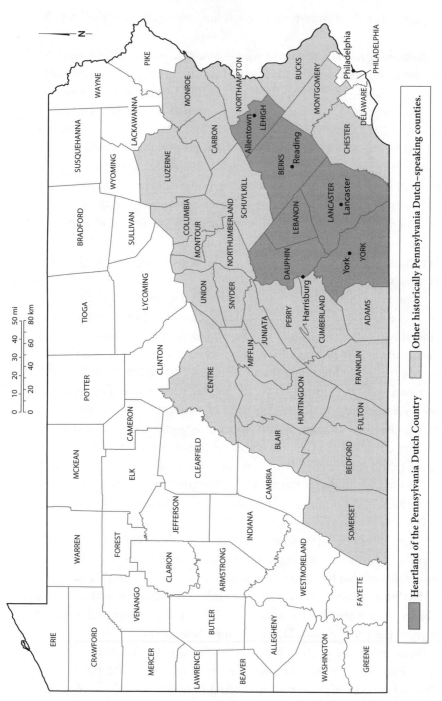

Pennsylvania counties in which Pennsylvania Dutch has been spoken historically.

Heartland of the Pennsylvania Dutch Country   Other historically Pennsylvania Dutch–speaking counties.

Table 2.1 German-speaking Radical Pietist (sectarian)
immigration into the thirteen colonies

Mennonites	1,536–4,200
Moravians	700–750
Amish	265–300
Dunkers	260–300
Schwenkfelders	206
Waldensians	110
Total	3,077–5,550

Fogleman 1995, 103.

ter, a significant distance between the two groups, what he calls an "isolationist interpretation" of early Pennsylvania history:

In the spirit of emphasizing differences, many who have written specifically about colonial Pennsylvania have assumed or argued that the German sectarians who settled there were quite isolated from the colony's social and political currents. They have often contrasted the "sects," or "meetinghouse people"—especially Dunkers, Mennonites, and sometimes Schwenkfelders—with the "church" Germans, mainly Lutheran and Reformed and sometimes Catholic. Their language sometimes implies a very high wall of separation between the meetinghouse people and the church Germans. One such overwrought interpretation in a recent college textbook[9] says that the sectarians were like " 'Protestant monks and nuns' with their quaint habits," while church Germans "dressed and, outside their homes, spoke as Americans." The church people, moreover, "entered politics" and "became merchants, and the numerous skilled craftsmen among them added much to Pennsylvania's prosperity. They rejected pacifism."[10]

With the exception of the Moravians, sectarians such as the Mennonites and Amish did not form distinct colonies in Pennsylvania but lived in communities in southeastern Pennsylvania in close proximity to Lutheran and Reformed Germans, as well as members of other ethnic groups. The Northkill Amish community, for example, was situated in the Tulpehocken region where Conrad Weiser's settlement was located. As MacMaster makes clear, the sectarians pursued livelihoods much like those of their nonsectarian and nonethnic German neighbors. The majority was involved with agriculture, and there is little evidence to suggest that their farming practices differed in any significant way from those of their fellow colonists. Aside from officeholding, innkeeping, ocean shipping, and military service, early Mennonites and other sectarians pursued the same occupations as their neighbors.[11]

Varieties of Pennsylvania Dutch spoken by sectarians and nonsectarians have always been completely mutually intelligible despite the fact that, beginning in the late eighteenth and early nineteenth centuries, when many sectarians moved west (and also north to Ontario), the two groups came to live apart from one another. If an Amish child from Kansas were to meet an elderly Dutch-speaking Lutheran from rural Berks County today, the two would have no difficulty communicating in their common mother tongue. That means that, early in the history of the language, relations among speakers across religious lines must have been close, especially among young people.

The most important agents of major change in any language are children and adolescents, who are able to learn new languages and restructure ones already acquired with greater facility than are adults. When considering German Pennsylvanian life in the eighteenth century, then, the function of schools in bringing children of diverse religious backgrounds together is especially significant.

> [E]ven in their churches and their schools—the very realms of life having more directly to do with nurture, worship, and the shaping of attitude and belief—Mennonites did not attempt nearly as much isolation as they might have. To organize and support elementary education for their children, Pennsylvania Germans, including Mennonites, worked through their churches. Yet they hardly ever tried to run schools along strictly denominational lines or to make them parochial in the modern sense. Mennonite school trustees, operating a school in or alongside their meetinghouse, might well hire a Reformed or Lutheran schoolmaster and gather pupils from both Mennonite and non-Mennonite homes. Or a Mennonite schoolmaster might teach as many children of church Germans as of Mennonites or other meetinghouse people.[12]

The relevance of schools to language development has less to do with formal instruction in language, which often does little to affect the naturally acquired habits of speech. Rather, schools are important in bringing children into close, informal verbal interaction with one another. When children learn and play together, both in school and outside of it, they grow up to talk like one another. In general, the striking similarity across varieties of Pennsylvania Dutch today—spoken by people whose ancestors have not been in contact with one another since the colonial period—strongly suggests that relations between church people and sect people in eighteenth-century Pennsylvania, especially children, were quite close.

The geographic cradle of the Pennsylvania Dutch language lies in what is known today as the Dutch Country of southeastern Pennsylvania. The facts of the settlement history of this region are not so neat as to identify a precise "ground zero" within the Dutch Country where Pennsylvania Dutch was born, but Berks County, located as it is in the heart of the region and originally the "Dutchiest" of the Dutch counties (85.4% of its inhabitants being of German extraction in 1790), occupies a place of prominence in the genesis of the language. Settlement history does, however, shed important light not just on the question generally where Pennsylvania Dutch was born, but also when.

As discussed earlier, most active speakers of Pennsylvania Dutch today are the descendants of what was originally one of the smallest religious subgroups to come to colonial Pennsylvania, the Amish. The Amish are also responsible for the fact that Pennsylvania Dutch is spoken by more people outside of the Commonwealth of Pennsylvania than within it: less than a quarter of the Amish in the United States and Canada live in Pennsylvania.[13] Most Amish live in midwestern states. Ohio and Indiana alone account for just over 40% of the total Amish population. Despite many external characteristics that connect the Amish to each other, especially the tenets and practice of their Christian faith, which includes maintenance of some form of German for worship, there is profound diversity that goes back to differing settlement and migration patterns in the eighteenth century.

Broadly speaking, today's Amish can be divided into two major groups: (1) those who are from Lancaster County, PA, or have close ties to coreligionists there; and (2) "Western" (midwestern) Amish, which includes nearly all Amish in the Midwest and other states, including settlements in New York and elsewhere. While relations between members of Lancaster-affiliated and midwestern communities are cordial, there is almost no intermarriage between the two, an expression of the fact that for most of the past two hundred years they have not lived in close proximity to one another. The roots of this separation go back to the second half of the eighteenth century. As mentioned earlier, the first Amish community in America, and the largest until the 1780s, was the Northkill settlement in Berks County. In the 1760s Amish began moving from Berks County south into Lancaster, establishing the first community there. Shortly thereafter, in the 1770s, Berks County Amish began moving westward, to Somerset County, PA. It was settlers from Somerset who in 1809 moved farther west to Holmes County, OH, which today is the nation's largest Amish settlement and the one to which most midwestern Amish can trace their roots.[14]

Thus, both major branches of the American Amish family tree, Lancaster and midwestern, have their origins in Berks County. With the establishment of the Lancaster and Somerset County settlements in the 1760s, 1770s, and 1780s, the divergence of the two groups that is so salient today began. The linguistic evidence from modern Lancaster and midwestern Amish varieties of Pennsylvania Dutch is crucial to date the genesis of the language. Despite nearly two and a half centuries of separation, the two varieties remain completely mutually intelligible, though with some interesting points of variation, especially lexical.[15] What this means is that, already in the second half of the eighteenth century, the immigrant dialects of German brought to Pennsylvania, especially Palatine, must have coalesced to yield the basis for the modern language. Given the separation between Lancaster Amish and their "western" cousins that set in at that early point, there is no other explanation for why the varieties they speak today are so uniform. The migration of Amish out of Berks County in the eighteenth century also marked the beginning of their separation from their historical Lutheran and Reformed neighbors, the Pennsylvania nonsectarians. Indeed, nonsectarian varieties of Pennsylvania Dutch also share the same basic grammatical structures and most of their vocabulary with forms of the language spoken by Amish sectarians, again, after almost two hundred and fifty years of no longer living close to each other.

The Amish were not the sole speakers of Pennsylvania Dutch to move westward. Into the nineteenth century, large numbers of nonsectarians did as well, but the language has survived only in sectarian communi-

ties. Nonsectarian Pennsylvania Dutch speakers never formed a large
enough critical mass in any given area outside of Pennsylvania to ensure the maintenance of their heritage language among their descendants.[16] Aside from the movement to western Pennsylvania and beyond,
there were other important migrations of Pennsylvania Dutch speakers,
north to Waterloo County, ON, and south into the Shenandoah Valley
of Virginia. The Ontario settlement, which consisted mainly of Mennonites, was part of a larger migration to Canada of Loyalist-minded
settlers from the new United States after the American Revolution. To
this day there are thousands of active speakers of Pennsylvania Dutch
in Ontario, virtually all of whom are members of Old Order Mennonite churches in the Kitchener-Waterloo area. Again, their Pennsylvania
Dutch, though distinctive, is entirely mutually intelligible with all other
varieties, including Lancaster and midwestern Amish dialects, varieties
spoken by other Old Order Mennonites in the United States, as well
as by nonsectarian Pennsylvania Dutch.[17] Migration from Pennsylvania
into Virginia (and West Virginia) began earlier in the eighteenth century
and extended somewhat later, relative to the movement to Ontario, but
the language is nearly gone there today, except among recent Amish migrants.[18]

"Do You Wish to Leave Your Children a Rich Inheritance? Then Teach Them German"

Crucial to understanding the development of Pennsylvania Dutch as a
distinct language in the late eighteenth and early nineteenth centuries
is an examination of the nascent culture in which the language was embedded. From the beginning, Pennsylvania Dutch culture was a fundamentally rural one. The earliest Pennsylvania Dutch perceived—and
asserted—themselves as different from their fellow Americans who
lived in cities and towns, where English rapidly became the dominant
language. Even Philadelphia was largely anglicized by 1800. A unique
language distinguished the Pennsylvania Dutch not only from their urban counterparts but also from their English-speaking neighbors in the
rural hinterlands, who were predominantly Quakers and other Anglo-
Americans, Scotch-Irish, and Irish. And although the Pennsylvania
Dutch spoke a vernacular language related to German and maintained

passive knowledge of a form of standard German, they felt little connection to contemporary European German speakers. To be sure, the
tumultuous experience of the Revolutionary era, which the Pennsylvania Dutch shared with members of other ethnic groups, went a long
way toward instilling in them a strongly American self-identity. But the
simple historical fact that immigration from German-speaking Europe
had dropped off dramatically after the mid-1750s was equally if not more
important in weakening the ties between the Pennsylvania Dutch and
their increasingly distant European cousins.

From the beginning, in the late eighteenth and early nineteenth
Writing of conditions in eighteenth-century Pennsylvania, Frederic
Klees characterizes the early Dutch Country as an "island of Rhenish
civilization in an English sea."[19] While it is true that much of what distinguished the culture of the early Pennsylvania Dutch from the ways of
their neighbors was inherited from Central Europe, including a Palatine
German–derived language, it is a mistake to think that the Pennsylvania
Dutch were eighteenth-century Rhinelanders living as a cultural isolate,
unchanging and frozen in time. In a similar way it is difficult for modern
observers of the Old Order Amish and other sectarian speakers of Pennsylvania Dutch to recognize the profoundly dynamic character of sectarian society; today's Amish and Old Order Mennonites do not live exactly
as their ancestors did, either in Europe or in early America. However,
there is a decidedly conservative element to be found in all Pennsylvania
Dutch–speaking groups, nonsectarian and sectarian. Their maintenance
of a language whose origins lie in eighteenth-century German-speaking
Europe is bound up with the preservation of a number of other cultural
patterns, both tangible, such as distinctive foodways, and intangible,
such as their belief systems, much of which they also inherited from the
European ancestors.

From the beginning, in the late eighteenth and early nineteenth
centuries Pennsylvania Dutch culture "rested on a foundation of language, religion, and agrarian mores," as the cultural geographer Walter
Kollmorgen puts it.[20] Indeed, Pennsylvania Dutch has remained a vital
language only in communities of farmers, craftspeople, and other country folk where a commitment to the Christian faith runs strong. The
robust use of Pennsylvania Dutch among rural-dwelling conservative
Anabaptist sectarians is evidence of this fact today, but this was equally
true of nonsectarian Pennsylvania Dutch in the eighteenth and nine-

teenth centuries. The religious convictions of active Pennsylvania Dutch speakers have long lent a moral imperative to the maintenance both of German (in some form) and of a traditional agrarian lifestyle.

Kollmorgen summarizes the basic message that early Pennsylvania Dutch Lutheran pastors conveyed to their congregants:

> We have made Pennsylvania the granary of the world; why should we not be proud of ourselves? . . . Do you wish to leave your children a rich inheritance? Then teach them German. Do you want your children to honor father and mother? Then see that they remain Lutherans. If they are to remain Lutherans, then they must remain Germans. But why remain German Lutherans or Lutheran Germans? Because if they do not remain Lutherans they will not remain farmers, and they are nothing if not farmers. Look at your farms and then look at the others! Do you want your children to fritter away what you have earned in the sweat of your brow? How long do you think they will hold on to the family farm once they have been Anglicized? Look at the Eiris[c]hdeutsche (English-speaking German farmers), you can tell the difference even now. Are their churches as prosperous as yours, their farms as well kept, their horses as sleek, their cattle as fat, their families as happy, their children as loyal as yours? Beware the beginning. The children cease speaking German, they stop going to church. . . . You won't know your children any more; they won't get up in the morning, but will loll in bed like ladies and gentlemen. Neither will they be ordered about. . . . But they will pester you from morn till night: Why don't you buy us a nice buggy so that we may do as the others do? Do what? Knock off long before *Feierabend* [quitting time], dress up and go to parties, where the girls dance and the boys gamble. But then it will be forever: Father, give us money.[21]

The association of real prosperity with an agrarian lifestyle, spiritual health, and maintenance of German is a profound one that runs through Pennsylvania Dutch culture right down to the present. Countless prose texts and poems produced by and for Pennsylvania Dutch, first in German and later in Pennsylvania Dutch itself, throughout the nineteenth century and beyond, deal with topics that alternately emphasize the salutary effects of living in a traditional Pennsylvania Dutch environment while warning parents and children of the ills among English-speaking gentlefolk in cities and towns. Much the same message is preached in many an Amish or Old Order Mennonite sermon today, often directed toward young people who may be tempted to leave the Old Order fold.

The central importance of the Christian faith in the lives of Pennsylvania Dutch in the late eighteenth and early nineteenth centuries is attested to by what they read, specifically the books, pamphlets, and broadsides that were printed for their consumption. The most comprehensive bibliography of German-language books and almanacs published in America between 1728 and 1830, most of which were from Pennsylvania, lists 3,151 titles, the great majority of which are religious in nature, including Bibles, hymnals, catechisms, and collections of sermons.[22] Of 1,682 German American broadsides published between 1730 and 1830 that form the basis for a recent study of their production and significance, 757 (45%) deal with spirituality in some way, by far the largest thematic category.[23] One of these is especially interesting since it speaks to the social status of farmers from a Christian perspective.

Der Bauernstand (also *Der Bauren-Stand*; The farmer class) was printed in Pennsylvania in at least twenty-one editions beginning as early as 1775, which attests to its popularity among the Pennsylvania Dutch.[24] The poem, which apparently traces its origins to the Rhineland around the time of the devastating Thirty Years' War (1618–1648),[25] begins as follows:

> Give ear, ye Christian people,
> To what I now sing:
>   About the farmer class,
>   It is well known
> What the farmers have to suffer
> Now, in these times of sorrow;
>   For they are also very much scorned,
>   Treated almost the same as dogs.
>
> All people in the land
> Are descended from the farmer class;
>   Everyone should dutifully
>   Take note of the proof of this,
> As we can read about Adam,

Who was the first farmer;
Eve was also a farmer's wife;
We are descended from her.

Everyone should bear in mind
That we are all, universally,
Very closely related
To the farmer class.
Whoever considers the matter properly
Will therefore not scorn the farmers;
All people in the land
Are nourished by the farmer class.[26]

The anonymous author of *Der Bauernstand* goes on to enumerate the many important ways in which city dwellers depend on farmers for their survival. The poet then scolds those who would scorn farmers and closes with the following prayer:

May God preserve the farmerfolk,
In peace forever,
So that there may be no want
Of dear bread;
May God further give
Farmers healthy bodies and long lives
Until we, freed from the cross and suffering,
Come to Heaven's bliss.[27]

While early Pennsylvania Dutch did not live in theocratic communities, the influence of their churches was strong in marking the boundaries between them, their English-monolingual rural neighbors, and city dwellers. The use of German in worship, which was viewed as vital to believers' spiritual health, went hand in hand with the maintenance of Pennsylvania Dutch as a vernacular language. *Die Mudderschprooch*, which encompassed both a form of standard German and the vernacular Pennsylvania Dutch, was at the center of their faith and culture:

In eastern Pennsylvania, the churches of the Pennsylvania Germans resisted the change to English, as long as the Pennsylvania German agrarian philosophy conditioned economy, education and religion and the ministers were drawn from a population reared in this philosophy, and often received their entire education in the section, even getting their theological training from fellow pastors instead of from a seminary. Of S. K. Brobst, militant Lutheran pastor and German editor of Allentown, the "English" in his congregation said once that he would like to erect a German wall around eastern Pennsylvania to keep the world out.[28]

The intertwining of German language maintenance with religious conservatism, especially in rural Lutheran, Reformed, and Anabaptist communities, was not unique to the Dutch Country of Pennsylvania. Indeed, later waves of German-speaking immigrants, especially but not only Lutherans who settled in rural communities throughout the Midwest as well as Texas, placed a similarly high value on maintaining German, such that the language was passed on to their descendants well into the twentieth century.

A crucial institution through which Pennsylvania Dutch churches exerted their influence on various aspects of community life, including the maintenance of German, was the school. To this day, an enduring stereotype about the Pennsylvania Dutch, including contemporary Amish and Old Order Mennonites, is that they are "antieducation." Underlying this stereotype is a long tradition of conflict between Pennsylvania Dutch parents and outside authorities who have sought to control the education of Pennsylvania Dutch children. Clyde Stine (1910–1968), who was born and raised in a traditional Pennsylvania Dutch community and became a leading expert on the Pennsylvania Dutch and schools, summarizes the conflict thus: "the history of the education of the Pennsylvania Germans has been largely one of struggle between the state and the Pennsylvania German agrarian spirit, each trying to further its own philosophy of life and education."[29] As far back as the middle of the eighteenth century, German Pennsylvanians made clear that they preferred locally controlled parochial schools to those overseen by outside authorities.

The earliest instance of conflict in the realm of education involved none other than Benjamin Franklin, who was a supporter of English-medium, free-tuition "Charity Schools" for children from German Pennsylvanian families in the 1750s. As Franklin wrote of Germans in Pennsylvania in 1753:

Those who come hither are generally of the most ignorant Stupid Sort of their own nation; . . . and as few of the English understand the German Language, and so cannot address them from the Press or Pulpit, 'tis almost impossible to remove any prejudices they once entertain. . . . Few of their children in the Country learn English. . . . In short unless the stream of their importation could be turned from this to other Colonies, . . . they will soon so out number us, that all the advantages we have, will not, in My Opinion, be able to preserve our language, and even our government will become precarious.[30]

It is no coincidence that Franklin expressed these fears, which foreshadowed the anti-immigrant rhetoric that endures today, precisely during the six-year period (1749–1754) when immigration to Pennsylvania from German-speaking Europe reached its zenith.[31] The Charity School movement, which was organized in London with Franklin's support in 1754, met with bitter resistance from German Pennsylvanians of all backgrounds, urban and rural, sectarian and nonsectarian, who (rightly) viewed these schools as an attempt to anglicize their children and more broadly to bring them into the fold of the Church of England.[32]

The successful fight against the Charity Schools led by German Pennsylvanian churches and sects meant that essentially the only schools that Pennsylvania Dutch children attended, for nearly a hundred years, from the middle of the eighteenth century until well into the first half of the nineteenth, were parochial schools. Pennsylvania Dutch families saw in the German school a vital institution to safeguard their linguistic, cultural, and spiritual heritage. Among tradition-minded Pennsylvania Dutch, the shift to English, especially in schools, heralded a moral decline. A March 12, 1819, editorial from the Sunbury *Nordwestliche Post* titled "German Schools" (*Deutsche Schulen*), captured this view well:

We had the pleasure to learn that the German language, for unknown reasons, is being resurrected from the dead, so to speak, through the establishment everywhere of schools for the instruction of the language of our ancestors. In the times of simple, hard-working, and upright people forty or fifty years ago, hardly anything but German was heard in our state. In those days the German spirit reigned universally and people enjoyed happy, prosperous times.—God showed his contentment with them by showering them with blessings. But since (for those who have paid attention) the German language has declined, pride, envy, and indolence have increased.—Everyone wants to become an Englishman, a gentleman or a lady. But look at the consequences: God is showing his zeal by pressing us from all sides and raining curses down on us gentlefolk.—Oh, how the English spirit has brought us down!—Is the rebirth of our language perhaps a harbinger of better times?—May our children seek not only to acquire the German language, but also the German spirit of years ago, a spirit of simplicity and faithfulness, surrounded by industry and wealth.[33]

Despite the ardent hopes of those Pennsylvania Dutch who feared the encroachment of "the English spirit" into their communities, German-medium schools, like most schools in early America, especially in rural areas, were beset by a number of challenges, including inadequate funding and a lack of qualified teachers. The most serious problem, however, was poor attendance, especially among children from farm families:

Frequently a child was sent to school for several weeks or months and then kept out an equal length of time. While the child was absent from school, he forgot nearly all he had learned, so that when he returned the teacher was compelled to go over the same work again. If the child made little or no progress, the teacher was blamed, and not infrequently, did the parents complain that they had sent their children to school for several years and yet they knew nothing, while as a matter of fact the actual attendance in school was only a few months.[34]

The subject matter taught in parochial schools serving Pennsylvania Dutch children reflected the modest expectations of their parents: "The early German immigrants did not regard it necessary to have their children taught more than the elementary subjects, that is, the three R's, and the catechism. They were taught to read the Bible, to write, and spell, and solve ordinary problems in arithmetic. Anyone who had an education beyond this was regarded as a scholar."[35]

The language of instruction in these early parochial schools was nominally German, but it would have been very difficult for most Pennsylvania Dutch children to have developed anything more than the ability to read and recite the Bible and other religious materials in German. Writing was more an exercise in calligraphy than learning to compose original texts, as pupils were expected mainly to copy words, sentences, and short texts from ABC books and primers. There is nothing in the historical record of early Pennsylvania Dutch schools to suggest that children were ever expected to learn to converse freely in German, which is understandable given that it was simply not communicatively necessary in the early Dutch Country: Pennsylvania Dutch and a measure of English were all that people needed to function orally in everyday life. The only individuals in Pennsylvania Dutch communities who would have been expected to actually speak and not just recite German were ministers, though what they used in the pulpit was more than likely a strongly Dutchified form of German, and outside of the pulpit they would have communicated with their parishioners in Pennsylvania Dutch. After the major decline in emigration from Europe after 1754, the number of European-born German speakers in the Dutch Country waned, thereby also limiting the pool of teachers in German-medium Pennsylvanian schools to US-born Pennsylvania Dutch speakers.[36]

The main pedagogical method in both German and English schools serving Pennsylvania Dutch children was recitation, known as *uffsaage*, 'to recite', in Pennsylvania Dutch. Abraham Reeser Horne (1834–1902), the leading expert on the education of Pennsylvania Dutch–speaking schoolchildren in the nineteenth century, had this to say about the nature of instruction in early Pennsylvanian schools:

The daily routine of school exercises consisted in "*ufsawga.*" This meant the reading and spelling of words, without regard to sense and expression. The exercise continued during all of the day, from 8 A.M. to 4 P.M., with an hour's recess at noon. There was ciphering and writing, but not in class. Each pupil constituted his own class, and when help was needed the slate was brought to the teacher, who looked over the "sums," while at the same time, the "*ufsawga*" went on. The writer received no attention, except an occasional mending of the goose quill pen.

The books in use were the *Testament*, the *English Reader*, *Comly's Spelling Book*, and the *American Tudor Arithmetic*. Geography, grammar, history, and kindred branches were not known. The teacher's knowledge of the branches taught was frequently very limited. Reading was a merely mechanical exercise, consisting of the pronunciation of a certain number of words. It was a practical solution of the problem of *maxima* and *minima*, pronouncing the greatest number of words in the shortest time possible. The pupil that could do this was considered the best reader. The teacher's knowledge of arithmetic was very meagre. One of the first superintendents of Lehigh County reports, that he found a teacher at his examinations who could add and subtract, but when he [was] requested to perform an operation involving multiplication and division, he excused himself, saying: *Des multiplizeera un defideera hawb ich nuch net gelernt.* "I have not learned yet to multiply and divide."[37]

An important firsthand account of the poor state of education among the Pennsylvania Dutch in early America is provided by William A. Helffrich, a prominent Reformed minister who was born in Weissenburg, Lehigh County, PA, in 1827 and died in 1894. Helffrich spent most of his life in the Dutch Country and produced an autobiography in German that was published posthumously by his sons in 1906. His recollection of the schools where he grew up in the early 1830s is illuminating:

The school system in those days was backward. Reading, writing, and figuring, at the blackboard or out of a few textbooks, was all that was practiced in school. And many teachers could not even teach that adequately. . . . About every tenth quarter-mile there was a school, four out of five of which were in bad shape. A sad situation for the school and the educational level of the community. I heard some farmers say that they had attended school for only four months. Among the poorer class there were people who could not read and only few who could write a letter. The state mandated that children in poor families should be taken care of, so each county had a poor fund from which disadvantaged children were to be educated. Later, each township assumed responsibility for these funds. But many parents regarded it as a shame for their children to be taught by the county or township; some poor children were reproached by other children because of this. In the end, the opportunity was no longer used. Some parents preferred to let their children run loose on the street, and many received almost no instruction at all.[38]

William Helffrich's family was exceptional in that his father, Johannes (1795–1852), also a Reformed minister, had been well educated as a child in Philadelphia and wanted to see that his own children be similarly trained. Johannes withdrew his two sons, William and his older brother, John, from the local parochial school when William was eight and engaged a series of six German-born private tutors to teach the Helffrich boys in their home, which became known as the Weissenburg Academy.[39]

Just one year before the Helffrich brothers began their private instruction, in 1834 the Pennsylvania legislature passed An Act to Establish a General System of Education by Common Schools, which went a long a way toward solidifying the reputation of the Pennsylvania Dutch as antieducation. The act was the most (in)famous in a series of laws passed by the Commonwealth of Pennsylvania aimed at establishing a system of free public schools to address the evident deficiencies across the state, including in the Pennsylvania Dutch Country. Although the school laws included no specific provisions about language of instruction, they were widely interpreted as mandating English, which raised the hackles of the Pennsylvania Dutch, who saw a direct threat to their culture. In fact, the bitter resistance on the part of most Pennsylvania Dutch to the establishment of publicly funded common schools was based on a number of factors.

Of major concern to the Pennsylvania Dutch was how these schools were to be financed. The Pennsylvania Dutch had expressed a classically rural American "antitax" spirit since the eighteenth century, which was never more visible than it was during the events surrounding the violent antitax uprising in 1799–1800 known as Fries's Rebellion.[40] The idea of the state taxing citizens to fund schools over which the state, rather than local communities, would have authority, was offensive to many rural Pennsylvanians, including the Pennsylvania Dutch. Further, the Pennsylvania Dutch attached a certain stigma to the idea of having to depend on the "charity" of the state to perform a duty so fundamental as the education of their children; they believed that indigent members of their communities, who were relatively few in any case, were already provided for. A typical sentiment was the following: "I am conscientious in regard to having my children taught at the expense of public charity, because I do not stand in need of such aid, for I can pay myself."[41]

Pennsylvania Dutch resistance to a common school system, as it was some eight decades earlier with the attempt to establish Charity Schools in Pennsylvania, was attributable to what L. S. Shimmell terms "the attachment to which the Pennsylvania-Germans had to the mother-tongue," intimately connected as it was with the Christian faith of their ancestors:

That their schools would become English was a foregone conclusion. Their preference for German schools was not alone due to a sentiment fostered by the segregated condition of their settlements. The reading and studying of the Bible, an indispensable part of the program of the German Reformers, made the mother-tongue the language of the schools. Luther's translation dignified the German language and made it revered and beloved by the common people. It became a great treasure to them, because it had become, as it were, a part of their religion. Educational reformers, after the Reformation, laid great stress upon the study of the vernacular. "Everything first in the mother-tongue" was a favorite principle with educational writers.

Having been taught in church and school to have a deep regard for the language of their fathers, the Pennsylvania-Germans looked upon it as a sacrilege to have it put out of their schools. They would never displace it in their churches until the oldest members were too few and feeble to make effectual resistance. *"Unser Herr Gott war ja deutsch"* [But our Lord God was German], said an old woman when English services were about to be introduced into her church.[42]

The religious significance for the Pennsylvania Dutch of maintaining their own schools extended beyond language to how they viewed their sacred duty as parents. Children were seen as first belonging to God, then to their parents, and only after that to the state. The Pennsylvania Dutch would have considered themselves to be failing in their calling as Christian parents if they had ceded responsibility for the education of their children to secular, outside authorities.[43]

Decades after the passage of the various school laws in Pennsylvania, George Mays (1836–1909), a native Dutchman who became a physician and wrote poetry in Pennsylvania Dutch, recalled the resistance of his people in verse, though unsympathetically.

Will ich bei der Woret bleiwe	*If I want to stay with the truth*
Muss ich eich au des noch schreiwe	*I have to yet write this to you;*
'S waar net de Ormut bei de Leit	*It was not the poverty among the people*
Das Schule raar mocht selle Zeit.	*That made school rare in those days.*

. . . .

Sie wisse os de frei Schul law	*They knew that the free school law*
Die greift yo ihre Geldsock au	*Hit them in their wallets;*
In fact 's waar nix os ihre Geld	*In fact, it was nothing but their money*
Os selli Leit so long z'rick held.	*That held those people back for so long.*

Sell Gsets mocht unser Toxbill gross	*"That law makes our tax bill big*
Un benefit die Schtatleit blos	*And benefits only the city people;*
Kauft uns ken Blotz net mol en Gaul	*Doesn't buy us a place, not even a horse*
Un mocht yusht unser Kinner foul.	*And just makes our children lazy."*

So waar's bi feeli Baure's Gschwetz	*That was the talk among many farmers,*
So hen si g'fuchte geges G'setz	*So they fought against the law,*
Un moncher glaubt er wert gedrickt	*And many thought they would be oppressed*
So bol mer mohl de freischul krickt.	*As soon as they got the free schools.*

(Hort hen sie g'fuchte geges Gsetz	*They fought hard against the law*
Un feel de mehne es ware letz	*And many thought it was wrong*
Sich en Larning au zu schoffe	*To get an education*
Weil es deht Foulenser moche.)	*Because that would make lazy people.*

Onri glauwe oni Zweifel	*Others believed without a doubt*
Ol de Lerning kumt fum Teifel	*That all education came from the devil,*
Un der wo'n Dorsht for Bicher hut	*And the one who was thirsty for books*
Wert efters shendlich ausgeschput.	*Was often scandalously mocked.*

. . . .

Uf der Bauerei zu schoffe	*"Working on the farm*
Un de Erwet leicht zu moche	*And making the work easy,*
Doh helft uns net de Schulgesets—	*There the school law doesn't help us";*
Sel waar of course en dummes	*That was of course silly talk.*
g'schwetz.	

'S gebt heit noch Leit de hases letz	*There are still people today who say*
	it was wrong
Un schteibere sich om Schulg'setz	*And are stubborn about the school law*
Doch wons net fer de Schullaw	*But if it hadn't been for the school*
wehr	*law*
Kemt moncher net so schmart do	*There would not be as many smart*
hehr.	*people.*[44]

To be sure, some early Pennsylvania Dutch, like George Mays, set their sights on professional careers away the farm, for which a good formal education was necessary. In virtually every case, such a move meant the loss of Pennsylvania Dutch over the course of their lives. While many formerly active speakers of Pennsylvania Dutch would not regret their decision to enter the English-speaking mainstream, it was not uncommon for them to wax nostalgic about their native language and culture years later.

Although the Pennsylvania Dutch were not able to stop the advance of a common school system in Pennsylvania during the nineteenth century in the same way their grandparents had ended the Charity School movement, German-medium parochial schools survived in the Dutch Country for decades after 1834, even receiving state funding until 1854.[45] There were also public schools in Pennsylvania Dutch communities that used German as a language of instruction, either solely or alongside English, well into the second half of the nineteenth century; as late as 1900 some such schools still existed.[46] The shift from German to English in schools serving Pennsylvania Dutch children, both parochial and public, was less the result of compulsion from the state than it was due to the attrition of Pennsylvania Dutch families from their *Mudderschprooch*, in both its forms, German in church and Pennsylvania Dutch at home, which accelerated in the decades following the Civil War. This eventual loss of Pennsylvania Dutch and German was, in turn, attributable to the weakening of the ties among language, faith, and an agrarian lifestyle, as increasing numbers of Pennsylvania Dutch left the farm and shop to enter an industrial workforce or white-collar professions that required advanced levels of formal education. While the Pennsylvania Dutch did not owe the state a huge debt of gratitude for having supported or protected their language and traditional culture, neither could they argue that they were the victims of a systematic policy of forced anglicization.

The protective isolation that early Pennsylvania Dutch created for themselves in which their *Mudderschprooch* thrived was reinforced not only by their commitment to their churches and control of how their children should be educated but also by their political activity. In the same way that the Pennsylvania Dutch were stereotyped as being opposed to education, they were also presumed to be apolitical, insufficiently patriotic, or, worse, subversive. Here again, Benjamin Franklin had such reservations regarding German Pennsylvanians. As early as the 1740s and 1750s, Franklin was openly critical of the migration of Germans to Pennsylvania, mainly out of concern that they would not take up arms in defense of their adoptive homeland. As the historian John B. Frantz has pointed out, however, it is likely that Franklin was misled into thinking that most German Pennsylvanians were sectarians, who, in addition to being pacifist also preferred to remain uninvolved in politics.[47] While it is true that sectarians were highly visible among German immigrants during the first half of the eighteenth century, they were later outnumbered by Lutheran and Reformed church people, many of whom were ardent supporters of the American Revolutionary cause and decidedly patriotic in the early decades of the new nation.

On the face of it, it seems paradoxical that an American minority group whose identity was grounded in a strong sense of patriotism would at the same time assert its difference from the social mainstream by maintaining a non-English language and distinctive folk culture with clear ties to Europe. This apparent conundrum is resolved by understanding what the historian Steven Nolt has termed the *peasant republicanism* of the early Pennsylvania Dutch:

[T]hey carried convictions associated with and supported by southwestern German Pietism, sentiments that paradoxically accented both the importance of personal freedom and the authority of local custom and

church structure to provide order and an effective measure of social control. Transferred to the political sphere, such attitudes and assumptions
amounted to what might be termed "peasant republicanism." Peasant republicanism regarded true liberty in negative terms—that is, as freedom
from intrusive agents of change. Its proponents resisted the efforts of
distant power brokers to meddle in their local and traditional affairs,
yet ancient privileges and the authority structures that guarded them
received honor and deferential respect, and peasant subjects dutifully
filled their roles in a vertically organized society. The system of reciprocal
relationships and localized mutual obligations that organized civic life
thus supported a delicate balance of obedience and vigilance. Peasant
republicanism endorsed a collective self-interest derived from a strong
local base. It could produce seemingly passive subjects who compliantly
yielded to hierarchies of merit, but its advocates actually based their actions on political principles that could also evoke stiff opposition and
vigorous protest.[48]

Early Pennsylvania Dutch, speaking the language of liberty with German words, asserted their right as Americans to practice their faith and
determine their own affairs, as well as to maintain a cultural identity at
the heart of which was a language all their own.

Countless poems written in German by and for Pennsylvania Dutch
in the eighteenth and early nineteenth centuries sang the praises of their
new "fatherland." Many, like the text of the *Bauernstand* broadside, cast
patriotism in a religious light. One example is "The Mournful Song
of Oppressed Freedom" (*Das Trauer Lied der unterdrückten Freyheit*),
which was apparently composed shortly after the Battle of Bunker Hill
in 1775. The song begins in a psalm-like way:

> Hear, oh Heaven, my cry,
>   For you know all;
> In these dark days of mourning
>   I am in anguish in my tender breast,
> I, who already two hundred years ago,
>   In order to become a free child,
> Traveled over the raging sea
>   To a barren land.[49]

The anonymous poet goes on to recall romantically the experience of the brave immigrants to America who "spared neither effort nor hard work" (*sparte keine Müh und Fleiß*) to cultivate the American "wasteland" (*Wüste*) to make a home for themselves and their descendants, which earned them the respect of the entire world. Now, however, many from the "motherland" (*Mutterland*), Britain, are baring their jealous teeth at America and drawing their bloodthirsty swords, breaking the "oath and seal" (*Eid und Siegel*) that once protected Americans' rights. The poet decries the injustice of the Stamp Act and the recent shedding of blood at Bunker Hill. By what right can a mother massacre her children? the poet asks.

Turning again toward heaven, the author of the "Trauer Lied" asks how this injustice can be allowed, wondering whether it is really a sin for "brave sons of freedom" (*tapfre Freyheits Söhne*) to defend "life, liberty, and property" (*Leben, Freyheit, Eigenthum*) in the face of evil. The poet answers his own question by saying that any blood that is shed in defense of the "dear fatherland" (*das liebe Vaterland*) will be on the enemy's conscience; "justice is our flag of victory, innocence our battle standard" (*Recht ist unsre Sieges-Fahne, Unschuld unser Feld-Panier*). His fellow Americans should have hope and courage in the virtuous fight on behalf of their beloved country. He closes the poem in a very secular way, even making reference to Mars, the Roman god of war, and in the last line he paraphrases Patrick Henry:

> Though the cannons may roar
>   And Mars appear in blood,
> Though bombs may churn up the ground horribly,
>   Smoke and fire together,
> Let it thunder, let it crack,
>   Let the ramparts cave in;
> This will be my motto:
> "I will be dead or free."[50]

If Anglo-Americans had been able to understand these verses, they would have had little need to fear the inaction of German Pennsylvanians, at least the nonsectarians among them, in the struggle against the British crown. Their peasant republican loyalty was twofold: to the faith, traditions, and language of their ancestors and to the emerging nation of which they felt fully a part.

Early Descriptions of the Speech of German Pennsylvanians

The era in which Benjamin Franklin was expressing his concerns about German Pennsylvanians and their stubborn loyalty to their heritage language was the critical period during which Pennsylvania Dutch developed. Between 1750 and 1780, the children of the immigrants who were part of the midcentury wave of immigration from German-speaking Europe reached maturity. Unfortunately, with a single exception, there is no evidence of texts produced in Pennsylvania Dutch by native speakers before 1800; those who did put pen to paper did so in German or English. There is, however, indirect evidence pointing to the existence of a distinctly Pennsylvanian form of German spoken in the rural Dutch Country by the early 1780s. One especially important source is an article from a German-language newspaper in Philadelphia, the *Gemeinnützige Philadelphische Correspondenz* (lit. 'Commonly useful Philadelphia correspondence'), that appeared on October 26, 1784.[51] The article is a satirical presentation made by three young men from prominent German Pennsylvanian families, Marcus Kuhl, George Lochman, and Frederick Augustus Conrad Muhlenberg (1750–1801), the latter of whom became notable in American history as the first Speaker of the House of Representatives in 1789. The three men had been students together at a German-Latin school in Philadelphia established by the German-born scholars and Lutheran ministers Justus H. C. Helmuth (1745–1825) and John Christopher Kunze (1744–1807). Kuhl, Lochman, and Muhlenberg delivered their presentation in a very Germanophile setting, at a meeting on September 20, 1784, honoring the incorporation of the German Society of Philadelphia (today, the German Society of Pennsylvania).

The beginning of the presentation, in German with English translation, is below. English-derived words, which were printed in roman type in the original, as opposed to the normal Fraktur (Gothic), are in italics here.

KUHL: Ich muß ihnen, meine theureste Freunde, einen wichtigen
   Artikel aus unserer Deutschen Zeitung vorlesen, er ist datirt, Stockholm, den 20sten April, und lautet wie folgt:

Fortsetzung der
Reden und Gespräche,
Welche am Montage, den 20sten September, dem
Gedächtnißtage der Incorporirung der Deutschen
Gesellschaft, von den Deutschen Studenten und
Schülern auf der hiesigen Universität, gehalten wor-
den.

Gespräche zwischen Kuhl, Mühlenberg, und
Lochman.

M. Ich muß ihnen, meine theureste Freunde, einen wichtigen Artikel aus unserer Deutschen Zeitung vorlesen, er ist datirt, Stockholm, den 20sten April, und lautet wie folget:

F. Mit ihrer Deutschen Newspaper, warum lesen sie
uns denn nicht rather diesen Artikel aus dem Englischen;
for you know the Dutch is out of Date amongst
us, and Gentlemen of our Abilities.

G. Ich wünsche sie geben uns einen Beweis von ihren
Geschicklichkeiten; mir deucht, ein junger Herr, der seine
Muttersprache nicht reden kan, sollte von keinen Geschick-
lichkeiten plaudern, und kan er sie reden, schämt sich aber
derselben, so verdient er nicht den Namen eines geschickten
Menschen, sondern er ist ein Thor.

F. Hey da! Certainly, wer sie jetzt reden hört, dem ist
easy zu wissen, daß sie ein grober Dutchman sind. Wissen sie nicht, daß ich ein Gentleman bin, und einen
Gentleman einen Thoren zu nennen, das ist meaner als
mean; aber es ist nicht worth while, viel Notice davon zu nehmen, was sie sagen, because ich werde doch bleiben, wer ich bin.

From the *Gemeinnützige Philadelphische Correspondenz*, October 26, 1784.

MUHLENBERG: Mit ihrer Deutschen *Newspaper*, warum lesen sie uns
denn nicht *rather* diesen Artikel aus dem Englischen; *for you know
the Dutch is out of date amongst us, and Gentlemen of our Abilities.*
LOCHMAN: Ich wünsche sie geben uns einen Beweis von ihren
Geschicklichkeiten; mir deucht, ein junger Herr, der seine Muttersprache nicht reden kan, sollte von keinen Geschicklichkeiten

plaudern, und kan er sie reden, schämt sich aber derselben, so verdient er nicht den Namen eines geschickten Menschen, sondern er ist ein Thor.

MUHLENBERG: Hey da! *Certainly,* wer sie jetzt reden hört, dem ist *easy* zu wissen, daß sie ein grober *Dutchman* sind. Wissen sie nicht, daß ich ein *Gentleman* bin, und einen *Gentleman* einen Thoren zu nennen, das ist *meaner* als *mean;* aber es ist nicht *worth while,* viel *Notice* davon zu nehmen, *because* ich werde doch bleiben, wer ich bin.

K: *I must read to you, my dearest friends, an important article from our German newspaper. It is dated Stockholm, April 20, and reads as follows:*

M: *Go on with your German* newspaper, *why do you not* rather *read us this article in English?* For you know the Dutch is out of date amongst us, and Gentlemen of our Abilities.

L: *I wish you would give us proof of your talents. It seems to me that a young gentleman who cannot speak his mother tongue has no business chatting about talents. And if he can speak his mother tongue but is ashamed of doing so, then he does not merit the title of a talented person; rather, he is a fool.*

M: *Hey there!* Certainly, *whoever hears you speaking now will know easily that you are a coarse* Dutchman. *Do you not know that I am a* gentleman, *and to call a* gentleman *a fool, that is* meaner *than* mean. *But it is not* worthwhile *to take much* notice *of this because I will remain who I am.*

In what follows, Lochman and Kuhl try to impress upon the foolish Dutchman portrayed by Muhlenberg the importance of the Enlightenment in Europe in improving the condition of Protestants in Catholic-majority lands. Joseph II of Austria, the progressive Holy Roman Emperor, and the Lutheran Gustav III of Sweden are singled out for special praise. Muhlenberg, in his uncouth Dutch alter ego, replies as follows:

I don't care much, was die grossen Herren mit der Religion vornehmen; alle meine Wünsche gehen dahin, daß wir nur unsere *Liberty preserviren* mögen: Ludwig der Sechszehnte, und Georg Waschington, das sind mir Männer die *admirable* sind.

I don't care much *about what the big guys do about religion. All I care about is that we are able to* preserve our liberty. *Louis XVI and George Washington, to me those are men who are* admirable.

Eventually, Muhlenberg switches to speaking standard German, reassuring his concerned interlocutors that he does indeed value religion above all other concerns and stating that he merely wanted to make a point for the benefit of some of the young people in the audience. After Muhlenberg departs, the relieved Lochman says:

Ich dachte halb, daß unser lustiger Freund nur spashaft seyn wollte, da er anfing den Pennsylvanischen Deutschen *Dialect* zu reden; denn ich weiß, daß er sonst so rein Deutsch spricht, als einer von uns.

I figured that our merry friend was just being silly when he began speaking the Pennsylvania German dialect, since I know that he otherwise speaks German just as purely as any of us.[52]

This latter statement by George Lochman is significant for the history of Pennsylvania Dutch, as it is the first known reference to a "Pennsylvania German dialect." Although Muhlenberg's speech is not Pennsylvania Dutch, rather standard German interspersed with many English loanwords and phrases, this parody is important in showing how the early Pennsylvania Dutch and their nascent language were viewed by outsiders. The stereotypical Dutchman is an ignorant rustic more concerned about the secular cause of American liberty than religion. He speaks a "dialect" rife with anglicisms that represents a linguistic fall from the grace of a "pure" standard German "mother tongue" (heritage language).[52] As the article goes on, Lochman and Kuhl make explicit their concern that the spiritual health of young German Pennsylvanians in rural communities is at risk because of the lack preachers and schoolmasters who could cultivate "pure" German and simultaneously check the forces of "faithlessness and godlessness" (*Unglaube und Gottlosigkeit*).

While Muhlenberg and his Philadelphia German friends may have gotten the details of early Pennsylvania Dutch speech wrong, they did observe correctly that the form of German being used in the hinterlands

S. Ich dachte halb, daß unser lustiger Freund nur spaß haft seyn wolte, da er anfing den Peunsylvanischen Deutschen Dialect zu reden; denn ich weiß, daß er sonst so rein Deutsch spricht, als einer von uns.

The first documented use of the expression "Pennsylvania German [Dutch] dialect";
Gemeinnützige Philadelphische Correspondenz, October 26, 1784.

of southeastern Pennsylvania differed significantly from the standard German that they used. And although the parodists captured the American self-identity of the rural Dutch accurately (as well as, incidentally, the poor quality of the schools that served Dutch children), their view that the patriotism of the Pennsylvania Dutch might undermine their commitment to the faith of their ancestors was misplaced. As peasant republicans, Pennsylvania Dutch could be both loyal Americans and true to the Christian faith they brought with them from Europe, the main vehicle of which was the German language. What Muhlenberg, Lochman, and Kuhl failed to understand was that although the Pennsylvania Dutch indeed did not speak "pure" German, their fidelity to a Germanic linguistic-spiritual heritage nonetheless remained strong. Had Muhlenberg and his friends asked their rural Dutch contemporaries why they had abandoned their "mother tongue," the Dutch would have replied they had done no such thing. True, their mother tongue was not the *Muttersprache* of European Germans and their urbane cousins in eighteenth-century Philadelphia. Rather, it was the *Mudderschprooch* of the rural Pennsylvania hinterlands, which included both a vernacular Palatine German–derived language and an Americanized form of "High German" for use in worship.

A second, more extensive source of information on the linguistic situation in late eighteenth-century German Pennsylvania comes from the two-volume work by the natural scientist Johann David Schöpf (1752–1800) mentioned in the previous chapter. Based on his experiences in Pennsylvania at precisely the same time the Kuhl/Lochman/Muhlenberg parody appeared, in 1783 and 1784, Schöpf's observations, colored as they are by the same Germanophile prejudice noted above, offer a valuable window on early Pennsylvania Dutch life and the place of language within it.

Johann David Schöpf (1752–1800).
Source: US National Library of Medicine, History of Medicine Division.

Regarding the speech of the German Pennsylvanians he encountered, Schöpf is quite harsh. He describes it as a "miserably broken mishmash of English and German" and a "bastard gibberish" (*Bastard-Kauderwelsch*).[53] Like Muhlenberg and his friends, Schöpf compares emerging Pennsylvania Dutch negatively to their "mother tongue," that is, standard German, the main difference between the two being the incorporation of elements from English in Pennsylvania Dutch. Both first-generation immigrants and their children come under fire from Schöpf: "Grown persons who come over from Germany partially forget their mother tongue as they attempt, in vain, to learn a new language; those born here almost never learn their mother tongue properly and purely."[54] Indeed, Schöpf goes so far as to accuse German Pennsylvanians of being doubly semilingual: "[a]mong themselves they often prattle on in bad German and worse English, for they have the unique distinction among other ethnic groups in that they quite truly have complete knowledge of neither the one language nor the other."[55] Schöpf continues, saying that Germans in rural areas have more limited proficiency in English than those in towns and cities, but their German is still bad: "[t]here are a small number of isolated communities and a few countrymen living in the mountains who have less contact with Englishmen and for that reason sometimes even do not understand English, but their German is still none the better for it."[56]

The characterization of rural German Pennsylvanians as falling between the linguistic chairs of English and "proper" German touches on the controversial concept of *semilingualism* or, more precisely, *double semilingualism*. Understood literally, this refers to a supposed lack of full knowledge of one or more languages. Already the question of what counts as "full knowledge" of a language is problematic. Does a gifted writer, for example, have a "fuller" knowledge of a language than an illiterate person in the same speech community? Linguists would reply that there is no qualitative difference between such individuals, *knowledge* or *competence* in a language being defined as the inventory of phonological, morphological, and syntactic rules and vocabulary that are acquired by children, usually without explicit instruction.[57] While an experienced writer and an illiterate person differ in their *facility* in their common language, they draw on the same basic inventory of structures regardless of whether what they produce is beautiful prose or a mundane comment about the weather. Apart from highly pathological cases in which children are deprived of crucial early language input, no human is semilingual.[58] It was quite likely that some of the German Pennsylvanians Schöpf encountered had incomplete knowledge of English, however their knowledge of a Pennsylvanian form of German, different though it was from prescriptive European standard German, was, psycholinguistically speaking, complete.[59]

Regarding standard German, Schöpf states that the only exposure German Pennsylvanians have to the language is in church, but to little positive effect: during sermons delivered in German, he says, the congregants converse in their "bastard gibberish."[60] The one exception Schöpf notes is in Moravian communities, where the "purest and most beautiful" German is spoken.[61] Somewhat later in his book Schöpf describes a visit to the Moravian settlement at Bethlehem, PA.[62] At the time of his visit, that community numbered approximately six hundred, the majority being Germans, though there were some English people there also. Interestingly, Schöpf mentions that nearly everyone in the community knew both languages and that sermons were occasionally delivered in

English. Most of the Moravian brethren, especially the ministers, were of Saxon origin, which explains, according to Schöpf, why the German spoken in Bethlehem and other Moravian communities was "the purest and best" in America.[63]

As far as written German goes, Schöpf is no more charitable about what he encountered in German-language publications in Pennsylvania than about the oral vernacular: "[i]t is not enough that they speak badly; they write and publish just as pitifully."[64] Schöpf goes on to mention one of Philadelphia's most famous German-language printers, Melchior Steiner (1757?–1807), who happened also to be the printer of the Philadelphia newspaper in which the Kuhl/Lochman/Muhlenberg parody of 1784 appeared. Speaking apparently of this very periodical, Schöpf says the following:

> The German press of Melchior Steiner (and at one time of Christoph Sauer), puts out weekly a German newspaper that contains just as frequent as sad examples of the pitifully deformed language of our American countrymen. These are mainly translations from English newspapers, but so stiff and so anglicized as to be nauseating. The two German clergymen [Justus H. C. Helmuth and John Christian Kunze] and Mr. Steiner edit the newspaper. If I am not mistaken, Mr. Kunze alone earns one hundred pounds for his work. "If we were to write the newspapers in pure German," the editors say in excuse, "our American farmers would never be able to read or understand them."[65]

Schöpf's disdain for the examples of published German he encountered in Pennsylvania did not extend to the three editors he named personally. The German-born John Christian Kunze and Justus H. C. Helmuth were in fact professionally dedicated to the promotion of German in Pennsylvania, and both occupied in succession a professorship in German and Oriental languages at the University of Pennsylvania, the first American university to have such a faculty position.[66] In an appendix to the first volume of his book, Schöpf includes the text of an address that Kunze delivered at the German Society of Philadelphia in 1782 on the history and goals of the organization.[67] In his speech Kunze states that the society's original work had been directed at aiding immigrants from Germany in their transition to life in America. Later, however, the

goals of the society shifted to improve the educational situation of Pennsylvanians of German descent. However, one challenge to achieving this,
according to Kunze, quoted below, is their language.

The ability to speak German is minimal among those born here, and
if that ability were greater, it would truly be a miraculous talent. Most
Germans do not speak German. If I did not add anything to this, I would
be neglecting the duties of an orator, for such a one may not lead his listeners into a labyrinth. You rightly ask, so what do those Germans speak
who do not speak German? And I reply, in order to be clear: America
is ahead of most of the other peoples of the earth. It has in it a group of
people who speak no language at all. It is not English, and it will never
be German.[68]

Kunze clearly shared Schöpf's assessment that eighteenth-century
German Pennsylvanians, especially those born in America, were semilingual, with deficient knowledge of both (standard) German and English.
But are there any examples of this "bastard gibberish," and how do they
compare to actual Pennsylvania Dutch? Recalling the speech of Muhlenberg in the parody, what he produced was in fact standard German with
numerous words and phrases borrowed from English, what might be
called "American Denglish." The grammatical structure of Muhlenberg's
speech shows none of the differences between real Pennsylvania Dutch
(or Palatine dialects) and standard German. Schöpf, however, devotes
one and a half pages to examples of what he claims to have heard directly
from a German Pennsylvanian farmer.[69] Although there are a number of
standard Germanisms in these examples, which are almost certainly due
to Schöpf's lack of knowledge of (and obvious disdain for) what was very
likely early Pennsylvania Dutch, they do include a number of nonstandard features that were (and still are) broadly characteristic of colloquial
spoken German, including many dialects and Pennsylvania Dutch itself.
His examples are thus not mere Denglish.

Schöpf's intent was to demonstrate the polluting influence of English
on the speech of German Pennsylvanians in the form of borrowed words
and phrases, similar to the Denglish of Muhlenberg's parody. Schöpf
goes further than Muhlenberg and makes an observation about two
types of lexical influence from English that are most definitely found

in Pennsylvania Dutch, as well as all other German American varieties and non-English heritage languages in the United States, namely calques (loan translations) and loan shifts.[70] One of Schöpf's examples of a calque is the verb *absetzen*, which is composed of the prefix *ab-*, meaning 'off, away', plus the root verb *setzen*, 'to set, place'. One of the multiple meanings of this word in standard German is 'to displace'; in Pennsylvania Dutch, however, *absetze* means 'to set off' in the sense of 'to detonate'.[71] Examples of loan shifts that Schöpf mentions include the verbs *gleiche[n]* (Ger. 'to resemble'; PD 'to like') and *belange[n]* (Ger. 'to punish, prosecute'; PD 'to belong').

While many of Schöpf's examples of English borrowings, calques, and loan shifts from the speech of the unnamed "German farmer" with whom he supposedly spoke are consistent with what is found in Pennsylvania Dutch, he, like Muhlenberg, exaggerates the extent to which English has affected Pennsylvania Dutch vocabulary and idioms. For example, *belange* has not displaced the older verbs *gheere* and *heere* inherited from Palatine German (related to std. Ger. *gehören*, 'to belong'). In modern Pennsylvania Dutch, *belange* is used only in the sense of property ownership, e.g., *Sell belangt zu mich (mir)*, 'That belongs to me'. Other senses of 'belonging' are rendered by *gheere* or *heere*, for example, *Sie (g)heere zu en annri Gmee*, 'They belong to a different church'; *Sell heert net datt*, 'That doesn't belong there'. Recall here the discussion of *waere/draage*, 'to wear / to carry', in the previous chapter: borrowings from English into Pennsylvania Dutch do not usually displace older, native lexical items. Older words fall out of use because of the changing real-world experiences of speakers, not their forgetfulness of German or their acquisition of English. Loanwords add nuance to a language by simultaneously reducing the polysemy of older, native vocabulary. The size of the Pennsylvania Dutch lexicon is increased by borrowings from English as the language is adapted to the circumstances of the New World.

Schöpf also distorts the lexical influence of English on Pennsylvania Dutch with one of the sentences he claims to have heard from his farmer consultant. This sentence was picked up by later observers of Pennsylvania Dutch who, like Schöpf, sought to illustrate the supposedly excessive degree to which the language was contaminated by English.[72] English-derived elements are underlined.

Mein <u>Stallion</u> ist über die <u>Fehnß</u> getsch[um]pt, und hat dem Nachbar sein' <u>Whiet</u> abscheulich gedämätscht.

My <u>stallion</u> <u>jumped</u> over the <u>fence</u> and <u>damaged</u> the neighbor's <u>wheat</u> terribly.

A comparison of this sentence with its rendering in modern Pennsylvania Dutch, however, suggests that Schöpf's claim to have actually heard it from a native speaker was likely fanciful. In the contemporary version below, the borrowings from English are again underscored.

Mei Hengscht is iwwer die <u>Fens</u> gschprunge (<u>getschumpt</u>) un hot em / der Nochber sei Weeze zimmlichi Schaade geduh.

Notably, the number of English-derived loans in the modern sentence is just one or two (see discussion below about the verb *tschumpe*), as compared to five in the original, which already casts doubt on the accuracy of Schöpf's example.[73] The overall influence of English on Pennsylvania Dutch vocabulary is more modest than he would lead his readers to believe. And, beyond that, the grammatical matrix into which English loans are inserted, even in Schöpf's example, is wholly Palatine German (Object > Verb) and not at all influenced by the sentence structure of English (Verb > Object): the conjugated verbs in the two main clauses *ist/is* and *hat/hot* and their participles *getschumpt* and *gedämätscht/ geduh* are separated from one another by the prepositional phrase in the first clause and the direct object in the second (the phrases meaning 'over the fence' and 'the neighbor's wheat', respectively). Further, borrowed verbs are made to conform to native Palatine German rules: the participial prefix *ge-* and the suffix *-t* are added to the English-derived stems (*tschump* and *dämätsch*), and the intransitive verb of motion *tschumpe* takes a form of the verb 'to be' (*ist/is*) as its auxiliary in the perfect tense, which corresponds in this instance to the English simple past tense (*jumped* rather than *has jumped*). A literal translation of the first clause—*My stallion is over the fence jumped*—shows just how different from English, and similar to Palatine German, the structure of the Pennsylvania Dutch expression is.

The motivation for borrowing the words for 'fence' and 'jump' in this shibboleth sentence reveals the naturalness of lexical influence from

English on Pennsylvania Dutch. The Pennsylvania Dutch word *Fens* is indeed an old borrowing from English, and one with a clear motivation. In eighteenth-century Central Europe, most properties, especially cultivated fields and pastures, were not enclosed by fence-like structures. Boundaries, if marked at all, were often indicated by hedges, rows of trees, or ditches. The closest thing to a fence in the modern sense was an enclosure around a small garden or yard, typically a paling or picket fence, the Palatine German word for which was *Zau* (std. Ger. *Zaun*). The circumstances encountered by immigrants to colonial Pennsylvania were different from the situation in Europe, both in Britain and on the continent. William Penn's statutes for his colony, which were passed in 1682 and dubbed collectively the Great Law, included the Law of Fences. According to this law, "all Cornfields shall be fenced, and all fences shall be at least five foot high, and for default thereof, such person shall be fined at the discretion of the County Court."[74] The novelty of man-made fences in Pennsylvania even attracted the attention of Johann David Schöpf, who devotes fully two pages to the topic.

One finds nowhere other than in America such many different kinds of enclosures. Practically every moment one encounters a different type and cannot avoid marveling at the ingenuity of the inhabitants. All the structures, however, seem to reflect a concern for economy of effort, rather than saving wood, space, or care in the long run. They are typically made of dead material, either thin stakes or split trees that are bound together in various ways, laid on top of one another, or set crosswise as overlapping upright poles. So-called worm-fences are the most common. Chestnut wood, when available, is selected because it is the lightest and lasts the longest when stripped of its bark.[75]

Given the novelty of fences as field enclosures in colonial Pennsylvania, it is entirely logical that German-speaking immigrants would borrow the English word for them. But what became of the Palatine-derived *Zau*, which originally meant 'paling fence'?[76] It retains its original meaning in the modern language, in the compound *Gaardezau*, 'garden fence'. Here again is an example where an English loanword does not supplant an older, native lexical item but expands the semantic field of which both the old and new words are a part.

As further evidence of how loan vocabulary reflect the changing situation of the speakers of a language, consider compound nouns in Pennsylvania Dutch that contain *Fens*. Some examples documented by C. Richard Beam in his monumental dictionary are given below.[77] English-derived nouns within the compounds are underlined.

<u>Bord</u>fens 'board f.'	Fensdor 'f. gate'
Dannefens 'briar f.'	Fenseck 'f. corner, cross-stitch'
Drohtfens 'wire f.'	Fensegift 'jewelweed'
<u>Glabbord</u>fens 'clapboard f.'	Fensemaus 'chipmunk'
Hinkelfens 'chicken f.'	Fenseposchde 'f. post'
Leinfens 'line f.'	Fenseschdraeme 'f. line'
Riggelfens 'rail f.'	Fenseposchde<u>schtamber</u> 'f. post stomper'
Schneefens 'snow f.'	Fenseschpringer 'f. jumper'
Schteefens 'stone f.'	Fenseschtippel 'f. staples'
Schdaagefens 'stake f.'	Fense<u>tschumper</u> 'f. jumper (fig.)'
Warremfens 'worm / snake f.'	Fenseweisse 'f. whitewashing'

Beam's dictionary lists twenty-eight compound nouns with *Fens*. Only five of those are formed with another English loanword; the rest contain Palatine German–derived nouns. While many of the fence compounds are calques of English nouns (e.g., *Schneefens*, 'snow fence'), a few are entirely innovative, for example, *Fenseck* for 'cross-stitch', *Fensegift*, 'jewelweed', and *Fensemaus*, 'chipmunk'. Thus, rather than being a symptom of semilingualism, lexical borrowing from English enables speakers of Pennsylvania Dutch to adapt to changed circumstances without diminishing the fundamentally Palatine German character of the language.

The second of two loanwords from English in the accurate rendering of Schöpf's stallion sentence, *tschumpe*, is another example of adoption of a verb into Pennsylvania Dutch that does not involve the replacement of an older one. In the Palatine source dialects for Pennsylvania Dutch, there was a verb *schpringe*, which meant both 'to run' and 'to jump'. In modern Pennsylvania Dutch *schpringe* has only the former meaning; *tschumpe* is used to describe the action of moving upward with one's legs (e.g., 'jumping in the air') or moving suddenly, as in 'jumping off the couch' or 'jumping when called'. In Schöpf's stallion sentence, *jumped* would be rendered better by *gschprunge*, since the action expressed necessarily involves movement both forward and upward (cf. the meaning of the related English verb 'to spring [over] something'). If, however, one were to emphasize that the horse *jumped over* the fence rather than *ran through* it, *tschumpe* would be used. Recalling the examples of fence compounds above, note that an animal that jumps over a fence is a *Fenseschpringer*. A *Fensetschumper*, in contrast, means 'fence jumper' in the figurative sense, referring to a person who changes church affiliations.

To sum up this section, accounts provided by outsiders of the speech of German Pennsylvanians suggest that by the early 1780s there existed a distinct form of language, a "Pennsylvania German dialect," thereby supporting the conclusion based on the settlement history of the Pennsylvania Dutch. The opinions about early Pennsylvania Dutch expressed by early observers were generally negative, the main stigma being the supposed contamination of the language by English. The reality, however, is that English influence on Pennsylvania Dutch was and still is relatively modest (estimated to be 10%–15% in the previous chapter). Words borrowed from English are fully adapted to the Palatine German–derived structures of Pennsylvania Dutch and ensure the expressive power of its vocabulary in the American context in which its speakers live. In the following section I consider some of the earliest examples of Pennsylvania Dutch, which set the stage for its development into a written medium in the nineteenth century.

The Emergence of Pennsylvania Dutch in Print

In his important study of early Pennsylvania Dutch life as documented in eighteenth-century newspapers, James Owen Knauss found just one item that could well be the earliest example of Pennsylvania Dutch in print. It is a short anecdote that appeared on April 30, 1794, in the *Neue Unpartheyische Readinger Zeitung* (New independent Reading newspaper) titled "Something about Fiddling and Dancing" (*Etwas vom Geigen und Tanzen*). It relates the story of a young Berks County farm boy. One day he comes into a small town and sees a group of people in a house dancing to music provided by a fiddler. The boy, who had never seen such a thing before, mistakes the violin, which has a head carved in the shape of a roaring lion, for a living creature. After witnessing this scene for some minutes, the boy runs several miles back home and reports to his father what he saw.

> Dadi was hun ich gseha!
> Was host du dan gseha?
> Ey ich hun a Ding gseha do isch a Kop druf und das bleckt die Zähn und der Man der zobelt dran, do knorrt's, dan streicht er, und do springa d'Leut in dem Haus rum und kaner kan die Thür finna.

> *Dad, guess what I saw!*
> *What did you see?*
> *Why, I saw a thing, there's a head on it and it shows its teeth, and the man is pulling on it, then it growls, then he plays, and then the people run around the house and no one can find the door.*

Unlike the Denglish of Muhlenberg and the marginally Dutchier samples of speech in Schöpf, "Something about Fiddling and Dancing" is written in something quite close to modern Pennsylvania Dutch, the few differences being features of Palatine German dialects that are not known to have survived in Pennsylvania Dutch (e.g., *ich hun* for *ich hab*, 'I have') or forms documented in earlier Pennsylvania Dutch that no longer exist (e.g., *isch* for *is*, 'is'). Thus, it is quite possible, given the overall accuracy of the text, that the anonymous writer was a native speaker of an early form of Pennsylvania Dutch. The function of this text was not to point out how ignorant country folk sounded but simply to entertain. Indeed, many of the earliest examples of written Pennsylvania Dutch had a similar function.

The first apparently native speaker of Pennsylvania Dutch to appear in print was an anonymous person who wrote letters to the editors of German-language newspapers under the pen name "Stoffel Ehrlich." *Stoffel* is a diminutive form of the name *Christoph* and was a common man's name among early German Pennsylvanians, but it also means 'dullard', 'blockhead', or 'stubborn person' in both German and Pennsylvania Dutch; *Ehrlich* is a German family name that derives from the adjective meaning 'honest'.[78] Stoffel's byline indicates that he was a resident of the *Canostogo-Kriek* (Conestoga Creek), in the heart of rural Lancaster County. In the second issue of the Lancaster newspaper *Der*

Etwas vom Geigen und Tanzen.

Ein Junge kam ohnlängst in ein kleines Städtgen in Berks Caunty und sahe allda einen Spiel-
man auf der Violine spielen und Leute darzu tanzen—
Der Junge war vorher noch nie über den Gränzen
seines Vaters Plantasche gewesen, und hatte noch
niemals eine Violin weder gesehen noch gehört und
auch noch nie tanzen gesehen. Des Spielmans Violine hatte vornen einen Kopf geschnitzt wie ein Löwen Kopf den Rachen auffsperrend, von diesem
muthmaßete der Junge die Violin müße ein lebendig Thier seyn. Nachdem er einige Minuten lang
mit Verwunderung und Furcht angehört und gesehen hatte lief er eilend weg und hielt sich nicht auf
bis er nach Hauße kam, welches etliche Meilen von
dem vorbedachten Städtgen entlegen war und er-
zehlte seinem Vater was er gesehen hatte auf nach-
folgende Weise :

Dadi was hun ich gseha ! Was hoft du dan
gseha? Ey ich hun a Ding gseha do isch a Kop
druf und das bleckt die Zähn und der Man der zo-
belt dran, do knorrt's, dan streicht er, und do sprin-
ga d'Leut in dem Haus rum und kaner kan die
Thür finna.

First documented example of early Pennsylvania Dutch,
Neue Unpartheyische Readinger Zeitung, April 30, 1794.

Wahre Amerikaner (The true American), on November 16, 1804, the following letter to the editor appeared:

> Mister Printer,
> We in Hempfield [Lancaster Co.] have gotten your newspaper, and as
> soon as we get into the city we will pay the subscription fee. . . . Since you
> are printing this newspaper every week, why don't you give us something
> fun every now and then. . . . Perhaps you could make the acquaintance
> of old Stoffel Ehrlich, not far from the Conestoga Creek, and get him to
> send you some articles. We used to laugh ourselves silly over his writ-
> ing, especially when he would take the big mouths down a notch. A few
> people in our neighborhood got angry over him and said he used too
> many English words without really understanding the language all that
> well. But they weren't on to his game [lit. 'up to his tricks']. We like to read
> different kinds of things in the newspaper.
> Signed: Various Subscribers[79]

This letter is written entirely in German with only a single English
loanword (*Tricks*), so it is not Denglish, but it does incorporate nonstandard forms that are obviously translated directly from Pennsylvania Dutch. The language of this letter, following Albert F. Buffington,
can therefore be called *Dutchified German*.[80] The Pennsylvania Dutch
features include two nouns, *Schreibens* (PD *Schreiwes*, 'writing') and
Großhansen (PD *Grosshanse*, 'big mouths'); two verb participles lacking
the standard *ge-* prefix, *kriegt* (PD *grigt*, 'gotten') and *worden* (PD *wadde*,
'become'); an adverb, *als*, 'used to'; one loan translation, *sie waren nicht
auf zu seinen Tricks* (PD *Sie waare net uff zu sei Tricks*, 'They weren't
up [on] to his tricks'); and one loan shift, *gleichen* (PD *gleiche*, 'to like').
Given that this was just the second issue of the newspaper, it is quite possible that the "various subscribers" were in fact the editors of the newspaper themselves, the brothers Henry (1777?–1814) and Benjamin Grimler
(1778?–1832), two Lancaster County natives who almost certainly spoke
Pennsylvania Dutch.[81] Even if the Grimler brothers were not the authors of this letter, their intent was to prepare their readers for the folksy
wisdom of Stoffel Ehrlich, who made his debut in the following issue.

   The entire first page of the November 23, 1804, issue of *Der Wahre
Amerikaner* was devoted to a humorous story told by Stoffel. In it, he

recounts how one day his daughter, Marei (*Mareia*, 'Mary'), and her "sweetheart from town" (*Swiethärt aus der Stadt*) quarreled. The boyfriend later supposedly spoke ill of Marei, prompting Stoffel to hire a lawyer to bring suit against him. After much back and forth, and a lot of attorney's fees, the case is dismissed, leaving Stoffel disgusted with the legal system. Stoffel compares lawyers to wagon wheels, stating that both have to be "greased" (*geschmiert*), a clever pun, since the verb *schmiere(n)* also means 'to bribe' in both German and Pennsylvania Dutch. Stoffel learns his lesson and vows to in the future "keep quiet and let the world go as it will." The text is written in Dutchified German, but his introduction includes extended quotes in (excellent) Pennsylvania Dutch. The introduction and first paragraph are given in translation below. Pennsylvania Dutch elements are italicized; English-derived words are underlined.

> Friend Grimler,
>
> Since you have already printed some of my letters, I am asking you to include the following in your newspaper. Leave *out* the English expressions as much as possible, *since my wife always scolds me: "Stoffel, if you want to write something, write correctly, or don't bother."* So I won't write anything, but just tell you what happened to me in court. And between you and me, I believe as strongly as ever:
>
> "Where women are in charge,
> "the outcome is rarely good!"
>
> And indeed, Mister Printer, to my greatest sorrow I experienced this at the last court. You can easily imagine how it goes when among us stubborn old Germans what today's world calls gentility wreaks havoc or becomes fashionable! What we used to call nonsense and foolishness *nowadays* so surely disturbs the contentment and happiness of an entire family. What *under the sun* could be worse than when discontent rules a house? As I *think* back to when *my* dear late father and we children lived so happily, I am almost forced to say, "People are not how they were in our times. Everyone gets worse with each passing day," and one could add, past common excluded![82]

What is striking about Stoffel's Dutchified German is how much it differs from the Denglish of non–Pennsylvania Dutch speakers such as

Excerpt from a letter by
"Stoffel Ehrlich," *Der Wahre*
Amerikaner, November 23, 1804.

> **Mittheilung.**
>
> **Freund Grimler,**
>
> Weilen du schon von meinen Stücker gesetzt
> hast, so ersuch ich dich mir folgendes in
> deine Zeitung zu thun—Laß die englische
> Expressions so viel als möglich haus;
> denn mei Fra zankt mich alsfort: „Du
> Stoffel, wann du ebes schreiben wit, so,
> schreib recht, oder laß die Finger da-
> von." Ich will also nichts schreiben, son-
> dern dir bloß erzählen, wie mirs an der
> Court gehappend ist—und zwischen uns
> gesagt, so glaub ichs so fest als ewer:
>
> „Wo Weiber führen das Regiment,
> Da nimmt es selten ein gutes End!"
>
> Und gewiß Meister Drucker, das hab
> ich bey der lezten Court zu meiner
> größten Sorrow erfahren. Du kannst,
> dir leicht einbilden wie es hergeht, wenn
> unter uns guten, ehrlichen, deutschen De-
> genknöp, was die jetzige Welt Gentiliti
> heißt, einreißt oder fashionable wird! Was
> wir vor Alters würden Flausen und Nar-
> rens-Possen geheißen haben, dis torb'l
> so schuhr alleweil die Happiness und Con-
> tentment von einer ganzen Familie. Was
> fah dann unter der Sun schlimmer seyn,
> als wenn in einem Haus Unzufriedenheit
> herrschet? Wenn ich dran denk wie mei
> seliger Vater und wir Kinder so gepliest
> lebten, so bin ich fast geforc'd zu sagen:
> „Die Menschen sind nicht wie sie in our
> Teims waren, iße werden von Tag zu
> Tag schlimmer," und man kan noch hinzu-
> setzen, päst common ausgelassen!

Muhlenberg and Schöpf. All the English loanwords are plausible in
Pennsylvania Dutch, and the occasional truly Dutch elements are used
in exactly the way a native speaker would use them. This is clearly the
work of a native Dutchman.

Stoffel's writing reappeared in a later issue of *Der Wahre Amerikaner*
(February 1, 1805), again taking up the entire first page. The content is
similarly humorous, and the language, Dutchified German, is the same.
Why the editors would choose to include (produce?) such writings is
hinted at in a letter published on January 18, 1805. Signed by an anony-

mous resident of New Holland, Lancaster County, the letter makes reference to the Pennsylvania gubernatorial election of 1799, in which the Jeffersonian Democratic-Republican candidate, Thomas McKean, defeated his Federalist opponent, James Ross, with crucial support from ethnic German voters angry over federal taxation. The unnamed *Neuholländer* devotes much of his letter to expressing gratitude that his fellow Pennsylvanians have now moved beyond the partisan strife of that earlier time and can enjoy the benefits of living in a free country under the rule of law.

> Who among us will complain? Who would prefer to live in slavery than under a government in which "*We the People*" is everything and bureaucrats are merely servants. Indeed, one who would choose the former must be a fool. I hope that in the future we can set aside all foolish partisanship (*Partheywesen*) and consider ourselves *as one family*. Then, and only then, may we laugh at the customs of other parts of the world and boldly cry:
> "We are a band of brothers,
> "united for the fatherland!"[83]

This partisan rancor of the late eighteenth century having now receded, the writer says that he and his neighbors "have been lying in wait for a long time for Stoffel Ehrlich" and "like to read something fun" in the newspaper. His letter concludes with the following postscript: "Don't forget to share entertaining material with us from time to time."[84]

It would appear that the editorial intent of featuring Stoffel Ehrlich's writings in *Der Wahre Amerikaner* was to entertain its predominantly rural Pennsylvania Dutch–speaking readership. Stoffel's everyman character is one that readers, especially older Pennsylvania Dutch males, could identify with. Stoffel is tradition minded and at times nostalgic and wary of social change, which often leads him to lock horns with his wife and daughter; he is not well educated but he is clever; and he is thrifty but able to indulge in simple pleasures, especially hearty food and drink. Linguistically, Stoffel's speech is a form of German that is as close as possible to being Pennsylvania Dutch without actually crossing that divide, employing numerous Pennsylvania Dutch expressions and English words that could be plausibly incorporated into Pennsylvania

Dutch by actual native speakers. This is not the constructed German-English "mishmash" of Muhlenberg and Schöpf, though, to be sure, standard German purists would have reacted to Stoffel's speech in a similarly negative way. The natural orality of Stoffel's text, as of Pennsylvania Dutch itself, is underscored in the introduction to his November 23, 1804, letter. Even though this is obviously a written text, Stoffel defers to his wife's objections that he cannot write properly and decides to "not write anything" and "just tell [erzählen] what happened."[85]

It will likely never be known who the real person was behind the character of Stoffel Ehrlich. Several letters under the same pen name appeared in an earlier German-language newspaper also from Lancaster, the *Neue Unpartheyische Lancäster Zeitung und Anzeigs-Nachrichten* (New nonpartisan Lancaster newspaper and advertiser; *NUL*), between 1787 and 1789, which was published by Anton Stiemer, Johann Albrecht, and Jacob Lahn. Clearly, the Stoffel of the early 1800s in *Der Wahre Amerikaner* was modeled after the same person from the 1780s, a "stubborn old German" (*deutscher Degenknopf*) husband and father from the *Canostogo-Kriek* in rural Lancaster County. The earlier Stoffel, however, writes not in Dutchified German but in the standard variety in which the rest of the newspaper was produced.[86] In terms of content, the 1780s Stoffel is still the down-to-earth Pennsylvania Dutch everyman, but his letters are not intended to entertain. Rather, they serve as foils to allow the editors to advocate certain positions on matters of concern to them. That is, the 1780s Stoffel Ehrlich, whose views were typical of those of many rural Pennsylvania Dutch of the time, serves as a straw man for the *NUL*'s progressive editorial line.

In six letters in the *NUL* signed by Stoffel Ehrlich that appeared between August 1787 and August 1789, several topics are discussed, including the value of higher education, superstitions, and the consumption of alcohol, coffee, and tea. In every instance, Stoffel holds traditional views that are later directly criticized by the editors or pseudonymous correspondents. Stoffel thinks higher education (most book learning, in fact) is a waste of time and money and believes strongly in the reality of the devil in the world. He considers having an occasional schnapps fine but bemoans the fact that his wife drinks coffee. In one letter he compares modern society to Sodom and Gomorrah.

In each of Stoffel Ehrlich's 1780s letters, its content and not its language marks the author as a conservative Dutchman. For example, his opinions on the founding of Franklin College in Lancaster, which began instruction in both English and German in the summer of 1787 and was aimed at elevating the educational status of German Pennsylvanians, are uniformly negative. In his letter of August 15, 1787, he writes:

> You tell us that Lancaster is to become the home of a German institution of higher learning; so I guess the idea is to make our children smarter than their fathers. Just don't get an idea like that. I am not highly educated either, but I don't need to know any more than what I already know. My dear late father didn't know nearly as much as I do, because he could neither read nor write, and when he wanted to figure, he counted everything on his fingers or made marks or x's above his parlor door. Aside from all that, he was, God bless his soul, an honest man, ate his piece of bacon and drank his cider daily, and passed away in his 86th year, peacefully, after he had bequeathed his entire place to me. So my two sons do not need to know anything more than he and I. For the egg should not want to be smarter than the chicken.[87]

One week later, on August 22, 1787, the editors reply to Stoffel as follows:

> We heartily welcome the contributions of Mr. Ehrlich, who seems to have a healthy intellect. Related to what we have discussed earlier, a good education establishes a foundation, because children grow up to become adults. We are thus puzzled that Mr. Ehrlich just cannot accept the idea of a German college here. Is it not true that if the head of a young man or woman is bereft of useful and healthy knowledge and the heart of each is stripped of the nobler sentiments of purer religion . . . how can the young man in such circumstances ever become a successful husband or the young woman a good housewife and mother? How can he serve his country in public office? Was this not the reason why the Germans were the woodcutters and waterbearers for their English neighbors?[88]

Regarding superstitions, in successive issues, on May 27 and June 3, 1789, the *NUL*'s editors published two articles debunking the legends of the Wandering Jew (*Der Ewige Jude*) and Doctor Faust, respectively. On August 12, 1789, Stoffel Ehrlich reacts as follows:

Misters Albrecht and Lahn!
No! I can't stand it anymore, this is driving me crazy. You consider everything fables and superstitions. According to you, the Wandering Jew and
Doctor Faust never existed, all ghosts exist only in the mind, and God
no longer works miracles. And in issue #101 of your newspaper you want
to show that the devil does not circulate among humans, putting evil
thoughts into their minds and affecting their souls so that they do things
they wouldn't otherwise do. Indeed, you call it a horrible morality, and to
make matters worse, you say that one could not conjure up the evil one in
order to receive hidden treasures from him. Don't hold it against me, but
you might be true atheists if you do not believe all of this.[89]

In their reply to Stoffel a week later, on August 19, 1789, the editors are
just as forceful in their criticism of traditional beliefs, especially hexing
and casting of spells.

To the honest Stoffel [Dullard].
My, my, the accusations Mr. Stoffel Ehrlich would heap upon us are a bit
too harsh. We won't refute him, but leave it to an enlightened public to
judge. But since he challenges us to explain what it means to be superstitious, because his mind is too simple to do so, we will tell him what, in
our humble opinion, it means to be superstitious: to claim or to expect
effects when causes are lacking. For example, if a person claims to be
able to hex or cast spells, or to be hexed or under a spell, such a person
is superstitious. One of two things is going on here. Either "to hex" or
"to cast spells" is meaningless (just as there are other words referring to
nonentities, or nothing), or it is possible for effects to come about without cause, which is also meaningless, since there is no such thing as an
effect without a cause.[90]

Returning to the question of language, the Stoffel Ehrlich of the 1780s
held views that were consonant with those of rural-dwelling, traditional
Pennsylvania Dutch men and women, but he expresses them in the same
way as his interlocutors, including the editors, not in Dutchified German or Pennsylvania Dutch but in eighteenth-century standard German. Stoffel's speech was not intended to reflect his character or way of
thinking.

Interestingly, one pseudonymous *NUL* subscriber from rural Lancaster County who gently takes issue with Stoffel, Hannickel Wahrheit (truth), adds the following postscript to one of his own letters to the editor, dated September 19, 1787.

Ey, noch eins, ihr Herrn Drucker! Was sagt man dann in der Stadt von der grossen <u>Eleckshen</u>? doch unsere <u>Hädt-männer</u> werden es wohl auch bey uns *storren*, so bald die Stadtherrn wort schicken was sie machen wollen, dann die Stadt ist doch der meister, und so wirds im Busch *allwann* seyn. *Adjes.*

Say, one more thing, Mr. Editors! What are they saying in the city about the big <u>election</u>? But I guess our <u>head men</u> will be stirring things up with us just as soon as the city fathers send word what they want to do. Because the city calls the shots, and in the country they don't care. Farewell.

Like the Stoffel Ehrlich letters that were to appear in the early 1800s, this postscript from Hannickel Wahrheit is an example of Dutchified German very likely produced by a native speaker of Pennsylvania Dutch. The English loanword *Eleckshen*, 'election', and the loan blend *Hädt-männer*, 'head men' (underscored above), are entirely appropriate in Pennsylvania Dutch, and the author inserts three words (italicized) that are derived from bona fide Pennsylvania Dutch: *storren* (modern PD *schtarre*; cf. Ger. *stören*), 'to stir up'; *allwann*, 'indifferent'; *adje(s)*, 'farewell'. Although Hannickel Wahrheit contradicts Stoffel Ehrlich in the main part of his letter, he maintains his credibility to the readership by identifying himself linguistically as a member of the Dutch tribe. The content of Hannickel's postscript is consistent with the image he aims to portray of himself in that he conveys the lack of interest on the part of rural folk toward the political goings-on in the city. This is a clever device on the part of the editors, to find a correspondent who shared their views but who was not as urbane as they were, someone who was more likely to connect with a reader sympathetic to Stoffel Ehrlich.

Recall that the two letters attributed to the early nineteenth-century Stoffel Ehrlich in *Der Wahre Amerikaner* (dated November 23, 1804, and February 1, 1805) served a function different from that of the six letters appearing in the 1780s. Written in Dutchified German, they were intended to entertain rather than to serve as foils for the editorial line. Although there is one letter to the editors of *Der Wahre Amerikaner* printed after Stoffel's letter of February 1, 1805, on March 23, 1805, whose author, from rural Manor Township ("Ein Mänorländer"), Lancaster County, mentions missing Stoffel in the newspaper, the editors of the newspaper decided from then on to focus on more serious news rather than humor, and Stoffel Ehrlich made no more appearances in their newspaper.

Other, shorter linguistically interesting material found its way into the pages of *Der Wahre Amerikaner* in 1805. A particularly important political issue throughout most of that year was the hotly contested gubernatorial race between incumbent Thomas McKean and his rival Simon Snyder, both Jeffersonian Democratic-Republicans. In the weeks leading up to and following the election on October 8, *Der Wahre Amerikaner* published many serious letters extolling the virtues of both candidates, though the editors leaned toward McKean. One curious letter appeared at the height of the McKean-Snyder race on July 20, 1805, and expressed support for the latter candidate. The letter, which was signed "A Goose" (*Eine Gans*),[91] is written not in Dutchified German but in Germanified Pennsylvania Dutch, that is, Pennsylvania Dutch with some standard Germanisms.

The tone of the Goose letter is definitely light-hearted, as those written by Stoffel Ehrlich, but this time the humorous content is underscored by strange graphic elements. Both the original and an English translation are given below.

Du Drucker Benjamin Grimler—Ich bin ahns von dein' Leser, und beschur auch ein deutsche "Gans," und schwätz bey meiner Sichel mit dir, just wie mirs um d' Leber ist—Was wet ihr mit dem M'Kean und den faule Dinte-SiFfer? Die plauderN und Schuhrigeln uns mit Der Kontuschin und sagen Vom volk—aber hol' mich der KukKuk, wann sie Mir e Loch in Kop blosa! iCH kenn' ihr Tricks! Das VOlk! ja halt a bissel— Offisen woll-a-sie, um ihr Ranzen ausZufüttern—und wie mei Reima-Macher auf mei Tisch schrieb:

Sie suchen und durch Plane zu gewinnen,

Und sich auf unsere Kosten hoch zu bringen!

Das Volk mag dann zum Teufel gehen!

He! du Drucker, wie g'fallt dir aber die reIm? Gelt, in einem Friestaat derf man Verdeufelt bold schwätzen? Hurrah dann vor unser *Simon Schneider* und Liberty! Was geb' ich drum, ob die Laier zu schaffen geforc'd werra—Ich schaff a, und denk mich beym Blitz so gut als eneger der sich den Kop in Mehlsack steckt.

Druck mir mei stück wie 's just steht—ich begehr Kein Bessermacher, veränder nix dran; sonst triet ich di net, wann ih in'd Stadt komm. Eine Gans.

You Printer Benjamin Grimler—I am one of your readers and for sure a German "goose," and talk with you by my sickle [on my honor], and just as I please.—What do you want with McKean and the lazy ink-drunkards? They prattle on and plague us with the constitution and speak of the people—but may the cuckoo take me if they don't blow a hole in my head! I know their tricks! The people! Now wait a minute—they want offices in order to fill their bellies—and as my rhyme-maker wrote on my desk:

They seek to win us through schemes,
And elevate themselves at our expense!
To the devil with the people!

Hey, you printer, how do you like this rhyme? In a free country one can speak darned boldly, right? So hurray for our Simon Snyder and liberty! What do I care if the lawyers [liars] are forced to work—I work, too, and consider myself by jiminy just as good as anyone who sticks his head in a flour sack.

Print my letter for me just as it is—I don't need anyone to correct me [a "better-maker"], don't change a thing; otherwise I won't treat you next time I come to town.
A Goose.

The editors append the following remarks to Mr. Goose's letter:

We followed the desire of our writer to the letter . . . but at the same time we wish that if he uses the pen again that he would at least use clean paper, since the letters and the paper had almost the same color, and the whole thing was very similar to our printer's ink![92]

In terms of its form, the Goose letter was intended to suggest someone with poor facility in standard German. Misspellings abound, and

Du Drucker Benjamin Grimler—Ich bin ahns von dein' Leser, und beschur auch ein deutsche "Gans," und schwätz bey meiner Sichel mit dir, just wie mirs um d' Leber ist—Was wet ihr mit dem M'Kean und den faule Dinte-Siffer? Die plaudern. und Schuhrigeln uns mit Der Kontuschin, und sagen Bom volk—aber hal' mich der Kukkuk, wann sie Mir e Loch in Kop blosa! Ich kenn' ihr Tricks! Das Volk! ja halt a bissel—Offisen woll-a-sie, um ihr Ranzen auszufüttern—und wie mei Reima-Macher auf mei Tisch schrieb:

Sie suchen uns durch Plane zu gewinnen, Und sich auf unsere Kosten hoch zu bringen! Das Volk mag dann zum Teufel gehen!

He! du Drucker, wie g'fallt dir aber die Reim? Selt, in einem Friestaat derf man verdeufelt bold schwätzen? Hurrah dann vor unser Simon Schneider und Liberty! Was geb' ich drum, ob die Laier zu schaffen geforch'd werra—Ich schaff a, und denk mich beym Blitz so gut als eneger der sich den Kop in Mehlsack steckt.

Druck mir mei Stück wie 's just steht—ich begehr kein Bessermacher, veränder nix dran; sonst triet ich di net, wann ih in Stadt komm.

Eine Gans.

[Wir folgten dem Begehren unsers Schreibers wörtlich....aber wünschen zugleich, so lange er die Feder mehr brauchen—doch säubres Papier zu nehmen, indem die Buchstaben und das Papier fast gleiche Farbe hatten, und das Ganze mit unserer Druckerfarbe Geschwisterkind war]

Pennsylvania Dutch letter to the editor from "A Goose," *Der Wahre Amerikaner*, July 20, 1805.

capitalization is at points wildly incorrect. Mr. Goose also creates childish-sounding collocations such as *Reima-Macher* (rhyme-maker) and *Bessermacher* (better-maker), misuses standard German words, and fails to rhyme his clumsy, three-line attempt at a poem. His ignorance extends to his knowledge of English, as his rendering of 'constitution' as *Kontuschin* would suggest. The use of *Laier* (pronounced like "liar") for 'lawyer' is a clever pun, though likely not intended to suggest native intelligence on Mr. Goose's part. As far as Mr. Goose's Pennsylvania Dutch goes, all indications suggest that the author was a native speaker of the language. He uses bona fide Pennsylvania Dutch words and idioms, and, importantly, the number of English loanwords is modest, in keeping with the un-Denglish-like character of the real language. Aside from *Kontuschin* and *Laier*, English-derived words include *beschur*, 'certainly' (lit. 'by sure'); *Tricks*; *Offisen*, 'offices'; *Liberty*; and *triet*, 'treat'. All are still used in modern Pennsylvania Dutch.

While Stoffel Ehrlich's earlier letters in *Der Wahre Amerikaner* entertained without necessarily serving up rural Pennsylvania Dutch for criticism or ridicule, Mr. Goose embodies multiple negative stereotypes. He is a rural dweller suspicious of politicians and lawyers and has a poor command of both German and English. And, importantly, he is a supporter of Simon Snyder. Snyder ended up losing the 1805 election to McKean, including in the heavily Dutch counties of southeastern Pennsylvania, but Snyder's political star rose quickly when Governor McKean made common cause with Federalists, the party of John Adams, against the more grassroots, populist Jeffersonian Democratic-Republicans, whose candidates most rural Pennsylvania Dutch favored. It makes sense that a rough-around-the-edges Dutchman like Mr. Goose would have been a Snyder man.

Simon Snyder's connection to Pennsylvania Dutch linguistic history is an interesting one. Born in 1759 in Lancaster County to Palatine German immigrants, Snyder was of humble background and almost certainly belonged to the first generation of Pennsylvania Dutch speakers.[93] A letter to the editor in *Der Wahre Amerikaner* of July 30, 1808, signed by "J. L., a loyal Republican and well-wisher of his fatherland" reads:

Is it not appropriate that we Pennsylvanians should finally have a governor who can also speak *German* with us? Do not let it be said that we Germans are against our fellow brother: If Mr. Snyder had ever voted for a Stamp Act, for excises and window taxes, for debts at eight-percent interest, and for war, then I would be just as opposed to him as to [James] Ross. But no, friends, Snyder is on the side of the farmers and craftspeople, which earns him our votes. Ross wants war and voted for oppressive taxes and slavery.[94]

In a later letter to the editors of *Der Wahre Amerikaner*, from September 24, 1808, another unnamed Jeffersonian Democratic-Republican, in a list of reasons why he was voting for Snyder, makes this comment about Snyder's language skills:

[Snyder] understands the German language, and our Germans in Pennsylvania have often had dealings with the governor, so through his election they will be able to take care of these matters in their own mother tongue.[95]

Yet another anonymous correspondent, writing in *Der Wahre Amerikaner* on November 7, 1807, defends Snyder against his rivals' criticism that he was not trained in classical languages:

The excessively ardent Federals are against Snyder because he speaks neither *Hebrew*, nor *Greek*, nor *Latin* and because he is a farmer and a craftsperson. Those are amazing reasons. If we should get their favorite as governor, woe unto us poor Germans and Englishmen in Pennsylvania: Would it be expected that we would be ruled in Hebrew, drilled in Greek, and have to dance in Latin or Spanish? Wouldn't that be fun?[96]

As Simon Snyder became more widely known among the Dutch after 1805, he went on to handily defeat the Federalist James Ross in the 1808

Simon Snyder (1759–1819), first Pennsylvania Dutch governor of Pennsylvania.
Source: Private collection.

Amerikaner,

Stämpelacten,

Fenstertaxen,

und Sclaverey

wollen wir nicht, sondern

Freyheit,

Simon Schneider,

Frieden und gleiche Rechte.

Advertisement urging voters to cast their ballots for Simon Snyder in the gubernatorial election of 1808, *Der Wahre Amerikaner*, October 8, 1808. Translation: "Americans, We Do Not Want Stamp Acts, Window Taxes, and Slavery, Rather Freedom, Simon Snyder, Peace, and Equal Rights."

gubernatorial election with overwhelming support from rural-dwelling Pennsylvanians across the ethnic spectrum, not just the Pennsylvania Dutch. The editors of *Der Wahre Amerikaner*, who had soured on Snyder's predecessor, Thomas McKean, came to express strong support for Snyder in his successful campaign. The advertisement above appeared in the last edition of the paper before the October 1808 election.

BY THE 1780S, when the children of German-speakers who arrived at the peak of immigration to Pennsylvania in the middle of the eighteenth century had reached maturity, the first descriptions appeared of a "bastard gibberish" form of German polluted by English that was spoken by people in the hinterlands of southeastern Pennsylvania. Since these descriptions came from outsiders, either Europeans or members of the standard German-speaking social elite in Philadelphia, the reliability of their "examples" of earliest Pennsylvania Dutch is questionable. However, such accounts make clear that a unique form of German was being spoken in the rural Dutch Country by the end of the eighteenth century. Support for this hypothesis comes from the facts of the history of the secondary settlements of Pennsylvania Dutch speakers, especially the communities in Ohio and further west, which were launched by settlers from Somerset County, PA.

Within a decade or two of the Muhlenberg and Schöpf accounts, during which time movement out of the traditionally Dutch counties, especially Berks, was underway, the first evidence of actual Pennsylvania Dutch appeared in print. Just as important as the actual evidence of early Pennsylvania Dutch words and structures are the sociolinguistic contexts in which these first texts emerged. Written Pennsylvania Dutch was not a neutral medium of communication in the way that standard German and English were. Rather, when Pennsylvania Dutch or Dutchified German was reproduced in print, it signaled a number of stereotypical, almost always humorous and often negative, characteristics attributed to the farmers and craftspeople of German extraction living in rural Pennsylvania, the kind of people who overwhelmingly supported one of their own, Simon Snyder, for the governorship in 1808.

As the following chapter will show, the stigma attached to Pennsylvania Dutch by outsiders, and not a few insiders, endured. However, active speakers of Pennsylvania Dutch themselves came to embrace their unique linguistic-cultural identity, bound up as it was with their conservative faith and peasant republicanism, and thumb their noses at both Yankees and more urbane German Americans. The covert prestige of Pennsylvania Dutch as a marker of positive virtues such as honesty, humility, and conservatism, leavened with a healthy dose of folksy humor, is crucial to understanding how the language has endured right up to the present day.

CHAPTER 3

Pennsylvania Dutch, 1800–1860

*Get lost with your "Sie." That ain't no language, everyone here
is equal. "You" is "du," and so it's no use for anyone to say "Sie."
I speak just as good German as you, I can tell you that.*
—FROM A CONVERSATION BETWEEN A PENNSYLVANIA DUTCH
SPEAKER AND A GERMAN SPEAKER, 1853

The *Independenz* of the Pennsylvania Dutch and Pennsylvania High German in the Early Nineteenth Century

The first half of the nineteenth century was a crucial period for the formation of a unique folk culture centered on the Pennsylvania Dutch language. After the middle of the eighteenth century, immigration from German-speaking Europe declined precipitously and largely came to a halt with the American Revolution. Few Germans came to America before 1830, but that number increased significantly in the 1840s and 1850s. An estimated 5.8 million German immigrants entered the United States between 1820 and 1930, with nearly 1.5 million arriving in the 1880s alone.[1] These immigrants, the *Deitschlenner*, had little impact on the *Deitsche*, the descendants of the approximately 81,000 eighteenth-century immigrants to colonial Pennsylvania, however.[2] Nineteenth-century immigrants who were farmers and rural-dwelling craftspeople looking to own their own property naturally went to where land was both available and affordable, which at that time was on the

American frontier, far west of the Pennsylvania Dutch Country. In the second half of the nineteenth century, millions of Germans settled in Ohio, Indiana, Michigan, Illinois, and especially the states of America's midwestern "German Belt," Wisconsin, Iowa, Minnesota, North Dakota, and Nebraska, as well as states farther south, including Kansas, Missouri, and Texas.[3] Those *Deitschlenner* who did make Pennsylvania their home were mainly urban dwellers who felt little kinship with their (very) distant cousins in the rural Dutch Country. And, for their part, the Pennsylvania Dutch also found their cultural and linguistic distance from the "new Germans" to be quite substantial.

One of the most detailed descriptions of Pennsylvania Dutch culture and language in the decades before the Civil War comes from Franz von Löher (1818–1892), a highly educated German jurist and historian who spent considerable time traveling in the United States. In a chapter titled "Formation of a New German Culture" in a book he published in 1847, Löher writes that after their arrival in America,

> [t]he German country folk retreated completely from the English. Either too weak or too poorly organized and led to be able to make their language and customs dominant, the German peasants were nonetheless too strong and too proud to give up their folkways. The thirty years during which they were as good as cut off from Germany created a chasm between themselves and countrymen who arrived later. So it happened in America the curious phenomenon that a new German cultural group formed, unique in language, customs, and outlook.[4]

Löher goes on to enumerate several tangible characteristics of this "new German cultural group," from their mixed-up language to their elongated noses.[5] Elsewhere in his book Löher, who was deeply disappointed by the level to which, in his opinion, German language and culture had degenerated in America, advances the myth that German was nearly declared the official language of Pennsylvania but for a single vote in the state House of Representatives, supposedly cast by none other than Frederick Muhlenberg, its Speaker from 1780 to 1783.[6]

As Löher's observations underscore, the divide between the Pennsylvania Dutch and other ethnic Germans was not just geographic (i.e., rural vs. urban) but also cultural and linguistic. The ancestors of the

Pennsylvania Dutch had come to America from what was an essentially premodern, feudal society. The more urbane *Deitschlenner*, by contrast, had grown up in a Central Europe influenced culturally and politically by ideas born of the Enlightenment and republican political movements. Nineteenth-century German Americans everywhere, including in the rural Midwest, identified with a transnational culture of *Deutschtum* (Germanness), an important part of which was a unified standard ("High") German language. Whereas the ancestors of the Pennsylvania Dutch had been receptively familiar with a written standard German variety in print media and especially in worship, as the nineteenth century progressed, the language of Goethe and Schiller came to be widely spoken as well as written among both European Germans and German Americans. As the star of the standard German language ascended, so too did its prestige vis-à-vis regional dialects increase. The rustic-sounding "bastard gibberish" spoken by the Pennsylvania Dutch elicited the same kind of reactions among many nineteenth-century German Americans as it had among earlier observers such as Johann David Schöpf, Franz von Löher's counterpart in the eighteenth century.

The shift to English monolingualism among the descendants of many later German immigrants, especially urban dwellers, widened the gap between *Deitschlenner* and the Pennsylvania Dutch even further. In the past as today, moving up socially was linked to proficiency in English. Bilingualism was in most situations transitory, usually associated with the children of immigrants but gone by the third generation, again, most often in towns and cities. Philadelphia is an apt example in this regard. Already by the early decades of the nineteenth century, the world of the German-speaking elite to which Marcus Kuhl, George Lochman, and Frederick Muhlenberg belonged was a thing of the past. Ironically, the scorned Pennsylvania Dutch had the last laugh sociolinguistically by successfully maintaining not only a German-derived vernacular language but also a form of standard German, receptively at least, for another two hundred years.

One important factor that promoted the cultural and linguistic isolation of the Pennsylvania Dutch from other Americans of German descent was the economic prosperity in the Dutch Country and many other parts of rural America in the first half of the nineteenth century. The twin forces of industrialization and urbanization that would later threaten that isolation and eventually, among the nonsectarians, bring about the shift to English monolingualism, were largely absent in the early 1800s. Farmers and craftspeople in rural southeastern Pennsylvania enjoyed economic security, with good access to markets in urban centers like Philadelphia and Baltimore, as well as in the smaller cities of York, Lancaster, Reading, and Allentown. Geographic and social isolation combined with economic success made southeastern Pennsylvania in the early nineteenth century an ideal crucible in which a distinct Pennsylvania Dutch culture could develop. The hybrid culture that emerged involved not only the innovation of tangible products such as pies, quilts, and the Conestoga wagon but also the preservation of practices and beliefs with antecedents going back many centuries, including superstitions, folk astronomical ideas, and traditional healing arts deeply rooted in premodern Europe. Earl F. Robacker, the author of an important survey of Pennsylvania Dutch literature, calls the decades between 1800 and the Civil War "the period of transition" in Pennsylvania Dutch culture, when the most popular secular German-language publications among the Pennsylvania Dutch were farmer's almanacs and the runaway bestseller, *Der Lang(e) Verborgene Freund* (The long lost friend), a powwowing manual first published in 1820 by John George Hohman.[7]

Robacker connects the "resurgence of primitive superstition" among Pennsylvania Dutch in the early nineteenth century to the "supplanting of a high type of spiritual religion," which coincided with the severing of most ties between European Protestants and their coreligionists in America at the end of the eighteenth century.[8] In a parallel way, the Pennsylvania Dutch language developed independently of influences from secular European German culture, and this was reflected in the increasing frequency with which it began to appear in print. The dominant medium of literacy among Pennsylvania Dutch in the early nineteenth century was still standard German, as demonstrated by the number of German-language newspapers published in several towns, including even very small communities. The most notable of these periodicals was the *Reading Adler* (Eagle), known as the "Bible of Berks County," which was published continuously in German from 1796 until 1913.[9] By contrast, the last German newspaper founded in the eighteenth century in Philadelphia, the *Neue Philadelphische Correspondenz*, ceased publication by at least 1812,[10] a reflection of both the rapid move toward English monolingualism in that city and the long-standing cultural and social, as well as linguistic, divide between it and the rural Dutch hinterlands. The German language, as both a spoken or written medium, receded quickly among German Philadelphians as the ties to Europe were weakened, while the Pennsylvania Dutch vernacular and Pennsylvania High German endure and continue to develop away from their European origins still today, more than two centuries later.

An articulate prophet of the anglicization of the German Philadelphian social and cultural elite was Frederick Augustus Conrad Muhlenberg, introduced in the previous chapter. Born in 1750 in Trappe, PA, in what was then Philadelphia County (now Montgomery County), Muhlenberg was a member of German Pennsylvania's most prominent family. His father, Henry Melchior Muhlenberg (1711–1787), is considered the father of the Lutheran Church in America, having emigrated to Pennsylvania in 1742 from Halle, Germany, the home of the Francke Foundations, a Pietist Lutheran enterprise devoted to education and social work.[11] On his mother's side, Frederick was the grandson of Conrad Weiser, the leader of the early Palatine settlement in the Tulpehocken region of Berks County. Muhlenberg grew up in a standard German–speaking home and became immersed in the language by spending much of his youth in Germany. When he was thirteen, he and two of his brothers were sent by their father to Halle for schooling at the Francke Foundations and later at the university there. Frederick returned to Pennsylvania in 1770, at the age of twenty, accompanied by John Christopher Kunze (1744–1807), who married Muhlenberg's sister, Margaret Henrietta, in 1771. Muhlenberg followed in his father's footsteps and was ordained a Lutheran minister, serving various pastorates in Pennsylvania and New York City from 1770 until 1779. In that year he entered politics, serving terms in the Continental Congress, the Pennsylvania House of Representatives, and the US House of Representatives, of which he was its first Speaker. In 1799 Muhlenberg retired from politics to Lancaster, where he died in 1801.[12]

On September 20, 1794, Frederick Muhlenberg, at the height of his career in the US Congress, delivered a speech to the German Society in Philadelphia that addressed the major goals of that organization. Whereas it had been founded in 1764 to protect the interests of eco-

Frederick Augustus Conrad Muhlenberg (1750–1801).
Source: http://upload.wikimedia.org/wikipedia/commons/8/88/Frederick_Muhlenberg.jpg.

nomically distressed German immigrants, especially redemptioners, by the 1790s the society had turned its attention to improving the educational situation of second- and third-generation German Pennsylvanian youth. In his remarks, Muhlenberg, who was also the president of the society at that time, devotes much attention to the question of language. Specifically, he expresses his view that the future success of German Pennsylvanians would depend on their mastery of English.

English is and will remain the language of the country. We in the United States are only a small minority. Even in this state, where the most Germans live, we make up barely a third of the population. By what right or justification may we expect the majority to accommodate us, the much smaller minority? All national laws and ordinances, all judicial matters, all commerce and contracts, and in fact all public affairs are conducted in the English language, and yet still there is a bias toward the German language. Which German among us in business or any other public occupation keeps his books in German, and if he does, must he not admit that this is bound up with numerous inconveniences? No one can deny that this causes the greatest harm for us, nor can one deny, on the contrary, that it is more advantageous in every respect for our youth if they acquire a thorough knowledge of the language of the country.[13]

Muhlenberg goes on to enumerate several reasons why it is incumbent on German Pennsylvanians to become proficient in English. He stresses the cost and inconveniences involved with having someone translate legal and business documents. And Muhlenberg points out that Germans are only one of several non-English-speaking immigrant groups in early America. If every group were to assert its right to educate their children in their native tongue, Muhlenberg speculates, the result would be a "linguistic chaos" (*Verwirrung der Sprachen*) comparable to the Tower of Babel.[14]

Muhlenberg's argument for the inevitable necessity for German Pennsylvanian youth to shift to English is amplified by his observations on what he viewed to be the abysmal quality of the German he heard spoken in Pennsylvania. In his speech he quotes at length from two people who had made similar observations on the language of German Pennsylvanians about a decade earlier, namely his brother-in-law, John Christopher Kunze, and none other than Johann David Schöpf:

There remains one other question, whether most of the so-called German spoken in Pennsylvania is actually German. If I overlook our sermons and the speech of those few Germans who have recently arrived in this country from respectable commercial centers, then the so-called Pennsylvania German language does not truly earn the right to be called German. The Swabian speaks differently from the Swiss, the Palatine from the Saxon, the Hessian from the Pomeranian, and the Low German from the High German. Out of all these diverse dialects, which are all called German, along with a considerable addition of corrupted English, the most ridiculous dialect of all developed: I mean the speech of my countrymen, Pennsylvania German.[15]

After quoting from Kunze's and Schöpf's earlier texts on the miserable state of German in Pennsylvania, Muhlenberg cites supposed examples of German Pennsylvanian speech, including the infamous sentence from Schöpf about the stallion jumping over the fence discussed in the previous chapter:

This is how a foreigner [Schöpf] laughs at the so-called German here, and his story is similar to the familiar one old [Christopher] Sauer told us in one of his newspapers or almanacs, namely *der Stallion sey über die Fence gejump'd und habe des Nachbars Wheat abscheulich gedamaged*. There is also the anecdote about the German girl who was hosting a respectable German minister. Wanting to invite him to eat in what she thought was the most polite manner, she said, in good Pennsylvania German: *Fress hearty, Herr Parr, du bis very willkumm* [Eat hearty, Mr. Pastor, you are very welcome].[16]

Muhlenberg's reference here to a publication by the "old" Christopher Sau(e)r (1695–1758) as the source of Schöpf's jumping stallion sentence underscores the fact that Schöpf apparently did not hear it (and likely the other examples of early Pennsylvania Dutch speech he cited in his 1788 book) directly from "an old German farmer."[17] The second sentence Muhlenberg mentions here, while closer to actual Pennsylvania Dutch, is still at odds with the real language both structurally and pragmatically. The word *Parr*, 'pastor', is very close to Pennsylvania Dutch (*Parre*), and *willkumm*, 'welcome', is identical, yet the Pennsylvania Dutch verb *fresse* refers to the consumption of food only by animals or human gluttons; no servant would ever have addressed a minister in this way. The two English words *hearty* and *very* are not used in Pennsylvania Dutch. Finally, if the servant girl had known enough standard German to use the honorific *Herr*, 'Mr.', which is not part of Pennsylvania Dutch, she also would have addressed him with a formal second person pronoun, either *Ihr* or *Sie*, not *du*.

Muhlenberg concluded his 1794 speech at the German Society by discussing at length what he saw as the appropriateness of using English in the one sphere of German Pennsylvania life where at that time loyalty to German still ran highest, the church. He pointed out that European American Protestant churches had shifted successfully to the use of English, including Swedish churches in Pennsylvania, as well as Dutch and German churches elsewhere. Muhlenberg bluntly stated that in his personal experience German Pennsylvanian youth actually got more out of sermons in English than those in German. Their spiritual needs could be adequately met in English, he argued, since important religious texts, hymns, catechisms, and other books were already available in translation, and experience showed that German American theologians and religious teachers could function well in both languages. Thus, for Muhlenberg there was little to argue against the inevitability—necessity, even—of German Pennsylvanians making the shift to English.[18]

Just months before Muhlenberg gave this speech in Philadelphia, on January 9, 1794, the US House of Representatives over which he presided received a petition from a group of German speakers in Augusta County, Virginia, requesting that "a certain proportion of the laws of the United States may be printed in the German language."[19] This petition was taken up and supported by two House committees, whose members happened to include a German Pennsylvanian born in Berks County, Daniel Hiester (1747–1804). After much back and forth into February 1795, the details of which remain murky, Congress never voted to authorize the publication of federal legislation in German, despite the support of the two committees. At one point in January 1795, the House, meeting as a committee of the whole, which meant that its Speaker, Frederick Muhlenberg, was not present, voted down a motion to allow a committee debating matters related to "promulgating the laws" to rise to report to the House. It is unclear whether this motion may have included a provision for the translation of laws into German, but the vote was 41 in favor of the motion and 42 opposed.[20]

Some years later, in 1813, Philadelphia's most prominent Lutheran leader at the time, the Rev. Justus H. C. Helmuth (1745–1825), pastor of St. Michael's and Zion congregation, of which Frederick Muhlenberg was a member, wrote the following:

What would Philadelphia be like in forty years if the Germans there remained German, if they preserved their language and customs? It would take no more than forty years and Philadelphia would be a German city, just as German as the counties of York and Lancaster are. The English would retreat further into the back country if they were not building up the southern parts of the city. And just imagine what all of Pennsylvania and the upper part of Maryland could become in forty or fifty years! A completely German state where, as years ago in Germantown, the beautiful German language would be spoken everywhere, even in government and the courts. Was it not an English lawyer twenty years ago who made the proposal that the German's affairs should be discussed in German? Did not General Hiester make the proposal in Congress in Philadelphia that all the laws of the land should be printed in German? He would have been successful had he not been outmaneuvered by a German, a proud German fool in the House, in fact, who by design undermined the best interests of his people and his constituents.[21]

Though confusing the details of the events of 1794 and 1795, Helmuth is clearly referring to Speaker Muhlenberg as the "proud German fool" who supposedly betrayed Daniel Hiester and all of German Pennsylvania. Helmuth had over several years fought a feverish and ultimately unsuccessful struggle with a pro-English faction in his home parish, St. Michael's and Zion, over the use of German or English in worship. Muhlenberg, as a particularly visible "anglicizer" in Helmuth's congregation and as someone who was in a position of considerable political power, became a convenient scapegoat for generations of Helmuth's Germanophile sympathizers who lamented the fact that the German language "lost out" to English in America.[22] Apparently Helmuth's bitterness, combined with the 41–42 vote of January 1795 (despite the fact that it was only on a motion related to the "promulgation of laws" and was taken in Muhlenberg's absence), gave rise to what is known today as the "Muhlenberg legend," according to which, but for a single vote cast by Speaker of the House Frederick Muhlenberg, German would have become the official language of the United States.

Decades later, the facts of history surrounding the Muhlenberg legend were distorted even further by Franz von Löher, who set the story in Pennsylvania rather than on the federal level, which was not a surprising switch, since in the 1790s Philadelphia was the seat of both the federal and Pennsylvania State governments. And, before he was elected to Congress, Muhlenberg had in fact been in the Pennsylvania House of Representatives and had also served as its Speaker. Quoting from Löher:

It is not surprising that English gradually came to play the leading role [in the United States] in politics, the courts, and other public affairs and imposed their language at least in the largest assemblies. In Pennsylvania, however, that was not easy. On a vote whether the dominant language in the State Assembly, in the courts, and in official documents in Pennsylvania should be German, the balloting was evenly split. One-half supported the introduction of German, and that was of great significance if one considers that this would have involved making a state German in which previously English had been the language of laws. The Speaker of the [Pennsylvania] House, a Muhlenberg, tipped the scales in favor of the English language through his vote.[23]

On balance, it is unfair to have cast Frederick Muhlenberg as an enemy of the German language, either in Pennsylvania or on the national level. He was a realist who understood that there was little hope of German—or any other language—ever enjoying equal status with English in the United States. This reality explains why there has never been any need for a vote at the federal level on whether English should be officially declared the national language. Since the colonial era, non-English speakers, including many Germans, and especially their children and grandchildren, have been voting with their feet (or tongues) in favor of English, making it the de facto, if not de jure, "language of the land."

The relatively rapid extinction of German among the descendants of both Justus H. C. Helmuth and Frederick Muhlenberg was, of course, not replicated among the Pennsylvania Dutch. Not only did they keep on speaking their "bastard gibberish"; they also maintained knowledge of a form of standard German known as Pennsylvania High German, which was used in periodicals such as *Der Wahre Amerikaner* and the *Reading Adler* as well as in religious worship. That there were differences perceived between European standard German and Pennsylvania High German is evident as early as the late eighteenth century. Recall Johann David Schöpf's disdain for the language of the German Pennsylvanian press, which he described as "pitifully deformed" and "nauseating," due mainly to the fact that he saw it as being influenced by English. Recall as well the response offered by the German-born Pastor Helmuth and Professor Kunze to Schöpf's charges, who said that if they did not publish German newspapers using the Americanized language that they did, "American farmers would never be able to read or understand them."[24]

Linguistically speaking, Schöpf was on the right track as to how Pennsylvania High German differed from its standard European counterpart. In the same way that Pennsylvania Dutch is influenced lexically and semantically by English, in the form of loanwords and calques, so Pennsylvania High German contains some anglicisms. Further, there are in Pennsylvania High German nonstandard German lexical items and expressions that are clearly derived from Pennsylvania Dutch, similar to what is found in Dutchified German. And Pennsylvania High German, especially in its contemporary form, contains words, phrases, and spellings that, though once common in earlier forms of standard German, are now archaic relative to the modern European language.

Across all these features of vocabulary and orthography, there is a notable lack of consistency in many Pennsylvania High German texts; that is, the same concept may be rendered by different words or phrases even within the same text, and multiple spellings for the same word often occur. Finally, in those areas of grammar where Pennsylvania Dutch and standard German differ (e.g., with the Genitive case for nouns, which was nonexistent in eighteenth-century Palatine German, as well as certain inflectional forms), Pennsylvania High German is also inconsistent, sometimes using standard grammatical forms, at other points Pennsylvania Dutch forms, and in still other instances so-called hypercorrect forms. Indeed, so different are Pennsylvania High German and European standard German today that contemporary Pennsylvania Dutch speakers can make sense of the latter in secular texts only with difficulty.

Some of the differences between European standard German and Pennsylvania High German are exemplified in various translations of the text of the American Declaration of Independence. Yet another popular legend in German American circles holds that the document was printed in German translation before it appeared in English. This is not correct. The text of the declaration was produced in broadside form in English in the shop of Philadelphia printer John Dunlap on the evening of July 4, 1776, distributed the following day, and printed in the *Pennsylvania Evening Post* on July 6. Three Philadelphia Germans,

Melchior Steiner, Carl Cist, and Heinrich Miller, produced a German translation of Dunlap's broadside, which appeared in Miller's *Pennsylvanischer Staatsbote* on July 9.[25] Over the next several decades, into the nineteenth century, German versions of the document appeared frequently in newspapers in the Dutch Country on or around the July 4 holiday. Interestingly, most if not all the editors of these various newspapers did not reprint the Steiner/Cist/Miller translation. In fact, a survey of six translations of the declaration in German in five newspapers between 1802 and 1828 shows several differences between them and the 1776 translation and also among each other, all of which exemplify both the divergence of Pennsylvania High German from European standard German, as well as the lexical, grammatical, and orthographic variation found within the former.

The opening sentence of the Declaration of Independence is given below, first in its original form and then in the 1776 translation by Steiner, Cist, and Miller. Following that first translation are two of the six different early nineteenth-century versions, from the *Harrisburger Morgenröthe* (Dawn), July 3, 1802, and from the Carlisle, PA, *Freyheits-Fahne* (Flag of Freedom), July 4, 1816.

When in the Course of human Events, it becomes necessary for one People to dissolve the Political Bands which have connected them with another, and to assume among the Powers of the Earth, the separate and equal Station[a] to which the Laws of Nature and of Nature's God entitle them, a decent Respect to the Opinions of Mankind requires that they should declare the causes which impel them to the Separation.

Wenn[c] es im Lauf[g] menschlicher Begebenheiten für ein Volk nöthig wird die Politischen Bande,[f] wodurch es mit einem andern verknüpft gewesen, zu trennen, und unter den Mächten der Erden eine abgesonderte und gleiche Stelle[a] einzunehmen,[d] wozu selbiges die Gesetze[h] der Natur und des GOttes der Natur berechtigen, so erfordern Anstand und Achtung[b] für die Meinungen[i] des menschlichen Geschlechts, daß es die Ursachen anzeige, wodurch es zur Trennung[e] getrieben wird. (*Pennsylvanischer Staatsbote*, July 9, 1776)

Wann[c] es in dem Lauf[g] der Zeiten nöthig wird, für ein Volk, die politische Banden[f] die sie zusammen hält, zu zerreissen, und unter den

Mächten der Erden eine abgesonderte und gleiche Station oder Stelle[a] anzunehmen,[d] zu welchem das Gesez[h] der Natur und dessen Schöpfer sie berechtiget hat, so erfordert die Bescheidenheit,[b] daß es Ursachen zu solcher Absonderung[e] angiebet. (*Harrisburger Morgenröthe*, July 3, 1802)

Wenn[c] es in dem Laufe[g] der menschlichen Begebenheiten, nothwendig für *ein* Volk wird die politischen Banden[f] aufzulösen, welche es mit einem *andern* verknüpft haben, und unter den Mächten auf Erden den abgesonderten und gleichen Rang[a] anzunehmen[d]; wozu die Gesetze[h] der Natur und des Gottes der Natur es berechtigen; so fordert ein bescheidener Respect[b] für die Meynung[i] der Menschen, daß es die Ursachen erklären sollte, welche es zu der Trennung[e] zwingen. (*Freyheits-Fahne*, July 4, 1816)

Two very straightforward differences between the 1802 and 1816 translations and the 1776 version involve borrowings from English. The original words *Station* and *Respect*, which are rendered by *Stelle*, 'position' (indicated by the superscript *a*), and *Anstand und Achtung*, 'propriety and esteem' (*b*), in the Steiner/Cist/Miller translation, appear as *Station oder Stelle*, 'station or position', in the 1802 version and as *Respect* in the one from 1816, which reflects the absence of native equivalents for these two English words in Pennsylvania Dutch.[26] A similar example of borrowing from English due to the lack of an appropriate word in Pennsylvania Dutch has to do with the title of the Declaration of Independence itself as it is rendered in Lancaster's *Der Wahre Amerikaner*. In an article published on July 1, 1809, that precedes a translation of the document, one finds the words *independent* and *Independenz* where one would expect *unabhängig* and *Unabhängigkeit*. Just paragraphs later, the standard German equivalents appear (in a quoted song and the title of the declaration, respectively). Here again Pennsylvania High German is being adapted to the linguistic knowledge of a Pennsylvania Dutch–speaking readership, whose native language lacks words cognate with *unabhängig* and *Unabhängigkeit*.

Other differences between the 1776 translation of the first sentence of the declaration and later versions point to influence from Pennsylvania Dutch. These include two lexical items, *wann*, 'if, when(ever)', for *wenn* (*c*); and *annehmen*, 'to assume' (Pennsylvania Dutch *aanemme*), for *einnehmen*, whose cognate in Pennsylvania Dutch, *einemme*, means 'to take in' (*d*). A third instance of Pennsylvania Dutch lexical influence has to

Der Wahre Amerikaner.

1809.]　　Eine Zeitung für den Bauer und Stadtmann.　　[No. 240.

[Newspaper facsimile columns in German Fraktur.]

Der Wahre Amerikaner, July 1, 1809. The loanwords *independent* and *Independenz* occur in the left column; *unabhängig* and *Unabhängigkeit* appear in the song and the heading below it in the middle column.

do with the substitution of *Absonderung* for *Trennung*, 'separation', in the 1802 translation (*e*). The cognate verb for the latter word in Pennsylvania Dutch, *drenne*, means 'to separate, sever, or rip' in reference to cloth, while the verb *absondere* is commonly used to describe the separation of groups of people from one another.

In the area of grammar, there are differences involving -*n*'s at the ends of nouns and adjectives. In German, -*en* is a common plural inflectional marker whose correlate is -*e* or ø in Pennsylvania Dutch. In the 1776 and 1816 translations, the English phrase *the Political Bands* is rendered prescriptively correctly as *die Politischen Bande* (*f*). The 1802 translation has *die politische Banden*, with the -*n* missing on the adjective but added to the noun. Finally, there are archaisms found in the Pennsylvania High

German translations that are absent in the 1776 version. These include an old Dative case ending on certain nouns (*Laufe* for *Lauf*, 'course'; [*g*]); the spelling of *Gesez*, 'law', without a *t* (*h*); and *ey* instead of *ei* in words such as *Meynung*, 'opinion' (*i*). Two other archaic spellings are also found in the 1802 translation, *berechtiget* for *berechtigt*, 'justified', and *angiebet* for *angi(e)bt*, 'declares'.

In the same way that Pennsylvania Dutch speakers paid little heed to those outsiders who stigmatized their vernacular language, from the early nineteenth century on they were content to use a form of standard German that diverged increasingly from the cultural language of Central Europeans and German Americans. This divergence was mainly due to the changes underway in European standard German. Norms that made clear what was "correct" and "incorrect" in grammar and vocabulary usage, and eventually also in pronunciation, became increasingly fixed in nineteenth-century German-speaking Europe, especially after the unification of the German states into an empire in 1871. Political unity within Germany, supported by increased mobility, higher literacy rates, and the need to communicate across a wide territory that came with industrialization and urbanization, made active knowledge of standard German a vital asset for both economic success and cultural and social progress. A reflection of the ongoing importance and utility of standard German is the fact that its lexicon continues to change: as with any living language, old words fall out of fashion while new ones are being coined, in step with the changing external circumstances of German speakers over the course of history.

The sociolinguistic situation of Pennsylvania High German in the nineteenth century and later was quite different from that of European standard German. Although many Pennsylvania Dutch were able to both read and write in German in the eighteenth century, by the nineteenth century very few Pennsylvania Dutch had the ability, need, or inclination to produce original writings in German, and still fewer had any occasion to speak it. Many if not most Pennsylvania Dutch did, however, retain the ability to read the language, but the texts they had at their disposal were for the most part religious works (the Bible, prayer books, and hymnals) and periodicals, mainly local newspapers and almanacs. Those few nineteenth-century Pennsylvania Dutch who were able to write in German were typically pastors and journalists. As farmers and craftspeople, average Pennsylvania Dutch, especially in the early nineteenth century, were not involved in occupations that required them to write much of anything, in any language, but, when they did write, it was increasingly in English.

Although the schools serving most Pennsylvania Dutch children in the early nineteenth century were nominally conducted in German, the language was used and taught in a limited manner. The previous chapter established that the educational situation of Pennsylvania Dutch children throughout the nineteenth century, especially in the decades before the Civil War, was beset by a number of challenges, especially poor attendance and deficient pedagogy (e.g., the method of [mindless] recitation, *uffsaage*). Accounts from Dutchmen who experienced rural education during that time, such as those of William A. Helffrich (1827–1894), underscore the many shortcomings of the schools, even if later in life these writers recalled their youth overall with nostalgia. Another firsthand observer of early Pennsylvania Dutch education and a contemporary of Helffrich was Henry Lee Fisher (1822–1909), the author of the poem in praise of the Pennsylvania Dutch language quoted at the end of chapter 1. In the same collection in which that poem appeared is another poem by Fisher recalling his days in a one-room German school near Waynesboro, Franklin County, PA. This very school was immortalized in verse by Fisher's second cousin, Henry Harbaugh (1817–1867), who had also been a pupil there just a few years before Fisher. "Das Alt Schulhaus an der Krick" (The old schoolhouse at the creek), which is discussed in the next chapter, is the best-known and most beloved product of Pennsylvania Dutch literature.[27]

Of special importance in Fisher's poem is his depiction of the language situation in his school. Fisher's German school is portrayed as a place of linguistic and intellectual stagnation led by an incompetent and unsympathetic schoolmaster whose charges are increasingly drawn toward English. The poem begins as follows:

> Dort hen m'r unser Schuling grügt,
>   Un hen dafor bezahlt;
> Es war 'n rechte Deutsche Schul—
> Der Meeschter, der, hot g'macht, e'n *Rule*—
>   Er hot's gedhu mit G'walt,—

Das *English* net drin glernt derf sei,
Schunscht gebt's zu'n grosse Hudelerei.

M'r sin all dorch's alt Rechel-Buch,
  Die Biewel un' d'r Psalter;
Die Summa hen m'r ufgesetzt,
Das jo ken Ziffer war f'rlezt—
  Sel war die *Rule* for alters;
'Nord isch's in Schwarz un Weis dort g'schtanne,
Das mir die *Business* hen f'rschtanne.

Doch hot'rs Englisch 's letscht erlaabt
  Weil fiel hen's lerne wölle;
Er hot un's A B C erscht g'lernt,
Was hot uns awer sel f'rzörnt,
  Nord hen m'r lerne schpelle;
Un dan war's Zeit for auszuschpanne,
For weiter hot'rs net f'rschtanne.[28]

That's where we got our schooling
  And paid for it.
It was a proper German school,
The teacher made a rule—
  And held to it with force—
That English was not to be learned there,
Otherwise there would be too much confusion.

We went all through the old arithmetic book,
  The Bible and the Psalter;
We added up the sums
So that no digit was misplaced.
  That was the rule, years ago.
In was in black and white back then;
So that we understood what we were supposed to do.

But he finally allowed English
  Because many wanted to learn it.

He taught us the ABCs first,
Did that ever upset us,
And then we learned to spell.
But then it was time to "unhitch the horse,"
Since he didn't know anything more.

A look at the typical curriculum in Pennsylvania's nineteenth-century German schools confirms what Fisher notes above, that is, it was largely limited to the "three Rs." In this respect, the schools that Pennsylvania Dutch children (occasionally) attended were little different from their English-medium counterparts. The typical text used in most early American schools was the traditional primer, of which the most famous in colonial America was the *New-England Primer*, first published in 1687.[29] A representative primer for Pennsylvania's German schools is *Das Neue ABC- und Buchstabir-Buch zum Gebrauch für Deutsche Volksschulen in Pennsylvanien und anderen Staaten* (The new ABC and spelling book for use in German public schools in Pennsylvania and other states), which was published in 1861 by Edwin M. Benner, the son of Enos Benner, an important Pennsylvania Dutch printer-editor discussed later in this chapter. After an introduction to the German alphabet, much of the book consists of syllabaries of increasing complexity, intended to lead Pennsylvania Dutch–speaking children toward literacy in German. There are a number of short texts, dealing with nature (especially animals) and moral and biblical topics, as well as a few longer poems. There is also a section of prayers: the Lord's Prayer, morning and evening prayers to be said at home, and prayers for the beginnings and ends of meals and of the school day. The book concludes with a comparison of the German and English alphabets and a multiplication table.[30]

Henry Lee Fisher's knowledge of Pennsylvania Dutch, German, and English was likely typical among his contemporaries, that is, those who were born in the rural Dutch Country in the early decades of the nineteenth century but who moved away and entered the professions. Pennsylvania Dutch remained his mother tongue, as the quality of his poetry reveals. Although he began to compose Pennsylvania Dutch poems only in 1875, when he was in his early fifties, Fisher's Dutch shows no attrition whatsoever.[31] At the same time, he was equally fluent in English, part of what distinguished him in his successful career as a jurist in York,

PA.[32] He also produced a volume of poetry in English.[33] No one reading
Fisher's English poems would suppose that English was not his first language. His German, however, was apparently deficient. There is nothing
in his biography to suggest that he had formal instruction in the language
beyond what he had received in the "old schoolhouse at the creek." The
spelling that he used in his Pennsylvania Dutch poetry, which he clearly
attempted to model on German, shows that his familiarity with the latter language was imperfect. While he knew, for example, to capitalize
nouns, write <sch> instead of <sh>, and distinguish correctly between
<ei> (for the diphthong that rhymes with *eye*) and <ie> (= "ee"), he wrote
only <f> where German uses both <f> and <v> (e.g., *f'rletzt*, 'damaged,
misplaced', and *fiel*, 'much, many', instead of *verletzt* and *viel*) and used
umlauts in a hypercorrect manner, as in the words *grügt*, 'gets' (PD *grigt*,
Ger. *kriegt*), and *wölle*, 'want to' (PD *welle*, Ger. *wollen*).[34]

 Fisher's poem on his time in school continues by saying that the push to
learn English came from the girls and that they were on the leading edge
of change generally: "[w]hen something new was discovered, / it wasn't
long before the girls took it up" (*Wan ebbes neues aus war g'funne / War's
net lang bis de Mäd's hen g'schpunne*).[35] Little by little the boys and the
girls would write English notes back in forth in school, and before long
they started using English words in their Pennsylvania Dutch. Their use
of English quickly exceeded that of their mean schoolmaster and spread
to domains outside of school, including with their horses.

> Anschtats fon kum, war's "*come along*,"
> Am Blatz fon Hot, war's "*jee;*"
> For Haa-rum hen m'r Wo! whaa! g'sad,
> Du *Bugger!* bischt so absanaad.
> Wu Deufels wid dan hi?
> Nau laaf m'r grad do in d'r Farich,
> Schunscht dresch ich dich noch dorich un dorich.

> *Instead of "kumm" it was "come along";*
> *In the place of "hott" it was "gee";*
> *For "haarum" we said "whoa, haw!"*
> *You "bugger"! You're so obstinate.*
> *Where the d——l do you want to go?*

Now walk straight in the furrow for me,
Otherwise I'll thrash you through and through yet.

According to Fisher, his peers' increasing preference for English over Pennsylvania Dutch was not well received by their elders. But, since English was associated with fashionability, it was almost inevitable that it would supplant Pennsylvania Dutch and German.

'S war juscht as wie's mit *Fashions* isch,
   Sei e'gneer Weg hot's g'numme;
Anschtats fon jerrem! war's "O, Lah !"
Am Blatz fon Krautselaad, war's "Schlaa,"
   Un *come*, anschtats fon kumme;
M'r hot als g'sad, in Deutsch, kumm rei;
Nau war's "*schtep in*, die Sus. kummt glei."

"*T-h-u-n-d-e-r-a-t-i-o-n!*" sagd die Betz,
   "Was fehlt nau dene Kuche?"
In *English* war nix g'schwinder g'lernt,
Abartig wan m'r war f'rzörnt,
   As bissel *English* fluche;
D'r Dan hot e'mohl g'sad "bi d——mnd
Wan ich nau so e' *Business schtand*."

D'r Fater war net weit eweck
   Un hot 'ns höre sage;
"Nau seenscht du Dan, was *English* koscht,
Wan du's net unnerwege loscht!
   Was dhun ich dich net schlage!
Seenscht du nau do, die Hick'ri-beitsch?
Wand' fluche muscht, dan fluch in Deutsch."

Krumbere hen m'r nimme g'sad,
   Des ware nau *Potatos*;
Kattun, war nix as *Calico*,
Mei Liewer Kerl, war nau mei *Beau*,
   Un Liewes-äppel, *Tomatos*;

For wan du wit, war's *if you please,*
Un Schmierkäs, der, war *Cottage-cheese.*

It was just as it is with fashions,
  It went its own way.
Instead of "Yerrem!" it was "Oh, la!"
In place of "Grautselaat" it was "shlaw,"
  And "come" instead of "kumme";
We used to say in Dutch, "kumm rei,"
Now it was "shtep in, die Sus kummt glei" [Susie's coming soon].

"Thunderation!" said Betty,
  "Was fehlt nau denne Kuche?" [What is wrong with those cakes?]
In English nothing was learned more quickly,
Especially when someone was angry,
  Than to curse a bit in English.
Dan said once, "[I'll] be d——d
If I can't stand that business."

Father was not far away
  And heard him say that.
"Now you see, Dan, what English costs,
If you don't leave it alone!
  I ought to beat you!
You see this hickory switch here?
If you have to curse, then curse in Dutch!"

We never said "Grummbiere" anymore,
  Those were now "potatoes."
"Gaduu" was nothing but "calico,"
"Mei liewer Kerl" was now my "beau,"
And "Lieweseppel," "tomatoes";
For "wann du witt" it was "if you please,"
And "Schmierkaes" was "cottage cheese."

Fisher's personal opinion on the attrition from Pennsylvania Dutch (and German) that he witnessed—and experienced—beginning in his youth is expressed in his writings, including the introduction to his 1879 anthology and some of the poems therein. There he defends Pennsylvania Dutch as a legitimate form of speech against the scorn it received from English and German speakers. His affection for the language was strong. Fisher was nostalgic about Pennsylvania Dutch and the culture in which it was embedded, yet nowhere does he express concern that the language might eventually die out. The last stanza of his poem on his German school is interesting in this regard:

> So dhun die Schprooche zamme laafe,
>   Juscht wie die Wässere a'h;
> So dhun die Buwe un die Mäd,
> Juscht weil sies gleiche, allebeed,
>   Un so gebt's Mann un Fraa;
> Un's Folk f'rmehrt sich in d'r Welt,
> Un so wert a'h die Schrift erfüllt.

> *That's how the languages flow together,*
>   *Just like waters.*
> *The boys and the girls do*
> *Just as they please, both,*
>   *And then they become husband and wife,*
> *And the people multiply in the world,*
> *And that is how Scripture is fulfilled.*

After devoting several verses to describing how boys and girls came to use more English than Pennsylvania Dutch over the protests of their parents, Fisher's concluding verse is remarkably dispassionate. He does not outright say that Pennsylvania Dutch has been supplanted by English; rather, he seems to convey that the vague "flowing together" of the two languages brought about by his generation was an inevitable and natural development in history.

Summing this section up, it is clear that in the early decades of the nineteenth century the productive literacy among the Pennsylvania Dutch went from being mainly in German to mainly in English, especially among those who, like Henry Lee Fisher, moved into social circles, often urban, in which Pennsylvania Dutch played less of a role. By the turn of the twentieth century other, less mobile nonsectarians also became less able to read and write in German, but they still kept speaking Pennsylvania Dutch. This describes the remaining nonsectarian speakers of Pennsylvania Dutch today, who are mostly elderly residents of southeastern Pennsylvania's traditionally Dutch counties. The German-language newspapers their grandparents read disappeared a century ago: the *Reading Adler* ceased publication in 1913, and Allentown's *Welt-Bote* followed suit just a few years later. And most Lutheran and Reformed churches in traditional Pennsylvania Dutch communities have not held regular services in German for decades.

The sociolinguistic situation of today's Amish and Old Order Mennonite sectarians is both similar and different. Pennsylvania Dutch remains the vital, rich language of everyday oral discourse, but nearly everything they write, and most of what they read, is in English, which is also the medium of instruction in their parochial schools. At the same time, although they maintain sufficient ability to read the Bible and other religious texts for worship in German, that is the extent of their German-based literacy. Many still purchase German-language farmer's almanacs each year, but almost no sectarians have the ability, inclination, or opportunity to read newspapers or other periodicals in German anymore.

During much of the nineteenth century, when Pennsylvania Dutch could still read Pennsylvania High German, if not necessarily write it, the German-language newspapers they subscribed to, like the *Adler* and the *Welt-Bote*, were a rich source of edification and entertainment. Today these periodicals offer us a fascinating window not only on early Pennsylvania Dutch culture but on early American life in general. The rest of this chapter picks up the thread of the discussion from the previous chapter about the emergence of Dutchified German and bona fide Pennsylvania Dutch in print. As their productive knowledge of German was gradually supplanted by English starting around 1800, some Pennsylvania Dutch chose a third path and began to put their oral vernacular to paper. As a distinct Pennsylvania Dutch folk culture fermented in the bucolic crucible of southeastern Pennsylvania in the first half of the nineteenth century, so too was the stage set during that time for the emergence of a body of folk literature in Pennsylvania Dutch that flowered in the decades after the Civil War. The German-language newspapers of the Dutch Country played a crucial role in that development, and they provide us with the richest documentation available of early forms of the Pennsylvania Dutch language. The following section considers samples from various newspapers and other sources that shed light on how Pennsylvania Dutch came to emerge as a vibrant medium of folk cultural and aesthetic expression.

From Dutchified German to Pennsylvania Dutch

Relatively few texts in Dutchified English or Pennsylvania Dutch from the earliest decades of the nineteenth century have been discovered. In a 1951 article titled "Early Use of Dialect," Alfred L. Shoemaker reprinted five short prose pieces, three of which appeared in the *Northumberland Republicaner* of Sunbury, PA, in 1814 and 1815; one in the *Nordwestliche Post*, also from Sunbury, in 1819; and one that was printed in an Allentown newspaper, *Der Unabhängige Republikaner* (Independent republican), in 1811.[36] In his article Shoemaker mentioned the existence of two other letters to the editor in *Der Wahre Amerikaner*, which were one of the Stoffel Ehrlich letters discussed in the previous chapter (from November 23, 1804) and the Goose letter of July 20, 1805. Stoffel, the "honest dullard" from the Conestoga region of rural Lancaster County, wrote on behalf of his fellow Dutch first in German in the 1780s in the *Neue Unpartheyische Lancäster Zeitung* and then in Dutchified German and Pennsylvania Dutch after 1800 in *Der Wahre Amerikaner*. "Dialect letters" such as Stoffel's became one of the most important vehicles through which later prose and poetry in Pennsylvania Dutch were disseminated. No letters bearing Stoffel Ehrlich's signature (from *Der Wahre Amerikaner*) have been identified after February 1, 1805. The last reference to him appeared almost exactly one year later, on February 8, 1806, in another letter to *Der Wahre Amerikaner*, written by a "Miss Schnips, from the country" (*Miß Schnips, aus dem Busch*). The name alludes to the Pennsylvania Dutch verb *schnippse*, which means 'to sob'. Miss Schnips's letter, which is in Dutchified German, begins as follows:

Mr. Editor Grimler,
Since there's not much news now, please do an old friend the courtesy of printing this in your next issue.

Don't put off until tomorrow what you can do today, so says Stoffel Ehrlich, and he's quite right there, for what good is there in drawn-out scheming? If someone enjoys doing something, then he gets right to it. Strike while the iron's hot and seize the opportunity when it's there, my step-sister says, who already had a husband when she was nineteen. I've complained (to myself) long enough, "Oh, how sick I am!" I've made myself up, preened myself, dressed up fancy, and for what? For nothing more than putting myself in the same situation that my mother was in before me. I see that I have had bad luck. I have to rethink my strategy, because otherwise I will join the class of old maids, and if that happens, that's it for me! All hope is lost, and all the preening and making myself pretty in the world will not do me any good. It's already hard for the young women, how will it be for the old ones?

It may be true that the *old bachelors* aren't worth much: they're stubborn simpletons who don't know what's good for them or what they want. For my part, I don't want a bachelor. Give me a widower instead. But the old fellows have better chances than we women do. And so, Mr. Editor, setting all embarrassment aside and speaking *plainly* [lit. 'German'], with the goal of finding a husband, would you do me the favor of placing the following *advertisement* in your newspaper? Just maybe someone will fall for me.[37]

In Miss Schnips's advertisement for a husband, she describes her manifold attributes as well as her desiderata in a husband: he should not be too fond of strong drink (though Spanish cigars are all right), and he must "understand the law." While the editorial intent of printing this letter is clearly to entertain and Miss Schnips's missal would not appear to contain a deeper message of social or political import, it does exemplify the familiar association of Dutchified German—that is, thinly veiled Pennsylvania Dutch—with straight-talking country folk.

Nearly all of the earliest writings in Dutchified German or Pennsylvania Dutch are humorous, at least superficially. That is not to say, however, that the subject matter of such writings is trivial. On the contrary, in the same way that the earliest Stoffel Ehrlich letters in German served as an editorial foil, so did writers of Dutchified English and Pennsylvania Dutch use vernacular language to connect more directly with their Dutch-speaking readership: to engage and entertain them, certainly, but also to sway them toward particular views on a range of topics of importance to the writers, especially social and political issues. To that end, one key genre employed by editors of early American newspapers generally, not just the German-language press, was dialog. In an era when media were limited to the printed word, reproducing oral language in dialogic form was an effective tool to reach readers. As such, dialog was well suited for the use of Dutchified German / Pennsylvania Dutch, *the* oral language most familiar to a German Pennsylvanian newspaper's intended audience.

Two examples of dialog from *Der Wahre Amerikaner* around the same time that Miss Schnips's letter appeared illustrate this point. The first, which was published on January 25, 1806, is in Pennsylvania Dutch, but it is framed by an introduction and a concluding paragraph in Pennsylvania High German. The conversation takes places in a tavern between a Drunkard (*Saufaus*) from the country and a So-called Gentleman (*sogenannter Gentelmann*) from the town. Since they both speak Pennsylvania Dutch to each other, the So-called Gentleman is presumably of rural background. After the two men stumble into one another in the tavern, the city slicker brags to his interlocutor that just the day before he had tricked a couple of "country boys" (*Buschbube*) out of several bottles of alcohol. The Drunkard takes offense at this story of trickery and points out that not only does he (the Drunkard) pay for his own drinks; he even has four dollars to spare, which he shows to the So-called Gentleman, who then tricks the Drunkard into paying for several rounds for them both and also into "lending" him two dollars. After receiving the money, the So-called Gentleman declares, "Now I can go on. I am a gentleman. Let whoever wants to work do so, that won't be me. Besides, who thinks anything of laborers? We certainly do not." Before he passes out on the floor of the tavern, the Drunkard rails at the So-called Gentleman, "You poor, drunken loser! Such fellows as you don't deserve to live. Anyone who wishes his parents were dead just to drink away his inheritance is a d——n rascal." The So-called Gentleman then departs and hires a sleigh in order to escort some "ladies of the evening from the town" (*Lädies des Abends aus der Stadt*) to another tavern, where he then brags about having cheated the Drunkard out of two dollars.

The anonymous person who relates this dialog (A Listener, *Ein Zuhörer*) concludes (in German) as follows:

And now, Mr. Editors, what do you think of the new, emerging, so-called gentlefolk who are embarrassed to work? What will become of this? I myself know parents who worked hard to raise their sons to be lazy. And with sadness I often see some men who live in poverty and misery: in their youth they were gentlefolk, but now they are beggars! How therefore utterly wrong are all such parents who do not have their children taught a trade, and who in fact expressly desire that their children *not* be taught a trade so that they may become gentlefolk. Only when it is too late will these parents realize, to their regret, how foolishly they acted.[38]

The moral of the brutally honest tale is clear: rural parents, don't let your sons grow up to be like gentlemen. The social divide between the country, the home of honest, hardworking (if sometimes also hard-drinking) farmers and craftspeople, and the town, where lazy, dissolute gentlemen and ladies career toward rack and ruin, is a theme that would be revisited frequently in later Pennsylvania Dutch literature, and it evokes the positive image that Pennsylvania Dutch speakers—who were by definition rural dwellers—held of themselves.

A second early dialog from *Der Wahre Amerikaner*, published on October 10, 1807, also takes place in a tavern. This time, the two interlocutors are considerably soberer, and the discussion centers on a political topic rather than a social or moral one. The dialog is conducted between members of the two major political parties at the time, the Federalists and the (Jeffersonian) Democratic-Republicans. The content of the dialog, which is in Dutchified German, leaves no doubt as to how the editors lean politically. Like the great majority of its rural Pennsylvania Dutch readers, *Der Wahre Amerikaner* ardently supported the party of the populist Thomas Jefferson, who was at the time in his second term as president, having handily defeated Federalist opponents in the elections of 1800 and 1804, the incumbent John Adams and Charles C. Pinckney, respectively.

Although this political dialog is more civil than the one between the Drunkard and the So-called Gentleman, it conveys in no less direct a manner the views of *Der Wahre Amerikaner*'s editors. It also echoes the salient dichotomy in early Pennsylvania Dutch society between honest farmers and craftspeople on the one side and deceitful gentlefolk, especially lawyers, on the other. And the political divide between Federalists and Republicans is apparently mirrored ethnically: the Republican in the dialog speaks of "we Germans," while the Federalist refers to "the Germans," who are equated with "the Democrats" and "Jefferson's friends," in the third person.

> FEDERALIST: Well, you Jacobin! This time we'll show you that we can do with you Republicans just as we please. We Federals are gentlefolk and have common sense, and you dumb fools are just about good enough to work.
>
> REPUBLICAN: I'm listening to you, but don't care what you say: I'm a farmer. I think it's good that we common people have the right to vote for whomever we want. You hear that?
>
> FEDERALIST: That doesn't matter, because we're going to convince the *Germans* of these nice things: That the Constitution will break down, that the country is headed for war and chaos, that lawyers are honest people and would be the most intelligent men for the Assembly, that only lawyers love wealthy farmers, that Jefferson wants war, and that robbery and stealing will ensue *if the Democrats (or Jefferson's friends)* win this time! I'll be darned if the Germans don't believe this like the Bible. They eat it up like sugar. And if there happens to be a McKean supporter nearby, we'll shout out "Hurrah for McKean and the Constitution!"
>
> REPUBLICAN: So, that's what you're "convincing the Germans of." One would have to be pretty dumb to believe such childish nonsense.
>
> FEDERALIST: All we want is to win the election. And because we Federals don't really believe in "McKean and the Constitution," many Quids are also voting for our ticket. Since we're trying to make the Constitution as important for the Germans as the New Testament, that's a good thing. And you must surely know that elections aren't lost on a couple of lies.
>
> REPUBLICAN: If the Constitution is so sacred, then why did you Federals want to amend it when the Assembly was still in Philadelphia?
>
> FEDERALIST: Be still and stop talking about old matters.
>
> REPUBLICAN: Do you people really think that we Germans are so dumb as to believe that the Assembly or Simon Snyder wants to overthrow the Constitution?

FEDERALIST: No, but be quiet. Come and drink a bit of wine and water, since I can't get anywhere with you.[39]

The tone of this dialog is thus more elevated than that of the one between the Drunkard and the So-called Gentleman, and that difference is nicely reflected in the choice of the somewhat more formal Dutchified German over the more obviously vernacular Pennsylvania Dutch in which the Drunkard and the So-called Gentleman converse. Both language varieties were comprehensible to a readership that spoke Pennsylvania Dutch and was literate in Pennsylvania High German, and, by having both forms of German at their disposal, writers were able to express themselves on multiple stylistic levels. The verbal repertoire of nineteenth-century Pennsylvania Dutch, which included knowledge of three linguistic varieties—Pennsylvania Dutch, Pennsylvania High German, and also English—allowed for a richness of expression in print of which writers took full advantage.

Keeping Dutch . . . and German

The first texts to appear in Dutchified German and Pennsylvania Dutch were in prose form. Poems, including the lyrics for songs, which were not infrequent in many German-language newspapers of Pennsylvania, were either reprinted from European German sources or were original compositions in Pennsylvania High German. Although at least some native speakers of Pennsylvania Dutch composed poetry in their native language in the first half of the nineteenth century (discussed in the next chapter), very little of it was published during that time. It might have been that Dutchified German and Pennsylvania Dutch were considered by newspaper editors too vernacular to be appropriate for versification, hence the restriction of these forms of language to prose texts that reproduced the speech of "common folk." Many poems in Pennsylvania High German nonetheless evoked classic nonsectarian Pennsylvania Dutch values of ethnic pride and American patriotism, as well as religious themes.[40]

One example from *Der Wahre Amerikaner* is the poem "The German in This Country" (*Der hiesige Deutsche*), which was published on November 10, 1804. It begins, in translation, as follows.

Joyfully I cry: German brethren!
Hail, America! Long may you live!
Let the echo resound:
Hail to the country that raised us!

Many years ago already
German integrity and renown reigned;
Courage and loyal people
Were consistently ours.

In Columbia's fold
Every art and skill thrive;
German spirit and language gladden
Even the stranger far and wide.

Where benign fathers rule,
A country blooms and conflict remains distant.
Germans like to live in peace,
And to respect good people.

Life passes gracefully
When one finds satisfaction:
German soil can give that,
How good it is that we are Germans!

Therefore, German brethren, swell
Your breast high with joy!
Let the echo resound:
Hail to the country that raised us![41]

Poems such as this embody a central aspect of Pennsylvania Dutch identity, that nonsectarian Pennsylvania Dutch saw themselves as the beneficiaries of two cultures, the German of their heritage and the American of their present. This dual identity, in which both cultures complemented rather than conflicted with one another, was also lauded by later generations of German Americans who were proud to proclaim "Germania our mother, Columbia our bride" (*Germania unsre Mutter, Columbia unsre Braut*).[42]

A later poem in Pennsylvania High German is of special interest since it deals with a number of things having to do with language. It is a poem titled "A New Year's Present" (*Ein Neujahrs-Geschenk*) that first appeared around January 1, 1829, in the *Greensburger Volksfreund* (People's friend), a short-lived German-language newspaper from Greensburg, Westmoreland County, in western Pennsylvania. The original is no longer extant, but it was reprinted twice in two Dutch Country newspapers, on January 28, 1829, in *Der Bauern Freund* (The farmers' friend), which was published in Sumneytown, Montgomery County; and on February 6, 1829, in *Die Republikanische Preße* (The republican press) of Easton, Northampton County.

The poem, whose author is identified only by the initials S.S.M., is in the form of a dialog between an uncle, Michael, and his nephew, Fritz. Michael begins by offering Fritz good wishes on the occasion of the new year. Fritz seems to not be able to understand his uncle and replies in mixture of English and grammatically incorrect and partly Dutchified German.

> Onkel, wat did ju seh?
> Ich kann sich nit versteh,
> Ju spohk in Dotsch tu mi,
> Ich wehs aber nit wie.
> Es war sich gar ein langes Ding,
> Und sind nur fremde Katzen-Spring.
>
> *Uncle, what did you say?*
> *I can't understand you.*
> *You spoke in Dutch to me,*
> *But I don't know what.*
> *It was something long*
> *And absurd-sounding.*[43]

Uncle Michael becomes upset with his nephew and chides him for his poor German. Fritz replies in marginally better German:

> Vetter Michael, was ist das?
> Ich glaube Ihr macht nur Spaß—
> Ich geb sich um die Deutsch nit viel,

Es is sich nur ein Kinderspiel,
Denn die hohen Tschentel-Leut,
Legen Deutsch ja ganz bey Seit.

Cousin Michael, what is this?
I think you're just joking.
I don't care much about German,
It's just a trifle,
Because the high-class gentlefolk
Are setting German aside.

But Michael is adamant about the importance of being German and the value of continuing to speak their heritage language; only foolish people would scorn it, he argues. Fritz responds, this time in prescriptively correct Pennsylvania High German, that he has to speak English in the company of gentlefolk, otherwise he would be mocked. The dialog then takes a decidedly Christian turn, with Michael identifying such mockery as a sin against God and the work of the devil. Fritz is sympathetic but frustrated because, as he says, he does not want to be left behind while his contemporaries "hang the German language on the wall." This is reminiscent of the situation described by Henry Lee Fisher in his poem recalling his school days, when members of his generation began to follow the "fashion" of using English, to the consternation of their elders. Fisher entered school around 1830, at essentially the same time the poetic dialog between Michael and Fritz appeared.

In the remainder of the poem, Uncle Michael extols the virtues of the German language and culture. It is the "queen of all languages" and "graces Christianity like the most beautiful flower." He reminds his nephew that it was Germans who (supposedly) invented gunpowder and book printing, and produced useful and exquisite clocks.[44] Fritz sees the wisdom in Michael's words and agrees with his uncle that what is considered fashionable, including preferring English over German, is idle vanity. Michael closes with a prayer:

We live in times of great adversity
Because many false prophets
Wrap themselves in sheep's clothing

And roar like lions.
They have the raging audacity
To deny us Heaven.
Hear, O Lord, my plea!
Send us comfort
So that virtue may again bloom
And that evil may flee.
Grant us for the new year
That we may praise you forever and ever.
Amen.[45]

As in other early texts produced by and for rural Pennsylvania Dutch readers, this poem refers to a familiar adversary, namely gentlefolk, and those Dutch men and women who would strive to emulate them. A symptom of their lack of moral rectitude, more specifically, the danger to their spiritual health, is the fact that they are abandoning the German language. The poem's author does not distinguish here between the vernacular language, Pennsylvania Dutch, and Pennsylvania High German, their main vehicle of literacy, since they were two sides of the same diglossic coin in the nineteenth century and later. Both were subsumed under the single concept of *die Muttersprache/Mudderschprooch*. In 1829, when this poem was published, active speakers of Pennsylvania Dutch still read and worshipped in German. They did not perceive knowledge of Pennsylvania Dutch to be a hindrance to maintaining standard German, as anglicizers such as Frederick Muhlenberg did. On the contrary, "keeping Dutch" for them meant preserving both their everyday language, which was so central to their secular identity, *and* High German, the tangible connection to their religious heritage.

In this way, S.S.M., the author of the Michael/Fritz poem, along with those rural Dutch who belonged to the generation of Henry Lee Fisher's parents, shared the views of urban conservatives such as Muhlenberg's critic, Pastor Helmuth of St. Michael's and Zion in Philadelphia, who made a direct connection between the maintenance of German and the spiritual health of German Pennsylvania's youth. Writing in 1813, Helmuth warned:

Now threatening the German Protestant churches is a mighty storm that is not merely a consequence of the natural course of things but is a sign of the times and one that will soon rob them of their well-being, with all of their joy, unless teachers and parents work against it as a united front. It is now generally happening, especially in towns and on the frontiers, that children are starting to be educated *completely* in the English language and irresponsibly neglected with respect to the German worship service. This is the result of the indifference and disrespect toward sound religious teaching, now, during this great hour of temptation that is engulfing the globe. True, no rational person could argue against teaching youth in English only, and entirely in English: their temporal welfare in this country makes that necessary. But to deprive young people of the German worship service and their church bespeaks an indifference to religion and a clear preference for the temporal that is truly striking.

Oh, dear guardians of the Protestant churches who are either indifferent to this evil or even promote it: consider what the sad outcomes will be![46]

A similar attitude exists among the main active speakers of Pennsylvania Dutch, the Amish and Old Order Mennonites today, who maintain both their vernacular idiom and Pennsylvania High German. Although Old Order sectarians no longer read secular literature in German (newspapers, for example), receptive literacy in German is essential for full participation in the life of their churches. Among contemporary sectarians, as among both sectarians and nonsectarians two centuries ago, keeping *Deitsch* means maintaining both "Dutch" and "German."

Some nineteenth-century Pennsylvania Dutch argued for conserving their Germanic linguistic heritage in the face of pressure to shift to English less for reasons specifically related to their Christian faith than on general moral grounds. In 1862, a pamphlet was printed in Allentown titled *German or English* (*Deutsch oder Englisch*), which consists of an extended prose dialog in standard German between two friends, Sebastian and Jacob. Sebastian pays a visit to Jacob and asks him why he sends his children to an English-language Sunday school. Jacob replies that they live in an English-speaking country; that English is a more beautiful language than German; and that if *Deutsche* (Pennsylvania Dutch or German Americans) want to amount to anything, they should learn English. Jacob replies that while the United States may be an "English country," it is also a free country. He regrets that his fellow Dutchmen / German Americans are committing linguistic suicide by favoring English and rejecting their mother tongue, their ancestral language. Reacting to Sebastian's claim that English is more beautiful than "cloddish" (*plump*) German, Jacob turns others' criticisms of Pennsylvania Dutch as a "bastard" form of speech on their head by claiming that English has been polluted by contact with other languages:

> An English-speaking scholar once said to me, "Our language is a piratical one. Pirates appropriate other men's property to themselves. So it is with our language. It has taken in and appropriated to itself words from almost every language." That's exactly how it is. It's hard to find another language in the world that is so cobbled together with all kinds of material than English. It is a daughter of German, but so terribly degenerated that one can no longer recognize in it the lovely features of its noble mother. In this way the language resembles—alas!—the children of noble German fathers and mothers who are becoming English. The language is ashamed of itself, which is why it has stolen whatever it pleases from the language of every other people to cover its own nakedness.[47]

Jacob goes on to make a number of other points in favor of maintaining their heritage language, including by linking it to the traditionally German virtues of industry, perseverance, simplicity, thrift, and modesty. Sebastian is finally convinced by Jacob's earnest arguments and decides that his children should learn German. Jacob closes by sharing a recent experience that shows what happens when Pennsylvania Dutch youth are lost to English society:

> I visited a home familiar to both you and me that I do not wish to name. On the bench in the corner sat the old Dutch mother of the house, who perhaps helped to carry on her head the boards to build that house in her younger years; whose lot it had probably been to carry on her head to and from the mill the grain and flour for her children's bread; and who in any case helped to lay the groundwork for and bring about her family's success through her hard work, thrift, and quiet modesty, content with her lot in life. As I mentioned, there she sat on the bench in the corner, mending with her usual diligence the torn work clothes of her now adult sons. And there, in the middle of the room, on an adorned rocking chair,

all decked out and fixed up, made up from head to toe, in a large, broad
hoop skirt, sat her English daughter-in-law, rocking such that her legs
came up into the air. And . . . and . . . do you know what? She was making lace! Take care, Sebastian, that this doesn't happen to you! Take care
that your children don't learn to say to you, "I don't like to go to Dutch
meetings!" Take care that in your old age you don't have to hear in your
own house, "I don't care for that old Dutchman! I don't care for that old
Dutch woman!"[48]

In the early nineteenth century, loyalty to both Pennsylvania Dutch
and Pennsylvania High German ran high among the conservative Dutch
who, unlike the lawyer-poet Henry Lee Fisher and others, chose to stay
on the farm or at least in the country. At the same time, the pressure to
anglicize if one chose to enter the class of gentlefolk was hard for many
to resist. Doubtless many Pennsylvania Dutch, including Fisher, were
indifferent to the attrition from their native language when they moved
up socially, an indifference that Pastor Helmuth, S.S.M., the author of
the dialog between Sebastian and Jacob, and others bitterly lamented.
In contrast, those who were content or even adamant about remaining
farmers and craftspeople took a dim view of the lives and morals of *Gen-
telmenner* and *Lädies*, and they were more likely to regard with suspicion
any attempt to compel their children to learn more English than was
absolutely necessary. This attitude clearly figured into the widespread
resistance to the Free School Law of 1834 mentioned earlier. Although
this and related laws did not explicitly seek to weaken the influence of
traditional German-medium parochial schools in the Dutch Country,
they did have the practical effect of hastening their demise.

As observed above, the deficient condition of German-medium
schools serving Pennsylvania Dutch children was reflected in their limited proficiency in Pennsylvania High German. Further evidence of the
imperfect command of German among early nineteenth-century Pennsylvania Dutch can be gleaned from personal letters produced during
this era by average Dutch men and women, that is, people other than
ministers and journalists whose livelihoods did not require active use of
German. One such letter was transcribed and translated by J. William
Frey in 1951. It was written in 1837 by a twenty-three-year-old woman
named Martha Leidig (1814–1888), who was born in Schaefferstown,

Lebanon County, PA.[49] At the time that Martha wrote this letter, she had recently moved with her family to Wayne County, OH, part of the westward migration of Pennsylvania Dutch and other Americans in the early nineteenth century. The letter begins as follows:

to Mr john Bomberger
levenen county
shefers town post offis

October th8 1837
Bachman taunschip ohio[50]
fiel geliete freund ich lasse euch wichen das ich gesund bin for dise zeit und ich winsche das dise paar zeilen euch augh gesund antreffen dethen weiter lasse ich euch wischen das die ohio mir sehr gut gefallen tut es war mir noch nicht verleth sinter das ich in ohio bin aber auf dem weg war mir es wunderful verleth die lite sind so gut fergnigt da als in Pensilvania si hawen alles da wi auch dort obs von alle sort hat es plente epfel pferschen und blaumen und bieren hat es alles genug und aber das stohr sach ist aber etwas deuer als dort. . . .

Much loved Friends,
I'm letting you know that I am well at this time, and I hope these few lines will find you the same. I'm letting you know that I like it very much in Ohio. I have not gotten tired of the place since I've been in Ohio, but I was wonderful tired of the trip out here. People are as happy here as back in Pennsylvania. They have everything that you have there. There are plenty of all kinds of fruit. There are enough apples, peaches, and plums and pears, but store-bought things are somewhat more expensive than there. . . .

Martha Leidig's letter is written in excellent Pennsylvania Dutch using more or less German orthography, but misspellings abound. There is no punctuation at all, and almost none of the nouns, including many proper nouns, are capitalized, contrary to the norms of High German, including its Pennsylvania variety. What this letter suggests is that its writer was trained in German to some degree but not enough to have acquired productive knowledge of the language; that is, she was unable to compose original texts in it. Had she been able to do so but simply chose instead to write in Pennsylvania Dutch, she would not have produced so many spelling errors, including multiple mistakes with the same word (e.g., *wichen* and *wischen* for Ger. *wissen*, 'to know').

If Martha Leidig's linguistic knowledge was typical for others of her generation, her letter provides evidence that literacy among average Pennsylvania Dutch was mainly receptive: they were able to read enough German to keep up the strong subscriber base for German-language newspapers that existed in nineteenth-century rural Pennsylvania but not to write in it. And this letter suggests that the writer may not have been particularly strong in her written English: the English words (*post*) *office* and *township* are spelled like German, and the place names *Lebanon*, *Schaefferstown*, and *Pennsylvania* are all misspelled.

Personal letters by other native speakers of Pennsylvania Dutch from this era paint a similar picture of their passive knowledge of German. In the archives at Ursinus College in Pennsylvania there is an important collection of correspondence written to Jacob Renno (1789–1865), an Amish man who lived his entire life in rural Berks County. The collection contains twenty-five letters by eight writers, produced between 1835 and 1843. In their form they are identical to the Martha Leidig letter in that they are written in Pennsylvania Dutch, with some influences from German. The spelling and punctuation are just as inconsistent as in the Leidig letter. Unlike that letter, though, the originals survive. The handwriting is German; that is, the correspondents employed the *Kurrent* script that was common at the time. While the actual spelling of the words is faulty, the handwriting is flawless. This suggests that young Pennsylvania Dutch of the time were taught to write in German more as a calligraphic exercise than with the goal of composing original texts in the language.

Below is an excerpt of an 1839 letter to Jacob Renno from Conrad Baver, a friend who had moved from Berks County to Ohio. An image of the original is also included.

Ein brief geschrieben den 4 den Augëst 1839
Ein freindlicher grus an Euch und an die god und an die Kinner und ich las Euch wissen das ich noch gesund bin und So lang der her wiel weider las ich Euch wissen das ich Euren brief Emfangen hab wu dör mir ge- schrieben habd und ich war Ser fro und wier haben dem Elias sein briief

auch Embfangen wu er uns geschrieben had und er Sol die anna mid raus
bringen und wan es eren nigt gefald in der ohiio dan wil ich Sie wieder
mid neu nemmen. . . .

A letter written on August 4, 1839
A friendly greeting to you and to my godmother and to the children. I am
letting you know that I am still healthy, as long as the Lord wills it. I am
letting you know further that I received your letter that you wrote me. I
was very happy. We also got Elias's letter that he wrote us. He should bring
Anna along out here, and if she doesn't like it in Ohio, then I will bring her
back. . . .

As in the Martha Leidig letter from two years earlier, Conrad Baver's letter shows considerable deviation from the norms of written German, including multiple misspellings of the same word, for example, *Emfangen*
and *Embfangen* for *empfangen*, 'to receive'. Punctuation is again nonexistent, and capitalization is faulty and inconsistent, even for proper names
(e.g., *Elias* but *anna* and *ohiio*). The handwriting, however, is completely
German and quite well executed. Conrad Baver and his contemporaries,
who were trained to produce German script but not to actually compose
in German, thus did their best to communicate in the one language they
knew best, Pennsylvania Dutch. In the same way that printed Dutchified
German was essentially Pennsylvania Dutch "dressed up" to look like
German, personal letters such as these were examples of the same basic
phenomenon.

Pennsylvania High German, Dutchified German, and Pennsylvania Dutch in *Der Bauern Freund*

The 1860s marked a turning point in the development of Pennsylvania
Dutch as a folk literary medium. At that time, especially in the years
immediately following the Civil War, German-language newspapers in
Pennsylvania began publishing regular features in the language, and in
1869 the first two books to include Pennsylvania Dutch literary texts appeared, Rachel Bahn's *Poems* and Ludwig A. Wollenweber's *Gemälde aus
dem Pennsylvanischen Volksleben* (Sketches of domestic life in Pennsylvania).[51] Pennsylvania Dutch literature, of course, did not emerge spon-

Excerpt from letter in Pennsylvania Dutch from Conrad Baver to
Jacob Renno, August 4, 1839.
Source: Pennsylvania Folklife Society Collection, Myrin Library, Ursinus College.

taneously. As noted above, its roots are to be found in texts that appeared in German-language newspapers that served the rural Dutch Country in the first half of the nineteenth century, such as *Der Wahre Amerikaner* in Lancaster. In a study of Pennsylvania Dutch material published between 1837 and 1857 in the *Reading Adler*, Mildred Runyeon found Pennsylvania Dutch texts appearing occasionally starting in 1849.[52] Over the second half of the nineteenth century, the *Adler* emerged as a prominent outlet for writings in Pennsylvania Dutch, which became a regular feature of the newspaper in the 1870s.

An equally important resource for students of Pennsylvania Dutch history is another German newspaper from the same era as the *Adler*, *Der Bauern Freund* (The farmers' friend, mentioned above, published in Sumneytown, Montgomery County). Its printer-editor, Enos Benner (1799–1860), was a fourth-generation American, his great-grandparents having come to Pennsylvania in the 1740s, just before the high point of immigration.[53] Benner edited *Der Bauern Freund* continuously for exactly thirty years, from 1828 to 1858. Like the *Adler* and contemporary

German-language newspapers published in Pennsylvania, *Der Bauern Freund* offers a fascinating window on early Pennsylvania Dutch culture, including the place of language in it.[54] The main language of the newspaper was Pennsylvania High German, but interspersed were a number of pieces in both Dutchified German and Pennsylvania Dutch, which are interesting both for their linguistic features and for their content.

In an editorial in the inaugural issue of *Der Bauern Freund* on August 6, 1828, Enos Benner makes clear that his newspaper will reflect decidedly Jacksonian Democratic sympathies. This time was a watershed in American political history, at the height of a presidential campaign that pitted the incumbent John Quincy Adams against the man whom he had defeated four years earlier under controversial circumstances, Andrew Jackson. Jackson's populist politics made him a folk hero among the Pennsylvania Dutch, even decades after his death.[55] As Benner writes:

We have already made known that we affirm Democratic-Republican principles, and now we cannot avoid saying that we are well-disposed to Gen. Jackson, that we regard as falsehoods the aspersions cast upon him, the anonymous pamphlets that are circulating, and that we strongly condemn the scornful speeches with which his enemies seek to bring him into contempt among the people. For according to the popular vote [in 1824], he was entitled to the presidency, so to promote his election [now] would appear reasonable to a fair-minded person.[56]

Despite his clear political leanings, Benner promises his subscribers that he will strive to uphold the principles of "moderation," "truth," "utility," "virtue," and "freedom" (*Mäßigung, Wahrheit, Nützlichkeit, Tugend,* and *Freyheit*) in his editorial work.

Immediately following this editorial in the first issue of *Der Bauern Freund* is a dialog in Pennsylvania High German between a *Jackson-Mann* and an *Adams-Mann*. Not surprisingly, the Jackson man makes the better arguments in favor of his candidate and also has the last (long) word in the conversation. The tone of the discourse is elevated, which makes the relatively formal Pennsylvania High German an appropriate linguistic medium. Later in the election season, though, Benner prints another dialog dealing with the presidential campaign (September 10, 1828), the content of which is considerably saltier. This conversation,

Bauern Freund print shop, Marlborough Township, Montgomery County, PA,
built in 1838 by Enos Benner.
Source: http://en.wikipedia.org/wiki/File:Bauren_Freund_Montco_PA.jpg.

like the earlier one, takes place between supporters of the rival candidates, but this time the interlocutors are identified by their occupations: the Jackson man is a farmer (*Bauer*), while the Adams supporter is a "lawyer from the town" (*Justus von der Stadt*). The two individuals symbolize the dual poles of the familiar "countryfolk-gentlefolk" dichotomy in depictions of early Pennsylvania Dutch society. A virtuous, honest Pennsylvania Dutch farmer is pitted against the epitome of the shifty urban dweller, a lawyer. The interaction between the two men is heated, with the *Justus* calling the *Bauer* a fool, who in turn calls his opponent a lying scoundrel. This time, the speakers address each other in Dutchified German, which is better suited for intemperate speech than High German. Indeed, throughout the thirty-year run of *Der Bauern Freund* under Benner's editorship, use of the three varieties, High German (both Pennsylvania and European forms), Dutchified German, and Pennsylvania Dutch, varies according to the formality of a text's content. In this way, Benner and other writers who knew both Pennsylvania Dutch and German drew on elements from both languages to produce texts of a wide stylistic range.

Interestingly, the very first text in *Der Bauern Freund* to contain actual Pennsylvania Dutch appeared on September 9, 1829, in an anecdote about a circuit-riding preacher traveling with his black servant, who is named Cuff. At one point, the travelers stop at a barn to rest, and the preacher sends Cuff to the upper level for corn. Cuff is inattentive (*nachläßig*) and spills some of the corn, which attracts a hungry, black pig. Later, when the preacher sends his servant back up to fetch a saddle, the pig, unseen by Cuff, grunts, scaring him. Cuff runs downstairs crying, in a mixture of Black English and Pennsylvania Dutch, "*Massa! de Deivel bi drowe, O Massa!*" (Massa! De debbil be up dere. Oh Massa!). The impatient preacher sends Cuff back up, who immediately runs back down again, yelling

De Deiwel bi Stek drowe, warhafdig. Massa hör em go eh, eh, he, he, nuh, drey vier mohl, so pleen kennuk puhr Nekar weiß sehna maka.

De debbil be stairs up dere, truly. Massa hear him go eh, eh, he, he, nuh, three, four times, plain enough to make Negro look white.

The preacher decides to investigate the situation for himself, leaving Cuff below to pray. When the pig sees the black-clothed preacher, the animal flees, running into the preacher's legs, which sends both tumbling down the stairs. The preacher shouts in German "*Der Teufel hat mich! um des Himmelswillen Cuff warum betest du nicht!*" (The devil has me! For Heaven's sake, Cuff, why aren't you praying?), to which the servant replies, "Amen!"

In Cuff's few lines in this anecdote, the writer displays a sophisticated familiarity with both Pennsylvania Dutch and stereotypical elements of Black English. Cuff's speech is essentially Pennsylvania Dutch, with certain grammatical errors that would have been due to interference from his native Black English, including the use of what is known in African American linguistics as "habitual *be*"; the absence of inflection on the verb *hör* (PD *heert*, 'hears'); no article before the noun *Nekar* (PD *Neger*, 'Negro'); and the use of the prepositional complementizer *puhr* (PD *fer*

... *zu*, 'for [in order] ... to'). Lexically, Cuff uses the verb *sehna*, 'to see' (PD *sehne*), to mean 'to look, appear' (PD *gucke*). In terms of pronunciation, Cuff substitutes *k*'s for *g*'s in the words *Nekar* and *kennuk* (PD *genunk*, 'enough') as well as for the *ch* sound in *maka* (PD *mache*, 'make'). Sociolinguistically, it is not surprising for Pennsylvania Dutch and Black English to be associated with one another in a text such as this, since both languages have long been negatively compared to higher-status linguistic varieties, German and standard English, respectively.[57]

Four months after the Cuff story appeared, on January 13, 1830, Benner printed another anecdote with a black protagonist titled "Neger Liebes Briefe" (Negro love letters). The narration is in Pennsylvania High German, but this time the black person's speech is more standard:

Ein Dändy Neger trat in einen Buchstohr und frug mit sehr ernsthafter Miene "Hab Sie ein paar Buch Briefpapier, von der aller vornehmst Art, für ein Schentelmann Liebs Brief drauf zu schreiben!"—"Ja," war die Antwort—"wie viel hättest du gerne?"—Er erwiederte "Ich denk, mein Aufhalt an den Springs mag seyn vielleicht zwey oder drey Woche, gib mich g'nug Buch, vier Brief zu schreiben."

A Negro dandy went into a bookstore and asked with a very serious expression, "You have a couple book of letter paper of the very finest kind for a shentleman to write love letter on?" "Yes," came the answer, "how much would you like?" He replied, "I think my stay at the Springs may be perhaps two or three weeks, give me enough book to write four letter."

As in the Cuff anecdote, the black customer has faulty control over the grammar and pronunciation of the language he is speaking, which, appropriate to his social status as a striving "dandy," is now High German instead of Pennsylvania Dutch. Inflections on verbs and nouns are missing (*hab* and *denk* for *haben*, 'have', and *denke*, 'think'; *Buch*, *Brief*, and *Woche* for *Bücher*, 'books', *Briefe*, 'letters', and *Wochen*, 'weeks'); standard German *Aufenthalt*, 'stay, sojourn', is rendered as *Aufhalt*; the word order is un-German in one sentence (*seyn*, 'be', should occur after *Woche*); and the prepositional complementizer *um*, 'in order (to)', is missing in the final clause. How the customer and proprietor address each other is also interesting: the black man uses both formal (*Sie*) and informal (*du*) second-person pronouns, while the store owner uses the less respectful *du* exclusively.

Looking beyond the offensive content of these two anecdotes, on the level of language, both underscore the complexity of the verbal repertoire at the disposal of early Pennsylvania Dutch writers. Not only did they have command of two distinct languages, Pennsylvania Dutch and Pennsylvania High German; their familiarity with variation in American English across different ethnic groups was sufficiently refined as to enable them to write texts of considerable linguistic sophistication. To be sure, most Pennsylvania Dutch during the *Bauern Freund* era would have not been able to *produce* such writings themselves, but they must have had sufficient passive familiarity with the language varieties in question to appreciate them, otherwise editors like Enos Benner would not have printed such linguistically diverse material.

A prominent feature of the mix of linguistic influences found in newspapers like *Der Bauern Freund* was the combination of elements from European and Pennsylvanian varieties of standard German. Editors during the time of Benner did not generate most of the material they ran in their weekly, four-page newspapers themselves. Rather, they drew on a range of sources, including guest contributors and other newspapers. Over the thirty years that Benner brought out *Der Bauern Freund*, he reprinted material not only from other German-language newspapers from Pennsylvania but also from German and English publications (in translation) from across the United States, including New England, the South, Southwest, and Upper Midwest, as well as from German-speaking Europe. Since many American German newspapers were edited by native Europeans, the considerable variation in the standard German vocabulary used in *Der Bauern Freund* was inevitable. Numerous words had two or more variants. The word 'railroad', for example, is rendered by five different German words. The two most frequent are *Eisenbahn* (lit. 'iron path/way') and *Riegelweg*, which is based on Pennsylvania Dutch *Riggelweeg* (*Riggel*, 'rail', + *Weeg*, 'road'); the blended forms *Riegelbahn* and *Eisenweg* occur also, as does *Riegelstraße* (*Straße*, 'street'). Not only was there variation across texts; even within a text, alternate forms were sometimes used. Another example are the words for 'public sale / auction', which was an event advertised in nearly every

Advertisements for public sales using both *Verkauf* and *Vendu, York Gazette*,
November 7, 1823.

issue of a newspaper. Both the standard German *Verkauf* and Pennsylvania Dutch *Vendu* were used, and the English *auction* also appeared on occasion. The image above, from the *York Gazette*, whose use of German was identical to that of *Der Bauern Freund* in this regard, shows two advertisements for public sales, using alternately *Vendu* and *Verkauf*.[58]

The lexical variation in the German of *Der Bauern Freund* and other contemporary newspapers, including the use of English loanwords common in the Pennsylvania Dutch of Benner and his readers, was derided by European-oriented German speakers. However, Benner and others paid little heed to prescriptivist norms in their Pennsylvania High German. On the topic of norms for German spelling and grammar, Benner published an article on January 26, 1848, which was written in the first person and titled "Driven Crazy by Spelling" (*Der Orthographische Narr*, lit. 'The orthographic crazy person'). It tells the story of an agitated newspaper editor who recently visited the narrator, who was himself apparently an editor also. The visitor is described as being normally "completely rational and intelligent" (*überaus verständig und gescheidt*) but has been driven mad by German spelling and grammar. Their interaction begins as follows:

> "Friend!", he calls out in great agitation. "Do you spell *Direktor* with a *c* or a *k*? And now I have to get a *Correktur* [revised text], but forgive me. How do you spell *Correktur*, with a *c* or a *k*? *Mir schwindelt der Kopf* [my head is spinning]. But how do you say it, *mir* or *mich schwindelt der Kopf*? *Mir* or *mich träumt* [I am dreaming]? *Mir* or *mich schwant* [I sense something]? *Mir* or *mich dünkt* [it seems to me]? I'm going crazy over these *mir*s and *mich*s, these *c*'s and *k*'s. How do you spell *Direktor*?"
>
> "As a rule, with a *k*," I replied, "but there are people who are perhaps just as correct in spelling the word with a *c*."
>
> "There we have it! 'As a rule,' you say, 'with a *k*'! Is that *Consequenz* [consistency]? Isn't it true that you yourself always spell it with a *c*?"
>
> "For the sake of convenience," I replied, "there is no specific rule for that."
>
> "Argh!", my friend shouted in complete anger. "There's no such thing as convenience in spelling. But wait. Do you spell *giebt* [gives] with or without an *e*?"
>
> "The author whose work I'm correcting consistently leaves the *e* out. But then he should write *libt* [loves] instead of *liebt* etc., or even *schrib* [wrote] instead of *schrieb*, *blib* [remained] instead of *blieb* etc."[59]

The conversation continues with a discussion of a number of examples of variation in German grammar, prompting the visitor to storm off in "anger and distress" (*Wuth und Verzweiflung*). The narrator concludes by saying that "it is true that the variability in German grammar and spelling is enough to drive anyone mad." What this story highlights is that German could not be written in an entirely consistent way, which helps explain the lack of norms in the Pennsylvania High German in newspapers such as *Der Bauern Freund*. At the same time, the writer points out that this phenomenon was not peculiar to America, but in fact partly a reflection of the situation in European German.

Apart from this discourse on German spelling and grammar, Benner devotes little attention to metalinguistic matters in *Der Bauern Freund*. He simply printed pieces in different forms of German, including Dutch-ified German and Pennsylvania Dutch, without concern for uniformity. He does, however, address the question of borrowed vocabulary in German twice. In the first instance, a short piece from January 28, 1835, titled "Linguistic Corrections" (*Sprach Verbesserungen*) Benner pokes fun at puristic tendencies of some European German speakers:

> At the time when people wanted to banish foreign words from the German language, for *Billard* [billiards] they came up with the following beautiful, bona fide German word, which is very much to be recommended for the way it rolls off the tongue: *Grüntuchsechslöcherstoßtafel* [green-cloth-six-holes-bounce-table].[60]

More seriously, on April 30, 1851, Benner wrote an editorial titled "*Bauer*, not *Farmer*," in which he took European-born German-language editors in America to task for using the English word *farmer* instead of *Bauer*, which is both German and Pennsylvania Dutch. His arguments are undergirded with an implicit defense of the social status of his fellow Pennsylvania Dutch:

> We have already drawn attention in this newspaper to the fact that almost all European German newspaper publishers in this country never use the fine word *Bauer* but instead always write *Farmer*. Perhaps these gentlemen think that *Bauer* is too *bäuerisch* [peasant-like], since in Europe the class of farmers [*Bauernstand*] is regarded as of very low social standing, and that only the aristocracy has noble people in its ranks. In America things are different. Here the aristocratic class gets lost in the class of farmers. The poorest person can work his way up to a place of honor and respect through hard work, virtue, and integrity, thereby earning respect as a noble person in the eyes of his fellow citizens. People here are proud to be called a *Bauer*, and no Pennsylvania farmer who speaks German says *Farmer*, but rather *Bauer*. In America the word *Bauer* sounds just as

good as "doctor," "lawyer," "professor," or "pastor." It is nice to see when, in the annual index of legislators, the majority identify themselves as farmers, since here the class of farmers is the most distinguished and the one on which all others in this country depend. And so, esteemed German newspaper editors, write *Bauer*, not *Farmer*, and *Thaler* instead of *Dollars*. We already have an abundance of English words in our German newspapers without having to use more, and without good reason.[61]

Thus, while Benner feels no particular inclination to discern or adhere to prescriptive rules in his German, when his *Deitschlenner* colleagues use words that are at odds with native Pennsylvania Dutch linguistic norms—especially when certain usages might also implicitly disrespect rural readers—Benner stands tall with his fellow Dutch.

Even though Pennsylvania Dutch material constituted only a small portion of the texts in *Der Bauern Freund*, Enos Benner, as a native speaker of the language, was clearly influenced by and respectful of it. As noted above, he drew on Pennsylvania Dutch (and Dutchified German) for stylistic effect, that is, when he aimed to strike an informal tone. There are also instances when using Pennsylvania Dutch allowed him and his contemporaries to express themselves more precisely when writing in German on formal topics. An example of this is found in an article from July 1, 1840, that was reprinted from a German newspaper from Lancaster, *Die Stimme des Volks* (The voice of the people). It bears a Pennsylvania Dutch title, "Es ist eppes letz" (Something is wrong), which was printed in quotation marks to signal its orality. The content deals with the familiar topic of tensions between the Democrats and their political rivals, at this time in the Whig Party. Although the article is written in German, the Pennsylvania Dutch word *letz*, 'wrong', written in quotation marks, appears throughout. The likely reason for this usage is that the German word meaning 'wrong' is *falsch*, which also exists in Pennsylvania Dutch but has connotations inappropriate to the content of the article. The Pennsylvania Dutch word *falsch* is used to mean 'false' in the sense of 'artificial', as, for example, in *falschi Zaeh*, 'false teeth'. It can also mean 'two-faced' or 'phony', or 'dishonest' in a religious context (as in 'to bear false witness'). *Letz*, however, means 'wrong' in the sense of 'incorrect', which fits the context of political article nicely. Quoting the first two paragraphs,

"*Es ist eppes letz*," cries the benchwarmer, now joined by the entire swarm of Federalists. "*Es ist eppes letz*," cries the fortune hunter who made just as bad a speculation with mulberry trees as the Whigs are now doing with their candidate Harrison, and along with him everyone who had others work for them for years on credit, never paying them their just wages.

Why is it that these people are only now recognizing that something is "*letz*"? Didn't President Jackson say many years ago already that there was "*eppes letz*"? It should be obvious to any casual observer that we went "*letz*" somewhere. Let's help the Federalists' poor memory and tell them what was "*letz*".[62]

Until about 1840, Pennsylvania Dutch appeared infrequently in articles in *Der Bauern Freund*, and then only embedded in standard German texts like the one quoted above. When Benner and other writers sought to strike a vernacular tone, they used Dutchified German. When Pennsylvania Dutch was used, it was usually in short, humorous anecdotes, as in the story of Cuff and the circuit-riding preacher from 1829. The earliest example of direct speech attributed to a native speaker of Pennsylvania Dutch is from July 7, 1830, in a brief story titled "Beware That First Step" (*Hütet euch vor dem ersten Schritt*).

One day, an old woman who attended church regularly and considered it a sin beyond measure for listeners to talk during the sermon was accompanied to church by her little dog. During the service, the dog started to look for the cookie that the old woman had brought with her as a snack. The old woman caught sight of the dog just as he was about to take the cookie in his mouth, when she screamed, "*Wid dä geh. Puttel!*" [Leave it, Puttel!] But, alarmed by her own voice, she said, "*Oh mei ich hab in der Kirch kschwätzt!*" [Oh my, I talked in church!]—"*Guk amol widder!*" [Oops, did it again!]—"*Un nach ämahl.*" [And again.]—"*Ey Herr Je, ich bappel jo di gans Zeit.*" [Oh my goodness, why I'm chattering the whole time.][63]

The comic effect is reinforced here by employing eye dialectal spellings, that is, writing the Pennsylvania Dutch words in a way that is clearly deviant from German, even when the words in question are identical to their cognates in German, as with *guk*, 'look' (Ger. *guck*), *di* (Ger. *die*), and *gans*, 'whole' (Ger. *ganz*).

Contrasting German and Pennsylvania Dutch for comic effect is nicely represented in an anecdote in *Der Bauern Freund* from December 7, 1836, that coincidentally also involves a female protagonist in church. The title of this story, "Ein Mistäk" (A mistake), signals right away the humorous content of what follows, since although the title is in German, *Mistäk* is an obvious loanword from English. The story is related in the first person by a hyperformal German speaker whose speech can be best described as purple prose.

> Slowly I ascended the shaded path leading to the church. I was of a very poetic mind as I entered the house of worship. At that moment a famous and beloved speaker was preaching. Every seat was filled, and many had to make do with standing in the crowded aisle. I, also, was compelled to remain in an upright position. For an instant I was the object of curiosity, as I was a stranger. Yet soon everyone's eyes were fixed on the speaker. I also listened to him with rapt attention, for he was a master of his subject matter, his language lofty. During the sermon I noticed that a beautiful young woman with large, soft, dark eyes was on occasion looking at me. I flattered myself by thinking that she found favor in me and that that was why she cast the friendliest of glances in my direction. . . .[64]

When the service concludes and the congregation is exiting the church, the young woman appears to linger, much to the delight of the gentleman. He approaches her and removes his hat in greeting. She, then, opens her mouth and asks, "*Bischt du net en Krämer?*" (Aren't you a huckster?), to which he replies, in the most elevated German, "No, my love, that is not my profession" (*Nein meine Liebe! das ist nicht mein Gewerbe*). She then growls, in flawless Pennsylvania Dutch, that he looks just like the good-for-nothing Yankee who recently stuck her with a leaden half dollar. Despite the man's protestations to the contrary, the Dutch girl is still mistrustful of him and warns him to watch out for her brother John (*Tschon*), since he promised to wring the shyster Yankee's neck when he finds him. Here again, Pennsylvania Dutch, set directly against exceptionally formal German, is employed for comic effect and visually reinforced by eye dialectal spellings.

Around 1840 lengthier texts written in Pennsylvania Dutch emerge in *Der Bauern Freund*, such as humorous stories/letters to the editor, dialogs, and poetry. These text types form the basis of the Pennsylvania

Dutch folk literature that blossomed in the second half of the nineteenth century. At the same time that Benner started publishing early Pennsylvania Dutch literary texts, he also reprinted similar texts from European German newspapers that featured diverse dialects from across German-speaking Europe, from Low German in the north to Bavarian-Austrian varieties in the southeast and Swiss dialects in the southwest. Examples of Yiddish-influenced German also appeared in anecdotes about Jews in *Der Bauern Freund*.

The growing popular interest in dialects in German-speaking Europe, as reflected in the humorous material found in their newspapers toward the middle of the nineteenth century, was paralleled among Americans who could read German, including the Pennsylvania Dutch. With the relative accessibility of print media from German-speaking Europe to editors such as Enos Benner, at least indirectly via other German American newspapers, texts in European German dialects found their way into Pennsylvania Dutch homes. The frequency with which these pieces appeared in *Der Bauern Freund* in the 1840s and 1850s suggests that they were popular among the Pennsylvania Dutch. Indeed, their appearance indicates a level of sophistication in the receptive familiarity of Pennsylvania Dutch readers with the German language, in all its structural, stylistic, and regional diversity. This is less true for modern speakers of Pennsylvania Dutch, who generally do not have access to print media in German beyond religious texts. Amish and Old Order Mennonites would have considerable difficulty making sense of, say, a dialog written in Berlin dialect. However, many modern Pennsylvania Dutch speakers still hold the folk linguistic belief that their language is descended from Swabian German (*schwäbisch*) dialects, which, though incorrect, is understandable given that Swabian material was not uncommon in German American newspapers in the nineteenth century.[65]

Another factor in the growing interest in, or at least familiarity with, European German dialects among the Pennsylvania Dutch in the 1840s and 1850s was contact with German immigrants, the New Germans or *Deitschlenner*. This was precisely the time when immigration from Europe was gaining speed again after a lull of more than half a century. Two dialogs in *Der Bauern Freund*, from March 6, 1850, and March 23, 1853, featured newly arrived European German speakers ("greenhorns") meeting up with Pennsylvania Dutch speakers. Interestingly, both these dialogs are set in Ohio and were originally published in German-language newspapers from that state, in the cities of Canton and Sandusky, respectively. It makes sense that Ohio, rather than Pennsylvania, would have been a meeting ground for Pennsylvania Dutch speakers and immigrants from Germany, since new arrivals to the United States at that time were more inclined to settle in the Midwest than in Pennsylvania.

Linguistically, there are some differences between the Pennsylvania Dutch in these dialogs and the varieties spoken back in southeastern Pennsylvania, which may reflect early variation within the language. There are also subtle differences in the content of these dialogs from Ohio as compared to similar material from Pennsylvania. For example, in dialogs featuring interactions set in Pennsylvania between typical Pennsylvania Dutch people and outsiders, the social and moral differences between the two groups are usually well defined: rural Dutch men and women are hardworking, honest, virtuous, and natively clever, while the gentlefolk from the town are lazy, untrustworthy, materialistic, and vain. In the Ohio dialogs, such clear dichotomies are lacking. For example, in both dialogs, there is nothing to suggest that the Pennsylvania Dutch speakers are farmers or even rural dwellers; in fact, the opposite appears to be true. In the 1850 dialog, for example, the Dutch speaker is called an *Eckensteher*, literally 'one who stands on a corner'; his interlocutor is identified simply as *Der Deutsche*, 'The German'. The second dialog, from 1853, is between the Pennsylvania Dutch-speaking *Herr Simpelmaier* and the German *Herr Witzhuber*. The German adjective *simpel* means 'simple(minded)', while the noun *Witz* evokes sharp-wittedness.

In the Ohio dialogs, linguistic differences between Pennsylvania Dutch (which is used to represent American varieties of German in general) and European German are addressed. The conversation featured in the 1850 article takes place somewhere in downtown Canton and begins with the German asking the American "corner-stander" for directions:

GERMAN: Good friend, can you tell me where the German debating society is holding its debates this evening?
CORNER-STANDER: You come from Germany, I heard that right away. Have you been in this country long?

G: About five weeks.

cs: So you don't know much about America. Can you talk English yet?

G: Very little.

cs: You'll have to learn that. I talk English just as good as German, both are the same. "How do you do," "never mind," "by jinks," "good-bye," "to be sure," "anyhow," "yes," "exactly," "plenty." Well! What do you want to do with the debating society?

G: I'd like to hear the debate.

cs: I don't care about that . . . what they have to say I've known for a long time already.[66]

Although the corner-stander is not a farmer, he does resemble a stereotypical Dutchman from Pennsylvania in other respects. He is uninterested in the "higher" culture symbolized by the German debating society, but he shows his street smarts in the way that he explains American culture to the German newcomer. The Dutch speaker expresses no shame that his speech is different from *die hoche deitsche Sproch* (the high German language) of his interlocutor. In fact, he even chides the German for the latter's inflated speech: *Mußt besser Deitsch schwetze, der Amerikaner schwetzt alles plain* (You'd better talk Dutch, the American says everything plain). And he makes no apologies for the English he intersperses throughout his speech. On the contrary, he prides himself on his knowledge of English as well as Pennsylvania Dutch since that is a sign of just how thoroughly American he is.

The second Ohio Dutch–German dialog, from 1853, focuses mainly on metalinguistic questions, including differences between Pennsylvania Dutch and German. In this interaction, the "green" German, Witzhuber, asks the Dutch-speaking Simpelmaier why the streets in Sandusky are so dirty. The discussion quickly devolves into a disagreement about the proper way of addressing someone, that is, with the formal pronoun *Sie* or the informal *du*.

WITZHUBER: Tell me, Mr. Simpelmaier, why is there is so much dirt on the streets around here? The authorities should do something about it.

SIMPELMAIER: Well, you know, here everything is free. Whoever

doesn't want to walk around in the mud can just walk on the side-
walk, as he pleases.

w: Would you [*Sie*] be so good as to speak German? What kind of
language is that?

s: You [*Ihr*] get lost with your "*Sie*". That ain't no language, everyone
here is equal. "You" is "*du*", and so it's no use for anyone to say "*Sie*."
I speak just as good German as you, I can tell you that.

w: So "you" supposedly means "*du*"? I know better than that: it's "*Sie*".
If you think that it should be "*du*" because Americans say "you" to
everyone, you're very wrong.

s: You can't teach me anything, you're a greenhorn. If you keep talking
to me like that, I don't want anything to do with you.[67]

One interesting aspect of this dialog is that even though Simpelmaier
insists that Witzhuber should say *du* instead of *Sie*, because that would
be more appropriate in egalitarian American society, Simpelmaier himself addresses Witzhuber with the archaic *Ihr* pronoun. Both *Ihr* and *Sie*
were used as formal pronouns in European German, standard and dialectal, and both are attested in Pennsylvania High German in eighteenth-
and early nineteenth-century Pennsylvania newspapers. There is no evidence to suggest that *Sie* was ever used in Pennsylvania Dutch, though
Ihr likely was. The speech of Simpelmaier here supports that speculation, but *du* has long been the preferred second-person singular pronoun among Pennsylvania Dutch and is the only form used today.[68] In
any case, the "simple" Dutchman in this dialog, like his counterpart in
the previous one, is, in contrast to the European, the embodiment of
the stereotypical self-assured, if somewhat rough-around-the-edges,
American. And even though he is able to communicate with a European
German, his Dutch (*Deitsch*) is as different from German (*Deutsch*) as
English is.

Pennsylvania Dutch was never used in a stylistically unmarked or
neutral way when it appeared in the pages of *Der Bauern Freund*, especially after 1840. That is, for straight reporting of news, legal notices, and
the like, Pennsylvania High German was the preferred medium. Political news was a major focus of all American newspapers at this time, the
unabashedly Jacksonian Democratic *Bauern Freund* being no exception,
and when it came to serious discussions of candidates and issues, Ger-

man was normally used. Benner and his fellow editors deployed Pennsylvania Dutch or Dutchified German for effect, to strike a vernacular, informal tone that would impact Pennsylvania Dutch–speaking readers in a more direct way than German would.

Given the association of German with serious and relatively formal content in *Der Bauern Freund*, it makes sense that it was also the main language of poetry in the newspaper. Nearly every issue during the thirty years of Benner's editorship contained at least one poem or the text of a song, and, with a single exception, all were either reprinted from European German sources or were Pennsylvania High German compositions. Most were intended to be aesthetically or morally uplifting, hence the inappropriateness of Pennsylvania Dutch as a medium. Even poems with superficially "lighter" content, such as the "New Year's Present" from January 28, 1829, mocking the faulty German of younger Pennsylvanians (*"Onkel, wat did ju seh?"*) still conveyed a serious message, which in that example was the importance to one's spiritual health of maintaining German. Most poems in *Der Bauern Freund*, if they did not deal with traditional topics such as the beauty of nature and the changing seasons, addressed political, social, moral, or religious themes that were consonant with the conservative values of its rural Pennsylvania Dutch readership.

The sole poem in Pennsylvania Dutch to appear in *Der Bauern Freund* between 1828 and 1858 was printed on August 15, 1849. Its content is not humorous. The unnamed poet delivers a message that was in line with the content of moralizing poems that were ordinarily in German. Titled "A Crab Complains about the World" (*Ein Krittler klagt über die Welt*), it addresses a theme that would be revisited numerous times in later Pennsylvania Dutch literary texts, both poetry and prose: a dissatisfaction with contemporary society. The poem begins as follows:

> It just makes me sick
> When I consider the world.
> It's a downright insane asylum,
> I just want to throw it out of the window.
>
> Just look around you,
> Everyone, despite being dumb,

Thinks he is the light of the world,
And is full of goodness.

Even someone with half a brain,
Brags and says, "I know something."[69]

The crabby narrator then launches into a litany of all that is wrong with the people around him, *Fritz* (Fred) with his new coat, *Sus* (Susie) with her fancy dress, *Hen* (Hank) with his wild horse, and of course "the lawyer with his hot air" (*der Lawyer mit sei'm lang Geschwätz*), among many others. Even though the topic of language does not come up in this poem, S.S.M., the author of the 1829 "New Year's Present" who lamented the preference of many younger people for English over German / Pennsylvania Dutch in their desire to be fashionable and modern, would have agreed with the message of the Crab in his poem from twenty years later.

The way in which many Pennsylvania Dutch writers looked askance at modernity and social progress was often complemented by nostalgic, romanticized views of bygone days. Just months after "A Crab Complains about the World" appeared in *Der Bauern Freund*, Benner printed an exceptionally lengthy poem in Pennsylvania High German (in two parts, on December 26, 1849, and on January 6, 1850) that blended an indictment of modern society with praise for a nobler, morally more upright past. The anonymously penned "Old and New Fashion" (*Alte und Neue Mode*) sets the black-and-white differences between today and yesteryear against an overtly Christian (more specifically, Lutheran) backdrop.

Years ago, Christendom
Was true and pure in Lutheranism,
Exactly after Luther's fashion.
But now it is completely distorted,
Mimicking modern trends;
That is the new fashion.

Preceptors in days of old
Taught students morality,
After the old fashion,

But now the trend is to jump and run
And scramble up the fence;
That is the new fashion.

One used to acquaint students with God
And teach them the Ten Commandments,
After the old fashion,
But now in the new era,
All of that is considered vanity;
After the new fashion.[70]

As fundamentally American as traditional Pennsylvania Dutch culture was and is, one way in which it has always stood apart from the English-speaking mainstream is the skepticism with which it regards progress. Whereas many Americans view change as inherently positive, especially materially, many Pennsylvania Dutch, especially those who have remained loyal to the language of their forebears, are more inclined to see change in society as a form of decline, especially morally. Even though "Old and New Fashion" and almost certainly also the "Crab" poem were written by members of the nonsectarian (Lutheran and Reformed) historical majority of Pennsylvania Dutch speakers, today's active speakers of the language, the Amish and Old Order Mennonites, would share the sentiments expressed by both poets.

AS THE DESCENDANTS OF THE HISTORIC German-speaking elite in Philadelphia assimilated with their English-monolingual neighbors in the early nineteenth century, residents of the hinterlands of the southeastern Pennsylvania not only "kept Dutch" but also maintained knowledge of a form of German that was free from norms of quality set down by Europeans. Pennsylvania Dutch speakers, as the newspapers they read show, were profoundly aware of what was going on in the larger world around them, in the United States and in Europe, but they enjoyed a level of material comfort that allowed them to feel good about who they were, culturally and linguistically, as a people distinct from both Yankees and Germans. True, some younger Dutch men and women were attracted to the ways of the town, and the pressure to speak English in order to join the ranks of gentlemen and ladies was certainly heightened by the decline of the status of German in Pennsylvanian schools, especially after 1834. Yet those who chose to keep Dutch were well served by newspaper editors like Enos Benner, whose publications promoted their traditional values, including giving those who were inclined to set their beloved native language to paper the opportunity to do so. The following chapter moves into the period during which the seeds of Pennsylvania Dutch literature sown in the cultural soil cultivated by Benner and others came into full bloom.

CHAPTER 4

Profiles in Pennsylvania Dutch Literature

[A]s far as we are concerned personally, believing that the
first word we ever uttered after getting out of the cradle was
either dawdy *or* mommy, *and having become very much accustomed*
to the term, we must confess that we rather prefer being called a
Pennsylvania Dutchman. *We like it because it is emphatic, simple*
and expressive, and everybody knows just what it means.
—EDWARD HENRY RAUCH, 1873

Ludwig A. Wollenweber and the Introduction of Pennsylvania Dutch Literature

The second half of the nineteenth century brought huge changes to the external circumstances in which all Pennsylvanians, including Pennsylvania Dutch speakers, found themselves. Active maintenance of Pennsylvania Dutch always correlated with rurality and limited geographic and social mobility. A child who grew up in a Pennsylvania Dutch–speaking family in a rural area populated by similar families was likely to maintain her heritage language into adulthood if she married another Pennsylvania Dutch speaker and pursued a rural livelihood similar to that of her parents. However, when the geographic and social isolation of linguistically distinct areas such as the Dutch Country of southeastern Pennsylvania was breached by in- and out-migration, marriage across ethnic lines, increased educational attainment, and entry into the professions, among other changes, the shift to English monolingualism was usually rapid. In the decades following the Civil War, many communities in rural America, including those in the Pennsylvania Dutch Country experienced just such an upheaval. Although the actual number of Pennsylvanians who were primarily engaged in agriculture and related occupations increased over this time, their percentage of the overall population of Pennsylvania dropped precipitously, from 68% in 1820 to just 17% by the turn of the twentieth century.[1] Industrial growth, especially in manufacturing, drew many young Pennsylvania Dutch men off the farm and into increasingly diverse workplaces where English was the dominant language. School attendance, which had been limited for most rural Pennsylvanian children to several weeks during the winter at best, improved dramatically in the second half of the nineteenth century. And the transportation network, which had formerly been dominated by canal and wagon travel, was revolutionized by railroads, which increased contact between town and country dwellers, thereby hastening the loss of Pennsylvania Dutch.[2]

Lester W. J. Seifert estimates that the Pennsylvania Dutch–speaking population peaked between 1870 and 1890, perhaps reaching as many as 750,000 speakers, of whom he speculates about 600,000 lived in Pennsylvania.[3] The vast majority of these speakers, likely upward of 95%, were still the descendants of Lutheran and Reformed church people; Mennonite and Amish sectarians were far fewer in number.[4] In the last decades of the nineteenth century and continuing into the twentieth, however, nonsectarians came to lose Pennsylvania Dutch, first in the secondary settlements in midwestern states such as Ohio, Indiana, and Illinois and then in Pennsylvania itself.[5] Few children born after 1940 to Pennsylvania Dutch–speaking parents who were neither Amish nor Mennonite acquired the language or maintained it into adulthood. The most conservative sectarians, by contrast, the Old Orders, successfully resisted the pressure to assimilate linguistically by consciously limiting the changes brought on by industrialization and urbanization, marriage across confessional lines, access to formal education, and entry into the professions.

The demographic high point of Pennsylvania Dutch–speaking society in the second half of the nineteenth century coincided with the appearance of a large body of folk literature in the language, during what Earl F. Robacker calls the "language-conscious period" in the history of Pennsylvania Dutch:

The tentative beginnings of dialect writing had already been made, and all that remained was for someone to shape the course of the new litera-ture—to stem the tide of the grotesque and to foster the appearance of the meritorious. The old way of life in the "Dutch" counties, seemingly so secure against the invasion of new ideas, could not much longer resist the quickening tempo of the age; and with the dawning realization of this fact came the attempt, perhaps unconscious in some cases, to preserve the memory of folk ways that seemed doomed to extinction. We there-fore face the unique spectacle in this period of a racial minority in the throes of national amalgamation, recording an existence many of them already believed past, in a language which was likewise losing ground year by year.[6]

Not surprisingly, many Pennsylvania Dutch texts produced in this pe-riod, which included both prose and poetry that appeared mainly in local newspapers, and also, for the first time, in books, had a nostalgic quality. Conversely, other Pennsylvania Dutch texts painted a critical picture of contemporary society in much the same ways that earlier texts in Dutchified German and Pennsylvania Dutch cast aspersions on the ways of the "so-called gentlemen" and ladies of the city.

The first book devoted to Pennsylvania Dutch writings was not pro-duced by a native Dutchman, but by a *Deitschlenner*, a German named Ludwig August Wollenweber who immigrated to Pennsylvania in 1832, at the age of twenty-four, and remained there for the rest of his life. Wollenweber was, coincidentally, a native of the Palatinate, having been born in 1807 in Ixheim, located near the city of Zweibrücken. Relatively well educated for his time, Wollenweber was apprenticed to a printer and bookseller after completing his studies at a *Gymnasium* but was compelled to leave Europe for his political activities in the wake of the liberal revolutions of 1830.[7] He settled in Philadelphia, where he edited a German-language newspaper, but he spent much time in the rural Dutch Country, married a Pennsylvania Dutch woman, and eventually relocated permanently to Berks County, where he died in 1888. Toward the end of his life, in 1877/1888, Wollenweber wrote his autobiography, which is especially important for the fact that he witnessed firsthand the changes in Pennsylvania Dutch society around the middle of the nineteenth century.

Shortly after his arrival in Philadelphia in the summer of 1832, Wollenweber headed out to Berks and Lancaster Counties in search of work and experienced the warm hospitality of a Pennsylvania Dutch farmer named Landis from Reinholds, Lancaster County, who welcomed him as a "good Democrat and Jackson man."

> I was highly delighted with the simplicity, the familiarity, and the warmth of the residents of Berks and Lancaster Counties at that time. To be sure, that was a different time than now. The German immigrant in particular was held in high regard and viewed as honest and hardworking, highly respected and sought after. Theft, flimflam, and fraud were almost unknown in the country. The doors of the farm houses were rarely locked, bolts and locks were seldom used. What an enormous change in 46 years! Today people have their hands full with rogues and tramps, and not just bolts and locks, but also sharp watchdogs and revolvers are used on farms to protect against thieves and burglars and attacks. The farmer has to exercise extreme caution so as not to be swindled or duped, even by his friends and neighbors.[8]

Linguistically, Wollenweber, as a native speaker of Palatine German, had no difficulty communicating with Landis and other Pennsylvania Dutch farmers, and, unlike most of his fellow *Deitschlenner*, he warmly embraced the language and culture of its speakers.

In 1869 Wollenweber brought out *Sketches of Domestic Life in Pennsylvania* (*Gemälde aus dem Pennsylvanischen Volksleben*), an anthology of Pennsylvania Dutch writings that was published in Philadelphia.[9] It consists of several examples of Pennsylvania Dutch prose and poetry, many of which he wrote himself, others of which he reprinted from three newspapers, the *Bucks County Express* and *Der Morgenstern* (Morning star), both of Doylestown, Bucks County, and the *Kutztauner Neutralist* of Kutztown, Berks County. In the introduction to the book, Wollenweber makes clear that he, unlike other educated European Germans such as Johann David Schöpf and Franz von Löher, is a sympathetic

Ludwig August Wollenweber (1807–1888).
Source: http://en.wikipedia.org/wiki/File:Ludwig_August_Wollenweber.jpg.

observer of the Pennsylvania Dutch. Writing in his nonnative Pennsylvania Dutch,[10] Wollenweber introduces his European and American readers to his subject:

> I have traveled many a year already through Pennsylvania and have gotten to know the country and people fairly well, have seen much good and some good-for-nothing, but when I add everything up and compare it, I find that Pennsylvania and the Pennsylvanians can beat most other countries and people that I have seen in my life on three continents, in every respect. And yet there are quite a lot of people in the world and even in America who do not yet know what a beautiful country Pennsylvania is and what intelligent people live there.[11]

Wollenweber continues in his preface to relate what is obviously an apocryphal story of how he came to write the book. He tells of climbing a mountain near Allentown, in Lehigh County, and meeting an old Dutchman from a few miles away. The old man speaks of how enchanted he is by the landscape of his home region, created as it is by God. Coming down to earth, the man then shares his idea of producing a book in "our own Dutch language" (*uns're egene deutsche Sproch*) about the country and its people that would include the kind of short humorous pieces that delight the readers of the *Express, Morgenstern,* and *Neutralist* so much. The old Dutchman is sure that all his neighbors would buy such a book and that its publisher would turn a decent profit. Wollenweber promises to go the next day to the offices of Schaefer and Koradi, German American publishers in Philadelphia, to discuss the project, even if it would be difficult to put Pennsylvania Dutch to paper, given how inconsistently people have written it. But Wollenweber has no difficulty convincing the publishers to bring out the book and realize the old man's dream.

Wollenweber wraps up the preface to his book with his most famous poem, "An Affirmation" (*Eine Beteurung*), in which he expresses his identity as an adoptive Pennsylvania Dutchman, though proud of his German ancestry:

> I am a Pennsylvanian,
> Of that I am proud and happy.
> The country is beautiful, the people are nice,
> By jinks! I'll make almost any bet
> That no country in the world can beat it.
>
> We come from the Germans,
> I am quite proud of that.
> The Germans are very good people,
> Thrifty, hardworking, and intelligent.
> No people in the world can beat them.
>
> Just look at the garden
> That Pennsylvania is called.
> Doesn't everything here grow nice and well
> And doesn't everyone have healthy blood?
> No country in the world can beat it.
>
> And not just on the ground
> Does everything grow nice and well.
> Also deep below there is as much as you want:
> Coal, iron—worth more than gold.
> No country in the world can beat it.[12]

Wollenweber's *Sketches* contains samples of all the major genres of the Pennsylvania Dutch folk literature that came to blossom in the second half of the nineteenth century and into the twentieth: short prose pieces, both serious and lighthearted, including letters to the editor, dialogs, and poems. While much of the content deals with fictitious stories set in the rural Dutch Country, Wollenweber also includes pieces on local history, lore, and legends. Despite the fact that he shared the Jacksonian Democratic leanings of most Pennsylvania Dutch, political themes are absent in Wollenweber's anthology, as are pieces with strongly moralizing or religious content.[13] Wollenweber does, however, reprint three letters to the editor of the Doylestown *Morgenstern* that address the familiar cultural divide between town and country.

In one letter, an anonymous writer takes aim at citified young women who are ashamed to be Pennsylvania Dutch. Reporting what he supposedly witnessed in Lower Salford Township, in Montgomery County just west of Doylestown, the correspondent declares that just as soon as they are out of diapers, young women are no longer *Mäd* (girls or unmarried women) but *Mißes* and *Lädies* who are embarrassed to be known by traditional Dutch names like *Betz, Pall, Mändie,* or *Kitti*: "Girls today are not like they were years ago. Full of pride and hooped up like a paper bellows, they're not made of the same material, they're designed and made completely differently. Around here they want to be as English as Queen Victoria, but if someone from town wants to talk to them, they stand there like a chicken who lost her egg."[14] The writer looks askance at such young women who would try to hide their Dutch identity by wearing fancy clothes and speaking English. He concludes his piece with a poem in the voice of one such lady:

> This is how I hide in my hoops,
>   And am a poor soul;
> Smooth on the outside and dirty on the inside,
>   This is how we are perfect.
>
> And whenever I have three cents left over,
>   I have to head to the store;
> I have to spend my last penny there,
>   That's how it goes year after year.

And if someone speaks to me in Dutch,
   And asks, "Kannst du des? [Do you know this?]"
   Then I say not "Ja,"
   I say in English, "Yes."[15]

The two other letters reprinted from the *Morgenstern*, "Fashions" (*Die Fäschens*) and "Tight Pants and Standup Collars Do Not Make the Man" (*Teite Hosen un Ständups mache der Mann net*), similarly criticize *Busch-mäd* (country girls) who move to town and act like *City-Ladies*, adopting their taste in clothing, for themselves and their beaus, again the tangible symbol of their citified identity.

The letter from Lower Salford is the only text in Wollenweber's book that touches on a metalinguistic question, namely the trend among upwardly mobile young women to prefer English. Interestingly, although Wollenweber's intended audience must have included both European and American German speakers, there is no comparison, negative or positive, of Pennsylvania Dutch to standard German. Pennsylvania Dutch is thus implicitly regarded as the legitimate idiom of a people with a culture and history that Wollenweber clearly respects. In this way, Wollenweber shares the values of native Dutchmen like Enos Benner, the editor of *Der Bauern Freund*.[16] Unlike Benner, though, Wollenweber includes numerous examples of Pennsylvania Dutch poetry in his *Sketches*. Recall from the previous chapter that in the entire thirty-year run of *Der Bauern Freund* under Benner's editorship, which ended in 1858, just one poem in Pennsylvania Dutch appeared. By the 1860s, however, tastes had clearly changed, as the numerous examples of poetry in Wollenweber's book attest.

One particular group of poems in *Sketches* sheds light on the emergence of Pennsylvania Dutch as a poetic vehicle. These are short poems that appeared in wedding announcements. Wollenweber includes eleven wedding poems reprinted from the *Morgenstern* and the *Express*, as well as one evidently fictitious one that he himself penned. Ten of the original poems are in Pennsylvania Dutch; the eleventh is in German, and it reads as follows:

Last Sunday, married by the Honorable Mr. John G., Mr. Samuel D., of Plumstead, with Miss Hannah L., of Bedminster, both from Bucks County.

> Cold is the winter night,
> So thought Sam!
>> And took for his better life
>> A wife who can keep him warm.
> And when the cradle comes into the house,
> He will not protest.
>> So live happily, young people,
>> From now until eternity.[17]

The Pennsylvania Dutch wedding poems in Wollenweber's anthology, unlike the one in German, are humorous. One especially clever poem celebrates the marriage of one Mr. John Apel and Miss Julian Weber, also from Bucks County. The family names *Apel* and *Weber* are homophonous with the Pennsylvania Dutch words for 'apple' (*Appel*) and 'weaver' (*Wewer*), which the anonymous poet exploits for effect:

> Julian, she did well,
> And took an apple for her husband;
>> One can eat it and besides
>> Make cider and also sauce.

> John, he does even better,
> He now has a weaver in the house;
>> For one always needs clothes,
>> John now doesn't have far to go for a weaver.[18]

Another example celebrates the union of Walter G. of Allentown, Lehigh County, with Elizabeth D. of Long Swamp, Berks County:

> Walter traveled
> For many years
>> Until he finally realized
>> What Betsy felt for him.
> Now when Walter's skin itches,
> He'll have Betsy by his side,
>> But that won't be so simple.
> Betsy has to be at home

> To scrub sturdy diapers
> When the baby cries in the rocker.
> But I wish him happiness and peace,
> Because he treated me well.[19]

Most of the other poems in the book are written by Wollenweber, on both serious and lighter themes. Two that he did not produce are notable for the fact that their author is identified: Reverend Henry Harbaugh, to this day the most well known Pennsylvania Dutch writer. The following section considers the life and work of Harbaugh in some detail.

Henry Harbaugh, Father of Pennsylvania Dutch Literature

Every depiction of Henry Harbaugh casts him as the embodiment of the Pennsylvania Dutchman. In an introduction to a biography of Harbaugh published in 1900, Nathan C. Schaeffer, a prominent educator in nineteenth-century Pennsylvania, writes the following:

> Dr. Harbaugh was a typical Pennsylvania German. The dialect and its range of ideas he acquired at his mother's knee and from the companions of his childhood and youth. His powers of work and his love of fun were developed under the tutelage of the old farm and under the influence of its customs, traditions and forms of speech. He was thoroughly familiar with the homes and habits, the social and religious life of the Pennsylvanians of German ancestry. He knew their merits, foibles, and shortcomings, their peculiar ways and superstitions, their highest hopes and noblest emotions. He admired their frankness and simplicity, their thrift and industry, their honesty and integrity. He shared their fondness for good meals, their sense of humor, their hatred of every form of sham and humbug. He summed up in his personality and exemplified in his life the best characteristics of these people.[20]

Born the tenth of twelve children near Waynesboro, Franklin County, PA, in 1817, to George and Annie Snyder Harbaugh, Henry showed an early inclination to become a Reformed minister. Before his nineteenth birthday, and without his father's blessing, Henry headed west to Ohio to work and pursue his education. In 1840 he returned to Pennsylvania and enrolled in Marshall College in Mercersburg, home to a preparatory school, college, and seminary sponsored by the German Reformed Church. After completing his studies there in just three years, he then spent the next twenty as a minister to congregations in Lewisburg, Lancaster, and Lebanon, PA. He returned to the Mercersburg Seminary in 1863 as a professor, where he remained until his death in 1867, at the age of just 50.[21]

Pennsylvania Dutch was Harbaugh's native language and the dominant idiom of his childhood and youth; however, he came to use English

Rev. Henry Harbaugh (1807–1857).
Source: Evangelical and Reformed Historical Society, Lancaster, PA.

more frequently as an adult. Recall that he attended the same German one-room school as Henry Lee Fisher, a second cousin of Harbaugh's five years his junior. The quality of German instruction at that school was no better when Harbaugh attended it. Even though Harbaugh had to use German in his professional life more than Fisher, he, like Fisher, came to master English much better than German. Nearly all of Harbaugh's copious writings on various topics were in English, including in the *Guardian*, a German Reformed church periodical for youth that he founded and edited. English was also apparently the everyday language used in his immediate family as an adult. Both his wives were English monolinguals of non–Pennsylvania Dutch background, and there is nothing in the historical record to suggest that any of his children used Pennsylvania Dutch as adults. Harbaugh knew standard German well enough to deliver sermons in it, but he did not begin formal study of the language until he entered college. Although he was a member of a German literary society there, he was chided by his fellow students for "his tendency to drift into the use of the Pennsylvania-German dialect—the language of his home."[22]

Harbaugh was said to have been more comfortable preaching in English,[23] though it is highly likely that he ministered to his congregants in Pennsylvania Dutch outside the pulpit in his two decades as a working pastor. Notes from one of Harbaugh's German sermons still exist, and while his command of the language is good, he makes a number of orthographic and grammatical errors. Below is an excerpt from the original followed by a corrected version, with points of difference underscored, along with an English translation.[24]

Die schönsten Gedichtin in der Englichen Spr[a]che sind Thompsons Yahrzeiten. Der Leser wird durch Labyrinten von Schoenheiten gefürt. Durch di gewald seiner einbildungsgraft, stelt er uns die bildhafte Natur vor, und besselt unseres ganzes Gesinn mit freudvoller entzickung. Alles das schön ist in der Natuhr wird gelobet in seinem sanftes Gesang.

Die schönsten Gedichte in der englischen Sprache sind Thomsons Jahreszeiten. Der Leser wird durch Labyrinthen von Schönheiten geführt. Durch die Gewalt seiner Einbildungskraft stellt er uns die bildhafte Natur vor, und beseelt unser_ ganzes Gesinn mit freudvoller Entzückung. Alles, was in der Natur schön ist, wird gelobt in seinem sanften Gesang.

The most beautiful poems in the English language are [James] Thomson's Seasons. The reader is led through labyrinths of beauties. Through the force of his imagination he introduces us to the picturesque nature and animates our entire sense with joyful delight. Everything that is beautiful in nature is praised in his gentle song.

As the content of the foregoing suggests, Henry Harbaugh was an admirer of poetry. He wrote many original compositions in English, though his native Pennsylvania Dutch at times left its phonetic imprint on what he produced.

> Ere I knew grief
> Or could belief
> That there was treachery[25]

Harbaugh's love of verse was well known to his friends and colleagues, and one of them, a fellow faculty member at Mercersburg, the eminent Reformed theologian Philip Schaff (1819–1893), states that it was he who encouraged Harbaugh to compose poems in Pennsylvania Dutch. Schaff was the editor of a German Reformed Church publication titled *Der Deutsche Kirchenfreund* (The German church-friend) that had published in August 1849 what many consider to be the "first piece of true literature" in Pennsylvania Dutch, a poem by Emanuel Rondthaler Sr. (1815–1848) that was originally given the German title "Abendlied" (Evening song).[26] Schaff, in a tribute to Harbaugh published just weeks after the latter's death on December 18, 1867, writes the following:

As the poet in the Pennsylvania-German dialect, [Harbaugh] stands alone, if we except an isolated attempt made before, namely, the touching evening hymn, "*Margets scheent die Sunn so schoe*," which was written by a Moravian minister (the late Rev. Mr. Rondthaler), and published, with some alternations, in Schaff's *Kirchenfreund* for 1849. I first directed his attention to this piece of poetry, and suggested to him the desirableness of immortalizing the Pennsylvania-German in song, before it dies out, as the Allemannian dialect has been immortalized by Hebel. He took up the hint and wrote his "Schulhaus an der Krick," which he modestly submitted to me, and which, when published in several newspapers, produced quite a sensation among the Pennsylvania-Germans, and found its way even to Germany. The "Heemweh" and other pieces followed from time to time in his *Guardian*, and were received with equal favor. These poems can, of course, only be fully appreciated in Pennsylvania; but in originality, humor, and genuine *Volkston* they are almost equal to the celebrated Allemannian poems of Hebel. They are pervaded, moreover, by a healthy, moral, and religious feeling. They deserve to be collected and published in book form either separately, or in connection with his volume of English poems.[27]

The "Allemannian dialect" author referred to by Schaff above was Johann Peter Hebel (1760–1826), an acclaimed German Romantic writer from Switzerland whose most famous work was a collection of poems written in the dialect of the northern Swiss–southwestern German border region where he was born and grew up.[28] Harbaugh was profoundly influenced by Hebel, describing him as "[t]he German [Robert] Burns," a Romantic contemporary of Hebel's whose renown in the English-speaking world also stemmed from his use of vernacular language, including Scots, in verse.[29] Introducing Hebel and his language to his youthful readers in the *Guardian*, Harbaugh in 1863 writes:

This dialect reminds one somewhat of what is known among us as Pennsylvania German, though most of its words are not known in our Pennsylvania dialect. Still it bears a striking similarity to it in its simplicity, heartiness, and adaptedness to express the droll and humorous, as well as the tender, touching, and sacred. Hebel has illustrated how well the peculiar life thoughts and feelings of the rural population can be expressed in the dialect which they use in everyday life; and we very much doubt whether this can be done at all by the use of the perfect and polished language, in which that kind of literature is embodied which is the fruit of scientific reflection. There is such an intimate connection between life and language, that the first will only live and feel at home in the forms of the last, which is its true correlative.[30]

Given Harbaugh's view that vernacular dialects were better suited to convey the "life thoughts and feelings" of country folk than more "perfect and polished" languages, it is not surprising that the content of his Pennsylvania Dutch verse differs from that of his English-language poems. Harbaugh composed at least seventy-five original poems in English, which is the total number included in his 1860 anthology. He produced another seventeen in Pennsylvania Dutch, fifteen of which were published in a single collection in 1870, two and a half years after his death. While many of Harbaugh's poems in both languages have a nostalgic, rustic quality reminiscent of the works of European Romantics such as Hebel and Burns, the range of emotions he expresses in his Pennsylvania Dutch poetry is broader than what he writes in "perfect and polished" English. In both languages Harbaugh expresses eloquently his love of nature, but the optimism and hope grounded in his strong Christian faith comes through more when he writes in English. His Pennsylvania Dutch poetry, by contrast, is often more melancholy, especially when he compares the present—negatively—to the halcyon world of his childhood.

An apt illustration of the difference between Harbaugh's poetic voices in English and Pennsylvania Dutch may be made by comparing his best-known poem, which is also the most famous Pennsylvania Dutch literary production ever, "Das alt Schulhaus an der Krick" (The old schoolhouse at the creek), with an English version that he wrote and was included in the *Harfe*, his posthumous collection of poems.[31] "Das alt Schulhaus" was the first Pennsylvania Dutch poem of Harbaugh's to appear in print, in the August 1861 issue of his journal, the *Guardian*. Two manuscripts of the poem written in Harbaugh's hand exist today, both of which he dated November 26, 1860. The poem consists of thirty-one five-line stanzas.[32] In it, the narrator recounts his return, after a twenty-year absence, to the old country schoolhouse of his boyhood, now empty. Standing in front of the school, he is flooded with memories of his and his classmates' experiences, some pleasant, others less so. Their teacher was a strict taskmaster who was not afraid to use his whip on the children, but at the same time the children could still play an occasional prank on him and have fun. The narrator's memories are bittersweet, however, since his classmates are all gone; some, like him, moved away to seek their fortune in the wider world, while others are now deceased. Concluding the poem, Harbaugh writes (in Pennsylvania Dutch):

My heart swells with thoughts,
   Until I nearly choke!
I could cry, I'm so sad—
And yet it gives me the greatest joy,
   This schoolhouse at the creek.

"Good bye, old schoolhouse!"—It echoes
   "Good bye! Good bye!" back;
O schoolhouse! Schoolhouse! Must I go?
And you just stand there all alone—
   You schoolhouse at the creek.

O listen, you people who will live after me,
   I will write you one more thing:
I warn you, threaten you, take care
And never forget
   This schoolhouse at the creek.[33]

Harbaugh's English-language "The Old School-House at the Creek" is just as nostalgic as the Pennsylvania Dutch poem, but much less bitter. When he addresses English readers Harbaugh is less sad reminiscing about bygone days, and he avoids anything like the somber warning that concludes "Das alt Schulhaus." In the concluding three stanzas of "The Old School-House," Harbaugh ends by encouraging his readers to recall the joys of innocent youth as a way to ease the cares of their adult lives:

My muse has struck a tender vein!
   And asks a soothing flow;
O Time! what changes thou hast made,
Since I around this school-house played,
   Just twenty years ago!

Good bye! Old school-house! Echo sad,
   "Good bye! Good bye!" replies;
I leave you yet a friendly tear!
Fond mem'ry bids me drop it here,
   'Mid scenes that gave it rise!

Ye, who shall live when I am dead—
Write down my wishes quick—
Protect it, love it, let it stand,
A way-mark in this changing land—
That school-house at the creek.[34]

On the language level, Harbaugh's English has an obviously more formal, "perfect and polished" quality in lines such as "My muse has struck a tender vein! / And asks a soothing flow." His Pennsylvania Dutch is much more natural, largely lacking in formal borrowings from standard German, which would have been the way to perfect and polish vernacular Pennsylvania Dutch. On the level of content, he is more somber and direct in Pennsylvania Dutch, as in the couplet just quoted: "My heart swells with thoughts, / Until I nearly choke!" (*Mei Hertz schwellt mit Gedanka uf, / Bis Ich schier gar verstick!*). And whereas Harbaugh "warns" and "threatens" the reader in the final stanza of the Pennsylvania Dutch original, in English he asks that the memory of the schoolhouse be "protected" and "loved."

Three years after Harbaugh's death in 1867, his friend and colleague Benjamin Bausman (1824–1909) brought out a collection of the fifteen Pennsylvania Dutch poems by Harbaugh, giving it the German title *Harbaugh's Harfe* (Harbaugh's harp). The language of these poems was "perfected and polished," however, to make them look and sound more like European German. It is not known who actually altered Harbaugh's poems, whether it was Bausman or one of six other men credited by Bausman with having helped bring the book to fruition.[35] At least five of these men were members of the Union of the German Press of Pennsylvania (*Verein der Deutschen Presse von Pennsylvanien*), which was founded in 1862 by a group of European Germans and educated Pennsylvania Dutchmen to promote the use of standard German in the press, schools, and cultural organizations.[36] Their attitude toward Pennsylvania Dutch, which they would have preferred to call *Pennsylvania German*, was an interesting one.

Capitalizing on a growing appreciation among cultural elites in German-speaking Europe for regional dialects, the *Verein* sought to emphasize the kinship of Pennsylvania Dutch with its distant rustic cousins abroad, but that meant de-emphasizing the influence of English, which was seen as corrupting. In an 1876 article in the *Reading Adler* looking back on the history of the *Verein*, an unnamed author summarized the organization's attitude toward Pennsylvania Dutch:

> Soon after its founding the *Verein* began to devote considerable attention to the German-Pennsylvanian language, and different members sought to investigate more closely and describe its unique character, as had been done previously. A high priority was to instill in the German Pennsylvanians themselves self-confidence and pride in their ancestry and then build on that by bringing them into the modern German development, from which they had remained apart through their long isolation from the intellectual life of Germany and through contact with English. After many debates and individuals' research, it became clear that the Pennsylvania-German language is Palatine German, with some Swabian elements, that it is easily expurgated of the admixture of English words, and that it deserves to be restored to its purity as a German dialect, like Alsatian, for example, whereby the old German-Pennsylvanians can and should be enlisted to cultivate High German. This is a special goal of the *Verein*, the full meaning of which it came to recognize and value only over the course of years.[37]

It is not clear whether Benjamin Bausman himself was a member of the *Verein*, but he is on record as having been skeptical about the utility of writing in Pennsylvania Dutch at all, as opposed to German or English. Unlike many of his fellow Pennsylvania Dutch, Bausman had actually traveled to Germany and Switzerland (for six months, in 1856–1857), and though not allied with the European German faction within the German Reformed Church in the United States, his knowledge of and appreciation for standard German was greater than that of Harbaugh.[38] Bausman enlisted Jacob M. Beck, a European German who was the editor of the *Reading Adler* from 1864 to 1881, to amend Harbaugh's orthography for the *Harfe*, which in the *Guardian* had been an inconsistent mix of German and English elements, to follow the norms of German phonetic spelling more closely. Beck also prepared a glossary at the end of the book, in the introduction to which he stated that "Harbaugh introduced an occasional High German word for the sake of the rhyme only, and the many English expressions with which he had originally overloaded some of his poems were, in accordance with his wishes, substituted with Pennsylvania German ones."[39]

Whether Harbaugh had truly wanted someone to edit out the English borrowings in his poetry is dubious and raises the question of why he had used them in the first place. In any case, Beck, Bausman, or one or more of the colleagues from the *Verein* rewrote a number of Harbaugh's poems to excise many of their English elements. In "Das alt Schulhaus," for example, Harbaugh's original included sixty-two Pennsylvania Dutch words and phrases derived from English.[40] In the *Harfe* version, that number was reduced by nearly half, to thirty-five. Below are the first four stanzas of "Das alt Schulhaus" as they originally appeared in the *Guardian* in August 1861 and in the *Harfe* version from 1870. Following is a translation of Harbaugh's original along with his own free rendering of the four stanzas in English. Lexical elements borrowed from English are underscored.

Harbaugh's 1861 published version[41]

Heit ishts exactly zwanzig Yohr,
 Das Ich bin Owa naus;
Nau bin Ich widder lewig z'rick,
Un' steh' am Schul-haus an der
  Krick,
 Yusht naekst an's [T]attys Haus.

Ich bin in hundert Haeuser g'west,
 Von marbel Stein un' Brick;
Un' alles was Ich hab' geseh,
Det Ich verschwappa any day,
 Fuer's Schul-haus an der Krick.

Wer mued da heme is, un' will fort,
 So los ihn numma geh;
Ich sag ihm awer forna naus,
Es is all Humbug Owa draus,
 Un' er werd's selver seh.

Ich bin draus rum in alle Eck'
 Getravelled high un' low;
Hab awer noch in kennem Spot,

Harfe **1870 edited version**[42]

Heit is 's 'xäctly zwansig Johr,
 Dass ich bin owwe naus;
Nau bin ich widder lewig z'rick
Un schteh am Schulhaus an d'r
  Krick,
 Juscht neekscht an's Dady's
  Haus.

Ich bin in hunnert Heiser g'west,
 Vun Märbelstee' un Brick,
Un alles was sie hen, die Leit,
Dhet ich verschwappe eenig Zeit
 For's Schulhaus an der Krick.

Wer mied deheem is, un will fort,
 So loss ihn numme geh'—
Ich sag ihm awwer vorne naus
Es is all Humbuk owwe draus,
 Un er werd's selwert seh'!

Ich bin draus rum in alle Eck',
 M'r macht's jo ewwe so;
Hab awwer noch in keener Schtadt

Uf e'mol so fiel <u>Joy</u> gehat,   Uf e'mol so viel Freed gehat
  Wie in dem Schul-haus do.   Wie in dem Schulhaus do.

Literal translation of Harbaugh **Free translation by Harbaugh in**
1861   **the *Harfe***

Today it is <u>exactly</u> twenty years   To-day it is just twenty years,
  that I headed out;   Since I began to roam:
Now I am back again alive   Now, safely back, I stand once more,
And stand at the schoolhouse at   Before the quaint old school-house
  the <u>creek</u>,   door,
    Just close by Dad's house.   Close by my father's home.

I have been in hundreds of houses,   I've been in many houses since,
  Of <u>marble</u>-stone and <u>brick</u>,   Of marble built, and brick;
And everything that I have seen   Though grander far, their aim they
    miss,

I would <u>swap</u> any day   To lure my heart's old love from this
  For the schoolhouse at the <u>creek</u>.   Old school-house at the creek.

Whoever is tired at home and   Let those who dream of happier
  wants to leave,   scenes,
  Just let him go;   Go forth those scenes to find;
But I'll tell him beforehand   They'll learn what thousands have
    confessed,
It's all <u>humbug</u> out there,   That with our home our heart's
    true rest
  And he will see it for himself.   Is ever left behind.

I've been out there in every corner, I've travelled long and travelled far,
  <u>Traveled</u> <u>high and low</u>,   Till weary, worn, and sick;
But I've never had in any <u>spot</u>   How joyless all that I have found,
So much <u>joy</u>   Compared with scenes that lie
    around
  As in this schoolhouse here.   This school-house at the creek.

Whoever rewrote Harbaugh's original poems to avoid English loans
was either a native or highly proficient speaker of Pennsylvania Dutch,

since the changes still involve Pennsylvania Dutch, as opposed to German, vocabulary. The overall effect was to "Hebelize" Harbaugh's Pennsylvania Dutch. Though Pennsylvania Dutch would never be able to rival the prestige of standard German, it could be admitted to the family of European German dialects, but only if it were de-anglicized as much as possible.[43]

The impact of Henry Harbaugh's Pennsylvania Dutch poetry on both average readers as well as later generations of Pennsylvania Dutch writers was profound. The popularity of his poems in the *Guardian* between 1861 and his death in 1867 was something Harbaugh himself had not anticipated. In an essay titled "The Poetry of German Pennsylvania," which was published in the *Guardian* just months after Harbaugh's death, Joseph Henry Dubbs, who, like Harbaugh, was a native Pennsylvania Dutchman, a Reformed clergyman, and an educator, pointed out that when Harbaugh published "Das alt Schulhaus," he did so anonymously, "fearful that his poem might not be appreciated. . . . It was, however, received with a perfect storm of applause, which certainly surprised no one as much as it did the author."[44] Years after Harbaugh's passing, Pennsylvania Dutch speakers could still recite "Das alt Schulhaus" from memory. Harry Hess Reichard (1878–1956), for example, a native Dutchman from Northampton County and a professor of German at Muhlenberg College, relates the following in his monumental study of Pennsylvania Dutch literature:

The present writer recalls the occasion when he was very young, a new schoolhouse near his home replaced an older one, and the new one was being dedicated by a Sunday School which made use of the building on Sundays; a very old man was one of the speakers; there were addresses in English and addresses in German, all of which he has forgotten, if he ever understood them; the old man had finished his address in German and had taken his seat when he suddenly jumped up and said, "Oh, ich het schier gar vergesse—Heit is es exactly zwanzig jahr" [Oh, I almost forgot—"Today it is exactly twenty years"] and recited the whole poem to the end, amid the smiles and winks of the younger men and the deep sighing and even tears of the older men and women, and so true, so realistic did it all seem that he did not know until years later that the old man had not spoken of himself and been describing the schoolhouse that had stood on that very spot in years gone by; and yet the schoolhouse of Harbaugh and the one where this occurred were as far apart as the most eastern and the most western counties of German Pennsylvania.[45]

At least as early as 1875 the poetry of "Heinrich Harbaugh" came to the attention of European scholars. In that year, Anton Birlinger, a professor of German philology at the University of Bonn and a native Swabian, published an article on Harbaugh, whom he called "a Pennsylvania German Hebel," drawing on a copy of the *Harfe* that he had acquired. Birlinger included in his article five poems, which he glossed for his European German readers, the first of which was, inevitably, "Das alt Schulhaus an der Krick."[46]

After Harbaugh's death in 1867, and into the twentieth century, hundreds of prose texts and poems in Pennsylvania Dutch appeared, a number of which were modeled directly after Harbaugh's works. This explosion of Pennsylvania Dutch literature after the Civil War might lead some to view it as a sign of the robust health of the language, but that was not the case. As Harbaugh himself notes in the third-person introduction to "Das alt Schulhaus" in 1861, already in his lifetime the future of Pennsylvania Dutch was in doubt:

> The following Poem is written in what is generally called "Pennsylvania German." This is a peculiar dialect, created by a strange mixture of all the European German dialects, with a large sprinkling of English words and pronunciations. It is passing away before the victorious progress of the English, and must ultimately become extinct. It will, however always remain as a curiosity in literature. This Poem, written by a Pennsylvania Pastor, is here inserted at the request of literary friends who saw it in manuscript. It has, we believe, the ring of the true vernacular.[47]

Harbaugh witnessed the displacement of Pennsylvania Dutch by English firsthand. Like his lawyer cousin, Henry Lee Fisher, Harbaugh left the farm both literally and figuratively, making the choice to enter into a world dominated by English. He moved away from the rural Pennsylvania Dutch–speaking community in which he had grown up, pursued higher education and a vocation in which English was the norm, and married two women who were not Pennsylvania Dutch speakers. Despite the popularity of his poetry, writing in Pennsylvania Dutch was for Harbaugh not a vocation but an avocation, as it was for all other Pennsylvania Dutch writers. For example, of the fifty-seven authors included in the two of the most comprehensive anthologies of Pennsylvania Dutch literature, fifty-three were highly educated professionals.[48] Not surprisingly, most of these white-collar Pennsylvania Dutch writers were engaged in professions in which the use of language is central, including the ministry, education, journalism, and the law. In every instance, these individuals acquired their knowledge of Pennsylvania Dutch language and culture in childhood, growing up, like Harbaugh, in Pennsylvania Dutch families in rural parts of the state. But, again like Harbaugh, they eventually moved *owwe naus* (up out), physically into towns and cities, socially into the professional world, and linguistically into English.

It is no wonder, then, that much of Pennsylvania Dutch prose and poetry, produced as it was by individuals who themselves were at the threshold of English monolingualism, had the same kind of nostalgic quality found in poems such as "Das alt Schulhaus an der Krick." These writers depict the past, the world of their childhood, in glowing terms. Conversely, when they turn their attention to the present, their views are often critical. Their jaundiced views of modern times can sometimes be lighthearted, but they are just as often harsh. In his "Country and Town" (*Busch un Schtettel*), for example, Harbaugh, writing in all seriousness, laments the "hankering" some Pennsylvania Dutch of his era (*Buschleut*, 'country people') have for the city, which he describes as the nineteenth-century equivalent of a concrete jungle, a noisy, built-up, hectic place where young men and women alike are unhealthy and lazy.[49] In another poem, "The New Kind of Gentlefolk" (*Die Neue Sart Gentleleut*),[50] he criticizes aspiring rural parents who take pride in seeing their sons drive fancy carriages drawn by silver-harnessed horses and their daughters prance around in silk dresses. In this way, Harbaugh echoes earlier Pennsylvania Dutch commentators who already in the first decades of the nineteenth century warned of the dangers of a English-speaking world where "so-called gentlemen" wear tight pants and stand-up collars and escort hoop-skirted women of questionable moral character to taverns.

What is striking about Harbaugh is the fact that his critical views of contemporary society are limited to his Pennsylvania Dutch poetry. For him, English was not an appropriate vehicle in which to uphold traditional Pennsylvania Dutch values. Ultimately, this says nothing about any inherent linguistic difference between Pennsylvania Dutch and English; rather, it all has to do with audience. When writing in English, Harbaugh was addressing a readership that held a generally positive, optimistic view of American life and times. With his fellow Dutch speakers, Harbaugh could bare his soul more and express a broader range of emotions when recalling their shared past and taking stock of the world of which they were now a part. Thus, in their original forms, poems like "Das alt Schulhaus an der Krick," "Busch un Schtettel," and "Die Neue Sart Gentleleut" convey not only Pennsylvania Dutch words but a Pennsylvania Dutch voice telling stories from a Pennsylvania Dutch world that was disappearing before the poet's eyes.

Edward H. Rauch, "Nestor of Pennsylvania Dutch"

Just over five years after the death of Henry Harbaugh in December 1867, the following announcement appeared in a Lancaster, PA, magazine:

> The editor of the *Dutchman* will deliver a lecture under the auspices of the Millerstown (Lehigh county) Lecture Association, on Saturday evening, March 15th, inst., in the Pennsylvania Dutch language, on the subject of "Allte un Neie T'zeita" [Old and new times]. He will also read Rev. Dr. Harbaugh's famous poem, "Dass Alt Schulhaus on der Kreek" and several other popular productions, including "De Alt Hehmet" [The old homestead] and "De Pennsylvania Millitz" [The Pennsylvania militia].[51]

The full name of the magazine in which this appeared was the *Pennsylvania Dutchman*, and its editor was Edward H. Rauch. In his 1918 study of Pennsylvania Dutch literature, Harry Hess Reichard writes that in Rauch "were centered a ceaseless activity, a wonderful initiative and an untiring energy that meant more for the growth of Pennsylvania-German literature than any other individual group of forces."[52] After Rauch's passing in 1902, none other than the *New York Times* devoted nearly an entire page to an obituary article on him, dubbing him "the Nestor of 'Pennsylvania Dutch,' a queer language spoken by five million Americans to-day." The *Times* declared that Rauch was a "soldier, energetic newspaper worker, proprietor and editor, political enthusiast, and an admirer of all that is good and ennobling in American citizenship, [and he] was moreover a scholar, and for years he devoted much of his time in studying, and in his writing keeping before the public Pennsylvania 'Dutch,' a living language which to him was a never-ending fund and storehouse of philological research."[53] Indeed, Edward H. Rauch occupies a place of singular importance in the history of Pennsylvania Dutch as its earliest defender in the face of skepticism of the language's inherent value among Pennsylvania Dutch and outsiders alike.

CAPT. E. H. RAUCH.

Edward Henry Rauch (1820–1902).
Source: Brenckman 1913, plate facing p. 548.

Born in 1820 in Warwick Township, near Lititz, Lancaster County, Edward Henry Rauch was a third-generation American, his paternal grandfather, Johann Heinrich Rauch, having immigrated to Pennsylvania in 1769. Young Edward, whose family spoke Pennsylvania Dutch, received an exceptionally good formal education for his time at the prestigious John Beck's Academy for Boys in Lititz. After an unpleasant apprenticeship with a cabinetmaker in Lancaster when he had completed his studies at the Beck Academy, Rauch was engaged in a number of professional capacities over his lifetime, mainly as a journalist and newspaper editor. He was drawn into politics during the 1840 presidential campaign between the incumbent Jacksonian Democrat Martin Van Buren, the favorite of most Pennsylvania Dutch, and William Henry Harrison, a Whig, who ended up defeating Van Buren (but dying after just thirty days in office). Rauch later became closely allied with Thaddeus Stevens, a Radical Republican congressman and ardent abolitionist from Lancaster. For a time in the 1840s, while employed as a secretary to a notorious (and illiterate) slave catcher in Lancaster, Rauch secretly aided the escape of runaway slaves via the Underground Railroad. During the Civil War Rauch served as a captain in the Union army, seeing much action and sustaining an injury at the Battle of Second Bull Run that led to his discharge in 1863. For most of his career thereafter, Rauch worked as a journalist and editor for Republican-leaning newspapers in Lancaster, Berks, and Carbon Counties, finally settling in Mauch Chunk (today, Jim Thorpe), Carbon County, where he remained from 1877 until his death in 1902.[54]

Like Henry Harbaugh, who was just three years his senior, Rauch was a fluent Pennsylvania Dutch speaker who had little formal instruction in German. German was part of the curriculum at the Beck Academy, but the medium of instruction at the school was English. While Rauch at one point founded a German-language newspaper in Reading, the *Berks County Zeitung*, he quit after just a few months, "conclud[ing] that he was unfitted to conduct a real German newspaper."[55] Rauch had in his various jobs no need for knowledge of German, unlike Harbaugh, who, as a pastor and theologian in the German Reformed Church, had to maintain at least receptive skills in the language. Rauch's relative distance from German compared to Harbaugh's situation was reflected in how the two men referred to and wrote in Pennsylvania Dutch. Though

Harbaugh was not at all a purist as far as English loanwords in Pennsylvania Dutch were concerned, he did refer to the language as Pennsylvania German, as in his introduction to "Das alt Schulhaus" in the *Guardian*, and also as a "peculiar dialect." Rauch, on the contrary, was adamant about identifying his native tongue as Pennsylvania Dutch, though he alternated between referring to it as a dialect and a language. An editorial in the *Reformed Church Messenger* announced the inauguration of Rauch's *Pennsylvania Dutchman* magazine in January 1873:

The enterprise of Mr. Rauch is a commendable one, and it will afford us pleasure to find it proving a success. We confess we do not exactly like the title given to his monthly. "The Pennsylvania German" would have sounded better in our ears, and been more correct in fact. We know that it is quite common to call Pennsylvania Germans "Dutch." The appellation, however, is not only a misnomer, but is more or less extensively used as a term of reproach. It is intended to fasten the stigma of ignorance and stupidity upon those to whom it is applied. Those properly acquainted with our Pennsylvania Germans know that the stigma is wholly unmerited by them as a class of citizens. Besides this, their language is a German dialect, imported from Germany, with a slight intermixture of English, and partakes of nothing that assimilates it to the language of the Dutch or Hollanders, beyond what is to be found in the pure German itself. We think the friends of Pennsylvania Germans ought to labor to correct the misnomer and remove the stigma of reproach it is often employed to convey, instead of legitimizing the term and affixing it permanently to those to whom it is commonly, but wrongfully, applied. This criticism, we doubt not, Mr. Rauch will appreciate, and we should be pleased to find him endeavoring to carry the suggestion it conveys into practical effect.[56]

In the February 1873 issue of his *Dutchman* magazine, Rauch reprinted the excerpt above, defending at length his preference for "Pennsylvania Dutch":

The best reason stated for endeavoring to "correct the misnomer" is the supposed stigma of ignorance and stupidity upon those to whom it is applied. But we believe the true way to remove such an impression, and to command the entire respect of the rest of mankind, is boldly and squarely to accept and adopt the inevitable title, and proudly and defiantly fling our *Pennsylvania Dutchman* banner to the breeze. . . . And, somehow, as far as we are concerned personally, believing that the first word we ever uttered after getting out of the cradle was either *dawdy* or *mommy*, and having become very much accustomed to the term, we must confess that we rather prefer being called a *Pennsylvania Dutchman*. We like it because it is emphatic, simple and expressive, and everybody knows just what it means.[57]

In the next (and final) issue of his magazine, Rauch astutely notes that the Dutch/German nomenclatural debate was ultimately moot when talking about the language in Pennsylvania Dutch itself: "[t]his question only arises when the language is referred to in English writing or speaking, all agreeing that 'Pennsylvania Deitsh' is correct, when referred to in 'Dutch' or 'German' writing or speaking."[58]

Rauch waved the banner on behalf of the Pennsylvania Dutch language in every possible way. Writing in English, he advocates for its legitimacy on numerous occasions, at times citing the work of Prof. Samuel Stehman Haldeman (1812–1880), a native Pennsylvania Dutchman from Lancaster County, who produced the first scholarly treatise on Pennsylvania Dutch in 1872.[59] In one instance, Rauch invokes Haldeman, whose monograph is titled *Pennsylvania Dutch*, in support of his own use of the term. Elsewhere, Rauch is clearly proud to note that Haldeman had brought Pennsylvania Dutch, and specifically some of Rauch's own writings in the language, to the attention of a distinguished British philologist, Alexander J. Ellis (1814–1890), who was researching the history of English pronunciation.[60] Ellis recounts the following in his introduction to Haldeman's treatise:

> While I was engaged with the third part of my *Early English Pronunciation*, Prof. Haldeman sent me a reprint of some humorous letters by Rauch. . . . Perceiving at once the analogy between this debased German with English intermixture, and Chaucer's debased Anglo-Saxon with Norman intermixture, I requested and obtained such further information as enabled me to give an account of this singular modern reproduction of the manner in which our English language itself was built up, and insert it in the introduction to my chapter on Chaucer's pronunciation.[61]

Ellis goes on to stress the importance of studying language change as it unfolds, pointing out that Pennsylvania Dutch, as a form of German in dynamic contact with English, presents just such an opportunity for scientific inquiry. Rauch, through his efforts to document and promote Pennsylvania Dutch in print, saw himself playing an important role in this philological work.[62] Ellis does, however, point out that Haldeman had taken Rauch to task for the way that he wrote Pennsylvania Dutch: "[t]he orthography is bad and inconsistent, sometimes English and sometimes German, so that it requires some knowledge of the dialect, and of English spelling to be able to read it."[63] Rauch does not acknowledge that he did in fact mix English and German spelling patterns in his writings. For example, the vowels in rhyming words like *Hoof*, 'hoof', and *uf*, 'on, upon', were written differently, as were the long <a> (phonetically [e:]) sounds in two grammatical forms of the same word, *sæ*, 'see', and *sana*, 'saw, seen'. Rauch's reaction to Haldeman's criticism centers instead on the practical utility of following English rather than German norms, arguing (rightly) that literacy in German among the Pennsylvania Dutch had declined precipitously in the nineteenth century.[64] It is striking that Rauch, unlike Wollenweber, Harbaugh, and the members of the *Verein der Deutschen Presse von Pennsylvanien*, regards the kinship of Pennsylvania Dutch with German as a fact of linguistic history and nothing more. Nowhere in his writings does Rauch seek to legitimize Pennsylvania Dutch by comparing it favorably to Palatine German or any other European German dialect. For Rauch, Pennsylvania Dutch is truly a language unto itself. Though he describes it as a "compound of German and English," it is, in his view, definitely autonomous from both.

While pleased that his work on behalf of Pennsylvania Dutch was validated by earning the attention of eminent scholars such as Samuel S. Haldeman and Alexander J. Ellis, Rauch seeks to demonstrate the legitimacy of his native language in a number of ways, not least of which is putting it to paper. Rauch stands out among all other Pennsylvania Dutch writers for the sheer range of genres in which he produced texts in his native language. These include short works of nonfiction, dialogs, poems, an original drama, translations of excerpts from English literature, and especially his "dialect letters," the antecedents for which can be found in the German and Dutchified German writings of late eighteenth- and early nineteenth-century newspaper correspondents such as Stoffel Ehrlich and Hannickel Wahrheit.

The earliest-known Pennsylvania Dutch writings of Rauch are from a newspaper he published in Reading during the election season of 1864. Titled *Father Abraham*, it was a fervently Radical Republican publication aimed at mustering support for Lincoln and other Republican candidates in Berks County, which was—and remained—a Democratic stronghold. Over the approximately four months that the Reading *Father Abraham* appeared, Rauch wrote Pennsylvania Dutch pieces for every issue, including dialogs featuring Democratic interlocutors who see the light and decide to vote Republican. Below is an excerpt from one dialog that appeared on October 18, 1864, days after state and local elections and two weeks before the presidential vote. Democrats had just triumphed everywhere in Berks County except in the city of Reading and there lost only by a small margin, but that did not deter Rauch from continuing to push for Lincoln.

Die Leckshun is Ewwa Ferlohra

JOHN—Well, du, sog amohl, husht shun g'hehrt wie die leckshun gonga is?

GODLIEB—Ei ich war letsht nacht in Reading un un about am nine uhr do hehr ichs emohl donnera—gontz immer un eawig hots gekracht. Well, ich bin don graud nye gonga un emohld nochgefroked was des ding mehnt—denk ich, desmohl hen mers doch emohl gewoona. Awer, holes mich der diefel wans net die Lincum's leit wara wu g'shussa hen. . . .

JOHN—Well, ich wehs net wie's is. Ich bin so an wenig gebottert. Ich glaub's besht ding das mer doo kennt wer emohl ach oof die onner seit shtimma.

GODLIEB—Koom, now, net so. Shtick zu der party.

JOHN—Stick zum deivel! Ich duhs net. Ich geh beim deihenker for der Lincoln, for er is anyhow der besht.

GODLIEB—Well, ich glaub auch sis eppas lets, was fehlt wehs ich net, un awer ich glaub so holwer dos unsery leeders nimmy exactly sin wie sie sei setta, soonsht deht net alles soonersht seversht geh.

JOHN—Well donn, los uns uf die onner seit shtimma. Sell deht ferleicht alles recht bringa.

GODLIEB—So sogt mei Alty [a]ch, un awer ich wehs net recht.

JOHN—Un awer ich wehs was ich duh—wie g'saht ich vote for der Lincoln.

GODLIEB—Well, donn, let her rib. Ich glaub ich wills ach prowiera. Kumm, los uns geh un emohl chirs drinka.

The Election Is Plain Lost

JOHN—*Say, have you heard already how the election went?*

GODLIEB—*My, I was in Reading last night and at about nine o'clock I heard it thundering, forever and ever cracking. So I went right on in and asked around what was going on. I thought, this time we actually won. But I'll be, if it wasn't the Lincoln people who were shooting. . . .*

JOHN—*Well, I don't know how it is. I'm just a little bothered. I think the best thing that one could do would be to vote for the other side.*

GODLIEB—*Come now, don't talk that way. Stick to the party.*

JOHN—*Stick my eye! I won't do it. I'm going for Lincoln, by crack, because he's anyhow the best one.*

GODLIEB—*Well, I also think that something's wrong, just what, I don't know, but I'm thinking that our leaders aren't exactly like they should be anymore, otherwise things wouldn't be so topsy-turvy.*

JOHN—*Well, then, let's vote for the other side. That might make everything right.*

GODLIEB—*That's what my wife says too, but I just don't know.*

JOHN—*But I know what I'll do. Like I say, I'm voting for Lincoln.*

GODLIEB—*Well, then, let 'er rip. I think I'll try it, too. Come on, let's go have a drink.*

Lincoln narrowly defeated his Democratic opponent, George B. McClellan, by less than 2% of the vote in Reading but lost everywhere else in Berks County by a two-to-one margin. In the November 15, 1864, Rauch overlooked that latter detail, trumpeting "Old Abe Re-enlisted for 4 years more! The Democratic Rooster Won't Crow!!! Victory! . . . Reading All Right!!"

Rauch made use of vernacular Pennsylvania Dutch to connect as directly with his readers as possible. As in his later writings, he favors English spelling patterns, though inconsistently, as variation in the example above shows in words with long and short *u* vowel sounds: *doo,* 'to do,' *koom*, 'come', and *oof*, 'on, upon', versus *duh*, *kumm*, and *uf*. The variation in the spelling of *Lincoln* in the dialog is also noteworthy. At first, the skeptic Godlieb mispronounces the name as *Lincum*, unlike John, who says *Lincoln*. And when Godlieb (whose old-fashioned German name connotes conservatism) uses the word *leeders*, Rauch similarly employs a misspelling for effect. In terms of the content, Rauch deftly creates characters whose personalities and ways of thinking closely resembled those of his Pennsylvania Dutch readers, then attempts to sway those readers toward his political leanings.

After the Civil War, when he started a new *Father Abraham*, this time in the city of Lancaster, Rauch invented a latter-day Stoffel Ehrlich named Pit Schwefflebrenner (Pete Sulfur-Burner), the Pennsylvania Dutch letters under whose name were to become a popular fixture in every newspaper Rauch edited for the rest of his life. Like John and Godlieb from Reading, Pit and his wife Bevvy, who were residents of the mythic Lancaster County community of Schliffletown (Rowdytown), were introduced to readers in May 1868 as typical Dutch Democrats, though by the end of the fall, first Bevvy, and then Pit, see the Republican light and become supporters of Ulysses S. Grant.

Most of Rauch's Schwefflebrenner letters deal with political content; those that do not often address technological advancements, especially the ultimate symbol of the industrial era, the railroad. Strikingly absent in Rauch's writings is any of the suspicion of progress, urban life, and related themes that permeate the writings of so many of Rauch's contemporaries, including Henry Harbaugh. When speaking of social and technological changes, Rauch's tone is more lighthearted. His progressive politics as a Radical Republican might well account for his apparent openness to progress in many aspects of life. And while Rauch does not lament the passing of bygone days, contrary to the more melancholy Harbaugh, neither does he in any of his writings even hint at the fact that progress might bring with it a shift to English monolingualism among the Pennsylvania Dutch. Though Rauch could not have been blind to the loss of Pennsylvania Dutch among his contemporaries in the professions, as well as almost certainly his own children, he never commented on it.

Rauch's implicit optimism about the health of Pennsylvania Dutch in the nineteenth century is exemplified by his most important work, his *Pennsylvania Dutch Hand-Book* (*Pennsylvania Deitsh Hond-Booch*), which he published in 1879. Its subtitle, *A Book for Instruction* (*En Buch for Inshtructa*), points to an intended didactic purpose. Rauch had two target audiences in mind with the *Hand-Book*: "business men who are located among Pennsylvania Dutch speaking people" and "the many thousands of native Pennsylvania girls and boys who attend the English public schools, and yet almost exclusively speak the Pennsylvania Dutch language at home."[65] In his preface he stresses the value of following (more or less) English rules of spelling to make what had historically been an oral vernacular also a medium of literacy.

Almost two-thirds of Rauch's *Hand-Book* consists of English–Pennsylvania Dutch / Pennsylvania Dutch–English word lists. This was the culmination of work Rauch had begun earlier in the 1870s and had started publishing in the three issues of his *Pennsylvania Dutchman* magazine in 1873, the first Pennsylvania Dutch dictionary project ever.[66] Following the word lists in the *Hand-Book* are several pages of Pennsylvania Dutch words in the context of actual usage. The linguistic value of Rauch's material is considerable. As someone who had no inclination to make Pennsylvania Dutch look or sound more like European varieties of German, Rauch presents the language as he naturally knew and loved it. Examples of his attitude are found in his sample sentences for the words *ouslender*, 'foreigner', *orrick*, 'very', and *nitzlich*, 'useful'.

De Deitshe <u>ouslender</u> sin goot om hoch Deitsh, awer Penn. Deitsh missa se larna.
The German <u>foreigners</u> are good with High German, but they must learn Pennsylvania Dutch.

Penn. Deitsh laisa un shtudya gait <u>orrick</u> leicht, un plesseerlich.
Studying and reading Pennsylvania Dutch goes <u>very</u> easily and pleasantly.

De shtudy fun Penn. Deitsh is net yoosht for ornament, awer es is <u>nitzlich</u>. Es is aw yoosht an tzeitsfroke wann es de shproach fun der welt si wærd.
The study of Pennsylvania Dutch is not merely ornamental, but <u>useful</u>. It is only a question of time when it will be the language of the world.[67]

Just as important for the purpose of linguistic documentation are Rauch's nine sample conversations in a section titled "Business Talk"

(*Bisness G'shwetz*). Set in everyday commercial settings, such as a book-store (that just happens to experience a rush on sales of Rauch's *Hand-Book*), a doctor's office, and a hotel, the conversations apply the familiar dialog genre to a pedagogical end. Following the business talk section is a discussion of the "progress of Pennsylvania Dutch literature," in which the question of orthography is central. To illustrate the advantages of an English-based system of writing, Rauch reprints verses from the German-oriented *Harfe* version of Harbaugh's "Das alt Schulhaus an der Krick" and rewrites them according to his method. With an air of self-confidence, Rauch establishes his authority on the matter of producing written texts in Pennsylvania Dutch: "[i]t is admitted by all, that the author of this book has had much more experience in writing Penn. Dutch than any other individual living."[68]

Aside from the practical aims of his *Hand-Book*, Rauch clearly also intended to establish Pennsylvania Dutch as a bona fide language rather than "just a dialect." According to popular linguistic thinking, then as now, languages are reified by being written, and then systematically, according to explicit rules. By assembling lists of words numbering in the thousands and then printing them in an orderly fashion in a hardbound book, Rauch was making a statement. Rauch's mention of the respect accorded Pennsylvania Dutch (and his own work) by philological scholars like Samuel S. Haldeman and Alexander J. Ellis further strengthens his case. And, to take matters one step further, Rauch renders excerpts from Shakespeare and the King James Bible, the most highly regarded works in the English language, into Pennsylvania Dutch. If such texts could be translated into Pennsylvania Dutch, Rauch surmised, no one could deny its linguistic legitimacy.

However, Rauch had no qualms about using Pennsylvania Dutch, including material translated from English, for humorous effect. For example, Rauch recognized that his Pennsylvania Dutch rendering of act 1, scene 5 of *Hamlet*, though linguistically accurate, ended up being "a burlesque rather than a translation." Below Rauch's version is Shakespeare's original.

HAMLET: Wo wid mich onna nemma? Shwetz, ich gæ nimmy weider.
GHOST: Now mind mich;
HAMLET: Ich will.

GHOST: My shtoond is sheer gor cooma
Os ich tzurick mus, in de shweffel's flomma,
Muss ich mich widder uf gevva.

HAMLET: Oh! du ormas shpook!

GHOST: Pity mich net, awer geb mer now di ora,
For ich will der amohl ebbas sawga.

HAMLET: Shwetz rous, for ich will 's now aw hara.

GHOST: Un wann du 's haresht don nemsht aw satisfaction.

HAMLET: Well, was is 's? Rous mit!

GHOST: Ich bin deim dawdy si shpook;
G'sentenced for a tzeit long rumm lawfa nauchts. . . .[69]

HAMLET: *Where wilt thou lead me? speak; I'll go no further.*

GHOST: *Mark me.*

HAMLET: *I will.*

GHOST: *My hour is almost come,*
When I to sulphurous and tormenting flames
Must render up myself.

HAMLET: *Alas, poor ghost!*

GHOST: *Pity me not, but lend thy serious hearing*
To what I shall unfold.

HAMLET: *Speak; I am bound to hear.*

GHOST: *So art thou to revenge, when thou shalt hear.*

HAMLET: *What?*

GHOST: *I am thy father's spirit*
Doom'd for a certain time to walk the night. . . .

Setting aside the humorous effect of hearing the dialog between Hamlet and his father's ghost in Pennsylvania Dutch, Rauch's translation was, on a linguistic level, excellent, as it aimed to provide not a verbatim rendering of the original but an adaptation befitting the language into which it was being translated. Below is a translation of Rauch's Pennsylvania Dutch version of the dialog.

HAMLET: *Where do you want to take me? Talk; I'm not going any farther.*

GHOST: *Now mind me.*

HAMLET: *I will.*

GHOST: *My hour has almost come,*
          That I have to go back, into the sulphurous flames,
          I have to give myself up again.
HAMLET: *Oh, you poor ghost!*
GHOST: *Don't pity me, but give me your ears now,*
          For I want to tell you something.
HAMLET: *Go ahead, talk; for I want to hear it now.*
GHOST: *And when you hear it, you'll take satisfaction, too.*
HAMLET: *Well, what is it? Out with it!*
GHOST: *I'm your father's ghost;*
          Sentenced to walk around for a while at night. . . .

In an instance of taking another earnest literary product and modifying it for comic effect, Rauch ends his treatment of Harbaugh's "Das alt Schulhaus" in an otherwise serious section on the "progress of Pennsylvania Dutch literature" by rewriting the first three stanzas of Harbaugh's English version of the poem from the *Harfe*. Since, in Rauch's view, Harbaugh's translation "fails to convey an idea as to the genuine Pennsylvania Dutch spirit of the original," he offers the following alternative version:

> To-day it vas joost dwendy years
>   Ven I out vesht dit go;
> Un now I's back, so nice, un shlick
> Un here's der shkool house on de creek
>   Joost close by daddy's house.
>
> I haf in hundred houses been,
>   Of marble, shtones un brick;
> But all of dem vat I dit see,
> I'd shwap 'm off on any day,
>   For 'd shkool house on der creek.
>
> Ven one don't vant to shtay at home,
>   So joost you led him go;
> But I can dell him—un I know besht—
> It is all hoombug out in 'd vesht
>   Un he vill find as dat ish so![70]

Rauch calls this an example of "'Dutchified' or broken English." Known more broadly in nineteenth-century America as *Dutch Dialect,* such constructed speech was the latter-day counterpart of the Denglish produced by eighteenth-century European German speakers who mocked Pennsylvania Dutch as bad German.[71] Although it is true that the English of Pennsylvania Dutch speakers has sometimes been influenced by their first language—that is, there is such a thing as Dutchified English—most of what goes by that name on countless postcards and tea trivets peddled in the Dutch Country today is as exaggerated as the jumping-stallion sentence quoted by Johann David Schöpf in 1788. In any case, literary Dutch Dialect, as a fanciful, wildly distorted form of Dutchified English, has no basis in real German-English bilingualism.

While it was misleading for Rauch to imply that Pennsylvania Dutch speakers actually said things like "I haf in hundred houses been," his employment of Dutch Dialect showed that he was influenced by larger trends in contemporary American popular literature. During the second half of the nineteenth century, "regional" or "local color" literature was in vogue. Many local color authors employed nonstandard language, stereotypically regional or ethnic forms of English ("dialects"), as a literary device. Although the works of writers such as Mark Twain and Willa Cather earned the respect of critics, other "dialect" pieces were more vaudevillian in nature. In rendering Harbaugh's poetry into Dutch Dialect, Rauch was emulating the productions of native English-speaking satirists, notably Charles Follen Adams (1842–1918) and Charles Godfrey Leland (1824–1903).[72]

In the first number of his *Pennsylvania Dutchman* magazine, Rauch reprinted one of Adams's most famous poems, "The Puzzled Dutchman," the first three stanzas of which are given below:

> I'm a proken-hearted Deutscher,
>   Vot's filled mit crief und shame;
> I dells you vot der drouble ish;
>   *I doesn't know my name.*

> You dinks dis fery vunny, eh?
>   Ven you der story hear,
> You will not vonder den so mooch,
>   It vas so shtrange und queer.

Mine modder had dwo leedle twins;
Dey vas me und mine broder:
Ve lookt so fery mooch alike,
No one knew vich vrom toder.[73]

Unfortunately, works such as this were often misidentified as examples of Pennsylvania Dutch (or Pennsylvania German), which fed the persistent misconception that Pennsylvania Dutch is not a German-derived language at all but a form of "broken" English.[74]

Rauch's use of Dutch Dialect material overall was minimal and limited to the occasional humorous item inserted into one of his publications. A more important influence on him was David Ross Locke (1833–1888), a fellow newspaper editor and Radical Republican, who created a literary persona that almost certainly served as a model for Rauch's Pit Schwefflebrenner. Like Pit, Petroleum V(esuvius) Nasby, a resident of "Confederit X Roads, Kentucky," was a rural Democrat in serious need of political and social enlightenment. Nasby's letters, which Locke began writing in 1861, were popular during and after the Civil War; President Lincoln himself was an admirer. In the second iteration of *Father Abraham*, which began in 1868, Rauch often included a Nasby letter on the same page as one of his own Schwefflebrenner pieces and even inserted a Nasby character (named Naspy) into a few of them.

While attending the 1868 Democratic National Convention in New York City, Pit and Petroleum meet up while carousing in a saloon. In a letter dated July 7, 1868, Pit writes:

[W]ie mer on der bar wara is ehner Naspy fun Kenducky derzu kumma un hut mer amohl de hond gevva un mich so ousgefroked wu ich wohn un was my nawma is. Donn hob ich noch amohl gedreat, un der Naspy hut ach close zu mer g'shtickt weil ich an gooter demokrat bin. Er hut mich ach uf a side genumma un gefroked eb ich ehm net finf dahler lehne kennt un, uf course, ich habs ehm gevva. Donn sin mer ivver de shtrose un in an onnerer saloon. . . .

When we were at the bar, this Nasby from Kentucky came up, shook my hand, and asked me where I live and what my name is. Then I bought another round, and Nasby stuck close to me because I'm a good Democrat. He

took me to one side and asked if I could lend him five dollars, and, of course,
I gave it to him. Then we went across the street into another saloon. . . .[75]

Distracted by the pretty girls waiting on their party, Pit loses his wallet to a pickpocket. When he asks Mr. Nasby for his five dollars back, the latter says he cannot make change. Eventually, Pit loses his watch also and is not allowed into the convention hall. By that time, his feckless Democratic friends, including Mr. Nasby, are long gone. Coincidentally, one of Locke's Nasby letters, dated July 13, 1868, makes reference to Nasby's own money woes at the same convention:

I didn't stay in Noo York till the Convenshen adjourned, for a most excellent reason, to wit, viz: my money run out. The Milesian female with whom I wuz forst to board required payment in advance, and uv coorse under sich an arrangement there wuz nothing left for me but to succum. The lenth uv my stay redoost itself to a mere matter uv money. I tried the borrowin dodge, and the cheekin dodge, but good Lord! wat cood I do with an entire Convenshen, all uv 'em more or less tryin to live in the same way? I left and come home while I cood, and before it was everlastingly too late.[76]

While the figures of Pit Schwefflebrenner and Petroleum V. Nasby both served as ignorant Democratic foils for their Republican creators, Pit is much more sympathetic than Petroleum. Already by the November 1868 election, Pit has experienced a political epiphany and switched parties. For the rest of his existence in Rauch's newspapers, he is an affable Pennsylvania Dutch everyman. Petroleum, however, remains an odious character in every respect and a permanent foil for Locke. When Pit pens his letters, his speech, which is both linguistically and visually accessible to like-minded Pennsylvania Dutch readers, has a positive value. Petroleum's writing, in contrast, while also vernacular, connotes ignorance, through the use of incorrect and eye dialectal spellings, and pretension, through pompous turns of phrase such as *to wit, viz., Milesian,* and *everlastingly*. While it is safe to say that the readers of Petroleum V. Nasby letters did not share Nasby's politics, Rauch's Pit Schwefflebrenner was a beloved literary figure among the people for whom Rauch had the greatest affection and respect, his fellow Pennsylvania Dutch, Republicans and Democrats alike.

Abraham Reeser Horne and Pennsylvania Dutch in Education

On the last page of the third and final issue of his short-lived *Pennsylvania Dutchman* magazine, published in March 1873, Edward H. Rauch inserted the following: "A writer in the Reading *Eagle* attempts to demolish Prof. Horne for advocating or suggesting the idea of teaching and using the Pennsylvania Dutch language in public schools, and for saying that it is really more practical and useful than pure German. We take it for granted the professor will attend to the fellow. Du 'm sein dicker dumm-cup t'zurecht setza [Set his thick dumb-head back in order]."[77] The professor whom Rauch was defending was Abraham Reeser Horne, a prominent educator and native speaker of Pennsylvania Dutch whose *Pennsylvania German Manual*, published for the first time in 1875, remains a classic work today.

Born in Bucks County, PA, in 1834, Horne was raised in a Mennonite family in which Pennsylvania Dutch was the dominant language. As was the case for most Pennsylvania Dutch children born in this era, Horne's early formal education was deficient. He learned English from a boy who was brought to live with his family and German from reading books that his father owned. At the age of twenty, Horne matriculated at the then–Pennsylvania College in Gettysburg, where he was baptized and confirmed in the Lutheran faith. He graduated in 1858 and two years later was ordained as a minister. Though he accepted calls to serve at various Lutheran congregations in the Dutch Country, most of Horne's professional life was devoted to public education, as a teacher and school superintendent, and as an administrator at the Keystone State Normal School in Kutztown, Berks County (from 1872 to 1877), and at Muhlenberg College in Allentown, Lehigh County (from 1877 to 1882). In 1860 he founded the *National Educator*, in which he wrote extensively on the educational situation of Pennsylvania Dutch–speaking children. Horne edited the journal until his death in Allentown in 1902.[78]

The year of Horne's birth coincided with the passage of the Free School Act in Pennsylvania discussed earlier, which was met with strong opposition from many Pennsylvania Dutch. Henry A. Muhlenberg (1782–1844), a Lutheran minister, politician, and diplomat who lived most of his life in Reading and was a nephew of Frederick A. Muhlenberg, wrote in 1836 that "[t]he Germans of our State are not opposed to education

Abraham Reeser Horne (1834–1902).
Source: Rohrbach Library, Kutztown University.

as such, but only to any system that to them seems to trench on their parental and natural rights."[79] Recall that many Pennsylvania Dutch opposed publicly funded schools for their children on religious grounds, fearing that such a system would undermine their moral and spiritual development. Maintenance of German and Pennsylvania Dutch figured into this equation as well, bound up as language was with the religious identity of nonsectarian and sectarian Pennsylvania Dutch alike. Other Pennsylvania Dutch, however, including educators like Horne, saw the benefits of improved formal education for Pennsylvania Dutch children. In 1876, when he was the principal at the Keystone State Normal School in Kutztown, he served on a committee with fellow Pennsylvania Dutch educators John S. Ermentrout and Samuel A. Baer to select inscriptions for the four sides of a centennial monument that is still standing today.[80] Rather than celebrating one hundred years of American independence, as one might expect, the monument honors the establishment of a free public school system in Pennsylvania. Each of the four inscriptions on the marker is in a different language: English, German, Latin, and Pennsylvania Dutch. The Pennsylvania Dutch text credits three governors of Pennsylvania Dutch extraction, George Wolf (1777–1840), Joseph Ritner (1780–1869), and Francis R. Shunk (1788–1848), for the eventual success of the 1834 school law.

> unser Freu
> schul wesa kumt
> fun da Pennsylfanish
> Deutsche har
> Dar govaner Wolf
> hots geplant
> un gestart un der
> Ritner un der
> Shunk hen's
> ausg'fehrt

Our free school system comes from the Pennsylvania Germans. Governor Wolf planned and started it, and Ritner and Shunk carried it out.[81]

Horne's *Pennsylvania German Manual* was born of what he saw as a crisis situation among Pennsylvania Dutch–speaking children in the nineteenth century caused by the failure of public schools to lead pupils toward proficiency in English, which all educators agreed was an essential foundation for academic success.[82] In an 1873 essay titled "Pennsylvania German," which appeared in Rauch's *Pennsylvania Dutchman,* Horne makes the following observation:

Every teacher in Eastern Pennsylvania is cognizant of the fact that many of our German pupils derive but little benefit from schools, because they are not conversant with the language in which their instruction is imparted. Their reading and other exercises are, to a great extent, mechanical and parrot-like on this account.

How to remedy this evil is a question of vast importance. Every child attending our schools should receive sufficient knowledge of English to be able to hold intelligent conversation and conduct correspondence in this language. Two-thirds of our Pennsylvania German pupils fail to do this at present. This is a great and crying evil, and demands an immediate remedy.[83]

Many of Horne's contemporaries placed the blame for this problem not on an educational system unequipped to meet the needs of Pennsylvania Dutch–speaking children but on the simple fact that children were growing up in families and communities where Pennsylvania Dutch predominated. Horne understood the situation differently. Rather than viewing knowledge of Pennsylvania Dutch as handicap to be overcome, he sought to promote a positive image of the language and the history and culture of its speakers. Horne saw children's native knowledge of Pennsylvania Dutch as an asset that, under the right conditions, could actually facilitate rather than hinder their acquisition of English as well as German. His *Pennsylvania German Manual*, the subtitle of which is *For Pronouncing, Speaking, and Writing English*, was the tool he created to promote this goal.

Even before Horne's *Manual* appeared in 1875, critics such as the "dumm-cup" Rauch referred to had their reservations about Horne's project. At some point between 1872 and 1875, Edward D. Leisenring (1816–1882), a fellow Dutchman from Allentown, who published the German-language *Welt-Bote* newspaper and was one of the supporters mentioned by Benjamin Bausman in the project to produce *Harbaugh's Harfe*, printed an open letter in Pennsylvania Dutch to Horne in the *Welt-Bote*. Though written in a humorous style, like so many other Pennsylvania Dutch "dialect letters" its content was serious:

A LETTER TO THE DISTINGUISHED PROF. HORNE
OF THE KUTZTOWN NORMAL SCHOOL

Distinguished Professor: I have read a lot about you in the *Friedensbote* and other newspapers and have seen that you defend our beautiful Pennsylvania German language to the ninth degree so that it would not be oppressed and destroyed by those English fellows who don't really know English or, my heavens, German either. It truly pleased me that such an educated fellow as yourself is taking our side. I am a Palatine, my grandfather come over from the Palatinate, and since scholars claim that the grandfather returns in his grandchild, that makes me my own grandfather who came over from the Palatinate. Of that I am proud, since he was an intelligent man.

What I actually wanted to say is this. I read in the newspaper that you're considering publishing a book and dictionary about Pennsylvania German. You know what? People here in Pennsylvania and everywhere else who speak the Pennsylvania German language would really like that, and my Nelly Ann jumped up in the air for joy when I read that article to her. . . .

I am, I think, not quite as sharp as Nelly Ann thinks, but if you want to write that book, I'd like to give you some advice, since I myself am a Pennsylvanian and a Palatine to boot, as I already proved to you. Now, the Palatine language and the Pennsylvanian language when cleanly spoken are the same thing, and there is hardly a difference between them. Just read *Fröhlich Palz, Gott erhalts* (Nadler),[84] then go out into the country and pay close attention to how the people talk—what the boys and girls say to each other at singing school, in front of the school house when it's dark; what the farmers say about horses, cattle, pigs, wheat, corn, and hay; all about the kinds of things that women discuss which concern just them—and you will soon learn what Pennsylvania German is. There are many fellows who think that if they write perfectly awful High German and include a whole bunch of English words, that's Pennsylvania German, and such crazy Germans who don't know any better then bestow on these writers great laurels for "this heavenly butchering of the noble German language." I want to warn you about that, Distinguished Professor.

No one has higher respect than I for those songs that Reverend Harbaugh wrote. I know how he felt when we wrote them: fearfully soft, nostalgic. Longing for the innocent years of childhood. And on such occasions something from on high affected him so that one cannot deny the poetry of his songs. But the language, well, I don't want to say anything about that; except, when there's just as much English as Palatine or High German in a text or song, that's not Pennsylvania German.

Now, if you want to go on and write that book, leave out that darned English gibberish that has no place in our language. I hit the roof every time such dumb stuff is printed and sent out into the world that is supposed to be Pennsylvania German but is actually a flat-out lie. We get lambasted when we don't deserve it. And when your book is ready and it reaches my hands and it turns out to be such miserable pile like one that came out again recently in Philadelphia,[85] then watch out, because I'll heckle you so much that you'll look like a tangled mess and people will look at you like you're a ghost.[86]

Leisenring was an active member of the *Verein der Deutschen Presse von Pennsylvanien* mentioned above and of the familiar puristic opinion that there were better and worse forms of Pennsylvania Dutch, depending on how many English-derived words and phrases a writer or speaker used. Horne was also a member of the *Verein* and agreed that English loan vocabulary "did not belong to" Pennsylvania Dutch, hence his preference for the term *Pennsylvania German*.[87] And on the title page of the first edition of his *Manual*, Horne includes an epigram from the German poet Friedrich Gottlieb Klopstock (1724–1803): "Our language: distinct, unadulterated, and unique" (*Unsere Sprache: Gesondert, ungemischt und nur sich selber gleich*). But Horne was not so puristically inclined as to edit English out of the Pennsylvania Dutch poetic selections he included in his *Manual*, as the editors of *Harbaugh's Harfe* had, nor does he avoid loanwords in his own writings in the *Manual*.[88] Horne's benign attitude toward English-derived vocabulary in Pennsylvania Dutch makes sense in light of the primary goal of his *Manual*, which was to enable children to become proficient in English.

The *Manual* appeared in four increasingly expanded editions in 1875, 1896, and 1905.[89] The third and fourth editions were issued posthumously by Horne's son Thomas. The evident popularity of Horne's *Manual* qualifies it as the first best seller in Pennsylvania Dutch language and literature. Each edition consists of three major parts, "English Pronunciation," "Pennsylvania German Literature," and "Pennsylvania German Dictionary." In his second edition Horne expanded the middle section substantially, which reflected the major growth of Pennsylvania Dutch literature in the twenty years after the appearance of the first edition. He left the first and third sections of the 1875 and 1896 editions largely intact, though he did double the length of the third by making the dictionary bidirectional, that is, both Pennsylvania Dutch–English and English–Pennsylvania Dutch.

Horne's ideas on various matters related to the place of Pennsylvania Dutch in schools, as well as his attitude toward the language generally, are reflected in his 1873 essay in Rauch's *Pennsylvania Dutchman*. Horne takes pains to emphasize the relatedness of Pennsylvania Dutch to German (hence his use of *Pennsylvania German* and not *Pennsylvania Dutch*). He argues that "German is cosmopolitan, nowhere a stranger, at home in every place, his fatherland everywhere," including in the United States, where, of all places, "as is well known, English was adopted as the language of the country, by a single vote, the decision of the speaker."[90] Horne declares Pennsylvania to be a "German state," claiming that one-half its population is of German background and estimating that at least a million residents of the state speak German. Though in much of the article Horne conflates Pennsylvania Dutch and (High) German, at points he does distinguish the two, even comparing the former positively to the latter:

> The Pennsylvania Germans speak a language, just as really as the high German or the English, though it is sometimes called Dutch and "Kauder Welsh," by the ignorant and prejudiced. Martin Luther chose the Misnian dialect, spoken in Saxony, the softest of all, for the translation of the Bible, and it has since become the basis of the modern literary high German.
>
> It does not follow, however, from this circumstance, that the Pennsylvania German is not a language. Without the admixture of English words, which do not belong to it, it can be used as purely, and in many cases, with more force and expression than the high German.[91]

In his 1873 essay Horne sought to elevate the status of Pennsylvania Dutch by alternately linking it to and distinguishing it from German. In schools, Horne saw knowledge of Pennsylvania Dutch as an advantage in learning German:

> That the Pennsylvania German is a great help to those who desire to study the high German is known to every one, who is familiar with the two forms of the language. Those who understand and pronounce Penn-

sylvania German find no difficulty in studying and understanding the high German. The Pennsylvania Germans make but few mistakes in terminations, and with the exception of two or three words, always give the correct gender. Here the English student finds his greatest difficulty, when commencing German. Pennsylvania Germans rarely make a mistake in applying the articles. It may be said, with truth, the Pennsylvania Germans do not make as many actual grammatical mistakes in their conversation, as the mass of Americans in talking English. We would by no means, therefore, disparage the Pennsylvania German, but employ it as the handmaiden, in acquiring the high German.

And, wherever the desire is felt for it, we would see the pure German introduced, and its rights accorded to it, by the side of the English. The two languages should complement each other, in this country, as do our right and left arms.[92]

For the acquisition of English, Horne advocates that Pennsylvania Dutch could likewise play the role of linguistic-pedagogical handmaiden. Rather than ignoring the language, teachers of Pennsylvania Dutch–speaking students should, Horne argues, take their knowledge of their native language as a starting point from which acquisition of English might proceed: "We wish to add yet [t]hat the German pupil must be made acquainted first with his own language, and be taught by a skillful teacher, who himself understands the subject, to note the differences between his own language and the English. In attempting, therefore, to teach our German children English, the knowledge they may have of their own tongue, be it small or great, constitutes the foundation on which the teacher must build."[93]

In his ideas on how to address linguistic diversity in schools, Horne prefigured much of the discussion in the field of bilingual (and bidialectal) education that took place in the twentieth century.[94] Horne was strongly influenced by European educational reformers, especially the Swiss Johann Heinrich Pestalozzi (1746–1826), who held a fundamentally positive view of children not as empty vessels to be filled by stern schoolmasters but as naturally endowed with cognitive gifts that could foster inductive learning under the right circumstances. Writing in an article published in 1884 titled "The 'How' and 'Why' of Teaching," Horne notes that a "child's mind is very inquisitive, and it is the teacher's business to encourage that faculty. Let children enquire for reasons, and far as it can be done with profit, let teachers give reasons to the children. One of the principles of Pestalozzi, 'The child should never be told anything he can find out for himself,' should be constantly in the mind of the teacher. By encouragement, reasons may be frequently ascertained by the children themselves."[95]

The main task of teachers, according to Horne, is to facilitate the development of the intellectual gifts with which children are innately endowed, though ideally not through explicit instruction. With regard to language and literacy, for example, Horne is skeptical of the value of teaching rules of grammar ("technical grammar"): "The best writers, Shakespeare, Milton, Addison, etc., used better language hundreds of years before there was an English grammar, than do we, who have studied it all our lives. We should read and study the works of the best authors. Grammar is evolved from language, and not language from grammar."[96] In line with this thinking, Horne left out any direct treatment of English grammar from his *Manual*, which may have seemed curious to some of Horne's contemporaries, since the goal of the book was to promote facility in English among Pennsylvania Dutch–speaking children. In his first edition, he did include a brief section titled "Pennsylvania German Grammar" as part of the dictionary, which consisted mainly of tables for the parts of speech in Pennsylvania Dutch modeled on those found in German grammars.[97] This section, which Horne omitted in his second edition,[98] was, like the dictionary, intended to serve only as a reference and not as a didactic tool. Additionally, its inclusion would have demonstrated to skeptics that, despite its oral vernacular character, Pennsylvania Dutch was structured according to the same grammatical categories as written and spoken German.

The only section of the *Manual* to employ an explicitly instructive methodology was the first one, "English Pronunciation." This section in the first edition was reprinted verbatim in the three later ones, with one exception. In the 1875 edition, Horne included a paragraph to the effect that teachers who themselves are native Pennsylvania Dutch speakers would be better able to help their pupils learn to pronounce English than English monolinguals: "No teacher can detect and remedy the errors in pronunciation as well, as the one who has himself mastered these defects, and who is able to combine his experience with theories. Printed rules are of but little value in comparison with personal experience. Besides, what may seem the greatest difficulties, to those familiar with a language from youth, are often less trouble to a learner than many others, which, a teacher, who has learned to remedy in himself, can most successfully correct in his pupils."[99] This paragraph was omitted from the later editions of the *Manual*, likely because of Horne's shifting views on the practicality of employing Pennsylvania Dutch in public schools.

It made sense for Horne to begin his *Manual* with a section of practical exercises aimed at improving children's pronunciation of English since speakers are typically judged more quickly on the basis of their accent than on other areas of language, such as grammar or word choice. The need for this kind of intervention was underscored by the pervasive stigmatization in Horne's day of Dutchified English. Horne's section on practical phonetics consists of twelve lessons targeting the most important points of difference between Pennsylvania Dutch and English pronunciation mentioned in chapter 1 that were the basis of a "Dutchy" accent in English.[100] Three of the lessons target vowels, eight focus on consonants, and the final lesson points out errors in the placement of stress and other features of polysyllabic words. The consonantal errors described include the substitution of <ch>, <s>, and <v> for <j>, <th>, and <w> such that *jump* would be pronounced like *chump*, *thing* like *sing*, and *wine* like *vine*. Horne also identifies errors due to hypercorrection, that is, overcompensating for phonetic differences between Pennsylvania Dutch in English, leading some speakers to say *jump* instead of *chump*, *thing* instead of *sing*, and *wine* instead of *vine*. Horne also notes the tendency for Pennsylvania Dutch speakers to pronounce words such as *zip* and *resign* like *sip* and *re-sign* (with an <s> sound), which is due to the absence in Pennsylvania Dutch of a <z> sound.

Horne mentions three other errors of pronunciation made by Pennsylvania Dutch children acquiring English that were not due to any apparent interference from their native language. These touch on interesting patterns of variation in the English spoken in southeastern Pennsylvania in the nineteenth century. The first has to do with words beginning with <wh>. In earlier forms of British and American English (and still today in many modern regional varieties), words such as *which* and *witch*, *where* and *ware*, were pronounced differently from one another. That is, some speakers pronounced the first words in these pairs as "hwich" and "hwere", while in the speech of others, the [hw] was lost and words such as *which/witch* and *where/ware* became homonyms, a historical process in the history of English known as the *wine–whine merger*. In contemporary Pennsylvania, this merger is the norm for most speakers; however, data from dialectological fieldwork conducted in the 1930s and 1940s in southeastern Pennsylvania show that [hw], though infrequent, was not yet completely lost and could well have been more widespread in Horne's lifetime.[101] In any case, Horne follows elevated norms and prescribes that words beginning with <wh> be pronounced as [hw].

The two other examples of pronunciation errors treated in Horne's *Manual* that were not due to interference from Pennsylvania Dutch deal with vowels. Horne prescribed the following:

1. The <e> in English words like *men*, *egg*, and *beg* should be a short "eh" [ɛ] and not a long <ey> [e:]; Pennsylvania Dutch speakers tended to pronounce these words like *main*, *aig*, and *baig*.
2. Words such as *due* and *dew* should not be pronounced with an <oo> [u:] vowel but with a <yoo> [ju:] sound, such that these words should sound more like *Jew* than *do*.

As was the case with the wine–whine merger, data from the early twentieth century show that southeastern Pennsylvania was subject to patterns of variation in pronunciation. On the one hand, Pennsylvania Dutch speakers preserved an archaic English dialectal feature, namely a long [e:] in words such as *men* and *egg*.[102] On the other hand, with words such as *do* [du:] and *due* [dju:], the tendency among Pennsylvania Dutch to pronounce them the same, as [du:], was actually a progressive trend; the merged pronunciation has since come to be the norm in southeastern Pennsylvania.[103]

The first section of Horne's *Manual* on pronunciation is the only overtly prescriptive material in the book. The second, more extensive section, "Pennsylvania German Literature," adopts a more Pestalozzian, inductive approach to promote literacy among Pennsylvania Dutch–speaking children. Quoting again from Horne's 1884 article, "The 'How' and 'Why' of Teaching":

The great father of object teaching is Pestalozzi. It is infinitely better to see an object than to hear about it. Impress into your service all objects and subjects at your command for illustration. Children learn by observation and examination, and should be given every opportunity to thus acquire knowledge. . . . In reading, everything possible should be illustrated by objects and pictures. The lesson should be thoroughly studied; to accomplish this result, the pupils should be interested in the work. Assign a lesson no longer than can be easily learned, and give special topics to each pupil. Make constant use of the dictionary, and pay special attention to the derivation of words.[104]

In the first edition of his *Manual*, Horne includes three pages of "object lesson exercises" consisting of pictures of everyday objects and their equivalents in Pennsylvania Dutch (using phonetic orthography), English, and German. In his second edition that section was increased to seventy-one pages and includes more complicated images that exemplify not only individual words but also phrases and short sentences. A sample page from this section is given below.

After teaching his students to read basic words and phrases that refer to familiar and interesting objects, Horne prepares them to tackle actual texts by providing them with sections of *Shprich-Werder* (proverbs), *Ratslă* (riddles), *Reimă* (rhymes), and *Shpichtă* (anecdotes) in only Pennsylvania Dutch in the first edition and with English translations added in the later ones. Selecting such short texts made good pedagogical sense, since the material would have been very familiar to Horne's pupils, deeply embedded as it was in Pennsylvania Dutch vernacular culture. Rather than starting right away with literary texts originally composed in English, Horne gradually leads his charges toward literacy by beginning with short texts on familiar subject matter in their native language. Examples from the four sections are given below:

Shprich-Werder (Proverbs)

13. Wŏs m'r nĕt was, mŏcht ĕm nĕt 'has. *What we know not burns us not.*

14. Wo shmok is, is feiăr. *Where there is smoke there is fire.*

73. Kla un schmărt is aw wŏs wărt. *Little and smart is of worth too.*[105]

Ratslă (Riddles)

Fŏr wŏs shbringt d'r fuks 'm bărg nuf?—Fŏr 'm shwŏns.
*Why [lit. 'for/before what'] does the fox run up the mountain?—
Before his tail.*[106]

PENNSYLVANIA GERMAN LITERATURE   43

Bŏberna bŭblĕn shneidă.
Cutting out paper dolls.
Papierne Puppen auschneiden.

Fawnă rasă.
Flag raising.
Fahne aufrichten.

Grŭttă hupsă.
Leap frog
Springfrosch.

Bănd shbelă.
Play band.
Musik spielen.

Page from *Horne's Pennsylvania German Manual*, 2nd ed., 1896, 43.

Reimă (Rhymes)

De ladi fŏn ďr rutsh,	*The dudish lady,*
Wŏn se fawră wil, hŭt se kĕn kŭtsh,	*When she wants to drive, has no carriage,*
Wŏn se reidă wil, hŭt se kĕn goul,	*When she wants to ride, she has no horse,*
Un wŏn se lawfă mus, is se zu foul.	*And if she must walk, she is too lazy.*[107]

Shpichtă (Anecdotes)

"De Nawmă, Hărmŏn un Yawkŭb"

'S is mol 'n kărl dŏrch 'n shwŏm g'lŭfă. D'nort is 'r im ă sumbichă blŏts nun'r g'sunkă bis ŏn d'r hŏls. We ăr drin g'shtŭkă hŭt, dŏs yusht nŭch d'r kŭp rous găgukt hŭt, is 'n ŏnĕrăr de shtros he gl'ŭfă. Sĕlĕm hŭt 'r no zugăroofă un hŭt gegrishă hăr, mŏn, hăr, mŏn! D'r ŏnăr hŭt yusht d'r kŭp g'sană, un hŭt g'mant's wăr niks we 'n kŭp un hŭt z'rik g'roofă, yaw, kŭp, yaw, kŭp! Uf dĕn wak sin de nawmă, Hărmŏn un Yawkŭb in d'r gong kumă.

"The Names, Harmon and Jacob"

Once upon a time a man was walking through a swamp, and getting into a marshy place, sunk down up to his neck. As he stuck in there with only his head out, another came along the road, and he called out to him: Hear, man; hear, man [hăr, mŏn; hăr, mŏn]. The other only saw the head, and thinking it was nothing but a head said: Yes, head; yes, head [yaw, kŭp; yaw, kŭp]. In this way came the names Harmon and Jacob [being the English for Hărmŏn and Yawkŭb].[108]

The linguistic and cultural familiarity of these short texts to emerging Pennsylvania Dutch readers was considerable. Horne was not guided by puristic or elitist notions with regard to content or language; he neither favored material that was of European German origin nor did he avoid anglicisms. In terms of content, the three selected proverbs, for example, are representative of the entire section. The first is derived from the German equivalent of 'What you know won't hurt you' (*Was man nicht weiß, macht einen nicht heiß*); the second is a loan translation of the English *Where there's smoke, there's fire* and includes the loanword *Schmook*; and the third, in which the borrowed and native words, *schmaert*, 'smart', and *wert*, 'worth', respectively, rhyme, is a Pennsylvania Dutch innovation. The rhyme about the "dudish lady" is entirely in line with classic Pennsylvania Dutch values, poking fun as it does at a pretentious, citified person. On the linguistic level, many of Horne's short texts display a high level of creativity beyond just rhyming, as do the riddle about the fox and the imaginative anecdote about the origin of the names *Harmon* and *Jacob*. The riddle makes clever use of the homophonous words *fer*, 'for', and *fer*, 'before, in front of', while readers of the Harmon and Jacob story can appreciate the punning humor in names that sound the same as entirely unrelated statements: the name *Harmon* was pronounced in the regional English of Pennsylvania like 'Hairmon', which rhymed with the Pennsylvania Dutch expression *heer, Mann,* 'listen, man'; and the native given name *Yaakob* rhymes with *ya, Kopp,* 'yes, head'.[109]

In the remaining sections of the second part of his *Manual,* Horne moves on to lengthier texts in Pennsylvania Dutch, both prose and poetry (again, with English translations added in the second, third, and fourth editions). As with the shorter texts, their focus is on content rooted in Pennsylvania Dutch culture. Many deal with historical topics, especially in the second and later editions, when Horne included an entire section titled "The Customs of the Pennsylvania Germans in the Olden Times" (*De G'Breichă fŭn D'Pĕnsilfawnish Deitshă in Ŏltă Zeită*) that discusses how holidays such as Christmas, New Year, and Easter were celebrated, along with "harvest home" (*Aerntkarich*), a fall thanksgiving church service of British origin; and "frolics" (*Fralicke*), gatherings combining socializing with collective work such as making apple butter, mowing hay in the middle of the night, quilting, corn husking, and helping families move in spring.[110] Battalion Day (*Bedallye*), an annual public holiday involving local militias, is also treated, as are "old games," including corner ball (*Eckballe,* still popular among Pennsylvania Amish youth), as well as more obscure games such as blue bird, plumsack, and figmill.[111] Wrapping up the second part are a number of Pennsylvania Dutch songs and poems, including works by Henry Harbaugh and Edward H. Rauch, as well as profiles of famous historical figures of Pennsylvania Dutch extraction.

In light of the evident popularity of Horne's *Pennsylvania German Manual,* appearing as it did in four editions, it is curious that the book found little resonance among its originally intended audience, educators. David S. Keck, for example, who was the superintendent of schools in Berks County from 1881 to 1890, in a letter from 1911, recalled of the *Manual,* "I only occasionally found a copy on a teacher's desk, the teacher sometimes consulted it to get the English names of common objects."[112] In his study of the education of Pennsylvania Dutch children, Clyde S. Stine notes, "[I]t is apparent that Horne's influence on his contemporaries was insignificant."[113] Who, then, did Horne's *Manual* appeal to? Almost certainly adult Pennsylvania Dutch speakers who were either loyal to or nostalgic about their mother tongue. At the turn of the twentieth century, when the second, third, and fourth editions of the *Manual* appeared, it would have been clear to most Pennsylvania Dutch (nonsectarians, at least) that the language of their heritage was endangered, and along with it the record of "olden times" that figures so prominently in the book's content. Rather tellingly, Horne himself, toward the end of his life, actually came to advocate prohibiting the use of Pennsylvania Dutch in schools. In an editorial from 1894 he exhorts his fellow educators to "[t]alk English and make everyone around you talk, regardless of blunders. Teachers place a sign over the entrance of their school grounds, even as our old friend Prof. O. S. Fell, did, at the Macungie Institute, thirty-five years ago: 'No German allowed to be spoken on these grounds.'"[114]

Just one published review has been found of Horne's *Manual* after the first edition appeared, a front-page letter to the *Reading Daily Eagle* on January 8, 1876, which was given the title "A Blast against Kutztown's Author." The correspondent is identified only by the initials "C.H.S."[115] He takes Horne to task for a number of supposed deficiencies in the *Manual*, including the absence of a section on English and German grammar, "something from which the student might infer that those languages have a grammar with fixed and unalterable rules of construction, that the vocabulary of each is a structure as perfect in its entirety as the human form, and, like it, as divisible into parts which have their separate functions to perform." C.H.S. goes on to slam Horne for producing a book that was probably intended to teach English speakers Pennsylvania Dutch, rather than the other way around:

> Mr. Horne's book is nothing more nor less than a futile effort to construct a language out of the Pennsylvania German, in other words to dignify into a language what is admitted by all to be but a mongrel dialect composed of several ancient patois which have sunk out of sight in Germany, and a mixture of English and German words with corrupted pronunciation. The effort will signally fail, as of course, it should, and the book will drift into the obscurity it deserves, and share the fate of all abortions and monstrosities. . . .
>
> For the good name of our own Pennsylvania German people whose desire for knowledge and literary culture is evidenced by the many institutions of higher learning scattered through Eastern Pennsylvania, not

least among which is the Keystone Normal School, we hope that Prof.
Horne's future efforts may be directed to a nobler method of teaching
"pure English and high German."[116]

It is not known whether anyone rose to Horne's defense in the pages
of the *Reading Daily Eagle*, but there was a reaction to C.H.S.'s letter a
few weeks later in the *Eagle's* German older sibling, the *Adler*. It was included in a column by one of the *Adler's* main Pennsylvania Dutch correspondents, Frank R. Brunner (1835–1908), a physician by profession
and Pennsylvania Dutch writer by avocation, who wrote under the name
of John Schumacher.[117] Writing in Pennsylvania Dutch about Horne's at-
tacker, Brunner remarks:

> I think he wanted to shave a horn and make deer horn schnapps from it,
> but he didn't succeed. He says the book has no nouns or verbs, no sub-
> stantives and predicates. What do I care about that? C.H.S. can go ahead
> and call his boys and girls Nouns and Verbs and Logical Subjects and
> Logical Predicates, that way he'll have those names in his family every
> day and they won't need to be in Horne's Pennsylvania German book.
> What good is a noun or a verb or a substantive to me for making shoes
> or boots? . . .
>
> Horne's book is good enough for me, for I cannot improve upon it,
> so it has to be good enough for me. But I am pleased that he did some-
> thing for the Pennsylvania German language, because that language is
> my mother tongue. When I used to cry in Pennsylvania German, my
> mother would sing this Pennsylvania German song to me "Sleep, baby,
> sleep . . ." Whenever I would cry for something to eat, she sang "Hush-
> abye, baby, . . ." I learned this by heart long before I could talk, and when-
> ever someone says something about the Pennsylvania German language
> nowadays, I get upset. But whenever you come into a city or one-horse
> town nowadays and talk Dutch, then the clueless city folks stand around
> and say, "Oh, the country Dutch." Tell that C.H.S. that he should now pay
> attention to whose brain [*Hern*] or what kind of horn [*Horn*] he starts to
> shave, or he could get into trouble. Tell him that he should go to a tannery
> and ask for an ox or cow horn and make sure that there's no live bone
> in it anymore and definitely not go to the Keystone Normal School in
> Kutztown, since that horn [*Horne*] is not safe for anyone to handle, and
> whoever doesn't know that could burn himself something bad.[118]

Brunner reacts by displaying the kind of native cunning (and clever word play, taking advantage of the homophony of Horne's name with the Pennsylvania Dutch words for 'horn' and 'brain') that traditional Pennsylvania Dutch prided themselves on, rather than bothering to debate intellectually the merits of C.H.S.'s views. Brunner, by writing in Pennsylvania Dutch, was addressing an audience who needed no proof of the value of their mother tongue.

Although Horne's *Manual* never lived up to its original intent as a "guide book for schools and families" to improve the educational situation of Pennsylvania Dutch–speaking children, in part because of its poor reception among educators and critics such as C.H.S., it did become exceptionally valuable as a documentary tribute to the language and culture of thousands of adult Pennsylvanians at the end of the nineteenth century, many of whose descendants were moving rapidly toward English monolingualism. The popular demand for the *Manual* even years after Horne's death is a testament to how meaningful it was to those Pennsylvanians, Horne's people.

WHEREAS THE NINETEENTH CENTURY BEGAN with Pennsylvania Dutch in a robust state of health across all generations, by the turn of the twentieth century fewer and fewer children—in nonsectarian families—were acquiring the language. Among the sect people, mainly Amish and conservative Mennonites, the situation was quite different, yet their numbers in 1900 were still quite modest compared to the much more numerous church people of Lutheran and Reformed background, who produced nearly the entire body of Pennsylvania Dutch literature. This includes hundreds of pieces of original poetry, prose, and even drama. With the exception of the texts in Rauch's *Hand-Book* and Horne's *Manual*, nearly all of these writings appeared exclusively in Pennsylvania Dutch, produced by Pennsylvania Dutch men and women for their fellow speakers alone. As essentially private conversations in literary form, these documents offer an invaluable insight into the history, traditions, values, and everyday life of a unique American cultural group. At the same time, the people engaging in these conversations were profoundly influenced by the larger culture they had chosen to join. Henry Harbaugh, the quintessential Dutchman, saw a connection between what he was doing in his poetry and the productions of European Romantics such as Hebel and Burns. Edward H. Rauch found in his beloved Dutch a perfect vehicle for the expression of his passionately held views about the world around him, much in the style of his contemporary Mark Twain. And Abraham R. Horne, progressive educator that he was, recognized in his work the fundamental validity of a language and culture deeply embedded in the American experience.

To be sure, the dozens of Pennsylvania Dutch writers whose works first began appearing in German-language local newspapers were best known among their fellow Dutch. Yet the upsurge in literary output of Pennsylvania Dutch writers in the second half of the nineteenth century fueled an increasing curiosity about them among Americans more widely. It is this growing popular attention directed toward the Pennsylvania Dutch and their language, as well as the Pennsylvania Dutch reaction to that attention, that is the focus of the following chapter.[119]

CHAPTER 5

Pennsylvania Dutch in the Public Eye

The tourist will encounter three types of Dutch in the
Pennsylvania Dutch Country: 1) Pennsylvania Dutch, the dialect
brought to Pennsylvania from the Palatinate between 1683 and
the time of the Revolutionary War; 2) Pennsylvania Dutch–English,
the English with a heavy accent, spoken by those Pennsylvanians
whose everyday language is still the Pennsylvania Dutch dialect;
and 3) Tourist Dutch, a much distorted Pennsylvania Dutch–English
which was invented in the past ten to fifteen years to make
"Amish Stuff" more palatable to the tourist-buying public.
—ALFRED L. SHOEMAKER, 1955

America Discovers Pennsylvania's "Curious Tongue" in the Popular Press

During the first half of the nineteenth century, Pennsylvania Dutch–speaking farmers and craftspeople prospered in relative isolation from the larger English-monolingual society. Their heritage language enjoyed widespread use among young and old in rural communities across Pennsylvania and beyond, including south of the Mason-Dixon Line in Maryland, Virginia, and West Virginia, as far north as Ontario, and in several midwestern states, especially Ohio. Pennsylvania Dutch was the dominant oral language in dozens of rural communities whose residents also had sufficient knowledge of German to be able to read and understand the Bible and hymn and prayer books, as well as farmer's almanacs and local newspapers. Limited school attendance among rural Pennsylvania Dutch children reinforced their distance from the English language. Their cultural and linguistic insularity was, of course, not absolute; they lived in close proximity to English speakers of diverse ethnic backgrounds with whom they interacted socially, transacted business, and, on occasion, married. Americans from outside of heavily Pennsylvania Dutch areas, however, were relatively unaware of their existence. Aside from the observations of a handful of outsiders, especially European-born Germans who, like Franz von Löher and Ludwig Wollenweber, were curious about their distant "countrymen" in America, there are few written descriptions, in German or English, of the language and social habits of Pennsylvania Dutch prior to the Civil War.

An interesting exception to the relative silence about the Pennsylvania Dutch and their language in early nineteenth-century media is a brief item that appeared in multiple English-language newspapers in 1840. It recounts an incident that occurred when the first American ambassador to what was then the Austrian Empire, Henry A. P. Muhlenberg (1782–1844), a nephew of Frederick Muhlenberg, presented his credentials to Emperor Ferdinand I (1793–1875) upon arriving in Vienna on November 7, 1838.

HON. HENRY MUHLENBURGH.—At the first interview [he] had with his majesty of Austria, as minister plenipotentiary, etc. of the United States, he was determined to show Ferdinand what stuff a Yankee was made of, and let him see, as the lamented Sam Patch said, "that some things can be done as well as others." After the ceremonial of the presentation was over, Muhlenburgh took his hands out of his breeches pockets, and made a long harangue to his Austrian majesty in praise of American institutions, etc., in *Pennsylvania Dutch*. Ferdinand was thunderstruck. Turning to Metternich, he quietly observed, in German, that he was not acquainted with the *American Language*, and begged to be favored with a translation of the Yankee minister's speech!

The above anecdote was related to us by the late Colonel White, of Florida, who was abroad at the time the occurrence took place. The Colonel stated that the affair caused much mirth among the *corps diplomatique*.[1]

Despite the fact that Henry Muhlenberg was a member of the most prominent German Pennsylvanian (as opposed to Pennsylvania Dutch) family, his biography suggests that he knew both German and Pennsylvania Dutch. Born in Lancaster in 1782, he was the pastor at Trinity Lutheran Church in Reading for more than a quarter century (1803–1829) before entering politics, and then not as a National Republican (the party of John Quincy Adams) but as a Jacksonian Democrat, like the vast majority of Berks County Dutch. In a memorial essay published one year after his death in 1844, his anonymous biographer notes that "German had been for so many years the language of his profession, and of his social intercourse, that he felt an embarrassment in the use of formal English, of which he could never entirely divest himself, though nothing in his diction or accent implied his German origin and education."[2] Given the marginal status of German as a language of "social intercourse" in early nineteenth-century Berks County, Muhlenberg's biographer must have been referring to his facility in Pennsylvania Dutch.

Henry Muhlenberg's display of Yankee moxie at an imperial court in Old Europe by using a quintessentially American language was repeated by another American ambassador some four decades later, in 1875, this time in the presence of Ferdinand I's nephew and successor, Franz Joseph I (1830–1916):

The Emperor of Austria speaks all the languages of his people (say thirteen), and yet does not understand Pennsylvania Dutch, the tongue employed by Minister ORTH. The following anecdote is good:
"A well known American, who was in Vienna, was presented to the Emperor, and the Emperor spoke in very complimentary terms of Mr. ORTH, and then asked: 'What was the dialect in which Mr. ORTH delivered his address? I know, of course, that it was not English, and I thought I detected some faint traces of the Teutonic tongue in some of the words.'"[3]

The ambassador in question was Godlove S. Orth (1817–1882), a native Dutchman from Lebanon County, who moved to Indiana as a young man and was, like Henry Muhlenberg, also a US congressman. The great-grandson of Palatine immigrants to Lebanon who came around 1730, Orth's encounter with Franz Joseph was one he enjoyed retelling and became a part of his official biography. In the spring of 1908, more than twenty-five years after Orth's death, the story was circulated in the German American press under the title "Sei deitsch Sprach" ('His German language', PD *Sei deitsch Schprooch*). At that time, President Theodore Roosevelt and Secretary of State Elihu Root were considering whom to appoint as US ambassador to Vienna. The article recommends finding someone like Godlove Orth, then goes on to "quote" from Orth's address to the Austrian emperor in 1875.

Mischter Emperor! Es freit mich exceedingly, von unserem honrable Präsident appoindet geworden zur sein, die glorreiche United Stätes bei Eure Court zu represente, und es gibt mer immenses Vergniege, Euch so g'sund und in ener first rate Condische begriße zu könne. Die Rie-läschens zwische dene beide Cuntries sind die beschte, und of cource werde sie aach so riemäne, jedenfalls werd nichts von meiner Seit' häppene, sie zu disturbe. Mischter Emperor! Ich hab' die Honor, Euch mei' Credentials zu hände!

Mister Emperor! I am exceedingly pleased to have been appointed by our honorable President to represent the glorious United States at your court, and it gives me immense pleasure to be able to greet you so healthy and in such a first-rate condition. The relations between these two countries are the best, and of course they will remain so, in any case nothing will happen from my side to disturb them. Mister Emperor! I have the honor of handing you my credentials![4]

The language of this address is closer to the Denglish used by European Germans, such as Johann David Schöpf, to stereotype Pennsylvania Dutch than to actual Pennsylvania Dutch. Yet the intent of the Orth story was not to mock him as an uncouth hick but to portray him as the model of an unpretentious American.

Another retelling of the meeting between Godlove Orth and the Austrian emperor, also in 1908, sought to emphasize the kinship between Pennsylvania Dutch and European Germans, rather than the distance between the two groups, as was the case with the Muhlenberg-Ferdinand meeting:

That [Orth] may be claimed in the great family of Pennsylvania-Germans is shown by the fact that when in his public life as Minister to

Vienna, he, upon his first presentation to the Emperor, was able to carry on conversation in German. According to Egle, "After a short conversation the Emperor asked: 'Tell me in what part of Germany were you born?' Mr. Orth replied, 'Not in Germany, but in Pennsylvania, in the United States.' 'But,' said the Emperor, 'you speak the pleasing accent of the Rhine.'" What was experienced by Mr. Orth has been the repeated experience of many others, Pennsylvanians by birth, in the home of their German fatherland.[5]

This account appeared in the *Pennsylvania-German* magazine, then edited by Howard W. Kriebel. Although this periodical was founded in 1900 by the Rev. Philip C. Croll, it came to follow under Croll's successors an avowedly Germanophile editorial line, and contained many important articles on Pennsylvania Dutch history and culture, as well as literary works in the language. It suffered from its sympathies with Imperial Germany on the eve of World War I and ceased publication in 1914.[6] Kriebel repeated the Orth story from an earlier source, whose author put a similar spin on it, concluding, "This shows that the so-called Pennsylvania German is a dialect of the great German language of Europe, from whence it was brought, and where, to this day, it is living in all its freshness and vigor as it did centuries ago."[7]

In the popular press of the nineteenth and twentieth centuries, depictions of the Pennsylvania Dutch language were rarely neutral. Some writers, such as the authors of the Muhlenberg and Orth anecdotes, sought to promote a positive image of the language by associating it with people of high status such as the politician-diplomats Henry Muhlenberg and Godlove Orth and by linking it in an affirmative way to either mainstream American or European German culture; the choice whether to refer to it as *Pennsylvania Dutch* or *Pennsylvania German* was often indicative of where a journalist's sympathies lay in this regard. However, Pennsylvania Dutch also always had its detractors, those who compared the language negatively to German or English (or both) and depicted its users as the opposite of the likes of Muhlenberg and Orth, as ignorant country bumpkins.

The following excerpt from an article titled "Local Prohibition in Pennsylvania," which appeared in the *Christian Union* on May 21, 1873, is an apt example. Edited by the famous clergyman, abolitionist, and social reformer Henry Ward Beecher, the newspaper published articles on a number of socially progressive causes, including temperance.

The twenty-three counties [of Pennsylvania] that have voted "for license" are largely populated by what are known as "Pennsylvania Dutch;" speaking a mongrel dialect—a hotch-potch of English and German. These people are very strongly conservative. They voted many years against common day-schools, which were left to the "local option" of counties. It is only about ten years since Northumberland county carried the establishment of common schools. Some farming districts in the state have made no provision yet for common schools. But, while opposed to day schools, they are in favor of liquor saloon night-schools; and have accordingly voted "for license."[8]

While the Pennsylvania Dutch language is not the focus of this article, it is invoked to denigrate its users, most of whom (nonsectarians, at least) happened to be decidedly antitemperance. Such negative side references to the language abounded in popular media in the nineteenth century and continue to the present.

An important watershed in the popular depiction of Pennsylvania Dutch culture, including its language, came in October 1869, the same year in which the first two books containing Pennsylvania Dutch writings were published (Ludwig Wollenweber's *Gemälde/Sketches* and Rachel Bahn's *Poems*). In that month, an article appeared in the *Atlantic Monthly* with the simple title "Pennsylvania Dutch." The author was Phebe Earle Gibbons (1821–1893). Born to a prominent Quaker family in Philadelphia, Gibbons lived most of her life with her husband Joseph (1818–1883) and their five children on a farm near Bird-in-Hand, located in the heart of a heavily Mennonite and Amish community in Lancaster County. Gibbons was an astute student of human culture and, though lacking in extensive formal education, became a prolific writer, including for the Quaker periodical edited by her husband, the *Journal: A Paper Devoted to the Interests of the Society of Friends*. Gibbons traveled extensively, including to Europe, always writing about what she observed, but her most memorable piece of journalism was her 1869 article, which she then expanded for publication in a collection of essays on various cultural groups in Pennsylvania. Her book, *Pennsylvania*

Dutch and Other Essays, garnered national attention and appeared in three editions, in 1872, 1874, and 1882. In many ways, Gibbons's lead essay put the Pennsylvania Dutch and their language on America's popular cultural map.[9]

A gifted writer in English, Gibbons also had excellent knowledge of German, which enabled her to understand Pennsylvania Dutch at least to some degree. The languages of the various groups of people who were her subjects figured prominently in many of her writings, and in fact the first section of her article on the Pennsylvania Dutch is titled "Language" and is reproduced in its entirety below. More accurate renderings of the Pennsylvania Dutch words and expressions she cites are given in square brackets; the comments in parentheses are from Gibbons.

The tongue which these people speak is a dialect of the German, but they generally call it and themselves "Dutch."

For the native German who works with them on the farm they entertain some contempt, and the title "Yankee" is with them a synonym for cheat. As must always be the case where the great majority do not read the tongue which they speak, and live in contact with those who speak another, the language has become mixed and corrupt. Seeing a young neighbor cleaning a buggy, I tried to talk with him by speaking German. "Willst du reiten?" said I (not remembering that *reiten* is to ride on horseback). "Willst du reiten?" All my efforts were vain.

As I was going for cider to the house of a neighboring farmer, I asked his daughter what she would say, under the circumstances, for "Are you going to ride?" "Widdu fawray?" [*Witt du faahre?*] "Buggy fawray?" [*Boggi faahre?*] was the answer (Willst du fahren?) Such expressions are heard as "Koock amul to," [*Guck emol do*] for "Guck einmal da," or "Just look at that!" and "Haltybissel" [*Halt ebissel*] for "Halt ein biszchen," or "Wait a little bit." "Gutenobit" [*Guder Owed*] is used for "Guten Abend." Apple-butter is "lodwaerrick" [*Lattwarick*] from the German *latwerge*, an electuary, or an electuary of prunes. Our "Dutch" is much mixed with English. I once asked a woman what pie-crust is in Dutch. "Py-kroosht" [*Pai/Boi-gruscht*], she answered.

Those who speak English use uncommon expressions, as,—"That's a werry *lasty* basket" (meaning durable); "I seen him yet a'ready;" "I knew a woman that had a good baby *wunst;*" "The bread is all" (all gone). I have heard the carpenter call his plane *she*, and a housekeeper apply the same pronoun to her home-made soap.

A rich landed proprietor is sometimes called *king*. An old "Dutchman" who was absent from home thus narrated the cause of his journey: "I must go and see old Yoke (Jacob) Beidelman. Te people calls me te kink ov te Manor (township), and tay calls him te kink ov te Octorara. Now, dese kinks must come togeder once." (Accent *together*, and pass quickly over *once*.)[10]

Elsewhere in her essay, Gibbons makes other, occasional comments on language, most of which are examples of Dutchified English, such as this quote attributed to an Amish man explaining the difference between his sect and the Mennonites: "[v]y, dey vears puttons, and ve vearsh hooks oont eyes."[11] Commenting on what she sees as the sorry state of their local public schools, Gibbons also shares the following anecdote, attesting to the strong influence of Pennsylvania Dutch in the classroom: "My little boy of seven began to go to school this fall. For a while I could hear him repeating such expressions as, 'Che, double o, t, coot' (meaning *good*). 'P-i-g, pick.' 'Kreat A, little A, pouncing P.' 'I don't like chincherpread.' Even among our 'Dutch' people of more culture, *etch* is heard for *aitch* (h), and *chay* for *jay* (j), and these rules are relics of early training."[12] At the end of the third edition of her book, Gibbons added a ten-page appendix titled "The Pennsylvania German Dialect" that includes a number of examples of the language (as well as Dutchified English), including from the works of Henry Harbaugh and Edward H. Rauch, and she cites contemporary scholarship on the language, especially an important article by Professor J. S. Stahr, president of Franklin and Marshall College in Lancaster.[13]

On the one hand, in the context of her entire essay, Gibbons's remarks on the Pennsylvania Dutch and especially the English spoken by her neighbors should be understood as having been made "sympathetically and without malice," as Don Yoder aptly comments.[14] On the other hand, her observations, which highlight the differences between Pennsylvania Dutch and German and between Dutchified and standard English, including her use of eye dialectal spellings, left some readers with the impression that Gibbons took a generally dim view of her neighbors and their language abilities. An anonymous reviewer of the second edition of Gibbons's book, writing in the February 8, 1874, issue of the *New*

York Herald, takes serious issue with much of what Gibbons said about language. Regarding Pennsylvania Dutch, he considers it inappropriate to compare it negatively to German. Although the language is mainly of German stock, the reviewer argues that it is in fact a New World phenomenon whose formation parallels that of English. "The Pennsylvania dialect is . . . almost a distinct tongue formed from the German, English and French vocabulary just as the English language was based upon Norman, Saxon and Latin speech. Its English words with their Germanic pronunciation and its German words with their semi-South German, semi-Anglicised sound are its essential ingredients."

Gibbons's reviewer, who may well have been of Pennsylvania Dutch background himself, is harsher when he reacts to her implication that the English skills of the Pennsylvania Dutch are woefully deficient:

The great body of the people speak English, pure and undefiled, at the same time that they are thoroughly conversant with the German dialect known as Pennsylvania Dutch. There are no better specimens of the genuine Pennsylvania Dutchmen than Congressmen [Hiester] Clymer and [John Weinland] Killinger. They were born and bred in the Dutchest of the Dutch districts, for in a homely Pennsylvania phrase the counties of Berks and Lebanon are "as Dutch as sour-kraut," but there is no provincialism in their speech, though both of them speak the dialect with fluency. The English vernacular in Pennsylvania is purer than either in New England or in the Cotton States, and the German dialect is just what it pretends to be, "Pennsylvania Dutch."

Gibbons's reviewer goes on to correctly point out that many of the supposed Dutchisms cited by Gibbons are in fact regional English forms ("provincialisms") that have nothing to do with interference from Pennsylvania Dutch. For example, as he says, " 'A lasty basket' is not a more remarkable phrase than Shakespeare's 'vasty deep.' " Overall, he concludes that "[w]ith such words as these with which to illustrate Pennsylvania provincialisms it is singular that Mrs. Gibbons should choose so many not peculiar to Pennsylvania, but our author evidently is not very profound in philological study, and any school girl could overturn her good natured chatter about the misuse of English words by the Pennsylvania Dutch."

Gibbons's "Pennsylvania Dutch" also attracted the attention of the contemporary German American press, including the leading German-language periodical of the era, *Der Deutsche Pionier* (The German pioneer), which was published in Cincinnati from 1869 to 1887. Its founder and editor was Heinrich A. Rattermann (1832–1923), a northern German who immigrated with his family to Cincinnati as a child. In the fall of 1872, a three-part article appeared in *Der Deutsche Pionier* on the occasion of the publication of Gibbons's essay in the first edition of her book.[15] Likely authored by Rattermann himself, the unsigned article is less a review of Gibbons's essay than an indictment of the people she wrote about.

The main thesis of the 1872 *Pionier* article is that the Pennsylvania Dutch, and especially the Mennonites and Amish, had cut themselves off from European German learning, especially the great works of German literature, to the detriment of their culture and language, which remained "just" a dialect. "Real language development, which takes place in writing and literature and becomes organized according to a grammar, never happened with Pennsylvania Dutch. It was also hardly corrected and expanded by a literary language, as was the case with dialects in Germany; only sporadically do writers use it, as [Johann Peter] Hebel and [Carl Borromäus] Weitzmann employ Alemannic and Swabian, in order to make their thoughts more accessible and interesting to certain people."[16] The *Pionier* reviewer compares the Pennsylvania Dutch negatively to Anglo-Americans who, in his view, were able to progress intellectually through their continued appreciation for the works of English writers, jurists, and physicians. According to him, this ongoing engagement with Britain not only benefited English speakers in America culturally; it even had positive consequences for their language: "[t]hrough the continued study of the literature of Great Britain by American scholars it came about that in America a purer pronunciation of English developed as native dialects were gradually discarded, while the Germans' disengagement from the written language of their fatherland led to the emergence of a fifty-fifty dialect, both parts bad."[17]

Although the author of the *Pionier* article on Gibbons's essay invokes scholars such as the eminent linguist Alexander von Humboldt (1769–1859) to buttress his speculations about the linguistic history of the Pennsylvania Dutch, his notion that American English is "pure" and lacking in dialectal diversity is unfounded. In any case, Gibbons's essay, focused as it is on Mennonite and Amish Pennsylvania Dutch speakers who indeed were very much unaware of the works of Goethe, Schiller, and Lessing, touched a nerve for its reviewer in *Der Deutsche Pionier* and underscored the profound distance between the Pennsylvania Dutch, especially the sectarians, and *Deitschlenner*. Though the reviewer scorns the Pennsylvania Dutch for their inability to "save their native tongue in America from contamination" (*ihre Heimathszunge in Amerika vor Verunreinigungen bewahren*), he finds other Americans of German stock just as guilty of polluting their speech with English.[18]

A number of the topics that Phebe Earle Gibbons focuses on in her essay were revisited in numerous other popular accounts of the Pennsylvania Dutch, including their speech, especially their supposed use of Dutchified English. Not surprisingly, given the fact that most curious readers were not German speakers, Pennsylvania Dutch sometimes came to be equated with Dutchified English. An example of this was the story of an aspiring actress from Pennsylvania who landed a part in a Broadway play in New York in 1916 for her supposed mastery of Pennsylvania Dutch:

Dutch Lingo Won Actress Her Job
Dialect She Once Mimicked Got Miss Longenecker Role in
"Erstwhile Susan"

"Ach, vy you vill? It iss no use!"

Miss Maud Longenecker, of 245 West Forty-fifth Street, daughter of Rear Admiral Edwin Longenecker, of Wernersville, Penn., and granddaughter of Jacob S. Haldeman, former United States Minister to Sweden, laughed as the Pennsylvania Dutch slid smoothly from her tongue.

"If I couldn't say that just so," she remarked, "I probably wouldn't be where I am to-day."

You see, it gives something nice to speak the Pennsylvania Dutch, already yet. It enabled Miss Longenecker to bridge the chasm between the dainty, trailing gowns of a rear admiral's daughter leading the biggest naval ball of the season and the sober black cashmere robes and bonnet of a little Mennonite maid. It transformed her from a society girl into plain Em Wackernagel of "Erstwhile Susan." . . .

"It gives much rain to-day," she said to Madison Corey, busy engaging the cast. "It's all, any more?" This was her Pennsylvania Dutch way of asking if the cast was complete.

"There's no room for you," declared Mr. Corey with emphasis.

So Miss Longenecker called to her aid Samuel Schmucker, New York artist, her childhood's playmate, and a descendant of old [Peter] Muhlenberg, the "Fighting Parson" of Revolutionary days, whose statue guards the City Hall in Philadelphia. Presently she was a full-fledged Em Wackernagel.

Vell, vell! it pays to know the languages, no?[19]

Erstwhile Susan was based on the 1914 novel *Barnabetta* by Helen Reimensnyder Martin (1868–1939), many of whose novels were set in Lancaster County and engendered much criticism for their demeaning view of Mennonite and Amish sectarians, which included stereotyping their English as being horribly Dutchified. Martin made no attempt to insert actual Pennsylvania Dutch into her novels, thus feeding the stereotype that Pennsylvania Dutch was the kind of English mimicked by Maud Longenecker and mocked in the article above.

The most famous instance of Pennsylvania Dutch being made synonymous with nonstandard English was in the lyrics of the 1956 song "Mama from the Train," a hit made popular by Patti Page (1927–2013):

Throw mama from the train a kiss, a kiss
Wave mama from the train a goodbye
Throw mama from the train a kiss a kiss
And don't cry, my baby, don't cry

How I miss that sweet lady with her old-country touch
Miss her quaint broken English called Pennsylvania Dutch
I can still see her there at the station that day
Calling out to her baby as the train pulled away

Throw mama from the train a kiss, a kiss
Dry mama all your tears, won't you try?
Throw mama from the train a kiss, a kiss
And eat mama up all her pie.

The song's composer was Irving Gordon (1915–1996), a native of Brooklyn who had no apparent firsthand connection to Pennsylvania Dutch but had to have been familiar with "ethnic" jokes that stereotyped the supposedly deficient English used by native speakers of other languages, including German and Yiddish.

Despite the assumption among some nineteenth- and twentieth-century Americans that Pennsylvania Dutch was simply a form of nonstandard English, others did recognize that it was a language in its own right, distinct from English. A number of the references to Pennsylvania Dutch in the popular press recount instances when it was used in unusual circumstances, as in the Muhlenberg and Orth episodes cited above. One very early such example appeared in an April 28, 1854, article in the *Kenosha (WI) Democrat* titled "Parrot Talk":

The bad Latin and French displayed in Congress, has passed into a proverb; and many a man, who might have held a respectable position in the House of Representatives and Senate, has been ruined by the display of his pedantry. The late Timothy Fuller, of Massachusetts, who was especially addicted to quotations, many years ago cover[ed] himself with confusion by concluding a speech with a long extract from Homer, which not a dozen men in the House could understand. The moment he resumed his seat, old George Kr[e]mer, of Pennsylvania, rose and by the way of ludicrous contrast and punishment, let off a volley of low Pennsylvania Dutch, to the amusement of every one, and to the chagrin and lasting mortification of the gentleman from Massachusetts.

Timothy Fuller (1778–1835) served in Congress from 1817 to 1825; George Kremer (1775–1854), a native of Dauphin County, represented Pennsylvania's Ninth Congressional District in the House from 1823 to 1829; thus, the incident related above would have occurred between 1823 and 1825. Fuller was a Harvard graduate from a prominent Massachusetts family, while Kremer, a rough-around-the edges Jacksonian and a nephew of Simon Snyder, had little formal education; thus, the contrast between the two men is nicely evoked by the languages they spoke.[20]

"Honest" George Kremer was by no means the only politician to use Pennsylvania Dutch publicly. As Harry Hess Reichard, writing in 1918, noted, "The politicians early learned to know the value of the dialect as a means of approach to the voters."[21] One of the most notable public figures associated with Pennsylvania Dutch, William H. Sowden (1840–1907), was in fact not an ethnic Dutchman. A native of Cornwall,

England, Sowden immigrated as a six-year-old to Pennsylvania, growing up mainly in Allentown, Lehigh County. After serving as an officer in the Civil War, Sowden attended Harvard Law School and had a distinguished career as a lawyer, solicitor, and district attorney in Allentown. He was elected to Congress as a Democrat in 1884, serving two terms (1885–1889).[22] Sowden's unabashed use of Pennsylvania Dutch became legendary in Pennsylvania politics, and the fact that he was not of Pennsylvania Dutch stock underscores the language's importance in public life at the turn of the twentieth century, even as its use was declining among nonsectarians.[23] Sowden's language abilities were mentioned in a *Philadelphia Inquirer* report on the 1896 congressional campaign of Henry Houck (1836–1917), a native Dutchman from Lebanon County: "Henry Houck is making Congressional campaign speeches in Lebanon county in German. The author of 'The Making of Pennsylvania' commends the foresight of those Pennsylvania Germans who insisted on their children learning English. But the foresight of the Englishmen who learned German might be equally commended. Store clerks cannot get a situation in many towns in Pennsylvania unless they can speak German as well as English. Even a Yankee like ex-Congressman Sowden, of Lehigh, is compelled to learn Pennsylvania Dutch."[24]

Sowden's close connection with Pennsylvania Dutch extended to the courtroom. In a November 22, 1888, article titled "Dutch vs. German," the *Philadelphia Inquirer* reported on the following "amusing scene in Judge Ermentrout's court in Reading":

In the Heffner will case before Judge Ermentrout this afternoon Lawyer Ruhl, who wrote the will, testified that he explained everything to Mr. Heffner in Pennsylvania Dutch before putting it on paper.

"Don't say Pennsylvania Dutch, I don't like it. Say Pennsylvania German," interrupted Judge Ermentrout.

"The highest authority has decided that it shall be called Pennsylvania Dutch," said Arthur Dewalt, Esq., of Allentown, one of the attorneys for the contestants.

"Who—Prof. Horne?" was asked.

"No, Congressman Sowden," was the answer.

A general laugh followed, and after this episode the case was adjourned to December 8.

The use of Pennsylvania Dutch in legal proceedings throughout the nineteenth century and into the twentieth is amply documented. Ludwig Wollenweber, for example, relates the following experience he had as a member of the jury in a Reading court in November 1876:

The proceedings naturally occurred in English, but since most of the residents of Berks County, especially those from outside of Reading, can express themselves more clearly in German than in English, even if they have been born here, plaintiffs, respondents, and witnesses often prefer to be examined in German. I convinced myself of the fact that most lawyers, as well as all the judges and court employees have command of German and must if a just verdict is to be reached.

After we Berks County jurymen had retreated to the deliberation room, I, as one who had never served on a jury before, was curious about how things would now proceed. I had thought that everything would be discussed in English, but I was greatly in error, for hardly had we taken our seats in the spacious room than one of the oldest members of our jury stood up and said: "Ich expect, daß wir Alle besser Deutsch als Englisch verstehn; ischt aber einer unner uns, bei dem es net der Fall ischt, so mag er es sage." [*I expect that we all understand German better than English, but if there is one among us for whom that is not the case, let him speak up.*] All twelve were silent. "Well," the old man continued, "dann ischt es verschtanne, weil alle schtill sind, daß wir unsere Sache in Deutsch abmache, es geht leichter wie in Englisch, obschon wir a All recht gut Englisch verschtehn. Nau, ich schlag Mr. Young als unsern Vormann vor: all wu davor sin, hebe die rechte Hand in die Höh!" [*Well, then it is understood, since everyone is quiet, that we will do our business in German; it is easier than in English, even though we all understand English quite well. Now, I nominate Mr. Young as our foreman: everyone in favor, raise your right hand!*][25]

Harry Hess Reichard, who was born in 1878 and whose documentation of Pennsylvania Dutch literature is unmatched, recalls the following about the use of Pennsylvania Dutch in the legal system:

In this connection it may not be out of place to cite from a newspaper of 1907. "Three different kinds of German were spoken recently in court at Harrisburg. A witness spoke High German, Judge Thomas Capp spoke the Pennsylvania Dutch of Lebanon County, and Senator John E. Fox, the defendant's counsel, spoke the Pennsylvania Dutch of Dauphin County." I have myself heard a lawyer review in the dialect before the jury, testimony that had been given in the dialect, at such length that the judge stopped him to inquire whether he purposed to give his entire plea in the dialect. Curiously enough, the lawyer in question was a native of Cornwall, England, [William H. Sowden] but he at least appreciated what [Edward H.] Rauch implied, that a knowledge of the dialect was a business necessity.[26]

One notable example of the use of Pennsylvania Dutch in court was in connection with a notorious case in 1903–1904 that drew national attention to Allentown, PA, where the crime occurred. In October of 1903, a young woman named Catharine Bechtel was brutally murdered. Five people were charged in her death, including her mother, Mabel; two of her brothers; and two men with whom Catharine had been romantically involved. All five defendants were eventually acquitted in January 1904. One sidelight of the trial was the fact that the proceedings were conducted in Pennsylvania Dutch, as the *New York Times* reported on page 1 of its January 22, 1904, edition: "Mrs. Bechtel is 'Pennsylvania Dutch' in race, and the entire proceedings were carried on in the 'Pennsylvania Dutch' dialect, which was understood not only by the judge, jury, and lawyers, but by most of the spectators in the crowded courtroom." The mystery of Catharine Bechtel's murder was never solved.[27]

Pennsylvania Dutch and the World Wars

It is widely believed that anti-German sentiments in America during the World War I era brought about the demise of the German language in education, media, and religion, as well as in families.[28] While it is true that legal measures were enacted in several states and communities forbidding the use or instruction of German, including in Pennsylvania, a close analysis of the facts of attrition away from German, especially in schools, the press, and churches, shows that the shift to English in German-speaking communities in the United States had been well underway by the time World War I came along and that the persecution of individuals and institutions for using German may have accelerated but did not generate that process.[29] Given the fact that Pennsylvania Dutch was spoken in public settings, such as the courtroom, into the twentieth century, what impact, if any, did the hostility that many Americans showed for all things German, including the language, during the years preceding and following World War I have on the use of Pennsylvania Dutch? Was the historical relationship between Pennsylvania Dutch and German close enough to have been a liability for the former language, or did the fundamentally American self-identity of Pennsylvania Dutch speakers protect them from anti-German sentiment? The following article, which originally appeared in the *Detroit Free Press* in the summer of 1918 and was widely reprinted in other newspapers across the nation that fall, addresses these very questions:

"Pennsylvania Dutch," that curious combination of German, English, and Yankee, which since revolutionary times has developed in parts of Pennsylvania and Ohio, is going into the discard. For more than a century it has been growing, just as languages always grow, with use. It has corrupted words, made words, created forms, one might say a grammar of its own. It has not, it is true, produced a literature. But it has been the speech of a considerable number of persons in their homes. It long since ceased to be recognizable as German, and English it never was. In it, students tell us, are mangled German, English, Welsh, French, and even Gaelic words. "Pennsylvania Dutch" has been the dialect of those German disciples of Peter Menno who came to America, some of them in pre-Revolutionary days, seeking religious liberty and political freedom. Some of those went into Ohio during Revolution days, others into Canada, some as late as Civil war days. Their religious beliefs contributed to isolation. And they were largely an agricultural people. Now the word has gone forth among the Mennonites that it is no longer patriotic to speak "Pennsylvania Dutch," and as fast and as thoroughly as possible these unbelievers in war are discarding the speech of their childhood and home associations. The task is not an impossible one for them, since all or nearly all of them have had some experience in the common schools. From among them 8,000 young men have gone overseas to fight the oppressors of their ancestors and the barbarians who threaten their own liberties. The banning of "Pennsylvania Dutch" is an impressive object lesson to all Americans. Let us resolve to speak English.[30]

On the surface, if this article is to be believed, it would appear that Pennsylvania Dutch speakers felt strong pressure to express their "patriotism" by giving up their heritage language and shifting to English. Further, the word *banning* raises the question whether perhaps some kind of legal measures might have been enacted to check the use of Pennsylvania Dutch during the World War I era. A review of what is known about what actually occurred in the Dutch Country during this time casts significant doubt about the veracity of this article.

The assertion in the 1918 *Free Press* article that it was rising patriotism that inspired Pennsylvania Dutch speakers to abandon their heritage language in favor of English is clearly false. To be sure, the author of the article got numerous other details wrong, for example, in assuming that all Pennsylvania Dutch were Mennonites (sectarians still constituted only a small fraction of Pennsylvania Dutch speakers in 1918), that they were led to America by a "Peter Menno" (the Mennonites take their name from Menno Simons, who had died more than a century before the first of his followers came to the New World),[31] and that the Pennsylvania Dutch lexicon includes words from Welsh, French, and Gaelic, in addition to English and German (simply false). It *was* true that many Pennsylvania Dutch speakers had shifted or were shifting to English by World War I, but, as was the case with German speakers across the United States at that time, the process of linguistic assimilation had begun long before then. The attrition of up- and outwardly mobile nonsectarians from Pennsylvania Dutch had been noted already in the middle of the nineteenth century, by Henry Harbaugh, for example, when he published "Das alt Schulhaus an der Krick" in the *Guardian* in 1861. Ironically, it was precisely in pacifist Mennonite and Amish sectarian communities where the use of Pennsylvania Dutch (and German in worship) remained the healthiest during the war years and beyond.

Still, some scholars writing about Pennsylvania Dutch have been inclined to think that anti-German prejudice during World War I did somehow have an impact on the language and its speakers, but without offering much in the way of evidence. Homer Tope Rosenberger, for example, devotes an entire chapter of his important history of the Pennsylvania Dutch to the World War I era, but much of the content of that chapter deals with the experiences of German Americans rather than specifically the Pennsylvania Dutch.[32] One exception is a report of harassment in the community of Emerald, Lehigh County, where some Pennsylvania Dutch were forced to kiss an American flag in public.[33] Rosenberger also quotes the Pennsylvania Dutch writer Pierce E. Swope (1884–1968), who attributed the switch to English in Reformed churches in Lebanon County during the war years to the anti-German mood at the time.[34] In general, Rosenberger was clearly influenced by the views of German American critics such as Carl Wittke who saw in World War I the beginning of the end for the German language in America.[35] Rosenberger also presumed—incorrectly—that the maintenance of Pennsylvania Dutch was somehow dependent on a solid knowledge of standard German:

The exclusion of German from the curriculum of public schools at the time of World War I almost sounded the death knell of the Pennsylvania German dialect. The exclusion was a punitive measure which cast a shadow upon German life and culture. Furthermore, with the next generation having little opportunity to learn German, the dialect spoken by the Pennsylvania Germans became corrupted because of too little familiarity with German sentence structure, and because of the natural tendency for one to use familiar English words when his vocabulary of German words was not adequate to complete a German conversation.[36]

It is true that actions were taken to ban or curtail the instruction of German in Pennsylvania schools, including in the Dutch Country, during the World War I years and immediately following. In May 1918, for example, it was reported that the school board in Lancaster banned the teaching of German in schools under its jurisdiction effective that fall.[37] However, an effort to do likewise in Allentown that same spring failed. Since 1858, German had been a required subject in Allentown high schools. In April 1918 the president of the Allentown Board of Education proposed the following:

I ask of the members of the Board of Education to divest our programme in the schools of Allentown of all the German studies, of all German propaganda, and that German kultur be eliminated from our schools; that we make our declaration that we have no use for German lies and Prussian murderers who control the German Government. Let us teach

our rising generation liberty and freedom. Let us despise all autocracy
and monarchy and teach our children to respect and obey the laws and
mandates of our noble country, that every promise made is sacred. Let us
be patriotic American citizens.[38]

At a contentious board meeting the following month, a compromise was
reached whereby German would be reduced to the status of an elective
in Allentown's high schools but not banned outright, which paralleled
a similar measure undertaken by Muhlenberg College, also located in
Allentown.[39]

The challenges to German in Allentown's schools had little impact on
the use of Pennsylvania Dutch in rural communities, however.

> More than in the schools, so far as the Pennsylvania German belt is con-
> cerned, German [= Pennsylvania Dutch] speech and thought are taught
> at home and in the churches. In many of the churches of the rural dis-
> tricts there is just as much German preaching as English, and some chil-
> dren take catechetical instruction in German. Occasionally the younger
> element in a church gains the upper hand and banishes German from
> the services, but there has not as yet been any general propaganda in
> the Pennsylvania German region to banish German from the churches
> altogether. The government has no complaint against the Pennsylvania
> Germans, but soon after the war began, in 1914, there was a loud wail
> from the German Government, which was totally and egregiously mis-
> taken in its estimate of the Pennsylvania Germans that they would side
> with Germany in the conflict.[40]

In any case, curtailment of the instruction of German in Pennsylvanian schools would have had little practical effect on the maintenance
of Pennsylvania Dutch for the important fact that German was taught
only in high schools, not grammar schools. The great majority of active
speakers of Pennsylvania Dutch in the early twentieth century were rural dwellers whose formal education ended before high school.

The movement against German in Allentown's schools in the spring
of 1918 was followed that summer by a directive from Allentown's city
government that municipal employees were forbidden to use "German
or other foreign languages," including Pennsylvania Dutch, unless abso-

lutely necessary.[41] However, there are no reports of anyone being sanctioned for violating this order, which came just months before the war ended in November. There also appears to have been little public support for the measure. An editorial in the *Allentown Democrat* published on September 4, 1918, titled "Putting the Ban on German and Pennsylvania German," made a strong case for moderation in the matter of language use in the city:

A representative of the *Democrat* has been asked this question: "Why do they permit German and Pennsylvania German to be spoken in Allentown, especially during the period of the war?"

The German language and the Pennsylvania German dialect are permitted to be spoken because there is no law that prevents their being spoken. Neither do we believe that any movement to prevent them from being spoken would be popular because it would mean a hardship for some people who are absolutely loyal.

We do not believe that either the German language or the Pennsylvania German dialect should be spoken where it is possible to use the English language. The city authorities were quite right when they instructed the city officials to use only English except in cases where English is not understood. All of us should strive to use only the English language. We must not be narrow minded or unreasonable, for the fact must not be lost sight of that there are still people among us, some German born and some native born, who are not as familiar with the English language as we might wish them to be. Particular is this true of some of the older Pennsylvania Germans. Let us illustrate: Some time ago a very reputable citizen who was born and reared in the country and whose knowledge of the English language is limited because his early associations were almost exclusively with people who spoke only Pennsylvania German, asked the writer to explain the meaning of a news story he had read. He can read English and he can speak it, though he is more familiar with German. What he had read was not perfectly clear to him, hence he sought enlightenment. We explained the meaning of the story, but we had to do it in Pennsylvania German. Was it disloyal on the part of the writer to speak the native vernacular? Would it have been more loyal to have permitted the citizen to remain in doubt as to the meaning of the story?

And here is another point: Several weeks ago in a neighboring village a native of Germany and his wife received the sad news from Washington that their son, who was with the American Expeditionary Force in France, had given up his life for his country. The parents are loyal Americans. They gave their son cheerfully. Memorial services were held for him. The sermon was in German. Should it have been in English? Hardly, because the parents would have received little benefit from the consolation given by the minister because they understand but very little English.

Let us be fair toward those who cannot understand English. It is undoubtedly a fact that there is more German and Pennsylvania German spoken than necessary, but to put the language and the dialect entirely under the ban would be unjust toward many people who are as loyal as those who insist that German and Pennsylvania German shall not be spoken. Let it be the rule of every establishment that German or Pennsylvania German shall be spoken only when absolutely a hardship on people, who, though they may have but a limited knowledge of English, are as loyal as anyone in the country. The *Democrat* is willing to advocate the dropping of German and Pennsylvania German when either is used needlessly, but we are not in favor of any movement which, for instance, will serve to deprive German-born parents of American soldiers the right to listen to words of consolation in the only language they understand if in case their soldier sons fall on the field of battle. To anything so narrow the *Democrat* can never subscribe. English is bound to be the language of the nation, but we cannot make the change over night. Until the change comes we must be patient with those who can best make themselves understood in German or Pennsylvania German, and in the meantime we should do all in our power to aid them in acquiring a better knowledge of English.

Though this editorial was not signed, it was almost certainly written by Charles W. Weiser (1863–1924), the *Democrat*'s editor at the time, who was not only a native speaker of Pennsylvania Dutch but also the author of a well-known humorous column in the *Democrat* (and a short-lived magazine) featuring the character "Sim Schmalzgsicht" (Simon Lardface).[42]

The views expressed by the editorship of the *Allentown Democrat* with regard to the use of German and Pennsylvania Dutch in public settings underscore the generally tolerant sociolinguistic atmosphere in southeastern Pennsylvania during the World War I era when it came to the Pennsylvania Dutch. Given their deep roots in America, it was hard for anyone who lived alongside them to question their loyalty to the United States in its conflict with Germany. A letter to the editor of the Lebanon *Evening Report* from August 24, 1918, by an Anglo-American resident of the Dutch Country reacting to suspicions of the Pennsylvania Dutch expressed by an outsider, illustrates what seems to have been the general sentiment of the time:

Sir—Referring to the article in the [Philadelphia] *Public Ledger* headed "Pennsylvania German Succumbs to War," the writer, in whose veins there is no German blood, but who thoroughly understands the Pennsylvania Dutch and speaks it fluently, would be very sorry should this be true.

Maybe it was a "mongrel" language 250 years ago, but today it is a "distinct" language spoken by a "very distinct" people. It is erroneous to speak of it as "Pennsylvania German"; it is Pennsylvania Dutch and is a development of the choicest and strongest and purest strains of English, French, Dutch, Welsh, Flemish, some Irish and Scotch, and here and there some German and quite a little Swiss. It is the most flexible language in existence; in fact those familiar with the Pennsylvania Dutch have little difficulty in acquiring the above-named languages. A Pennsylvania Dutchman is never embarrassed, no matter in what language he is addressed, and likewise he is misunderstood in no language than there is of other tongues, and therefore no reason at all why it should be thrown into the discard. There are numerous other strong reasons why it should be extensively cultivated.

As to patriotism, the Pennsylvania Dutch are the Americans of all Americans. Their advent into this country antedates Plymouth Rock by only a very few years. In the wake of the Revolution they bore their full share of the burden in army contributions and supplies. With the Boones and Lincolns they "trekked" to the South and West, and were the pioneers who opened to civilization these territories of boundless wealth and resources which now figure so strongly in the present crisis. They were the immortal sharpshooters with Jackson at New Orleans, and still vote for him (bless their honest Democratic hearts). They furnished their full quota of men in the Mexican war. When Lincoln called for volunteers in '61 the Pennsylvania Dutch were on the march before the ink was dry on the paper on which it was penned. When Wilson foresaw the necessity of supplying the French with hope, courage, and help, his first call went out to the Pennsylvania Dutch, and let me tell you that Beelzebub himself is a mere tyro in his profession compared to what the Pennsylvania Dutch will do with "Schrecklichkeit"—not because they love war, but because they love peace.

Don't be ashamed of your language, you Pennsylvania Dutchman. The language, as well as your personality, stand for what is most precious in life: "stick to it."

Chas. S. Hill

Though Pennsylvania Dutch speakers had little to fear in the way of harassment in their home communities, where everyone understood the difference between them and Germans, outside of Pennsylvania the situation was somewhat different. In the first half of 1917, there were accounts in Pennsylvania newspapers of three separate incidents in which native speakers of Pennsylvania Dutch traveling out of state were suspected of being German spies because of their language. On January 26, 1917, the *Allentown Democrat* reported that a school administrator from Nesquehoning, Carbon County, who was vacationing in Canada was detained for three days on charges of espionage because he spoke Pennsylvania Dutch. A few months later, on May 16, the same newspaper told the story of three Pennsylvania Dutch–speaking Lutheran pastors who had made a "botanical visit" to Virginia. In the woods near a reservoir serving the community of Buena Vista in the Blue Ridge Mountains, the suspicions of local residents were aroused when they heard the men speaking a German-like language and saw them digging in the ground and scanning the skies with binoculars. It took some time before the local police believed that the clergymen were simply enjoying the natural beauty of the area and not spying for the enemy.

A third incident of Pennsylvania Dutch speakers coming under scrutiny for possible espionage in 1917 occurred in Minnesota and was reported in the April 21 issue of the *Gettysburg Times*:

To be held up as suspected German spies and placed in a station house for a day, was the rather unpleasant experience of Charles Keagy, of Oxford Road, near McSherrystown, and Albert Kline, of Midway, while returning from a two months' Western jaunt.

The young men left February 27 on a sight-seeing trip. They first stopped at Dayton, Ohio. From there they went to St. Louis, Kansas City, and St. Paul. From this point they went North to Anoka, Minnesota, where they spent some time.

Last Tuesday they decided to return home and went to the North Western railroad depot. Before they could purchase tickets, however, three Secret Service men felt sure they had trailed two of the "Kaiser's lieutenants," and placed them under arrest as suspects. Messrs. Keagy and Kline were then taken to the city police station, where they were searched from head to foot.

Fortunately for the young men, they had nothing on their person that would arouse suspicion, and the following morning they were liberated. The condition, however, was that they were to go to the depot and purchase tickets for "Hanover, Pennsylvania." Even the word "Hanover" looked suspicious and the fact that the boys could speak a little Pennsylvania Dutch didn't help matters either.

To be sure that the two "American Kaiser-Wilhelms" would not run at large, the Secret Service men accompanied the boys to the depot and witnessed the purchase of their tickets.

They are now at their homes.

While knowledge of Pennsylvania Dutch may have been a liability for some of its speakers who ventured outside of southeastern Pennsylvania during the World War I era, for others it proved advantageous. Many young men from the Dutch Country served in the US Army in Europe, and their ability to speak a language closely related to German dialects was on occasion put to strategic use by their superiors:

The story of how his knowledge of the Pennsylvania German dialect netted him a responsible position on the fighting lines in France is one of the interesting sidelights in the war diary of Captain John E. Dillinger, formerly commander of Company D, Fourth Pennsylvania Infantry, of Allentown, who is now at Camp Dix, N.J. awaiting his discharge from military service. Captain Dillinger visited friends in this city for a few hours on Sunday.

It all happened while Captain Dillinger and several Allentown boys were enjoying a much deserved rest outside of their billets, just behind the lines of France. The aggregation was comfortably seated on improvised chairs, all chatting in that dialect that is peculiar to this locality. Everything was going along nicely, when an American general officer came along, and overhearing part of the conversation being conducted in German, he ordered Captain Dillinger to report at his headquarters at a stated hour, presumably for the purpose of demanding an explanation as to the conversation.

At the appointed hour, Captain Dillinger reported to his superior officer, quaking in his boots, for fear of being accused of being a spy, or for most anything else. Imagine his surprise, when the general told him that he wanted him to take charge of a large German prison camp, as he was the logical man for the job. Thus, the quaking in the boots reduced, a smile played on the corners of the captain's mouth, and he about-faced and walked out of the general's headquarters, thankful that for once his knowledge of the Pennsylvania lingo did him a good turn.[43]

Dillinger and his fellow soldiers from Allentown also put their native language to use in combat:

"Pennsylvania Dutch" spoken by American soldiers in the AEF [American Expeditionary Forces] caused some amusing complications in France, but none greater interest to the men concerned than when an entire company of Iron Division machine gunners, surrounded by Huns in a night attack, were mistaken by an enemy regiment for fellow Germans and escaped from what looked like certain attack. It was in a big movement in the fighting near Chateau-Thierry that Company C, of the 109th Machine Gun Battalion, commanded by Captain Dillinger, of Allentown, Pa., well in advance, found itself suddenly enveloped in an enemy maneuv[er].

According to the casuals who [we]re returning ahead of the 28th Division, the Germans started to rush the company when the central Pennsylvanians in the excitement of defending themselves, began to shout in [the] German language.

Fritz mistook this for a warning from friends; German officers called off the charge and C Company officers were able to extricate their command and rejoin the battalion a little later.

"It was of no significance to Fritz that we wore American uniforms," says an Iron Division veteran. "Many of the attacking Germans were rigged out in uniforms of French and British soldiers and there even a few American uniforms in their line."[44]

Decades later, during the Second World War, another young soldier from Pennsylvania fighting in Europe was not as fortunate as Captain Dillinger and his men had been. Corporal Gilbert J. Beamesderfer (1918–1991), a native speaker of Pennsylvania Dutch from Ephrata, Lancaster County, and a member of I Company, 320th Infantry, Thirty-Fifth Division, was wounded in combat against German forces in France in September 1944. While recovering in an American evacuation hospital, he tried his Pennsylvania Dutch out with a captured German medic, and the two were able to communicate well. A nurse overheard their conversation and presumed that Beamesderfer was in fact a German spy. Beamesderfer's American uniform (worn by many a real German spy at that time, as during World War I) and vigorous protestations were of no use, and he was held with wounded German soldiers in France and England for a month before American officers finally accepted his story. It was eventually Beamesderfer's knowledge of local Pennsylvania lore, not his mastery of English, that suggested to an interrogating officer that he might really be who he said he was:

"Colonel," he said, "did you know that Lancaster County is officially listed as the Garden Spot of the World?"

"No, I didn't," the colonel said.

"And that Lancaster is the Red Rose City and York the White Rose City?"

The colonel didn't know that either, but he was impressed. He called in a nurse who came from Philadelphia and Beamesderfer told the nurse more things about Pennsylvania, how when an Amish family, for example, has a marriageable daughter in the house they paint the fence white and the gate green.

When Beamesderfer had finished, the colonel sat in silence for a while. The he said: "OK. We'll send your fingerprints to Washington."[45]

Gilbert Beamesderfer returned to Lancaster County, where he remained for the rest of his life. His story was widely reported in newspapers across the country in June of 1945. It is not known how actively he continued to use Pennsylvania Dutch over the course of his life, but an April 15, 1950, article in the *Reading Eagle* reported that Beamesderfer and his wartime experience were featured at a local fersommling, a festive social gathering consisting of a banquet and program conducted in Pennsylvania Dutch.

A somewhat different experience of contact between European Germans and Pennsylvania Dutch during World War II is related in collection of documents pertaining to the life of an Amish man, Amos J. Stoltzfus (1872–1947) from Morgantown, PA, which is located on the border between Lancaster and Berks Counties. German prisoners of war being held in Reading were permitted to assist local farmers, including Amos Stoltzfus, during harvesttime. Stoltzfus and his family befriended a number of these prisoners and were apparently able to communicate in something between Pennsylvania Dutch and German, at least to some degree. The collection of Stoltzfus family documents includes four letters written to Stoltzfus by former POWs after the war, two of which are in German and two in English. There is also a copy of a letter written by Stoltzfus to one German and his family in a blend of Pennsylvania Dutch and Pennsylvania High German that is reminiscent of the early nineteenth-century correspondence considered in chapter 3:

Willi Nolden und Frau und Kinder
August 22, 1947
Ein Gruss aus das aller Herzlichter das ziat au denn brunen den Lebligen wasser, das ihn das evign quellet. Une zu dem wahran tuhr denn shaaf-stall so wei wir lessen ihm Testament.

Hoffen desen Zeilen wirt einen gesunt antriffen. Bei mir gehet das arbeiten nicht, und ich fiel als wenn ich am warden wer auf den zukunft Christi wo wir lessen in Thessolanung das 4 Kapitel 13 durich 18 und auf am Offonbaruing 10 Kapitel das 6 farst. Ich glaube ihr ihn Deutchland kennt dieser zeit besser bekriefen als wie wir kennen hier ihn Amerika wo alles darft listig leben, und der Herr Gott giebt als nach fruchbarn zeiten zu uns. Aber Gott wird gedankt sein, und er weist was am besten ist. Wir sind Schuldig wahrlich Dankbar zu sein.

Den letzen brief haben wir einor Christum Pflucht buchlein senten darin kannst du finden unssern Glauben Article auf gesetz, hoffen is

Cpl. Gilbert J. Beamesderfer, whose story ("Mistaken Identity") was
featured in *True Comics*, November 1946.

wirt dir zu dem gerechtigkeit weisen. Lasst uns fleis thun um einzukom-
men zu dieser ruhe, nicht es versaumen als das unsern Keinor dahinder
bleiben.

Gegrusst gute gesund am Leib und Seel.

Amos J. Stoltzfus

*A most heartfelt greeting that draws from the well of living water flowing
to eternity and to the true gate, the sheep pen, as we read in the New Testament.*

*I hope these lines find you healthy. I am not able to work, and I feel as if
I were waiting for the future of Christ, as we read in 1 Thessalonians 4:13–18
and Revelation 10:6. I think that you in Germany can understand this time
better than we can in America, where everyone lives happily and the Lord
God still gives us fruitful times. But thanks be to God, He knows what is
best. We are obliged to be truly thankful.*

*In the last letter we sent you a Christenpflicht [Die Ernsthafte Christen-
pflicht, 'Prayer book for earnest Christians']. In it you can find our articles
of faith, I hope it will guide you to justice. Let us work hard to enter into
this rest, not neglect it, lest our children stay behind.*

Be well greeted in body and soul.[46]

Marketing the Pennsylvania Dutch and Their Language

Reports in the media about the Pennsylvania Dutch and their language in the early twentieth century, including during the World War I years, were dominated not by stories of repression or discrimination but by the novels of Helen Reimensnyder Martin (1868–1939). A native of Lancaster County, Martin, despite her Pennsylvania Dutch–sounding name, was the daughter of a German American Lutheran pastor, Cornelius Reimensnyder, and his wife, Henrietta Thurman, and she was not a speaker of Pennsylvania Dutch. In addition to having grown up in a *Deitschlenner*-leaning cultural milieu, she was college educated and held progressive social and political views (including feminism and socialism), all of which led her to form a strongly negative image of the Pennsylvania Dutch, especially conservative Anabaptist sectarians.[47] Her most popular novel, *Tillie: A Mennonite Maid*, appeared in 1904. The basic plot line of this work, repeated in many other of her novels, is this: a sweet, natively intelligent Pennsylvania Dutch girl, Tillie Getz, is born into a backward and benighted family dominated by her father. Tillie suffers further as a member of a "New Mennonite" church she joins. Her escape from these oppressive circumstances is facilitated by two Yankee outsiders, first her schoolteacher, Miss Margaret from Kentucky, and then by her knight in shining armor, the Harvard-educated Walter Fairchild, whom she ends up marrying and with whom she lives happily ever after.

Language occupies a central place in Martin's depictions of Pennsylvania Dutch characters in her novels, but it was not Pennsylvania Dutch she used, rather a fanciful form of English so Dutchified as to be nearly incomprehensible to outsiders. Already in the first few pages of *Tillie*, the supposedly deformed speech of the Pennsylvania Dutch is prominently displayed:

> Miss Margaret always made Tillie feel that she *liked* her. Tillie wondered how Miss Margaret could like *her*! What was there to like? No one had ever liked her before.
>
> "It wonders me!" Tillie often whispered to herself with throbbing heart.
>
> "Please, Miss Margaret," said the child, "pop says to ast you will you give me the darst to go home till half-past three this after?"

"If you go home till half-past three, you need not come back, honey— it wouldn't be worthwhile, when school closes at four."

"But I don't mean," said Tillie in puzzled surprise, "that I want to go home and come back. I sayed whether I have the darst to go home till half-past three. Pop he's went to Lancaster, and he'll be back till half-past three a'ready, and he says then I got to be home to help him in the celery beds."

Miss Margaret held her pretty head on one side, considering, as she looked down into the little girl's upturned face. "Is this a conundrum, Tillie? How can your father be in Lancaster now and yet be home until half-past three? It's uncanny. Unless," she added, a ray of light coming to her—"unless 'till' means *by*. Your father will be home *by* half-past three and wants you then?"

"Yes, ma'am. I can't talk just so right," said Tillie apologetically, "like what you can. Yes, sometimes I say my we's like my w's, yet!"[48]

The linguistic knowledge of Martin's Pennsylvania Dutch characters is limited entirely to this nonsensical English; nowhere does Martin suggest that real Pennsylvania Dutch people might speak a language related to German. For Martin, deficient English is *the* most tangible hallmark of her subjects' intellectual, cultural, and spiritual shortcomings.

Martin made this clear not only in her novels themselves but also in her discussions about the Pennsylvania Dutch in interviews. For example, on the occasion of the adaptation of her novel *Barnabetta* for the Broadway stage as *Erstwhile Susan* in 1916, Martin shared the following in an interview in the *New York Post*:

You can tell the Pennsylvania Dutchman by his speech even after he sheds his queer clothes and barbering, and takes on the outward American guise in the bigger cities in southeastern Pennsylvania. A bellboy in Allentown disarmed my wrath once when I had been ringing for him in vain for an hour, with "Was yu bellin' for me? I didn't hear it make." I knew him then as coming from my people. His father would probably say, cocking his weather eye, "It looks for rain. I'm sure it's going to make something down." Or his mother, pricing at market, would ask, "For what do you sell your chickens at? I want to wonder. I feel for getting that fat one." Your washer-woman with all the deference in the world will refer to your husband and hers: "Does your Charlie like his shirt ironed? My mister don't."[49]

Martin's depictions of Pennsylvania Dutch and their "queer speech," which became familiar across America in the early decades of the twentieth century, fed the misguided belief that Pennsylvania Dutch was not so much a distinct language as a bizarre form of English. But for those curious outsiders who knew that the Pennsylvania Dutch spoke a German-derived language, the fanciful notions about their mangled English fed the long-standing view, going back to the very genesis of Pennsylvania Dutch, that the language was similarly garbled German.

Helen R. Martin's works appeared just at the time that tourism in America was becoming a leisure activity for people of average means, not just the wealthy. The Ford Model T was introduced in 1908, and the second and third decades of the twentieth century witnessed the rapid increase in personal mobility through affordable automobiles and a network of highways on which to drive them. Pennsylvania's Dutch Country, especially Lancaster County, is still today an easy day's drive for travelers from large urban centers such as New York, Philadelphia, and Baltimore. Although Martin's novels were not solely responsible for the development of Dutch-themed tourism in Pennsylvania, they certainly whetted the appetites of visitors to the Dutch Country. By the 1930s a number of popular stereotypes about the Pennsylvania Dutch coalesced into a tourist's canon of sorts. These included the notion that most Pennsylvania Dutch were either Mennonites or Amish who dressed distinctively, ate specific foods, and spoke in a humorous way. Further, it was believed that the Pennsylvania Dutch were profoundly superstitious, practicing forms of witchcraft (*Hexerei*), weather prognostication, and traditional healing arts (powwowing, *Braucherei*), as well as painting decorative symbols on their barns ("hex signs") to ward off evil spirits.[50] These stereotypes were shaped by an emerging body of popular literature that went beyond the Dutch-themed fiction of authors such as Helen R. Martin and purported to present the facts of Pennsylvania Dutch life and culture, including their language, in an objective way.

For many years, the most prolific and successful popular writer on Pennsylvania Dutch cultural topics was a Harrisburg bookseller-publisher and native Dutchman named A. Monroe Aurand Jr. (1895–1956).[51] Aurand's publications ranged widely, from *The Animal Nature of Man, or Modern Laws on Public Morals and Decency* to *Little Known Facts about the Witches in Our Hair* to *The Privy Builder and the Art of*

Wiping, but most dealt with Pennsylvania Dutch history and culture, especially themes related to witchcraft (including powwowing) and bundling (more formally known as "bed courtship," which Aurand called "America's greatest indoor sport").[52] In 1939 Aurand brought out two pamphlets on language: *Pennsylvania-German Dialect: Stories and Poems* and *Quaint Idioms and Expressions of the Pennsylvania Germans.*[53]

Unlike his writings on witchcraft and bundling, which clearly cross the line from folklore into *fakelore,*[54] what Aurand wrote about Pennsylvania Dutch verbal behavior is overall not too far from what is known today to be accurate. For example, in *Pennsylvania-German Dialect* his account of the historical development and maintenance of Pennsylvania Dutch is largely correct, and he does not fall victim to describing it as a German-English mishmash.[55] Most of this pamphlet is devoted to a sampling of good quality Pennsylvania Dutch prose and poetry, though one poem, the anonymously authored "En Drawm" (A dream), subtitled "A Song on 'Bundling,' " notably reflects Aurand's fascination with bed courtship. Aurand also includes a good translation into Pennsylvania Dutch of President Lincoln's Gettysburg Address ('M President Lincoln Si Dedication Address) that he made himself:

Sivva und auchtzich yohr tzurick hen unser fodder uf den neue welt 'n neue lond-lite foregabrucht, in freiheit aw-g'fonga und g'dedicate tzu de gadonka os de lite oll gleich g'maucht wara.

Fourscore and seven years ago our fathers brought forth upon this continent a new nation, conceived in Liberty, and dedicated to the proposition that all men are created equal.[56]

In his *Quaint Idioms and Expressions,* Aurand built on the well-established popular belief that Pennsylvania Dutch people spoke "broken" English. While it is quite likely that at least some of what he wrote was derived from his direct observations as a native Dutchman, the overall picture he painted was intended more to entertain than to inform. Although not a linguist, Aurand did make some sociolinguistically valid observations about Pennsylvania Dutch bilingual behavior, but they almost inevitably were put in such a way that objective information was embellished or distorted for entertainment purposes. The following is excerpted from the first section of *Quaint Idioms*, which is titled "On Making Ourselves Understood!":

> While it may be a novelty to hear Pennsylvania-Germans speak in the "dialect," it is no less entertaining to hear, shall we say, two such women, who might perchance be gossips, speaking in their rural English, occasionally including one, or perhaps several of those odd words that seemingly have no orthodox origin.
>
> Surely some of these, when used in conversation in a community where they are understood, find their usage justified—especially when to all intents and purposes they express so much better than English or German, what the speakers have in mind.[57]

Aurand divides his examples of "quaint idioms and expressions" into three types: (a) Pennsylvania Dutch words directly borrowed into English, (b) words and idioms that may or may not be the result of Dutch influence ("Just Poor English, That's All"), and (c) random expressions of excitement ("The 'Dutch' Will Come Out"). Most of the featured words in all three sections are embedded in sample sentences, which are, for the most part, intended to be humorous. In the first section, he offers these examples:

> That fellow is the darndest BLABBERMAUL (talkative)—he sure takes the cake.

> FERSHITT (to spill, or spilled), as you will note, is not corrupt; but it is used frequently to express other ideas—as "darn" is synonymous for "damn."

> Whack him good on his HINNERDALE (hinder part). "Hinnerdale" is used frequently in conversation.[58]

Aurand includes these examples of "poor English" in the second part:

> It wasn't in print ANYMORE in 1928.

> I BACH myself. (I am a bachelor; I live alone).

You MIND (recall) old Fenstermacher? He was at Ensminger's STILL (formerly).[59]

Even the most far-fetched depictions of Dutchified English, such as those of Aurand and even Helen R. Martin, are of interest to dialectologists, as they often contain examples of nonstandard forms that were and in some cases still are found in regional varieties of American English; the use of *anymore* and *still* above are examples, as well as *darst*, 'permission', in the excerpt from Martin's *Tillie* quoted above.

The proliferation of fakelore in literature available to visitors to the Dutch Country, especially as pertained to the Amish, was one major motivation for three gifted young scholars who were also native Pennsylvania Dutchmen—Alfred L. Shoemaker (1913–?)[60] and J. William Frey (1916–1989), both of Franklin and Marshall College in Lancaster, and Don Yoder (1921–2015), later of the University of Pennsylvania—to found the Pennsylvania Dutch Folklore Center (PDFC) in 1949, which was based at Franklin and Marshall. Among the center's most notable achievements was the publication of the *Pennsylvania Dutchman* newspaper (later *Pennsylvania Folklife* magazine) in 1949, which was named after Edward H. Rauch's short-lived publication of 1873, and the founding of the Pennsylvania Dutch Folk Festival in Kutztown, Berks County, the following year. While the center, and especially Shoemaker, took great pains to present a more accurate picture of Pennsylvania Dutch language and culture than the one A. M. Aurand and others were selling, the pressure to actually participate in the commodification process already underway was difficult to withstand. Aurand became a particular lightning rod for the ire of two of the PDFC's founding codirectors, Shoemaker and Frey. Shoemaker, for example, wrote of Aurand, "There is no one in America who has done as great a disservice to the Pennsylvania Dutch country . . . as has he."[61] Unfortunately, some of the PDFC's own publications on language only added to the lighthearted image of the bilingual behavior of the Pennsylvania Dutch perpetuated by Aurand and the tea-towel and switch-plate manufacturers in the burgeoning Dutch-themed tourist industry.[62]

In 1951 J. William Frey produced a pamphlet titled *That* Amazing *Pennsylvania Dutch Language*. The title page introduces "a description of the most expressive tongue in the world, including some of its outstanding features, unlimited freedoms, unique idioms, borrowings from English, and a modest supply of cuss words." To be sure, Frey is one of the most important figures in the history of serious Pennsylvania Dutch linguistics, and this pamphlet contains much important and accurate information on the origins, development, and use of Pennsylvania Dutch.[63] His corrective to popular misunderstandings about the relationship between English and Pennsylvania Dutch, for example, is grounded in solid linguistic scholarship, pointing out that the German spoken in Europe is just as susceptible to "foreign" influences, if not more so, than Pennsylvania Dutch is in America:

> Pennsylvania Dutch, having been located in an English-speaking territory for over 250 years, has naturally absorbed some words from that language. But this fact enhances the beauty and quaintness of the language, rather than corrupts it. Sometime, somewhere, somebody spread the vicious rumor that Pennsylvania Dutch was simply broken English spoken by a group of ignorant farmers who threw in a German word now and then for the heck of it. We would like to hold a conversation in Pennsylvania Dutch with the nitwit who made such claims—we are sure we could buy him and sell him before he knew it! The use of English words in Pennsylvania Dutch is done quite naturally and without any sort of affectation. This is not true of a single other language. Take English, for example, in which a French or Spanish word is employed with a dramatic air, an overstrained pronunciation and is always put on a pedestal in writing by being placed between quotation marks. In German this disease is worse—Germans riddle their speech and printed pages with scores of French words and expressions. History tells us that they imitated French for a 100 years back in the 17th and 18th centuries. This has left its mark today, though few Germans will admit it. Nevertheless, I'll wager that a one-hour conversation in Pennsylvania Dutch with someone who really speaks the language well will not contain nearly so many English words as you would find French words in a similar conversation in German.[64]

Frey's remarks are grounded in linguistic-scientific reality, yet the scholarly substance of his booklet is difficult to discern amid the humor that at points exceeds even what is found in Aurand's writings, as the example below, taken from a section titled "Different Terms for the Same Thing," shows:

The potatoes are ALL!

Hér hair are so shtroovly!

That *Amazing*
Pennsylvania Dutch
Language

By

J. William Frey

Konsht du Deitsh shwetza?

Du dummer aisel!

Nix-kooma-rous

Ya, ferdommt-sei!

Dunnerwedder noach a-mole!

Don't rootch off your chair!

Cover of *That* Amazing *Pennsylvania Dutch Language.*
Source: Frey 1951.

But this example [words for a "sowbug"] does not demonstrate the freedom of expression nearly so well as do the various terms for the oil-gland,
or uropygial gland of the chicken—that's the part, you know, in which
the tail feathers are stuck, or we say, "the piece that went over the fence
last!" Very well, here's what you may call it in Pennsylvania Dutch: TSIP-
PEL, BOTZEL, SHWONS-GRIP, SHMELS-PON, AIL-KENNLY, AIL-
KEVVICH, AIL-TSEPPLY, FETT-SHNEPPEL, SHMOOTZ-HEFFLY,

SHMOOTZ-KENNLY, FETT-HEFFLY, FETT-PON, SHNEVLY, and last but by no means last, POOP-NOCKER!!![65]

Frey concludes his pamphlet by arguing that, in light of the numerous "virtues and possibilities" of Pennsylvania Dutch, the language should be adopted, Esperanto-style, as "the universal language." Musing about how United Nations gatherings would proceed if this were to happen, Frey states, "One good barnyard story at the beginning of each meeting would give all members a hearty laugh and a good send-off for better understanding among themselves!"[66]

The humorous excesses in Frey's 1951 pamphlet aside, the PDFC made impressive attempts to offset the ubiquitous fakelore served up to tourists, which paved the way for other scholars similarly concerned with dispelling popular misunderstandings about Pennsylvania Dutch culture, especially the Amish. A contemporary of Shoemaker, Yoder, and Frey, for example, John A. Hostetler (1918–2001), a sociologist at Temple University in Philadelphia who grew up in an Amish family and played a leading role in the emergence of the modern field of Amish studies, published a popularly accessible pamphlet on the Amish in 1952.[67] In 1954, the PDFC began producing substantial tourist guides to the Dutch Country that contained several short essays on various aspects of Pennsylvania Dutch culture, including language. "The Dutch Tongue," apparently written by Alfred L. Shoemaker, clarifies many of the most prevalent myths about Pennsylvania Dutch and Dutchified English in a single page:

The tourist will encounter three types of Dutch in the Pennsylvania Dutch Country: 1) Pennsylvania Dutch, the dialect brought to Pennsylvania from the Palatinate between 1683 and the time of the Revolutionary War; 2) Pennsylvania Dutch English, the English with a heavy accent, spoken by those Pennsylvanians whose everyday language is still the Pennsylvania Dutch dialect; and 3) Tourist Dutch, a much distorted Pennsylvania Dutch English which was invented in the past ten to fifteen years to make "Amish Stuff" more palatable to the tourist-buying public. Remember, then, as you pick up the thousand and one Dutch gift items flooding the Pennsylvania countryside that Tourist Dutch is not a spoken language, but the brain child of the bric-a-brac manufacturers. You see there is a strong belief in certain circles that the queerer the Dutch can be made out to be, the easier it will be to extract the tourist dollar.[68]

Shoemaker's essay goes on to give specific examples of fanciful Tourist Dutch (e.g., "Pop's on the table and half et already") and compares them to the much less exotic reality of Dutchified English, including Dutch loanwords in Pennsylvania English—*spritz*, 'to water', and *all*, 'all gone'—and loan translations such as "Eat your mouth empty before you say something." Concluding his brief description of the linguistic reality of the Dutch Country, Shoemaker provides a sample of actual Pennsylvania Dutch, "a dignified language that has been the cradle tongue of millions of Americans—of the Hoovers and the Eisenhowers—from Colonial times to the present," an original folk rhyme:

> Der monn un der hund kaira nouse,
> Der monn fer shoffa
> Der hund fer bloffa.
> De fraw un de kotz kaira ins house,
> De fraw fer housa
> De kotz fer mousa.

> *A husband and dog belong in the barn,*
> *the husband to work*
> *and the dog to bark.*
> *A wife and a cat belong in the house,*
> *the wife to keep house*
> *and the cat to catch mice.*[69]

Shoemaker, Yoder, and Frey aimed to combine scholarly research with public outreach, an unusual and forward-looking orientation for academics of their generation. They were part of a cohort of young scholars who not only grew up in Pennsylvania Dutch families but also pursued careers in the nascent field of Pennsylvania Dutch studies. Two of these founders of the Pennsylvania Dutch Folklore Center, Shoemaker and Frey, wrote their doctoral dissertations on the Pennsylvania Dutch language, both, coincidentally, at the University of Illinois. Shoemaker's thesis, completed in 1940, was a pioneering study of a midwestern Pennsylvania Dutch variety spoken by Old Order Amish in Arthur, IL.[70] Frey, a native of eastern York County, PA, finished his dissertation on the Pennsylvania Dutch of that region one year after Shoemaker, in 1941.[71]

A contemporary of Shoemaker, Yoder, and Frey, who also was a native speaker and concentrated his PhD research on the Pennsylvania Dutch language, was Albert F. Buffington (1905–1980), who did his graduate work at Harvard University and taught at Penn State University.[72] Among Buffington's achievements was coauthoring a grammar of Pennsylvania Dutch in 1965 with Preston A. Barba (1883–1971), a professor of Pennsylvania German language and literature for nearly three decades at Muhlenberg College. Barba's signature contribution to Pennsylvania Dutch studies was founding and editing 'S Pennsylfawnisch Deitsch Eck (The Pennsylvania German corner), a weekly column devoted to the language, history, and culture of the Pennsylvania Dutch that appeared weekly from 1935 to 1969 in the Allentown *Morning Call*.[73] The Eck, which was revived in 1975 by C. Richard Beam (b. 1925), a former student of Buffington's and a professor of German at Millersville (PA) University, became a leading outlet for quality work in and on Pennsylvania Dutch.[74]

Pennsylvania Dutch Present Their Language and Culture to the Public

The passion that Shoemaker, Yoder, Frey, Buffington, Barba, and Beam brought to their scholarship and to their public work on behalf of the culture and language of the Pennsylvania Dutch was kindled early in their lives, growing up as they did in Dutch communities. Their ethnic loyalty, however, never compromised the quality of their scholarship; they were participant-observer researchers whose work advanced the frontiers of academic research and simultaneously helped elevate public respect for American vernacular culture generally. Their way had been paved in the previous century by Edward H. Rauch, the first native Dutchman whom one could consider to be a kind of grassroots advocate for his heritage language. Whereas the production of prose and poetry in Pennsylvania Dutch was an *a*vocation for most Pennsylvania Dutch writers, for Rauch such work was part of his *v*ocation, a calling to promote publicly the language of his people.

A clear expression of Rauch's sympathies lay in his use of *Pennsylvania Dutch* over *Pennsylvania German* when referring to the language. Rauch notably advocated for this preference at a gathering in the city of Lancaster on February 26, 1891, of sixteen representatives from the various Pennsylvania counties with substantial Pennsylvania Dutch populations to plan the "preliminary organization of a Pennsylvania German Society."[75] Rauch, a resident of Mauch Chunk (today, Jim Thorpe), represented Carbon County; among the other delegates was Abraham Reeser Horne, one of two representatives from Lehigh County. One of the various questions discussed at that planning meeting was what to call the organization. Only Rauch is on record for supporting naming it the Pennsylvania Dutch Society. All others, Horne included, thought that Pennsylvania German Society was more appropriate. The society, which was formally inaugurated on April 15, 1891, was not motivated to refer to itself as *German* out of a desire to align itself with European German culture; membership in the society was explicitly limited to those whose German and Swiss ancestors had settled in Pennsylvania before 1800. Rather, the ostensible justification for the use of *German* rather than *Dutch* in the organization's name was historical clarity; in the words of the Reverend E. K. Levan, of Luzerne County, "In literature we are spoken of as descendants of Germans and not the Dutch."[76]

A deeper reason for the choice of *Pennsylvania German* over *Pennsylvania Dutch* in the name of the newly formed society, which still exists today, had to do with the makeup of its membership and their attitudes toward the Pennsylvania Dutch language. To a man, the founding members of the society were educated professionals, mainly clergymen, jurists, and editors whose primary interest was the promotion of an appreciation for the noteworthy achievements of "the Pennsylvania German-Swiss element" in American history. They cared little about the language and everyday culture of the majority of their rurally dwelling kin. Yet Edward H. Rauch, despite his status as a journalist and editor, never lost the connection to his humbler roots, hence his consistent preference for *Pennsylvania Dutch*.

At the founding meeting of the Pennsylvania German Society on April 15, 1891, Rauch was one of two speakers to address the gathering in Pennsylvania Dutch, the second being Henry Lee Fisher, who recited a poem. Rauch's speech, titled "De Olta un Neia Tzeita" (The old and new times), which he regularly delivered at public gatherings in southeastern

Pennsylvania, stood out from the others not only for the language in which it was presented but also for its content. After a number of formal addresses and discussion of business matters in English, the seventy-year-old Rauch rose to speak, beginning as follows:

Ich con on nix bessers denka os a pawr wardt sawga weaga de olta un neia tzeita. Suppose mer mista now widder tzurick gæ ivver fooftzich yohr, un laiva we sellamohls? Denk a mohl drau, ainer het business in Pittsburg, un mist dort si in dri odder feer dawg. Ar kent's net du in wennicher os sex dawg in der stage we se ols gatraveled sin sellamohls. Un suppose eber het in sella dawga bahawpt os de tzeit yeamohls coomd wann ainer mit feer odder finf hoonert onnera, all in ainer foor ob shtarta con fun doh om sivva uhr ovets, un im same grossa foorwaisa, os runn'd ona geil, ins bet gæ, un goot shlofa, un der naigsht morya om sivva uhr uf wecka un grawd ous der foor in de shtadt Pittsburg shteppa, . . . un ins grose wærtshouse, esst'n morya-essa un don si bisness tenda in a pawr shtund, un d'no widder in der shteam foor tzurick un by siner fraw un fomelia aw landa un si naucht essa nemma derhame alles inside fun feer un tzwansich shtoond! Wann aner for fooftsich yohr tzurick contend het os mer yeamohls so travella con, sex, odder sivva hoonert mile in ame dawg, so ainer hetta se grawd ei gshpart im norra house.

I can think of nothing better than to say a few words about the old and new times. Suppose one would now have to go back more than fifty years and live as in those days? Think about it, one would have business in Pittsburgh and have to be there in three or four days. He wouldn't be able to do it in less than six days on the stagecoach, as they used to travel back then. And suppose someone would have claimed back then that the time would ever come when one could leave from here at seven in the evening with four or five hundred others in the same carriage, and in the same big carriage that runs without horses, go to bed and sleep well and wake up the next morning at eleven o'clock and step right out of the carriage in the city of Pittsburgh and into the big tavern, eat breakfast and then attend to his business in a couple of hours, and then head back in the steam carriage and get back home to his wife and family and eat supper all in less than twenty-four hours! If somebody had contended fifty years ago that one could ever travel that way, six or seven hundred miles in a single day, right away they would have locked him up in the insane asylum.[77]

In his speech, Rauch goes on to wax nostalgic about the old days, when a jigger of decent whiskey cost just three cents, people had less money and fewer material possessions yet still lived well, and there were no thieves in elected offices. And then Rauch takes direct aim at "the exceedingly intelligent people who speak only English" (*de ivver ous shmarta leit os yusht English shwetza*). Where do they live? In miserable places like New Jersey (*drunna in der Jrsey*), where the only crops one can raise are weeds and cobblestones, and livestock consists of opossums, owls, rattlesnakes, and hogs that are so skinny one has to tie knots in their tails to keep them from slipping under the door into the house. In places like New Jersey, Rauch continues, there are no "dumb or clumsy Dutchmen" (*dumma odder dobbicha Deitsha*), just "well behaved and intelligent" (*hoch awrtich un shmart*) people who speak English. Rauch ends his remarks by saying that he is not the least bit ashamed when a skinny, pathetic "dude" accuses him of being nothing more than "a common Pennsylvania Dutchman" (*'n commoner Pennsylvania Deitsher*).

There is no record of how the English-speaking "dudes" who heard Rauch's remarks reacted. The next speaker to ascend the rostrum was Col. Thomas C. Zimmerman, from Reading, who delivered a speech titled "Puritan and Cavalier? Why Not the Pennsylvania-German?" This was the only address at the meeting other than Rauch's that made any mention of language. Several minutes into his remarks, Zimmerman said the following:

[L]ittle can be said in favor of the perpetuation of the Pennsylvania-German dialect. In other words, notwithstanding the extraordinary vitality of the vernacular, which has survived the wreck of centuries, there need be no undue solicitude about its gradual, but ultimate disappearance from the languages of the earth. Its somewhat limited capabilities have been fully tested by Harbaugh, Fisher, Rauch and others, all of whose writings show that while the dialect is ample for the ordinary needs of expression, from its inherent limitations it lacks compass and flexibility. But the compulsory teaching of English in our public schools must eventually displace it as a medium of intercourse, even in this section where its lodgment has been so deep-seated and its use so general.

While I yield to none in reverence for the associations of childhood—and the Pennsylvania-German dialect is interwoven with every warp and woof of my early days—and while admitting the value of the vernacular as a help to the understanding of the pure German, with opportunities for appropriating something from its store-house filled with treasures of human intelligence, it is not a growing indifference to its merits which prompts me to say that, in the category of living tongues, it should take its place as a purely secondary lingual accomplishment.[78]

Zimmerman's favorable attitude toward the eventual disappearance of Pennsylvania Dutch was one widely held by the society's membership for many years. Eventually, though, the organization opened its membership to nonethnic Pennsylvania Dutch and came to appreciate the value of the language as a vital part of the cultural heritage of its speakers.[79]

Although Rauch's sympathies toward the Pennsylvania Dutch language were evidently not shared by the broader membership of the Pennsylvania German Society, that did not deter Rauch from continuing to take a public stand in defense of his beloved mother tongue. On March 22, 1891, the *Philadelphia Inquirer*, which had endorsed the idea of the Pennsylvania German Society, reprinted three short articles from other sources under the title "Pennsylvania Dutch: How the Language Is Still Growing." One of these items referred to plans to found the Pennsylvania German Society in Lancaster. Another was drawn from the *Easton Express*, a newspaper published in Northampton County, which borders on Lehigh and Carbon Counties:

Last week a Pennsylvania Dutch Literary Society was organized at Mauch Chunk by prominent citizens of that place. This is a literary society of a new kind. Everything was done in the Pennsylvania German—or Dutch, as they insist upon it up there—language. Naturally there was a strong influence of English, in sentences of Parliamentary phraseology. For instance, a motion to appoint the committee on by-laws was made and disposed of substantially in this form, as given by the Mauch Chunk *Democrat*:

"Mr. President, ich move for'n committee appointa for 'n constitution un by-laws prepara un reporta on der naigsht meeting."

"Ich second de motion," came from another voice.

Then, by the president—"Es is gamoved un g'second 'n committee tzu appointa for 'n constitution un by-laws prepara un reporta an der naigsht meeting. Is de society ready for de froke? All os in favor sin fun der motion sawg yaw." All responding in the affirmative, the president announced the result: "De majority sawga yaw, un de motion is g'dopt."

The *Express* article goes on to defend Pennsylvania Dutch against the familiar criticism that the language borrowed words from English by pointing out that English does precisely the same thing, incorporating loanwords derived from Latin and Greek. As it happens, all but two of the seventeen English loans in the discourse quoted from the Mauch Chunk meeting—*president, move, committee, appoint, constitution, bylaw, prepare, report, second, motion, society, favor, majority,* and *adopt*—are themselves borrowings in English (all are Latinate, except for *bylaw,* which is of Norse provenance); only *meeting* and *ready* are of native Anglo-Saxon stock. The article concludes by declaring the value of Pennsylvania Dutch for philological scholarship as "the linguistic wonder for the age" and "the best language ever used by man." There is no doubt that Edward H. Rauch was the driving force behind the creation of this group in Mauch Chunk (he was also the editor of the *Democrat* referred to above), which occurred between the planning meeting for the Pennsylvania German Society on February 26 and its actual founding on April 15. Unfortunately, there is no indication that Rauch's Pennsylvania Dutch Literary Society ever got off the ground.

Some four-plus decades after the founding of the Pennsylvania German Society (and Rauch's short-lived rival organization), in the 1930s nonsectarian Pennsylvania Dutch who shared Rauch's ardor for their vernacular language moved to rectify its neglect in the public sphere. A major turning point occurred in 1933, when the first Pennsylvania Dutch fersommling (gathering, meeting) was held in Selinsgrove, Snyder County. Still a fixture on the Pennsylvania Dutch folk cultural landscape some eighty years later, fersommling is an umbrella term that describes a number of different types of events devoted to bringing together Pennsylvania Dutch speakers in celebration of their language and culture.[80]

Among the most notable of the fersommlinge are the *Grundsow* (Groundhog) Lodges, all-male fraternal organizations whose members gather annually on or around February 2, Groundhog Day.[81] In an early study of fersommlinge, Alvin F. Kemp (1896–1961), who himself was a founding member (in 1937) and president of the Berks County fersommling in Reading, identified seven objectives of fersommlinge, which are quoted here:

1. A night of wholesome entertainment.
2. A substantial Pennsylvania "Dutch" meal.
3. Familiarity with Pennsylvania German history and traditions.
4. Appreciation of Pennsylvania German folklore.
5. A renewal of pride in the soul of the Pennsylvania Germans.
6. Curbing of unjust and undeserved criticism of writers and speakers.
7. Revitalization of the Pennsylvania German language.[82]

Originally, all fersommling activities were to be conducted strictly in Pennsylvania Dutch; use of "literary 'High German'" or English was prohibited, with violators often receiving a ticket, such as the one below, for infractions. Today, as the number of fluent nonsectarian Pennsylvania Dutch speakers dwindles (sectarians avoid participation in fersommlinge), such a rule is becoming increasingly difficult to enforce.

The Pennsylvania Dutch language has always figured prominently in all major elements of a fersommling program. Every address, including the main speech after the meal, is entirely in Pennsylvania Dutch, as are all items on the menu (*Fuder Tzettle*, lit. '[animal] feed broadside'), many of which have creative (nonliteral) translations, such as *Appedit Macher*,

---

Tza Sent Resade

Die-Der ——————————————————————————

ISS NET FULSHDENSICH DEITSH

Ar hut sich fershnopt on d'
**Pennsylfawnish Deitsh Fersommling un hut tzu
fiel English g'shwetzt**

Citation for speaking English at a *fersommling*.
Translation: *Ten Cent Receipt / [Name] / is not completely Dutch. / Er got caught at the*
— */ Pennsylvania Dutch fersommling and / spoke too much English.*
Source: Kemp 1946, 215.

'appetizer' (lit. 'appetite maker'); *'M Adam Sei Unnergong,* 'apple dessert' (lit. 'Adam's downfall'); *Uff Shtose Mints,* 'after dinner mints' (lit. 'burp mints'); *Bauch Dicher* or *Bobierna Schlower Dicher,* 'napkins' (lit. 'belly cloths', 'paper slobber cloths'); and *Tzae Blicker,* 'toothpicks' (lit. 'teeth pickers'). Other examples of creatively translated material include the Pledge of Allegiance (*Versprechnis zum Flag,* lit. 'promise to the flag') and the lyrics of the patriotic song "America," which was rendered into Pennsylvania Dutch by the poet John Birmelin (1873–1950) and is sung at nearly every fersommling.

Mei Land, ich sing fun dir,	*My country, I sing of you,*
Siess is die freiheet mir,	*Sweet is freedom to me,*
Do will ich sei;	*Here is where I want to be;*
So wie die alde leit,	*Just like the old folks,*
So fiel ich aw noch heit,	*I still feel that way today,*
Bin dir tzu yader zeit	*I am to you at all times*
Immer gedrei.	*Always faithful.*

Like Birmelin's "America," most fersommling songs are popular American songs translated into Pennsylvania Dutch—but always creatively, that is, not literally, thereby allowing the translator to produce texts that are original and appropriate to a Pennsylvania Dutch cultural context; examples include "O Bolly Melinda" ('O Polly Melinda' = "Sweet Rosie O'Grady"), "Dot Geht Da Kauder" ('There Goes the Tomcat' = "Pop Goes the Weasel"), and "D'haem Uff Die Alt Bauerei" ('Home on the Old Farm' = "Home on the Range"). Other fersommling songs are "Dutchified German spirituals," nineteenth-century gospel hymns set to German texts that are heavily influenced by Pennsylvania Dutch, such as "Ich Brauch Dich Alle Schtunn" ("I Need Thee Every Hour") and "Naycher Mei Gott Zu Dir" ("Nearer, My God, to Thee").[83] There are also a handful of songs of European German origin that were originally familiar among German Americans and that then became popular among other Americans, including the Pennsylvania Dutch, such as "Du, Du Liegst Mir im Herzen" ('You, you lie in my heart') and "Die Schnitzel Bonk" (Ger. "Die Schnitzelbank," 'The whittling bench').

The strict upholding of a Pennsylvania Dutch–only rule at fersommlinge fostered linguistic creativity among the various writers who composed texts for popular American (including German American) songs. Such creativity reached its zenith in the focal point of a fersommling, the main speech, "'S Fesht Rade" (The festival speech). The structure and content of many of these speeches are not unlike what is found in Rauch's "De Olta un Neia Tzeita," which made sharp observations about life from the vantage point of Pennsylvania Dutch culture, delivered in a lighthearted way. Russell Wieder Gilbert (1905–1985), one of the early leaders in the fersommling movement and a German professor for forty years at Susquehanna University,[84] describes the importance of the Pennsylvania Dutch language as a rhetorical vehicle in fersommling speeches:

> Most speeches at the *Versammlinge* have a distinct conversational quality; after all, dialect is essentially spoken language. Historical facts, customs, folklore, mores, the humorous and the serious, fun and home-spun philosophy are cleverly woven into the fabric of the speeches. Sometimes the conversational trend turns into an oratorical glorification of Pennsylvania German greatness or into an emotional appeal to reminiscence and moral principles. The dialect hardly leans toward heaviness of structure, artificiality, exhibitionism, or clumsy cluttering of words, but rather lends a naturalness of manner, a simplicity of form, a succinctness and forcefulness of expression, and genuine strength through portrayal in connotative terms. True and fictional humor visualize for the listener the original story or idea.[85]

Gilbert's insights capture the essence of Pennsylvania Dutch literature from its beginnings, as reflected in the poems of Henry Harbaugh and those after him who produced hundreds of works of poetry and prose dealing with every aspect of Pennsylvania Dutch life, past and present. And like Pennsylvania Dutch prose and poetry, fersommling speeches, though publicly presented, still have the quality of private discourse: they are produced by Pennsylvania Dutch people for their fellow Pennsylvania Dutch. Outsiders, be they English or German speakers, are not intended to be privy to these conversations. Gilbert notes further:

> Almost automatically, the use of dialect creates a positive speaker-audience relationship. Dialect is superlatively closer to the soil than the literary language. The conversational and colloquial quality, difficult to

translate, produces a cordiality and unanimity of feeling unprecedented in speech annals. The bond between speakers and listeners is perfect. Try to sell a Pennsylvania German something in English, and mistrust may forbid the sale. The companionship of the dialect will warm the cockles of his heart. Ideas glorifying Pennsylvania German accomplishments in his own *Mundart*, simple, unhewn, and unsophisticated, can engender uncommon enthusiasm for even the commonplace.[86]

What Gilbert says of the atmosphere created by fersommling speeches just as accurately characterizes the intimate bond between any two individuals speaking Pennsylvania Dutch to each other. Use of the Pennsylvania Dutch language, in whatever medium, connotes emotional intimacy and trust.

Few complete transcripts of fersommling speeches were ever published. One exception, however, is an address made by Harry Hess Reichard (1878–1956), a native Dutchman and professor of German at Muhlenberg College from 1924 to 1948, whose scholarly achievements in the documentation of Pennsylvania Dutch literature are of singular importance.[87] Reichard was also active in the Grundsow Lodges, and on February 2, 1951, he delivered the main address at the Grundsow Lodge *Nummer Drei* (number three), which met at Temple University in Philadelphia. His remarks were published in full in Preston Barba's Pennsylfawnisch Deitsch Eck in the Allentown *Morning Call* on February 27, 1954. Reichard's speech was titled "Die Wedderberichte" (The weather reports) and dealt with the central symbol of the Grundsow movement, and of nonsectarian Pennsylvania Dutch culture more generally, the groundhog. Whereas the bald eagle is considered an appropriate emblem of the United States for its "majestic beauty, great strength, and long life,"[88] the lowly groundhog evokes a blend of humility and native intelligence. He is a "weather prophet" whose knowledge is derived not from book learning but from his proximity to the earth. A Pennsylvania Dutch poet from Montgomery County, Henry C. Detweiler, expresses the traditional affection for the groundhog in his poem "Oh Du Grundsow" (Oh, you groundhog), to be sung to the tune of "Oh, Susanna":

Do is en shai Farsommeling.   *This is a nice fersommling.*
  Do hucka mir all rum,   *Here we all sit around together,*
All Pennsylfawnisch Deitscha Leit.   *All Pennsylvania Dutch people.*

Mir gooka net so dum.	*We don't look so dumb.*
Mir hen en shaine Grundsow Lodge.	*We have a nice Grundsow Lodge.*
Mir wissa aw ferwos.	*We also know why.*
Mir macha net en langes G'sicht.	*We don't make long faces.*
Mir gleicha wenich G'shposs.	*We like a little fun.*

Chorus:

Oh du Grundsow,	*Oh, you Groundhog,*
Du bisht unser Brofate.	*You are our prophet.*
Du saicht uns was es Wedder gebt.	*You tell us what the weather will be.*
Ebs reggert oder schnate.	*Whether it will rain or snow.*

Dar Weddermon is net feel vart.	*The weather man isn't worth much.*
Fum Wedder vase ar Nix.	*About the weather he knows nothing.*
Von mir usht uf een haricha date,	*If we would just listen to him,*
Don wair mir in ra Fix.	*Then we'd be in a fix.*
Mir wissa vas die Grundsow saicht,	*We know what the groundhog says,*
Un vas os sie baricht.	*And what it reports.*
Mir halta sie in grosse Ehr.	*We hold it in high honor.*
Farfaila dut sie nicht.	*It never fails.*[89]

Reichard's audience at the Philadelphia lodge, because of its location at Temple University, had a more intellectually inclined membership than lodges in the rural Dutch hinterlands. Addressing his "dear Brother Groundhogs" (*liewe Brieder Grundsei*),[90] Reichard recounts the history of weather prognostication, beginning in the Garden of Eden, when Farmer Adam paused from his ploughing to gaze up at the sky, wondering whether the nice weather would hold until he had sown his oats or whether it would rain just after he had gotten his field ready to plant potatoes. Then, striking a more scholarly tone, Reichard reminds his audience that in those days all humans were farmers, shepherds, or hunters whose very livelihoods depended on their ability to read the signs of nature in order to know what the weather would be. Likewise, animals learned to become weather prophets, sharing their wisdom with humans, including with "a smart old Jew" (Noah) who correctly predicted forty days and nights of bad weather, thereby saving the human race.

Reichard goes on to enumerate twenty different signs (*Zeeche*) related to weather prognostication derived from the work of "an old Greek high school teacher" (*en alder griechischer Hochschul-meeschder*), Aristotle.[91] And none other than Jesus, Reichard points out, had the ability to predict meteorological phenomena, quoting the Luther German versions of Matthew 16:2–3 and Luke 12:54–55. Reichard then adds the following aside:

Des hot nau net graad ebbes zu duh mit der Widdering, awwer die Schtelle aus der Biwel warre alsemol aagfiehrt fer weise, ass Jesus Deitsch gschwetzt hot. Ennihau, ich hab sie eich yuscht vorgelese aus em Nei Teschtament, wu's gsaat hot "und er antwortete und sprach" un noh geht's weider in Deitsch. Un wann Jesus Deitsch gschwetzt hot, dann denk ich, dutt er aa Pennsylveeni Deitsch verschteh. Un Parre Slifer, waar's net zu dir ass selli alt deitsch Fraa ihre Biwel gebrocht hot un im aerschte Buch Mose, der 9t Vaerscht im 3te Kabittel gelese hot: "Und Gott der Herr rief Adam und sprach zu ihm, 'wo bist du?'" fer prufe, ass der liewe Gott aa Deitsch schwetzt? Ennihau, sell waar in der Biwel, waar's nau net?

Now this does not exactly have anything to do with the weather, but these passages from the Bible are sometimes quoted to show that Jesus spoke German. Anyway, I just read them to you from the New Testament, where it said "and he answered and said" and then it goes on in German. And if Jesus spoke German, then I guess he can understand Pennsylvania Dutch, too. And, Pastor Slifer [the president of the Grundsow Lodge at Temple University], wasn't it to you that that old Dutch woman brought her Bible and read in Genesis 3:9 "And the Lord God called to Adam and said to him 'Where are you?'" in order to prove that dear God also spoke German? Anyway, that was in the Bible, wasn't it?[92]

Reichard's lighthearted observation that God must have spoken German, since that is how he is quoted in the Luther Bible, is one still familiar to sectarians, who frequently hear Genesis 3:9 recited in church.[93]

Overall, the structure of Reichard's address is an excellent example of classic Pennsylvania Dutch oratorical (and literary) style. Beneath the at-times silly veneer of his remarks lies real substance, in this instance, the significance, both real and symbolic, of weather prognostication in traditional Pennsylvania Dutch culture. The leading researcher on fersommlinge, Kutztown University professor William W. Donner, compares gifted fersommling speakers, among whom Harry Hess Reichard can be counted, favorably to Will Rogers and Mark Twain, who similarly conveyed important messages in clever, homespun ways.

Orators as well those who present skits at fersommlinge are carrying on a tradition of dramatic performances in Pennsylvania Dutch that extend as far back as the early nineteenth century. Beginning in 1823, Hugh Lindsay (1804–1860), a Pennsylvanian of Scotch-Irish background who had learned Pennsylvania Dutch as a teenager by working on Pennsylvania Dutch farms, began presenting Punch and Judy–style puppet plays in Pennsylvania Dutch that were wildly popular in rural southeastern Pennsylvania for nearly a quarter century.[94] Two firsthand accounts of Lindsay and his performances exist, both by men who had seen Lindsay's shows as boys and later grew up, coincidentally, to become physicians and Pennsylvania Dutch authors, George Mays (1836–1909) and Ezra Grumbine (1845–1923).[95] Writing in 1909, Grumbine recalled:

[Lindsay] came to Fredericksburg [in Lebanon County] in the forties and fifties. His Punch and Judy puppets were Pennsylvania German characters, and were named Mr. and Mrs. Waffelbach, or as expressed in the vernacular, "der alt Waffelbach un' sei Fraw die alt Waffelbachsy." Lindsay was quite a ventriloquist and the coarse and often vulgar jokes he put into the mouths of his puppets were greatly enjoyed by the large crowds that gathered under his canvas. His tent was pitched on the Pine Grove Road, a short distance north of the easternmost hotel, then kept by John Foesig, on the occasion of his last visit to Fredericksburg in 1857.[96]

George Mays shares his memories of Linday's puppet shows in the form of an extended poem in Pennsylvania Dutch titled "Der Honsworsht" (The clown).[97] The following few verses describe the back and forth between Mr. and Mrs. Waffelbach:

Er bloudert feel fom Wofelboch,   *He chatted much about Waffelbach,*
(En alte un bekonde soch)   *(An old and familiar matter)*

Translation: *Third Annual Fersommling and Festival of Grundsow Lodge Number One on the Lehigh, Monday evening after Groundhog Day, at 6:30 p.m., February 3, 1936.*

Un seiner, wieschte behse frau,	*And his nasty, mean wife,*
Fom lezte immer naive drau.	*Of the wrong kind, always alongside.*

We ich mich nuch erinre duh,	*As I still recall,*
Hut selli frau net recht gedu	*That woman did not act right.*
Ich wehs der mon guckt uft ferschaicht	*I know, her husband often looked terrified*
Un scheind gons mechtich ufgeraicht.	*And seemed to be quite upset.*

So bol os ehr sei ricke wend	*As soon as he turned his back,*
Don hut si gleich sei naume g'nend	*Then she said his name right away.*
Ihr zung waar hinne un fonne los,	*Her tongue was loose in front and back,*
Un auge mocht si shrecklich gros.	*And she made her eyes scarily large.*

Saugt ehr, "Mer hehrt si meile weit	*He said, "You can hear her miles away*
Un mehnd si wehr yusht holver g'scheit.	*And you'd think she's not quite right.*
Un won mer denkt, now is si schdil	*And just when you thought, now she's quiet,*
Don kumt ufs frish sel same gebrill."	*The same roaring would start right up again."*

"Husht g'saugt won ich dich heire du'	*"You said that if I'd marry you,*
Don kumt mier olles guhte zu,	*Then everything good would come to me*
Breicht net im kolde wosser weshe,	*And I wouldn't need to wash in cold water.*
Ich hob sel au nuch net fergesse."	*I haven't forgotten that."*

"Yah well," saugt ehr, "Don mocht ders worm,	*"Fine," he said, "then warm yourself up,*
Wesht guht genunk ich bin zu orm	*You wash good enough, I'm too poor*
Epper zu kriege der immer,	*To get someone who will*
Olles bringe duht ins zimmer."	*Be a house-servant."*

Sel hut de rechte eidruck gmocht,	*That made the right impression,*
De crowd hut drivver shendlich g'locht	*The crowd laughed uproariously.*
Don jumpt si uf un ruld ihr aug,	*Then she jumped up and rolled her eye*
We'n g'schtuche kolb, so g'wiss ich saug.	*Like a stuck calf, I tell you truly.*[98]

In the latter decades of the nineteenth century, original plays in Pennsylvania Dutch were composed and performed. The first published Pennsylvania Dutch play was written by Ezra Grumbine in 1880 and was titled *Die Inschurens Bissness*.[99] The play, which Grumbine called a "serio-comic drama in the Pennsylvania German vernacular," enjoyed considerable popularity into the twentieth century. The drama centers on the family of Yokle and Frany Brownshweiger, who are heavily indebted to their neighbor, Henner Hoffman, who holds the mortgage on their farm. A shifty insurance agent, William Schwinefelt, talks Yokle into taking out a life insurance policy on his elderly mother-in-law, Granny Aunschitz (*die grossmommy*), which involves altering her *daufschein* (baptismal certificate) to make her eligible for the policy. Schwinefelt sells Yokle the policy and convinces him to sign a confession of judgment giving Schwinefelt considerable financial control over Yokle. Two years pass, Granny Aunschitz is still living, and financial pressures are mounting on Yokle, who lets Schwinefelt talk him into buying mouse poison to slip into Granny's tea. Fortunately, disaster is averted, Granny survives, and the beau of the Brownshweigers' daughter Sallie, Augustus "Gust" Eslinger, comes into an inheritance and assumes responsibility for the Brownshweigers' mortgage. Gust draws a pistol on Schwinefelt, gets him to tear up the insurance papers, and sends him packing. All ends happily ever after, and Granny, with outstretched hands, utters the final words of the play: *Liebe kinner. Empfongt my säga* (Dear children. Receive my blessing). While this play echoes the traditional Pennsylvania Dutch suspicion of dishonest and immoral city dwellers, the drama is not nearly so black and white, given that farmer Yokle, true to his name, is portrayed as not much better than the insurance agent Schwinefelt.

Arguably the most popular dramatic production in Pennsylvania Dutch ever was an adaptation of Gilbert and Sullivan's comic opera *H.M.S. Pinafore*. The English-language original opened in London on

May 25, 1878, to huge success, and the opera made its way quickly to stages in the United States, where it enjoyed similar acclaim. In 1882, two Allentown natives, Alfred Charles Moss, a composer and director, and Elwood L. Newhard, a singer and stage manager, collaborated to create a Pennsylvania Dutch version of *Pinafore*, which premiered in Allentown on November 23, 1882.[100] Performances in Bethlehem and Reading followed. The production was wildly popular everywhere, and Newhard, who sang the role of Sir Joseph "Sir Joe" Porter, organized a touring company to take the Pennsylvania Dutch *Pinafore* to other cities and towns across Pennsylvania. It was revived twice, in 1901 and 1910, with similar success. Like most "translations" of works from English into Pennsylvania Dutch, including a Pennsylvania Dutch dramatic adaptation of *Rip Van Winkle* by Edward H. Rauch in 1883,[101] Moss and Newhard's *Pinafore* was far from a verbatim rendering of the original. Newhard was a fluent speaker of Pennsylvania Dutch, and Moss had good receptive knowledge of the language. Both were also familiar with the fanciful Dutch Dialect, the pseudo-Germanized English employed in works such as *Breitmann's Ballads*. Moss and Newhard's *Pinafore* is of considerable linguistic complexity, incorporating lyrics from four separate varieties, Pennsylvania Dutch, English, Dutch Dialect, and even a small amount of standard German, which reflects the diversity of the verbal repertoire of the Pennsylvania audiences who flocked to see it.

A comparison of some of the lyrics from Sir Joe's famous song "When I Was a Lad" in the original English with Moss and Newhard's Pennsylvania Dutch version demonstrates the originality with which the two collaborators approached the task of adapting the work for Pennsylvania Dutch audiences. The Pennsylvania Dutch version of the first stanza appears to generally follow the sense of the original, but whereas the ambitious young English aristocrat Joe smarmily recounts how he is able to become the First Lord of the Admiralty without any naval experience, in Pennsylvania Dutch his character is not at all insipid:

English Original
When I was a lad I served a term
As office boy to an attorney's firm.
I cleaned the windows and I swept the floor,

And I polished up the handle of the big front door.
I polished up that handle so carefullee,
That now I am the Ruler of the Queen's Navee!

Pennsylvania Dutch

We ich 'n chap un 'n pre'ntis wawr,
Hawb ich obg'wawrt for 'n lawyers pawr;
Ich hab d'r dish ufg'romd un de shbouboxa g'butst,—
Un die, ken'r denka wawrn orrik f'rshmutst—
Die butz'rei wawr grensalos,
Dos ich g'rebell'd hawb noch un noch.

When I was a boy and an apprentice,
I served a pair of lawyers;
I cleared the table and cleaned the spittoons,—
And those, you can imagine, were very dirty—
That confounded cleaning was limitless,
Such that I gradually came to rebel.[102]

In the British original, Joe works hard to impress his employers, who hire him into their firm. He becomes rich and is voted by a "pocket borough" into Parliament, where he "always voted at his party's call" and "never thought of thinking for myself at all." The English Joe ends his song by advising others to do as he did: "Stick close to your desks, and never go to sea, / And you all may be Rulers of the Queen's Navee!" The Pennsylvania Dutch Joe's experiences are somewhat different. Like his English counterpart, the Dutch Joe is hired full time by the law firm he works for, but he becomes so successful that the lawyers end up firing him. The cocky Dutch Joe happily strikes out on his own (after cursing his former employers), decking himself out "like a Bethlehem dude" (*we'n Bedlahem "dude"*) with polka-dotted pants and a high hat. And since his fancy attire now makes up for his lack of formal education, he decides to run for Congress (*Mei larning wawr net gons uf zu meim dress, / No bin ich g'luffa f'r in d'r Congress*). After he is elected, he makes so much money as a congressman that he is able to retire and move to England, where he is given a naval commission. The Pennsylvania Dutch Joe's advice is as follows:

Nou fum shbouboxa butsa in a lawyer firm
Bin ich advanc'd in an'm term.
In d'm lond do hasa ses: "go it pretty quick"
"and when you have a place don't too long stick."
So nem mei advice un kum in de roi
No moch'n 'r ol geld so long wie hoi.

Now from cleaning spittoons in a law firm
I advanced in a single term.
In this country they call it "going pretty quick"
"and when you have a position, don't stay in it too long."
So take my advice and get in line
Then you will all make money as tall as hay.[103]

While Gilbert and Sullivan's Sir Joe is an obsequious toady, Moss and Newhard's Pennsylvania Dutch Joe displays a measure of classic American cleverness, which gives his character more depth (and appeal) than the British Joe has. Apart from Joe's lines in the script, the native Dutchman Elwood Newhard's portrayal of Sir Joe was one of the greatest highlights for audiences seeing the Pennsylvania Dutch *H.M.S. Pinafore*.

The Pennsylvania Dutch public's appetite for dramatic entertainment in their native language was amply met by clever, well-written and effectively produced works such as Moss and Newhard's adaptation of *H.M.S. Pinafore*. In the 1930s and succeeding decades, the rise and growth of fersommlinge, including the Grundsow Lodges, intersected with and fueled numerous other scripted performances in Pennsylvania Dutch, including over the airwaves. The most successful Pennsylvania Dutch radio show was *Asseba un Sabina Mumbauer im Eihledaahl* (Asseba and Sabina Mumbauer of Owl Valley), which was broadcast from 1944 to 1954 in Allentown.[104] The show's main protagonists were an older Pennsylvania Dutch couple in a typical rural Dutch Country community. The writers and actors, all native speakers of Pennsylvania Dutch, were singularly talented; they included Harry Hess Reichard, who played the role of Asseba. The fifteen-minute weekly *Asseba un Sabina* sketches were so well loved that they were often featured at various public venues, including fersommlinge, even into the twenty-first century, thereby enhancing the popularity of such gatherings.

While the fersommlinge, conducted as they were entirely in Penn-

PENNA. GERMAN PINAFORE TAKES READING BY STORM

Allentown Company Invades Stronghold of German Dialect With
a Stirring Rendition of the Old-Time
Popular Opera

From the *Philadelphia Inquirer*, February 12, 1901.

sylvania Dutch, offered a natural outlet for gems of Pennsylvania Dutch
folk theater like *Asseba un Sabina*, the interest of nonethnic Pennsylvania Dutch in such cultural products grew rapidly. Beginning in the
late 1940s, larger events showcased Pennsylvania Dutch culture and language for nonnative speakers, both locals and tourists. The two most
prominent of these were Pennsylvania Dutch Days, which began in 1949
and ran for thirty years in Hershey, Dauphin County, and the Pennsylvania Dutch Folk Festival, the first of which was held in 1950 in Kutztown, Berks County. Pennsylvania Dutch Days grew out of a popular
evening-school Pennsylvania Dutch language course taught by Berks
County native Pierce E. Swope (1884–1968), a minister by profession and
a prominent Pennsylvania Dutch columnist (for the *Lebanon News*).[105]
The festival in Kutztown was begun by the Pennsylvania Dutch Folklore
Center led by Alfred L. Shoemaker, Don Yoder, and J. William Frey and
continues today as the Kutztown Folk Festival, one of America's oldest and largest celebrations of local culture.[106] While English has always
been the predominant language of the Kutztown festival presenters and

Bilingual advertisements from the program for the 15th Annual Pennsylvania Dutch Days, Hershey, PA, 1963.

visitors, some events still feature the Pennsylvania Dutch language, including humorous stories told by native speakers.

OVER MOST OF ITS HISTORY, the Pennsylvania Dutch language has attracted the attention of outsiders, some of whom have been more sympathetic than others. The representations of the verbal behavior of

Pennsylvania Dutch speakers in the writings of Phebe Earle Gibbons and Helen R. Martin give a sense of the wide range of views observers have had, from fairly accurate portrayals to fanciful and even hostile depictions of the language and the people who speak it. Complementing outsiders' views of and pronouncements about Pennsylvania Dutch have been the efforts of native speaker insiders such as Edward H. Rauch and many others after him on behalf of their mother tongue, both for their own, private benefit, as in the Grundsow Lodges, and for non-Dutch audiences at public gatherings like the Kutztown Festival. In the twentieth century, the efforts of people like Alfred L. Shoemaker, Don Yoder, and J. William Frey were of special importance, as these scholars sought, quite successfully in many ways, to legitimize the study of vernacular culture and language within the academy and simultaneously present reliable information in an accessible way for a curious public. Although the efforts of organizations such as the Grundsow Lodges did not impede the overall shift of nonsectarian Pennsylvania Dutch away from the use of their heritage language in everyday life, the survival of the lodges to the present, some eight decades after they were founded, is a testimony to the important role they continue to play in promoting the Pennsylvania Dutch cultural heritage.

Largely absent from such public celebrations of Pennsylvania Dutch, however, are the Amish and Mennonite sectarians. Though they found themselves being thrust into the spotlight of public curiosity about Pennsylvania Dutch very early on, in the tradition of their spiritual ancestors, who sought to maintain a measure of distance from "the world," they have rarely paid much attention to outsiders' views of them and their heritage language, either positive or negative. Nor do they feel any particular need to promote the vitality of Pennsylvania Dutch in an intentional way, since they maintain the language effortlessly within their communities. Indeed, the present and likely future of Pennsylvania Dutch are bound up with the faith and life of conservative Amish and Mennonite sectarians, who are the focus of the next chapter.

CHAPTER 6

Pennsylvania Dutch and the
Amish and Mennonites

Es ist nix letz mit die English Sproch, awer won die Deutsche
leit mohl English warre welle, sel is Hochmut!

There's nothing wrong with the English language, but when
German people want to become English, that's pride!

—M.S.Z., OLD ORDER MENNONITE MINISTER

Sectarians and the History of Pennsylvania Dutch

D uring the boom in the production of writings, public presenta-
tions, and events centered on the Pennsylvania Dutch language
in the second half of the nineteenth century and the first half of
the twentieth, Mennonite and Amish sectarians were conspicuously absent as participants. None of the identified Pennsylvania Dutch authors
during this time was a member of an Anabaptist congregation.[1] There
is no evidence to suggest that Mennonites or Amish were involved in
any of the organizations devoted to the documentation of Pennsylvania
Dutch history and culture, such as the Pennsylvania German Society
and the Pennsylvania German Folklore Society, nor did they engage in
the promotion of the language through attendance at venues like the
fersommlinge or Grundsow Lodges. Although sectarians avoided direct
involvement in these various activities, they did figure prominently as

subjects in the writings on Pennsylvania Dutch culture and language produced by outsiders such as Phebe Earle Gibbons, Helen R. Martin, and A. Monroe Aurand Jr., and their "exotic" character among the various Pennsylvania Dutch–speaking groups attracted the special attention of tourists and other observers. Their images were—and still are—everywhere on the salt-and-pepper shakers, trivets, and countless other Pennsylvania Dutch–themed items marketed to consumers, many of which include examples of what Alfred L. Shoemaker called "Tourist Dutch," or fanciful Dutchified English. Notably, however, nonsectarian "insiders" who wrote in and about Pennsylvania Dutch for their fellow native speakers, such as Edward H. Rauch and Abraham Reeser Horne, rarely if ever mentioned anything related to Mennonites or Amish. The sect people were simply not on the radar of Pennsylvania Dutch writers, virtually all of whom were descended from or affiliated with Reformed, Lutheran, and other Protestant churches.

Recall that when Pennsylvania Dutch was emerging as a distinct language in the eighteenth century, relations between the church people and the sect people were relatively close; they had to have been, otherwise Pennsylvania Dutch would not be as structurally and lexically homogeneous as it is across the various groups of people who use it to this day. Mennonite historian Theron F. Schlabach claims that the ties that bound sectarians and nonsectarians to one another in the eighteenth century endured into the nineteenth:

> As the nineteenth century began, Mennonites were somewhat buffered from the world. In eastern Pennsylvania, where most resided, one buffer was English-speaking Quakers and other fellow pacifists. Even more effectively, they lived in a womb of Pennsylvania-German culture. Scholars write of different kinds of Pennsylvania Germans: the "church" people (primarily Lutheran and Reformed); sectarians (mainly Mennonites, Dunkers, Amish, and Schwenkfelders); and, by the 1790s, the revivalists (Methodist-oriented groups, especially the United Brethren, and after 1800 the Evangelical Association).
>
> Such distinctions are often useful, yet they can make the Mennonites and other "sectarians" seem more separated than they were. With other Pennsylvania Germans, Mennonites shared a dialect learned in the Palatinate and known in America as "Pennsylvania German" or "Pennsyl-

vania Dutch." Religiously they shared broadly the language of Pietism. Sometimes they shared pulpits, especially at funerals. In their schools (often in or by their meetinghouses) they frequently cooperated with Pennsylvania-German neighbors, including the "church" people. The schools in turn taught the language and outlook of Pietism. Intermarriage was extensive, with intricate family networks across church and sectarian and revivalist lines. And in daily life Mennonites and Amish constantly mixed with their neighbors in mills, distilleries, markets, and shops.[2]

Schlabach goes on to note that in the early 1800s, as Mennonites and Amish began expanding out of Pennsylvania, to Ontario in the north, southward along the eastern edge of the Appalachian mountains, and especially to Ohio and points farther west, they did so with Pennsylvanians of different backgrounds. "They were not highly separated," Schlabach states.[3]

The relatively proximity of Pennsylvania Dutch–speaking sectarians and nonsectarians in early America was not a new phenomenon; rather, it continued a pattern of interaction that had already been present in Europe, especially the Palatinate, before the ancestors of both groups came to colonial Pennsylvania. The majority of Mennonite and Amish immigrants to Pennsylvania in the eighteenth century were of Swiss ancestry, yet very few arrived directly from Switzerland. Most came from the Palatinate and other territories east and west of the Rhine, where their ancestors had lived for nearly a century before migrating to North America. In the Palatinate there was considerable intermarriage between Anabaptists from Berne and Zurich, for example, and collectively they lived in sufficient proximity to their non-Anabaptist neighbors to shift from Swiss to Palatine German within a single generation.[4] In contrast, Bernese Mennonites who settled in the French Jura mountain region had very little interaction with their French-speaking neighbors and instead formed Swiss German speech islands.[5] The close ties that bound nonsectarian and sectarian Pennsylvania Dutch speakers to one another in eighteenth- and early nineteenth-century America thus paralleled the conditions under which their ancestors had lived alongside one another in the Palatinate, while the linguistic and cultural divide between (Swiss) German and French speakers in seventeenth- and eighteenth-century

Europe was repeated in America between the Pennsylvania Dutch collectively, sectarians and nonsectarians, and their English-speaking neighbors.

As the nineteenth century proceeded, however, nonsectarian and sectarian Pennsylvania Dutch grew apart, a main factor being differences in settlement patterns. In Pennsylvania, Mennonites and Amish came to be concentrated in areas where there were relatively few church people. Lancaster, Mifflin, and Somerset Counties, for example, had and still have sizable Anabaptist presences, whereas in the "Dutchiest" counties of Berks, Lehigh, and Lebanon nonsectarians predominated. The separation between the two groups was even more pronounced outside of Pennsylvania. In places such as Ohio, Indiana, and Illinois, as well as in Ontario, where sizable Mennonite and Amish communities developed, most nonsectarian Pennsylvania Dutch shifted relatively quickly to English; there is little evidence that the language has been maintained among the descendants of church people outside of those counties in southeastern Pennsylvania where their roots were deepest.

Over time, the divide between the two groups of Pennsylvania Dutch speakers became as great as that between English-speaking Americans and Pennsylvania Dutch people generally. Today, for example, the average Pennsylvania Dutch nonsectarian knows no more about who the Amish and Mennonites are than their non–Pennsylvania Dutch neighbors do, sometimes even mispronouncing the name *Amish* as "Ay-mish." What is more, contemporary speakers of midwestern varieties of Pennsylvania Dutch, mainly Old Order Amish and Old Order Mennonites, are largely unaware that there are people in Pennsylvania who speak their language and are not of Anabaptist background. Likewise, the writings of Henry Harbaugh and the dozens of other Pennsylvania Dutch authors are unknown to sectarians everywhere today, including those living in Pennsylvania.[6]

While geographic separation is an important reason for the cultural divide between sectarian and nonsectarian speakers of Pennsylvania Dutch since the nineteenth century, the nearly complete lack of Mennonite or Amish involvement in the development of a Pennsylvania Dutch folk culture, including its literature, is due to a number of other factors, the most important of which is the way they choose to live out their Christian faith. Above all, Mennonites and Amish see a direct connection between the ideals grounded in their strong faith and everyday life, and most of what they choose to read and write is expected to provide useful knowledge or promote Christian virtues. In general, most of the Pennsylvania Dutch writings of nonsectarians deal with secular rather than religious themes. While even the most conservative Amish and Mennonites are avid readers, their tastes tend to be more inclined toward spiritually uplifting reading matter, and many of the secular texts most popular among them are works of history or historical fiction. Although many of the hundreds of prose and poetic texts written in Pennsylvania Dutch would be generally in line with sectarian values, others are not. Writings with substantial political content, for example, such as Rauch's Pit Schwefflebrenner letters, would hold little appeal for Mennonite and Amish readers, who avoid involvement in partisan politics and take only minimal interest in national and world affairs. Lighthearted or humorous texts whose primary purpose is to merely entertain, rather than to enlighten or inspire readers, which describes some of Pennsylvania Dutch literature, would be considered of little value by many sectarians. Further, many sectarians are uncomfortable with fiction overall as a genre, because of the blurred line between fabricating stories and lying.[7]

There are additional, more practical reasons sectarians have been so disconnected from the production and consumption of Pennsylvania Dutch literature and celebrations of its culture. Until the twentieth century, Mennonites and Amish constituted only a tiny fraction of the total Pennsylvania Dutch–speaking population. And even among nonsectarians, those individuals who wrote in Pennsylvania Dutch were relatively few in number and exceptional among their fellow speakers of the language, who were mainly rural dwellers of limited social and geographic mobility. The typical Pennsylvania Dutch writer was a highly educated professional male who had grown up in a traditional Pennsylvania Dutch–speaking community but had moved away, physically and intellectually, and then wrote in his native language only as an avocation. Amish or Mennonites who grow up speaking Pennsylvania Dutch and leave their communities later in life typically show little interest in maintaining their mother tongue. Furthermore, most Pennsylvania Dutch, sectarians and nonsectarians alike, have always had difficulty reading their native language, since Pennsylvania Dutch literacy has never figured into school curricula. Finally, many aspects of the organized, public activities devoted to the promotion of Pennsylvania Dutch, such as the Grundsow Lodges, run directly counter to sectarian values. It would be unthinkable for Amish and Mennonites, including most modern or progressive Mennonites, whose members are forbidden from joining fraternal organizations and secret societies, to swear an oath of loyalty to an oversized groundhog, even playfully.[8]

One Pennsylvania Dutch–speaking sectarian in the nineteenth century did produce texts in his native language, an early Mennonite leader named John H. Oberholtzer. Born in rural Berks County in 1809, Oberholtzer moved to Milford Square, Bucks County, and became a locksmith by trade and was an ordained minister in the Mennonite Church. He also edited and printed the first Mennonite periodical in America, the German-language *Der Religiöse Botschafter* (The religious messenger), which was published from 1852 to 1855, as well as its successor *Das Christliche Volks-Blatt* (The Christian people's paper), which he brought out from 1856 to 1866.[9] Oberholtzer was a vocal advocate for a number of changes in American Mennonite practice, including religious instruction for children, and he also supported the progressive idea that Mennonite ministers should be formally trained rather than simply chosen by lot in their congregations, which is still the practice among Old Order Mennonites and Amish today. Associated with the first schism in the American Mennonite church, in 1847, Oberholtzer was one of the founders of the Eastern District Conference of the Mennonite Church, which split from the more conservative Franconia Conference, whose origins go back to the very first American Mennonite congregation, founded at Germantown in 1683. Oberholtzer occupied a prominent place in nineteenth-century Mennonite life, preaching into his ninth decade at West Swamp Mennonite Church, in rural Bucks County. He died in 1895, at the age of eighty-six.[10]

John Oberholtzer's periodicals, which were important outlets for his views on Mennonite faith and life, consisted mainly of content he himself wrote in Pennsylvania High German, but he did include a few items in Pennsylvania Dutch. His Pennsylvania Dutch material, just as the texts he wrote in German, dealt almost exclusively with matters pertaining to the faith and life of his fellow Mennonite readers. Like other early native speakers who included occasional Pennsylvania Dutch material in

John H. Oberholtzer (1809–1895).
Source: Mennonite Library and Archives, Bethel College, North Newton, KS.

their writings, such as his contemporary Enos Benner (1799–1860) from nearby Sumneytown, Montgomery County,[11] Oberholtzer used Pennsylvania Dutch to connect more directly with his readership. One example is an article he published titled "Marrying outside the Faith" (*Vom naus Heira*), which appeared on April 2, 1862, in *Das Christliche Volks-Blatt*. Oberholtzer precedes the article with a brief statement, in German, begging the readers' pardon for writing in Pennsylvania Dutch: "The following was submitted in the name of an old 'Pennsylvanian,' and we hope that although he wrote in such a coarse and simple Pennsylvania style our readers will not be offended, since he makes a number of points that are of no little importance, if one reflects on them with common sense."[12]

The "old Pennsylvanian," who was almost certainly Oberholtzer himself, begins his discourse by striking an informal tone, saying that in the course of pondering a number of things the other morning, he came to dwell on the question of marrying outside of one's faith. In his mind he debated the wisdom of writing something for the *Volks-Blatt* out of concern that some "blockheaded readers" (*dickköpfige Leser*) might try to twist his words around, but in the end he decided he would go ahead anyway, no matter what the reaction might be.

Wegem naus heira hab ich kment wollt ich schreiwa. Ich kann net versteh daß sell ganz recht ist. Ich hab mol klesa im a dicka Buch das ener "Büchner" kschriwa hot, der ment sie sollten, wo möglich enerle Religion sein; aber guck just a mol des geheier in der Welt a. es wert ja nimme uf Vater und Mutter, nimme uf Freund oder Bekannter und bei viel am allerwenigsta uf Religion geguckt wanns numma keiert ist. freilich uf reich und sche gukt alt und jung. die ältera saga als zu ihra Kinner selli dort sin reich und ich denk sie sin a schmert und verstehns Geldmacha, selli det ich heira wan ich euch wer. do kommt es awer nau a noch druf a ob er oder sie scheh is. nau wann des beinanner ist, dann hen sie's geriß als wenn sie die letzta in der Welt wera und Gott und Religion wird ganz hinta dra gestellt.

I thought I'd write about this marrying outside the faith. I just can't accept that that is quite right. I read once in a fat book by some guy named Büchner, who thinks that everyone should have the same religion. But just look at what goes on in the world. No one pays attention anymore to father and mother, friend or acquaintance, and most definitely not to religion when it comes to getting married. Old and young folks alike just think about whether someone is rich and good looking. Parents say to their children, "Those ones are rich and I'll bet they're smart, too, and know about making money, I'd marry them if I were you." And then it's important whether he or she is good looking, too. Now, when they're at this, they go and on as if they were all alone in the world, and God and religion end up getting pushed off to the side.[13]

Oberholtzer's anonymous Pennsylvania Dutch–speaking correspondent is reminiscent of Stoffel Ehrlich from the turn of the nineteenth century, whose vernacular speech enabled newspaper editors to make their arguments in favor of certain positions more effectively to their readers.

Oberholtzer draws on Pennsylvania Dutch in a similar way in an extended dialog he created between two farmers, "A" and "B," which appeared in two issues of *Das Christliche Volks-Blatt*, on September 3 and 17, 1862. At that time, Oberholtzer was deeply involved with national efforts to raise the funds necessary to create a Mennonite institution of higher learning. The campaign was ultimately successful, leading to the founding of the Wadsworth Mennonite School in Ohio in 1868.[14] Oberholtzer's farmers are two typical Mennonites. One day, the two friends meet up and start chatting about their families and how things generally are going. Then Farmer A mentions that a man has been visiting local churches recently to raise money for a school. Farmer B scoffs at this effort:

Was! far a Schul!! Hemmer dann nach net Schula knunk! Was far a Schul soll dann des nau gewa? Vermuthlich sin widder so a paar Faullenzer ergets uferstanna die ebbes a bartiges ufstella wolla. Do wer ich awer, denk ich mol, mei Geldsack zuschrauwa.

What?! For a school?! Don't we have enough schools?! So what kind of school is this supposed to be? Apparently there are a couple of lazybones running around who want to start up something very special. Well, I think I'll just close up my money purse good and tight.[15]

Farmer A tells his friend that he actually heard this visitor preach in church. B's tone softens, and he asks A to tell him more about what he heard. A then goes on to talk about how the Mennonite church in America is suffering for a lack of trained ministers. B, like many of his Mennonite and nonsectarian Pennsylvania Dutch contemporaries, questions the value of formal education, saying that it can make people crazy. But A persists, eventually raising important questions in B's mind about the ability of uneducated ministers to lead their flocks effectively. Here again Oberholtzer, like his predecessors who created the Stoffel Ehrlich persona, makes effective use of constructed but realistic discourse to convince those who would identify with Farmer B to reconsider their views.

John Oberholtzer's decidedly reform-minded attitudes about the Mennonite church in America were reflected in the range of material he published in his periodicals, which included articles from German Reformed and Lutheran outlets, something that could not have sat well with his more conservative coreligionists. Among these articles from other sources are a number of pieces decrying the casual attitude of some Americans of German descent with regard to the maintenance of the German language. Too many people, especially youth, are shifting to English, the writers warn. One article, titled "Speak German! (*Sprich deutsch!*), which appeared in *Das Christliche Volks-Blatt* on February 3, 1862, takes German speakers to task for including "foreign" words in their speech and concludes by saying, "Hold fast to your mother tongue, understand it and you will make yourself understood with it" (*Halten Sie sich an ihre Muttersprache, die verstehen Sie und mit ihr werden Sie verstanden*). In light of these pro-German-language sympathies, one might surmise that Oberholtzer was espousing traditional Mennonite values. On the contrary, he was aligning himself with a more *Deitschlenner* way of thinking, oriented toward the supposedly "better" German spoken by Europeans. Although there is no evidence to suggest that Oberholtzer shared the *Deitschlenners'* views that Pennsylvania Dutch was a degraded form of German, he clearly saw proficiency in German as important.

What was the state of knowledge of the standard German language among sectarian Pennsylvania Dutch during John Oberholtzer's lifetime? In brief, mixed. Oberholtzer himself, despite having had very little formal education as a boy, which was typical for Pennsylvania Dutch children in the first decades of the nineteenth century, actually became quite proficient in German, as his writings demonstrate. In the 1930s, Harold S. Bender, a prominent Mennonite theologian at Goshen College, discovered a letter sent by Oberholtzer in 1849 to European Mennonites. The German in this letter, which provides a detailed description of the situation of American Mennonites at that time from Oberholtzer's perspective, is well written both in its penmanship, using the old German script, and in its structural form. Although Oberholtzer's German shows some influence from his native Pennsylvania Dutch, it is not dramatically different from other examples of Pennsylvania High German, and the few English loanwords he uses he glosses for his European readers:

Zuerst als die Väter von Europa hieher gelangten, fanden sie ein Land, bewohnt von Wilden (Indianern) welche die Europäer und andere als Feinde ansahen, und deswegen sie vielfältig mit ihrem Tomehaak (Strei-

taxt) und Scalpier-Messer verfolgten, plünderten und umbrachten. Hie-
raus lässt sich schon schliessen dass die ersten Ansiedler unsers Volks sich
nicht ordnen haben können wie sie (ganz natürlich) gewünscht hätten.

*At first when the forefathers from Europe came here they found a land oc-
cupied by savages (Indians) whom the Europeans and others regarded as
enemies, and for that reason they often pursued, robbed, and killed them
with their tomahawk (battle axe) and scalping knife. From this one can
conclude that the first settlers of our people could not organize themselves
as they (quite naturally) would have wanted to.*[16]

In his letter Oberholtzer correctly uses grammatical forms that are part
of standard German but not Pennsylvania Dutch, including the simple
past (preterite) tense for verbs (e.g., *gelangten*, 'came (to)', *fanden*, 'found',
ansahen, 'regarded') and the Genitive case for nouns (*unsers Volks*, 'of our
people'). The one clearly Pennsylvania Dutch (and nonstandard German) feature in this passage is the arrangement of the three verbs in the
cluster *ordnen haben können*, 'were able to organize' (std. Ger. *haben
ordnen können*). Overall, Oberholtzer's mastery of German is impressive
compared to that of his contemporaries, including Henry Harbaugh,
who was just seven years younger than he and had received postsecond-
ary instruction in German at the Reformed seminary he attended.

John Oberholtzer was not the only prominent sectarian speaker of
Pennsylvania Dutch in the nineteenth century whose progressive opinions on church matters included placing special value on knowing German well. Another was S(amuel) D. Guengerich, a prolific Amish writer
and German-language publisher who was born in Somerset County, PA,
in 1835 and died in 1929 in Iowa. Guengerich's biography was somewhat
unusual for an Amish person. Although he had little in the way of formal
education as a child, he attended Millersville Normal School in Lancaster
County (today, Millersville University), became a certified teacher, and
taught for many years in Iowa public schools. Guengerich held progressive views on a number of matters pertaining to Amish faith and life,
including his avid support for Sunday schools. In general, Guengerich
was concerned about what he saw as poor educational circumstances for
Amish youth, most of whom at that time attended public schools, and

he became a strong advocate for the establishment of parochial schools. One particular concern of Guengerich's was what he saw as poor knowledge of standard German among his fellow Amish, including ministers. In an 1897 pamphlet arguing for parochial education, Guengerich wrote, "It has happened often that the lot has fallen to brethren who could read German either poorly or not at all and therefore found themselves practically having to start with the ABCs, which they should have learned as children before the evil years come."[17]

One might think that the strong emphasis S. D. Guengerich placed on improving German knowledge among the Amish would have marked him as a conservative in the Amish church, but that was not the case. His advocacy of formal religious instruction outside of worship services, in line with John Oberholter's thinking, put him at odds with some of his Old Order brethren, and eventually his own Iowa congregation became affiliated with the more progressive Conservative Amish Mennonite Conference, a denomination that was formed in 1910.[18]

Some of Guengerich's fellow Amish Mennonites not only expressed concerns about the lack of proficiency in German among their brethren but went further to blame Pennsylvania Dutch for weakening the position of German in their churches, thereby promoting poor spiritual health. Guengerich wrote the introduction and served on an editorial committee for an anonymously authored collection of essays directed at Amish Mennonite families that was published in 1907. The author, an Amish Mennonite who wrote under the name "A Friend of Humanity," had harsh words for what he called "the Pennsylvania language":

What would my readers think if I were to find fault with the Pennsylvania German? Perhaps that is what it will amount to before I get through with what I have to say. I imagine I hear you say, "This language has been in use so long, and is so entirely satisfactory in all of our settlements that we can not understand why you should find any fault with it."

What you say is true so far as it goes. This Pennsylvania German answers our purpose so far as the things of this world are concerned (except that it is in a measure responsible for the growing aversion to German in print), but when it comes to spiritual matters is where its greatest lack is felt.

I believe that this dialect was first originated when our people began to prosper in this world's goods, and to be "at ease in Zion," and take plenty of time for local gossip, and not while they were reading their Bibles or holding prayer meetings as our Martyr forefathers used to do. You see it was when we began to be more worldly minded and less spiritual in our talk that this careless way of speaking was first considered good enough.

But what hurts my conscience most is to listen to some of our people trying to preach the Gospel almost entirely in this dialect, for it is my conviction that such attempts greatly lower the standard of the Scriptures. By this means we drag our careless, every-day twaddle into the Scriptures, or drag the Scriptures into it, and the result is disastrous to our spiritual life. I think it is due to carelessness on the part of parents that our young people can not better understand the Scriptural German, and would advise our people to make a heroic effort to get out of these ruts and then keep out. However, I am of the opinion that if sermons were preached in the Scriptural German, and in the power of the Spirit, our young people would understand them, even now.

I do not mean that a preacher's language may not be slightly modified, or blended with this dialect without injury, but it is when an effort is made to preach entirely in it that the Word of God is robbed of its power. This is how I find fault with the above mentioned language.[19]

The views of the Friend of Humanity on "Scriptural German" notwithstanding, progressive churches that broke from the Old Order Amish, such as the Conservative Amish Mennonite Conference, ended up moving fairly quickly to the use of English in worship and in their homes over the course the twentieth century. Numerous factors underlay this shift, but one major one was the inclination among these churches to pursue mission work, which maintaining German (or Pennsylvania Dutch) did nothing to facilitate.

The gradual shift among progressive Amish and Mennonite sectarians away from Pennsylvania Dutch as an everyday language and German for worship was set in motion in the second half of the nineteenth century, at precisely the same time that the attrition of nonsectarian Pennsylvania Dutch speakers from their heritage language was accelerating. During the 1860s and 1870s, approximately two-thirds of Amish in North America, for example, became affiliated with progressive groups, virtually all of whom eventually shifted to English, while the remaining third, who became known as the Old Order Amish, have maintained Pennsylvania Dutch and German to the present.[20]

Among Mennonites, similar divisions occurred between 1872 and 1901, with the most conservative churches, who acquired the name *Old Order Mennonite*, also continuing to use Pennsylvania Dutch and German.[21] Many issues, not just differences of opinion about language use, divided Amish and Mennonite progressives and conservatives, all having in some way to do with the degree to which they wanted to assimilate—or not—with the larger society, both materially and spiritually. The maintenance of Pennsylvania Dutch and German became an important symbol of Old Order identity, which stressed a greater degree of nonconformity with "the world" than was found among other Anabaptist groups. For the Old Orders, the use of English, not just with outsiders but within their communities, connoted the sin of pride (*Hochmut* in both Pennsylvania Dutch and German), whereas continuing to speak the heritage language of their ancestors, the lowly Pennsylvania Dutch, was a marker of humility (*Demut*), still today a cardinal virtue in Old Order faith and life. Historian Amos B. Hoover, himself an Old Order Mennonite, notes the connection between the shift from German to English and a shift in theology, with English making its first inroads among Mennonite churches through music:

In all of the three hundred years of history of Mennonites in America, there were those of ability who could communicate to their neighbors in English. This was always considered a special "gift" not to be suppressed. But now in the 1880's to forfeit the native tongue in worship service for the English tongue was too much for those who wanted the old ground. The leaders who claimed that the English language leads "high" were right in that it partly changed the theology from a submissive theology and lifestyle to an aggressive one. The language change is so intricately interwoven with lifestyle that a lengthy thesis could be written on the subject, too long for full treatment here. Briefly stated, a new type of hymns, mostly Methodist in background, was introduced, shifting from brotherhood ideology and centered more on individual pietism. Along with these new hymns came an entire new system of melodies with a new tempo and part singing, to the point that we began to think of these

melodies as being "English tunes" versus "German tunes." This new type
of hymnody called for new types of songleading and new types of church
furniture and eventually renovation of church buildings.[22]

An Old Order Mennonite preacher who lived from 1854 to 1941, and
who therefore witnessed firsthand the major schisms within his church
in the late nineteenth century, expressed the negative valuation of shifting toward English as follows: "*Es is nix letz mit die English Sproch, awer
won die Deutsche leit mohl English warre welle, sel is Hochmut!*" (There's
nothing wrong with the English language, but when German people
[i.e., sectarians] want to become English, that's pride!).[23]

For their part, modern Mennonites have tended to view the Old Order maintenance of Pennsylvania Dutch and German negatively. The
contemporary understanding of nonconformity among modern Mennonites in North America differs substantially from that of the Old Orders. Outward symbols of nonconformity, including distinctive dress
and grooming and the selective use of technology, which are still important among the Old Orders, have been given up by most modern Mennonites. Nonresistance, the renunciation of violence in all forms (on the
model of Jesus's injunctions to "turn the other cheek" and to love one's
enemies), is still equated with nonconformity by modern Mennonites,
but the tangible boundaries between the Old Orders and the larger society are largely absent among modern Mennonites, who tend favor a
more engaged witness to the world.

Modern Mennonites have tended to see Pennsylvania Dutch as a
handicap to intellectual and spiritual development. Especially because
Pennsylvania Dutch is a primarily oral language distinct from both standard German and English, English-speaking Mennonites have feared
that a mismatch between what one speaks and the language(s) in which
one is literate poses a problem not only for understanding Scripture and
other religious texts but even for one's abililty to think effectively. In
his 1937 history of the Franconia Conference of the Mennonite Church,
J(ohn) C. Wenger (1910–1995), has this to say about language:

The Mennonite pioneers brought a German dialect with them from the
Palatinate. The Bible was read in high German, but the spoken language
was this Palatine dialect, "Pennsylvania German." It is considerably used

even today in parts of Bucks, Montgomery, Lehigh, Berks, Northampton, Lancaster, and other counties. In the territory covered by the Franconia Conference it is still spoken by many people. It is not a denominational dialect; Lutherans and Reformed use it as much as the Mennonites. It is a household dialect, lacking cultural richness. In the Mennonite services a modified high German was used. Luther's Bible was read, but the exposition of the text was largely in Pennsylvania German. . . .

Many of the older people have their richest religious memories bound to their "Muttersproch" (mother tongue), Pennsylvania German. Some Mennonites strenuously resisted the change from German to English in the church service. On the other hand, the use of Pennsylvania German seems to tend to an intellectual poverty, for when a great part of a person's thinking is done in a language in which he does no reading (as is the case with the typical Pennsylvania German farmer), what he does read in English is not grasped as quickly and fully as it should be. This is not due to an inherent mental weakness, but to the language barrier. Further when Pennsylvania Germans speak English certain sounds (the cognates) are poorly distinguished. For example it is difficult for a Pennsylvania German to distinguish some of the following words: *search, serge; char, jar; vary, wary; bag, back; rib, rip; mate, made; face, phase*; and even in some cases, *worth* and *worse*. When two consonants are involved, the case is still worse, as *ragged, racket!* This language barrier helps to account for the charge of plain stupidity sometimes brought against Mennonites (Pennsylvania Germans).[24]

An articulate exponent of the critical attitude many modern Mennonites have toward the preservation of an in-group language among the Old Orders and similar groups was the Mennonite historian and theologian Harold S. Bender (1897–1962), a close friend and colleague of J. C. Wenger.[25] Among Bender's many accomplishments was his founding of the *Mennonite Quarterly Review*, as well as *The Mennonite Encyclopedia* (today, the *Global Anabaptist Mennonite Encyclopedia Online*), which he edited and for which he wrote several entries. One of these was an article he published in 1957, "Language Problem," whose title already points to his critical views on language maintenance patterns among conservative Anabaptist groups.[26]

Bender begins his article by conceding, on the one hand, that "the maintenance of the language of the motherland has aided in maintaining separation from the surrounding culture in the new homeland and thus strengthened the sense of nonconformity to the world."[27] This, in turn, has helped foster a distinctive Mennonite identity more generally. "On the other hand," Bender continues,

> the language breach has usually prevented a program of active evangelism and outreach, and has imposed a necessary system of private or parochial schools. As long as the breach with the surrounding culture and language was complete and continuous, problems of adjustment, either of the group with the outside world, or of individuals to individuals within the group, seldom arose. However, when the breach has been only partial, or when individuals or a subgroup within the larger group become wholly or partially assimilated to the "outside" language, serious problems of internal adjustment have arisen. At times this has been a problem of adjustment between the generations, so that youth has come into conflict with age, and usually large numbers of the youth have been lost to the group and its faith and way of life. At other times factionalism has arisen, resulting in serious schisms. Conservative groups attempting to hold the language line have died out because of failure to adjust to the new environment. Successful maintenance of small language enclaves detached from any larger language culture body has resulted in cultural and intellectual impoverishment, frequently with attendant religious losses. The battle to maintain the language has usually been fought with religious sanctions which have at times gone to the extreme of claims of higher spiritual values for the mother tongue as compared with the new tongue and of forfeiture of group principles and even faith in God in case of surrender of the language. Usually the transition from one language to another has required two or more generations of confusion and turmoil with considerable loss of membership en route, as well as the diversion of much energy from constructive work. The effect in literary production and consumption by the group is also usually very detrimental.[28]

Time has proved Bender's assessment of the detrimental effects of minority language maintenance among the Old Orders largely wrong. Bender thought that "partial assimilation" with the larger society, which in a linguistic context would mean bilingualism, would lead to conflict and confusion, especially among youth. In reality, however, the Old Orders' knowledge of both Pennsylvania Dutch and English (as well as German, receptively) has proved highly advantageous to them, facilitating their selective interaction with the larger society, which is necessary for survival, without having to assimilate completely and lose their distinctive identity. This is part of what the sociologist Donald B. Kraybill has termed the Old Orders' "bargain with modernity," an effective strategy of charting a middle course between tradition and progress.[29] The exceptionally high growth rate among the Old Orders today, a half century after Bender was writing, is a function not only of large average family sizes but also high retention rates: approximately 85% of children born to Old Order Amish and Old Order Mennonite parents make the decision as young adults to formally join the church. Thus, for Bender to say that "[c]onservative groups attempting to hold the language line have died out because of failure to adjust to the new environment" is incorrect; the tremendous growth of the Old Orders outpaces that of any other Anabaptist group in North America today.

Old Orders themselves value their bilingualism in a strongly positive way. They all recognize the necessity of making certain compromises in order to maintain the ways they live out their faith, one of which is learning English alongside Pennsylvania Dutch and German. They are profoundly aware of the advantages that knowing more than one language brings, including to their spiritual life. They recognize that their ability to understand and interpret Scripture, for example, is enhanced because they can read not only Luther's German translation of the Bible but also the numerous English-language versions available. This appreciation of the benefits of bilingualism is typically lost on those, including Harold Bender, who function exclusively or primarily in one language and assume that bilingualism must lead to cognitive confusion or "semilingualism." Quoting again from Bender's 1957 essay:

> Sometimes the theory of the cultural value of using two languages has been propounded to support retention of the "mother tongue." Actually it is probable that only highly intelligent persons who diligently pursue both languages on a literary level profit from this dualism. More common outcomes are the failure to master either language adequately, confusion of vocabulary and ideas, undesirable carryover of idioms from

one language to the other (Germanisms in English and Anglicisms in German), and undesirable foreign accents which handicap individuals in their speaking and other expression as they move in public life.[30]

Here again, time has proved Bender wrong. As I explore in depth in the following section, having not one but two (actually, three) languages at their disposal enables Old Orders to fully meet all their communicative needs, both oral and written, and without interference or confusion. As one thoughtful Amish man expressed it, "Knowing two languages is a privilege God has provided for us, and we can put them to good use."[31]

There are some individuals who leave the Old Order Amish and Mennonites and would agree with Harold Bender that maintenance of Pennsylvania Dutch and German is spiritually problematic since it is an impediment to outreach and evangelism. One of the most articulate exponents of this view was Elmo Stoll (1944–1998), a former Old Order Amish bishop from Aylmer, ON, who left the Amish in 1990 to form a communal Christian community in Cookeville, TN, that attracted disaffected former members of diverse Plain Anabaptist churches, as well people of other backgrounds. The common language of Stoll's new community, including in worship, was English.

In an unpublished essay titled "The Language Barrier," Stoll expresses his view that the maintenance of Pennsylvania Dutch and German by the Amish violated Scripture:

God intends, in the New Testament era, that languages serve as a means of communication, and not as barriers or a method of separation. This is verified by the special miracle of tongues at Pentecost (Acts 2:6–11) and Paul's statement to the Corinthians, "In the church I had rather speak five words with my understanding, that by my voice I might teach others also, than ten thousand words in an unknown tongue" (1 Cor. 14:19). To continue to perpetuate and practice our language separation system without any Scriptural precedence or principle is an on-going burden on my conscience.[32]

In his essay Stoll makes clear that he is not opposed to learning or maintaining multiple languages, just as long as they serve as "bridges to get people together," and not as barriers to communication, which would be "selfish and clannish."[33]

As a former Amish bishop, Stoll knew well the arguments made by those in leadership positions in the church justifying the maintenance of Pennsylvania Dutch and German, but to Stoll these were mostly "sentimental reasons." For example, it is difficult to argue the necessity of being able to read the Bible and early Anabaptist writings, including those of Menno Simons, in German when that was not the original language in which they were written. And even for those texts that were originally composed in German, such as the hymns in the *Ausbund*, one could consult English translations. Stoll also responds to those who argue against the appropriateness of using English in the Amish church:

> Others have said, "English is the nearest thing to a world language. It is the language people do business in the world over."
>
> That is true. So maybe we should be different than the world and refuse to do business in English. Would it not be more Scriptural if we had a church *Ordnung* that we would only make business deals in German? Whenever we did any buying and selling, we would speak only German. If we ran any ads in the paper, they would be in German, or if we had any salebills printed, they would be in German. If we refused to do any business in English, this would provide the needed separation from the world. We are always getting too involved in making money anyhow, so no harm would be done. And if the world really wanted to do business with us, they could learn German.
>
> Of course, we all think that would be ridiculous. We would have a hard time selling our products, and we might lose a few dollars. Does it bother us when we erect barriers to communicating our faith, and we lose a few souls?[34]

Underlying Stoll's critical views on the preservation of Pennsylvania Dutch and German by the Amish is a fundamentally different outlook between them and him regarding the life of the church. For Stoll, it is a Christian's duty to actively witness to others and to encourage those who would join the body of believers. By requiring those seeking to join the Amish church to learn Pennsylvania Dutch and German, which is indeed a practical barrier (among several others), the Amish risk becoming a "cultural church, and so much less a 'fellowship of faith,'" in Stoll's opinion. In other words, Stoll believes strongly in the necessity for Christ-followers to actively share their faith with others. The Old Orders, on the contrary, including the Amish, prefer to be "silent witnesses" to their faith of discipleship rather than engaging in overt evangelization and proselytization. In the words of one Amish person, "We try to let our light shine, but not shine it in the eyes of others."[35]

To be sure, outsiders are allowed to join Old Order churches, and some have done so successfully and learned Pennsylvania Dutch and German. However, some seekers have joined and then left again, which is painful for those left behind. Thus, sectarians are quick to point out how difficult it is for outsiders to join and stress that one need not be Amish or Old Order Mennonite to be saved. The Amish and horse-and-buggy Mennonites do indeed have a linguistic fence around their communities, but a fence that is not insurmountable and one that can serve as test of seekers' sincerity. More importantly, the Old Orders see maintaining Pennsylvania Dutch and German as being less about keeping people out and more as a means of helping to preserve their spiritual heritage. As one Amish man puts it, "For the safety of our church, I think we need to keep the German language. I don't know of a place where they changed from German to English that they didn't start drifting. It seems that in North America, the English language is style, since that is what the worldly people use. If we aren't careful, the styles of the world can draw more people than what the ministers preach."[36]

Unser Leit, unser Schprooch—Our People, Our Language

The earliest scholarly descriptions of Pennsylvania Dutch, going back to the 1872 treatise by Samuel S. Haldeman, and including the doctoral dissertations of Marion Dexter Learned, Albert F. Buffington, J. William Frey, Carroll E. Reed, and Lester W. J. Seifert, make no reference to sectarian speakers other than mentioning in passing that they were among the many religious groups who were part of the Pennsylvania Dutch founding population in the eighteenth century. This is understandable for multiple reasons, including the fact that Mennonites and Amish constituted a relatively small percentage of the total Pennsylvania Dutch–speaking population until the second half of the twentieth century. The reticence of sectarians to being interviewed by researchers was likely also a factor. Into the early twentieth century, discussions of the verbal behavior of Mennonite and Amish speakers of Pennsylvania

Dutch were limited to the nonscholarly writings of outsiders such as Phebe Earle Gibbons and Helen R. Martin who, despite the clear difference in the overall quality of what they produced, both focused on sectarians' use of English.

That situation changed in 1938 with the appearance in Preston A. Barba's Pennsylfawnisch Deitsch Eck of an article by a young professor of German at Rockford College in Illinois, Herbert Penzl, on language use in an Old Order Amish settlement located near Arthur, IL.[37] In the same year that Penzl's article was published, he received an appointment at the University of Illinois at Urbana-Champaign, which is just forty miles from Arthur. At Illinois, Penzl served on the doctoral committee of Alfred L. Shoemaker, who ended up writing his dissertation on the Pennsylvania Dutch spoken by the Arthur Amish.[38] Shoemaker was a native Pennsylvania Dutch speaker from Lehigh County, PA, who returned to his home state after completing his studies and, as discussed in the previous chapter, went on to found the Pennsylvania Dutch Folklore Center at Franklin and Marshall College with J. William Frey and Don Yoder.

Penzl's article and Shoemaker's dissertation are important because they addressed two gaps in the previous scholarship on Pennsylvania Dutch by, first, focusing on a sectarian community and, second, choosing one that was located far outside of the historic cradle of the language in southeastern Pennsylvania. Penzl described the overall sociolinguistic situation in the Arthur settlement, discussing the status of the three languages in the verbal repertoire of the Amish: Pennsylvania Dutch, English, and Pennsylvania High German. Shoemaker complemented Penzl's study by focusing in depth on the linguistic features of the Pennsylvania Dutch spoken by Arthur Amish, which he compared to his own Lehigh County variety.

Building directly on Penzl's and Shoemaker's work, J. William Frey wrote an article titled "Amish 'Triple-Talk,'" which was published in 1945 and grew out of fieldwork he conducted in the Amish settlement in Lancaster County.[39] As the title of Frey's article suggests, his focus was on the trilingualism of sectarian Pennsylvania Dutch speakers, which Frey considered noteworthy in the study of Pennsylvania Dutch, since the third of their three languages, German, was no longer part of the sociolinguistic mix among nonsectarians. Frey, like Shoemaker, was a nonsectarian speaker of Pennsylvania Dutch who hailed from eastern York County, the focus of his own dissertation at Illinois, which he completed just one year after Shoemaker finished his degree.[40]

The 1930s, when Penzl, Shoemaker, and Frey began directing the attention of their fellow scholars to sectarian speakers of Pennsylvania Dutch, was an important turning point in the history of the language. This was the era during which the last generation of fluent nonsectarian speakers was born; after the 1930s there were very few nonsectarian Pennsylvania Dutch who acquired the language fully during childhood, and even fewer who maintained it actively into adulthood. This was the culmination of a process of language shift that had been underway at least since the time of Henry Harbaugh in the middle of the nineteenth century. As discussed earlier, maintenance of Pennsylvania Dutch had always correlated with the limited geographic and social mobility of its speakers. By the 1930s, the traditional isolation of rural southeastern Pennsylvania was largely gone as most Americans' physical and social mobility dramatically increased, with the result that Pennsylvania Dutch speakers came into closer contact than ever before with English monolinguals in their communities, workplaces, and even families through intermarriage.

Modern Mennonites and members of other relatively progressive sectarian groups experienced much the same assimilation to the English-speaking majority during this time, minus the intermarriage, but their Old Order cousins did not. The most conservative Amish and Mennonites, as members of endogamous, rurally based communities who intentionally set very clear boundaries between them and the larger society, including in the area of education, were able to successfully maintain Pennsylvania Dutch and, receptively, German.

The changes in American society that marked the beginning of the end for Pennsylvania Dutch among nonsectarians were not without effect on the Old Orders, however, who were brought into closer contact with English-monolingual outsiders, which now included relatives who were members of a growing number of more progressive Anabaptist churches. The increased pressure on the Old Orders to use English more often did not compel them to abandon their heritage language, as the nonsectarians had, but it did leave its mark on the varieties of Pennsylvania Dutch that they speak. In the remainder of this chapter, I consider in some detail the status of each of the three languages used by Old Order sectarians today, Pennsylvania Dutch, English, and German.

As native speaker–scholars of Pennsylvania Dutch, Shoemaker and Frey were intimately familiar with something even outsiders knew, which was that, despite the striking homogeneity across all subvarieties of Pennsylvania Dutch, which is still true today, there were differences in the way the language was spoken in different regions. In particular, Carroll E. Reed, Lester W. J. Seifert, and Albert F. Buffington produced a number of publications documenting patterns of variation in Pennsylvania Dutch in southeastern Pennsylvania and elsewhere.[41] Simplifying greatly, going back at least to the early nineteenth century, there was a general east-west division within the traditional Dutch Country, with the greatest differences to be found between the Pennsylvania Dutch spoken in what is today Lehigh County, in the northeast, and the Lancaster and York County varieties, in the southwest. Berks County, located between Lehigh and Lancaster, was a transitional area, alternately patterning with eastern and western varieties.[42] Although there had been an Anabaptist presence in Berks County in the earliest days of German settlement in southeastern Pennsylvania, sectarians soon came to be concentrated more heavily in Lancaster County, certainly to a much greater degree than in Lehigh County. Most sectarian varieties today, including those spoken outside of Pennsylvania, bear a greater resemblance to the historically western Dutch Country varieties than to eastern ones.

Already in the late eighteenth century, Mennonites and Amish began migrating out of southeastern Pennsylvania, including to Ontario in the north, and especially westward to counties in central and western Pennsylvania, and eventually to Ohio and other midwestern states. Somerset County, which is located in southwestern Pennsylvania, some 150 miles west of Lancaster County, played an especially important role in the development of Pennsylvania Dutch in the Midwest; most of the contemporary Amish and Mennonite settlements in Ohio, Indiana, Illinois, and other midwestern states have a historical connection to migration from or by way of Somerset County. Although the earliest Amish settlers had moved to Somerset in the 1760s from Berks County,[43] settlers came there from other communities in eastern and central Pennsylvania, as well as directly from Europe. A leveling-out of differences appears to have occurred in the Pennsylvania Dutch spoken in Somerset County, with variants from Lancaster and other western counties winning out.[44]

The result is that contemporary midwestern varieties of Pennsylvania Dutch are more similar to what is spoken in Lancaster than in other parts of the traditional Dutch Country in Pennsylvania, especially Lehigh County. This means that the Pennsylvania Dutch varieties spoken by Mennonite and Amish sectarians, regardless of whether they live today in Pennsylvania or the Midwest, share more in common with each other, grammatically and lexically, than they do with the eastern-county varieties. Examples of pansectarian Pennsylvania Dutch words and phrases that differ from historically Lehigh County variants include the following:[45]

English	Sectarian PD	Lehigh County PD
'lantern'	Ladann/Licht	Lutzer
'to bark'	gautze	blaffe
'lard'	Fett	Schmals
'pastor'	Breddicher	Parre
'drunkard'	Siffer	Sauflodel
'midnight'	Middernacht	Halbnacht
'you should'	du settscht	du sottscht
'you (pl.) can'	dir kennet	ihr kennt
'we were'	mir waare	mir warn
'orchard'	Baamgaarde	Bungert
'little cup'	Koppli	Koppche
'church'	Gmee	Karrich
'noise'	Yacht	Zucht
'to smell'	schmacke	rieche
'to set the table'	Disch rischde	Disch setze

Aside from vocabulary, there is one important area of Pennsylvania Dutch grammar that is shared across nearly all contemporary sectarian varieties and that serves to differentiate them as a group from historical and nonsectarian varieties. This has to do with the case systems for Pennsylvania Dutch nouns and pronouns. Throughout most of the history of the language, pronouns were inflected for three cases: Nominative for subjects, Accusative for direct objects, and Dative for indirect objects. Definite articles preceding nouns were inflected for one of two cases, a Common case (for both subjects and direct objects)[46] and a Dative case (for indirect objects).[47] The grammars of all varieties of Pennsylvania Dutch, nonsectarian and sectarian, were identical with respect to case into the twentieth century; this is amply documented in descriptive linguistic work based on data from speakers from both groups, for example, in the dissertations of Buffington, Shoemaker, and Frey, as well as in Frey's 1945 "Amish 'Triple-Talk'" article. Today, however, the Dative case has disappeared from most sectarian varieties, existing only in isolated relic forms, yielding a case system that is identical to that of English: two for pronouns and one for definite articles.[48]

The disappearance of the Dative case in sectarian Pennsylvania Dutch may be dated precisely to the first decades of the twentieth century, on the basis of interviews made with sectarian and nonsectarian speakers of Pennsylvania Dutch in the 1980s as part of a research project overseen by Wolfgang W. Moelleken of the State University of New York at Albany.[49] The Moelleken Collection of recordings includes interviews made with Amish from Lancaster County and Arthur, IL, among many other communities, who were born between 1904 and 1958, and 1905 and 1958, respectively. Frey and Shoemaker, who did their fieldwork in these two Amish communities in the 1930s (Shoemaker in Arthur) and 1940s (Frey in Lancaster), drew their data from adult speakers who would have been born between the 1860s and the 1910s; thus, the oldest speakers interviewed by the Moelleken team would have been young adults during the time of Frey's and Shoemaker's fieldwork. The data in the Moelleken Collection that were collected from speakers from the Lancaster and Arthur Amish communities show that the loss of the Dative began in Lancaster with at least a few speakers born in 1910. No Dative forms are attested in Lancaster speakers who were born after 1924. In the Moelleken recordings from Arthur, the oldest Dative-free speaker was born in 1933; in speakers born after 1933, the Dative is completely gone. These data strongly suggest that the first Amish to acquire Pennsylvania Dutch without a Dative case were born in the 1920s and 1930s, at precisely the time their contact with English monolinguals intensified.

Given that the resulting Pennsylvania Dutch case system became identical to that of English, it is quite plausible that an increase in their proficiency in English at least promoted the loss of the Dative. Further

support for the role of English bilingualism in leading to the convergence of the Pennsylvania Dutch case system with that of English comes
from a modern sectarian variety in which the Dative is still used. This is
the Pennsylvania Dutch spoken by the so-called Swartzentruber Amish,
the most conservative Amish group, whose ancestors split from the Old
Orders in eastern Ohio in 1913.[50] The Swartzentrubers, who currently
account for approximately 7% of the total Amish population,[51] in many
areas have very little contact with non-Swartzentrubers, both Amish
and non-Amish. The use of English is therefore much less widespread
among the Swartzentrubers than among other sectarian groups, hence
it is not surprising that their Pennsylvania Dutch shows less structural
influence from English.[52]

Despite the strong resemblance of Mennonite and Amish varieties
of Pennsylvania Dutch to one another in terms of vocabulary and
grammar (e.g., their Dative-less case system), two major parameters
of variation serve to differentiate sectarian varieties from one another,
one geographic and the other having to do with church affiliation. The
most salient regional differences distinguish the speech of Amish from
or affiliated with congregations in Lancaster County, PA, on the one
hand, and midwestern Amish, on the other. One phonetic feature in
particular is a shibboleth that quickly reveals one's origin, namely the
pronunciation of the diphthong /ai/ in words such as such as *drei*, 'three',
deitsch, 'Pennsylvania Dutch / German', and *Weibsleit*, 'women'. Historically, in Palatine German, and still among Lancaster Amish, the vowel
rhymes with the English word *eye*. Most midwestern Amish pronounce
the vowel differently, as a monophthong, somewhat like the vowel in
the English *badge*. So a Lancaster Amish person would refer to three
Pennsylvania Dutch–speaking women as "*dry dytchi Vypslyt*," while a
Midwesterner would say, "*dræ dætchi Væpslæt*."[53]

A second major phonetic shibboleth distinguishing the Pennsylvania Dutch spoken by sectarians (both Amish and Mennonites) from
Lancaster County from the varieties used by midwestern Amish has
to do with the pronunciation of /r/. Lancaster speakers have adopted
the "American" (retroflex) /r/, while Midwesterners are somewhat more
conservative, continuing to articulate this sound with a tap of the tip of
the tongue, as Palatine German speakers and most nonsectarians used
to do also, though only in certain phonetic environments. Midwestern

Amish produce this "tapped" /r/ between vowels in the middle of a word (e.g., *faahre*, 'to drive') or after another consonant at the beginning of a word (e.g., *griege*, 'to get, receive'); when an /r/ is the first sound in a word, as in *Riewe*, 'beets', *ruhich*, 'quiet', and *Ratt*, 'rat', most midwestern Pennsylvania Dutch speakers now use the retroflex /r/.[54]

Aside from differences in the speech of Amish from Lancaster and from the Midwest, there are also differences between the Pennsylvania Dutch spoken by Amish and Old Order Mennonites, including within Lancaster County. Here, the differences are generally lexical rather than pronunciational. Examples of familiar vocabulary differences between Amish and Mennonites in Lancaster are given below.

English	Lancaster OOM	Lancaster OOA
'dress'	Frack	Rock
'coat'	Rock	Wammes
'buggy'	Fuhr/Karritsch	Dachweggli
'to comb'	schdreele	kemme
'lawn'	Hoof	Heefli
'communion'	Nachtmohl	Grossgmee

Regional (Lancaster versus Midwest) and intrasectarian (Old Order Amish versus Old Order Mennonite) differences aside, the domains in which Pennsylvania Dutch is used among Old Orders are largely the same. It is the primary medium of oral communication with other Pennsylvania Dutch speakers. In the same way that the language always connoted trust and intimacy among nonsectarians, Pennsylvania Dutch continues to have strong symbolic power by connecting speakers with one another, even across lines of sectarian affiliation. A brief anecdote illustrates this point. An Old Order Mennonite man who is close friends with a Pennsylvania Dutch–speaking modern Mennonite once remarked how strange it was for him to hear his friend speak English. "When you speak Pennsylvania Dutch, you sound like my brother; in English you sound like a different person," he said.

The use of Pennsylvania Dutch among sectarians is a marker of humility (*Demut*), the cardinal virtue that sectarians very intentionally aim to live by. If Old Orders speak English rather than Pennsylvania Dutch among themselves and no English monolinguals are present, it is often viewed as a sign of pride (*Hochmut*), which all sectarians would agree must be avoided. Old Orders are keenly aware that Pennsylvania Dutch has long been compared negatively to German, but its "low" status in the view of outsiders, "the world people" (*Weltleit*; also *die Hohe*, lit. 'the high ones'), makes it an appropriate symbol, along with dress and limitations on the use of technology, for people who intentionally strive to be "lower" (*niddrer*) than the rest of society.[55]

Although Pennsylvania Dutch is the primary oral language within Amish and Old Order Mennonite communities, sectarians rarely read or write in the language; their literacy needs are met mainly by English and, secondarily, German. Though personal letters will often contain an occasional Pennsylvania Dutch word that is not easily rendered into English, that language, the sole medium of instruction in sectarian parochial schools, is essentially the only one that sectarians use for writing. The large body of Pennsylvania Dutch literature from the nineteenth and twentieth centuries is largely unknown to Old Orders, and when they do occasionally come across written Pennsylvania Dutch, as for example in the successor column to Preston Barba's Pennsylfawnisch Deitsch Eck, which was edited for many years by C. Richard Beam of Millersville University and printed in the two English-language newspapers serving Amish and Mennonite readers, *Die Botschaft* and the *Budget*, many sectarians admit they can read Pennsylvania Dutch prose and poetry only with considerable effort.

As mentioned above, John H. Oberholtzer was the only nineteenth-century sectarian known to write complete texts in Pennsylvania Dutch. There were only a few more such writers in the twentieth century, two of whom both happened to have grown up in Old Order Mennonite communities in Ontario.[56] The lengthiest single example of written sectarian Pennsylvania Dutch is a translation of the Bible, *Di Heilich Shrift*, that was produced by a committee of native speakers from Old and New Order Amish communities in Ohio coordinated by Henry D. Hershberger.[57] The same committee also produced *Vella Laysa* (Let's read), a collection of Bible stories for children.[58] Although the Pennsylvania Dutch translation of the Bible is not used in Old Order Amish worship services (the Luther German version continues to serve that purpose), many Amish do own copies and appreciate having a translation in a third language, in addition to German and English, in order to deepen their understanding of Scripture.

To give a more detailed sense of how sectarians express themselves in Pennsylvania Dutch, four versions of the same Scriptural passage, Luke 2:8–12, are given below: the King James English version; an older, Lehigh County–oriented Pennsylvania Dutch translation made by Ralph Charles Wood (1905–1984), a nonsectarian native speaker; the *Heilich Shrift* translation; and the *Vella Laysa* paraphrase for children. Verbatim English translations for the latter three follow each.

King James English

And there were in the same country shepherds abiding in the field, keeping watch over their flock by night. And, lo, the angel of the Lord came upon them, and the glory of the Lord shone round about them: and they were sore afraid. And the angel said unto them, Fear not: for, behold, I bring you good tidings of great joy, which shall be to all people. For unto you is born this day in the city of David a Saviour, which is Christ the Lord. And this *shall* be a sign unto you; Ye shall find the babe wrapped in swaddling clothes, lying in a manger.

Nonsectarian Pennsylvania Dutch (Ralph C. Wood)

Un 's waare Schoofhieder in sellre Gegend im Feld, die hen in der Nacht ihre Schoof ghiet. Un sehnt, em Harr sei Engel is zu ne kumme un die Glori vum Harr hot um sie geleicht un sie hen sich arrick gefarricht. Awwer der Engel hot ne gsaat: Farricht eich net. Sehnt, ich verkindich eich groosi Freed, as far all die Leit in der Welt bschtimmt is. Far heit is eich der Heiland gebore, Grischdus der Harr, in em Daavid seinre Schtatt. Un des nemmt fer en Zeeche: ihr finne es Kindche in Windle gewickelt un in em Fuderdroog leie.[59]

And there were shepherds in that area in the field who were taking care of their sheep at night. And see, the Lord's angel came to them, and the glory of the Lord shone around them, and they were very afraid. But the angel said to them: "Don't be afraid. See, I am announcing to you great joy, which is meant for all the people in the world. Because today the Savior is born for you, Christ the Lord, in David's city. And take this for a sign: you will find the little child wrapped in diapers and lying in a feed trough."

Ohio Amish Pennsylvania Dutch (Committee for Translation)

Un in selli landshaft voahra shohf-heedah draus im feld am iahra shohf heeda deich di nacht. Un's is en engel fumm Hah zu eena kumma, un di hallichkeit fumm Hah hott um si rum ksheind, un si henn sich kfeicht. No hott da engel ksawt zu eena, "Feichet eich nett, fa ich bring eich goodi zeiya vo eich froh macha zayla, un vo zu awl di leit kumma zayla. Fa zu eich is heit da Heiland geboahra vadda in di shatt fumm Dawfit. Eah is Christus da Hah. Un dess zayld en zaycha sei fa eich: diah finnet's kind eigvikkeld imma duch un am imma foodah-drohk leiya."[60]

And in the same area were shepherds out in the field taking care of their sheep through the night. And an angel of the Lord came to them, and the glory of the Lord shone around them, and they were afraid. Then the angel said to them: "Don't be afraid, because I bring you good witnesses that will make you happy and which will come to all the people. For to you is born today the Savior in the city of David. He is Christ the Lord. And this will be a sign for you: you will find the child wrapped up in a cloth and lying in a feed-trough."

Ohio Amish Pennsylvania Dutch Paraphrase for Children
(Vella Laysa)

Di saym nacht es Jesus geboahra voah, voahra samm mennah am iahra shohf heeda nayksht an Bethlehem. Es is en engel fu'm Hah zu eena kumma un's is gans hell vadda datt um si rumm. Di shohf-heedah henn sich gans shlimm kfeicht. Avvah da engel hott gsawt, "Feichet eich nett. Heichet mol! Ich habb samm vundahboahri goodi sacha es ich eich fazayla vill un dess soll sei fa awl leit. Heit is da Heiland geboahra vadda in di shtatt fu'm David. Eah is Christus da Hah! Dess zayld en zaycha sei fa eich: diah finnet's kind gvikkeld in en duch un in en foodah-drohk leiya."[61]

The same night that Jesus was born, there were some men taking care of their sheep near Bethlehem. An angel from the Lord came to them and it got really bright around them there. The shepherds were really afraid. But the angel said, "Don't be afraid. Listen! I have some really good things to tell you, and this should be for all people. Today the Savior has been born in the city of David. He is Christ the Lord! This will be a sign for you: you will find the child wrapped in a cloth and lying in a feed-trough.

Although the Luther German Bible is the only translation that is employed in Old Order Amish and Old Order Mennonite worship services,

Pennsylvania Dutch is nonetheless used in church as the main language of sermons. It is common for individual words and longer quotations from the Luther Bible and other religious texts to be recited, yet all original speech during worship is in Pennsylvania Dutch. The use of the language in one of the most sacred contexts in Old Order life demonstrates that its appropriateness is not limited to informal domains. Overall, Pennsylvania Dutch is not subject to prescriptive standards of quality; that is, speakers do not have explicit norms to distinguish "good" from "bad" Pennsylvania Dutch in the way that speakers of languages with established literary traditions such as English, German, Spanish, and the like have.

The consensus among Old Orders is that there are more and less appropriate ways of expressing oneself in both Pennsylvania Dutch and English, which derive from their spiritual values. In a book written to clarify what Amish people believe and how their beliefs are grounded in Scripture is a section titled "Our Speech." It does not refer to any specific language, but it does offer guidelines for appropriate speech that are reflected in how sectarians express themselves in Pennsylvania Dutch and English.[62] In general, there is an awareness that speech can be put to good and bad use, and sectarians cite references to both from the Old and New Testaments. To the question "Do words really matter?" the anonymous authors of the book on Amish doctrine respond, "Yes, for God will judge us accordingly. Jesus said, 'Every idle word that men shall speak, they shall give account thereof in the day of judgment. For by thy words thou shalt be condemned'" (Matt. 12: 36–37). This question and answer are followed up with specific examples of what constitutes "idle words," namely "swearing," "cursing," "blasphemy," "profanity," "bywords or 'softer' versions of profanity," and "lightminded or silly chatter."[63]

Above all, sectarians never invoke God, Jesus, heaven, hell, the devil, and related concepts (e.g., damnation) in the casual ways that many outsiders do. They will utter *Gott, Yesus, Himmel, Hell,* and *der Deifel* but only in serious religious discussions, never in vain. On occasion God is referred to as *der gut Mann,* 'the good man', and the devil as *der wiescht Mann,* 'the evil man'. However, the use of bywords is somewhat more common than many sectarians would prefer. Examples include *jiminy kratz* (≈ Jesus Christ), *was der Hund* (≈ *was die Hell,* 'what the hell'), and *verderbt* (≈ *verdammt*, 'damned'). These are not frequent, however, and are overtly stigmatized. Interestingly, Pennsylvania sectarians who happen to have had contact with nonsectarian speakers of Pennsylvania Dutch, from Berks County, for example, stereotype them as using profanity with some frequency (*Selli Barricks Kaundi Leit kenne rieli fluche*, 'Those Berks County people can really curse').

Sectarians place considerable value on speaking honestly, which is reflected in their tendency to speak in ways that outsiders often view as especially understated. For example, many Amish and Mennonites will not use the adjective *hees*, 'hot', in reference to the weather, out of a desire not to inadvertently compare the Earth to hell. Even on brutally hot days, sectarians will typically describe the weather as something like *addlich waarm*, 'pretty warm'. *Hees* can, however, be used to speak of substances such as boiling water, when there is no risk of comparison to hell. Other examples of sectarian understatement include their avoidance of expressions such as *ich bin an verhungere*, 'I am starving', or *ich kennt ebaut doot gehe*, 'I could just about die', because such statements are patently false and therefore tantamount to lying, which is a serious transgression. And although many sectarians have a hearty (and often earthy) sense of humor, the jokes or funny stories they tell almost always refer to real or plausibly real rather than imaginary events, and then only when there is no risk of causing offense or embarrassment to another person. The Old Order concern to avoid telling untruths partly explains their discomfort with literary fiction, especially "lighter" texts, like much of the humorous material produced by nineteenth- and twentieth-century nonsectarian Pennsylvania Dutch writers.

An additional example of moderation in Amish and Mennonite use of language has to do with expressions of love and affection. In sectarian Pennsylvania Dutch, the verb meaning 'to love', *liewe*, which is attested for nonsectarian varieties, is never used. Its German counterpart, *lieben*, is, but only in reference to Christian love or agape. The related noun *Liebe* is used in both sectarian German and Pennsylvania Dutch (rendered in Pennsylvania Dutch as *Liebi* or *Liewi*) but, again, only in the sense of agape. Sectarians who feel more than brotherly love for each other will prefer to let their actions rather than their words express their emotions, but on occasion parents and children will say to each other *ich gleich dich*, literally, 'I like you' (meaning 'I love you') at bedtime.[64]

Hochdeitsch, not Hochdeutsch

Even though there is a clear difference in Amish and Mennonite sectarians' proficiency in Pennsylvania Dutch, which is their main oral language for everyday interactions, and Pennsylvania High German, which they can read, sing, and recite but not converse in spontaneously, symbolically the two languages are intertwined. The maintenance of German for religious purposes correlates with the continued use of Pennsylvania Dutch in both informal and formal domains. There is no Anabaptist sect that uses German in worship and English in all other situations; members of churches that maintain German also keep speaking Pennsylvania Dutch. However, the converse is not always true: there are groups that split from the Old Order Amish and horse-and-buggy Old Order Mennonites, notably the Beachy Amish and the Horning Mennonites,[65] who have switched to English in worship, some of whose members continue to speak Pennsylvania Dutch at home. In general, though, the bilingualism in families who belong to churches separate from but with close historical ties to the Old Orders is transitional. Though it may take a generation or two, when German is displaced from the church, the shift to English monolingualism at home becomes almost inevitable.[66]

The extent to which Pennsylvania High German and Pennsylvania Dutch are inextricably linked to one another in the sociolinguistic ecology of sectarian life is nicely expressed in a poem written in Pennsylvania High German by an anonymous Amish sectarian titled "Die Muttersprache" (The mother tongue).[67] The poem begins with the poet expressing his community's "love" (here is an example of how *lieben* may be used in sectarian German) for its "mother tongue," the preservation of which is equated with upholding the fifth commandment ("Honor your father and your mother").

> We love our mother tongue
> That we learned on her [mother's] lap,
> So honor your parents
> With the language, as they would like you to.[68]

As the poem proceeds, it becomes clear that *die Muttersprache* refers to both Pennsylvania Dutch and German. In the second verse, the

Die Muttersprache

Wir lieben doch die Muttersprache
Die wir lernten auf ihren Schoß,
So tut doch eure Eltern ehren
Mit der Sprache wie sie es begehren.

Wo kommt das her daß unsre Knaben
Ein andere Sprach im Gebrauch haben
Wenn sie also zusammen kommen,
Haben wir dies schon wahr genommen?

Was möchte dann der Treiber sein
Andre Sprach zu gebrauchen in der
  Gemein,
Welcher Geist tut zu diesem führen,
Daß die Muttersprach sie tun verlieren?

Wenn an der Gemein man das muß
  hören,
Wünsch ich mir würden alle wehren.
Daß nicht eine Sprach kommt herein
Daß uns nicht ziemt in der Gemein.

Wir wollen das doch recht betrachten,
Und das doch nicht so gar leicht achten,
Daß wir das nur walten lassen,
Das Rechte dann zu viel vergessen.

Der Hochmuts-Geist, der liebt das sehr,
Wer Demut liebt, dem fällt es schwer,
Und nimmt doch solches tief zu Herzen,
Wie das in Zeit uns macht zu stürzen.

Ich will uns alle hier noch recht warnen
Daß wir die Kinder recht Deutsch lernen
Daß sie recht können lesen und singen,
Für den Herrn ein Dankopfer bringen.

Wo möchte das uns dann hinführen?
Wenn wir unsere Sprach verlieren,
O warnet sie doch recht in Zeit
Und nehmt es wahr, ihr liebe Leut'.

Wer mit der Muttersprache
  nicht zufrieden ist
Geißt er noch wirklich dann
  ein „Christ"?

—Anonymous

"Die Muttersprache" 1983.

poet asks his readers whether they have noticed that their young people sometimes use a different language (*ein andere Sprach*, i.e., English) when they socialize with one another. And then, in the next two verses, the writer questions the encroachment of that "other language" into the realm of *die Muttersprache* in church and expresses his desire for his fellow Amish to hold the line "so that a language does not come in that is not appropriate in our church" (*daß nicht eine Sprach kommt herein daß uns nicht ziemt in der Gemein*). Since both German and Pennsylvania Dutch are used in church, *die Muttersprache* could refer here to either language or both.

In the sixth verse, the author makes clear what is at risk with the loss of German / Pennsylvania Dutch for his community and links language shift to the dichotomy of *Hochmut* (pride) versus *Demut* (humility), which is so salient in everyday sectarian life.

> The spirit of pride loves it [shifting to English] much,
> But whoever loves humility is hurt by it
> And takes very seriously
> How it, in time, could make us fall.[69]

The poet urges his readers to "teach children German properly" (*die Kinder recht Deutsch lernen*) so that they are able to read and sing in order to please God. Here *Deutsch* is clearly referring to German and not Pennsylvania Dutch, since the latter language is neither explicitly taught nor read nor sung. The poem concludes with a warning that echoes the serious tone at the conclusion of Henry Harbaugh's "Das alt Schulhaus an der Krick":

> Where might this lead us then,
> If we lose our language?
> O, warn them in time
> And take this seriously, dear people.
>
> Can whoever is with his mother tongue
>   not satisfied
> Really still be called
>   a "Christian"?[70]

The undeniable spiritual-symbolic importance attached by Old Orders to maintaining German in church does not mean that their use of it is made to conform to explicitly prescriptive standards of correctness, as is the case with Modern Standard German in Europe. The situation of contemporary sectarian German is thus similar to that of largely uncodified Pennsylvania High German in the nineteenth century as used by nonsectarians, especially in the press. This lack of normativity often surprises contemporary European German speakers, who are struck by the many differences, both structural and orthographic, between their language and sectarian German in texts like the poem above.[71]

Another example of sectarian German that is even more different from European German than the language in "Die Muttersprache" is the editors' preface (*Forrede*; Eur. Ger. *Vorrede*) to a reference manual for Amish ministers and bishops.[72] In this text there are numerous divergences in grammar and spelling from what one would find in standard European German, many of which are due to influence from Pennsylvania Dutch. Yet its "faultiness" as measured against modern European German criteria is irrelevant for sectarian users of German, for

Die Forrede

Liebe Lefer! Nach-dem das fiele Bischofe und Prediger, fo-wohl wie auch Brüder, ein herzlicher zu-fpruch gegeben haben für dies Buch in der druck bringen, haben wir es mit fleiß unterfucht und es gefunden unter die alte-Bischofe angefehet (notwendig) und kann nach eine große hilfe fein für die deutfche fprache Gemeinden mit helfen. Da das diefe fprache eine der fchönften, wortreichften und vollkommenften, unter allen fprachen ist und nach am meiften die Mutterfprache, da wollen wir, Amifhe Leute, mehr fleiß a-wenden fie auf-halten.

Ihr lefer werdet auch fiele verwechfeln und unfolkommene auf-fetene finden in die- fem Buch, da wollen wir es haben das ihr uns anfagen und mechten die veränderung machen im nachten druck etc.

Wir hofen auch nach das alle lefer es zu herzen nehmen das die Leiden Lehr, an Jefu Chrifti, im diefem Buch verzügelt ist von die beftimmte Bischofe die da beftimmt fein mit rat von Holmes, Bahne und Cochocton County Bischofe welche zum Bischop Amt Erwählt warten im jahr 1961 und eher. Auß Liebe.

Die Berfaffer.

Die Forrede (Preface).
Source: Miller and Raber 1976.

whom it is not necessary to be able to write original texts and converse spontaneously in German. All an Old Order sectarian needs to know—and should know—is enough German to be able to understand the Bible, hymnals, and prayer books. It makes no difference how one might choose to write it, since that is a superfluous linguistic exercise. There is thus nothing ironic when the editors explain their intent to promote the maintenance of German through their manual:

Da das diese sprache eine der schönsten, wortreichsten und vollkommensten, unter allen sprachen ist und nach am meisten die Muttersprache, da wollen wir, Amishe Leute, mehr fleiß a-wenden sie aufhalten.

European German translation

Da diese Sprache eine der schönsten, wortreichsten und vollkommensten unter allen Sprachen ist, und noch vor allem unsere Muttersprache, so wollen wir Amische Leute mehr Fleiß anwenden und sie aufrechterhalten.

Since this language is one of the most beautiful, most rich in vocabulary, and most advanced of all languages, and above all our mother tongue, let us Amish people apply more diligence and keep it up.

Differences in spelling between words in the Forrede and their European German equivalents abound, for example, *fiele* ≈ *viele*, 'many'; *nach* ≈ *noch*, 'still, yet'; *Amishe* ≈ *Amische*, 'Amish'; *mechten* ≈ *möchten*, 'might'; *hofen* ≈ *hoffen*, 'hope'; *verzügelt* ≈ *versiegelt*, 'sealed'; *yahr* ≈ *Jahr*, 'year'. Capitalization of nouns, which is required in European German, is also largely absent in the sectarian text. The text includes many hyphenated words that in European German are written without hyphens. There are also a number of grammatical divergences between the Forrede and how European German speakers would write it, many of which are directly due to influence from Pennsylvania Dutch, including the use of two elements instead of one to introduce certain dependent clauses, for example, PHG *nach-dem as* ≈ PD *nochdem as* ≈ EG *nachdem*, 'after'; and the use of *für*, 'for' (PD *fer*), instead of EG *um . . . zu* to express the meaning 'in order to'. Several individual words in the sectarian text are also modeled directly after Pennsylvania Dutch words, for example,

PHG *auf-halten* ≈ PD *uffhalde* ≈ EG *aufrechterhalten*, 'to keep up'; PHG *mechten* ≈ PD *mechte* ≈ EG *würden vielleicht*, 'might (bring)'; and PHG *warten* ≈ PD *waarde* ≈ EG *wurden*, 'were (chosen)'.

Despite the orthographic, grammatical, and lexical deviations from European German norms in this sample of written sectarian German, the text is completely comprehensible to its intended audience, Amish ministers, which is the only goal of its writers. *Hochdeitsch* enjoys considerable prestige among sectarians as the language of the Bible and other religious works, but like its vernacular counterpart, Pennsylvania Dutch, it is free of codified norms of correctness. The fact that a standard variety of German may be written as one pleases, as long as the meaning is accurately conveyed, is anomalous for people who read and write standard European German.

The lack of normativity in sectarian German is not a new phenomenon. Going back to the earliest days of the Pennsylvania Dutch presence in North America, Pennsylvania High German was largely autonomous from the rules set down for standard European German, the criticisms of outsiders such as Johann David Schöpf notwithstanding. Amish and Mennonite sectarians today are thus carrying on a very old tradition that was once shared by all Pennsylvania Dutch groups who employed German in worship. The strongly "Dutchified" character of Pennsylvania High German extends beyond how it is written to how it is recited and sung. Albert F. Buffington, a native nonsectarian Pennsylvania Dutch speaker and Harvard-trained linguist, described in detail the phonological patterns of oral Dutchified German he heard growing up in the early decades of the twentieth century.[73]

Although the prayer and revival meetings Buffington attended as a child were sponsored by Evangelical and United Brethren churches with no direct connection to Anabaptist sects, the way German was pronounced by members of those groups was largely the same as among today's Amish and Mennonites. Examples of German words pronounced according to the rules of Pennsylvania Dutch phonology include *Herr* = *Harr*, 'Lord'; *schöne* = *scheeni*, 'beautiful'; *Freund* = *Freind*, 'friend'; *Tag* = *Daag*, 'day'; *bereiten* = *bereide*, 'to prepare'; and *Christus* = *Grischdus*, 'Christ'.[74] J. William Frey made similar observations about "Amish High German" in his fieldwork in Lancaster County but commented extensively on the pronunciation of /r/ at the end of a word.[75] While it is articulated as an *ah*-like vowel in Pennsylvania Dutch, in sectarian German it is pronounced like the "American" (retroflex) /r/, even by speakers who still use the original /r/ produced by a tap of the tongue. *Unser Vater*, 'our Father', which would be pronounced like "oonsah fahdah" in Pennsylvania Dutch, is rendered in sectarian German as "oonser fahder".

The lack of standardization in sectarian German is reflected in how the language is taught in parochial schools.[76] Overall, there is considerable variation across Amish and Old Order Mennonite schools as to how German is taught, usually depending on the ability of the teacher. Unlike other subjects, though, it is expected that parents share at least some of the responsibility for their children to learn German, as a manual for Amish teachers points out:

> The privilege of teaching German is ours if we use it, and it can be and certainly should be a very important part of our school program. How much, when, and in what way depends entirely on the teacher, the board, and the parents. For the parents to depend entirely on the teacher to teach their children German is about as wrong as for the teacher to refuse to teach any German at all, for here is one subject that can be taught at home to a good advantage.
>
> There is no better place to learn the German ABC's than at the family fireside.[77]

At most, German is taught for a small portion of each school day, but more commonly Amish and Mennonite school teachers set aside Friday afternoons for German instruction. Since adult sectarians need only to read, understand, sing, and recite in German, that is all that is taught in parochial schools. Children learn the German ABCs and basic phonic patterns of the language but nothing more. In this way, sectarian pupils continue to learn German today much as their ancestors—indeed all Pennsylvania Dutch children—did in the nineteenth century. Although Old Order pupils learn the fundamental elements of English grammar, often in a very prescriptive way (i.e., with a clear sense of what is "proper English" and what is not), their metalinguistic understanding of the building blocks of German word and sentence structure (e.g., noun cases, verb tenses, word order, etc.) is nonexistent. Again, this is because such knowledge is superfluous for them, since they have no need to converse or produce original texts in the language.

However, many sectarians do recognize that there is room for improvement even in their receptive knowledge of German to enable them to maintain the vital connection to their spiritual tradition. As one Amish woman has noted, "These hymns and prayers are sacred to us, written under conditions we can hardly imagine. We would not wish to lose this part of our heritage. Yet we must admit, we are not as much at home in the German language as our forefathers were. Therefore it takes more of an effort, yes, a real dedication, to keep the true spirit of these songs, prayers, and our German heritage alive. And to do this, we must understand what they are saying."[78] In response to such needs, some sectarians have produced English translations of key German texts, and many families own bilingual Luther German–King James English Bibles.

One very recent development in Old Order churches has compelled some of their members to do something highly unusual with German, namely learn to speak it. Beginning in 2000, a number of Amish and Old Order Mennonite school teachers, mainly unmarried women, started going to northern Mexico to assist a group of Mennonites living there improve their parochial schools. These Mennonites are known as the Old Colony Mennonites, whose migration history has been especially complicated. Ethnically, they trace their origins to Netherlandic-speaking northwestern Europe, but their ancestors migrated eastward, eventually ending up in Russia, thus they are sometimes referred to as *Russian Mennonites*. On the way east the ancestors of the Old Colony Mennonites shifted from Dutch to German; still today they use standard German in worship and speak a form of Low German known as *Plautdietsch* (Mennonite Low German). From Russia they emigrated to North and South America, including to northern Mexico, where they are now in contact with Old Order sectarians. In recent decades, the Old Colony Mennonites in Mexico have been beset by a number of challenges, both external and internal, one of which has been a problematic school system. Traditionally, Old Colony Mennonite parochial schools have been conducted in High German. In recent decades the quality of instruction in these schools has suffered, in part because of the teachers' low levels of proficiency in German. Inspired in the mid-1990s to help their spiritual brethren south of the border, Amish and Old Order Mennonites have started an outreach program, Old Colony Mennonite Support, an important part of which has been the service of Old Order teachers in Old Colony schools.

Pennsylvania Dutch and Plautdietsch are not mutually intelligible, since their linguistic roots lie in disparate parts of the European German dialectal area; the Palatinate is on the western periphery of modern Germany, while the source dialects for Plautdietsch were once spoken at the opposite end of German-speaking Europe, in former East Prussia, a territory that is today spread over Russia and Poland. One of the many challenges facing Old Order teachers in working to improve Old Colony schools is developing enough proficiency in German to be able to use it spontaneously in the classroom, as well to read nonreligious texts, with which they have had no experience as North American sectarians who work in English-medium schools. High German is also a means of communication between the Old Order teachers and members of the Old Colony community, who all speak Plautdietsch; some also know Spanish, but few are proficient in English. Many Old Colony Mennonites have difficulty speaking High German, in large part because of its neglect in their parochial schools.

Despite these challenges, the outreach program has shown real successes, which is gratifying to both the Old Colony Mennonites and their Old Order partners, who work hard to accommodate one another linguistically.[79] Two Amish teachers shared some of their thoughts on the language situation in Mexico:

> Continued contact with the Amish is one factor to overcoming the language barrier, but the more important factor is obviously our own education in High German. This is especially important for those who teach in Mexico. It is not a small task. German grammar is very complicated, with lots of rules and word lists to be memorized. And there are hundreds of new words to learn. While many words are related to our previous knowledge of German, many more remain to be learned.
>
> Learning German is one of the benefits that we can take home with us. But in Mexico our primary reason for learning it is so that we can teach it. Reading books in modern German is one way we can teach ourselves to use the language properly. Yet no matter how properly we speak, our efforts are wasted if the teachers and children we work with do not catch on. We need to speak properly, but in a way these Plattdeutsch speaking folks can understand.[80]

Old Order teachers in Mexico find themselves not only expanding their German vocabulary greatly but also acquiring metalinguistic knowledge about German grammar that they have never been exposed to before. To be sure, their task is eased somewhat by the fact that German, Pennsylvania Dutch, and Plautdietsch have structures in common because of the languages' shared ancestry. For example, the structures of main and dependent clauses, which are the basic building blocks of sentences, are largely the same across all three varieties: in main clauses the conjugated verb is placed in the second position, while in dependent clauses it is at the end. The verb tense systems are also quite similar in the three languages. If a Pennsylvania Dutch speaker learning to speak High German does not worry about structural details that are not essential to getting the point across (e.g., gender, number, and case endings on articles and adjectives), being able to communicate in German becomes largely a matter of learning new words that can then be inserted into familiar sentence structures. Hence the teachers' intuition expressed above that much of what they have to do to speak German involves vocabulary building.

Inevitably, these gifted and highly motivated Old Order teachers in Mexico find themselves making connections between what they learn about German and what they already know from Pennsylvania Dutch: "In studying High German, we are often excited to learn that some of our Pennsylvania German terms are actually correct. Because we are teachers and love words, we like to see the High German word in our minds when we use its rounded-off Pennsylvania German equivalent. For example, we Pennsylvanians say *Kivel* for bucket. In High German it is *Kübel*. An *Eimer* is a bucket, but so is a *Kübel*! That is the excitement of the word world. There are always new things to be learned."[81]

The enthusiasm that Amish and Old Order Mennonite teachers bring to the adventure of learning German carries over into an affection for Plautdietsch, which in turn reinforces their appreciation for maintaining their own vernacular language, Pennsylvania Dutch:

Learning Plattdeutsch allows you to feel more connected with the Russian Mennonite culture. It also opens the door to a very fascinating language. My impression is that Plattdeutsch is somehow more colorful and descriptive than either High German or English. For example, the Plattdeutsch poem and song that the first graders learned one Easter were so alive with meaning. The clear word pictures, the powerful way the emotions of Good Friday and Easter were portrayed in the poetry, seemed singular to me. I have grown to appreciate the beauty of the language.

Speakers of Plattdeutsch seem also to be aware of this beauty and therefore treasure it enough not to lose it. To us, as conservatives from the States, this stands out because of the trend towards English and away from Pennsylvania German in our circles. Among our people, one of the first things lost in a more liberal move is the German language. In Mexico, even the most liberal of the Russian Mennonites retain the speaking of their mother tongue. There are many beautiful Plattdeutsch songs and hymns, and recently Plattdeutsch Bibles and dictionaries are available. Plattdeutsch is still their favorite language to speak, even for those who know High German, Spanish, and English.[82]

The experience of Old Order teachers in the Old Colony communities of Mexico not only brings tangible benefits to their Old Colony pupils and their families; it leaves a lasting impact on the teachers themselves, including a deeper respect for their German linguistic heritage: "I personally find the German language to be a beautiful language. I love it for its depth and simplicity. Learning to speak and understand it better has enriched my appreciation for the German literature passed down to us by our forefathers. They must have been well educated to be able to preserve their faith and convictions in writing. Where would we be if they had not been so literate?"[83]

"There's Nothing Wrong with the English Language, But . . ."

Sectarian attitudes toward proficiency in English differ considerably from their view of how German should be used, which may seem paradoxical given that German is so closely bound up with their spiritual heritage, while English is the language of "the world." Indeed, one of the most common ways for Old Orders to refer to non–Amish and Mennonites, even those who may have grown up in sectarian families but later left, is as "English" (*englisch*). However, the status of English in the sociolinguistic ecology of Old Order communities is quite different from that of German. Whereas the latter language has profound spiritual-symbolic significance, English is above all regarded as a necessary tool for sectarians' economic well-being. Uria R. Byler, the Amish author of the teacher's manual quoted above, stressed to his fellow sectarian readers in 1969 the critical importance of proficiency in English and left no doubt as to the necessity of it being taught, and taught well, in parochial schools:

> English is too vital a subject to be relegated to the "only-when-there-is-time" duties. By neglecting it the teacher is failing to provide an adequate education for his pupils after they graduate and meet the general public. And let's not delude ourselves and think that we can insulate ourselves against the world today. It is impossible to shut ourselves off completely and be isolated from our fellow citizens, the non-Amish.
>
> Years ago it was not so important to stress English as it is now. The same can be said for any other school subject. Back in Grandfather's day the country schools ran only about six months of the year, and for their type of living Grandfather got along fine with little education. Not so today.
>
> In our day and age we must face the fact that our educational patterns have changed. For better or worse, our life is more complicated, more complex, and we need to keep records, learn how to figure and tabulate correctly. We need to know how to write business letters and mail orders to a far greater extent than our ancestors did. Not knowing how to transact a business deal can be expensive: Ignorance may be bliss in some cases but in others it may cost dollars and cents and embarrassment.
>
> For these reasons a thorough course in English is very important.[84]

Byler's "Grandfather's day" was the era before the 1920s and 1930s, when the major changes affecting rural America brought on by increasing urbanization, industrialization, and social and geographic mobility marked the beginning of the end for Pennsylvania Dutch among the nonsectarians, while Amish and Old Order Mennonites who clung to both Pennsylvania Dutch and German were compelled to engage with English speakers to a degree never experienced in their history before. An Amish man is said to have remarked once, "If we were to disappear from the face of the Earth tomorrow, no one would miss us. But if the rest of society were to disappear tomorrow, we would disappear with them." The English language is not a secondary player in the sociolinguistic ecology of modern Pennsylvania Dutch speakers; it is essential to their economic survival.

The importance of English among today's sectarians goes well beyond its utility as a means of communication with outsiders for business and other purposes. It serves important functions within Old Order society as well, primarily through its status as the main medium of active literacy. Although Amish and Mennonite sectarians are able to read the Bible, prayer books, and hymnals in German, all other reading matter, books and other print media, including religious works (children's Bible stories, for example), is in English. And when Old Orders themselves write anything, from grocery lists to letters to diaries to poems written to honor loved ones who have passed away, it is almost always in English. A language that serves to express the most personal and intimate thoughts, as in private correspondence between sectarians, is not merely an impersonal tool employed for communication only when absolutely necessary; it is an important part of Old Order identity. Not only in writing but also in their speech sectarians use English to convey much more than mundane information. For example, essentially all sectarian families today have at least a few close relatives, often modern Mennonites, who are either not able or choose not to speak Pennsylvania Dutch, which means that oral communication between Old Orders and non–Old Orders, including family members, typically happens in English.

The central place of English in Old Order society is reflected in the fact that the majority of Amish and Mennonites are natively ambilingual; that is, they have equal oral mastery of Pennsylvania Dutch and English. If an English monolingual were to converse with an Old Order sectarian without knowing that person's religious affiliation and linguistic background, the English speaker would likely have no clue that the person she is talking to acquired another language before English. Without a doubt, Old Order parochial schools play a crucial role in promoting the proficiency of sectarians in English. English is the sole medium of instruction in schools, and many teachers also require English to be used on the playground. Old Order children thus acquire the language naturally and well within the critical or sensitive period for psycholinguistic development, which is crucial for the development of native knowledge of a language, even if it is not the first language a child is exposed to.

Historically, sectarian ambilingualism was not as widespread as it is today. In his seminal 1945 "triple-talk" article, which was based on his experience with Amish in Lancaster County, J. William Frey notes,

"The English used by the Amish—this language being employed only on 'forced' occasions such as talking with non-Amish in towns and cities, or in the public schools—has all the earmarks of the type of speech found among any other Pennsylvania Dutch group. It can be briefly described as American English built on a framework of Pennsylvania Dutch phonemic patterns and interjected continually with whole or part loan-translations from the dialect."[85]

In essence, Frey is describing the English spoken by Amish as being just as Dutchified, phonologically and lexically, as that spoken by nonsectarians. The main reason for the linguistic dominance of Pennsylvania Dutch over English, for nonsectarians and sectarians alike, was an inverse correlation in the use of the two languages. People who were proficient in Pennsylvania Dutch and spoke the language frequently by definition did so at the expense of English. Their bilingualism was imbalanced, with Pennsylvania Dutch being the dominant of the two languages. As himself a nonsectarian native speaker of Pennsylvania Dutch and a linguist who was one of the leading experts of his time on the language, Frey can be trusted to have provided an accurate description of the sociolinguistic reality among adult sectarians in Lancaster County in the 1930s and 1940s.

The English of most sectarian speakers of Pennsylvania Dutch is quite different today. The first scholarly documentation of this fact came in 1980, with the appearance of the first of many articles written by Marion Lois Huffines, a linguist and professor of German at Bucknell University. In a study that was the first of its kind, Huffines interviewed nearly one hundred Pennsylvania Dutch speakers of varying proficiency levels, as well as another twenty-five who were ethnic Pennsylvania Dutch people but not speakers of the language. Huffines's pool of consultants included sectarians and nonsectarians and examined both their English and their Pennsylvania Dutch.[86] One of Huffines's most striking findings is that her Old Order Amish and Old Order Mennonite consultants showed far fewer phonological influences from Pennsylvania Dutch in their English than the fluent nonsectarian speakers did. In other words, nonsectarian Pennsylvania Dutch speakers tended to speak English with a "Dutchy" accent, while the sectarians as a group did not.[87] This is counterintuitive, since one would expect the people who are most distant from the social mainstream, the Old Orders, to speak the most divergent English.

One year after Huffines first reported her findings, a German scholar, Joachim Raith, offered independent confirmation of the same basic phenomenon. In his study, Raith interviewed sixteen Pennsylvania Dutch speakers from Lancaster County of different religious affiliations, three Old Order Amish, five Conservative Mennonites, six Mennonite Church Mennonites, one member of the Church of the Brethren, and one Lutheran/Reformed (nonsectarian). After asking each consultant to read aloud an English text that targeted major phonological contrasts between English and Pennsylvania Dutch, Raith found that speakers fell into one of three groups in terms of the "Dutchiness" of their English. The first group was those who spoke English essentially accent-free, and it included all three of the Amish consultants and three of the Conservative Mennonites. The second group showed minimal interference from Pennsylvania Dutch in their English and consisted of two Mennonite Church Mennonites. The remaining consultants, two Conservative Mennonites, four Mennonite Church Mennonites, and the Brethren and Lutheran/Reformed speakers, all spoke English with a heavy Dutch accent. In other words, the interviewees who were members of the most conservative sect, the Old Order Amish, spoke the "best" English, while the speech of members of the most assimilated churches (the Brethren and Lutheran/Reformed speakers) displayed the greatest influence from Pennsylvania Dutch on their English.[88] Raith notes that what he discovered about the English of the Old Order Amish is at odds with Frey had observed some three and a half decades earlier. Taken together and compared with older research, Huffines's and Raith's studies confirm that the English proficiency of most Old Order sectarians improved dramatically at some point between approximately 1940 and 1980.[89]

Anecdotal evidence of a historical difference between sectarians and nonsectarians with regard to English proficiency is provided by the following item from a collection of documents connected to a Lancaster County Amish family. It is given the title "Pennsylvania Dutch Accent."

Why don't the Amish in Lancaster County have an accent like Berks County, and some other places where Pennsylvania German is spoken? It has been quoted by some of the old Grandpas that the teachers in Lancaster County schools not only spoke, but taught very good English. An example of the caliber of some of the teachers in the public schools a hundred years ago, where my Granddad [Amos J. Stoltzfus (1872–1947)] attended, would be to note their professions: bankers, preachers, engineers, and so on. We are told that years ago when the farm work was finished in the Fall, sometimes families who had grown sons that they did not really need in winter time would send them to other farms just to work for their board and lodging because it took so much food. Many of these young men would come to Lancaster County to work in the winter so that they could learn good English.[90]

Herbert Penzl, who had studied the trilingual situation of the Amish living near Arthur, IL, at roughly the same time that Frey did his work in Lancaster, also commented on the contact between English and Pennsylvania Dutch in their community, but he found something quite different than did Frey:

Outsiders near Arthur learn the dialect very rarely. An English farmer living among the Amish, who, incidentally, called them "the world's best neighbors," picked up some Pennsylvania German, and so did one drugstore clerk in Arthur. The Amish in Arthur all speak English too; they have the rare and valuable experience of being bilingual. Their English does not show any sound-substitutions; it is not "broken." Not even any accent is noticed by the people in Arthur. When their little children are sent to the small one-room country school-houses, they understand hardly any English. In some cases they learned a little English from older children in the family, or the parents taught them a few words, not to make it too "unhendig" (unhandy) for the teacher, as I was told. But, as a rule, the children hear nothing but Pennsylvania German in their homes, before they go to school. This is the only practicable method of making them bilingual. Any foreigner living in this country, who wants his children to be bilingual, can only get a similar result by imitating the Amish. Very few have had the energy and consistency to go through with this method.[91]

Clearly, the Amish in Arthur, and likely in other midwestern sectarian communities in the 1930s, were ahead of Lancaster County in the degree to which their members had become ambilingual in Pennsylvania Dutch and English. This may have had to do with lower population density of sectarians relative to their English-monolingual neighbors in midwestern settlements at the time, in contrast to the situation in Lancaster. Recall that when nonsectarians moved west in the nineteenth century, to Wisconsin, for example, the shift to English was rapid, as they moved into communities in which they comprised only a small minority.[92] Notably, Penzl makes special mention of how well integrated (and respected) the Arthur Amish were in the larger community, which clearly fostered their strong English skills.

As the Dutchiness of sectarians' English has decreased over the past few generations, the influence of English on their Pennsylvania Dutch has increased. While the grammatical changes discussed above, especially the loss of the Dative case, have gone largely unnoticed by sectarians, there is a widespread perception among Amish and Mennonites that the amount of English loan vocabulary in their Pennsylvania Dutch is increasing. It is common for parents and grandparents to express the view that younger sectarians today use more English than did earlier generations; the English words for numbers and days of the week are often mentioned as examples of recent change in the Pennsylvania Dutch lexicon. As an Amish man from Arthur, IL, notes in a booklet directed at his fellow church members:

English is displacing [Pennsylvania] German in many areas, but of special concern are basic words which children use to describe the world around them. Sentences such as *"I[ch] bin Heem kumme Monday am Ten O'Clock"* reveal a thought pattern which relies heavily on English. Many of our young people do not understand time, such as *halwer Sechs.*

Teach your children the colors, numbers, days of the week and time in Pennsylvania German. Make a conscious effort to use those words in your sentences and expect your children to do the same. Language purity is not a reasonable goal, but the foundational words for describing and defining our world should be German if we are speaking German, and English if we are speaking English.

When using [High] German songs or scriptures for family devotions, take time to discuss (in Pennsylvania German, not English) the meaning of the words. Rephrase the verse in PA German. This brings the language to life![93]

Given the close relationship between German and Pennsylvania Dutch as two halves of the same *Mudderschprooch* coin, the Amish author continues, striving to check the influence of English on the latter language can improve facility in the former: "Avoid treating PA German and High German as separate languages. Improvement in a child's PA German will often lead to an improvement in High German comprehension. That's because they are just two flavors of the same language. Just as there is a difference between written and spoken English, PA German is for speaking and High German is for reading and writing."[94]

It is an open question as to what extent recent English borrowings actually displace older, Palatine German–derived vocabulary or whether they enhance the expressive power of the language by existing side by side with native synonyms. One interesting example of situation-specific variation in the use of native and borrowed words in Pennsylvania Dutch has to do with what is known as *child-directed speech* (also *caretaker speech, motherese, baby talk*), the speech used by sectarian adults and older children when addressing infants and toddlers.[95] Frequently, individual English lexical items are inserted into Pennsylvania Dutch sentences directed at babies and small children when native words would be used if the same sentences were directed at older persons. Examples are given below:

BABY PD:	Witt (du) sleepe?
ADULT PD:	Witt (du) schloofe?
	Do you want to sleep?
BABY PD:	Welle mer night-night / bye-bye gehe?
ADULT PD:	Welle mer ins Bett / fatt gehe?
	Shall we go to bed / away?
BABY PD:	Bis a sleepy boy!
ADULT PD:	Bischt en schleefricher Buh!
	You're a sleepy boy!
BABY PD:	No, no!
ADULT PD:	Nee, nee!
	No, no!

BABY PD: Hos du di(ch) verpoopt?
ADULT PD: Hoscht du dich vermesst / verschisse?
             Did you soil your diaper?

BABY PD: Guck mol Bossy / Puppy / Kitty!
ADULT PD: Guck mol die Kuh / der Hund / die Katz!
             Look at the cow / dog / cat!

One of the most frequent instances of using English in sectarian child-directed speech occurs when quieting a group of people down to pray silently before or after a meal. Two expressions are especially common: *Welle / lets mer pretty sei* (lit. 'Let's be pretty') and *Paddies nunner* (lit. 'Paddies down'). One would not refer to older children as *pretty* or to their hands as *Paddies*; the native words *braav*, 'well-behaved', and *Hend*, 'hands', would be used. The child-directed expressions have become so frequent, however, that this has almost become a substitute for saying *Mir welle / welle mer nau bede*, 'We'd like to / let's pray now'. Some adults will say to a mixed-age gathering, *Zeit fer Paddies nunner duh*, 'time to do paddies-down'.

It would be challenging to quantify the extent to which the English-derived component in the sectarian Pennsylvania Dutch lexicon has increased, in part because variation in the frequency of English borrowings depends on the topic of conversation.[96] As previously discussed, a count of the exact number of words in any language, borrowed or native, is impossible. Nonetheless, a sample of naturally occurring speech can convey a general impression of the English lexical influence on modern sectarian Pennsylvania Dutch. The following is an excerpt from an interview with a young Amish woman from northern Indiana who taught parochial school, a domain in which English dominates. English borrowings are underscored:

Ins Yaahr vun <u>seventy-seven to seventy-nine</u> dann waar ich an Schul <u>tietsche</u> gwest. Mir hen als browiert in die Schul geh bis ... net schpeeder as halwer acht hen mer gegliche datt sei, so as mir die <u>Lessons</u> un Schtoff <u>schtuddye</u> kenne fer seller Daag un alles <u>reddi</u> hawwe bis die Kinner kumme an acht Uhr. Sie waare als net <u>supposed</u> kumme eb die acht Uhr. Noh hen sie als <u>usually</u> gschpielt bis halwer nein wann unser Schul noh

gschtaert hot. Noh hen mer als die <u>Bell</u> grunge. S'waar en eeschtubbich
Schulhaus un mir hen all acht <u>Grades</u> ghatt, es waare zwee von uns <u>Tie-</u>
<u>tschers</u>. Ich hett die <u>five</u> <u>through</u> <u>eight</u> ghadde. Un s'erscht Ding meigeds,
dann hen mir als unser <u>Devotions</u> ghatt, mir hen als en <u>Prayer</u> ghatt,
noh hen mer als en <u>Bible Story</u> glese oder dann hen mir als gsunge. <u>Usu-</u>
<u>ally</u> hen mir Englisch gsunge, alsemol hen mer Deitsch gsunge. Noh hen
mer <u>usually</u> gschtaert mit <u>Rithmetic</u> un noh <u>Reading</u>. Zehe Uhr hen mer
<u>Recess</u> ghatt. Noh waer's . . . halwer zwelf hedde mer Middag ghatt noh
hen sie als en Schtund schpiele daafe. Un mer hen <u>Rithmetic</u> un <u>Reading</u>
un <u>Writing</u> un <u>Spelling</u>; <u>History</u> . . . <u>7th</u> un <u>8th</u> hot <u>History</u> ghatt. Un <u>5th</u>
un <u>6th</u> hot <u>Geography</u> ghatt. Noh hen mer . . . alli Freidaag hen mer <u>Ger-</u>
<u>man</u> ghatt. Mundaag meigeds hen mer als browiert en <u>Bible Verse</u> uffs
<u>Board</u> schreiwe as die Kinner <u>supposed</u> waare <u>memorize</u> bis freidaags,
noh waare sie all <u>supposed</u> 's wisse <u>by heart</u>. In die <u>Classes</u>, dann . . . wann
mer <u>Classes</u> ghadde hot, dann hen sie immer misse Englisch schwetze,
s'waar alles Englisch. Un uff <u>Recess</u>, dann waare sie aa <u>supposed</u> Englisch
schwetze. Alsemol waare . . . sin sie <u>sadde</u> wegge<u>carried</u> wadde un hen
als Deitsch gschwetzt. Noh hen mer als misse <u>sadde</u> . . . <u>sadde</u> en <u>Game</u>
schpiele mit sie fer, oh, vielleicht sie so viel Schticker Welschkann gewwe
adder ebbes, un wann mer sie ge<u>catch</u>t hen Deitsch schwetze dann hen
mer . . . hot seller <u>Person</u> daafe en Welschkannkann wegnemme von sie
un noh vielleicht bis End vun die Woch gucke wer s'menscht ghadde hett.
Awer noh fer en <u>Treat</u> alsemol dann hen mer sie glesst <u>baut</u> die letschte
sechs Woche vun's Schuljaahr hen mer sie glesst Deitsch schwetze.

From '<u>77</u> to '<u>79</u> I was <u>teaching</u> school. We would try to go to school by . . .
we liked to be there no later than seven-thirty, so that we could study the
<u>lessons</u> and stuff for that day and have everything <u>ready</u> by the time the
children came at eight o'clock. They weren't <u>supposed</u> to come before eight
o'clock. Then they <u>usually</u> played until eight-thirty when our school <u>started</u>.
Then we would ring the bell. It was a one-room schoolhouse and we had all
eight <u>grades</u>. And the first thing in the morning we had our <u>devotions</u>, we
would have a <u>prayer</u>, then we would read a <u>Bible story</u> or then we would
sing. We usually sang in English, sometimes we sang in German. Then we
usually <u>started</u> with <u>arithmetic</u> and then <u>reading</u>. At ten o'clock we had <u>re-</u>
<u>cess</u>. Then it would be . . . at eleven-thirty we would've had lunch, then they
would be allowed to play for an hour. And we had <u>arithmetic</u> and <u>reading</u>

and _writing_ and _spelling; history_ . . . _7th_ and _8th_ had _history_. And _5th_ and
_6th_ had _geography_. Then we . . . every Friday we had _German_. On Monday
mornings we would try to write a _Bible verse_ on the board that the children
were _supposed_ to _memorize_ by Friday, then they were all _supposed_ to know
it by heart. In the _classes_, then . . . when we had _classes_ they always had to
speak English, everything was English. And at _recess_ they were _supposed_ to
speak English also. Sometimes . . . they would get sort of _carried_ away and
would speak Pennsylvania Dutch. Then we would have to _sort of_ . . . _sort
of_ play a _game_ with them to, oh, give them maybe so many pieces of corn
or something, and if they got _caught_ speaking Pennsylvania Dutch then we
. . . that _person_ was allowed to take a kernel of corn from them and maybe
by the end of the week see who had the most. But sometimes as a _treat_, for
about the last six weeks of the school year, we would let them speak Pennsylvania Dutch.[97]

In this speech sample, all _function words_ (e.g., articles, pronouns,
prepositions) are completely native (i.e., not English-derived). Looking,
then, at only the _content words_ (nouns, verbs, adjectives, and adverbs),
the numbers of English loans in this sample are as follows:

nouns:	22/43	(51%)
verbs:	6/25	(24%)
adjectives:	1/5	(20%)
adverbs:	4/15	(27%)
total:	33/88	(38%)

At first glance, these appear to be considerable percentages, but, looking
at each borrowed word individually, nearly every one refers either to an
object or concept that was unknown to eighteenth-century immigrants
from Central Europe (e.g., _lesson, grade, recess_) or otherwise enriches
the Pennsylvania Dutch lexicon without displacing an older vocabulary
item. _Tietsche_ and _schtaerde_, for example, complement the older words
lehre and _aafange_, which today have church-specific meanings, 'to teach
religious content' and 'to deliver an opening sermon', respectively. And
the names of specific school subjects, such as _reading, writing_, and _Ger-
man_, are practically proper nouns; the native verbs _lese_, 'to read', and
schreiwe, 'to write', also occur in this text, as does the noun _Deitsch_.

Pennsylvania Dutch is not "watered down" by the borrowing of such words but enhanced both in terms of the overall size of its vocabulary and the range of meanings its words can express. In the same way that Amish and Mennonites have had to strike "bargains with modernity" in order to survive, the language they speak has made similar accommodations. But, in both instances, change is kept within clear limits. In terms of Old Order life, their Christian faith—the core of their society—is not the least bit compromised by the fact that they make selective use of certain aspects of technology and modern life. Similarly, the core grammatical structures of their heritage language, Pennsylvania Dutch, remain unaffected by the selective adoption of words from English.

One caveat about the place of English in Old Order communities is called for, and that has to do with the sociolinguistic situation of the Swartzentruber Amish. The Swartzentrubers, who distanced themselves from more mainstream Old Order Amish in the early twentieth century, are today the most conservative Amish group and, as a community, have the least interaction with outsiders. As a result, the English proficiency of many of their members is more limited than what is typical for most other Amish and Old Order Mennonite sectarians. Not surprisingly, Swartzentruber parochial schools place much less emphasis on developing fluency in English than schools in other Old Order communities do. The Swartzentrubers' situation is thus similar to what J. William Frey found to be the case for mainstream Lancaster Amish born in the early twentieth century in that many speak a fairly "Dutchy" English. Conversely, Swartzentruber varieties of Pennsylvania Dutch are less affected by contact with English than those spoken by other Old Order sectarians: they use fewer English borrowings in their Pennsylvania Dutch and still use the Dative case productively, as discussed earlier. The Swartzentrubers' distance from English means that it is not uncommon for them to require the assistance of English interpreters in some official situations, in court, for example. Of course, many English monolinguals also have difficulty understanding "legalese" (and medical and other forms of jargon); however, Swartzentruber Amish experience special challenges when compelled to use English in formal settings outside their community.[98]

THE TWENTIETH CENTURY MARKED an important turning point in the history of Pennsylvania Dutch. The language has now all but disappeared as an active medium of communication for nonsectarians, but, among the Old Order Amish and Old Order Mennonites, it is thriving. Comparing the sociolinguistic situation of the Old Orders today with that of nonsectarians in the nineteenth century, when both groups still spoke Pennsylvania Dutch actively, there are both similarities and differences. For sectarians and nonsectarians alike, the basic requirements for language maintenance have been largely the same: active speakers of Pennsylvania Dutch are rural dwellers of limited social and geographic mobility who live in heavily Pennsylvania Dutch communities and marry within their group; those who move away, pursue higher education, enter the professions, and marry outsiders usually shift to English.

For both sectarians and nonsectarians, Pennsylvania Dutch has been at the center of a group identity, though in different ways. For nonsectarians, the language was a hallmark of an ethnic-cultural identity distinct from that of their English-speaking neighbors, especially Anglo-Americans and other descendants of immigrants from the British Isles. The association of nonsectarian Pennsylvania Dutch language and culture with rural as opposed to urban life was also highly salient. However, the nonsectarians' Protestant Christian faith was never premised on maintaining clear boundaries between them and the rest of society, as is the situation among today's Old Orders. For Amish and Mennonite sectarians, the preservation of a mother tongue that includes two "flavors," Pennsylvania Dutch and German, has become a tangible symbol of their distinct socioreligious identity apart from "the world." And, unlike the nonsectarians, maintenance of Pennsylvania Dutch / German does not come at the expense of being proficient in English. Back in the middle of the twentieth century, it would have been difficult for observers of Old Order life, such as Harold S. Bender and perhaps also J. William Frey, to predict that English would come to occupy such an important and natural place in Amish and Old Order Mennonite verbal behavior without displacing their Germanic mother tongue.

It is in many ways unfortunate that the rich vernacular culture of the nonsectarian Pennsylvania Dutch, the banner of which was the Pennsylvania Dutch language, is now largely limited to specific events like the fersommlinge and Grundsow Lodges, public celebrations such as the annual Kutztown Folk Festival, and the activities of groups such as the

Pennsylvania German Society, the Pennsylvania German Cultural Heritage Center, and the German-Pennsylvanian Association. As laudable as the efforts of these organizations to preserve and promote the fruits of Pennsylvania Dutch culture are—and their members do important and meaningful work—one cannot help, on the one hand, but mourn the loss of the Pennsylvania Dutch language in nonsectarian homes and communities in rural Pennsylvania where it thrived for some two centuries. On the other hand, the incredible vitality of Pennsylvania Dutch in Old Order communities as far flung as Maine, Florida, Texas, Colorado, and Montana, whose populations are doubling every twenty years, suggests a bright future for the language. In the following chapter, I offer some concluding thoughts on the modern success story that is Pennsylvania Dutch among the Old Orders.

CHAPTER 7

An American Story

Knowing two languages is a privilege God has provided for us. . . .
—ANONYMOUS AMISH MAN

A Sturdy Pennsylvania Hybrid

The healthy sociolinguistic situation of Pennsylvania Dutch is linked to the social-spiritual vitality of the faith communities for whom it has become a central part of their identity. The Old Order Amish and Old Order Mennonites are profoundly aware of the significance of preserving their mother tongue, Pennsylvania Dutch and their variety of standard German, but their language maintenance has proceeded largely effortlessly when compared to other situations of language preservation. Among the Old Orders, Pennsylvania Dutch is for the most part not written down, not taught in schools, and not subject to norms of "correctness." It enjoys neither governmental support nor legal protection nor much respect from outsiders. And most of its speakers are fully fluent in the language of the larger society in which they live, English. In the same way that so many outsiders find it difficult to grasp how the Amish and Old Order Mennonites are able to not just survive but thrive in the twenty-first century, it may be just as hard for those dedicated to the preservation of the myriad endangered minority languages around the world to understand how a language such as Pennsylvania Dutch can beat the odds. Underlying the modern success story of Pennsylvania Dutch among the Old Orders is, of course, the symbolic value it holds, externally as a tangible marker of Old Orders' difference from the social mainstream and internally as the glue that bonds its speakers to one another. Above all, it is the link between language and a spiritual past, present, and hoped-for future that ensures the vitality of Pennsylvania Dutch today.

Some years ago I asked an Austrian ethnomusicologist friend who studies the Amish what impressions he, as a European, had about the existence of such a religious-cultural group in the heart of the United States. He replied that, to him, the Amish phenomenon was an expression of American tolerance. Only in America, he said, could one imagine that such a religious community would not only endure but flourish. Indeed, many Central Europeans find it hard to imagine that groups like the Amish could ever live in their societies today. Horse-drawn transportation would be anomalous on many European roads, if not banned outright. For their part, the Amish would chafe at the lack of freedom they would have to operate their own parochial schools, which in most European countries are subject to government oversight. And their non-Amish neighbors, especially those with direct experience of the privations of the World War II and postwar eras, would be utterly baffled that anyone in his or her right mind would voluntarily forgo the use of something so fundamental to modern life as electric power. Overall, the highly secular character of modern Europe would not incline citizens of countries like Germany and Switzerland to embrace social-religious communities for whom faith is at the very center of their daily lives, avowedly trumping all allegiances to secular authorities. It is telling that the German word for *sect* is *Sekte*, which can express the concept of *sect* in a neutral sense, but actually means *cult* for most people.

In spite of the fact that today's active speakers of Pennsylvania Dutch, members of Old Order Anabaptist groups, place their ultimate trust in God and not in any secular authority, including the US government, their success in America, which entails also their ability to maintain Pennsylvania Dutch, is due to a number of circumstances that are particular to American society. To be sure, the Amish and related groups are the beneficiaries of a heritage that includes tolerance, even at times a celebration, of cultural and religious diversity that is absent in many other societies. However, American tolerance has its limits. Many religious minority groups, including those indigenous to the United States, such as the Mormons, Jehovah's Witnesses, and Christian Scientists, are viewed by some with suspicion. Old Order Anabaptist faith communities are no exception in this regard. While many Americans are "enchanted" by the sight of cute Amish children at play on the grounds of their parochial country schools, still others are frustrated that those same children will not pursue formal education beyond the eighth grade. And, when it comes to linguistic diversity, the threshold of American tolerance is decidedly low. Although the story of Frederick Muhlenberg casting a deciding vote paving the way for English to become the official language of the United States is a fiction, some twenty-eight US states and many more counties and municipalities have declared English their sole official language, which reflects a deep-seated concern on the part of many English-monolingual Americans about the supposed ill effects of multilingualism.[1]

The sociolinguistic health of Pennsylvania Dutch in America has never been dependent on any support it has received from outsiders, including governmental authorities. If that had been necessary, the language would never have survived past 1800. However, Pennsylvania Dutch, unlike many Native American languages, was never the target of formal policies aimed at cultural and linguistic eradication. The key to understanding the successful maintenance of Pennsylvania Dutch is to be found in a mix of internal and external factors. Those groups who have "kept Dutch" the longest are those who have created a measure of distance, both physical and spiritual, between them and their English-monolingual neighbors. This was easier in the early nineteenth century, when most Americans were country folk and the spirit of American democracy, in both its Jeffersonian and Jacksonian expressions, allowed for distinctive local cultures—including non-English languages—to thrive, especially in rural areas.

It is tempting to think that the survival of distinctive cultures in rural America with European roots is due to their social and cultural stasis, that they are somehow frozen in time, holdovers from another era. While groups such as the Pennsylvania Dutch are indeed conservative in the literal sense of *conserving* cultural attributes with a clear historical connection to the Old World, most especially their Palatine German–derived language, all American cultures, including that of the Pennsylvania Dutch, are profoundly blended. Speaking at the first Pennsylvania Folk Life Conference, held at Franklin and Marshall College on March 31, 1951, Don Yoder had this to say about cultural synthesis in Pennsylvania:

[A] unitive movement has been prepared for in Pennsylvania's folk-culture. We are now in the second half of the 20th Century. The Holy Experiment of Father Penn is two and a half centuries old. The major assimilation of the colonial and 19th Century emigrant groups has already taken place, both in the realm of intermarriage between groups and the realm of cultural exchange. Get the picture! If you will only stop to examine your own family heritage, most of you will find that intermarriage has already taken place in your own background between the various nationalities that once made up Pennsylvania's colorful populace. How can I, for example, call myself a "Pennsylvania Dutchman" when my delightful little mother contributed so important an English, Welsh, and Irish Quaker strain to my makeup? Although it was perhaps not strong enough to cancel out the Berks and Lehigh County Dutch background of my father, it makes me *less*—or should I say *more*?—than a "Pennsylvania Dutchman." I am what most of you are, an example of this Pennsylvania hybridization. Whether we are more drought-resistant or rust-resistant, or corn-borer resistant than the parent varieties I can't say; but the truth remains that we are now a new people, a sturdy Pennsylvania hybrid![2]

Both materially and spiritually, the culture of the Pennsylvania Dutch, while conservative in some aspects, has been dynamic in many others, incorporating influences from its neighbors. No area of Pennsylvania Dutch life has been unaffected by contact with other American groups: technology (e.g., the Conestoga wagon), arts and crafts (e.g., quilts), religion (e.g., revivalism), architecture (e.g., house and barn styles), foodways (e.g., pies), and folklore (e.g., Groundhog Day). Even the distinctive garb of Amish and Old Order Mennonites has changed over time: though women's prayer coverings have their origins in Central Europe, the practice of wearing bonnets over those coverings outside the home was something Pennsylvania Dutch sectarians borrowed from their Quaker neighbors in the nineteenth century.[3] Less tangibly but no less important to understanding the culture in which the Pennsylvania

Dutch language is embedded is the notion of peasant republicanism, the synthesis of Old and New World political ideologies that justified the preservation of cultural and linguistic patterns inherited from Europe by invoking the American ideal of liberty. Hybridity is not a symptom of cultural impurity but rather a sign of the adaptability of a cultural group to changing circumstances, which in turn promotes survival. The Old Order sectarians' "bargain with modernity" is an excellent example of the dynamic character of cultural and linguistic preservation. Their willingness to make compromises on certain aspects of modern life allows them to preserve the nonnegotiable spiritual core of their existence.

To be sure, the conservative Christian faith that is at the heart of contemporary Old Order life is one of the strongest factors accounting for their maintenance of Pennsylvania Dutch. Although sectarians are quick to point out that knowledge of Pennsylvania Dutch and German is not necessary for a believer to be saved, the symbolic connection between their *Mudderschprooch* and their spiritual heritage is strong. The fact that Pennsylvania Dutch is healthiest among those sectarian groups who continue to use German in worship speaks to how tightly interwoven the two languages are in a spiritual-linguistic ecology. Although the link between faith and language has been lost among nonsectarian Pennsylvania Dutch, as established in chapter 2, early nineteenth-century Lutheran and Reformed preachers considered the spiritual health of their congregants dependent on maintaining German in some form and in an agrarian context. This view is completely consonant with modern Old Order values. While sectarians readily acknowledge that it is possible to be a faithful Christian and live in a city, in their view the salutary effects of country living on one's spiritual health are many: "[W]e find in the country a much closer communion with God. Life in the country is awake to the natural order of daylight and dark, sunshine and rain, the swing of the seasons, and the blessings with which God has ordered our world."[4] The history of Pennsylvania Dutch shows that it has from its very genesis been a fundamentally rural language; thus, to associate it not only with a spiritual heritage but also with an agrarian lifestyle has been crucial to its continued health over time. In the same way that Old Order sectarians argue that is easier to live a godly life in the country, so too do they say it is easier to "keep Dutch" outside of the city.

The essentially hybrid character of Pennsylvania Dutch culture, which is mirrored in all other American ethnic and regional cultures, including, for example, African American culture, whose roots also extend far back in American history, is of course aptly exemplified in the language itself. While the basic structural building blocks of Pennsylvania Dutch retain a strong resemblance to Palatine German, as I have shown throughout this book the language's vocabulary, though still also basically Palatine German, shows clear influence from English, both in the form of outright borrowings as well as less obvious loan translations and loan shifts. This leads to the somewhat paradoxical situation that today's Pennsylvania Dutch speakers construct utterances that are composed mainly of Palatine German–derived elements and are at the same time incomprehensible to speakers of European German. A simple sentence will illustrate this: *Sell hot mich aardlich uffgschafft grigt* is a verbatim translation of the English expression 'That got me really worked up'. Every one of the six words in that sentence is of Palatine German provenance, as is the grammatical template into which those words are inserted, yet even a German speaker from the Palatinate would have no clue what is being conveyed if that person did not know English well. Pennsylvania Dutch is a linguistic machine made in America but with most of its parts imported from Germany.

Portable Pennsylvania Dutch

An enduring stereotype held by Americans and non-Americans alike is that Americans are highly mobile, even "rootless." This supposed rootlessness is viewed, especially in the popular media, as a cause of numerous social ills. For example, a 1995 article in the *Chicago Tribune* titled "America, the Rootless," bore the ominous subtitle "Our Eroding Sense of Community Could Imperil the Democracy Founded on the Activism of Regular Citizens."[5] While it is true that migration, especially westward, was considerable throughout the nineteenth century and into the twentieth, since the end of World War II most Americans have in fact become steadily *less* mobile, meaning that the reasons for any social instability in the United States need to be sought elsewhere.[6] One group of Americans who have defied this general trend and become in fact more mobile in recent decades are the active speakers of Pennsylvania

Dutch, the Old Order sectarians. The rapid growth of their populations due to the twin factors of high birth rates and low attrition means that especially younger sectarian families are compelled to move in search of affordable farmland and economic opportunities, among other reasons. An analysis of reports of Amish migration between 2006 and 2010 shows the five US states to gain the most new families during this period to be New York, Kentucky, Illinois, Kansas, and Virginia. Conversely, the top five "losing states" during that time were Pennsylvania, Wisconsin, Delaware, Ohio, and Michigan.[7]

Earlier I noted that, among nonsectarian Pennsylvania Dutch, their heritage language endured the longest where it originated in the eighteenth century, in the historically Dutch counties of southeastern Pennsylvania; the farther west Pennsylvania Dutch migrated, the more rapidly their descendants became assimilated to their English-speaking neighbors. This raises the question of why nineteenth-century migration out of Pennsylvania had such a negative impact on the maintenance of Pennsylvania Dutch among nonsectarians but not among the most conservative Amish and Mennonites. The answer lies in a crucial difference between the two groups regarding their interactions with coreligionists in nineteenth-century America who were either new arrivals from German-speaking Europe or their immediate descendants. The longstanding cultural and linguistic differences between Pennsylvania Dutch and *Deitschlenner* extended to religion, which was especially clear in the divide between Lutherans and German Reformed who were Pennsylvania Dutch–speaking and members of "New German" congregations.

One important difference had to do with the spirit of *unionism* that was widespread among members of Pennsylvania Dutch Lutheran and Reformed congregations in the eighteenth and nineteenth centuries. Like their sectarian neighbors, many nonsectarian Pennsylvania Dutch had little concern for theology. Many Lutheran and Reformed pastors received no formal seminary training, and they and their congregants enjoyed close ties across what was a largely nominal confessional divide, often sharing buildings that are known to this day as *union churches*. William A. Helffrich, the Reformed pastor introduced in chapter 2, served in such a church, in Longswamp Township, located in Berks County at the border with Lehigh County. In 1852 it was decided that it was time for the two congregations to build a new church, which inspired Helffrich

and his Lutheran colleague, Rev. Jeremiah Schindel, to mark the occasion in a special way:

> The old church had to be torn down; therefore, Schindel and I decided
> on May 4 and 5 as days for the last services in the old church in the form
> of a joint communion service for both congregations, Reformed and Lu-
> theran. On Saturday afternoon we had our preparatory service. Schindel
> preached and I conducted the liturgical service at the altar. It was a solemn
> occasion when the whole congregation knelt for the last time in the old
> church. After the benediction I gave a talk looking back on the many and
> rich blessings God had in this house poured out onto those slumbering
> in the churchyard and the congregation assembled here for the last time;
> I spoke also of how our last service and communion celebration would
> be held here. Few eyes remained dry. On Sunday morning I preached and
> Schindel conducted the liturgical service. Then we took communion, I
> extended it to Schindel and Schindel to me, whereupon the members of
> the congregation came and took part, more than four hundred of them.
> Oh, how I felt at that time the separation of the two churches! Why is this
> cleft? Why not one church as far as the German language resounds? And
> the whole congregation felt the same way. Many expressed that senti-
> ment to us after the service. Schindel responded: If it were up to Brother
> Helffrich and me, things would definitely be different.[8]

As Helffrich's comments suggest, an important factor underlying
unionism in the Pennsylvania Dutch country was a shared desire to
maintain German as a language of worship. This loyalty to German was
similar to the situation among Old Order Anabaptist groups today. As
Ralph Charles Wood puts it, "The Pennsylvania German churchgoers
did not prefer German because it was German, but because they thought
it was the language in which the eternal truths of their faith were better expressed."[9] At the same time, the preference among Pennsylvania
Dutch Lutheran and Reformed congregations for German was an expression of the widening cultural and spiritual divide between them and
their rapidly anglicizing coreligionists in cities such as Philadelphia and
Lancaster.[10] Pennsylvania Dutch resistance to the use of English in both
Lutheran and Reformed congregations in particular was reinforced by a
concern that their churches might thereby come under the sway of the
Church of England, a fear that was not misplaced.[11]

When *Deitschlenner* Lutherans and Reformed encountered their American brethren in the nineteenth century, the language question was turned on its head, and some rural nonsectarian Pennsylvania Dutch actually came to favor English as a language of worship:

> One of the contributing factors to the spread of English in the churches was the fear of many pastors that an exclusively German church in eastern Pennsylvania would be dominated by the "High German" ministers, who sometimes showed less understanding for the Pennsylvania German population than did the Anglo-Americans. Many who thought that the Anglicized sections of their denominations preached a superficial, showy Christianity, the result of a compromise with worldliness, also felt that European German Protestantism was no longer the old-time religion and that European German ministers tried to dazzle congregations with their erudition rather than preach the word of God in language that the simple man could understand. Many who smarted under the ridicule of New German pastors for the Pennsylvania High German pulpit language with its archaic vocabulary and pronunciation dating from pre–Classic Germany, went over to English, or, if this was too difficult for them, or their congregations would have none of it, they had their sons trained only in English. Thus the last of a long line of German clergymen—it is surprising how the profession runs in single families in German Pennsylvania—would propagate English in his church because he had no command of "Schriftdeutsch."[12]

The tendency for nonsectarian Pennsylvania Dutch to prefer English over German as a sign of their resistance to being "Germanized" by recent arrivals from Europe was more pronounced in the Midwest, where conservative groups such as the Missouri Synod of the Lutheran Church were demographically much stronger than migrants from Pennsylvania. In essence, the encounter between Pennsylvania Dutch and *Deitschlenner* Lutherans and Reformed in the nineteenth century pointed up just how Americanized the former had become relative to the latter.[13] Pennsylvania-style unionism was anathema to later Protestant immigrants from German-speaking Europe, many of whom explicitly rejected the so-called Prussian Union of 1817, whereby Lutheran and German Reformed Churches in Central Europe's dominant kingdom were compelled to merge. The loss of Pennsylvania High German as a language of worship among nonsectarians, especially in the Midwest, but also in Pennsylvania, then led to attrition of the oral vernacular half of their mother tongue, Pennsylvania Dutch.[14]

Anglicization for reasons related to faith was not limited to nonsectarian Pennsylvania Dutch in the nineteenth century; many Amish and Mennonites also moved toward English during that time, especially in the decades after the Civil War. It is estimated that just one-third of the sectarians who identified as Amish Mennonites in 1850 eventually came to be affiliated with the conservative Old Order faction, which emerged around 1870 and whose descendants are the largest sectarian group to maintain Pennsylvania Dutch and German actively today.[15] Also in the second half of the nineteenth century, North American Mennonites experienced similar divisions, again with a small, archconservative minority choosing to "keep the Old Order," which in most cases has also meant "keeping Dutch." In the case of the descendants of historically Pennsylvania Dutch–speaking Anabaptist sectarians, the move to become English monolingual was not influenced by conflicts with *Deitschlenner*. Rather, their shift to English was a consequence of their increasing assimilation to the American Protestant mainstream. John H. Oberholtzer, discussed in chapter 6, was a prominent early figure in this movement, with his advocacy for improved education for Mennonites, including formal training for ministers, Sunday schools for children, the production of periodicals aimed at edifying all Mennonites, mission work, and mutual aid.[16] Other characteristics that came to distinguish more progressive Mennonites and Amish from their Old Order cousins included a greater value placed on the autonomy of individual believers and the importance of their personal conversion and "upright" behavior (e.g., avoidance of tobacco use and "youthful rowdiness"), stronger regional and national organizations and institutions, and a de-emphasis on legalistic rules aimed at promoting outward uniformity (e.g., related to dress and grooming).[17]

The heritage language of nonsectarians was always truly *Pennsylvania Dutch*; only in exceptional cases did it survive for longer than a generation when they migrated out of Pennsylvania. To be sure, Pennsylvania Dutch did serve as a cultural line of demarcation between the church people and their English-speaking fellow Pennsylvanians of various ethnic backgrounds, but the maintenance of that border did not remain vitally connected to their Christian faith in the way that it has always been for the sect people. A useful concept for understanding the dynamics of how Pennsylvania Dutch has been spread by conservative Anabaptist sectarians from southeastern Pennsylvania across the American Midwest and beyond is what linguist Steven Hartman Keiser, building on the work of historian Steven Reschly, describes as *portable community*.[18]

Since the inception of the Anabaptist movement in the sixteenth century, Mennonites, Amish, and related groups have been "pilgrims and exiles" in the diverse lands where they have lived, or, to adapt a common phrase applied to them, they are "in the world, but in no one part of it permanently."[19] Their faith and identity have been profoundly portable as they have migrated in response to changing external circumstances. Wherever Old Orders move, certain things remain constant, including what they believe, how they worship, and what they speak. As Keiser has aptly noted, "Pennsylvania German is a language that has outgrown its name."[20] Indeed, like its communities of users, Pennsylvania Dutch has become a "portable language" whose connection to the Commonwealth of Pennsylvania is an increasingly distant one.

Other Portable Languages

The connection between spiritual and linguistic preservation among contemporary Pennsylvania Dutch–speaking Old Orders is neither new nor unique. Today there are two other Anabaptist groups whose sociolinguistic situations bear a strong resemblance to that of the Amish and Old Order Mennonites, despite the fact that the three faith communities have no direct historical connection with one another and even now have little contact. The first of these is a group discussed briefly in chapter 6, the Old Colony Mennonites.[21] These Mennonites trace their origins to Netherlandic-speaking northwestern Europe. In the sixteenth century, their ancestors migrated eastward to the Vistula Delta region of Prussia, eventually shifting, by the end of the eighteenth century, from Dutch to German. As Dutch speakers living in German territory, the distinct linguistic identity of these Mennonites promoted their spiritual doctrine of separation from the world. In 1759, a German-speaking Lutheran pastor who was interested in preaching in Prussian Mennonite congregations recalled the resistance with which his offer was met by the Dutch-speaking Mennonites, whom he quoted as saying, "Let this strange preacher with his black frock and his proud devil's language preach where he wants to, but not in our congregations."[22]

Eventually, in the second half of the eighteenth century, the Mennonites in the Vistula Delta did come to adopt the East Low German speech of their neighbors and began using High German in worship as well as in their schools, a practice that continues today. Shortly after making the transition from Dutch to German, beginning in 1789, these Mennonites moved farther east, to the Russian Empire, where their vernacular form of Low German, Plautdietsch, constituted along with High German for worship a bipartite mother tongue that served as a salient barrier between them and their Slavic neighbors, in much the same way that Pennsylvania Dutch and (High) German do among Old Orders today. Experiencing a tumultuous and often tragic history in the Russian Empire and then the Soviet Union, the people who became known as the Old Colony Mennonites migrated westward, to Canada, and then south, mainly into Latin America. The most conservative Old Colony communities today include the settlements in northern Mexico, where the outreach program sponsored by the Amish and Old Order Mennonites is active, and in South America, especially in Bolivia and Paraguay. For these Mennonites, maintenance of Plautdietsch and German remains as central to their sociolinguistic identity as Pennsylvania Dutch and German are for the Old Orders.

The second Anabaptist group whose sociolinguistic situation parallels that of the Old Orders and the Old Colony Mennonites is the communal Hutterites.[23] Taking their name from an early Anabaptist leader, Jakob Hutter, the Hutterites originated in Tyrol, a region that today is divided between southern Austria and northern Italy. Like the Dutch ancestors of the Old Colony Mennonites and the mainly Swiss forebears of the Amish and Old Order Mennonites, the Hutterites were persecuted and compelled early on to become portable communities, migrating into mainly Slavic-speaking lands, first to Moravia and later into the western part of the Russian Empire where, coincidentally, the Dutch-descended Mennonites lived. In the 1870s the Hutterites, like many of their Mennonite neighbors, moved to North America, settling in the Canadian provinces of Alberta and Saskatchewan and the states of Montana and the Dakotas, where they are still concentrated today. Like the

Old Orders, the Hutterites are trilingual. Their vernacular language is Hutterisch (Hutterite German), while High German is used in church and both English and (High) German are media of instruction in their parochial schools. Also like the Amish and Old Order Mennonites, as well as the Old Colony Mennonites, maintenance of a dual-variety Germanic mother tongue is a salient marker of a social-spiritual identity distinct from that of their Canadian and US neighbors.

Despite numerous differences in specific aspects of life and culture, these conservative Anabaptist groups have much in common with another people of faith whose complex history of migration has also been indelibly marked by survival in the face of often incredible hardship, namely the Jews of the Diaspora. In the same way that the Christian faith of the Anabaptists became a profoundly portable one, Jews replaced the ancestral Palestinian homeland from which they were dispersed with the Word of God as embodied in the Torah, which the geographer Emanuel Maier describes as *movable territory*.[24] "The Talmud (i.e., Torah and commentaries) gave the landless and persecuted Jew of the diaspora another world into which he could escape and survive when the vicissitudes of the real world had become too great to bear. 'It gave him a fatherland, which he could carry about with him when his own land was lost.'"[25]

Many groups of diasporic Jews, especially the most conservative ones, lived as "pilgrims and exiles" in majority-Gentile communities from which they maintained a measure of distance, both by compulsion and by choice. In the Diaspora, many Jews came to express their faith in outward symbols such as distinctive dress and grooming, as well as language, very much like what we find today among the Old Orders, the Old Colony Mennonites, and the Hutterites. The Jewish people today who most closely resemble the conservative Anabaptists are the Haredim, Orthodox Jews who are mainly of Ashkenazic (Western and Eastern European) origin.[26]

In the United States, where approximately a half-million Haredim live, theirs is a situation of "Jewish triple-talk": Yiddish, a German-derived language affectionately called the *mame-loshn* (mother tongue) is the dominant medium of everyday discourse; Hebrew, a Semitic language, is used for religious purposes; and English is used mainly to communicate with non-Haredim. Coincidentally, Yiddish and Pennsylvania

Dutch share a common historical connection with Palatine German dialects, meaning that the two languages today resemble each other to some extent, though other dialects also played an significant role in the genesis of Yiddish. There is also an important sociolinguistic parallel between Yiddish and Pennsylvania Dutch. Until the Holocaust, the majority of Yiddish speakers were non-Haredim Jews, who were more assimilated into the larger culture. These more secular Jews were comparable to nonsectarian Pennsylvania Dutch and, like the nonsectarians, produced a considerable body of literature in Yiddish. Unlike Pennsylvania Dutch literature, however, Yiddish prose and poetic works by such luminaries as Sholem Aleichem and I. L. Peretz, as well as the Nobel laureate Isaac Bashevis Singer, have gained international acclaim and are widely accessible in translation.

There is an interesting paradox with regard to the languages situations of all four faith communities, the Old Orders, the Old Colony Mennonites, the Hutterites, and the Haredim. All are profoundly conservative in a literal sense: they seek to conserve a revered spiritual heritage that has enabled them to not just survive but to prosper, a heritage that extends back many generations. And yet the faith that they have inherited transcends the historical experiences of their ancestors. In each of the four cases, there is a mismatch between their ethnic backgrounds and the geographic origins of the languages they speak. The Old Orders are of mainly Swiss ethnicity, yet they speak a Palatine German–derived language. The Old Colony Mennonites trace their roots to Germanic northwestern Europe yet speak a language that derives from the far eastern reaches of German-speaking territory. The ethnic-linguistic mismatch among the Hutterites is not as great as for the other Anabaptist groups, but no less real: they are of Tyrolean descent while their in-group language most closely resembles Austrian German dialects from the central-southern region of Carinthia. For the Haredim, the difference between their ethnicity and their *mame-loshn* is the greatest: their Semitic roots lie in ancient Palestine, while the seeds of their Germanic tongue sprouted in the Rhineland area of Central Europe.

In some ways, the lack of a connection between ethnicity and language history among these four faith communities allows their languages to become "supraterritorial" varieties that are as easily moved from place to place as their speakers. Ask an Amish or Old Order Mennonite, Old

Colony Mennonite, Hutterite, or Haredi Jew where Pennsylvania Dutch, Plautdietsch, Hutterisch, or Yiddish comes from, and he or she will be hard pressed to respond. Then ask that person where those languages are spoken, and he or she will say, "everywhere where our people live." Just as God accompanies God's people wherever they may go, so do the portable languages of God's Anabaptist and Haredi followers go with them.

The following thoughts about language shared by an Amish person would likely be echoed by his brothers and sisters of faith, Jew and Christian alike.

> Knowing two languages is a privilege God has provided for us, and we can put them to good use. Although we have a knowledge of two languages, it would be wrong not to make an effort to express ourselves better in the English language. But it would be just as wrong to fail to keep and pass on the German to our children—that rich language our forebears left for us. It is a well-known fact that losing our mother tongue and drifting into the world usually go together.
>
> Any time we speak English around the home when just family members are around, or while working or visiting with others who know Pennsylvania Dutch, we put in a vote to drop a rich heritage that will never be brought back if we lose it.
>
> The value of that heritage is so great that we can't afford to lose it.[27]

THE STORY OF PENNSYLVANIA DUTCH, as I have shown, is a profoundly American one. It began in the colonial era, and now, nearly three centuries later, it is continuing to add new chapters. The language, though preserving a fundamentally Palatine German character, has been indelibly influenced by American English. Indeed, Pennsylvania Dutch would be something entirely different were it not a fact that to speak it one has to "think in English." The history of the speakers of Pennsylvania Dutch is marked by alternate patterns of distance from and proximity to the English-speaking American mainstream, with now only the Old Order sectarians having reached a state of sociolinguistic equilibrium between their *Mudderschprooch* and English that is an apt expression of their "bargain with modernity." Yet as much as Pennsylvania Dutch is truly an "American language," its Old Order speakers, as "pilgrims and exiles" everywhere they live, demonstrate how languages, like the communities that use them, transcend classification according to national or political categories. Pennsylvania Dutch has always belonged to its users, be they elderly attendees at a fersommling in Pennsylvania or Amish kids at play in Oklahoma.

It is fitting to close this exploration of the odyssey of Pennsylvania Dutch by letting a pastor-poet, Rev. Adam Stump (1854–1922), have the last, lyrical word.

Die Muttersproch	***The Mother Tongue***
Die erschte Worte, die mer weess,	*The first words we learn*
Die's diefscht in unsre Herze g'sunke,	*Which sink the deepest into our hearts*
Die immer gut un niemols bees,	*And are always good and never bad,*
Hen mir mit Muttermilch getrunke—	*We drank with our mother's milk.*
Wie doch des arme, schwache Kind	*How this poor, weak child*
Die Sproch so siess un lieblich find!	*Finds the language so sweet and dear!*
Wie kenne mir die liewe Sproch	*How can we abandon the dear language*
So leichtsinnig im Stolz verlosse!	*So frivolously in pride!*
Der alte Strom, so noch un noch,	*The old stream, little by little,*
Is noch net ganz un gar verflosse.	*Has not yet completely flowed away.*
Mir henke fescht am alte Stamm,	*We are holding fast to the old tree trunk,*
So wie die Braut am Breitigam.	*Like the bride to the bridegroom.*
Es gebt en Sproch, die is nix wert:	*There is a language that is worthless:*
Die roschtig Flint is glei versprunge.	*The rusty gun is soon exploded.*
Lateinisch, Greek sin g'schwind verkehrt;	*Latin and Greek are quickly confused,*
Ei, sie verdrehe jo die Zunge!	*My, how they twist tongues around!*
Ja, Englisch un Hebreisch ah—	*Yes, English and Hebrew, too;*
Mit denne is mer iwwel dra'.	*You're bad off with those two.*

Die Muttersproch, die lebt un geht	*Our mother tongue, she lives and goes*
So gut wie Brod un Salz im Esse;	*As well as bread and salt in a meal.*
Un wie der Fels am Berg dra' steht,	*And like the rock on the mountain,*
So kenne mir sie net vergesse.	*So we cannot forget her.*
Wie uns die Mammi g'sunge hot,	*How Mother sang to us,*
So denke mir noch all'gebot.	*That's what we think of now and again.*
So wie mer g'heilt hen, hen mir g'lacht	*As we cried, so did we also laugh*
In selle siesse Kindheits-Dage,	*In those sweet days of childhood,*
Wie Gott die Blum in d' Welt gebracht;	*Like God brought the flower into the world—*
Ja, eppes will ich dir grad sage;	*Yes, I want to tell you something now—*
Die Blum vergesst den Dau nie net,	*The flower never forgets the dew*
Der sie gekisst—wann sie ah wet.	*That kissed her, even if it wanted to.*
Die Traub, die hasst die Rank jo nie,	*The grape never hates the vine,*
Wann mir sie ah vun ihr wegreisse.	*Even if we pluck it from it.*
Mir sin net schlimmer wie des Vieh:	*We are no worse than cattle:*
En Hund dut nie sei Friend wiescht beisse!	*A dog never bites his friends!*
O Muttersproch, du bischt uns lieb!	*Oh mother tongue, you are dear to us!*
In deinem Ton is sel'ger Trieb.	*In your tones is blessed desire.*
Weit z'rick in unsrer Zeitgebert	*Long ago at the time of our birth*
Bischt du schun uns entgege kumme,	*You already met us,*
Un wann des Dodes Lewe plärrt,	*And when death comes calling*

Dann gebscht du uns ah siesse
Wonne.
Uf deinem Bussem schlof ich ei—
Der erscht Kumrad, der bleibt
getrei!

You give us sweet bliss.

Upon your bosom I fall asleep;
One's first friend remains loyal!

Un wann ich mol in meinem
Grab,
In meinem kiehle Bett ei
'kehre,
Ja, Esch zu Esch, un Staab zu
Staab—
Dann mag mei Grasdach sich
vermehre.
Die Ihm, der Vogel, ohne Drang,
Die singe mir ihr Lewe lang.

And when I go to my grave,

To my cool bed,

Yes, ashes to ashes, and dust to dust,

Then may my roof of grass cover
me.
The bee and the bird, without effort,
Sing to me their whole life long.

Ja, in der Schockel, in der Lad,
Bleibt unsre liewe Sproch
dieselwe;
So peift der Wind, so brummt's
Spinnrad;
Von dere Erd bis ans Gewelwe

Yes, in the cradle and the coffin,
Our dear language remains the
same;
So whistles the wind and the
spinning wheel hums;
From this Earth to the arch of
Heaven

Schwetzt alles zu uns jo so klar,
Wie's als daheem ah eemol war.

Everything speaks to us so clearly,
As it always once was at home.

O sanfte, deire Muttersproch!
Wie Hunnig fliesst sie darch
mei Sinne!
Un wann ich mol im Himmel hoch
Mei scheene Heemet duh
gewinne,
Dann heer ich dart zu meinem
Wohl
En Mutterwort—ja, ah ebmol.[28]

Oh gentle, dear mother tongue!
Like honey she flows through my
senses!
And when I find in Heaven
My beautiful home,

Then I will hear for my comfort

A mother's word—yes, sometimes, too.

Notes

Preface

1. Reichard 1940, xx. See Reichard (1940, xix–xxiii) for a good review of the debates over Pennsylvania Dutch orthography; see also Beam 2004–2011. The various writers mentioned in this poem are among the most prominent in Pennsylvania Dutch literary history.

Chapter 1. What Is Pennsylvania Dutch?

1. When referring to the vocabulary of a language, linguists distinguish between *native* and *nonnative* words. Native lexical items are those that are descended from an ancestral form of a language; nonnative words are *borrowings* or *loan vocabulary*, which enter a language through contact. In Pennsylvania Dutch, native vocabulary items are words that derive from the German dialects originally spoken by the earliest progenitors of the Pennsylvania Dutch; nonnative words are, in the case of Pennsylvania Dutch, borrowings from English.

2. Adding to the German/Dutch confusion in Pennsylvania is the name of the borough of New Holland in northern Lancaster County. This name was chosen by early German settlers who immigrated to America by way of the Netherlands and were grateful for the hospitality they received there.

3. The first definition of the adjective *Dutch* in the Oxford English Dictionary reads as follows: "Of or pertaining to the people of Germany; German; Teutonic. *Obs.* exc. as a historical archaism, and in some parts of U.S." See Yoder 1980 for a discussion of the different terms used in earlier America to describe people of German ancestry. Notably, the use of *Dutch* as a synonym for *German* in America is not limited to the Pennsylvania Dutch. It is also common in other areas of German settlement, including the Midwest. Numerous place names, for example, incorporate the word *Dutch*, many if not most of which derive from a historically German rather than Netherlandic presence. In addition, the word *Dutch* itself is of ancient Germanic provenance. *German* and *Teuton(ic)*, by contrast, are borrowings from Latin. Since many Latinate words in English, as well as

those derived from Greek, are used in more formal registers of the language (cf. *domicile* or *residence* versus *home*), it makes sense that *Dutch* should have a more vernacular or colloquial sense to it than *German*.

4. See Yoder 1988. Today, the term *Deitschlenner* is much less common among active speakers of Pennsylvania Dutch, in part because the number of immigrants from Germany or US-born speakers of German whom they encounter is quite low. Pennsylvania Dutch speakers will now more typically use the English word *German* when referring to speakers of European German.

5. Shryock 1939, 265.

6. See Reichard (1918, 216–220), for information on Keller's Pennsylvania Dutch literary output.

7. Reichard 1940, 162.

8. Bekanntlich gibt es hier zu Land
   Viel', die sich Deutsche nennen;
   Die aber, ei, welch' große Schand'!
   Kein Wort Deutsch lesen können.

   Auch ist die Sprache gar zu schlecht,
   Die viele Deutsche führen;
   "Buhtschäck" heißt man den Stiefelknecht,
   Und "spellen" 's Buchstabiren.

   Wie hat der Gaul so arg "gekickt",
   Die "Hinkel" laut "gekrischen";
   Der "Butscher" hat das "Bief" geschickt;
   Mein "Freddy" ist "gehn fischen".

   "Well" rufet "nau" den "Däd" herein,
   Ich hab' das "Bräckfäst reddy";
   Grüß mir den "Tschäck", die "Emmelein",
   Die "Horses" ziehen "steddy".

9. Ist's nun nicht eine Schand und Schmach,
   Wie man an vielen Orten
   Die liebe schöne deutsche Sprach'
   Verketzert in den Worten?—

   Sprich "ja" und "nein" für "yes" und "no",
   Statt "kicken" sage "schlagen",
   Und statt des lustigen "Window"
   Kannst du ja "Fenster" sagen.

   Dein "Hinkel" wandle um sofort
   In "Hühner" oder "Hennen";

Dein "Bräckfäst" kannst mit deutschem Wort
Dein "Morgenessen" nennen.

In Deutschland würden Viele ja
Dein Deutsch gar nicht verstehen;
Sie dächten: "In Amerika
Muß traurig es aussehen."—

Ein Deutscher bist geboren Du;
Ein Deutscher sollst Du bleiben;
Drum lerne fröhlich immerzu
Deutsch sprechen, lesen, schreiben.

10. Another member of the Germanic language family, Afrikaans, has a sociolinguistic history similar to that of Luxembourgish. For centuries considered a dialect of Dutch called *Cape Dutch*, Afrikaans was elevated to the status of a distinct language by an act of Parliament in 1925. Prior to that time, it was often stigmatized by European Netherlandic speakers as "bad" or "incorrect" Dutch in ways that were similar to how standard German speakers scorned Pennsylvania Dutch. See Deumert 2004 for an excellent review of the history of Afrikaans.

11. Most German speakers, as well as the Pennsylvania Dutch, believe that High German is so called because of its "high" social status. In fact, the modifier derives from an originally geographic distinction; see n19 below.

12. The term *diglossia* was coined by the linguist Charles Ferguson (1959). Of the many case studies of diglossic speech communities around the world, an important one in Germanic linguistics is Rash 1998, which deals with Switzerland.

13. The parallel between the Arabic and Pennsylvania Dutch situations extends further. In the same way that there are actually multiple forms of standard German (e.g., Pennsylvania High German and Swiss Standard German), so too are there regional varieties of Modern Standard Arabic.

14. See Labov 2006.

15. In modern standard German, there are two words for 'dialect', *Mundart* and *Dialekt*. The former is of Germanic etymology (meaning, literally, 'mouth type'), while the latter is a nineteenth-century loanword from Greek. Although *Mundart* was in existence in the eighteenth century and earlier, many regional dialects, including Palatine German, did not have separate words for 'language' and 'dialect'. Pennsylvania Dutch thus inherits this semantic uniformity from its European German source dialects. Interestingly, the words *language* and *dialect* in English are both borrowed: the former comes from French, the latter from Greek. The original Germanic word in English used to describe all linguistic varieties was *tongue*.

16. See Wokeck 1999, 44–47.

17. See Kuhns 1900, 55; and Wokeck 1999, 2–3.

18. See Eshleman 1935; Buffington 1938, 1939; Christmann 1950; Haag 1956; Veith 1968; and Buffington 1970. Very useful are the maps in Veith (1968, 272–283) showing where key phonological and lexical features of Pennsylvania Dutch match those of the

Palatinate, especially the composite maps 6 and 12 on pp. 277 and 283, respectively. The most comprehensive reference work on Palatine German, which includes discussion of Pennsylvania Dutch, is Post 1992.

19. German dialects are divided into two major groups, Low and High, terms that derive from the physical landscape of the areas in which they are spoken. Low German dialects are spoken in relatively flat northern Germany, while High German dialects extend from the hillier central German-speaking regions south- and eastward to alpine Switzerland and Austria. The reason the standard (written and spoken) variety of German is called *High German* is because of its origins in High German dialects mainly from the East Central area. Tradition holds that the translation of the Bible made by Martin Luther (1483–1546), who hailed from this region, provided the basis for the modern standard German language, yet the situation was considerably more complex (Salmons 2013, 264–274). In any case, what is called High German is a linguistic cousin to spoken German dialects, including those from the Palatinate and their distant relative in North America, Pennsylvania Dutch, and not, as some people believe, the ancient source from which regional varieties of German descended.

20. We have no direct evidence of how dialect contact unfolded in colonial Pennsylvania; see Seifert (1971, 17–20) for a discussion what might be plausibly speculated about this process and the importance of Palatine German dialects. Although there has never been complete homogeneity across Pennsylvania Dutch varieties, especially in its vocabulary, the sound and grammatical structures of the language are strikingly consistent across regions and groups of speakers, even after two centuries of separation among many of them.

21. See Seifert 2001.

22. There is a subgroup of Old Order Amish whose ancestors came to America from Switzerland and Alsace in the early nineteenth century and who still speak a form of Bernese Swiss German. Many of these "Swiss Amish," a number of whom live near the southern Indiana town of Berne, also speak Pennsylvania Dutch, but they often resort to English when communicating with Pennsylvania Dutch–speaking Amish, since Amish Swiss German and Pennsylvania Dutch are not mutually intelligible.

23. See Karch (1973, 90–97). The speaker grew up in a farming family in the village of Gimmeldingen. He was sixty-two years old when interviewed in 1956, so he was born in either 1893 or 1894. The digitized interview with this speaker is part of the Zwirner-Korpus (speaker identification number I/1595), which is accessible through the Datenbank für Gesprochenes Deutsch at the Institut für Deutsche Sprache–Mannheim, Germany (dgd.ids-mannheim.de). A complete analysis of Gimmeldingen Palatine German is given in Karch 1973.

24. In the Pennsylvania Dutch translation, forms in the Dative case occur as in the Palatine German original. Until the twentieth century, the Dative was fully productive in all varieties of Pennsylvania Dutch; however, in the twentieth century it has been lost in the speech of most Old Order Amish and Old Order Mennonite sectarians.

25. A common stereotype about rural forms of speech, including languages spoken by the descendants of immigrants who move far away from a language's homeland, holds

that such "rustic" languages are unchanging or at least highly conservative. Cf. Michael Montgomery's 1998 essay debunking the myth that "in the Appalachians they speak like Shakespeare." The reality is that while some extraterritorial or colonial varieties of a language may be conservative in some features with respect to an ancestral homeland, they are progressive in others. So it is with Pennsylvania Dutch: it has some features that are no longer used in Palatine German, while developing others that are novel and not found in any European German dialect.

26. See Becker 1808. There is no detailed biographical information on Becker available, though he did sign one pamphlet addressed to Pennsylvania governor Simon Snyder, "Christian Becker, *Teacher* Beyers schoolhouse, Bethlehem township, Northampton county, state of Pennsylvania, November 7, 1812" (Becker 1812). Information on Becker's impact as a German and English language textbook author can be found in Cazden (1984, 270–273).

27. *Cook-shop* is an archaic word for an establishment selling prepared food; the *Oxford English Dictionary* definition of *ordinary* is "an inn, public house, tavern, etc., where meals are provided at a fixed price."

28. Becker 1808, 138–139.

29. To be sure, it is impossible to assess the precise extent to which any written representations of earlier Pennsylvania English, including Becker's dialogs, resembled linguistic reality. However, Becker's goal was a practical one, namely to teach German Pennsylvanian farm children English. His book was a language textbook and not a prescriptive manual of style intended to hone the skills of fluent English speakers. Therefore, it is likely that his dialogs, which dealt with topics set in everyday communicative situations (including shopping, asking for directions, and chatting about the weather), are reasonably close to how early Pennsylvanians actually communicated with each other orally. In general, research on early American English confirms the basic similarity between it and modern varieties of the language, relative to British English, with most changes involving vowels and vocabulary. See Wolfram and Schilling-Estes (1998, 92–107).

30. This was reprinted in A. L. Shoemaker 1951a.

31. As mentioned in the introduction, there is no system for writing Pennsylvania Dutch that all writers follow, but the one most common in academic publications was developed by Pennsylania Dutch studies scholars Albert F. Buffington, Preston A. Barba, and C. Richard Beam (see Beam 2004–2011). The Buffington-Barba-Beam system is based mainly on German orthographic norms.

32. The verb *darichgeh*, 'to abscond, run away', as it was used in this text is documented in varieties spoken in Pennsylvania in the early twentieth century, as well as in Ontario (see Beam 2004–2011), but it is no longer common in the speech of younger Old Order Amish or Mennonite speakers with this meaning. Modern *darichgeh* means 'to go through'.

33. The Accusative, Dative, and Genitive cases are also used in German for objects of prepositions.

34. Learned (1888/1889, 431) and Frey (1941, 158) observe that the Accusative masculine definite article *den* was preserved in the Pennsylvania Dutch that they documented

only when the article was used demonstratively, that is, when used to mean 'this (noun)' as opposed to 'the (noun)'.

35. A comparison with the history of English is apt here. Old English, which was spoken between roughly the fifth and twelfth centuries, had five cases: Nominative, Accusative, Dative, Genitive, and Instrumental. In modern English, cases are nonexistent for full nouns. Only certain pronouns still show case, and even there the system has been reduced to just two cases, Subjective (derived from the old Nominative) and Objective (a blend of historical Accusative and Dative forms). Few observers would argue that modern English speakers are somehow communicatively disadvantaged relative to their Old English predecessors because of the loss of nominal case in the history of their language.

36. Many southern German dialects, like Pennsylvania Dutch, similarly employ compound rather than synthetic (one-word) forms to express past tense, for example, *Ich habe gehen wollen*, 'I wanted to go'.

37. See Louden 2011b for a discussion of verb clusters in modern Pennsylvania Dutch and their historical development.

38. "Die Sprache, deren sich unsere deutsche Landesleute bedienen, ist ein erbärmlich geradebrechter Mischmasch der englischen und deutschen, in Ansehung der Worte sowohl, als ihre Fügungen. Erwachsene Personen, welche aus Deutschland hinüber kommen, vergessen ihre Muttersprache zum Theil, indem sie eine neue zu lernen sich vergeblich bemühen; die eingebornen lernen ihre Muttersprache fast niemalen ordentlich und rein" (Schöpf 1788, 155).

39. Schöpf 1788, 156.

40. The description was made by William C. Reichel, cited in Reichard (1918, 50).

41. Mencken 1965, 616–697.

42. This expression is taken from a description of the Creole French spoken in New Orleans in Hearn and Bronner (2002, 127), cited in Jackson (2010, 177).

43. The concept of loan shift goes back to Haugen (1969, 391).

44. The number of English borrowings in the Pennsylvania Dutch translation of the Palatine German sample discussed earlier is similarly modest. There are only two, *well* and *Daed*, 'dad'.

45. Vella Deitsh 1997.

46. I received a photocopy of this unpublished story from Amish friends in Indiana.

47. Both oral samples are from the (Wolfgang W.) Moelleken Collection in the North American German Dialect Archive of the Max Kade Institute for German-American Studies, University of Wisconsin–Madison. Both interviews were conducted in 1984. The first interviewee, speaking on Pennsylvania Dutch traditions, was from Northampton County, PA, and was born in 1897 (MOE 092). The second sample is taken from an interview with a speaker (MOE 204) from Kosciusko County, IN, who was born in 1967.

48. Lambert (1977, ix) estimates an upper limit of 15% loan vocabulary in Pennsylvania Dutch.

49. Swadesh lists are named for the linguist Morris Swadesh. There are multiple lists in use, but the 207-item list referred to here is the one currently used for the lexical comparison of Germanic languages. See http://ielex.mpi.nl./; and http://en.wiktionary.org/wiki/Appendix:Swadesh_lists_for_Germanic_languages. I am grateful to Joseph

Salmons and Andrew Wedel for fruitful discussions about the utility of analyzing a Swadesh list of Pennsylvania Dutch vocabulary.

50. In nineteenth-century Pennsylvania Dutch, the conjunction *fer*, 'because', which was modeled on the English *for*, was also used to introduce to main clauses. As the English conjunction *for* to mean 'because' has become archaic in contemporary American English, so too has the Pennsylvania Dutch causative conjunction *fer* fallen out of use.

51. Retroflex, which means literally 'bending back', describes the position of the tongue when pronouncing the sound at the beginning of words like *rough* and *ready*.

52. The status of /r/ in midwestern Pennsylvania Dutch varieties is somewhat more complex. The older /r/ produced with the tip of the tongue is still the norm between vowels in the middle of a word, but, at the beginning of a word, the retroflex /r/ that speakers from Lancaster also use is increasingly common.

53. In older Pennsylvania Dutch, *lehre* was used (cf. Ger. *lehren*, 'to teach'). Among Amish and Mennonite speakers, this verb is now used to refer to religious instruction only.

54. The asterisk is used in linguistic notation to mark a form that is not directly attested. In historical linguistics, it used to indicate reconstructed forms, that is, forms from ancient languages for which firsthand documentation is lacking. When the asterisk precedes a form from a modern language, as is the case here, that means that the form in question is *ungrammatical*, that is, not produced by native speakers under natural circumstances.

55. The basic order of verbs and their objects in Pennsylvania Dutch, is Object > Verb (OV), which is a typological characteristic of other Germanic languages, namely German, Dutch, and Frisian, as well as Afrikaans and Luxembourgish. English and the Scandinavian languages are Verb > Object (VO). Regarding Yiddish, there is a lack of consensus among scholars whether it is fundamentally OV or VO.

56. See Salmons (2013, 337–340) for a brief overview (in English) of the controversy surrounding Denglish in Germany. Another, more popularly oriented treatment of the topic in English is accessible here: http://german.about.com/od/vocabulary/a/denglish .htm. There is a considerable body of literature about Denglish, both scholarly and popular, published in German, including Hoberg 2000. Interestingly, concerns about Denglish, which are largely unfounded scientifically, are more frequently heard in the Federal Republic of Germany than in German-speaking Switzerland or Austria.

57. *Guardian*, April 1868, pp. 125–126.

58. See Anderson 2014 for an analysis of contemporary Pennsylvania Dutch English, including a comparison to what she terms *South Central Pennsylvania English*.

59. See Struble 1935.

60. See Page 1937.

61. See Frey 1940.

62. See Kreider 1957, 106–122, reprinted as Kreider 1962. The examples of Dutchified English vowels are found in Kreider (1957, 111–112) and (1962, 41).

63. As Anderson (2014, 31) notes, the monophthongization of [aɪ] in contemporary Pennsylvania Dutchified English is documented mainly before what are known as liquid sounds, namely [l] and [r], as in the words *tire* and *tile* (pronounced like "tar" and "tal[ly]"). Kreider's observation that her Lebanon County consultants had the monophthongal [æ]-pronunciation before [t] also is important.

64. See Huffines 1980b, 358; also Anderson 2014, 25–26.

65. See Page 1937, 205.

66. Examples are from Struble 1935 and Frey 1940.

67. In modern Pennsylvania Dutch, the infintival marker *zu*, 'to', has been lost.

68. See Kreider 1957, 112; Kreider 1962, 41.

69. See Struble 1935, 167.

70. *Ferhoodled English* 1964.

71. Not all Pennsylvania Dutch–speaking sectarian groups aim to develop native-like proficiency in English. Among the Swartzentruber Amish, for example, one of the most conservative Amish subgroups, as linguist and anthropologist Karen Johnson-Weiner has observed, English "is not meant for general communication" (2007, 57). This has the effect that the English they use with outsiders is often subject to interference from their Pennsylvania Dutch; in other words, it is Dutchified. See Johnson-Weiner 1993, and 2007, 53–57; 62–63.

72. Reliable information on the Amish, including updated population estimates, can be found at the Amish studies website maintained by the Young Center for Anabaptist & Pietist Studies at Elizabethtown College: http://www2.etown.edu/amishstudies/. The premier print reference work on the Amish is Kraybill, Johnson-Weiner, and Nolt 2013.

73. Old Order proficiency in English varies, often according to how conservative a particular subgroup is. In general, members of more progressive Pennsylvania Dutch–speaking Amish and Mennonite churches are more proficient in English than those affiliated with more conservative groups, such as the Swartzentrubers mentioned above. Even within the same community, there can be individual differences in English proficiency, depending on how regularly sectarians interact with English monolinguals. Business owners who have more frequent contact with non-Amish / Mennonites may speak more native-like English than those who farm and have fewer dealings with outsiders (Johnson-Weiner 2007, 260–261n11).

74. See Keiser 2012 for an excellent study of Pennsylvania Dutch in the Midwest, where most speakers currently reside.

75. See http://www2.etown.edu/amishstudies/Population_by_State_2014.asp.

76. See Fogleman 1996, 102–103; and Wokeck 1999, 45–46.

77. Hostetler 1993, 97.

78. The 2000 US Census found the number of Pennsylvania Dutch speakers in Pennsylvania to be 39,605 (http://www.usefoundation.org/view/29), but there is no way of knowing how many of these speakers might have been Old Order sectarians. It seems reasonable, then, to assume that the nonsectarian Pennsylvania Dutch–speaking population is today lower than 40,000.

79. See Louden 2003b.

80. The experience of non-English-speaking immigrant groups to America has been relatively benign in comparison to what indigenous Americans have undergone. Into the twentieth century, American Indians were the victims of governmental efforts to eradicate their traditional cultures, including their languages. The most disturbing of these programs was the establishment of boarding schools, in which Native youth were prohibited from using their heritage languages. See D. W. Adams 1995.

81. There is a sizable body of literature on language endangerment. Two important book-length treatments of the topic are Crystal 2000 and Nettle and Romaine 2000. A more popularly oriented book on endangered languages is Abley 2003. The United Nations Educational, Scientific, and Cultural Organization (UNESCO) maintains a website devoted to the topic: http://www.unesco.org/new/en/culture/themes/endangered-languages/.

82. Klees 1950, 279.

83. See Bronner 1996 for a study of the life and career of Henry W. Shoemaker.

84. See H. W. Shoemaker 1926.

85. See H. W. Shoemaker 1930.

86. The ability to "speak" Pennsylvania Dutch extended not only beyond those of Germanic ancestry but in at least one case to an animal. With evident tongue-in-cheek delight, J. William Frey, a pioneer in the academic field of Pennsylvania Dutch studies, reported the following in the March 15, 1951, issue of the *Pennsylvania Dutchman* newspaper:

> According to the Allentown *Sunday Call-Chronicle*, a Kunkletown, Pennsylvania, woman possesses a pet of rare ability.
>
> The pet, a parakeet (commonly referred to as a love-bird) owned by Mrs. Erastus Borger, is believed to be the only parakeet in the United States able to speak and understand two languages, English and Penna. Dutch.
>
> Buddy, as the bird is called, was raised by Mrs. Borger's daughter, Mrs. Gladys Eckhart. Mrs. Eckhart raises parakeets as a hobby, but says that Buddy has been the only one of 200-odd parakeets she has raised to display such an unusual talent.
>
> His owner states that the bird sometimes argues with himself in Dutch, disguising his voice so that it sounds like a conversation. The first phrase Buddy learned to say in Dutch was one he heard Mrs. Borger repeat to her late husband several times a day when on the way to his coal truck, "Gehst du fa kola?" [*Gehscht du fer Kohle?* 'Are you going for coal?']
>
> Buddy's most common English phrase is a plea for freedom from his cage. When he says, "Buddy wants to come out," Mrs. Borger can seldom refuse the bird's request.
>
> Buddy is quite polite, too. All visitors to the Borger home are greeted with a cheery "hello" and bid farewell.
>
> Kannscht du Deitsch schwetza? *Der Buddy kann!* [Can you speak Dutch? Buddy can!]

87. Fisher 1879, 198.

Chapter 2. Early History of Pennsylvania Dutch

1. The Germantown Mennonite immigrants were predominantly Dutch or Low German speakers; Germantown is considered a "German" settlement because of the location of Krefeld in northwestern Germany. Most settlers were not farmers, unlike many if not most of the later German and Swiss immigrants to Pennsylvania. Also, the size of the Germantown congregation remained quite small, not exceeding one hundred baptized members during the colonial era. Thus Germantown played no significant role in the genesis of Pennsylvania Dutch. See H. S. Bender 1956.

2. See Friesen 1990, especially pp. 23–39, on the early group of settlers to which the Herr family belonged.

3. See Weiser 1899/2004 for a biography of Conrad Weiser by one of his descendants. Weiser, who had lived apart from his family while immersed in a Mohawk Indian community in New York as a teenager, occupies an important place in American history for his career as an interpreter-diplomat among and between Native Americans and European colonists.

4. See Rupp 1844, 95.

5. Wokeck 1999, 44–46.

6. See Seifert 1971, 17–19.

7. See Purvis 1987, especially table 2, p. 115, which shows that ethnic Germans in Pennsylvania comprised 38% of the population of Pennsylvania in 1790. The percentages for each county are given here also. Multiplying the total population of 434,373 (http://en.wikipedia.org/wiki/1790_United_States_Census) by 38% yields an estimated 165,062 residents of Pennsylvania in 1790 of German descent.

8. Although Fogleman's figures are for all American colonies, most sectarians settled in Pennsylvania.

9. Gruver 1981, 66.

10. MacMaster 1985, 139.

11. See ibid., 140.

12. Ibid., 150.

13. According to statistics maintained by the Young Center for Anabaptist & Pietist Studies at Elizabethtown College, in 2014 there was an estimated total of 290,009 Amish living in thirty-one states and Ontario, of whom 67,045 lived in Pennsylvania. Source: http://www2.etown.edu/amishstudies/Population_by_State_2014.asp.

14. The main resources for the history of the various Amish settlements cited here are Mast 1953 for Berks County; Umble and Yoder 2011 for Lancaster-Chester Counties; A. J. Beachy 1954 and I. J. Miller 1959 for Somerset County; and Bender and Yoder 2011 for the Holmes-Wayne-Tuscarawas (OH) settlement. Another secondary settlement of Amish from the eastern core of Pennsylvania Dutch–speaking counties, which was also started in the late eighteenth century, was located in the Kishacoquillas ("Big") Valley in Mifflin County, PA (Hostetler 1957). This compact area is distinguished today by its great diversity of sectarian Pennsylvania Dutch–speaking groups (Brown 2011).

15. Keiser's 2012 monograph is the key study on the analysis and interpretation of similarities and differences between Lancaster and midwestern varieties of Pennsylvania Dutch.

16. An example of the rapid loss of Pennsylvania Dutch among nonsectarians who migrated westward is documented for Wisconsin. Fancy Dutch had settled there well before statehood in 1848 (Dundore 1954). Regarding the language, Dundore (1954, 162–163) states, "As settlers in Wisconsin the Pennsylvania Germans left behind them their dialect as a means of communication, for many had lived previously in Ohio, Indiana, and Illinois and thus lost their fluency. Others lost their native tongue because their neighbors hailed from Wales, Ireland, Germany, France, Belgium, and from the American states of New York, New Hampshire, Connecticut, Kansas, and Iowa. The best means of communication seem to have been American-English." One interesting exception is the

Pennsylvania Dutch poet, Louisa Weitzel, who was born in Green Bay, WI, in 1862 but moved with her family to Lititz, PA, where she became one of the few prominent female writers in Pennsylvania Dutch (Reichard 1918, 275–278).

17. There is a considerable literature on the history and language of the Pennsylvania Dutch in Ontario, e.g., Graeff 1946, Kratz and Milnes 1953, Anderson and Martin 1977, and Burridge 1989. Buehler 1977 contains much primary data of the language, as it is an autobiography written in Pennsylvania Dutch.

18. Works on Pennsylvania Dutch in Virginia and West Virginia include Hays 1908, Kyger 1964, Pulte 1971, Kehr 1979, and Van Ness 1990.

19. Klees 1950, 2.

20. Kollmorgen 1942, 48.

21. Ibid. 49–50. Kollmorgen cites this as coming from Maurer 1932, but I was unable to locate the page(s) from which this quote derived.

22. See Arndt and Eck 1989.

23. Wellenreuther 2013, 259.

24. See Wellenreuther 2013, 115–117; also Yoder 2005, 32–33.

25. See Schmitz 1856, 146–149. The tune to which this poem was set can be found in von Zuccalmaglio (1840, 540–542).

26. Merket auf, ihr Christenleut,
    Was ich sing zu dieser Zeit
        Vom Bauern-Stand.
        Es ist wohl bekannt
    Was die Bauern müßen leiden
    Jezt in den betrübten Zeiten.
        Dennoch sind sie sehr veracht,
        Einem Hund schier gleich geacht.

    Alle Menschen in dem Land
    Kommen her vom Bauernstand,
        Jeder mit Fleiß
        Merk den Beweiß,
    Wie von Adam ist zu lesen,
    So der erste Bau'r gewesen,
        Eva auch ein' Bäurin wär
        Von ihr sind wir kommen her.

    Jedermann bedenke fein,
    Daß wir alle insgemein
        Dem Bauernstand
        Gar nah verwandt.
    Wer die Sach thut recht betrachten,
    Wird die Bauern nicht verachten;
        Alle Menschen in dem Land,
        Nähren sich vom Bauernstand. (Yoder 2005, 32)

27. GOtt erhalt die Bauers-Leut
Nur im Frieden allezeit,
So hat's kein Noth
Ums liebe Brod.
Weiter wolle GOtt ihn'n geben
G'sunden Leib und langes Leben,
Bis wir aus dem Kreuz und Leid
Kommen zu der Seligkeit. (Yoder 2005, 32)

28. Wood 1942, 90.

29. Stine 1942, 107.

30. Morgan 2006, 162–163.

31. See figures in Wokeck 1999, 45. For more background on Benjamin Franklin's complicated relations with German Pennsylvanians, see Frantz 1998.

32. See Weber 1905; also Stine 1938, 29–35.

33. "Wir hatten die Freude wahrzunehmen, daß die deutsche Sprache wieder, durch unbekannte Ursache, wie zu sagen, von den Todten auferweckt wird, durch deutsche Schulen, die allerwegen errichtet werden, zur Erlernung der Sprache unserer Vorältern. In den Zeiten der Einfältigen, Fleißigen und Rechtschaffnen vor 40, 50 Jahren wurde in unserem Staat kaum etwas anders als Deutsch gehört—dazumal regierte der deutsche Geist durchgängig und sie hatten auch frohe glückliche Zeiten—Gott zeigte seine Zufriedenheit mit ihnen, dadurch, daß er sie mit Seegen überschüttete. So wie aber seither (wers bemerkt hat) das Deutsche abnahm, so nahm Hochmuth, Neid und Faulenzerey zu—jeder will jetzt ein Englischman, ein Gentelman und Lädy werden—aber, seht die Folgen—Gott zeigt seinen Eifer, da er uns auf allen Seiten drängt und uns Gentelleute mit Unseegen begüßt—O, der englische Geist hat uns gestürzt!—Ist das Aufleben unserer Sprache, wohl ein Vorbothe von bessern Zeiten?—Möchten unsere Kinder nicht nur die Deutsche Sprache, sondern auch den Deutschen Geist suchen zu erlangen, wie er vor Alters bestand aus Einfalt und Treue, umgeben von Fleiß und Reichthum."

34. Maurer 1932, 223.

35. Ibid., 224.

36. See Stine (1938, 36–53) for a good overview of the state of parochial education in rural Pennsylvania between 1750 and 1834, especially pp. 43–44 for details of the pedagogy in schools during this time. There are striking parallels between parochial education among the early Pennsylvania Dutch and Swartzentruber Amish schools today, especially as regards the teaching of English and German and the use of English and Pennsylvania Dutch in the classroom. See Johnson-Weiner 2007, 40–71.

37. *National Educator*, February 1, 1884, p. 4.

38. "Das Schulwesen war damals noch sehr zurück. Lesen, Schreiben und Rechnen, an der Tafel, wie auch aus einigen Textbüchern, war alles was in der Schule geübt wurde. Und viele Lehrer konnten dies nicht einmal gründlich lehren. . . . Auf je zehn Geviert-Meilen kam etwa eine Schule, deren vier aus fünf schlecht besetzt wurden. Ein trauriger Zustand für die Schule und Bildungsgrad der Gemeinde. Habe manche Bauern sagen hören, sie wären vier Monate in die Schule gekommen. Bei der ärmeren Klasse gab es

Leute, die gar nicht lesen und wenige nur, die einen Brief schreiben konnten. Man hatte wohl von Seiten des Staates Anordnung getroffen, die Kinder der Armen zu versorgen. So hatte jedes County eine Armenkasse, woraus die Kinder der Unbemittelten unterrichtet wurden. Später nahm jedes Township die Verwaltung dieser Kasse selbst über sich. Man achtete es aber als eine Schande, seine Kinder vom County oder Township lehren zu lassen; wurde auch manchen Kindern von den andern vorgehalten. Zuletzt wurde die Gelegenheit nicht mehr benutzt. Lieber liess man seine Kinder auf der Strasse laufen und viele blieben beinahe gänzlich ohne Unterricht" (Helffrich 1906, 24–25).

39. Johannes Helffrich also took a strong interest in homeopathy, which was developed by a German, Samuel Hahnemann (1755–1843). One of Hahnemann's students, Wilhelm (William) Wesselhöft (1794–1858), whose family counted Johann Wolfgang von Goethe among their friends, emigrated to Pennsylvania some time before 1830, when he met Johannes Helffrich, who had come to him seeking homeopathic treatment. The two men became close friends, and Wesselhöft recommended a number of other well-educated, German-born students of homeopathy as teachers in the Helffrich home. William Helffrich's older brother, John Heinrich, later became a homeopathic physician. See Helffrich 1906, 27–38; also Peabody 1859.

40. See Newman 2005. An obscure but important article on Fries's Rebellion written in German is Trexler 1880–1886, which is based in part on firsthand accounts of the event.

41. See Shimmell 1907. The quote is on p. 571.

42. Ibid., 572–573.

43. Ibid., 572.

44. Reichard 1918, 153–154.

45. See Stine 1938, 64.

46. See ibid., 64–71.

47. See Frantz 1998.

48. Nolt 2002, 31.

49. Hör o Himmel, meine Klagen,
    Weil dir alles wohl bewust,
In den schwartzen trauer Tagen,
    Aengstet sich die zarte Brust,
Die schon vor zwey hundert Jahren
    Um ein freyes Kind zu seyn,
Durch die wilde See gefahren,
    In ein wüstes Land hinein. (Anonymous 1775[?])

50. Wann gleich die Cartaunen brüllen,
    Wann der Mars im Blut erscheint,
Wann die Bomben gräulich wühlen,
    Dampf und Feuer sich vereint.
Laß es donnern, laß es krachen,
    Laß die Wälle fallen ein,
Diesen Wahl-Spruch will ich machen,
    Tod oder frey, will ich seyn. (Ibid.)

51. See Knauss 1922, 106–107; and Louden 2008, 6.

52. In linguistics, *mother tongue* normally refers to the first language (L1) a child acquires, usually the language of her parents. Lochman was using the word *Muttersprache* to refer to the language of one's immediate ancestors, essentially what linguists would call a *heritage language*, though that term implies at least some knowledge of the language. See Van Deusen-Scholl 2003. A standard German mother tongue, in the sense that the word was used by Lochman and contemporaries, serves as what Einar Haugen calls a *rhetorical norm* or ideal or preferred way of using language (1977, 91).

53. Schöpf 1788, 156, 157.

54. "Erwachsene Personen, welche aus Deutschland hinüber kommen, vergessen ihre Muttersprache zum Theil, indem sie eine neue zu lernen sich vergeblich bemühen; die eingebornen lernen ihre Muttersprache fast niemalen ordentlich und rein" (ibid., 156).

55. "[Sie schwäzen] auch unter sich vielfach, bald elend deutsch, bald noch elender englisch, denn sie haben den besondern Vorzug vor andern Nationen, daß sie im eigentlichen Verstand weder der einen noch der andern vollkommen mächtig sind" (ibid., 157).

56. "Es sind einige wenige abgesonderte Ortschaften, und einzelne wohnende Landleute im Gebürge, die weniger Umgang mit Engländern pflegen, und dahero zwar zuweilen ganz und gar kein Englisch verstehen, aber deswegen doch auch nicht besser deutsch sprechen" (ibid., 157).

57. The naturalness of first language acquisition is a universal phenomenon across the human species, an expression of our "language instinct" (Pinker 1994). We acquire most of the basic structural rules of our language within the first five or six years of life, and it becomes difficult to alter our native phonological, morphological, and syntactic habits after puberty. The acquisition of vocabulary and the largely unconscious rules of usage (i.e., the situational norms governing when we use certain constructions, words, or expressions; *pragmatic* knowledge) is not age sensitive.

58. For a discussion of cases of true pathological linguistic deprivation, see Curtiss 1977 and Schaller 1991.

59. Martin-Jones and Romaine 1986 and MacSwan 2000 discuss in detail the conceptual and practical problems associated with (double) semilingualism, especially in educational settings involving the children of families in minority-language communities.

60. Schöpf 1788, 157.

61. Ibid.

62. Ibid., 203–205.

63. See ibid., 204–205. This confirms what others have noted, namely that the Moravians, though German-speaking sectarians, spoke a form of standard German and were not really a part of Pennsylvania Dutch–speaking society (Rauch 1873, 58).

64. "Nicht genug aber, daß man elend spricht, man schreibt und druckt eben so erbarmenswürdig" (Schöpf 1788, 159).

65. "Die deutsche Buchdruckerey des Melchior Steiners, (und ehemals des Christoph Sauers) liefert wöchentlich ein deutsches Zeitungsblatt, welches eben so häufige, als traurige Beweise der erbärmlich verunstalteten Sprache unserer amerikanischen Landsleute enthält. Es sind hauptsächlich nur Übersetzungen aus englischen Blättern, aber so steif, und so englisirt, daß sie ekelhaft werden. Die beyden deutschen Geistlichen und

Herr Steiner selber besorgen das Blatt. Wenn ich nicht irre, erhält Herr Kunze allein 100 Pfund Pens. für seine Arbeit. Wenn wir sie rein deutsch schrieben, entschuldigen sich die Verfasser, so würden sie unsere amerikanische Bauern weder verstehen noch lesen können" (ibid., 159–160).

66. See McCarthy 2001.

67. Schöpf (1788, 161) gives the citation for Kunze's complete speech, which was published by Melchior Steiner in 1782.

68. "Die Fähigkeit, Deutsch zu sprechen, ist in hier gebohrnen gering, und wenn sie größer wäre, müßte auch wirklich die Gabe wunderthätig seyn. Die meisten Deutschen reden nicht deutsch. Wenn ich nichts weiter hinzu thue, so werde ich die Pflichten eines Redners diesmal übel erfüllen, denn dieser darf seine Zuhörer in kein Labyrinth führen. Sie fragen mit Recht, was reden die Deutschen denn, die nicht deutsch reden? und ich antworte, um deutlich zu seyn: Amerika hat vor allen Völkern des Erdbodens etwas voraus: es hat ein Volk in sich, das gar keine Sprache redet. Englisch ists nicht und deutsch solls nicht seyn" (ibid., 623–624).

69. Ibid., 158–159.

70. Recall the discussion in the previous chapter of the example of the Pennsylvania Dutch expression on the Old Reading Beer coaster.

71. Schöpf gave the English equivalent of the verb *absetzen* as 'to set off', meaning 'to depart'. Since this English phrasal verb is somewhat archaic in modern spoken English, contemporary Pennsylvania Dutch *absetze* means only 'to detonate'. Note that all the examples of verbal infinitives Schöpf cites end in *-en*, as in standard German. In Pennsylvania Dutch, the correct suffix is *-e*.

72. For example, the sentence was reproduced in slightly modified form, without attestation, by H. L. Mencken in his classic *American Language* (1965, 618): "[s]ome astounding examples of Pennsylvania-German are to be found in the humorous literature of the dialect, *e.g.*, 'Mein *stallion* hat über die *fenz getschumpt* und dem nachbar sein *whiet* abscheulich *gedämätscht*.'" Though Mencken cited Haldeman 1872 elsewhere in his remarks on Pennsylvania Dutch, it would appear not to be the source of the stallion sentence, since Haldeman rendered Schöpf's original accurately. Interestingly, a different author, Nils Flaten, a Norwegian-American scholar at St. Olaf College, did draw on Haldeman in this context. In an article from 1900 on American Norwegian, Flaten echoed the sentiments of Schöpf and others in decrying the mixture of Norwegian with English in the Midwest, referring to it as "a horrible jargon of mutilated English words" (Flaten 1900, 119). To exemplify this he translated Schöpf's stallion sentence into "Minnesota Norse," in which precisely the same five English loanwords (*stallion, jump, fence, wheat, damage*) occur.

73. S. S. Haldeman, in the first scholarly treatise on Pennsylvania Dutch, made this very point, noting that Schöpf's original was "probably spurious and a joke" since "'hengscht' and 'weetse' (instead of *stallion* and *wheat*) are in common use" (1872, 29).

74. George, Nead, and McCamant 1879, 207.

75. "Umzäunungen wird man sicher nirgends von so vielerley verschiedenen Arten sehen, als in Amerika, wo man jeden Augenblick beynahe eine neue Manier davon antrift, und nicht umhin kan, den erfinderischen Geist der Einwohner zu bewundern. Bey allen

aber verräth die Einrichtung, daß man auf Ersparniß der Mühe mehr, als auf Ersparniß des Holzes, des Raums, und auf Dauer Bedacht genommen habe. Gewöhnlich sind es nur todte Befriedigungen; entweder dünne Stangen, oder gespaltene Bäume, auf verschiedene Weise unter einander verbunden, oder übereinander gelegt, oder aufrecht stehende Pfäle gegen- und ineinander, so und anders, geschränket. Die sogenannten Wurmzäune (Worm-fences) sind die allergemeinsten; man wählt, wenn es zu haben ist, Kastanienholz dazu, weil es das leichteste ist, und geschält lange dauert" (Schöpf 1788, 195–196).

76. Lambert 1977, 182.

77. Beam 2004–2011.

78. The name thus can be translated as 'honest dullard', a collocation that is documented in eighteenth- and nineteenth-century British and American English. Although the proper name *Stoffel* is no longer common among Pennsylvania Dutch, perhaps because of its association with the homophonous 'dullard' word, it appears as a man's name in numerous early Pennsylvania Dutch texts, often with the same humorous intent. Regarding *Ehrlich*, a search of the 1790 federal census rolls for Lancaster County shows that there was at least one person with this family name, a Christian Ehrlich (http://usgwcensus.org/cenfiles/pa/lancaster/1790/pg035.txt). Interestingly, there is a poem titled "Stoffel" that was written in another form of extraterritorial Palatine German, namely the dialect spoken by the descendants of Palatines who migrated in the eighteenth century not west to America but east into the Bukovina region of the eastern Austro-Hungarian Empire. "Stoffel" was written by the Bukovina German poet Heinrich Kipper (1875–1959) and centers on a henpecked character that is strikingly similar to the Stoffel Ehrlich figure in eighteenth- and early nineteenth-century Pennsylvania. The parallels between the Bukovina and Pennsylvania Stoffels strongly point to a shared Palatine source for this literary figure. Kipper's poem appeared originally in Kipper (1925, 167–168) and was reproduced in Christmann and Kloss (1937, 24–25).

79. "Meister Drucker, Wir haben in Hempfield eure Zeitung kriegt, und sobald wir in die Stadt kommen, wollen wir das Einschreib-Geld bezahlen.... Da ihr jezt doch die Zeitung alle Woche druckt, so gebt uns auch dann und wann etwas Spaßiges.... Vielleicht könnet ihr mit dem alten Stoffel Ehrlich, nicht weit von der Canostogo-Kriek, bekant werden, euch Stücker zuzuschicken. Wir haben als pommerisch über sein Schreibens gelacht, besonders wie er die Großhansen abgenommen hat. In unserer Nachbarschaft sind einige bös über ihn worden, und gesagt daß er zu viel Englische Wörter vorbringe, und es auch nicht besser verstünde. Aber sie waren nicht auf zu seinen Tricks. Wir gleichen ein wenig von allerhand in der Zeitung zu lesen. Verschiedene Subscribenten."

80. Buffington (1905–1980) was a native speaker of Pennsylvania Dutch who wrote one of the first doctoral dissertations on the language, at Harvard University (Buffington 1937). He uses the term *Dutchified German* to describe the language of spirituals popular among the Pennsylvania Dutch in the nineteenth and early twentieth centuries; see Buffington (1965, 18–24).

81. Their father, Heinrich Augustus Grimler, immigrated to Pennsylvania in 1754. Their mother, Hannah, was a native of Charleston, SC, and an acquaintance of Benjamin Franklin (Harris 1872, 241–242).

82. "Freund Grimler, Weilen du schon von meinen Stücker gesezt hast, so ersuch ich dich mir folgendes in deine Zeitung zu thun—Laß die englische Expressions so viel als möglich haus; denn mei Fra zankt mich alsfort: 'Du Stoffel, wann du ebes schreiben wit, so schreib recht, oder laß die Finger davon.' Ich will also nichts schreiben, sondern dir blos erzählen, wie mirs an der Court gehäppend ist—und zwischen uns gesagt, so glaub ichs so fest als ewer:

"'Wo Weiber führen das Regiment,
"Da nimmt es selten ein gutes End!'

"Und gewiß, Meister Drucker, das hab ich bey der lezten Court zu meiner größten Sorrow erfahren. Du kanst dir leicht einbilden wie es hergeht, wenn unter uns guten, ehrlichen, deutschen Degenknöp, was die jetzige Welt *Gentiliti* heißt, einreißt oder fäshinable wird! Was wir vor Alters würden Flausen und Narrens-Possen geheißen haben, *distorb'd* so schuhr alleweil die Häppiness und Contentment von einer ganzen Familie. Was kan unter der Sun schlimmer seyn, als wenn in einem Haus Unzufriedenheit herrschet? Wenn ich dran denk' wie mei seliger Vater und wir Kinder so *gepließt* lebten; so bin ich fast geforc'd zu sagen: 'Die Menschen sind nicht wie sie in *our Teims* waren ... alle werden von Tag zu Tag schlimmer,' und man kan noch hinzusetzen, päst common ausgelassen!"

83. "Wer also unter uns wird murren? wer will lieber unter der Sclaverey als unter einer Regierung leben, wo '*Wir* ... *das Volk*' ... alles, und die Beamten blos die Diener sind; gewiß müßte derjenige, welcher das erstere erwählen würde, ein Thor seyn. Ich hoffe daß in Zukunft wir alles thörichte Partheywesen auf die Seite legen, und uns als *eine Familie* betrachten werden; dann, und nur dann, können wir über die Costüme der andern Welttheile lachen, und beherzt ausrufen:

"Wir sind hier wie ein Bruderband,
"Und sind vereint fürs Vaterland!"

84. "Wir haben schon lange auf den Stoffel Ehrlich gelauert"; "[Wir] gleichen etwas Spaßiges zu lesen"; "Vergesset mittlerweile nicht bey Gelegenheit uns etwas zum Zeitvertreib in der Zeitung mitzutheilen."

85. "Ich will also nichts schreiben, sondern dir blos erzählen, wie mirs an der Court gehäppend ist."

86. To be sure, the standard German in eighteenth-century Pennsylvania itself was somewhat Dutchified, as it included borrowings, loan translations, and calques from English, including an occasional word from Pennsylvania Dutch that may not have had a standard equivalent. Cf. in the text in the following note the borrowing *seider*, 'cider'; the calque *platz*, 'place, property'; and the Pennsylvania Dutch word *hinckel*, 'chicken'.

87. "Ihr sagt uns, daß Lancäster zum sitz einer Deutschen Hohen Schule ersehen worden; da will man vielleicht unsere kinder kluger machen als wir väter sind; daß laßt euch nur nicht in den sinn kommen. Ich bin auch nicht hochstudirt; aber ich brauch auch nicht mehr zu wissen als ich weiß. Mein vater seeliger wuste lange nicht so viel als ich weiß, denn der konte weder lesen noch schreiben, und wenn er rechnen wolte, so zählte er alles an den fingern ab, oder machte striche und kreutze über seine stubenthür.

Bey alle dem war er, GOtt hab ihn selig, ein herzens braver mann, aß sein stück speck, trank täglich seinen seider, und entschlief im 86sten jahr seines alters, sanft und selig, nachdem er mir seinen ganzen platz vermacht hatte. Meine beiden jungen brauchen also nicht mehr zu wissen als er und ich; denn das ey muß nicht klüger seyn wollen als das hinckel."

88. "Die beyträge des Meister Ehrlichs, der uns scheinet einen gesunden menschenverstand zu haben, sollen uns herzlich willkommen seyn. Zu unserm oben angeführten, muß nun der grund durch eine gute erziehung gelegt werden, denn aus Kindern werden Leute. Es befremdet uns dahero von dem Meister Ehrlich sehr, daß ihm die anlegung einer Deutschen Hohen Schule dahier nicht recht in den kopf will. Ist es nicht eine wahrheit, daß wann der kopf des jünglings oder mädchen leer von brauchbaren und gesunden kentnißen, und das herz entblößt von edlen empfindungen der reinern religion ist . . . Wie kan jener hernach ein glücklicher mann, und dieses eine gute hausfrau oder mutter werden? Wie kan er seinem lande in ämtern dienen? War dieses nicht die ursach daß die Deutschen bisher ihrer Englischen mitbürger, holzhauer und wasserträger gewesen?"

89. "Meister Albrecht und Lahn! Nein! nun kan ichs nicht mehr aushalten, die laus läuft mir endlich über die leber. Alles haltet ihr für fabeln und aberglauben, was! keinen ewigen Juden, keinen Docter Faust solte es gegeben haben, alle gespenster sollen in der einbildung bestehen, Gott thue zu unsern zeiten keine wunder mehr, ja in Num. 101 eurer zeitung, wollet ihr beweisen, daß der teufel nicht mitten unter den menschen herum gehe und denselben die bösen gedanken eingebe, noch auf ihre seele wirke, daß sie thun müssen, was sie sonst nicht würden gethan haben; ja, ihr nennet es eine abscheuliche moral, und um dem faß den boden auszustossen sagt ihr daß man den bösen feind nicht citiren könne, um verborgene schäze von ihm zu bekommen: nehmt mirs nicht übel, rechte Atheisten mögt ihr seyn wann ihr dieses alles nicht glaubet."

90. "An den ehrlichen Stoffel. Ey! ey Herr Stoffel Ehrlich seine beschuldigungen die er uns aufbürden will sind ein wenig zu hart; wiederlegen wollen wir ihn zwar nicht, sondern es ledig einem aufgeklärten publicum überlassen, da er uns aber auffordert, ihm zu erklären was abergläubisch seyn heiße, weil sein verstand darzu zu rund sey, so sagen wir ihm hiermit daß unserer einfältigen meynung nach abergläubig seyn, so viel bedeute: würkungen behaupten, oder erwarten, darzu die ursachen fehlen, zum beyspiel, wenn ein mensch hexen oder zaubern zu können, oder selbst behext oder bezaubert zu seyn, vorgiebt, so ist ein solcher mensch abergläubig. Denn entweder, hexen und zaubern heißt gar nichts, (wie es denn mehr solche wörter giebt, die undinge, oder nichts, bezeichnen,) oder es heißt, ohne ursach, wirkungen hervor bringen, welches wieder so viel als nichts heißt: denn ohne ursach sind auch keine wirkungen."

91. *Goose* was a term of opprobrium used by Thomas McKean to describe his political opponents and was applied more generally to supporters of Thomas Jefferson. http://www.pasleybrothers.com/jeff/writings/Pasley1800.htm.

92. "Wir folgten dem Begehren unsers Schreibers wörtlich . . . aber wünschen zugleich, solte er die Feder mehr brauchen, doch sauberes Papier zu nehmen, indem die Buchstaben und das Papier fast gleiche Farbe hatten, und das Ganze mit unserer Druckerfarbe Geschwisterkind war!"

93. As is the case for essentially all German Pennsylvanians of the late eighteenth and early nineteenth centuries, while it is possible to know whether they spoke "German" (*Deutsch*, pronounced as *Deitsch*; see the quote below), there is often little information about exactly what kind of German they spoke. However, it is reasonable to assume that most ethnic German children born to typical families in the Dutch counties of Pennsylvania in the second half of the eighteenth century spoke Pennsylvania Dutch. In the case of Simon Snyder, his official biography states that he had no formal education until he was seventeen and before his entry into politics had been trained as a tanner and then operated a store and gristmill in Selinsgrove, in what later became Snyder County (named for him). Snyder County was overwhelmingly Pennsylvania Dutch, having been settled by migrants from Berks and Lancaster Counties. It is thus entirely plausible that, when observers described Snyder as knowing German, that meant he spoke Pennsylvania Dutch.

94. "Ist es nicht billig daß wir Pennsylvanier doch einmal einen Gouverneur haben solten, der mit uns auch *Deutsch* reden kan? Laßt es nicht gesagt werden, daß wir Deutsche gegen unsern Mitbruder sind: Hätte Hr. Schneider jemal für eine Stämpel-Acte—für Accise und Fenstertaxen—für 8 pro Cent Schulden, und für Krieg gestimmt, dann wäre ich so gut gegen ihn als Roß; aber nein, Freunde, Schneider ist auf der Seite der Bauern und Handwerksleuten, welches ihn zu unsern Stimmen berechtiget. Roß wünschte Krieg, und stimmte für sclavische Taxen und Sclaverey."

95. "Er verstehet auch die Deutsche Sprache, und oft haben unsere Deutschen in Pennsylvanien Geschäfte mit dem Gouverneur, und durch seine Erwählung können sie dieselben dann in ihrer eigenen Muttersprache ausrichten."

96. "Die zu hitzigen Federals sind gegen den Schneider, weil er nicht *Hebräisch*— nicht *Griechisch*—und nicht *Lateinisch* spricht und ein Bauer und ein Handwerker ist. Das sind erstaunliche Ursachen—Solten wir ihren Liebling zum Gouverneur krigen, so wehe uns, armen Deutschen und Englischen in Pennsylvanien: Wäre nicht zu erwarten, daß wir Hebräisch regiert—Griechisch exercirt—und Lateinisch oder Spanisch tanzen müßten? Wäre das nicht Spaß?"

Chapter 3. Pennsylvania Dutch, 1800–1860

1. See Luebke 1990, 95.

2. One exception worth noting is the migration of ethnic Swiss and Palatine German Anabaptists from Switzerland, Alsace, and the Palatinate to mainly western Pennsylvania, Ohio, Indiana, Illinois, and Iowa between 1815 and 1860. Although the total number of Anabaptist arrivals during this time is estimated to have been around 3,400, a tiny fraction of the nearly 1.5 million German immigrants to America between 1820 and 1860, some, mainly those who settled in Somerset County in western Pennsylvania, merged with Pennsylvania Dutch–speaking sectarian groups (see H. S. Bender 1959 on nineteenth-century Anabaptist immigration to the United States and Luebke [1990, 95] for statistics on German immigration generally).

3. There is a considerable body of literature on the impact of nineteenth-century German immigration to the Midwest, Plains States, and Texas, including studies on the

maintenance of forms of the German language in many, especially rural, communities for generations after immigration ceased. See, for example, Eichhoff 1971 on German in Wisconsin and Boas 2009 on Texas German.

4. "Das deutsche Landvolk zog sich nun gänzlich von den Englischen zurück. Zu schwach oder zu schlecht geordnet und geführt, um ihre Sprache und Sitten herrschend zu machen, waren die deutschen Bauern doch zu stark und zu stolz, als daß sie ihre volks-thümliche Weise hätten aufopfern können. Die dreißig Jahre, aber, während welcher sie von Deutschland so gut wie abgeschnitten waren, zogen eine Kluft zwischen ihnen und später kommenden Landsleuten. Es begab sich in Amerika die merkwürdige Er-scheinung, daß sich ein neuer Volksstamm bildete, eigenthümlich in Sprache, Sitten und Anschauungsweise" (Löher 1847, 199–200).

5. See ibid., 201–202.

6. See ibid., 198.

7. See Hohman 1820. See also Hohman 2012, which is a reprint of another German-language folk-healing manual published by Hohman in 1813, which includes an intro-duction, translation, and annotations by Patrick J. Donmoyer.

8. See Robacker 1943, 70.

9. See Arndt and Olson 1961, 587–588; also Runyeon 1936. The English-language *Reading Eagle* began appearing in 1868 and continues today.

10. See Arndt and Olson 1961, 565.

11. In an 1870 article on Pennsylvania Dutch that was actually written in the lan-guage, historian Israel Daniel Rupp (1803–1878) quotes from a letter supposedly written by Henry Melchior Muhlenberg in 1745 to colleagues in Halle commenting negatively on the intermingling of German and English among German Pennsylvanians: "The Ger-mans, who are mainly in Chester County, and live among the English, speak half Ger-man and half English" (*Die Teutsche, welche meistens in Chester Grafschaft sind, und bei den Englischen wohnen, reden halb-Teutsch, und halb-Englisch*) (Rupp 1870, 309). I was not able to confirm the existence of such a letter, but if Muhlenberg did in fact write this, his would be one of the very earliest commentaries on the language contact situation among German Pennsylvanians in the colonial era.

12. See Seidensticker 1889.

13. "Die Englische ist und bleibt die Landes-Sprache. Wir sind in den Vereinigten Staaten überhaupt nur eine geringe Anzahl, selbst in diesem Staat, indem die meisten Deutschen wohnen, kaum ein Drittheil, mit welchem Recht oder Billigkeit können wir erwarten, daß jene die weit grössere Anzahl sich nach uns, der weit geringern, rich-ten solte. Alle Landesgesetze und Verordnungen—alle Gerichtssachen—aller Handel und Vergleiche, und überhaupt alle öffentiche Angelegenheiten werden in Englischer Sprache verrichtet, und dennoch herrscht das Vorurtheil für die Deutsche Sprache. Welcher Deutsche unter uns, der in der Handlung, oder irgend einem öffentlichen Gewerbe stehet, führt seine Bücher in Deutscher Sprache, und wenn er es thut, muß er nicht eingestehen, daß es mit vielen Unbequemlichkeiten verknüpft ist? Daß dieses uns selbst in der Folge den größten Schaden zufügt, kan niemand in Abrede seyn, und daß es im Gegentheil für unsere Jugend in aller Absicht weit vortheilhafter ist, wenn sie

eine gründliche Erkenntniß der Landessprache erlangen, kan nicht geläugnet werden" (Muhlenberg 1795, 8–9).

14. Ibid., 10.

15. "Endlich ists noch eine Frage, ob das mehreste sogenannte Deutsche, welches in Pennsylvanien gesprochen wird, wirklich Deutsch ist. Wenn ich unsere Kanzelreden, und vielleicht die Sprache derer wenigen Deutschen ausnehme, die von angesehenen Handlungsstädten kürzlich in dis Land gekommen, so verdient die sogenannte Pennsylvanisch-Deutsche Sprache wirklich den Namen der Deutschen nicht. So spricht der Schwabe anders als der Schweitzer, der Pfälzer anders als der Sachse, der Hesse anders als der Pomeraner, und der Nieder- oder Plattdeutsche anders als der Hochdeutsche. Aus allen diesen verschiedenen Mundarten, die doch alle Deutsch heissen, und einem merklichen Zusatz von verdorbenem Englisch ist endlich die posierlichste von allen entstanden—ich meyne die Sprache meiner Landesleute, das Pennsylvanisch-Deutsche" (ibid.).

16. "So lacht ein Ausländer über das hiesige sogenannte Deutsch, und seine Historie ist der bekannten Geschichte ähnlich, die uns ehemals der alte Saur in einer Zeitung oder Calender erzelte: Nämlich, der Stallion sey über die Fence gejump'd und habe des Nachbars Wheat abscheulich gedamaged; oder auch der Anecdote von einer Deutschen Jungfer, die einen angesehenen Deutschen Prediger zu Gast hatte, den sie ihrer Meinung nach aufs höflichste zum Essen nöthigen wolte, und auf gut Pennsylvanisch-Deutsch sagte: Freß hearty, Herr Parr, du bis very willkumm" (ibid., 12).

17. Christopher Sauer (also spelled Saur, Sower) was the most famous German printer in colonial America. Based in Germantown, he published the first German-language periodical and the first German-language Bible in America.

18. Ibid., 13–14.

19. See Arndt 1976, 140.

20. See Feer 1952, 400; and Arndt 1976, 140–143.

21. "Was würde Philadelphia in vierzig Jahren seyn, wenn die Deutschen dort deutsch blieben; wenn sie Sprache und Sitten beybehielten? Es brauchte keine vierzig Jahre, so wäre Philadelphia eine deutsche Stadt, so gut als York und Lancaster deutsche Grafschaften sind. Die Engländer würden sich weiter ins Gebüsch begeben, wenn sie nicht in den südlichen Theilen der Stadt mehr anbaueten. Und was würde in dem Fall nicht aus ganz Pennsylvanien und dem oberen Theil von Maryland in vierzig oder fünfzig Jahren werden können! Ein ganz deutscher Staat, wo man einst allgemein, wie vor Alters in Germantaun, auch im hohen Staatsrath und in den Gerichten die schöne deutsche Sprache redete. Hat nicht vor etwa zwanzig Jahren, selbst ein englischer Advocat im Gericht den Vorschlag gethan, daß des Deutschen Sache, in deutscher Sprache verhandelt werden sollte? Hat nicht Herr General Hiester, zu Philadelphia im Congreß den Vorschlag gethan, daß alle Gesetze der Union in Deutsch gedruckt werden sollten; und hätte seinen Zweck gewiß erreicht, wenn er nicht durch einen Deutschen—sogar durch einen deutschen stolzen Thoren im Haus, wäre hintergangen worden, der das Beste seiner Nation und seiner Constituenten mit Vorsatz vereitelte" (Helmuth 1813b, 175–176). See also Arndt 1976, 139.

22. See Baer 2008 for an excellent study of the division within Philadelphia's St. Michael's and Zion congregation between those who favored the use of English in worship and those who, like Pastor Helmuth, preferred German. An important fact that Baer brings out is the correlation of class with language preference. Generally speaking, congregants of more modest social standing tended to prefer German, while the English party tended to be more affluent. The loyalty of urban Lutheran craftspeople to German parallels directly the situation of Pennsylvania Dutch / German maintenance among rural dwellers. And that both urban and rural advocates for the preservation of German framed their arguments in the language of American ideals of freedom and self-determination is crucial to understanding how assimilated ideologically, if not linguistically, those loyal to the German language in America were. See also Roeber 1994 for an in-depth look at Pastor Helmuth's (ultimately fruitless) ideas and activities on behalf of strengthening the status of German in education in Philadelphia. In 1789 Helmuth founded the von Mosheim Society with the express purpose of furthering interest in the German language. Notably, the society's membership included Marcus Kuhl and George Lochman, Frederick Muhlenberg's friends in the parody discussed in chapter 2. It is all but certain that Muhlenberg was not a member of the society.

23. "Man konnte sich daher nicht mehr wundern, daß auch in Politik, in den Gerichten und bei den andern öffentlichen Verhandlungen die Englischen nach und nach die Leitung erhielten und ihre Sprache wenigstens bei den bedeutendsten Versammlungen einführten. In Pennsylvanien war das gleichwohl nicht leicht. Bei der Abstimmung über jene Frage: ob die herrschende Sprache auf dem Landtage, an den Gerichten und in den Urkunden in Pennsylvanien die deutsche sein solle,—waren die Stimmen gleich. Die Hälfte war für Einführung der deutschen Sprache, und das war schon von großer Bedeutung, wenn man bedenkt, daß es darauf ankam, einen Staat deutsch zu machen, in welchem die englische Sprache vorher die Gesetzessprache gewesen war. Da gab der Sprecher des Landtages, ein Mühlenberg, durch seine Stimme den Ausschlag zu Gunsten der englischen Sprache" (Löher 1847, 198).

24. See Schöpf 1788, 159–160; and the discussion in chapter 2.

25. See Arndt 1986.

26. Note that both *Station* and *Respect* are also attested in eighteenth-century German, both loanwords from French.

27. The school that Harbaugh and Fisher attended was located close to the Harbaugh farmstead southeast of Waynesboro, just north of the Maryland state line. A historical marker dedicated to Henry Harbaugh is located near where the home and school were situated, at 14301 Harbaugh Church Road.

28. Fisher 1879, 191. The entire poem is on pp. 191–195. In his 1882 collection of Pennsylvania Dutch poems, Fisher includes a slightly modified version of this first stanza:

> Do hen mer unser Schuling grigt
>   Un' hen dafor bezahlt;
> Es war so 'n Schproch-fermixte Schul—
> Der Meschter, König, uf seim Schtuhl—
>   Hot g'sad mit Ernscht un' G'walt,

Das Englisch net drin g'lernt sol sei,
Sunscht gebt 's zu 'n grosze Hud'lerei."

Here we got our schooling
And paid for it.
It was a linguistically mixed-up school,
The teacher, a king, on his chair
Said with seriousness and force
That English should be not learned in there,
Otherwise there would be too great a confusion. (Fisher 1882, 227)

29. See Ford 1897/1962. For an excellent study of German-language ABC books used by German Pennsylvanians and Pennsylvania Dutch, see Klinefelter 1973.

30. There are two details of linguistic interest in the description of the letters of the English alphabet (*Das Neue ABC- und Buchstabir-Buch* 1861, 46). For the letter *r*, the author writes the English name as *ar* and then renders it phonetically in German as *ärr*, which would mean that the letter name rhymed with *air*, with the vowel [æ], rather than with *are*, whose vowel is transcribed as [a]. This was an originally British English dialectal feature that was also found in many varieties of early American English, including those spoken in Pennsylvania, which explains why most English-derived loanwords in Pennsylvania Dutch containing <ar> are pronounced in with the [æ]. *Hardly, smart,* and *charge,* for example, are rendered into Pennsylvania Dutch as *haerdly, schmaert,* and *tschaerdsche.* Many early descriptions of early American English make reference to this pronunciation of <ar>, including one from none other than Benjamin Franklin (1779; see p. 476, in which *hardly* is written "hardli"; Franklin's <a> had the phonetic value of [æ]). See Penzl 1938b for a thorough discussion of the pronunciation of <ar> in English loanwords in Pennsylvania Dutch. A second phonetic detail of interest in the English alphabet list in this primer concerns the English letter *v*. Its English name is written as *ve*, but in German it is *v'wi*, which reflects the Pennsylvania Dutch voiced bilabial fricative [β] mentioned in the description of Dutchified English in the first chapter.

31. See Haag 1988, 68; also Betz 1910. Betz notes that Fisher's knowledge of Pennsylvania Dutch ("German") was a professional asset to him in his career as a lawyer in York, as he was often called upon to interpret between Pennsylvania Dutch and English in court (Betz 1910, 7).

32. Fisher "was a man who could think and express himself while on his feet. He was never at a loss for words and had command of a vigorous Anglo-Saxon vocabulary. Like Carlyle and Whittier he was a passionate admirer of the poet Burns. Like Ingalls he was a student of the dictionary and Roget's 'Thesaurus of English Words'" (Betz 1910, 5).

33. See Fisher 1888. These poems are as important for their content as many of his Pennsylvania Dutch poems, especially the second part of Fisher 1879 (titled "Die Alte Zeite" [The old(en) times]), since they also deal with the early life and customs of his people.

34. The confusion between <ü> and <ö> and <i(e)> and <e(e)> was understandable for anyone learning German in the eighteenth and early nineteenth centuries in both

America and Europe, since in many central and southern dialects the front rounded vowels [y] and [ø] corresponding to <ü> and <ö> had merged with unrounded [i] and [e]. Another orthographic archaism in Fisher's German-influenced Pennsylvania Dutch orthography is the silent <h> in *gedhu*, 'done' (PD *geduh*, earlier Ger. *gethan*, modern Ger. *getan*).

35. Fisher 1879, 191. This gender difference in social and linguistic behavior is an example of what sociolinguists, notably William Labov, have observed in a number of studies of language change: "Women conform more closely than men to sociolinguistic norms that are overtly prescribed, but conform less than men when they are not" (Labov 2001, 293). In Pennsylvania Dutch society, English has long enjoyed overt prestige, hence it makes sense that females would be more inclined to shift away from Pennsylvania Dutch, whose maintenance is linked to its covertly prestigious status, as discussed in chapter 1.

36. A. L. Shoemaker 1951a.

37. "Mr. Drucker Grimler,

"Weil anjezo wenig Neuigkeiten vorhanden sind, so zeiget einer alten Freundin die Gefälligkeit, uns setzet folgendes in eure nächste Zeitung.

"Was heute gethan werden kan, muß man nicht auf Morgen verchieben—so sagt Stoffel Ehrlich—und darin hat er auch ganz vollkommen Recht; denn wozu hilft das lange getricks? Wenn man doch eine Sache gern thut, so schlägt man eben sowohl gleich zu. Schlage weil das Eisen heiß ist, und nehme Notis von der Gelegenheit weil sie da ist, sagte als meine Stiefschwester, die schon im 19ten Jahre einen Mann hatte. Ich habe lang genug (bey mir selber) geklagt: 'O wie krank bin ich!' Ich habe mich lang genug geschmiert, gepuzt und aufgeschleckt: Und für was? um weiter nichts, als in den nemlichen Stand zu kommen, worin meine Mutter vor mir war: Ich sehe daß es mit mir schlechte Numren hat—Meinen Plan muß ich anders angreifen; denn ich denk daß ich sonst unter die Classe der alten Jungfern (*Old Maids*) komme, und wann das so eintrift, so ist es bey mir verspielt! Hopfen und Malz sind dann verloren; Alles Puzen und Schönmachen hilft also nichts mehr. Es geht ja anjezo schon den Jungen hart—wie wirds denn erst mit den Alten gehen?

"Es ist wohl wahr, daß mit den *alten Bätschelors* nicht viel ist—sie sind halsstarrige Tröpf, und wissen nicht was ihnen gut ist oder was sie wollen: Ich verlange meines Theils keinen—gebe mir lieber einen Witmann. Aber doch haben die alten Kerls viel bessere Aussichten wie wir—Und mich, Mr. Drucker, aus aller Verlegenheit zu setzen, und *Deutsch* zu reden, in der Absicht einen Mann zu krigen, so beliebet mir folgendes *Adverteismen* in eure Zeitung zu setzen—vielleicht vergaft sich doch einer" (*Der Wahre Amerikaner*, February 8, 1806).

38. "Und nun, Herren Drucker, was denkt ihr von den neuen, heranwachsenden, sogenannten Gentelleuten, die sich schämen zu schaffen? Was wird am Ende daraus werden? Ich selbst kenne Eltern, welche sich hart plagten, deren Söhne in der Faullenzerey auferzogen werden. Und mit Wehmuth sehe ich öfters einige, die in Armuth und Elend ihr Leben zubringen—in ihrer Jugend waren sie Gentelleute, jezt aber Bettler!—Wie höchst unrecht handeln dahero alle solche Eltern, die ihren Kinder kein Handwerk lernen lassen, und zwar unter dem Gedanken, kein Handwerk lernen lassen, daß sie

deswegen keine Gentelleute seyn können. Wann es zu spät ist, werden sie's zu ihrem Leidwesen, einsehen, wie thöricht sie gehandelt haben" (*Der Wahre Amerikaner*, January 25, 1806).

39. "FEDERALIST. Well, du Jakobiner! aber dismal wollen wir euch weisen, daß wir mit euch Republikaner just machen können was wir wollen. Wir Federals sind Gentelleut und haben Verstand—und ihr dumme Tölpel seyd gut genug zum schaffen.

"REPUBLIKANER. Ich hör' dich—gehe nur an; ich bin ein Bauer. Aber es ist doch gut, daß wir gemeine Leute ein Recht haben zu stimmen, für wen wir wollen—Hörest du auch das?

"F. Ja das hilft alles nichts; denn wir machen den *Deutschen* folgende schöne Sachen weiß: 'Daß die Constitution zu Grund gehe—daß es Krieg und Verwirrung im Lande giebt—daß Lawyer ehrliche Leute und die gescheitsten Männer für die Assembly wären—daß nur Lawyer die reichen Bauern lieb haben—daß Jefferson für Krieg sey —und daß das Rauben und Stehlen angeht, *wann die Democraten, (oder Jeffersons Freunde)* diesesmal gewinnen! Hols der Teufel, die Deutschen glauben dies wie die Bibel —und sie veschlucken es wie Zucker. Und wann etwa ein M'Keaner in Companie ist, so rufen wir laut: *Hurra für M'Kean und die Constitution!*

"R. So, ihr macht nur 'den Deutschen so weiß!' Aber dumm muß der seyn, der so einfältig Kinderwesen glaubt.

"F. Die Wahl zu gewinnen, ist alles was wir wollen—Und da wir Federals nur so zum Schein für M'Kean und die Constitution rufen, so stimmen viele Quids auch für unser Ticket. Da wir die Constitution den Deutschen so wichtig als das Testament zu machen suchen, so thut's gut—und du mußt wissen, daß es bey Wahlen auf eine Handvoll Lügen nicht ankommt.

"R. Wann die Constitution so heilig ist, warum habt ihr Federals sie verbessern wollen, als die Assembly noch in Philadelphia war?

"F. Halts Maul von alten Sachen.

"R. Glaubt ihr denn daß wir Deutsche so dumm sind zu glauben, daß die Assembly oder Simon Schneider die Constitution umstoßen will?

"F. Nein—aber sey still; komm und trink ein bissel Wein und Wasser; denn mit dir kan ich nichts thun" (*Der Wahre Amerikaner*, October 10, 1807).

40. Overt expressions of patriotism among Pennsylvania Dutch people, historically as well as today, are largely limited to nonsectarians. Most Anabaptists, especially the Amish and Mennonites, avoid the display of political and patriotic symbols, including flying and pledging allegiance to the American flag, in order to stress the ultimate loyalty they have as Christians not to a secular authority but to God.

41.   Freudig ruf ich: Deutsche Brüder!
Heil Amerika! lebe hoch!
Lauter Echo halle wieder:
Heil dem Land, das uns erzog!

Krönte schon vor alten Zeiten
Deutsche Redlichkeit und Ruhm;
Tapferkeit und treue Leuten
War stets unser Eigenthum.

In Columbia's Schoos gedeihet
Jede Kunst und Fertigkeit;
Deutscher Geist und Sprache freuet
Auch den Fremdling weit und breit.

Da wo milde Väter thronen,
Blüht das Land, ist Zwietracht fern.
Deutsche gern in Ruhe wohnen,
Ehren gute Menschen gern.

Anmuthsvoll verstreicht das Leben,
Wo man volle Gnüge findt;
Deutsche Erde kan sie geben,
Wohl uns, daß wir Deutsche sind!

Drum so schwelle, Deutsche Brüder,
Freudensang den Busen hoch!
Lautes Echo halle wieder:
Heil dem Land, das uns erzog! (*Der Wahre Amerikaner*, November 10, 1804)

42. See Sutro 1912.

43. The translation of this verse is from Robacker (1943, 61). The glaring errors in Fritz's German both involve the use of the third-person reflexive pronoun *sich*, 'oneself', in the second line, when he should have used *dich*, 'you (object)', and in the fifth line, when it is superfluous. This is intended to reflect the tendency for some nonfluent learners of German to overgeneralize *sich* during the acquisition process. The Pennsylvania Dutch elements include *nit* for *nicht*, 'not'; *versteh* for *verstehen*, 'understand'; and *wees* for *weiß*, '(I) know'.

44. The supposedly German origin of gunpowder is associated with the legend of a fourteenth-century alchemist named Berthold Schwarz.

45. Wir sind in großen Nöthen,
Weil viel falsche Propheten
Sich schlau in Schaaf-Fell' hüllen,
Und wie die Löwen brüllen,
Wie wüthend sich erfrechen
Uns den Himmel abzusprechen.
So hört, Herr! doch meine Bitte;
Sende Trost in unsrer Mitte,
Daß die Jugend wieder blühe,
Und das Übel von uns fliehe—
Schenk uns das zum neuen Jahr,
Daß wir dich preißen immerdar.—
Amen. (*Die Republikanische Preße*, February 6, 1829).

46. "Aber nun drohet den deutschen protestantischen Kirchen ein gewaltiger Sturm, der nicht blose Folge des natürlichen Ganges der Dinge, sondern ein Zeichen dieser Zeit ist; und ihnen ihren kirchlichen Wohlstand sammt aller ihrer Freude bald rauben wird, wenn nicht Lehrer und Eltern mit vereinten Kräften dagegen arbeiten. Man fängt fast allgemein an, besonders in Städten und an den Grenzen, die Kinder **ganz** in der englischen Sprache zu erziehen und für den deutschen Gottesdienst ganz unverantwortlich zu vernachlässigen. Dies ist Folge der Gleichgültigkeit und Verachtung der heilsamen Lehre, in der großen Versuchungsstunde, die jetzt über den Erdkreis ergehet. Wenn man die Jugend blos englisch lernen ließe, und vollkommen englisch; dagagen könnte kein Vernünftiger etwas sagen—ihre zeitliche Wohlfahrt in diesem Lande macht es nothwendig; aber sie ganz dem deutschen Gottesdienst und ihrer Kirche zu entziehen, setzt bey den Eltern eine Religions-Gleichgültigkeit und eine so große Vorliebe zum Zeitlichen voraus, die sicherlich auffallend ist.

"Ach, ihr theure Wächter der protestantischen Gemeinden, die ihr entweder gleichgültig gegen dieses Übel seyd, oder es gar unterstützt; bedenken Sie, was die traurigen Folgen seyn werden!" (Helmuth 1813a, 67).

47. "Zu mir hat einmal ein englischer Gelehrter gesagt: 'Our language is a piratical one. Pirates appropriate other men's property to themselves. So it is with our language. It has taken in and appropriated to itself words from every language.' Gerade so verhält es sich. Schwerlich giebt es in der ganzen Welt eine so geflickte und aus allerlei Stoff zusammen gestoppelte Sprache, wie die englische. Sie ist eine Tochter der deutschen, aber so entsetzlich entartet, daß man die lieblichen Züge ihrer edlen Mutter nicht mehr erkennt. Hierin gleicht sie leider! vielen englisch werdenden Kindern edler deutscher Väter und Mütter. Sie schämt sich ihrer selbst, darum hat sie jedes Volk um das in der Sprache beraubt, was ihr schön dünkt, damit sie ihre eigene Blöße decken möchte" (*Deutsch oder Englisch* 1862, 5).

48. "Ich kam in ein mir und Dir bekanntes Haus, das ich aber nicht nennen will. Auf der Bank in der Ecke saß die alte deutsche Mutter des Hauses, die möglicherweise die Bretter zu demselben in ihren jungen Jahren auf ihrem Haupte herbeitragen geholfen haben mochte; deren Loos es wahrscheinlich gewesen war, das Getreide und das Mehl zum Brode ihrer Kinder auf dem Haupte nach und von der Mühle zu tragen, und die jedenfalls durch ihren Fleiß, ihre Sparsamkeit und stille, mit ihrem Loos zufried[e]ne Bescheidenheit den Wohlstand der Familie hatte begründen und erschaffen helfen;— dort saß sie, sage ich, auf der Bank in der Ecke und flickte mit gewohntem Fleiß die zerrissenen Arbeitskleider ihrer nun erwachsenen Söhne; und dort—mitten in der Stube, auf geschmücktem Schaukelstuhl, aufgewichst und aufgefixt, bis über die Ohren in Putz gewickelt, mit großem weitem Reifrock, saß die englische Schwiegertochter und schaukelte sich, daß die Beine in die Höhe kamen, und—und—nun?—sie strickte eine Spitze! Sieh' dich vor, Sebastian, daß es Dir nicht so geht! Sieh' dich vor, daß deine Kinder nicht zu Dir sagen lernen: 'I don't like to go to dutch meetings!' Sieh' dich vor, daß Du nicht in deinen alten Tagen in deinem eigenen Hause hören mußt: I don't care for that old dutchman! I don't care for that old dutch woman!" (*Deutsch oder Englisch* 1862, 10).

49. *Pennsylvania Dutchman*, November 15, 1951, p. 4. See also http://www.geni.com /people/Martha-Leidig/6000000000628268964.

50. John Bomberger lived from 1803 to 1889. Source: http://records.ancestry.com /John_Bomberger_records.ashx?pid=62877322&te=1.

51. See Robacker (1943, 72–118), who identifies 1861 as the beginning of the "language-conscious period" for Pennsylvania Dutch literature, a flowering of prose, poetry, and dramas in the language that extended into the early years of the twentieth century.

52. The very first item was a short dialog between a child and his or her father titled "Humbug," which appeared on October 16, 1849 (Runyeon 1936, 83).

53. Enos Benner's great-grandfather was Ludwig Benner (1728–1791). No information on Ludwig's wife is available, but his first child, the sister of Enos's grandfather John (1750–1823), was born in 1748, apparently in Pennsylvania. Source: http://www.find agrave.com/cgi-bin/fg.cgi?page=gr&GRid=73727457.

54. See Wood 1940 for an engaging history of *Der Bauern Freund*, which actually spanned two eras. When Benner retired in 1858, he sold the newspaper to a European-born German speaker, Albrecht Kneule, who merged it with the *Pennsburg Demokrat*. In 1896 Kneule's son, Henry A., took over. *Der Bauern Freund und Demokrat* ceased publication in 1908. Under all three editors, *Der Bauern Freund* was an ardently Democratic newspaper. As Wood discusses, during Benner's editorship, the Democratic Party enjoyed considerable success at the national level, but that changed during and after the Civil War. The reactions of Pennsylvania Dutch to the changing conditions in American politics are well documented in the pages of *Der Bauern Freund*.

55. Though Jackson won a plurality of the popular vote in 1824, the House of Representatives voted for Adams, allegedly because of the machinations of Speaker Henry Clay, who was named Adams's secretary of state. Clay was a target of regular criticism in the pages of *Der Bauern Freund*.

56. "[Wir haben] schon bekannt gemacht daß wir democratische republikanische Grundsätze behaupten, und jezt können wir nicht umhin zu sagen daß wir freundlich gegen Gen. Jackson gesinnt sind—daß wir die Verläumdungen gegen ihn, die Pamphlets ohne Druckers Name welche im Umlauf sind als Unwahrheiten betrachten, und die Schimpfreden womit ihn seine Feinde suchen bey dem Volk in Verachtung zu bringen höchst mißbilligen, denn der Volkswahl gemäß war er zur Presidentenstelle berechtiget gewesen, und seiner Erwählung günstig zu seyn kann uns in der Achtung eines billig denkenden Mannes um so weniger herabstimmen" (*Der Bauern Freund*, August 6, 1828).

57. See Rickford and Rickford 2000 for an accessible history of Black English.

58. Pennsylvania Dutch *Vendu* has an interesting history. It is a borrowing from regional English *vendue*, which, during the New Netherland era in American colonial history, inherited it from Dutch, which in turn had borrowed it from French.

59. "'Freund!' ruft er in großer Aufregung aus: 'Schreiben Sie Direktor mit einem c oder k? Da habe ich eine Correktur zu besorgen, doch um Vergebung; wie schreiben Sie Correktur, mit einem c oder k? Mir schwindelt der Kopf—oder wie sagen Sie: mir oder mich schwindelt der Kopf? Mir oder mich träumt? Mir oder mich schwant? Mir oder mich dünkt? Ich werde noch verrückt über diese Mir oder Mich's, diese k's und c's? Wie schreiben Sie Direktor?'

" 'In der Regel mit einem k,' antwortete ich, 'es gibt aber Leute, die das Wort, vielleicht mit demselben Rechte mit einem c schreiben.'

" 'Da haben wir's: in der Regel, sagen Sie, mit einem k! Ist das Consequenz? Heißt das nicht: Sie schreiben es ausnahmsweise auch wohl mit einem c?'

" 'Nach Bequemlichkeit,' antwortete ich, 'man hat keine bestimmte Regel dafür.'

" 'Zum Teufel!' rief mein Freund in vollster Wuth, 'in der Orthographie gibt es keine Bequemlichkeit. Doch halt: schreiben Sie "giebt" mit oder ohne ein e?'

" 'Der Verfasser, dessen Werk ich hier korrigire, läßt in toller Consequenz das e fort; da müßte er doch auch "libt" statt "liebt" u. s. w. schreiben, oder gar "schrib" statt "schrieb," "blib" statt "blieb" u. s. f.' " (*Der Bauern Freund*, January 26, 1848).

60. "Für das Wort 'Billard' erfand man in der Zeit, wo man alle Fremdwörter aus der Deutschen Sprache verbannte, das schöne ächtdeutsche wegen seiner Geläufigkeit sehr zu empfehlende Wort, Grüntuchsechslöcherstoßtafel" (*Der Bauern Freund*, January 28, 1835).

61. "Wir haben schon früher in dieser Zeitung darauf aufmerksam gemacht, daß fast alle europäische deutsche Zeitungs-Herausgeber in diesem Lande das schöne Wort *Bauer* in ihren Zeitungen nie gebrauchen, sondern immer *Farmer* schreiben. Vermuthlich glauben diese Herren, das Wort *Bauer* sei zu *bäuerisch*, weil in Europa der Bauernstand als auf einer sehr niedern Stufe stehend betrachtet wird, und nur der *Adelstand Edelleute* in sich fassen könne.—In Amerika ist die Sache umgekehrt. Hier verliert sich der adelige Stand im Bauernstand. Der Ärmste kann sich durch Fleiß, Tugend und Rechtschaffenheit zu Ehren und Ansehen emporschwingen, und somit sich die Achtung seiner Mitbürger als Edelmann erwerben. Man ist hier stolz darauf, Bauer zu heißen, und kein pennsylvanischer Bauer, der deutsch spricht, sagt *Farmer*, sondern *Bauer*.—In Amerika ist das Wort *Bauer* so wohlklingend als Doctor, Advokat, Professor oder Pastor. Man sieht es gern, wenn auf dem Verzeichniß der Glieder der Gesetzgebung, deren Professionen gewöhnlich jährlich bekannt gemacht werden, eine Mehrheit steht, die sich Bauern nennen, denn der Bauernstand ist hier der Vornehmste und derjenige, von welchem alle andern Stände dieses Landes abhängig sind. Also nur Bauer nicht Farmer geschrieben, und *Thaler* anstatt *Dollars*, ihr werthe deutsche Zeitungsschreiber, denn wir haben ohnehin schon einen Überfluß englischer Wörter in unsern deutschen Zeitungen, ohne daß wir noch, mehr ganz und gar ohne Ursache, gebrauchen sollten" (*Der Bauern Freund*, April 30, 1851).

62. "'Es ist eppes letz' ruft ein Bankdrucker, und sogleich stimmt der ganze föderalistische Schwarm dasselbe Lied an. 'Es ist eppes letz' ruft ein Glücksjäger, der mit Maulbeerbäumen eine eben so schlechte Spekulation gemacht hat, als die Whigs mit ihrem Candidaten Harrison, und sogleich stimmen ihm alle Leute bei, die seit Jahren auf Credit haben arbeiten lassen, und ihren Arbeitern den sauverdienten Lohn nicht bezahlten.

"Wie kommt es, daß diese Menschen jetzt erst einsehen, daß etwas 'letz' ist? Hat doch President Jackson schon vor mehreren Jahren gesagt, daß 'eppes letz' sei! Mußte doch jeder unbefangene Beobachter längst einsehen, daß wir 'letz' giengen! Wir wollen dem schwachen Gedächtniß der Föderalisten nachhelfen und ihnen sagen, was 'letz' war" (*Der Bauern Freund*, July 1, 1840).

63. "Eine alte Frau welche sehr regelmäßig die Kirche besuchte, und es für eine unvergleichliche Sünde von Zuhörern hielt während der Predigt zu reden, wurde eines Tages von ihrem Hündchen nach der Kirche begleitet. Während dem Gottesdienst suchte der Hund den Kuchen auf den die alte Frau zu besserer Erfrischung mit genommen hatte, und wurde erst gesehen als er denselben in das Maul nehmen wollte: 'Wid dä geh. Puttel!'—schrie die Dame: Aber erschrocken über ihre eigene Stimme, wiederholte sie, 'O mei ich hab in der Kirch kschwätzt!'—'Guk amol widder!'—'Un nach ämahl,'—'Ey Herr Je, ich bappel jo di gans Zeit'" (*Der Bauern Freund*, July 7, 1830).

64. "Langsam gieng ich den schattigten Gang hinauf, der zur Kirche führte. Sehr dichterisch war mein Gemüth gestimmt, als ich den Tempel betrat. So eben predigte ein berühmter und beliebter Volksredner. Alle Stühle waren besetzt und Viele mußten mit Stehen im gedrängten Gange vorlieb nehmen. Auch ich war gezwungen, meine senkrechte Stellung zu behalten. Für einen Augenblick war ich der Gegenstand der Neugierde, denn ich war ein Fremdling. Doch bald hefteten sich Aller Augen auf den Redner. Auch ich hörte ihm mit steigender Theilnahme zu, denn er war Meister seines Subjekts und seine Sprache oft erhaben. Während dem Vortrag bemerkte ich, daß ein schönes Mädchen, mit großen sanften schwarzen Augen mich zuweilen ansah. Ich schmeichelte mir, sie hätte Wohlgefallen an meiner Person, und warf ihr daher die freundlichsten Blicke zu. . . ." (*Der Bauern Freund*, December 7, 1836).

65. As previously mentioned, Pennsylvania Dutch is most closely related to Palatine German dialects, which are spoken in an area to the north and west of the Swabian region. Because of their geographic proximity, there are similarities between Palatine and Swabian German, which likely made texts in the latter more accessible to nineteenth-century Pennsylvania Dutch readers. Further, the German linguist Rudolf Post, a leading expert on Palatine German, notes that *Swabian* was a blanket term for many dialects and their speakers originating southwestern Germany, similar to the way that *Saxon* has been applied to people hailing from east-central Germany.

66. "Der Deutsche. Guter Freund, können Sie mir sagen, wo der deutsche Redeverein heute Abend seine Debatten hält?

"Eckensteher. Du kummst von Deutschland, des hab ich gleich gehert. Bist schon lang im Land?

"Deutscher. Etwa fünf Wochen.

"Eckenst. Do weßt Du noch nit viel von Amerika. Kannst schon Englisch schwetze?

"Deutsch. Sehr wenig.

"Eckenst. Das mußt Du lerne, ich schwetz Englisch so gut as Deitsch, macht' mir ken Unterschied. Hau du ju du, newer meind, bai schinks, gut bai, tu by schur, enne hau, jes, axekle, plente. Well! was willscht beim Redeverein mache?

"Deutsch. Ich möchte einmal die Debatte hören.

"Eckenst. Ei dont kehr.—Was die do sage welle, weß ich schon lang" (*Der Bauern Freund*, March 6, 1850).

67. "Witzhuber. Sagen Sie einmal, Herr Simpelmaier, wie kommt es denn, daß hier so viel Dreck auf den Straßen ist, da sollten sich doch die Behörden drein legen.

"Simpelmaier. Well, wissener, hier ist Alles zamma frei, wer net im Mutt laafen will, der kann juscht auf die Seidwaak gehne, wies ehm pliescht.

"Witzhuber. Sind Sie doch so gut, und sprechen Sie deutsch. Was ist denn das für eine Sprache?

"Simpelmaier. Gehen mer mit Eurem Sie eweg, das ischt keh Sprooch net, alle sind hier gleich. Juh heeßt du, und deß wege ischts aa keh Juhs net, daß man Sie sagt; ich spreche juscht so e guts Deitsch as ihr dohn, da laß ich mich net lang fuhle.

"Witzhuber. Juh soll Du heißen, daß weiß ich besser; es heißt Sie. Wenn Sie aber glauben, es heiße deßwegen Du, weil die Amerikaner zu allem Juh sagen, so sind Sie sehr irre.

"Simpelmaier. Ihr werre mich doch net titsche wolle, Ihr sein a Grünhorn wenn Ihr immer so vorlaut schwäzet, so kann ich Euch net päterneise" (*Der Bauern Freund*, March 23, 1853).

68. Some contemporary Pennsylvania Dutch speakers believe that *Ihr* was used in the nineteenth century to address only clergymen.

69.   Es hot mich schon verdollt gekränkt,
Wann ich die Welt so recht bedenkt;
Sie is en rechtes Narrenhaus,
Ich schmeiß sie bal zum Fenster naus.

Guck just emol recht um dich rum,
Ein Jeder, wenn auch noch so dumm,
Meent er wär selbst ein Licht der Welt,
Das lauter gutes in sich hält.

Ist einer ah just halb gescheid,
So brummt er doch: ich wees Bescheid. (*Der Bauern Freund*, August 15, 1849)

70.   Vor Alters war das Christenthum
Ächt und rein im Lutherthum,
    Ganz nach Luther's Mode,
Jetzt wird es aber ganz vernefft,
Dem Seelenwesen nachgeäfft,
    Das ist neue Mode.

Präzeptoren alter Zeit
Lehrten Schüler Sittsamkeit,
    Nach der alten Mode.
Jetzt aber heißt es Spring und Lauf
Kletter an der Fens hinauf,
    Das ist neue Mode.

Man machte sie bekannt mit Gott
Und lernte sie die zehn Gebot,
    Nach der alten Mode.
Jetzt aber in der neuen Zeit
Hält man dies für Eitelkeit,
    Nach der neuen Mode! (*Der Bauern Freund*, December 26, 1849)

Chapter 4. Profiles in Pennsylvania Dutch Literature

1. See Cuff 1989, 92.

2. Robacker (1943, 72–73) also points to the upheaval brought on by the Civil War as opening up the Pennsylvania Dutch to outside influences. Quoting Weygandt (1938, 337), "The Civil War played its part in the upsetting of the old order of things. Men from all parts of the country were forced to fraternize through the exigencies of campaigning and so learned of one another's different ways."

3. See Seifert 1971, 16–17. It is not clear how Seifert arrived at this number, but population statistics for 1890 for the four "Dutchiest" counties of Berks, Lancaster, Lebanon, and Lehigh show a combined total population of 411,184, of whom 130,624 lived in the cities of Reading, Lancaster, Lebanon, and Allentown. Ten additional counties with historically large concentrations of Pennsylvania Dutch—Bucks, Dauphin, Franklin, Juniata, Montgomery, Northampton, Northumberland, Snyder, Union, and York—had a combined population of 653,478 in 1890, of whom 92,661 were residents of Harrisburg, York, Doylestown, Norristown, Bethlehem, and Sunbury, the largest cities for which census data are available. Subtracting the city data from the total populations of these fourteen counties produces a total of just over 841,377 residents of nonurban communities in the greater Pennsylvania Dutch Country, where most active speakers of the language would have lived. Thus, the estimate of 600,000 is between two-thirds and three-quarters of that total. This figure is likely somewhat generous, since the combined average percentage of residents of these counties who were of German ancestry in 1790 had been 47% (Purvis 1987, 115). All 1890 census data are drawn from the Wikipedia entries for the counties and cities listed above.

4. Hostetler (1993, 96–97) estimates the total Amish population in the United States to have been around 3,700 in 1890, of whom roughly 1,000 lived in Lancaster County, the largest Amish settlement in the state. This includes both church members (adults) and their children at a rate of 100 to 131. Baptized Mennonites in Pennsylvania in 1890, a group that would have included at least some English monolinguals, numbered approximately 15,330 (Loewen and Nolt 2012, 342). Adding the estimated number of children calculated at the same rate as Hostetler does for the Amish in 1890 yields a total of 27,832 persons in Pennsylvania Mennonite families at that time. Amish and Mennonites combined would have thus accounted for fewer than 5% of the estimated 600,000 Pennsylvania Dutch speakers in Pennsylvania in 1890.

5. See Seifert 1971, 16.

6. Robacker 1943, 72.

7. Wollenweber's biography and republican political activities in Germany are discussed in a German-language newspaper article by Martin Baus, "Kämpfer für die Demokratie, Ludwig August Wollenweber flüchtete kurz vor Hambacher Fest in USA" (Fighter for democracy, Ludwig August Wollenweber fled shortly before the Hambacher Festival to the USA), *Pfälzischer Merkur*, October 12, 2013; http://www.pfaelzischer -merkur.de/lokales/lokalimport/lokales/Noch-mehr-Lokales-Kaempfer-fuer-die -Demokratie;art27906,4975162. A street, Wollenweberstraße, has been named for him in Ixheim, which is now part of the city of Zweibrücken.

8. "[I]ch war hoch erfreut über die Einfachheit, das Zutrauliche und Gemütliche der damaligen Bewohner von Berks und Lancaster County. Freilich war es damals eine ganz andere Zeit wie die jetzige; der deutsche Einwanderer besonders war wohl gelitten und galt als ehrlich und fleißig, war hoch geachtet und gesucht. Von Diebstahl, Schwindel, Betrug hörte man auf dem Lande fast gar nichts. Die Haustüren der Farmhäuser waren selten geschlossen, Riegel und Schloss waren selten in Gebrauch. Eine ungeheure Veränderung in 46 Jahren! Heute hat man seine liebe Not mit Spitzbuben und Bummlern (Tramps), nicht nur Riegel und Schloss, sondern auch scharfe, wachsame Hunde und Revolvers sind auf den Farmen in Gebrauch, um sich gegen Diebe und Einbrecher und Gewalttätigkeiten zu schützen, und höchste Vorsicht muss der Bauer anwenden, um nicht beschwindelt und überlistet zu werden, selbst von Freunden und Nachbarn" (Wollenweber 1977, 12).

9. On the title page of Wollenweber's book, two places of publication are given: Philadelphia and Leipzig. It is not clear that the publisher, the firm of Schaefer & Koradi, actually printed books in Leipzig as well as in Philadelphia.

10. Despite his best efforts, Wollenweber's Pennsylvania Dutch falls short of native norms, influenced as it is by his knowledge of standard and Palatine German. Heinz Kloss (1957) describes his Pennsylvania Dutch as "Wollenweberisch."

11. "Bin ich doch schun gar manches Johr durch Pennsylvenie geträwelt, (gereist) un hab das Land und die Leut, so ziemlich gut kenne gelernt, hab viel Gutes aber a manch' Nixnutziges gesehne, doch wann ich so Alles zusammengerechnet und vergliche hab, do hab ich doch ausgefunne, das Pennsylvenie un die Pennsylvenier, die merste Länder und Volk, die ich in meinem Leben in drei Weltthel gesehene hab, in jeder Hinsicht biete könne. Un doch gebt es in der Welt, un selber in Amerika noch arg viel Leut, die noch net wisse, was for ä schö's Land Pennsylvenie ischt, un was for schmate (tüchtige) Leut drinn wohne" (Wollenweber 1869, 3).

12. Ich bin e Pennsylvänier
D'ruff bin ich stolz un froh.
Das Land ist schö, die Leut sin nett
Bei Tschinks! ich mach' schier en'ge Wett,
'S biets ke' Land der Welt.

Mir stamme vun de Deutsche her,
Druff bin ich a recht stolz,
Die Deutsche sin arg brave Leut
Sin sparsam, fleißig und gescheut,
Sie biet ke Volk der Welt.

Do guk nur ens de Garte an,
Wie Pennsylvänie heßt,
Wachst do net Alles schö un gut
Un hot net jeder g'sundes Blut
'S biets ke' Land der Welt.

Un net allenig uf der Erd'
Wachst Alles schö un gut,
A drunne gebts so viel ihr wollt,
Kohle, Eise,—meh werth wie Gold,
'S biets ke' Land der Welt. (Ibid., 5–6)

13. In a postscript to his biographical reminiscences titled "My Last Wish" (*Mein letzter Wunsch*), written in 1880, eight years before his death, Wollenweber makes explicit that although he believed in "an eternal and inscrutable God" and strove in life to help his fellow man wherever possible, he was not a member of any Christian denomination and therefore did not want a church funeral or any clergyman to speak at his graveside. His brothers from Masonic and Odd Fellows lodges, however, as well as other German American organizations with which he was affiliated, were to be invited to attend his funeral (Wollenweber 1977, 88). A detailed account of Wollenweber's funeral appeared in the *Reading Adler* on August 7, 1888. In fact, one clergyman, Pastor F. K. Huntzinger from Reading's St. Luke's Lutheran Church, delivered a short eulogy at the service. All of the organizations formally represented there with which Wollenweber had been affiliated were secular German American groups, mainly from Philadelphia, whose members would have been *Deitschlenner*.

14. "Heutigs Tags sen die Mäd gar nit meh wie vor Alters; lauter Hochmuth, ufgehuppst wie a papirner Blohsbalg; sie sen gar nit meh vom säme Stofft, sie sen ganz annerster gemustert un ganz annerster gemacht. Bei uns do rum wolle sie englisch sei wie die lebendig Viktoria, but wann epper vun der Stadt kummt for mit sie zu schwätze, stehen sie do wie a Hinkel wu a Ei verlore hot" (Wollenweber 1869, 64).

15. So steck ich do in meine Hupps,
    Un bin a arme Seel;
Auße glatt, un inne Schmutz,
    So sin mer ohne Fehl.

Un wann ich auch drei Cents noch hab,
    So muß ich doch in Stohr;
Dort muß der letzte Kupper fort,
    So geht's vun Johr zu Johr.

Un schwätzt zu mir epper deutsch,
    Un frogt: Kannst du des?
So sag ich, awer, jo nit, ja,
    Ich sag in Englisch—*Jes*. (Ibid., 65)

16. It is very likely that Wollenweber and Benner were personally acquainted. Benner reprinted a few of Wollenweber's writings in his newspaper, and Wollenweber also sent Benner a letter that was printed in the May 17, 1854, issue of *Der Bauern Freund*.

17. Kalt ist's bei Wintersnacht,
    So hat der Säm auch gedacht!
        Und nahm zu seinem besseren Leben,
        Ein Weib, das ihm mag warm geben.

Und kommt die Wiege einst in's Haus,
So macht er sich auch nichts d'raus.
  So lebet glücklich, junge Leut,
  Von nun bis in die Ewigkeit. (Wollenweber 1869, 38)
18. Julian, die hat wohlgethan,
  Sie nahm en Apel for ihr Mann
    Den kann man esse un dabei
    Seider draus mache un a Brei.

Der John, der macht noch besser aus
Der hat a Weber nau im Haus
  Dann Kleder brauch man jederzeit,
  John hat zum Weber nau net weit. (Ibid., 38–39)
19. Der Walter is gefahre
  Gar viele lange Jahre
    Bis es endlich in ihm hot gewühlt,
    Was die Betz für ihn gefühlt.
  Wann nau der Walter Häut thut schabe
  Möcht er die Betz bei sich habe,
    But sell geht net so leicht,
  Die Betzi hot derhehm zu bleibe,
  Muß dort stoti Windle reibe,
    Wann's in der Schockel kreischt.
  Doch wünsch ich ihm Glück und Fried,
  Bekahrs er hot mich gut getriht. (Ibid., 39)
  20. L. Harbaugh 1900, 7.
  21. Henry Harbaugh's life and work are amply documented in a number of secondary sources, the most extensive of which are the biographies written by his son, Linn (L. Harbaugh, 1900), and Elizabeth Clarke Kieffer (1945). Henry Harbaugh himself produced a family history (1856); see Cooprider and Cooprider 1947 for a more thorough genealogy. Harry Hess Reichard's discussion of Harbaugh's Pennsylvania Dutch writings (1918, 54–73) also contains a list of source material on Harbaugh. See Nolt (2002, 133–139) for an analysis of Harbaugh as an exemplar of an assertive Pennsylvania Dutch ethnic identity in nineteenth-century America. With regard to the history of the Harbaugh family, a modern descendant and economist at the University of Oregon, William Harbaugh, has refuted the long-held belief that the original Harbaugh immigrant to colonial Pennsylvania, Yost Harbaugh (Jost Herbach), came from Switzerland. In fact, the Harbaughs emigrated from the Palatinate, near the city of Kaiserslautern, though they could have been descended from Swiss Mennonites who had come to the Palatinate by way of the Netherlands. Source: http://harbaugh.uoregon.edu/History/WHH%20on%20Harbaugh%20History,%202000.pdf.
  22. L. Harbaugh 1900, 147.
  23. See Reichard 1918, 72.

24. These sermon notes from Harbaugh, as well as materials related to his poetry discussed below, are contained in the archives of the Evangelical and Reformed Historical Society in Lancaster, PA, Ms. Coll. 009. The Harbaugh file also contains three pages of what appear to be lecture or study notes on Ezekiel 34:16. Unlike the sermon notes, which are written in English cursive, these notes are written in German script, which Harbaugh would have had to have learned when he studied German in college. The fact that he did not use German script for his sermon notes underscores the secondary status of standard German in his verbal repertoire.

25. Kieffer 1945, 56.

26. The quote in this sentence is from Haag (1988, 31), which also gives the provenance of Rondthaler's poem and a version of it rewritten according to the contemporary Buffington-Barba-Beam spelling system (32). Though first published in 1849, Rondthaler's daughter believed her father to have composed the poem around 1835 for the purpose of demonstrating that Pennsylvania Dutch could serve as a vehicle for serious literature. As I have already established, humorous texts containing Pennsylvania Dutch began appearing in German-language newspapers in the first decades of the nineteenth century. Speaking specifically of poetry in Pennsylvania Dutch, Rondthaler's is indeed a very early specimen, though it is an odd coincidence that the one Pennsylvania Dutch poem in the entire thirty-year run of Enos Benner's *Der Bauern Freund* appeared in precisely the same month as Rondthaler's "Abendlied," namely on August 15, 1849. This was the poem "Ein Krittler klagt über die Welt" (A crab complains about the world) mentioned in the previous chapter. The Crab poem must have been reprinted in other newspapers, since it was included decades later in the second volume of an anthology of classic Pennsylvania Dutch literature (Daniel Miller 1911, 130–131), in which Rondthaler's "Abendlied" (renamed "Morgeds un Oweds" [Mornings and evenings]) also was reprinted. The author of the Crab poem is unknown, as are others in Daniel Miller 1911. Likely the oldest known Pennsylvania Dutch poem whose author is identified was written by Lewis (also Louis, Loui) Miller, an important early American folk artist from York, PA (Historical Society of York County 1966). Born in 1796, Miller was almost a generation older than Rondthaler. His poem, which was published apparently for the first time in 1886, four years after his death, was titled "The Wagoner's Song" (*Das Fuhrman's Lied*) and told of how early Pennsylvania Dutch farmers used to bring their products by Conestoga wagon to market in cities like Baltimore (Fisher 1886, 238–239). It is probable that this poem was composed before 1835.

27. Schaff's memorial to Harbaugh appeared on January 9, 1868, in the periodical the *Christian World*; this excerpt was reprinted in L. Harbaugh (1900, 235–236). The book of English-language poems by Harbaugh referred to by Schaff is Harbaugh 1860. This volume includes translations made by Harbaugh from Latin, German, and French.

28. Hebel's classic *Allemannische Gedichte* (Alemannic poems) first appeared in 1803. It is still popular today and has served as a model for later generations of German dialect poets. *Alemannic* describes the German dialects spoken in Switzerland, southwestern Germany (e.g., Swabian), and eastern France (e.g., Alsatian). In the north the Alemannic region borders on the Rhine-Franconian family of dialects that includes

Palatine German, the main European source of Pennsylvania Dutch. It is not surprising that Philip Schaff would have appreciated Hebel's work, since Schaff himself was a native Swiss.

29. See H. Harbaugh 1866b.

30. H. Harbaugh 1863, 69.

31. "Das alt Schulhaus an der Krick" was one of the two poems cited by Philip Schaff in his 1868 tribute to Harbaugh, the other being "Heemweh" (Homesickness). These poems were also the two Harbaugh works that Ludwig Wollenweber included in his 1869 *Sketches*.

32. Harbaugh's English-language "The Old School-House at the Creek," which appeared posthumously in *Harbaugh's Harfe*, contains four more stanzas than the Pennsylvania Dutch original (thirty-five total). The reason for this difference was explained by Preston A. Barba in his weekly column on Pennsylvania Dutch, *'S Pennsylfawnisch Deitsch Eck* (The Pennsylvania German corner) in the Allentown *Morning Call*, February 15, 1947. A man named William J. Rupp wrote to Barba that he found what was apparently Harbaugh's personal copy of the bound issues of the *Guardian* magazine for 1861, in the August issue of which "Das alt Schulhaus" first appeared. To this issue Harbaugh appended a note stating that he had composed four extra stanzas, which were intended to be the twenty-first through twenty-fourth in the poem. Barba dutifully reprinted them in the Eck, and they are given below:

> Sell is eme net yuscht gar zu lieb!
> M'r hot ke luschta dra;
> Die boes Natur is bom'rish blaed,
> Sie will net was zum guta g'schaet,
> Un nemmt's net dankbar a'!

> Hen mir e neuer Maeschter krickt,
> Dann war die Frog zuersht:
> "Sag, is er Irish?—is er boes?
> Denkst net verleicht die Mamme wees—
> Bass uf obt Eppes hoersht!"

> Wann nord die Schul a g'fanga hot,
> Dann war m'r Meschter-scheu!
> Sei Rules—sei Wip—hen klor gezeicht,
> Das er net weit vom alta weicht—
> Im Sinn war gar nix neu!

> Doch war net fiel zu klaga so
> S'war a Blaesier dabei;
> In derra Welt is nix das geht
> Yusht grad so wie m'r's gleicha det—
> M'r mus geduldig sei!

[The schoolmaster] did that only too gladly
> *No one liked it;*
Our evil nature is quite reluctant,
It doesn't like what is good for us
> *And doesn't accept it willingly.*

If we got a new schoolmaster,
> *Then the first question was,*
"Say, is he Irish? Is he mean?
Do you think Mom might know?
> *Keep your ears open!"*

And when school started again
> *We were shy around the schoolmaster!*
His rules and his whip showed clearly
That he wasn't any different from the old one.
> *Basically nothing changed.*

But there wasn't that much to complain about,
> *We had fun, too;*
In this world nothing goes
Just as we'd like it to;
> *You have to be patient!* ('S Pennsylfawnisch Deitsch Eck, *Morning Call*, February 15,
1947)

33. Mei Hertz schwellt mit Gedanka uf,
> Bis Ich schier gar verstick!
Konnt heula's dut mir nau so leed—
Un' doc[h] gebt mir die groschte Freed,
> Des Schul-haus an der Krick!

Good bye! alt Schul-haus—echo Kreischt
> Good bye! Good bye! zurueck;
O Schul-haus! Schul-haus! mus Ich geh?
Un du stehst nord do alle' aleh—
> Du Schul-haus an der Krick!

O horcht ihr Leut wo nach mir lebt,
> Ich Schreib euch noch des Stick:
Ich warn euch, droh euch, gebt doch acht
Un' nemmt for ever gut enacht,
> Des Schul-haus an der Krick! (H. Harbaugh 1861, 235–236)

34. H. Harbaugh 1870, 93–94. In his 1860 collection of English-language poems, Harbaugh wrote another poem, "Our School-Boy Days," which, though much shorter than
"The Old School-House at the Creek," also evokes a relatively upbeat mood (H. Har-

baugh 1860, 160–161). Prior to composing both these poems, Harbaugh published an essay in the *Guardian* in 1854 titled "The Old School-House" (H. Harbaugh 1854). The content of this essay parallels that of "Das alt Schulhaus," beginning and ending with reflections on the significance of the abandoned schoolhouse as a symbol of both his own past and more generally a bygone era. And, as in "Das alt Schulhaus," in the middle of his 1854 essay Harbaugh shares detailed descriptions of what schooldays were like in his youth. In the poem, however, Harbaugh waxes bitter about the world beyond the old schoolhouse, which he dismisses as "all humbug," saying that he was never happier than when he was a schoolchild. By contrast, the tone in the essay, as in "The Old School-House at the Creek" and "Our School-Boy Days," is still quite nostalgic but not bitter:

> All that I can remember is so connected with the innocence of childhood, that memory attaches no sorrow to it. Though tinged with the mellow-mournful, yet pleasant as the music of Ossian, are all the reminiscences associated with that old school-house.
>
> I turned away; but looking back once more from a little distance I said, with the pilgrim at the tomb of the patriarchs,
>
> "How many pleasant memories
> Glide o'er my spirit now."
>
> I found that my fingers were wet as I drew my hand down from over my cheek! Only the softest words escaped my lips; it was something like, "Farewell, old school-house!" I was back in the world again. (H. Harbaugh 1854, 102)

35. Five of these colleagues were from Allentown, Lehigh County: E. D. Leisenring and Benjamin F. Trexler, German-language newspaper editors; Rev. Samuel Kistler Brobst and Rev. A. J. G. Dubbs, prominent clergymen and educators; and Prof. Friedrich W. A. Notz, a German-born faculty member at Muhlenberg College. The sixth was Jacob M. Beck, the European-German editor of the *Reading Adler*.

36. Leisenring, Trexler, Brobst, Notz, and Beck were all members of the *Verein*. Brobst was also its president.

37. "Der Verein hat bald nach seiner Gründung angefangen, der deutsch-pennsylvanischen Sprache große Aufmerksamkeit zu widmen, und verschiedene Mitglieder sich beeifert, deren Eigenthümlichkeit genauer zu ergründen und darzustellen, wie das früher geschehen war. Es geschah Das vor allen Dingen, um den Deutsch Pennsylvaniern selbst Selbstbewußtsein und einen Stolz auf ihre Abstammung einzuflößen und sie zum Anschluß an die moderne deutsche Entwicklung heranzuziehen, von welcher sie durch lange Abgeschlossenheit vom geistigen Leben Deutschlands und durch englische Einmischung abseits getreten waren. Man kam nach vielen Debatten und Studien Einzelner in das Klare, daß die pennsylvanisch-deutsche Sprache das Pfälzische ist, mit weniger schwäbischer Beimischung; daß es sehr leicht von dem Zusatz englischer Wörter zu reinigen ist und daß es seine Wiederherstellung zu seiner Reinheit ebenso verdient, wie z.B. das Elsässische, als ein deutscher Volks Dialekt, wodurch die alten Deutsch-Pennsylvanier zur Pflege des Hochdeutschen herangezogen werden können und sollen. Dies ist eine besondere Aufgabe des Preß-Vereins, welche er erst im Verlauf der Jahre in seiner vollen Bedeutung erkannt und gewürdigt hat" (*Reading Adler*, January 25, 1876).

38. See Yoder 1992.

39. "Die hie und da vorkommenden hochdeutschen Worte hat HARBAUGH nur des Reimes halber eingeführt, und viele englische Ausdrücke, mit denen er einige seiner Gedichte überladen hatte, sind auf seinen Wunsch durch pennsylvanisch-deutsche ersetzt worden" (H. Harbaugh 1870, 113).

40. This count is based on types rather than tokens. That is, each borrowed word or phrase that is repeated (e.g., *Krick*) in the poem is counted only once.

41. H. Harbaugh 1861, 233.

42. H. Harbaugh 1870, 13–14.

43. The *Verein* had ultimately little success in realizing its goal of elevating the status of standard German in Pennsylvania (or purging Pennsylvania Dutch of its English vocabulary) and declined rapidly after the death of its president, Rev. Samuel Kistler Brobst, in 1876. Kloss (1931, 238) states that the organization had ceased to exist entirely by 1889.

44. See Kieffer 1945, 363. Harbaugh's initial caution about publishing his Pennsylvania Dutch poetry does not mean that he was embarrassed about using the language in public settings. Nathan Schaeffer, quoted earlier, recalled the following event in the year before Harbaugh's death:

> I saw and heard Harbaugh but once. It was a rare privilege. It deepened the impression which his articles in the *Guardian* had made, and greatly enhanced the high estimate which I had formed of his genius. The occasion was the commencement banquet of Franklin and Marshall College in the year 1866. We undergraduates were not allowed to participate in the feast; but when the part of the program which consisted of toasts was reached, the alumni adjourned to the main auditorium of Fulton Hall (since converted into an opera house), and this gave me the opportunity to hear Dr. Harbaugh's response to the toast, "The Mercersburg Review." Its humor and delivery made a deeper impression than the oratory of all the eminent men at home and abroad whom I have had the good fortune to hear at banquets, in the pulpit or from the rostrum. This may be due to the fact that the speech was delivered in the dialect of my boyhood. He had shown the poetic possibilities of the Pennsylvania German in the pages of the *Guardian*; he was now to prove its power and fitness for the purposes of an after-dinner speech. When the toast was announced, he attracted attention by walking forward after the manner of an old farmer, pulling off a slouch hat with both hands, and catching a red bandanna handkerchief as it dropped from his forehead. His first sentence, "*Es gebt gar greislich gelernte Leut, und Ich bin awe aner dafun* (There are some very learned people, and I am one of 'em)," sent a flash of merriment through the assemblage. When he proceeded to enumerate the learned languages—"*Es gebt sieva gelehrte Sproche, Englisch und Deutsch, Lateinisch und Griechish und Hebraeisch; sell sin fünf. Die sechst haest Pennsylvania Deutsch, die sievet is German Reformed* (There are seven learned languages, English and German, Latin and Greek and Hebrew; these are five. The sixth is called Pennsylvania German, the seventh is German Reformed)"—there were shouts of laughter over the entire hall. The merriment reached its climax when he referred to the venerable Dr. John W. Nevin as "*Der Chon Nevin, do navig mir* (John Nevin, here aside of me). The applause then was like that of a great convention and lasted for some time." (L. Harbaugh 1900, 5–6)

45. Reichard 1918, 60–61.

46. Birlinger 1875.

47. H. Harbaugh 1861, 233.

48. The two anthologies are Reichard 1918 and Haag 1988. The four non-white-collar Pennsylvania Dutch writers were Lewis Miller (1795–1882), who was nominally a carpenter but also an accomplished folk artist who even traveled to Europe; Rachel Bahn (1829–1902), a distant cousin of Henry Harbaugh, who was disabled and confined most of her life to her home; Edwin Gehman Weber (1904–1995), a farmer; and Ernest Waldo Bechtel (1923–1988), a barber.

49. H. Harbaugh 1862.

50. H. Harbaugh 1866a.

51. *Pennsylvania Dutchman*, March 1873, p. 95.

52. Reichard 1918, 74.

53. *New York Times*, September 21, 1902. Obviously, the figure of five million speakers of Pennsylvania Dutch in 1902 was wildly inflated.

54. See Pennsylvania German Society 1893; Brenckman 1913, 546–552; and A. L. Shoemaker 1949 for general biographical information about Rauch. This latter source contains the text of an autobiography written shortly before his death. See also Reichard (1918, 74–99); and Louden 2003c, 2006, and 2008 for discussions of Rauch's contributions to Pennsylvania Dutch studies.

55. Brenckman 1913, 551. See also Arndt and Olson 1961, 590.

56. *Reformed Church Messenger*, January 15, 1873, p. 4.

57. *Pennsylvania Dutchman*, February 1873, p. 63.

58. *Pennsylvania Dutchman*, March 1873, p. 96.

59. See Haldeman 1872. See also Hart 1881 for a biography of Haldeman. Haldeman was an exceptional polymath, a gifted natural scientist as well as philologist. He produced more than one hundred publications and held numerous professorships, including the chair of comparative philology at the University of Pennsylvania.

60. Aside from his multiple scholarly distinctions, Ellis was also George Bernard Shaw's inspiration for the character of Prof. Henry Higgins in *Pygmalion*.

61. Haldeman 1872, v.

62. See Rauch 1879, 237. Ellis (1871, 652–663) includes an extensive discussion of Pennsylvania Dutch, with data from Rauch's writings.

63. Haldeman is quoted in Ellis 1871, 655n2.

64. It is not clear whether Rauch knew how harsh Haldeman was in his criticism of Rauch's spelling as he was quoted in Ellis 1871. Rauch mentioned receiving a letter from "our esteemed friend" about 1869, in which Haldeman was quoted as saying, more mildly, "In order to read your Dutch, a German must first learn to read English". *Pennsylvania Dutchman*, January 1873, p. 31.

65. Rauch 1879, iii.

66. See Beam (2004–2011, ii–vi) for a chronology of Pennsylvania Dutch lexicography.

67. Rauch 1879, 168, 169.

68. Ibid., 209.

69. Ibid., 220.

70. Ibid., 214.

71. To be clear, *Dutch Dialect*, sometimes also known as *German Dialect*, refers to (supposedly) German-influenced English. By contrast, *Denglish* (or *Germerican*) is the reverse: German with English elements interspersed. The most prominent German American writer of Denglish/Germerican works was Kurt M. Stein (1894–1967); cf. Stein 1925, 1927, 1932.

72. See Kersten 1996 and 2000 on the use of Dutch Dialect in American literature. White 2012 deals with the general phenomenon of the social and political implications of the use of nonstandard language in nineteenth-century American literature. Adams's most famous collection is *Leedle Yawcob Strauss and Other Poems* (1878); *Hans Breitmann's Ballads* is Leland's signature Dutch Dialect work (Leland 1871).

Dutch Dialect writings, since they were targeted at a mainly English-speaking audience, required no knowledge of German to be understood. In the same era in which they were produced, the late nineteenth and early twentieth centuries, there were other humorous texts written not in a fanciful English supposedly warped by German but in a latter-day form of Denglish that was clearly intended to resemble Pennsylvania Dutch. One of the most well-known German Americans to produce such writings was a Catholic priest from Milwaukee, WI, Rev. Michael J. Lochemes (1860–1924). Born in New York City to German immigrants, Lochemes gained notoriety for humorous works written under the pen name of "Meik Fuchs" (Mike Fox). His best-known work was an anthology of prose and poetry titled *Dreiguds un Noschens* (Dry goods and notions; Fuchs 1898), which many readers believed to be written in Pennsylvania Dutch.

Although Lochemes grew up and lived most of his life in southeastern Wisconsin, where he would have had no direct contact with Pennsylvania Dutch speakers, he was able to approximate Pennsylvania Dutch well enough to have been mistaken for a speaker of the language. Earl F. Robacker, for example, included a reference to Lochemes's works in his excellent study of Pennsylvania Dutch literature (Robacker 1943, 102). However, nowhere in his writings did Lochemes himself identify the language he used as Pennsylvania Dutch, nor did his poems and stories deal with Pennsylvania Dutch people or their culture, or even the state of Pennsylvania. The editors of the *Pennsylvania-German* magazine, when introducing a short story by Fuchs/Lochemes titled "Charlie Grien's Expirienz Mit eme Skunk" (Charlie Green's experience with a skunk), identified the language as "Western German-American Dialect" and not Pennsylvania Dutch (*Pennsylvania-German*, April 1907, 184–186).

Given Lochemes's apparent lack of direct contact with Pennsylvania Dutch speakers, how might he have been able to approximate their speech? First, as an American born around the middle of the nineteenth century, Lochemes lived in the era when Pennsylvania Dutch literary productions reached their zenith, thus he could have had easy access to writings in the language through the media of the day. Further, his mother was a native of the western Palatinate; she was born in the community of Steinbach (today, Steinbach am Glan), in the county of Kusel, which is located fifty to sixty miles west of the Vorderpfalz region where the closest Palatine German cousins of Pennsylvania

Dutch are spoken (Watrous 1909, 789). Finally, as a US-born speaker of both German and English, Lochemes would have had a good intuitive sense for how German American and Pennsylvania Dutch bilinguals might naturally intersperse English in their German or Pennsylvania Dutch. Taken together, these factors would have been sufficient to enable Lochemes to produce texts that were similar enough to Pennsylvania Dutch that his readers, German speakers, at least, could have taken them for actual Pennsylvania Dutch writings.

73. *Pennsylvania Dutchman*, January 1873, p. 8. This was Adams's first Dutch Dialect poem. It first appeared in 1872 and was reprinted in a collection of his works (C. F. Adams 1878, 27–29). Rauch's version, which is what is given here, diverges orthographically from the original in a few places.

74. The Wikipedia entry for Charles Follen Adams, for example, states, "In 1872, he began writing humorous verses for periodicals and newspapers in a Pennsylvania German dialect." Source: http://en.wikipedia.org/wiki/Charles_Follen_Adams.

75. *Father Abraham*, July 10, 1868, p. 4.

76. *Father Abraham*, July 31, 1868, p. 4.

77. *Pennsylvania Dutchman*, March 1873, p. 96.

78. Donner 1999 and 2000 are the best resources on Abraham R. Horne's biography and career. Reichard (1918, 118–128) provides a valuable overview of Horne's significance for the history of Pennsylvania Dutch literature.

79. Kuhns 1900, 149.

80. See Kutztown Centennial Association 1915, 161.

81. Stine 1942, 118.

82. See Stine 1938 for a thorough study of the educational situation of Pennsylvania Dutch–speaking children from the colonial period to the early twentieth century.

83. Horne 1873, 78.

84. *Fröhlich Palz, Gott erhalts* is a classic collection of poems written in Palatine German by Karl Gottfried Nadler (1809–1849) (Nadler 1847).

85. Leisenring is referring here to Ludwig Wollenweber's 1869 *Gemälde*.

86. " 'N Brief an der Hochwerdig Prof. Horne von der Kutztauner Normalschul.

"*Hochwerdiger Professor:* Ich hab schon viel von d'r gelese im Friedensbote und annere Zeidinge, un g'sehne, dass du dich bis uf die neunt Haut wehre dhust for unser schöne Pennsylvania Deutsche Sprach ufzuhalte, dass sie net unnerdrückt un vernicht sott werre von dene Englishe kerls, wo doch net English kenne un leeber Gott, ah kenn Deutsch. 'S hot mich werklich gepläsirt, dass so'n gelernter Kerl, wie du eener bist, unser Part nemmt. Ich bin 'n Pfalzer, mei Grossdadi is aus der Palz rüwer kumme, un dieweil die gelernte Leut behaupten, der Grossdadi dhat alsfort widder im Enkel raus kumme, do bin ich dennoch mei grossdadi selwert, wo von der Palz rüwer kumme is. Uf sell bin ich stolz, vonwege er war'n schmarter Mann.

"Was ich awer eegentlich hab sage wolle is des: Ich hab in der Zeidung gelese, du dhatst mit dem Gedanke umgeh, 'n Buch un 'n Dickschonary üwer Pennsylvanisch Deutsch rauszugewe. Weest was—so 'n Buch dhat 'n die Leit do in Pennsylvania un sunst üwerall wo die Pennsylvanisch Deutsch Sprach schwatze gewiss arg gleiche, un die Nellyänn is recht in die Höh g'huppst for Freede wie ich sell Stückel in der Zeidung vorgelese hab. . . .

"Ich bin, denk ich net ganz so g'scheidt wie die Nellyänn meent awer wann du sell Buch schreiwe wit, mocht ich d'r eppes von Adveis gewe, vonwege weil ich selwert 'n Pennsylvanier un noch newebei 'n Palzer bin wie d'r bewisse hab. Nau die Palzer Sprooch un die Pennsylvanisch Sprooch sauwer g'schwetzt, sin eens, un is schier keen Unnershied dazwische. Les mol 'Fröhlich Pfalz, Gott erhalts' (Nadler) noh geh ufs Land un geb gut acht wie di Leut schwätze; was die Buwe un die Mäd zu nanner sage an der Singschul, vor'm Schulhaus wann's dunkel is: was die Baure sage von de Gäul, vom Rins-vieh, von de Sau, vom Weeze, vom Welshkorn un vom Hai; was un wie die Weibsleut mit-nanner dischkurire üwer allerhand Sache, die juscht sie alleen a'belange, un du werscht bal erfahre, was Pennsylvanisch Deutsch is. Do sin viel von dene kerls wo's prowirt hen, die meene, wann sie recht hunsgeschmee schlecht Hoch Deutsch schreiwe un fer-chterlich viel Englische worte drunner dhate, sell war Pennsylvanisch, un so narrische Deutsche, wo's net besser verstehen, spend 'ne dann grosse Lorbeere for 'dieses Göttliche Verhunzen der so edlen deutschen Sprache.' Vor selle, hochwerdiger Professor, mocht ich dich gewarnt hawe.

" 'S kann gewiss niemand hoherer Respect hawe vor selle Lieder, wo der Parre Har-bach g'schriwe hot, wie ich. Ich wees, wie's'm um's Herz war, wie'r alsemol selle Lieder g'schriwe hot—dotlich weech, heemwehrig. Herzweh noch de unschuldige Kinner-johre un bei so Gelegenheite hot noch eppes von owerunner aus der annere Welt uf'n gewerkt—so dass m'r viel von seine Lieder die Poesie gewiss net ablegle kann; awer die Sproch, well ich will nicks drüwer sage—just, wo in're Schrift oder in'me Lied so viel Englisch wie Palzich oder Deutsch vorkummt, is net Pennsylvanisch Deutsch.

"Nau wann du dra' gehst, for sel Buch zu schreiwe los des verhenkert Englisch Kau-derwelsch haus, wo gar net in unser Sproch g'höre dhut. Ich arger mich allemol schwarz und blo, wann so dumm stoff gedruckt un in die Welt g'schickt werd wo Pennsylvanisch Deutsch sei sol, awer lauter geloge is. 'S is uns verlaschtert wo m'r's net verdient hen. Un wann dei Buch mol fertig is, un 's kummt mir unner die Finger un 's is so'n elendiger Wisch wie kerzlich wieder eener im Fildelfi raus kumme is, dann ufgebasst for dann verhechel ich dich, dass du aussehnst wie verhudelt Schwingwerk, un die Leut dich for'n Spuk a'gucke" (Reichard 1918, 123–125).

87. *Pennsylvania Dutchman*, March 1873, p. 76.

88. By way of comparison, Leisenring's lengthy letter to Horne quoted above contains just three English borrowings (*part*, *smart*, and *dictionary*), and he includes a number of High Germanisms (e.g., *hochwerdig*, 'distinguished', *Lorbeere*, 'laurel(s)', and *Poesie*, 'poetry').

89. See Kopp 2010 for an excellent discussion of the contents Horne's *Manual* over the four editions. Donner 2000 situates the *Manual* against the backdrop of Horne's evolving educational philosophy. See also Donner 2010.

90. Horne 1873, 74, 75.

91. Ibid., 76.

92. Ibid., 78.

93. Ibid.

94. See, for example, Rickford 2005, for an interesting discussion of how a nonstandard and highly stigmatized vernacular variety of English, Ebonics or African American Vernacular English (Black English), can be employed in the classroom to the educational advantage of children who speak it. There are a number of parallels between the situation of Pennsylvania Dutch in nineteenth-century schools and African American children today.

95. Horne 1884.

96. Ibid.

97. Horne 1875, 83–94.

98. Interestingly, Horne's son Thomas saw fit to reintroduce the grammatical sketch from his father's first edition in the posthumous third and fourth editions.

99. Horne 1875, 5.

100. Horne 1896, 7–17.

101. See Kurath and McDavid 1961, 178.

102. See ibid., 132–133.

103. See ibid., 174.

104. Horne 1884.

105. Horne 1896, 49, 53.

106. Ibid., 56.

107. Ibid., 60.

108. Ibid., 65–66.

109. See the discussion in chapter 3, n30.

110. See A. L. Shoemaker 2000 and 2009 for fascinating studies of the history of the celebration of Easter and Christmas in Pennsylvania, respectively, including distinctively Pennsylvania Dutch folk traditions. It surprises many people to learn that these and other Christian holidays were not celebrated publicly in many parts of America until the nineteenth century. Writing of the situation in colonial Pennsylvania, Don Yoder notes, "[T]here was no uniform eighteenth-century 'Pennsylvania Christmas.' If one belonged to the Episcopalians or Lutherans or some other pro-Christmas denomination, one celebrated Christmas; if one was a Quaker or a Mennonite or a Presbyterian, one did one's best, like the Puritans, to ignore it" (Shoemaker 2009, 2). Many of the Pennsylvania Dutch holiday traditions described in Horne's *Manual* were associated with the nonsectarian (mainly Lutheran and Reformed) majority rather than with the Anabaptists.

111. Horne 1896, 69–78.

112. Reichard 1918, 127.

113. Stine 1938, 81.

114. From an article in the *National Educator* by A. R. Horne (September 8, 1894, p. 4), quoted in Donner (2000, 539).

115. Recall Rauch's reference to a "dumm-cup" mentioned at the start of this section who, two years earlier, also in the *Eagle*, had criticized Horne's plans to produce his *Manual*. It may well be that this person was C.H.S., but the 1873 article to which Rauch referred has not been located.

116. *Reading Daily Eagle*, January 8, 1876.

117. See Haag 1988, 107.

118. "[I]ch denk er hot g'meent er wolt emol en Horn schäffe un wott Herschhorn Geist mache, awer es [is] ihm net g'gluckt. Er sagt es Buch hett keen Nouns un keen Verbs, keen Substantives un keen Predicätes. Was macht sell aus zu mir. Der C. H. S. kann jo sei Buwe un Mäd Nouns un Verbs un Logical Subjects un logical Predicätes heeße, dernoth hot er selle Name alle Tag in seiner Familie un brauche sie net im Horne seim pennsylvanisch-deitsch Buch zu sei. Was batt mich en Noun oder en Verb oder en Substäntive for Schu oder Stiwwel zu mache? . . .

"Em Horne sei Buch is mer gut genunk, for ich kann's net verbessere, un do muß es mir gut genunk sei. Ich bin awer froh daß er eppes geduh hot for die Pennsylvanisch Deitsch Sproch, for selle Sproch is mei Mutter Sproch. Wann ich Pennsylvanisch Deitsch g'heult hab, hot mei Mäm des Pennsylvanisch Deitsch Lied als for mich g'sunge—'Schloff Bewi schlof, der Daddy hiet die Schof, die Mammie hiet die Lämmer, ihr liewe kleene Kinner.' Wann ich als g'heult hab for Esse, hot sie g'sunge—'Husche bei Bewi des Breule schmackt gut, wann die Mämmie em John recht viel Zucker druf duht.' Sell hab ich ausewennig g'wißt lang eb ich schwetze hab könne, un wann epper alleweil eppes üwer die Pennsylvanisch Deitsch Sproch sächt, wer ich unzufriede. Doch wann mer alleweil ergens in en Stadt oder in so en kleen Lumpe Städtel nei kummt un schwetzt deitsch, dann stehne die unverstännige Stadtleit hie un sage: 'Oh die Kountrie Dutsch'. Sag zu sellem C. H. S. daß noch dem selt er acht gewe an wem seim Hern oder an was vorm Horn er anfange deet zu Schäffe, oder er könnt unglücklich werre. Sag er sett noch dem an ere Gerwerei geh un sett froge for en Ox oder Kuh Horn, daß es schur wär daß keh Lewe meh drin wär, awer jo nimme noch der Keystone Normal Schule an Kutztown, for sell Horn is net säf for eenig epper zu händle, un wer's net versteht, könnt sich wüscht verbrenne" (*Reading Adler*, February 1, 1876).

119. The treatment of Pennsylvania Dutch literature in this chapter and elsewhere in this book is far from exhaustive; there are many other important writers working in the nineteenth and early twentieth centuries not mentioned here. Classic, out-of-print books that contain quality early Pennsylvania Dutch writings include Bahn 1869 (see also Lockyer 1979 for biographical information on Rachel Bahn); Fisher 1879, 1882; E. Grumbine 1917; L. L. Grumbine 1903; Harter 1893; Light 1928; H. Miller 1906, 1907, 1911, and 1939; Weitzel 1931; and Ziegler 1891. Helffrich 1906 is a rare and good example of a book written entirely in Pennsylvania High German. The works of Harry Hess Reichard are of singular importance in the documentation of Pennsylvania Dutch literature (Reichard 1918, 1940; Buffington 1962), as is Earl F. Robacker's 1943 study. The anthologies of Daniel Miller (1904, 1911) and Haag (1988) are also excellent resources. See also the collection of translations in Troxell 1938.

Chapter 5. Pennsylvania Dutch in the Public Eye

1. This anecdote appeared in the *Cabinet* newspaper of Schenectady, NY, May 12, 1840. Another newspaper, the *Morning Chronicle* (location unknown) is cited as the source of the original report. The "Colonel White" referred to as the witness to this incident was almost certainly Joseph M. White (1781–1839), who was a delegate from

the Florida Territory to the US House of Representatives from 1825 to 1837. He was a colleague in Congress of Henry A. P. Muhlenberg, who represented Pennsylvania's Seventh and Ninth Districts from 1829 until his appointment to the ambassadorship to Austria in 1838. The Sam Patch (1799–1829) mentioned in the article was a daredevil and national celebrity whose catchphrase, "some things can be done as well as others," was popular in nineteenth-century America. Source: http://en.wikipedia.org/wiki/Sam_Patch.

2. "J." 1845, 76.

3. *Cincinnati Commercial*, December 20, 1880.

4. The original article, which has not been located, seems to have appeared in the *Illinois Staatszeitung* sometime prior to May 25, 1908, when it was reprinted on page 4 of the *Erie (PA) Tageblatt*. It was printed again on June 12, 1908, in the *Highland (IL) Union*, page 4. There are slight differences in the language of Orth's speech in these two reprintings. The *Highland Union* version is slightly less influenced by standard German than the one from the Erie newspaper, hence the decision to quote the Highland version here.

5. Kriebel 1908, 435; see Rosenberger (1966, 103–106) for a discussion of the history of the *Pennsylvania-German*, including Kriebel's editorship.

6. See Rosenberger 1966, 103–106. In January 1912, the magazine changed its name to the *Penn Germania*.

7. Egle 1886, 510.

8. Mowatt 1873, 405.

9. The third and final edition of Gibbons's book is reprinted in Gibbons 1882/2001, with an extensive introduction by Don Yoder (pp. iii–xx), which provides an excellent discussion of Gibbons's biography and significance for the documentation of nineteenth-century Pennsylvania folklife.

10. Ibid., 11–12. Gibbons's parenthetical comment here about placing the sentence stress on *togeder* and de-emphasizing *once* almost certainly refers to the distinctive "rise-fall" intonation pattern associated with Dutchified English discussed in chapter 1.

In a footnote at the end of her discussion of language, Gibbons (1882/2001, 11) makes an interesting observation on the language of Henry Harbaugh's poems: "The most elegant specimens of Pennsylvania German with which I have met, are the poems of the late Rev. Henry Harbaugh; but, as the English words introduced by Mr. H. have since been in general substituted by German, the poems are not a perfect specimen of the spoken language." Gibbons is apparently referring to the editing out of a number of English loanwords in Harbaugh's original verse by the editors of his posthumous *Harfe*. Gibbons's astute observation underscores the rightful place of English-derived vocabulary in naturally spoken Pennsylvania Dutch.

11. Ibid., 15.

12. Ibid., 48–49.

13. See ibid., 381–391; also Stahr 1870. A large portion of the Stahr essay was also quoted by Henry Lee Fisher in the introduction to his 1879 compendium of Pennsylvania Dutch poems (1879, xii–xvi). Regarding the essay, Fisher writes, "It is pre-eminently the best description and ablest defence of our Pennsylvania-German Dialect I have ever

seen. It needs no better. It is able, impartial, perfect. Every Pennsylvania-German should be proud of it" (xvi).

14. Gibbons (1882/2001, iii).

15. "Pennsylvania Dutch" 1872.

16. "Die eigentliche Sprachbildung, welche sich in der Schrift und Literatur vollzieht und grammatikalisch geordnet wird, ist für das Pennsylvanisch-Deutsche nie einge-treten; auch wurde es nur sehr wenig, wie die Dialekte in Deutschland, durch eine Buch-sprache berichtigt und erweitert, und nur sporadisch benutzen es Schriftsteller, wie Hebel das Alemannische und Weitzmann das Schwäbische, um ihre Gedanken gewis-sen Leuten zugänglicher und interessanter zu machen" (ibid., 274).

17. "Durch dieses fortgesetzte Studium amerikanischer Gebildeten in der Literatur Großbritanniens kam es, daß sich in Amerika eine reinere Aussprache des Englischen ausbildete, indem hier die heimathlichen Dialekte nach und nach abgelegt wurden, während aus dem Entziehen der Deutschen von der Schriftsprache ihres Vaterlandes, sie hier einen halb und halb Dialekt, und beides schlecht, entstehen ließen" (ibid., 251).

18. Ibid., 275.

19. *New-York Tribune*, March 3, 1916, p. 3.

20. In 1873, the story was told that George Kremer had reacted to a speech in the House by Rep. John Randolph (1773–1833) from Virginia that was "larded with copi-ous quotations from Latin and Greek" by "pour[ing] forth a torrent of Pennsylvania German" (Forney 1873, 202–203); see also the *Guardian*, February 1877, p. 52. Historian William A. Russ Jr., writing in 1940, cast doubt on that account, noting that based on congressional records the probable speech in question, which was delivered on March 13, 1824, was made by Rep. Joshua Cushman of Maine and that, according to those records, Kremer's response to Cushman's use of Latin had been more tempered (Russ 1940, 202–203n8); see also Ellis and Hungerford 1886, 1561. Russ seems not to have been aware of the reported Fuller-Kremer encounter, which should also have taken place between 1823 and 1825. It must be noted that the Homer supposedly quoted by Fuller would have been in Greek. See also the article, "Pennsylvania Dutch in Congress," *Pennsylvania Dutch-man*, May 19, 1949, p. 5.

21. Reichard 1918, 44.

22. See http://bioguide.congress.gov/scripts/biodisplay.pl?index=S000692.

23. At least one person, none other than Edward H. Rauch, suggests that Sowden's use of Pennsylvania Dutch in his campaigns may also have been a liability. Sowden was not re-elected in 1888 and mounted at least one another unsuccessful attempt to gain the Democratic nomination from his Lehigh County district in 1894. In an article on the possible reasons behind Sowden's loss, the *Philadelphia Inquirer* reported on August 22, 1894, "Editor E. H. Rauch, of the Mauch Chunk 'News,' than whom there is no bet-ter authority, attributes Sowden's defeat to an entirely different cause. Sowden has been in the habit of making speeches in Pennsylvania German, and in the present campaign depended for his success entirely upon the jokes and stories which he told his Pennsylva-nia German audiences in their native tongue. They came to the conclusion that he was a buffoon and nothing else, a mistake as great as Mr. Sowden himself made in shooting by

his mark." However, there is evidence from the German-language press of Pennsylvania, that Sowden, affectionately known as "Der Billy," enjoyed considerable support from rank-and-file Pennsylvania Dutch Democrats (*Pennsylvania Dutchman*, August 25, 1949, p. 5). It is quite possible that the Radical Republican Rauch's view of Sowden was colored by their differing party affiliations.

24. *Philadelphia Inquirer*, June 9, 1896. Houck's 1896 campaign was unsuccessful, though he was later elected to statewide office, including as Pennsylvania's secretary of internal affairs from 1906 until his death in 1917. Writing of Houck's oratorical gifts, Samuel W. Pennypacker, governor of Pennsylvania from 1903 to 1907, recalled, "Houck had the disposition of a Celt with the name and intonations of the Pennsylvania Dutch, and in his speeches, with his anecdotes, his tears, his native wit and his accent, was inimitable" (Pennypacker 1918, 304–305).

25. "Nachdem wir Berks County Jurymänner uns zur Berathung des obengenannten Falles zurückgezogen hatten und eingesperrt waren, war ich, da ich, wie gesagt, noch nie zuvor als Jurymann gedient hatte, neugierig über die Verhandlungen, die jetzt vorgenommen werden sollten. Ich dachte, daß nun Alles in englischer Sprache verhandelt werden müßte, aber ich irrte mich sehr, denn kaum hatten wir in dem geräumigen Zimmer Platz genommen, so stand einer der Ältesten in unserer Jury auf und sagte: 'Ich *expect*, daß wir Alle besser Deutsch als Englisch verstehn; ischt aber einer unner uns, bei dem es net der Fall ischt, so mag er es sage.' Alle 12 schwiegen. 'Well', fuhr der Alte fort, 'dann ischt es verschtanne, weil alle schtill sind, daß wir unsere Sache in Deutsch abmache, es geht leichter wie in Englisch, obschon wir a All recht gut Englisch verschtehn. Nau, ich schlag Mr. Young als unsern Vormann vor: all wu davor sin, hebe die rechte Hand in die Höh!' " (*Reading Adler*, December 5, 1876).

26. Reichard 1918, 80.

27. For more information on the Catharine Bechtel murder, see the article by Frank Whelan, "Bloody Tale of Rebellious Allentown Woman Unearthed," *Morning Call*, March 28, 2004, http://articles.mcall.com/2004-03-28/entertainment/3516780_1_silk-industry -unsolved-murder-pennsylvania-german.

Although Pennsylvania Dutch has always been healthiest in rural areas, stories of urban families such as the Bechtels who favored the language demonstrate that it was also used in Dutch Country cities into the twentieth century, especially in Allentown, even across ethnic lines. For example, the *Allentown Leader*, in a brief item on page 8 of its March 12, 1903, issue, describes a prominent citizen, John R. Dougherty, as a "native of the famous Sixth Ward of Allentown, a ward wherein every resident is Irish and everyone can talk the Pennsylvania German dialect." As late as 1918, help wanted advertisements in Allentown newspapers sought Pennsylvania Dutch–speaking workers, as, for example, this one from the *Allentown Democrat* (March 25, 1918, p. 10): "Wanted—One more salesman (must be able to speak Pennsylvania German) with auto, to call on retail merchants in Allentown and vicinity." There are similar stories mentioning active speakers of Pennsylvania Dutch in Reading. In one instance, an obituary in the *Reading Times* (September 19, 1933, p. 3) for Edward J. Morris, a former city assessor (and a Democrat), reports, "Thrown into close association all his life with neighbors, friends, and business and political associates of German descent, Mr. Morris, himself a second-generation Irishman, learned to speak Pennsylvania German fluently. He took considerable pride in this achievement."

28. One of the most familiar expressions of this thesis was made by Carl Wittke (1936, 33–34), who famously likened the effect of the war on German America to a "thunderclap from a cloudless sky."

29. See Nollendorfs (1988, 184); Adams 1993 (especially ch. 7); and Salmons 2002.

30. *Grand Forks (ND) Herald*, August 24, 1918. The original article from the *Detroit Free Press* appeared some time shortly before this date, as this is the earliest of several reprintings in American newspapers.

31. It is likely that the author of the Detroit *Free Press* article was thinking here of Peter Minuit (1580–1638), an early leader in the New Netherland settlement in what is now New York.

32. See Rosenberger 1966, 129–151.

33. See ibid., 146–147.

34. The *Reading Times* reported on May 3, 1918, that the Lancaster Classis of the Reformed Church had voted unanimously to discontinue services in German after July 1, 1918, which may have coincided with the same change in Lebanon County churches referred to by Pierce Swope. Though the church may have felt some pressure to no longer use German in worship, contemporary sources underscore the fact that the transition to English in historically German churches in Pennsylvania had been underway long before World War I by regularly pointing out a generational gap in attitudes toward language: older parishioners favored German, while younger ones preferred English. Cf. the following excerpt from another *Reading Times* article one week later (May 10, 1918):

> Now as a matter of fact the German teaching we are trying to eradicate from our schools is not Pennsylvania-German or "Dutch" at all, but high German, the German of the kaiser's court and "kultur." Our Pennsylvania-German is a mere mongrel of English and German; perhaps it were better if it did not exist at all, but you cannot abolish the spoken word of generation at one fell swoop. Many East Pennsylvanians, not only those of Berks and Lehigh counties, but of Lancaster and Lebanon and York and Northampton and Schuylkill and others as well, will go on speaking Pennsylvania-German because it is the only language they know. This is especially true of the older generation; as far as the younger generation is concerned, it is gradually becoming acclimated and discarding the mother tongue for English. Long before the war German services in Berks churches were being eliminated or reduced to a minimum because the young folks were growing up and demanding English.

Yet another *Reading Times* article, which appeared on May 19, 1918, makes much the same point: "The younger members of the churches of the upper end of Montgomery and neighboring parts of Berks, Lehigh and Bucks counties are strongly in favor of eliminating German services from the churches, but they are met by staunch opposition on the part of older members, and since the pastors claim the older members of the church are really the financial backing of the congregations, it looks as if German would remain in this Pennsylvania-German community." The same article quotes the priest at Most

Blessed Sacrament Catholic parish at Bally in rural eastern Berks County: "As far as my congregation comes in the question of the elimination of the German from the church service, I may state that it would create a great revolution in my flock if I would make a change in my church and forbid them to speak in their mother tongue. They are all Pennsylvania-Germans, born and reared in this country, and nobody can convince them that the German language has anything to do with the war."

35. See Wittke 1936.

36. Rosenberger 1966, 149.

37. See *Reading Times*, May 31, 1918, p. 3.

38. *Philadelphia Inquirer*, April 20, 1918, p. 9.

39. See the article by Frank Whelan, "Call to Ban Teaching German Language Split Allentown Board during WWI," *Morning Call*, March 27, 2000, http://articles.mcall .com/2000-03-27/news/3284846_1_german-ancestors-board-members-foreign-lan guage. This article also notes that German *was* banned statewide a year later, in April 1919 (six months after the end of the war), by the Pennsylvania legislature, though that law lapsed some time later. The change in the status of German in Muhlenberg College's curriculum was reported in the April 20, 1918, *Philadelphia Inquirer* article cited above.

40. *Philadelphia Inquirer*, April 20, 1918, p. 9.

41. See *Reading Times*, July 20, 1918, p. 14.

42. See Robacker 1943, 141.

43. Harrisburg *Patriot*, March 8, 1919, p. 4. Capt. Dillinger (1885–1928), who was later promoted to the rank of major, commanded Company C (not D) of the 109th Machine Gun Battalion, Fourth Infantry Regiment, Pennsylvania National Guard (States Publications Society 1921, 465).

44. *Philadelphia Inquirer*, April 6, 1919, p. 17.

45. *Yank: The Army Weekly*, August 10, 1945, p. 17.

46. C. J. Stoltzfus 1984, 295–296.

47. See Weaver-Zercher (2001, 34–39) for an excellent discussion of Martin and her writings, her popularity, and her detractors, especially as her work relates to popular images of the Amish that were emerging in the early twentieth century. Although some believe that Martin's father was a German immigrant, Cornelius Reimensnyder was actually a third-generation American; his paternal grandfather came to America from Germany (Bell 1891, 833). Martin herself made no attempt to hide her disdain for Pennsylvania Dutch people, especially sectarians, and defended her negative portrayals of them (Martin 1913).

48. Martin 1904, 5.

49. Excerpts from the *New York Post* interview with Helen R. Martin appeared in the Harrisburg *Patriot*, February 3, 1916, p. 12.

50. The myth that hex signs were talismans used by Pennsylvania Dutch is one of the most persistent in Dutch-themed tourism. Folklorist Alfred L. Shoemaker's 1953 booklet *Hex, No!* refutes that myth strongly. See Yoder and Graves 2000 for a definitive analysis of the history and significance of hex signs. The marginal status of hex signs in earlier Pennsylvania Dutch culture is underscored by the fact that there is no word for *hex sign* in Pennsylvania Dutch.

51. See Deibler 1988/1989 and 1989.

52. Bundling (bed courtship) was a not uncommon practice in early America, including among the Pennsylvania Dutch, whereby a dating couple spends the night together in the same bed, yet clothed. Bed courtship is still practiced among some Amish groups, though it has been criticized by other Amish as morally inappropriate (Kraybill, Johnson-Weiner, and Nolt 2013, 222–223).

53. See Aurand 1939a and 1939b.

54. The term *fakelore* was coined by folklorist Richard Dorson (1977) and refers to fictional descriptions of folk cultural individuals and practices. In America, fakelore is often disseminated by popular media and commercial enterprises catering to tourists. Much Pennsylvania Dutch– and Amish-themed literature targeted at visitors to the Dutch Country, especially from the early twentieth century, is infused with fakeloric content.

55. See Aurand 1939a, 3–5. In a section titled "Our Dialect Common In Europe," Aurand (1939a, 4) notes, "During the world war it was a very easy matter for our Pennsylvania-German-spoken soldiers of the AEF, to enter into conversation with the natives in Alsace-Lorraine. Likewise, it was with little difficulty that these Pennsylvania 'Dutch' could get along in conversation in numerous other instances when occasion presented itself with German soldiers or towns-people during the period of American occupation at Coblentz."

56. Aurand 1939a, 18–19.

57. Aurand 1939b, 3–4.

58. Ibid., 11, 14, 15.

59. Ibid., 22, 25.

60. It is not known when Alfred L. Shoemaker died. After experiencing legal and mental health problems in the mid-1960s, he was believed to have moved to New York City, lived on the streets, and passed away there, though the circumstances of his death are unknown. See the article by Ron Devlin, "Founder of Kutztown Folk Festival Vanished in Mid-1960s, But His Legacy Lives On," *Reading Eagle*, June 27, 2009, http://www2.readingeagle.com/article.aspx?id=145809.

61. Shoemaker 1951b, 29.

62. See Weaver-Zercher (2001, 114–115) for an analysis of the challenges faced by the Pennsylvania Dutch Folklore Center.

63. Frey's doctoral dissertation on the Pennsylvania Dutch spoken in his native eastern York County, completed in 1941, remains a classic work today.

64. Frey 1951, 9.

65. Ibid., 6.

66. Ibid., 12.

67. John Hostetler's former doctoral student, Donald B. Kraybill of Elizabethtown College, has inherited Hostetler's mantle and, together with other scholars, has produced sensitive, objective works on Amish faith and life that are accessible to a nonscholarly readership. See Hostetler 1952 and Kraybill 2008.

68. Shoemaker and Yoder 1955, 39.

69. Ibid.

70. See A. L. Shoemaker 1940. Shoemaker's was just the second academic study of a sectarian variety of Pennsylvania Dutch, the first being a 1929 master's thesis on the Pennsylvania Dutch spoken in Johnson County, IA, by Ruth Bender (1929).

71. See Frey 1941.

72. Buffington's 1937 Harvard dissertation on the Pennsylvania Dutch language, along with those of Shoemaker and Frey, is an outstanding piece of scholarship. The very first PhD thesis on the subject was completed at Johns Hopkins University in 1888 by Marion Dexter Learned (1888/1889), also an excellent study. Two contemporaries of Buffington, Frey, and Shoemaker, who produced dissertations on Pennsylvania Dutch dialectology while graduate students at Brown University, were Carroll E. Reed (1941) and Lester W. J. Seifert (1941). See Louden 2001 for a review of the history of linguistic research on Pennsylvania Dutch. Albert Buffington, like Shoemaker, Frey, and Yoder, was engaged in public outreach related to Pennsylvania Dutch, including producing a weekly radio program in Pennsylvania Dutch as *Der Nixnutz* (The Good-for-Nothing). See *Pennsylvania Dutchman*, June 2, 1949.

73. See Haag 1988, 209-210; and Hanson 2009.

74. See Rosenberger 1966, 202-206.

75. *Reformed Church Messenger*, March 12, 1891, p. 2.

76. Ibid.

77. Pennsylvania German Society 1891, 33-34.

78. Ibid., 45.

79. The lack of emphasis that the Pennsylvania German Society placed on the language and vernacular culture of Pennsylvania Dutch inspired a group of scholars and laypersons to found the Pennsylvania German Folklore Society (PGFS) in 1935, whose membership was open to persons of any ethnic background; see Rosenberger (1966, 206). The annual volumes of the PGFS complemented those of the Pennsylvania German Society, and although the organizations were in some ways rivals, many individuals were members of both. The societies formally merged in 1966. In the foreword to the first yearbook of the PGFS, which was published in 1936, the importance of the Pennsylvania Dutch language in the planned work of the society was acknowledged:

> On Saturday, May the fourth, 1935, The Pennsylvania German Folklore Society was formed with the purpose of preserving for future benefit the folklore of the Pennsylvania German past. Cognizant of the fact that with the passing of the years the Pennsylvania German dialect was slowly losing its hold in the life of the people, conscious of the necessity of preserving in scholarly fashion the culture of our people, and aware of the interest in the formation of an organization to carry out such a program, a group of interested individuals took the initiative and issued a call for a society. (Pennsylvania German Folklore Society 1936, 5)

Appropriately, the lead contribution in the first yearbook was devoted to the poetry of Pennsylvania Dutch poet Charles C. Ziegler (1855-1930).

80. For a definitive study of the history and cultural significance of fersommlinge, see Donner forthcoming.

81. The premier reference on all themes related to the groundhog in Pennsylvania Dutch culture, including the Grundsow Lodges, is Yoder 2003. See also Donner 2002. A leading figure in the establishment of the Grundsow Lodges and the promotion of the Pennsylvania Dutch language in the twentieth century more generally is William S. "Pumpernickle Bill" Troxell (1893–1957). A tireless advocate for Pennsylvania German culture, Troxell was especially important for continuing the nineteenth-century tradition of "dialect columns" in local Pennsylvania newspapers. Troxell's column appeared in the Allentown *Morning Call* six times a week for more than three decades, earning him distinction as "the most prolific writer of the dialect of all time" (Yoder 2003, 66). When Troxell passed away in 1957, a memorial poem composed in Pennsylvania Dutch by James A. Koch appeared in the *Call*, the last three verses of which are reproduced below, followed by a lightly amended translation by Troxell's lifelong friend and fellow language advocate, Melville J. Boyer (Rosenberger 1966, 310–311).

> Die Mudderschprooch war ihm im Hatz,
> Er schreibt sie dann uff weiss un schwatz,—
> Er eschdimiert sie hoch.

> Mer kennt viel schreiwe un viel saage,—
> Doch heit sin Dreene in viel Aaage,—
> Mer duhne nix dezu.

> Die Fedder un Babier leit schtill,—
> Dann saag ich: Pumpernickle Bill
> Gott geb dir selichi Ruh.

> *The mother tongue was in his heart,*
> *In black and white he penned it,—*
> *Held it in high esteem.*

> *Much might we write and say,*
> *Full of tears are many eyes,—*
> *We will add no more.*

> *His pen and paper quiet lie,—*
> *Then I say: "Pumpernickle Bill,*
> *God grant you peaceful rest!"*

82. Kemp 1946, 218.
83. See also Buffington 1965.
84. See Haag 1988, 275–276.
85. Gilbert 1956, 4–5.
86. Ibid., 5.
87. See Buffington (1962, ix–xviii) for biographical information on Harry Hess Reichard and his wife, Ida Ruch Reichard.

88. See http://www.statesymbolsusa.org/National_Symbols/Bird_bald_eagle.html.

89. From the program for the ninth annual meeting of Grundsow Lodge Nummer 4 on the Tohickon (Creek), Quakertown, Bucks County, February 5, 1957. See also Yoder 2003, 102.

90. 'S Pennsylfawnisch Deitsch Eck, *Morning Call*, February 27, 1954.

91. Reichard referred implicitly here to Aristotle's *Meteorology*, an important work of ancient science.

92. 'S Pennsylfawnisch Deitsch Eck, *Morning Call*, February 27, 1954.

93. A similar version of this story was told in 1979 by Ernest G. Gehman (1901–1988), a Mennonite pastor and longtime member of the Eastern Mennonite University German faculty (*Pennsylvania Mennonite Heritage*, January 2015, p. 33; translation by K. Varden Leasa):

> Der Schtorkieper Abram Glemmer vum Schteddel Line Lexington, net weit vun der Schtadt Lansdale in Oscht-Pennsylvanie, hot mir die Gschicht verzaehlt wie ich en yunger Mann waar. Er hot gsaat as en aldi Gremmemm vun der mennischde Gmee datt im Schteddel mol bei ihm im Schtor waar und gsaat hot, "Ich kann gaar net verschteh ferwas so viel vun unsre Gmeesglieder so englisch warre wolle heidesdaags, wann doch der liewe Herr Gott deitsch is."
>
> Der Glemmer hot die Aage uffgerisse, "Wie hoscht du sell ausgfunne, Schweschder?"
>
> Sie hot graad geantwatt, "Ei, er hot doch sellemols im Gaarde gerufe: 'Aadam, wu bischt du?'"

> *The storekeeper Abram Clemmer from the village of Line Lexington, not far from the town of Lansdale in eastern Pennsylvania, told me this story when I was a young man. He said that an old grandmother from the Mennonite congregation there in the village was in his store once and said, "I can't understand at all why so many of our church members want to become so English nowadays, when, after all, the dear Lord God is German."*
>
> *Clemmer opened his eyes wide, "How did you find that out, Sister?"*
>
> *She answered right away, "Yes, after all, he called that time in the garden: 'Aadam, wu bischt du?'"*

94. See Buffington 1962, 1–4.

95. For biographical information on George Mays, see Reichard (1918, 150–154); and for Ezra Grumbine, see Reichard (1918, 192–202).

96. E. Grumbine 1909, 1; quoted also in Buffington 1962, 2.

97. Reichard 1940, 175–176.

98. Ibid. A broadside of Mays's original poem is included in the German-American Imprint Collection of the Franklin and Marshall College Library, box 2, item number H-287.

99. See Buffington 1962, 20–41.

100. See ibid., 97–131; also Reichard 1918, 254–266.

101. The first performance of Rauch's "Dutch Rip," in 1884, was produced by none other than Alfred Charles Moss, who also composed original music for it (Buffington 1962, 44–45).

102. Buffington 1962, 110–111.

103. Ibid., 111.

104. See Fetterman 1988/1989 for an excellent review of the history and significance of *Asseba un Sabina*.

105. See Rosenberger 1966, 295–298. Haag (1988, 268–269) provides biographical information on Pierce Swope. Among Swope's many achievements is the fact that he became first person formally licensed to teach Pennsylvania Dutch in public schools.

106. See Rosenberger 1966, 298–303.

Chapter 6. Pennsylvania Dutch and the Amish and Mennonites

1. One exception is the Mennonite educator and writer Joseph W. Yoder (1872–1956), who produced at least one poem; see Reichard (1940, 292–293). The leading reference works on the Old Order Amish and Old Order Mennonites are Kraybill, Johnson-Weiner, and Nolt 2013; and Kraybill and Hurd 2006, respectively.

2. Schlabach 1988, 22.

3. Ibid., 27.

4. See Gratz 1953, 167.

5. See ibid., 83.

6. Interestingly, in a collection of documents related to the family of an Amish man from Lancaster County, Amos J. Stoltzfus, is a transcription of one of Henry Harbaugh's most beloved poems, "Heemweh" (Homesickness; H. Harbaugh 1870, 77–85; C. J. Stoltzfus 1984, 121–126). It was made from a copy embellished with a bird drawn by an Amish girl in 1892 for another Amish girl, a friend or possibly a relative. The transcription deviates from the original in *Harbaugh's Harfe*, and has a different title, "Der Alte Heimet" (The old home). The girl who copied the poem was evidently not aware that Harbaugh wrote it.

7. See Kraybill, Johnson-Weiner, and Nolt (2013, 369–377) for a discussion of the kinds of literature that Amish people tend to read and write.

8. The overtly patriotic content of much fersommling programming is also something that does not appeal to sectarians. Although most Mennonite and Amish express gratitude for the various freedoms they enjoy as citizens of the United States (or Canada), they avoid expressions of patriotism that might imply loyalty to a worldly authority rather than to the kingdom of God. All Amish and most Mennonites do not display political symbols, such as the American flag, nor do they say the Pledge of Allegiance or sing patriotic songs, both of which are staples of fersommlinge.

9. See Arndt and Olson 1961, 545–546.

10. See Fretz 1987.

11. Milford Square and Sumneytown are less than ten miles apart; thus, is it is highly likely that the two printer-editors, Oberholtzer and Benner, were acquainted with one another.

12. "Das Folgende ist zum Einrücken mitgetheilt worden im Namen eines alten 'Pennsylvaniers,' und wir hoffen, so plump und einfach pennsylvanisch er auch geschrieben hat, werden's unsere Leser doch nicht übel aufnehmen, da er gewiß Punkte in

seiner Mittheilung hat, die nicht von geringer Tragweite sind, wenn man mit gesunder Vernunft darüber nachdenkt" (*Das Christliche Volks-Blatt*, April 2, 1862).

13. *Das Christliche Volks-Blatt*, April 2, 1862, p. 71. In this excerpt Oberholtzer refers to Georg Büchner (1813–1837), a German writer known for his views critical of religion. The content of Oberholtzer's article is also interesting for historical reasons, since it brings out the fact that intermarriage between Mennonites and non-Mennonites was sufficiently common as to be a matter of concern for him. This underscores the closeness between sectarians (at least Mennonites) and their nonsectarian neighbors in the nineteenth century.

14. See Shelly 2002. The Wadsworth Institute lasted only ten years, closing in 1878, but had a significant impact on the growth of the General Conference Mennonite Church, founded in 1860, and also the theological training of American Mennonites.

15. *Das Christliche Volks-Blatt*, September 3, 1862, p. 8.

16. Oberholtzer 1937, 157.

17. "Da kam es schon öfters vor, daß solches Loos auf Brüder fiel die nur ärmlich, oder fast gar nicht deutsch lesen konnten; und daher genöthigt waren fast in dem A, B, C, anfangen zu lernen; welches sie schon hätten lernen sollen in ihrer Kindheit, ehe die bösen Jahren kommen" (Guengerich 1897, 32).

18. See Swartzendruber 1956.

19. "A Friend of Humanity" 1907, 231–232.

20. See Hostetler and Meyers 2012; also Nolt 2003, 157–192.

21. See J. C. Wenger 2002.

22. A. B. Hoover 1982, 30.

23. Ibid., 593–594. See also Johnson-Weiner 1989, 1992, and 1998 for thorough analyses of language maintenance and shift among sectarian Pennsylvania Dutch speakers.

24. J. C. Wenger 1937, 29–30, 31.

25. See Gross 1990 for biographical information on Harold S. Bender.

26. See H. S. Bender 1957.

27. Ibid.

28. Ibid.

29. See Kraybill, Johnson-Weiner, and Nolt 2013, 8–10.

30. H. S. Bender 1957.

31. Igou 1999, 58.

32. E. Stoll n.d., 1.

33. Ibid., 1.

34. Ibid., 6.

35. Kraybill, Johnson-Weiner, and Nolt 2013, 74. The most powerful example of the potential impact of the Amish silent witness to the world was their reaction to the tragedy at the schoolhouse in Nickel Mines, Lancaster County, in 2006. See Kraybill, Nolt, and Weaver-Zercher 2010b.

36. Igou 1999, 268.

37. See Penzl 1938a. Herbert Penzl (1910–1995) was a native of Austria who had a long and distinguished career as a Germanic linguist in the United States. After teach-

ing briefly at Rockford College (today, Rockford University), he held appointments at the University of Illinois, the University of Michigan, and the University of California, Berkeley. Penzl's 1938 article was not the first scholarly treatment of a sectarian variety of Pennsylvania Dutch; that distinction is held by Ruth Bender, whose 1929 master's thesis consisted of a list of selected vocabulary in the variety spoken by Amish and Mennonites living near Kalona, IA (R. Bender 1929).

38. See A. L. Shoemaker 1940.

39. See Frey 1945.

40. See Frey 1941. Not surprisingly, Herbert Penzl also served on Frey's doctoral committee. Frey has warm words of gratitude for both Shoemaker and Penzl in the preface to his dissertation.

41. See Reed 1941; Seifert 1941; Buffington 1948; and the various articles reprinted in Seifert 2001.

42. See Seifert 1946.

43. See A. J. Beachy 1954, 264–266.

44. See Buffington 1980. Somerset County was also a point of arrival for some early nineteenth-century Amish immigrants from Europe. It is estimated that 2,700 Amish from eastern France, Hesse, and Bavaria came to Somerset, as well as communities in Ohio, Illinois, and Iowa, between 1815 and 1860 (H. S. Bender 1959). Some of these newcomers assimilated culturally and linguistically with the older Pennsylvania Dutch–speaking Amish, including the father of S. D. Guengerich, Daniel P. (1813–1889), who was born in Waldeck, Hesse, and came to America in 1833. Many other immigrants, perhaps the majority, ended up in the nineteenth century becoming Mennonites who eventually shifted to English. These would include the descendants of S. D. Guengerich, whose own Iowa congregation left the Old Order Amish to become affiliated with the more progressive Conservative Amish Mennonite Conference in 1912. There is no evidence of linguistic influence from the European German varieties spoken by these nineteenth-century Amish (viz., Alsatian, Hessian, or Bavarian German) on Pennsylvania Dutch. Also during the first half of the nineteenth century, some five hundred Mennonites and Amish of Bernese Swiss background settled in Ohio and Indiana (H. S. Bender 1959). Some "Swiss" Amish (known as *Schwyza* or *Shwitsa*) to this day speak languages that are distinct from Pennsylvania Dutch, varieties of Bernese Swiss German (e.g., in Adams County, IN) and Alsatian German (e.g., in Allen County, IN). Owing to historical and modern contacts and some intermarriage with Pennsylvania Dutch speakers, these Alemannic German varieties show some influence of Pennsylvania Dutch. See M. R. Wenger 1969 for discussion of Swiss varieties spoken in two settlements in Ohio and one in Indiana (Adams County). Humpa 1996 is an excellent, in-depth study of Adams County Amish Swiss German, including a comparison with related European dialects. See also Fleischer and Louden 2011, which supports the observation that Pennsylvania Dutch has influenced the Swiss German of Adams County. Thompson 1994 demonstrates that the German spoken by some Amish in Allen County, IN, is descended from Alsatian German rather than Bernese varieties. An important area for future investigation would be an analysis of the Pennsylvania Dutch spoken in Daviess County, IN, which was settled

by Amish from Allen County, as well as diverse other midwestern and Ontario Amish communities (J. Stoll 1997). Anecdotal evidence suggests that there may be Alemannic (Swiss or Alsatian) features to be found in modern Daviess County Pennsylvania Dutch.

45. These examples are drawn from the maps in Seifert 2001 and the word list in Shoemaker's dissertation (A. L. Shoemaker 1940, 72–75).

46. The Common case for definite articles in Pennsylvania Dutch is a historical merger of older Nominative and Accusative cases. Recall that a single Accusative form (*den*, the emphatic article for masculine nouns) existed in earlier Pennsylvania Dutch, but this was eventually lost.

47. The three main uses of the Dative case in Pennsylvania Dutch, as in German, were for simple indirect objects, objects of certain prepositions, and in expressions of possession. The semantics of *indirect affectedness* of the nouns marked in the Dative applies in all three instances.

48. See Huffines 1987, 1989; and Keiser 2012, 152–155.

49. See Moelleken 1988. Professor Moelleken generously donated the recordings made for this project to the Max Kade Institute for German-American Studies at the University of Wisconsin–Madison, where they are a part of the MKI North American German Dialect Archive.

50. See Kraybill, Johnson-Weiner, and Nolt 2013, 148 and references.

51. See Kraybill, Johnson-Weiner, and Nolt 2013, 146.

52. Burridge (1992, 226–233) documents Dative case forms in the speech of Old Order Mennonites from Ontario, though it is not clear just how widespread the Dative was among all generations of speakers at the time she did her fieldwork there.

53. See Louden 1997, 81; also Keiser 2012, 75–115.

54. See Keiser 2012, 117–129.

55. See Johnson-Weiner 1998 for an excellent discussion of the symbolic value of Pennsylvania Dutch among sectarians relative to English.

56. Allan M. Buehler (1899–1981) grew up in an Old Order Mennonite family but eventually joined a Baptist church. His book, Buehler 1977, contains an extensive autobiography and information on the variety of Pennsylvania Dutch he grew up with. Horst 2001 was written by Isaac R. Horst (1918–2008), who remained an Old Order Mennonite all his life. Horst's book provides a fascinating description of Canadian Old Order Mennonite life.

57. See *Di Heilich Shrift* 2013. This translation of the complete Bible was preceded by a translation of the New Testament (*Es Nei Teshtament* 1993).

58. See Vella Deitsh 1997. A number of other books have appeared that aid in the comprehension of *Di Heilich Shrift* as well as teach nonnative speakers the fundamentals of the Pennsylvania Dutch language as used by midwestern Amish: T. Beachy 1999, 2011; D. Miller 2013a, 2013b, 2014. Lillian Stoltzfus, a sectarian from Lancaster County, PA, has also produced a fine textbook with a CD introducing learners to the variety of Pennsylvania Dutch spoken by Lancaster Amish (L. Stoltzfus 2013).

59. Wood 1968, 94.

60. *Di Heilich Shrift* 2013, 2314–2315.

61. Vella Deitsh 1997, 50.

62. See *1001 Questions and Answers on the Christian Life* 1992, 111–115. See also Kraybill, Nolt, and Weaver-Zercher 2010a, 213–217.

63. *1001 Questions and Answers on the Christian Life* 1992, 112–113.

64. The tendency of Amish and Mennonite sectarians to express their love for each other in a verbally understated way is a habit that is almost certainly inherited from Europe. Modern German speakers today also say *ich liebe dich* much more infrequently to each other, including to their children, than speakers of American English say *I love you*.

65. Technically, the Horning Mennonites also identify as Old Order, but their worship services are in English and their members own and operate automobiles.

66. See especially Fuller 1997 and 2005 on the sociolinguistic situation of Pennsylvania Dutch among progressive Anabaptist groups who have split from the Old Orders.

67. "Die Muttersprache" 1983.

68. Wir lieben doch die Muttersprache
Die wir lernten auf ihren Schoß,
So tut doch eure Eltern ehren
Mit der Sprache wie sie es begehren. (Ibid.)

69. Der Hochmuts-Geist, der liebt das sehr,
Wer Demut liebt, dem fällt es schwer,
Und nimmt doch solches tief zu Herzen,
Wie das in Zeit uns macht zu stürzen. (Ibid.)

70. Wo möchte das uns hinführen?
Wenn wir unsere Sprach verlieren,
O warnet sie doch recht in Zeit
Und nehmt es wahr, ihr liebe Leut'.

Wer mit der Muttersprache
nicht zufrieden ist
Heißt er noch wirklich dann
Ein "Christ"? (Ibid.)

71. See Enninger 1986 for a thorough analysis of what he terms *Amish High German*.

72. See Miller and Raber 1976.

73. See Buffington 1946; also Wood 1945; Kreider 1957; and Raith and Lehmann 1989.

74. See Buffington 1946; also Frey 1945, 91–97.

75. See Frey 1945, 94.

76. See Johnson-Weiner 2007 for a study of Amish and Old Order Mennonite parochial education. For important observations on differences in the status of German in Swartzentruber and Old Order Mennonite school curricula, see Johnson-Weiner (2007, 183–186).

77. Byler 1969, 36.

78. M. N. Miller 2008, v.

79. Old Colony Mennonite Support 2011 offers fascinating overview of the work of this project, including many firsthand accounts from teachers.

80. Ibid., 311. Note that *Plattdeutsch* is the standard German word for *Plautdietsch*, which simply means 'Low German'. *Niederdeutsch* is yet another word with the same meaning. The German word *nieder*, 'low', refers to the low elevation of northern Central Europe, where Low German originated. Somewhat confusingly, the Low German adjective *platt* means 'flat', but in reference to language, in earlier times it also meant 'in a clear or easily comprehensible way'. Thus, the original meaning of *Platt(deutsch)* was something like 'clear, straightforward speech (German)'.

81. Ibid., 315. Coincidentally, the words *Kiwwel* and *Eemer* (cognate with standard German *Eimer*) are shibboleths for west-east dialectal differences in the southeastern Pennsylvania heartland of Pennsylvania Dutch. *Kiwwel* is used by Lancaster-origin Amish and Old Order Mennonites, but Lehigh County nonsectarians and midwestern Amish prefer *Eemer*.

82. Ibid., 318.

83. Ibid., 317.

84. Byler 1969, 34.

85. Frey 1945, 86.

86. See Huffines 1980a.

87. See Huffines 1980b.

88. See Raith 1981.

89. See also Kopp 1999, whose in-depth study of the English of Pennsylvania Dutch sectarians and nonsectarians complements the findings of Huffines and Raith.

90. C. J. Stoltzfus 1984, 167.

91. Penzl 1938a.

92. See Dundore 1954, 162–163.

93. L. M. Miller 2014, 10.

94. Ibid.

95. See Louden 1992, 275.

96. See the discussion of English loan vocabulary in Pennsylvania Dutch in chapter 1.

97. This woman was an Amish speaker of Pennsylvania Dutch who was born in Elkhart, County, IN, in 1956. She was interviewed by Jürgen Eichhoff in April 1984 in conjunction with the atlas project overseen by Wolfgang W. Moelleken. The recording is part of the Moelleken Collection in the North American German Dialect Archive at the Max Kade Institute for German-American Studies at the University of Wisconsin–Madison (MOE 203).

98. See Johnson-Weiner 1993; and Johnson-Weiner 2007, 40–71.

Chapter 7. An American Story

1. Crawford 1992 and 2000 are good references on the official English movement in the United States. A website maintained by James Crawford (www.languagepolicy.net) is a useful resource on various aspects of language policy in the United States, including updated information on language legislation in individual states (http://www.language policy.net/archives/langleg.htm).

2. *Pennsylvania Dutchman*, May 1, 1951.

3. See Yoder 2001, 162.

4. *1001 Questions and Answers on the Christian Life* 1992, 138–139.

5. *Chicago Tribune*, December 25, 1995.

6. See C. S. Fischer 2002.

7. See Kraybill, Johnson-Weiner, and Nolt 2013, 181–183.

8. Die alte Kirche musste niedergerissen werden; da bestimmten Schindel und ich den 4. und 5. Mai als Tage zum letzten Gottesdienst in der alten Kirche, und zwar zu einer gemeinschaftlichen Abendmahlsfeier für beide Gemeinden, reformirt wie lutherisch.—Auf Samstag Nachmittag hatten wir unsere Vorbereitung. Schindel predigte und ich hielt den liturgischen Gottesdienst am Altare. Es war feierlich, wie sich die ganze Gemeinde zum letztenmal in der alten Kirche niederknieete. Nach der Einsegnung hielt ich noch eine Rede im Rückblick auf den vielen und reichen Segen, den Gott in diesem Hause über die da draußen auf dem Gottesacker schlafende und die hier zum letztenmal versammelte Gemeinde ausgegossen hatte; und wie nun hier unser letzter Gottesdienst und Abendmahlsfeier gehalten würde. Wenige Augen waren trocken.—Am Sonntag Morgen hielt ich die Predigt und nach der Predigt Schindel den Altargottesdienst. Dann nahmen wir das Abendmahl, ich reichte es Schindel und Schindel mir, worauf die Gemeindeglieder kamen und Antheil nahmen. Mehr als 400 Glieder genossen das Mahl.—O, wie fühlte ich damals die Trennung der beiden Kirchen! Warum ist diese Spaltung? Warum nicht eine Kirche so weit die deutsche Zunge klingt? Und die ganze Gemeinde fühlte so. Viele sprachen es aus zu uns nach dem Gottesdienst. Schindel antwortete: Wenn es an Bruder Helffrich und an mir läge, dann wäre es gewiss anders" (Helffrich 1906, 203).

A slightly different English translation is found in Wood (1942, 93). The church is today Longswamp United Church of Christ (http://www.longswampucc.org/). The building in which the congregation worships is the same one that was built in 1852.

9. Wood 1942, 91.

10. Recall the conflict over language in Philadelphia's largest Lutheran church, St. Michael's and Zion, touched on in chapter 3, which was resolved in favor of English. See Baer 2008.

11. See Wood 1942, 89.

12. Ibid., 92.

13. See Wood 1942; also Ludwig 1947, 46.

14. See also Schiffman 1987 for a review of the eventual shift from German to English among the two largest German American denominations in nineteenth-century America, the Lutheran Church–Missouri Synod and the Evangelical (Reformed) Synod. Kamphoefner's 1994 study of 1940 US Census records shows the strongest correlate of maintenance of German among midwestern German Americans was rurality. Louden 2011a discusses the sociolinguistic history of Wisconsin's oldest German settlement, Freistadt, Ozaukee County. Founded in 1839 by Old Lutherans (believers who rejected the Prussian Union of 1817) from Pomerania, Freistadt residents were originally bidialectal, speaking a Low German dialect at home and in the community and using standard German in their Lutheran church and parochial school (today affiliated with the Missouri Synod; http://www.trinityfreistadt.com/). Around the turn of the twentieth century, many Frei-

stadt families began to prefer standard German over Low German as a home language, though most children born after 1930 grew up to be dominant in English. This shift from (dialectal) German to English indirectly, by way of standard German for one or two generations, was not uncommon in rural midwestern German American communities at the turn of the twentieth century, especially those with a large Lutheran presence.

15. See Hostetler and Meyers 2012.

16. See Fretz 1987; also Schlabach 1988, 118–127. Chapter 8 of Schlabach (1988, 201–229) provides an excellent summary of the divergence in the latter half of the nineteenth century between the conservative Mennonites and Amish who came to be known as Old Order and more progressive groups.

17. See Schlabach 1988, 202–203.

18. See Keiser 2012; also Keiser 2006. Keiser's analysis of the sociolinguistic relevance of portable community for Amish speakers of Pennsylvania Dutch complements Steven Reschly's (2000) research on the historical (and contemporary) mobility of Amish in America, especially in the Midwest.

19. The term "pilgrims and exiles" derives from the title of a focus issue of *Christian History Magazine* (#84, 2004) on Anabaptist groups.

20. Keiser 2012, 1.

21. See Redekop 1969. See Moelleken 1992 for a review of the linguistic history of Old Colony Mennonites. Siemens 2012 is an excellent reference work on the grammar, history, and sociolinguistic situation of Plautdietsch.

22. Loewen 1986, 2. Loewen presumes that the Mennonites quoted were already Low German–speaking and therefore were referring to High German when speaking of the "devil's language." That is unlikely, since Low German was never used by Mennonites as a sacral language; when they shifted from speaking Dutch and using it in worship, they spoke Low German among themselves and then also switched to High German in church. That is, the Mennonites would not have viewed Low and High German as linguistic adversaries in the way that Dutch and German were.

23. See Hostetler 1974; and Kraybill and Bowman (2001, 20–59) for an overview of Hutterite faith and life. Rein's (1977) comparative study of Hutterite German, Amana German, and Swiss Volhynian German includes a thorough description of the linguistic features of Hutterite German; see also W. B. Hoover 1997.

24. See Maier 1975.

25. Maier 1975, 20. The quote in this passage is from Roth (1953, 132).

26. The best single overview of Haredi verbal behavior is Isaacs 1999; see also Glinert and Shilhav 1991. An accessible history of the Yiddish language is Weinstein 2001; Jacobs 2005 is a comprehensive reference work for Yiddish linguistics.

27. Igou 1999, 57–58.

28. Reichard 1940, 256. For biographical information on Adam Stump, see Reichard (1918, 269–274).

Bibliography

Abley, Mark. 2003. *Spoken Here: Travels among Threatened Languages*. New York: Houghton Mifflin.

Adams, Charles F. 1878. *Leedle Yawcob Strauss, and Other Poems*. Boston: Lee and Shepard.

Adams, David Wallace. 1995. *Education for Extinction: American Indians and the Boarding School Experience, 1875–1928*. Lawrence: University Press of Kansas.

Adams, Willi Paul. 1993. *The German-Americans: An Ethnic Experience*. American ed., trans. and adapted by LaVern J. Rippley and Eberhard Reichmann. Indianapolis: Max Kade German-American Center, Indiana University–Purdue University at Indianapolis.

Anderson, Keith O., and Willard M. Martin. 1977. "Language Loyalty among the Pennsylvania Germans: A Status Report on Old Order Mennonites in Pennsylvania and Ontario." In *Germanica-America 1976*, ed. Erich A. Albrecht and J. A. Burzle, 73–80. Lawrence, KS: Max Kade Center.

Anderson, Vicki Michael. 2014. *Bidialectalism: An Unexpected Development in the Obsolescence of Pennsylvania Dutchified English*. Publications of the American Dialect Society 98. Supplement to *American Speech*, vol. 88.

Anonymous. 1775[?]. "Das Trauer Lied der unterdrückten Freyheit." N.p.

Arndt, Karl J. R. 1976. "German as the Official Language of the United States of America?" *Monatshefte* 68: 129–150.

———. 1986. "The First German Broadside and Newspaper Printing of the American Declaration of Independence." *Pennsylvania Folklife* 35 (Spring 1986): 98–107.

Arndt, Karl J. R., and Reimer Eck. (eds.) 1989. *The First Century of German Language Printing in the United States of America*. Göttingen: Niedersächsische Staats- und Universitätsbibliothek Göttingen.

Arndt, Karl J. R., and May E. Olson. 1961. *German-American Newspapers and Periodicals, 1732–1955: History and Bibliography*. Heidelberg: Quelle & Meyer.

Aurand, A. Monroe, Jr. 1939a. *Pennsylvania-German Dialect: Stories and Poems*. Harrisburg: Aurand Press.

————. 1939b. *Quaint Idioms and Expressions of the Pennsylvania Dutch.* Harrisburg: Aurand Press.

Baer, Friederike. 2008. *The Trial of Frederick Eberle: Language, Patriotism and Citizenship in Philadelphia's German Community, 1790–1830.* New York: New York University Press.

Bahn, Rachel. 1869. *Poems.* York, PA: H. C. Adams.

Beachy, Alvin J. 1954. "The Amish Settlement in Somerset County, Pennsylvania." *Mennonite Quarterly Review* 28: 263–292.

Beachy, Thomas. 1999. *Pennsylvania Deitsh Dictionary.* Sugarcreek, OH: Carlisle Press.

————. 2011. *Ich kann PA Deitsh Shreiva.* Sugarcreek, OH: Carlisle Press.

Beam, C. Richard. (ed.) 2004–2011. *The Comprehensive Pennsylvania German Dictionary.* With assistance of Joshua R. Brown, Jennifer L. Trout, and Dorothy Pozniko Beam. Millersville, PA: Center for Pennsylvania German Studies.

Becker, Christian. 1808. *Der Deutschen allgegenwärtiger Englischer Sprachlehrer des Wortes Gottes.* Easton, PA: C. J. Hütter.

————. 1812. *A communication to His Excellency Simon Snyder governor of the state of Pennsylvania concerning a new method of teaching.* Pennsylvania: n.p.

Bell, Herbert C. (ed.) 1891. *History of Northumberland County, Pennsylvania.* Chicago: Brown, Runk.

Bender, Harold S. 1956. "Germantown Mennonite Settlement (Pennsylvania, USA)." *Global Anabaptist Mennonite Encyclopedia Online.* Retrieved 25 April 2014, from http://gameo.org/index.php?title=Germantown_Mennonite_Settlement_(Pennsylvania,_USA)&oldid=121096.

————. 1957. "Language Problem." *Global Anabaptist Mennonite Encyclopedia Online.* Retrieved 22 April 2014, from http://gameo.org/index.php?title=Language _problem &oldid=83047.

————. 1959. "United States of America." *Global Anabaptist Mennonite Encyclopedia Online.* Retrieved 17 November 2014, from http://gameo.org/index.php?title=United _States_of_America&oldid=121761.

Bender, Harold S., and Samuel L. Yoder. 2011. "Holmes-Wayne-Tuscarawas Counties Old Order Amish Settlement (Ohio, USA)." *Global Anabaptist Mennonite Encyclopedia Online.* Retrieved 25 April 2014, from http://gameo.org/index.php?title=Holmes -Wayne-Tuscarawas_Counties_Old_Order_Amish_Settlement_(Ohio,_USA) &oldid=120936.

Bender, Ruth. 1929. "A Study of the Pennsylvania German Dialect as Spoken in Johnson County, Iowa." MA thesis, University of Iowa. [Edited and reprinted as *The Kalona/ Iowa Pennsylvania-German Dialect,* ed. C. Richard Beam and Rachel Cornelius, 2003. Millersville, PA: Center for Pennsylvania German Studies, Millersville University of Pennsylvania.]

Betz, I. H. 1910. "The Career of Henry Lee Fisher." *The Pennsylvania-German* 11: 2–9.

Birlinger, Anton. 1875. "Heinrich Harbaugh, ein Pennsylvanisch-deutscher Hebel." *Alemannia* 2: 240–253.

Boas, Hans C. 2009. *The Life and Death of Texas German.* Durham, NC: Duke University Press.

Bräutigam, Kurt. 1934. *Die Mannheimer Mundart.* Walldorf: Lamade.

Brenckman, Fred. 1913. *History of Carbon County, Pennsylvania.* Harrisburg: James J. Nungesser.

Bronner, Simon J. 1996. *Popularizing Pennsylvania: Henry W. Shoemaker and the Progressive Uses of Folklore and History.* University Park: Pennsylvania State University Press.

Brown, Joshua R. 2011. "Religious Identity and Language Shift among Amish-Mennonites in Kishacoquillas Valley, Pennsylvania." PhD dissertation, Pennsylvania State University.

Buehler, Allan M. 1977. *The Pennsylvania German Dialect and the Life of an Old Order Mennonite.* Cambridge, ON: Allan M. Buehler.

Buffington, Albert F. 1937. "A Grammatical and Linguistic Study of Pennsylvania German." PhD dissertation, Harvard University.

———. 1938. "Characteristic Features of Pennsylvania German: An Attempt to Correct Some Erroneous Impressions Concerning the Dialect." 'S Pennsylfawnisch Deitsch Eck. *Morning Call,* December 10 and 17, 1938.

———. 1939. "Pennsylvania German: Its Relation to Other German Dialects." *American Speech* 14: 276–286.

———. 1946. "'Dutchifed' German." 'S Pennsylfawnisch Deitsch Eck. *Morning Call,* June 1, 1946.

———. 1948. "Linguistic Variants in the Pennsylvania German Dialect." *Pennsylvania German Folklore Society* 13: 217–252.

———. (ed.) 1962. *The Reichard Collection of Early Pennsylvania German Dialogues and Plays.* Vol. 61 of *Pennsylvania German Society.* Lancaster: Pennsylvania German Society / Fackenthal Library, Franklin and Marshall College.

———. 1965. *"Dutchified German" Spirituals.* Vol. 62 of *Pennsylvania German Society.* Lancaster, PA: Commercial Printing House.

———. 1970. "Similarities and Dissimilarities between Pennsylvania German and the Rhenish Palatine Dialects." *Pennsylvania German Society* 3: 91–116.

———. 1980. "The Pennsylvania German Dialect and Folklore of Somerset County." *Ebbes fer Alle-Ebber—Ebbes fer Dich: Something for Everyone—Something for You,* ed. Albert F. Buffington et al., 3–33. Breinigsville, PA: Pennsylvania German Society.

Buffington, Albert F., and Preston A. Barba. 1965. *A Pennsylvania German Grammar.* Allentown: Schlechter's.

Burridge, Kathryn. 1989. *Pennsylvania-German Dialect: A Localized Study within a Part of Waterloo County, Ontario.* Waterloo, ON: Pennsylvania German Folklore Society of Ontario.

———. 1992. "Creating Grammar: Examples from Pennsylvania German, Ontario." *Diachronic Studies on the Languages of the Anabaptists,* ed. Kate Burridge and Werner Enninger, 199–241. Bochum: Universitätsverlag Dr. N. Brockmeyer.

Byler, Uria R. 1969. *School Bells Ringing: A Manual for Amish Teachers and Parents.* Aylmer, ON: Pathway.

Cazden, Robert E. 1984. *A Social History of the Book Trade in America to the Civil War.* Columbia, SC: Camden House.

Christmann, Ernst. 1950. "Das Pennsylvaniadeutsch als pfälzische Mundart." *Rheinisches Jahrbuch für Volkskunde* 1: 47–82.

Christmann, Ernst, and Heinz Kloss. 1937. *Pälzer Stimme in aller Welt*. Bad Dürkheim: Verlag Deutsche Volksbücher.

Cooprider, Cora Bell Harbaugh, and Joseph L. Cooprider. 1947. *Harbaugh History: A Directory, Genealogy, and Source Book of Family Records*. Evansville, IN: n.p.

Crawford, James. (ed.) 1992. *Language Loyalties: A Source Book on the Official English Controversy*. Chicago: University of Chicago Press.

———. 2000. *At War with Diversity: U.S. Language Policy in an Age of Anxiety*. Clevedon: Multilingual Matters.

Crystal, David. 2000. *Language Death*. Cambridge: Cambridge University Press.

Cuff, David J. (ed.) 1989. *The Atlas of Pennsylvania*. Philadelphia: Temple University Press.

Curtiss, Susan. 1977. *Genie: A Psycholinguistic Study of a Modern-Day "Wild Child."* Boston: Academic Press.

Das Neue ABC- und Buchstabir-Buch zum Gebrauch für Deutsche Volksschulen in Pennsylvanien und anderen Staaten. 1861. Sumneytown, PA: E. M. Benner.

Deibler, Barbara E. 1988/1989. "The Bookish Aurands." *Pennsylvania Portfolio* 6 (2): 27–31.

———. 1989. "The Aurands in Print." *Pennsylvania Portfolio* 7 (1): 21–25.

Deumert, Ana. 2004. *Language Standardization and Language Change: The Dynamics of Cape Dutch*. Amsterdam: John Benjamins.

Deutsche oder Englisch. Ein Gespräch zwischen zwei Nachbarn, Sebastian und Jacob, über Die deutsche Sprache in Nord-Amerika. 1862. Allentown: Druck und Verlag von Trexler, Harlacher & Weiser.

"Die Muttersprache." 1983. Gordonville, PA: Pequea Publishers.

Di Heilich Shrift. 2013. Wycliffe Bible Translators.

Donner, William W. 1999. "Abraham Reeser Horne: To the Manor Born." *Der Reggeboge / Journal of the Pennsylvania German Society* 33 (1/2): 3–17.

———. 2000. "'We Are What We Make of Ourselves': Abraham Reeser Horne and the Education of Pennsylvania Germans." *Pennsylvania Magazine of History and Biography* 124: 521–546.

———. 2002. "Loss uns Deitcha wos m'r sin: Leave Us Dutch the Way We Are: The Grundsow Lodges." *Pennsylvania German Review*, Spring 2002, 39–47.

———. 2010. "The First College Course in Pennsylvania German." In *Festschrift for Earl C. Haag*, supplement, *Yearbook of German-American Studies* 3: 15–26.

———. Forthcoming. *Serious Nonsense: Groundhog Lodges, Versammlinge, and Pennsylvania German Heritage*. University Park: Pennsylvania State University Press.

Dorson, Richard M. 1977. *American Folklore*. Chicago: University of Chicago Press.

Dundore, M. Walter. 1954. "The Saga of the Pennsylvania Germans in Wisconsin." *Pennsylvania German Folklore Society* 19: 33–166.

Egle, William Henry. 1886. *Pennsylvania Genealogies: Scotch-Irish and German*. Harrisburg: Lane S. Hart.

Eichhoff, Jürgen. 1971. "German in Wisconsin." In *The German Language in America: A Symposium*, ed. Glenn G. Gilbert, 43–57. Austin: University of Texas Press.

Ellis, Alexander J. 1871. *On Early English Pronunciation, with Especial Reference to Shakspere and Chaucer.* Part III. London: Philological Society.

Ellis, Franklin, and Austin N. Hungerford. 1886. *History of That Part of the Susquehanna and Juniata Valleys, Embraced in the Counties of Mifflin, Juniata, Perry, Union and Snyder in the Commonwealth of Pennsylvania.* Vol. 2. Philadelphia: Everts, Peck, & Richards.

Enninger, Werner. 1986. "Structural Aspects of Amish High German." *Studies on the Languages and the Verbal Behavior of the Pennsylvania Germans I,* ed. Werner Enninger, 61–105. Stuttgart: Franz Steiner Verlag.

Eshleman, Cyrus H. 1935. "The Origin of the Pennsylvania German Dialect." 'S Pennsylfawnisch Deitsch Eck. *Morning Call,* November 2, 9, and 16, 1935.

Es Nei Teshtament. 1993. South Holland, IL: Bible League.

Feer, Robert A. 1952. "Official Use of the German Language in Pennsylvania." *Pennsylvania Magazine of History and Biography* 76: 394–405.

Ferguson, Charles A. 1959. "Diglossia." *Word* 15: 325–340.

Ferhoodled English. 1964. Gettysburg, PA: Conestoga Crafts.

Fetterman, William. 1988/1989. "Asseba un Sabina: The Flower of Pennsylvania German Folk Theater." *Pennsylvania Folklife* 38: 50–68.

15th Annual Pennsylvania Dutch Days Program, Hershey Park, Hershey, PA, 1963. N.p.

Fischer, Claude S. 2002. "Ever-More Rooted Americans." *City & Community* 1: 177–198.

Fisher, Henry Lee. 1879. *'S Alt Marik-Haus Mittes in D'r Schtadt un Die Alte Zeite.* York, PA: York Republican.

——. 1882. *Kurzweil un Zeitfertreib.* York, PA: Fischer Brüder.

——. 1886. "The Pennsylvania Germans: Their Ancestry, Character, Manners, Customs, Dialect, Etc." In *History of York County, Pennsylvania,* ed. John Gibson, 219–277. Chicago: F. A. Battey.

——. 1888. *Olden Times; or, Pennsylvania Rural Life, Some Fifty Years Ago, and Other Poems.* York, PA: Fisher Brothers.

Flaten, Nils. 1900. "Notes on American-Norwegian, with a Vocabulary. *Dialect Notes* 2: 115–126.

Fleischer, Jürg, and Mark L. Louden. 2011. "Das Amish Swiss German im nordöstlichen Indiana: eine alemannisch-pfälzische Mischmundart?" In *Alemannische Dialektologie—Wege in die Zukunft,* ed. H. Christen, S. Germann, W. Haas, N. Montefiori, and H. Ruef, 231–244. Stuttgart: Franz Steiner Verlag.

Fogleman, Aaron Spencer. 1996. *Hopeful Journeys: German Immigration, Settlement, and Political Culture in Colonial America, 1717-1775.* Philadelphia: University of Pennsylvania Press.

Ford, Paul Leicester. (ed.) 1897/1962. *The New-England Primer.* New York: Teachers College, Columbia University.

Forney, John W. 1873. *Anecdotes of Public Men: Originally Published in the "Washington Sunday Chronicle" and "Philadelphia Press."* New York: Harper & Brothers.

Franklin, Benjamin. 1779. "A Scheme for a New Alphabet and Reformed Mode of Spelling." In *Political, Miscellaneous, and Philosophical Pieces,* 467–478. London: J. Johnson.

Frantz, John B. 1998. "Franklin and the Pennsylvania Germans." *Pennsylvania Biography* 65: 21–34.

Fretz, J. Herbert. 1987. "Oberholtzer, John H. (1809–1895)." *Global Anabaptist Mennonite Encyclopedia Online*. Retrieved 19 April 2014, from http://gameo.org/index.php?title=Oberholtzer,_John_H._(1809-1895)&oldid=120989.

Frey, J. William. 1940. "The English of the Pennsylvania Germans in York County, Pa." 'S Pennsylfawnisch Deitsch Eck. *Morning Call*, May 18, 1940.

———. 1941. "The German Dialect of Eastern York County, Pennsylvania." PhD dissertation, University of Illinois.

———. 1945. "Amish 'Triple-Talk.'" *American Speech* 20: 85–98.

———. 1951. *That Amazing Pennsylvania Dutch Language*. Lancaster: Pennsylvania Dutch Folklore Center.

"A Friend of Humanity." 1907. *Glimpses of Amish-Mennonite Homes and Some Plain Talks to the Inmates*. Scottdale, PA: Mennonite Book and Tract Society.

Friesen, Steve. 1990. *A Modest Mennonite Home*. Intercourse, PA: Good Books.

Fuchs, Meik [Michael J. Lochemes]. 1898. *Dreiguds un Noschens*. Milwaukee: M. H. Wiltzius.

Fuller, Janet M. 1997. "Pennsylvania Dutch with a Southern Touch: A Theoretical Model of Language Contact and Change." PhD dissertation, University of South Carolina.

———. 2005. "The Sociopragmatic Values of Pennsylvania German ('Dutch'): Change across Time, Place, and Anabaptist Sect." In *ISB4: Proceedings of the 4th International Symposium on Bilingualism*, ed. James Cohen, Kara T. McAlister, Kellie Rolstad, and Jeff MacSwan, 800–807. Somerville, MA: Cascadilla Press.

George, Staughton, Benjamin M. Nead, and Thomas McCamant. (eds.) 1879. *Charter to William Penn, and Laws of the Province of Pennsylvania, Passed between the Years 1682 and 1700*. Harrisburg: Lane S. Hart, State Printer.

Gibbons, Phebe Earle. 1882/2001. *Pennsylvania Dutch and Other Essays*. With an introduction by Don Yoder. Mechanicsburg, PA: Stackpole Books.

Gilbert, Russell W. 1956. "Pennsylvania German Versammling Speeches." *Pennsylvania Speech Annual* 13: 3–20.

Glinert, Lewis, and Yosseph Shilhav. 1991. "Holy Land, Holy Language: A Study of an Ultraorthodox Jewish Ideology." *Language in Society* 20: 59–86.

Graeff, Arthur D. 1946. "The Pennsylvania Germans in Ontario, Canada." *Yearbook of the Pennsylvania German Folklore Society* 11: 1–80.

Gratz, Delbert L. 1953. *Bernese Anabaptists and Their American Descendants*. Scottdale, PA: Herald Press.

Gross, Leonard. 1990. "Bender, Harold Stauffer (1897–1962)." *Global Anabaptist Mennonite Encyclopedia Online*. Retrieved 22 April 2014, from http://gameo.org/index.php?title=Bender,_Harold_Stauffer_(1897-1962)&oldid=104575.

Grumbine, Ezra. 1909. *Stories of Old Stumpstown*. Fredericksburg, PA: Lebanon County Historical Society.

———. 1917. *Der Prahl-Hans and Other Rhymes*. Lebanon, PA: Sowers.

Grumbine, Lee L. 1903. *Der Dengelstock*. Lancaster, PA: New Era Printing Press.

Gruver, Rebecca Brooks. 1981. *An American History*. New York: Addison-Wesley.

Guengerich, S. D. 1897. *Deutsche Gemeinde Schulen, ihren Zweck, Nutzen und Nothwendigkeit zum Glaubens-Unterricht, deutlich dargestellt*. Amisch, IA: S. D. Guengerich.

Haag, Earl C. 1956. "A Comparison of the Pennsylvania-German and Mannheim Dialects." MA thesis, Pennsylvania State University.

———. (ed.) 1988. *A Pennsylvania German Anthology*. Selinsgrove, PA: Susquehanna University Press.

Haldeman, Samuel Stehman. 1872. *Pennsylvania Dutch: A Dialect of South German with an Infusion of English*. London: Trübner.

Hanson, Gregory J. 2009. "'S Pennsylfawnisch Deitsch Eck: A Journalistic Success Story." *Der Reggeboge / Journal of the Pennsylvania German Society* 43 (1): 20–32.

Harbaugh, Henry. 1854. "The Old School-House." *Guardian* 5: 97–102.

———. 1856. *Annals of the Harbaugh Family in America, from 1736 to 1856*. Chambersburg, PA: M. Kieffer.

———. 1860. *Poems*. Philadelphia: Lindsay and Blakiston.

———. 1861. "Das Alt Schul-Haus an der Krick." *Guardian* 12: 233–236.

———. 1862. "Busch un Schtettel." *Guardian* 13: 86.

———. 1863. "The Alemanian Poet: John Peter Hebel." *Guardian* 14: 69–73.

———. 1866a. "Die Neue Sart Gentleleut." *Guardian* 17: 64.

———. 1866b. "The German Burns." *Hours at Home* 3: 553–561.

———. 1870. *Harbaugh's Harfe: Gedichte in Pennsylvanisch-Deutscher Mundart*, ed. Benjamin Bausman. Philadelphia: Reformed Church Publication Board.

Harbaugh, Linn. 1900. *Life of the Rev. Henry Harbaugh, D.D.* Philadelphia: Reformed Church Publication Board.

Harris, Alexander. 1872. *A Biographical History of Lancaster County, Pennsylvania*. Lancaster, PA: Elias Barr.

Hart, Charles Henry. 1881. *Memoir of Samuel Stehman Haldeman LL D*. Philadelphia: Edward Stern.

Harter, Thomas H. 1893. *Boonastiel: A Volume of Legend, Story, and Song in "Pennsylvania Dutch."* Middleburg, PA: T. Harter.

Haugen, Einar. 1969. *The Norwegian Language in America: A Study in Bilingual Behavior*. Bloomington: Indiana University Press.

———. 1977. "Norm and Deviation in Bilingual Communities." In *Bilingualism: Psychological, Social, and Educational Implications*, ed. Peter A. Hornby, 91–102. New York: Academic Press.

Hays, H. M. 1908. "On the German Dialect Spoken in the Valley of Virginia." *Dialect Notes* 3: 263–278.

Hearn, Lafcadio, and Simon J. Bronner. 2002. *Lafcadio Hearn's America: Ethnographic Sketches and Editorials*. Lexington: University Press of Kentucky.

Hebel, Johann Peter. 1803. *Allemannische Gedichte*. Carlsruhe: Macklors Hofbuchhandlung.

Helffrich, William A. 1906. *Lebensbild aus dem Pennsylvanisch-Deutschen Predigerstand: oder Wahrheit in Licht und Schatten*. Allentown, PA: N. W. A. & W. U. Helffrich.

Helmuth, Justus Henry Christian. 1813a. "Zuruf an die deutschen protestantischen Kirchen in Nord-Amerika." *Evangelisches Magazin, unter der Aufsicht der Deutschen Evangelisch-lutherischen Synode* (1811–1817), January 1, 1813, 65–71.

——. 1813b. "Dritter Zuruf an die Deutschen in Amerika." *Evangelisches Magazin, unter der Aufsicht der Deutschen Evangelisch-lutherischen Synode* (1811–1817), April 1, 1813, 174–177.

Historical Society of York County. 1966. *Lewis Miller: Sketches and Chronicles. The Reflections of a Nineteenth-Century Pennsylvania German Folk Artist.* York, PA: Historical Society of York County.

Hoberg, Rudolf. 2000. "Sprechen wir bald alle Denglisch oder Germeng?" In *Die deutsche Sprache zur Jahrtausendwende. Sprachkultur oder Sprachverfall?*, ed. Karin Eichhoff-Cyrus and Rudolf Hoberg, 303–316. Mannheim: Duden.

Hohman, Johann Georg. 1820. *Der lange verborgene Freund.* Reading, PA. N.p.

——. 2012. *Ein Freund in der Noth; or, The Friend in Need.* An annotated translation of an early Pennsylvania folk-healing manual. Introduction, translation, and annotations by Patrick J. Donmoyer. Kutztown, PA: Pennsylvania German Cultural Heritage Center, Kutztown University of Pennsylvania.

Hoover, Amos B. 1982. *The Jonas Martin Era.* Denver, PA: Amos B. Hoover.

Hoover, Walter B. 1997. *The Hutterian Language.* Saskatoon: Walter B. Hoover.

Horne, Abraham Reeser. 1873. "Pennsylvania German." *Pennsylvania Dutchman* 1: 74–79.

——. 1875. *Pennsylvania German Manual.* Kutztown, PA: Urick & Gehring. 2nd ed., 1896, Allentown, PA: National Educator Print. 3rd ed., 1905. Reprint 1910, Allentown, PA: T. K. Horne.

——. 1884. "The 'How' and 'Why' of Teaching." *National Educator*, April 1, 1884, 2.

Horst, Isaac R. 2001. *Separate and Peculiar: Old Order Mennonite Life in Ontario.* Waterloo, ON: Herald Press.

Hostetler, John A. 1952. *Amish Life.* Scottdale, PA: Herald Press.

——. 1957. "Mifflin County (Pennsylvania, USA)." *Global Anabaptist Mennonite Encyclopedia Online.* Retrieved 21 February 2014, from http://gameo.org/index.php?title =Mifflin_County_(Pennsylvania,_USA)&oldid=113521.

——. 1974. *Hutterite Society.* Baltimore: Johns Hopkins University Press.

——. 1993. *Amish Society.* Baltimore: Johns Hopkins University Press.

Hostetler, John A., and Thomas J. Meyers. 2012. "Old Order Amish." *Global Anabaptist Mennonite Encyclopedia Online.* Retrieved 21 April 2014, from http://gameo.org/in dex .php?title=Old_Order_Amish&oldid=113857.

Huffines, Marion Lois. 1980a. "Pennsylvania German: Maintenance and Shift." *International Journal of the Sociology of Language* 25: 43–57.

——. 1980b. "English in Contact with Pennsylvania German." *German Quarterly* 53: 352–366.

——. 1987. "The Dative Case in Pennsylvania German: Diverging Norms in Language Maintenance and Loss." *Yearbook of German-American Studies* 22: 173–181.

——. 1989. "Case Usage among the Pennsylvania German Sectarians and Nonsectarians." In *Investigating Obsolescence: Studies in Language Contraction and Language Death*, ed. Nancy C. Dorian, 211–226. Cambridge: Cambridge University Press.

Humpa, Gregory J. 1996. "Retention and Loss of Bernese Alemannic Traits in an Indiana Amish Dialect: A Comparative Historical Study." PhD dissertation, Purdue University.

Igou, Brad. (ed.) 1999. *The Amish in Their Own Words: Amish Writings from 25 Years of Family Life Magazine.* Scottdale, PA: Herald Press.

Isaacs, Miriam. 1999. "Haredi, *haymish*, and *frim*: Yiddish Vitality and Language Choice in a Transitional Multilingual Community." *International Journal of the Sociology of Language* 138: 9–30.

"J." 1845. "Biographical Memoir of the Late Henry A. Muhlenberg." *United States Democratic Review* 16 (79): 67–78.

Jackson, Korey B. 2010. "Literatures of Language: A Literary History of Linguistics in Nineteenth-Century America." PhD dissertation, University of Michigan.

Jacobs, Neil G. 2005. *Yiddish: A Linguistic Introduction.* Cambridge: Cambridge University Press.

Johnson-Weiner, Karen M. 1989. "Keeping Dutch: Linguistic Heterogeneity and the Maintenance of Pennsylvania German in Two Old Order Communities." In *Studies on the Languages and Verbal Behavior of the Pennsylvania Germans II*, ed. Werner Enninger, Joachim Raith, and Karl-Heinz Wandt, 95–101. Stuttgart: Franz Steiner Verlag.

———. 1992. "Group Identity and Language Maintenance: The Survival of Pennsylvania German in Old Order Communities." In *Diachronic Studies on the Languages of the Anabaptists*, ed. Kate Burridge and Werner Enninger, 26–42. Bochum: Universitätsverlag Dr. N. Brockmeyer.

———. 1993. "Community Expectations and Second Language Acquisition: English as a Second Language in a Swartzentruber Amish School." *Yearbook of German-American Studies* 28: 107–117.

———. 1998. "Community Identity and Language Change in North American Anabaptist Communities." *Journal of Sociolinguistics* 2: 375–394.

———. 2007. *Train Up a Child: Old Order Amish and Mennonite Schools.* Baltimore: Johns Hopkins University Press.

Kamphoefner, Walter D. 1994. "German American Bilingualism: *Cui malo*? Mother Tongue and Socioeconomic Status among the Second Generation in 1940." *International Migration Review* 28: 846–864.

Karch, Dieter. 1973. *Gimmeldingen Kr. Neustadt an der Weinstrasse; Mutterstadt Kr. Ludwigshafen am Rhein.* Phonai, vol. 13, monograph 6. Tübingen: Max Niemeyer Verlag.

Kehr, Kurt. 1979. " 'Deutsche' Dialekte in Virginia und West Virginia (U.S.A.)." *Zeitschrift für Dialektologie und Linguistik* 46: 289–319.

Keiser, Steven Hartman. 2006. "Portable Community: The Linguistic and Psychological Reality of Midwestern Pennsylvania German." In *Language Variation and Change in the American Midland: A New Look at "Heartland" English*, ed. Thomas Murray and Beth Simon, 263–274. Amsterdam: John Benjamins.

———. 2012. *Pennsylvania German in the American Midwest.* Publications of the American Dialect Society 96. Supplement to *American Speech*, Volume 86.

Kemp, Alvin F. 1946. "The Pennsylvania German Versammlinge." *Pennsylvania German Folklore Society* 9, 187–218. Allentown, PA: Schlechter's.

Kersten, Holger. 1996. "Using the Immigrant's Voice: Humor and Pathos in Nineteenth-Century 'Dutch' Dialect Texts." *MELUS* 21 (4): 3–17.

———. 2000. "The Creative Potential of Dialect Writing in Later-Nineteenth-Century America." *Nineteenth-Century Literature* 55: 92–117.

Kieffer, Elizabeth Clarke. 1945. *Henry Harbaugh, Pennsylvania Dutchman, 1817–1867.* Vol. 51 of *Pennsylvania German Society*. Norristown: Pennsylvania German Society.

Kipper, Heinrich. 1925. *Die Enterbten*. Vienna: Österreichischer Bundesverlag.

Klees, Fredric. 1950. *The Pennsylvania Dutch*. New York: MacMillan.

Klinefelter, Walter. 1973. *The A B C Books of the Pennsylvania Germans*. *Pennsylvania German Society* 7: 1–104.

Kloss, Heinz. 1931. "Die pennsylvaniadeutsche Literatur." *Mitteilungen der Deutschen Akademie* 4: 230–272.

———. 1957. "En Bissel Wollenweberisch." 'S Pennsylfawnisch Deitsch Eck. *Morning Call*, October 19, 1957.

Knauss, James Owen, Jr. 1922. *Social Conditions among the Pennsylvania Germans in the Eighteenth Century, as Revealed in the German Newspapers Published in America*. Lancaster: Pennsylvania German Society.

Kollmorgen, Walter M. 1942. "The Pennsylvania German Farmer." In *The Pennsylvania Germans*, ed. Ralph Wood, 27–55. Princeton: Princeton University Press.

Kopp, Achim. 1999. *The Phonology of Pennsylvania German English as Evidence of Language Maintenance and Shift*. Selinsgrove, PA: Susquehanna University Press.

———. 2010. "Abraham Reeser Horne's *Pennsylvania German Manual*." *Yearbook of German-American Studies* 45: 107–127.

Krahn, Cornelius, Harold S. Bender, and John J. Friesen. 1989. "Migrations." *Global Anabaptist Mennonite Encyclopedia Online*. Retrieved 20 April 2014, from http://gameo .org/index.php?title=Migrations&oldid=113734.

Kratz, Henry, and Humphrey Milnes. 1953. "Kitchener German: A Pennsylvania German Dialect." *Modern Language Quarterly* 14: 274–283.

Kraybill, Donald B. 2008. *The Amish of Lancaster County*. Mechanicsburg, PA: Stackpole Books.

Kraybill, Donald B., and Carl Desportes Bowman. 2001. *On the Backroad to Heaven: Old Order Hutterites, Mennonites, Amish, and Brethren*. Baltimore: Johns Hopkins University Press.

Kraybill, Donald B., and James P. Hurd. 2006. *Horse-and-Buggy Mennonites: Hoofbeats of Humility in a Post-Modern World*. University Park: Pennsylvania State University Press.

Kraybill, Donald B., Karen M. Johnson-Weiner, and Steven M. Nolt. 2013. *The Amish*. Baltimore: Johns Hopkins University Press.

Kraybill, Donald B., Steven M. Nolt, and David L. Weaver-Zercher. 2010a. *The Amish Way: Patient Faith in a Perilous World*. San Francisco: John Wiley & Sons.

———. 2010b. *Amish Grace: How Forgiveness Transcended Tragedy*. San Francisco: John Wiley & Sons.

Kreider, Mary C. 1957. "Languages and Folklore of the 'Hoffmansleit' (United Christians)." MA thesis, Pennsylvania State University.

———. 1962. "'Dutchified English'—Some Lebanon Valley Examples." *Pennsylvania Folklife* 12: 40–45.

Kriebel, H. W. 1908. "Godlove S. Orth." *The Pennsylvania-German* 9: 435–442.

Kuhns, Otto. 1900. *The German and Swiss Settlements of Pennsylvania: A Study of the So-Called Pennsylvania Dutch*. New York: Henry Holt.

Kurath, Hans, and Raven I. McDavid Jr. 1961. *The Pronunciation of English in the Atlantic States*. Tuscaloosa: University of Alabama Press.

Kutztown Centennial Association. 1915. *The Centennial History of Kutztown, Pennsylvania*. Kutztown, PA: Kutztown Publishing.

Kyger, M. Ellsworth. 1964. "Variants in the Pennsylvania German Dialect Spoken in the Valley of Virginia and Nearby Sections." In *The Pennsylvania Germans of the Shenandoah Valley*, ed. Elmer L. Smith, John G. Stewart, and M. Ellsworth Kyger, 243–278. Allentown, PA: Schlechter's.

Labov, William. 2001. *Principles of Linguistic Change*. Vol. 2, *Social Factors*. Malden, MA: Blackwell.

———. 2006. *The Social Stratification of English in New York City*. Cambridge: Cambridge University Press.

Lambert, Marcus Bachman. 1977. *Pennsylvania-German Dictionary*. Exton, PA: Schiffer.

Learned, Marion Dexter. 1888/1889. "The Pennsylvania German Dialect." *American Journal of Philology* 9: 64–83, 178–197, 326–339, 425–456, 517; 10: 288–315.

Leland, Charles G. 1871. *Hans Breitmann's Ballads*. Philadelphia: T. B. Peterson & Brothers.

Light, Joseph H. 1928. *Der Alt Schuhlmeshter*. Lebanon, PA: Frank G. Light.

Lockyer, Timothy J. 1979. "Walking with the Lord: Rachel Bahn." *Pennsylvania Magazine of History and Biography* 103: 484–496.

Loewen, Jacob A. 1986. "The German Language, Culture, and Faith." Unpublished paper presented at the conference "Dynamics of Faith and Culture in Mennonite Brethren History," Centre for Mennonite Brethren Studies, Winnipeg, MB, 14–15 November 1986.

Loewen, Royden, and Steven M. Nolt. 2012. *Seeking Places of Peace*. Intercourse, PA: Good Books.

Löher, Franz. 1847. *Geschichte und Zustände der Deutschen in Amerika*. Cincinnati: Eggers & Wullkop.

Louden, Mark L. 1992. "Old Order Amish Verbal Behavior as a Reflection of Cultural Convergence." In *Diachronic Studies on the Languages of the Anabaptists*, ed. Kate Burridge and Werner Enninger, 264–278. Bochum: Universitätsverlag Dr. N. Brockmeyer.

———. 1997. "Linguistic Structure and Sociolinguistic Identity in Pennsylvania German." In *Languages and Lives: Essays in Honor of Werner Enninger*, ed. James Dow and Michèle Wolff, 79–91. New York: Peter Lang.

———. 2001. "The Development of Pennsylvania German Linguistics within the Context of General Dialectology and Linguistic Theory." In *A Word Atlas of Pennsylvania German*, by Lester W. J. Seifert, 7–52. Madison, WI: Max Kade Institute.

———. 2003a. "An Eighteenth-Century View of Pennsylvania German and Its Speakers." In *German Language Varieties Worldwide: Internal and External Perspectives,* ed. William D. Keel and Klaus J. Mattheier, 69–85. Frankfurt am Main: Peter Lang.

———. 2003b. "Minority-Language 'Maintenance by Inertia': Pennsylvania German among Nonsectarian Speakers." In *"Standardfragen": Soziolinguistische Perspektiven auf Sprachgeschichte, Sprachkontakt und Sprachvariation,* ed. Jannis K. Androutsopoulos and Evelyn Ziegler, 121–137. Frankfurt am Main: Peter Lang.

———. 2003c. "Edward Henry Rauch." *Pennsylvania German Review,* Fall 2003, 27–40.

———. 2006. "Edward H. Rauch's *Pennsylvania Dutch Hand-Book.*" In *Preserving Heritage: A Festschrift for C. Richard Beam,* ed. Joshua R. Brown and Leroy T. Hopkins Jr., supplement, *Yearbook of German-American Studies* 2: 111–122.

———. 2008. "Die Alde un Neie Zeide: Old and New Times for the Pennsylvania Dutch Language." *Der Reggeboge: Journal of the Pennsylvania German Society* 42 (2): 3–18.

———. 2011a. "Amerikanisches Missingsch: syntaktische Folgen des Kontakts zwischen Niederdeutsch und Hochdeutsch in Wisconsin." In *Dynamik des Dialekts—Wandel und Variation: Akten des 3. Kongresses der Internationalen Gesellschaft für Dialektologie des Deutschen (IGDD),* ed. Elvira Glaser, Jürgen Erich Schmidt, and Natascha Frey, 207–220. Stuttgart: Franz Steiner Verlag.

———. 2011b. "Synchrony and Diachrony of Verb Clusters in Pennsylvania Dutch." In *Studies on German-Language Islands,* ed. Michael T. Putnam, 59–76. Philadelphia: John Benjamins.

Ludwig, G. M. 1947. "The Influence of the Pennsylvania Dutch in the Middle West." *Yearbook of the Pennsylvania German Folklore Society* 10: 1–101.

Luebke, Frederick C. 1990. *Germans in the New World: Essays in the History of Immigration.* Urbana: University of Illinois Press.

MacMaster, Richard K. 1985. *Land, Piety, and Peoplehood: The Establishment of Mennonite Communities in America, 1683–1790.* Scottdale, PA: Herald Press.

MacSwan, Jeff. 2000. "The Threshold Hypothesis, Semilingualism, and Other Contributions to a Deficit View of Linguistic Minorities." *Hispanic Journal of Behavioral Sciences* 22: 3–45.

Maier, Emanuel. 1975. "Torah as Movable Territory." *Annals of the Association of American Geographers* 65: 18–23.

Martin, Helen Reimensnyder. 1904. *Tillie: A Mennonite Maid.* New York: Century.

———. 1913. "American Backgrounds for Fiction—I: The Pennsylvania 'Dutch.'" *Bookman,* November 1913, 244–247.

Martin-Jones, Marilyn, and Suzanne Romaine. 1986. "Semilingualism: A Half-Baked Theory of Communicative Competence." *Applied Linguistics* 7: 26–38.

Mast, C. Z. 1953. "Berks County (Pennsylvania, USA)." *Global Anabaptist Mennonite Encyclopedia Online.* Retrieved 15 January 2014, from http://gameo.org/index.php?title=Berks_County_(Pennsylvania,_USA)&oldid=91061.

Maurer, Charles Lewis. 1932. *Early Lutheran Education in Pennsylvania.* Philadelphia: Dorrance.

Mays, George. 1904. *Why the Pennsylvania German Still Prevails in the Eastern Section of the State.* Reading, PA: Daniel Miller.

McCarthy, John A. 2001. "'An Indigenous and Not an Exotic Plant': Toward a History of Germanics at Penn." In *Teaching German in Twentieth-Century America*, ed. David Bensler, Craig W. Nickisch, and Cora Lee Nollendorfs, 146–172. Madison: University of Wisconsin Press.

Mencken, H. L. 1965. *The American Language*. New York: Alfred A. Knopf.

Miller, D. 2013a. *Pennsylvania German Dictionary*. Chesterbrook, PA[?]: Deitsh Books.

———. 2013b. *Pennsylvania German Phrases*. Chesterbrook, PA[?]: Deitsh Books.

———. 2014. *Pennsylvania German: Vitt Du Deitsh Shvetza?* Chesterbrook, PA[?]: Deitsh Books.

Miller, Daniel. (ed.) 1903. *Pennsylvania German*. Reading, PA: Daniel Miller.

———. (ed.) 1904. *Pennsylvania German*. 2nd ed. Reading, PA: Daniel Miller.

———. (ed.) 1911. *Pennsylvania German*. Vol. 2. Reading, PA: Daniel Miller.

Miller, Emanuel, and Ben J. Raber. (eds.) 1976. *Von dem Christlichen Glauben und Leiden Jesu Christi*. Baltic, OH: Raber's Book Store.

Miller, Harvey. 1906. *Pennsylvania German Poems*. Elizabethville, PA: Hawthorne Press.

———. 1907. *Pennsylvania German Stories*. Elizabethville, PA: Hawthorne Press.

———. 1911. *Pennsylvania German Stories: Prose and Poetry*. Elizabethville, PA: Hawthorne Press.

———. 1939. *G'shbos und Arnsht*. Elizabethville, PA: Hawthorne Press.

Miller, Ivan J. 1959. "Somerset County (Pennsylvania, USA)." *Global Anabaptist Mennonite Encyclopedia Online*. Retrieved 5 February 2014, from http://gameo.org/index .php?title=Somerset_County_(Pennsylvania,_USA)&oldid=112648.

Miller, Lynn Marcus. 2014 (rev. 2015). *Ferwass mer Deitsch Schwetze dun* [Why we speak German]. Arthur, IL: n.p.

Miller, Mary N. (ed.) 2008. *Our Heritage, Hope, and Faith*. Topeka, IN: Mary N. Miller.

Moelleken, Wolfgang W. 1988. "Linguistic Atlas of Pennsylvania German." *Monatshefte* 80: 105–114.

———. 1992. "The Development of the Linguistic Repertoire of the Mennonites from Russia." In *Diachronic Studies on the Languages of the Anabaptists*, ed. Kate Burridge and Werner Enninger, 64–93. Bochum: Universitätsverlag Dr. N. Brockmeyer.

Montgomery, Michael. 1998. "In the Appalachians They Speak Like Shakespeare." In *Language Myths*, ed. Laurie Bauer and Peter Trudgill, 66–76. London: Penguin Books.

Morgan, Edmund S. (ed.) 2006. *Not Your Usual Founding Father: Selected Readings from Benjamin Franklin*. New Haven: Yale University Press.

Mowatt, James Alexander. 1873. "Local Prohibition in Pennsylvania." *Christian Union*, May 21, 1873, 404–405.

Muhlenberg, Frederick A. C. 1795. *Rede vor der incorporirten Deutschen Gesellschaft in Philadelphia, im Staat Pennsylvanien, am 20sten September, 1794*. Philadelphia: Steiner und Kämmerer.

Nadler, Karl G. 1847. *Fröhlich Palz, Gott erhalts! Gedichte in Pfälzer Mundart*. Frankfurt am Main: H. L. Brönner.

Nettle, Daniel, and Suzanne Romaine. 2000. *Vanishing Voices: The Extinction of the World's Languages*. New York: Oxford University Press.

Newman, Paul Douglas. 2005. *Fries's Rebellion: The Enduring Struggle for the American Revolution.* Philadelphia: University of Pennsylvania Press.

Nollendorfs, Cora Lee. 1988. "The First World War and the Survival of German Studies." In *Teaching German in America*, ed. David P. Benseler et al., 176–196. Madison: University of Wisconsin Press.

Nolt, Steven M. 2002. *Foreigners in Their Own Land: Pennsylvania Germans in the Early Republic.* University Park: Pennsylvania State University Press.

———. 2003. *A History of the Amish.* Rev. and updated ed. Intercourse, PA: Good Books.

Oberholtzer, John H. 1937. "A Letter from John H. Oberholtzer to Friends in Germany, 1849." *Mennonite Quarterly Review* 11: 156–162.

Old Colony Mennonite Support. 2011. *Called to Mexico: Bringing Hope and Literacy to the Old Colony Mennonites.* Walnut Creek, OH: Carlisle.

1001 Questions and Answers on the Christian Life. 1992. Aylmer, ON: Pathway.

Page, Eugene R. 1937. "English in the Pennsylvania German Area." *American Speech* 12: 203–206.

Peabody, Elizabeth. 1859. *Memorial of Dr. William Wesselhöft.* Boston: Nathaniel C. Peabody.

"Pennsylvania Dutch." 1872. *Der Deutsche Pionier* 4: 218–220, 249–251, 272–277.

Pennsylvania German Folklore Society. 1936. *The Pennsylvania German Folklore Society.* Vol. 1. Allentown, PA: Schlechter's.

Pennsylvania German Society. 1891. *Proceedings and Addresses.* Vol. 1. Lancaster: Pennsylvania German Society.

———. 1893. *Proceedings and Addresses.* Vol. 3, 171–174. Lancaster: Pennsylvania German Society.

Pennypacker, Samuel W. 1918. *The Autobiography of a Pennsylvanian.* Philadelphia: John C. Winston.

Penzl, Herbert. 1938a. "A Pennsylvania German 'Sprachinsel' near Arthur, Illinois." 'S Pennsylfawnisch Deitsch Eck. *Morning Call*, March 12, 1938.

———. 1938b. "Lehnwörter mit ä vor r im Pennsylvanisch-Deutschen Dialekt." *Journal of English and Germanic Philology* 37: 396–402.

Pinker, Steven. 1994. *The Language Instinct: How the Mind Creates Language.* New York: Harper Perennial Modern Classics.

Post, Rudolf. 1992. *Pfälzisch: Einführung in eine Sprachlandschaft.* 2nd ed. Landau / Pfalz, Germany: Pfälzische Verlagsanstalt.

Pulte, William J., Jr. 1971. "German in Virginia and West Virginia." In *The German Language in America: A Symposium*, ed. Glenn G. Gilbert, 58–69. Austin: University of Texas Press.

Purvis, Thomas L. 1987. "Patterns of Ethnic Settlement in Late Eighteenth-Century Pennsylvania." *Western Pennsylvania Historical Magazine* 70: 107–122.

Raith, Joachim. 1981. "Phonologische Interferenzen im amerikanischen Englisch der anabaptistischen Gruppen in Lancaster County (Pennsylvania). Unter Berücksichtigung von Sprachgemeinschaftstyp und Erwerbskontext." *Zeitschrift für Dialektologie und Linguistik* 48: 35–52.

Raith, Joachim, and Uwe Lehmann. 1989. "The Pronunciation of Amish High German." In *Studies on the Languages and the Verbal Behavior of the Pennsylvania Germans II,* ed. Werner Enninger, Joachim Raith, and Karl-Heinz Wandt, 81–93. Stuttgart: Franz Steiner Verlag.

Rash, Felicity. 1998. *The German Language in Switzerland: Multilingualism, Diglossia, and Variation.* Bern: Peter Lang.

Rauch, Edward H. 1873. "Litiz." *Pennsylvania Dutchman* 1: 55–58.

———. 1879. *Rauch's Pennsylvania Dutch Hand-Book: A Book for Instruction.* Mauch Chunk, PA: E. H. Rauch.

Redekop, Calvin Wall. 1969. *The Old Colony Mennonites: Dilemmas of Ethnic Minority Life.* Baltimore: Johns Hopkins University Press.

Reed, Carroll E. 1941. "The Pennsylvania German Dialect Spoken in the Counties of Lehigh and Berks: Phonology and Morphology." PhD dissertation, Brown University.

Reichard, Harry Hess. 1918. *Pennsylvania-German Dialect Writings and Their Writers.* Vol. 26 of *Pennsylvania German Society.* Lancaster: Pennsylvania German Society.

———. 1940. *Pennsylvania German Verse. An Anthology of Representative Selections in the Dialect Popularly Known as Pennsylvania Dutch with an Introduction.* Vol. 48 of *Pennsylvania German Society.* Norristown, PA: Pennsylvania German Society.

Rein, Kurt. 1977. *Religiöse Minderheiten als Sprachgemeinschaftsmodelle: Deutsche Sprachinseln täuferischen Ursprungs in den Vereinigten Staaten von Amerika.* Wiesbaden: Franz Steiner Verlag.

Reschly, Steven. 2000. *The Amish on the Iowa Prairie, 1840 to 1910.* Baltimore: Johns Hopkins University Press.

Rickford, John R. 2005. "Using the Vernacular to Teach the Standard." In *Ebonics: The Urban Education Debate.* 2nd ed., ed. J. David Ramirez, Terrence G. Wiley, Gerda de Klerk, Enid Lee, and Wayne E. Wright, 18–40. Cleveland, OH: Multilingual Matters.

Rickford, John Russell, and Russell John Rickford. 2000. *Spoken Soul: The Story of Black English.* New York: John Wiley & Sons.

Robacker, Earl F. 1943. *Pennsylvania German Literature: Changing Trends from 1683 to 1942.* Philadelphia: University of Pennsylvania Press.

Roeber, Anthony Gregg. 1994. "The Mosheim Society and the Preservation of German Education and Culture in the New Republic 1789–1813." In *German Influences on Education in the United States,* ed. Henry Geitz, Jürgen Heideking, and Jürgen Herbst, 157–176. Cambridge: Cambridge University Press.

Rosenberger, Homer Tope. 1966. *The Pennsylvania Germans 1891–1965 (Frequently Known as the "Pennsylvania Dutch").* Vol. 63 of *Pennsylvania German Society.* Lancaster: Pennsylvania German Society.

Roth, Cecil. 1953. *History of the Jewish People.* London: East and West Library.

Runyeon, Mildred. 1936. "Pennsylvania-German in the 'Reading Adler': 1837–1857." MA thesis, Pennsylvania State University.

Rupp, Israel Daniel. 1844. *History of the Counties of Berks and Lebanon.* Lancaster, PA: G. Hills.

———. 1870. "Eppes über Pennsylvanisch-Deutsch." *Der Deutsche Pionier* 2: 307–309.

Russ, Willam A., Jr. 1940. "The Political Ideas of George Kremer." *Pennsylvania History* 7: 201–212.

Salmons, Joseph. 2002. "The Shift from German to English, World War I, and the German-Language Press in Wisconsin." In *Menschen zwischen zwei Welten: Auswanderung, Ansiedlung, Akkulturation*, ed. Walter G. Rödel and Helmut Schmahl, 179–193. Trier: Wissenschaftlicher Verlag Trier.

———. 2013. *A History of German: What the Past Reveals about Today's Language*. Oxford: Oxford University Press.

Schaller, Susan. 1991. *A Man without Words*. New York: Summit Books.

Schiffman, Harold. 1987. "Losing the Battle for Balanced Bilingualism: The German-American Case." *Language Problems and Language Planning* 11: 66–81.

Schlabach, Theron F. 1988. *Peace, Faith, Nation. Mennonites and Amish in Nineteenth-Century America*. Scottdale, PA: Herald Press.

Schmitz, J. H. (ed.) 1856. *Sitten und Sagen, Lieder, Sprüchwörter und Räthsel des Eifler Volkes*. Vol. 1. Trier: Fr. Lintz'sche Buchhandlung.

Schöpf, Johann David. 1788. *Reise durch einige der mittlern und südlichen vereinigten nordamerikanischen Staaten nach Ost-Florida und den Bahama-Inseln unternommen in den Jahren 1783 und 1784*. Vol. 1. Erlangen: Johann Jacob Palm.

Seidensticker, Oswald. 1889. "Frederick Augustus Conrad Muhlenberg, Speaker of the House of Representatives, in the First Congress, 1789." *Pennsylvania Magazine of History and Biography* 13: 184–206.

Seifert, Lester W. J. 1941. "The Pennsylvania German Dialect Spoken in the Counties of Lehigh and Berks: Vocabulary." PhD dissertation, Brown University.

———. 1946. "Lexical Differences between the Four Pennsylvania German Regions." *Pennsylvania German Folklore Society* 11: 155–176.

———. 1971. "The Word Geography of Pennsylvania German: Extent and Causes." In *The German Language in America: A Symposium*, ed. Glenn G. Gilbert, 14–42. Austin: University of Texas Press.

———. 2001. *A Word Atlas of Pennsylvania German*, ed. Mark L. Louden, Howard Martin, and Joseph C. Salmons. Madison, WI: Max Kade Institute.

Shelly, Maynard. 2002. "Creating the Wadsworth Mennonite Seminary." *Mennonite Life* 57 (4).

Shimmell, L. S. 1907. "The Pennsylvania-Germans and the Common-School Law of 1834." *The Pennsylvania-German* 8: 571–577.

Shoemaker, Alfred L. 1940. "Studies on the Pennsylvania German Dialect of the Amish Community in Arthur, Illinois." PhD dissertation, University of Illinois.

———. 1949. "Rauch's Dialect Writings." *Pennsylvania Dutchman*, July 7, 1949, p. 1.

———. 1951a. "Early Use of Dialect." *Pennsylvania Dutchman*, January 15, 1951, 7.

———. 1951b. *Three Myths about the Pennsylvania Dutch Country*. Lancaster: Pennsylvania Dutch Folklore Center.

———. 1953. *Hex, No!* Lancaster: Pennsylvania Dutch Folklore Center.

———. 2000. *Eastertide in Pennsylvania*. With a foreword and afterword by Don Yoder. Mechanicsburg, PA: Stackpole Books.

————. 2009. *Christmas in Pennsylvania*. 50th anniversary ed. With an introduction and afterword by Don Yoder. Mechanicsburg, PA: Stackpole Books.

Shoemaker, Alfred L., and Don Yoder. 1955. *1955 Tourist Guide through the Dutch Country*. Lancaster: Pennsylvania Dutch Folklore Center.

Shoemaker, Henry W. 1926. "The Language of Pennsylvania German Gypsies." *American Speech* 1: 584–586.

————. 1930. *Thirteen Hundred Old Time Words of British, Continental or Aboriginal Origins, Still or Recently in Use among the Pennsylvania Mountain People*. Altoona, PA: Times Tribune Press.

Shryock, Richard H. 1939. "The Pennsylvania Germans in American History." *Pennsylvania Magazine of History and Biography* 43: 261–281.

Siemens, Heinrich. 2012. *Plautdietsch: Grammatik, Geschichte, Perspektiven*. Bonn: tweeback verlag.

Stahr, J. S. 1870. "Pennsylvania German." *Mercersburg Review*, October 1870, 618–634.

States Publications Society. 1921. *Pennsylvania in the World War: An Illustrated History of the Twenty-eighth Division*. Vol. 2. Pittsburgh: States Publications Society.

Stein, Kurt M. 1925. *Die Schönste Lengevitch*. Chicago: Pascal Covici.

————. 1927. *Gemixte Pickles*. Chicago: Pascal Covici.

————. 1932. *Limburger Lyrics*. New York: Covici-Friede.

Stine, Clyde S. 1938. "Problems of Education among the Pennsylvania Germans." PhD dissertation, Cornell University.

————. 1942. "Pennsylvania Germans and the School." In *The Pennsylvania Germans*, ed. Ralph Wood, 103–127. Princeton: Princeton University Press.

Stoll, Elmo. n.d. "The Language Barrier." N.p.

Stoll, Joseph. 1997. *The Amish in Daviess County, Indiana*. Aylmer, ON: Joseph Stoll.

Stoltzfus, Christian J. (ed.) 1984. *Golden Memories of Amos J. Stoltzfus*. Gordonville, PA: Pequea.

Stoltzfus, Lillian. 2013. *Speaking Amish: A Beginner's Introduction to Pennsylvania German*. Bird-in-Hand, PA: Eckschank.

Struble, George G. 1935. "The English of the Pennsylvania Germans." *American Speech* 10: 163–172.

Sutro, Theodor. 1912. "Germania und Columbia." *Penn Germania*, March 1912, title page.

Swartzendruber, A. Lloyd. 1956. "Guengerich, Samuel D. (1836–1929)." *Global Anabaptist Mennonite Encyclopedia Online*. Retrieved 21 April 2014, from http://gameo.org/index.php?title=Guengerich,_Samuel_D._(1836-1929)&oldid=113400.

Thompson, Chad L. 1994. "The Languages of the Amish of Allen County, Indiana: Multilingualism and Convergence." *Anthropological Linguistics* 36: 69–91.

Trexler, Benjamin F. 1880–1886. "Die Schreckenszeit von '99." In *Skizzen aus dem Lecha-Thale*, ed. Benjamin F. Trexler, 251–259. Allentown: Trexler & Härtzell.

Troxell, William S. (ed.) 1938. *Aus Pennsylfawnia: An Anthology of Translations into the Pennsyvania German Dialect*. Philadelphia: University of Pennsylvania Press.

Umble, John S., and Samuel L. Yoder. 2011. "Lancaster-Chester Counties Old Order Amish Settlement (Pennsylvania, USA)." *Global Anabaptist Mennonite Encyclopedia Online*.

Retrieved 14 April 2014, from http://gameo.org/index.php?title=Lancaster-Chester
_Counties_Old_Order_Amish_Settlement_(Pennsylvania,_USA)&oldid=121198.

Van Deusen-Scholl, Nelleke. 2003. "Toward a Definition of Heritage Language: Sociopo-
litical and Pedagogical Considerations." *Journal of Language, Identity, and Education*
2: 211–230.

Van Ness, Silke. 1990. *Changes in an Obsolescing Language: Pennsylvania German in West
Virginia.* Tübingen: Gunter Narr Verlag.

Veith, Werner H. 1968. "Pennsylvaniadeutsch: Ein Beitrag zur Entstehung von Sied-
lungsmundarten." *Zeitschrift für Mundartforschung* 35: 254–283.

Vella Deitsh. 1997. *Vella Laysa: Bivvel Shtoahris Fa Kinnah. (Let's Read: Bible Stories for
Children).* Sugarcreek, OH: Schlabach.

Watrous, Jerome A. (ed.) 1909. *Memoirs of Milwaukee County.* Vol. 2. Madison: Western
Historical Association.

Weaver-Zercher, David L. 2001. *The Amish in the American Imagination.* Baltimore:
Johns Hopkins University Press.

Weber, Samuel Edwin. 1905. *The Charity School Movement in Colonial Pennsylvania.*
PhD dissertation, University of Pennsylvania. Philadelphia: George F. Lasher.

Weinstein, Miriam. 2001. *Yiddish: A Nation of Words.* New York: Ballantine Books.

Weiser, C. Z. 1899/2004. *The Life of (John) Conrad Weiser, the German Pioneer, Patriot,
and Patron of Two Races.* Reading, PA: Daniel Miller. Reprint Whitefish, MT: Kes-
singer.

Weitzel, Louise A. 1931. *Shpecktakel.* Lititz, PA: Record.

Wellenreuther, Hermann. 2013. *Citizens in a Strange Land: A Study of German-American
Broadsides and Their Meaning for Germans in North America, 1730–1830.* University
Park: Pennsylvania State University Press.

Wenger, John C. 1937. *History of the Mennonites of the Franconia Conference.* Telford, PA:
Franconia Mennonite Historical Society.

———. 2002. "Old Order Mennonites." *Global Anabaptist Mennonite Encyclopedia Online.* Retrieved 21 April 2014, from http://gameo.org/index.php?title=Old_Order
_Mennonites&oldid=113859.

Wenger, Marion Roy. 1969. "A Swiss-German Dialect Study: Three Linguistic Islands in
Midwestern U.S.A." PhD dissertation, Ohio State University.

Weygandt, Cornelius J. 1938. *Philadelphia Folks.* New York: D. Appleton / Century.

White, Thomas. 2012. "'Languages for America': Dialects, Race, and National Identity
in Nineteenth-Century American Literature." PhD dissertation, University of Oklahoma.

Wittke, Carl F. 1936. *German-Americans and the World War.* Columbus: Ohio State Ar-
chaeological and Historical Society.

Wokeck, Marianne S. 1999. *Trade in Strangers: The Beginnings of Mass Migration to North
America.* University Park: Pennsylvania State University Press.

Wolfram, Walt, and Natalie Schilling-Estes. 1998. *American English: Dialects and Variation.* Oxford: Blackwell.

Wollenweber, Ludwig A. 1869. *Gemälde aus dem Pennsylvanischen Volksleben: Schilderungen und Aufsätze in poetischer und prosaischer Form, in Mundart und Ausdruckweise der Deutsch-Pennsylvanier.* Philadelphia and Leipzig: Schäfer & Koradi.

———. 1977. *Aus den Aufzeichnungen von L. A. Wollenweber über seine Erlebnisse in Amerika, namentlich in Philadelphia.* Pennsylvania Dutch Studies 10. Collegeville PA: Institute on Pennsylvania Dutch Studies. Reprinted from *Mitteilungen des Deutschen Pionier-Vereins von Philadelphia,* 1909–1910.

Wood, Ralph Charles. 1940. "*Der Bauernfreund*: A Newspaper of the Pennsylvania-Germans." *Bulletin of the Historical Society of Montgomery County, Pennsylvania* 2: 175–213.

———. 1942. "Lutheran and Reformed, Pennsylvania German Style." In *The Pennsylvania Germans,* ed. Ralph Wood, 85–102. Princeton: Princeton University Press.

———. 1945. "Pennsylvania 'High German.'" *Germanic Review* 20: 299–314.

———. 1968. "The Four Gospels Translated into the Pennsylvania German Dialect." *Publications of the Pennsylvania German Society* 1, 3–184. Allentown: Pennsylvania German Society.

Yoder, Don. 1980. "Palatine, Hessian, Dutchman: Three Images of the German in America." In *Ebbes fer Alle-Ebber—Ebbes fer Dich: Something for Everyone—Something for You,* ed. Albert F. Buffington et al., 105–129. Breinigsville, PA: Pennsylvania German Society.

———. 1988. "The 'Dutchman' and the 'Deitschlenner': The New World Confronts the Old." *Yearbook of German-American Studies* 23: 1–17.

———. 1992. "The Reformed Church and Pennsylvania German Identity." *Der Reggeboge: Journal of the Pennsylvania German Society* 26 (2): 1–16.

———. 2001. "Sectarian Costume Research in the United States." In *Discovering American Folklife: Essays on Folk Culture and the Pennsylvania Dutch,* ed. Don Yoder, 143–171. Mechanicsburg, PA: Stackpole Books.

———. 2003. *Groundhog Day.* Mechanicsburg, PA: Stackpole Books.

———. 2005. *The Pennsylvania German Broadside: A History and Guide.* University Park: Pennsylvania State University Press.

Yoder, Don, and Thomas E. Graves. 2000. *Hex Signs: Pennsylvania Dutch Barn Symbols and Their Meaning.* Rev. and expanded 2nd ed. Mechanicsburg, PA: Stackpole Books.

Ziegler, Charles Calvin. 1891. *Drauss un deheem.* Leipzig: Hesse und Becker.

Zuccalmaglio, Anton Wilhelm von. 1840. *Deutsche Volkslieder mit ihren Original-Weisen.* Vol. 2. Berlin: Vereins-Buchhandlung.

Index

"Abendlied" (Evening song; poem), 191

Adams, Charles Follen, 215–216

Adams, John, 115, 146

Adams, John Quincy, 160

"Affirmation, An" (*Eine Beteurung*; poem), 184

African Americans: hybrid culture, 360; Pennsylvania Dutch–speaking, 54–56; speech of, represented in Pennsylvania Dutch and German, 162–164

African American Vernacular English (Black English, Ebonics), 10–11, 417n94

Afrikaans language, 375n10

agrarian spirit, and Pennsylvania Dutch identity, 71–76, 359

/ai/: in Dutchified English, 379n63; in Pennsylvania Dutch, 324

Albrecht, Johann, 108

Aleichem, Sholem, 368

Allentown, Lehigh County, PA, 122, 404n3; *Allentown Democrat*, 257–258; *Asseba un Sabina Mumbauer im Eihledaahl* broadcast from, 294; Bechtel murder case in, 252; efforts to ban German and Pennsylvania Dutch in, 255–258; German-language publishing in, 142, 143, 153, 221; Grundsow

Lodge gathering in, 289; Alfred Charles Moss from, 292, 427n101; Muhlenberg College in, 199, 218, 256, 276, 285, 411n35, 422–423n39; Elwood L. Newhard from, 292; reported use of Dutchified English in, 267; use of Pennsylvania Dutch in, 294, 421–422n27, 423n39; World War I soldiers from, 261–263

Allentown Democrat (newspaper), 257–258

almanacs, farmer's, 122

Amana German, 435n23

"America" (song), 283

American Sign Language, 53

Amish: Amish Mennonites, 309–310; in Arthur, IL, 275–276, 319, 323, 346–347; Beachy, 331; division between progressives and Old Orders, 310–311, 364, 430–431n44, 435n16; division between Swartzentrubers and Old Orders, 324; early settlement history, 382n14, 430–431n44; Lancaster vs. midwestern affiliations, 69–70; New Order, 326; Northkill (Berks County) settlement, 64, 67, 70; Old Order population and growth, 50–51, 65–67, 315, 380n72, 380n75, 382n13, 404n4;

Amish (cont.)
popular image of, 72, 423n47; Swartzentruber, 324, 352, 380n71, 380n73,
384n36, 432n76; "Swiss," 376n22, 391n2,
430–431n44. See also sectarians
Amish High German. See Pennsylvania
High German
Amish Mennonites, 309–310
"Amish 'Triple-Talk'" (scholarly article),
319–320, 343–344
/ar/, in early American English and Pennsylvania Dutch, 231–232, 395n30
Arabic language, 11–12, 28, 375n13
Asseba un Sabina Mumbauer im Eihledaahl (Asseba and Sabina Mumbauer of Owl Valley; radio show), 294
/aʊ/ (Pennsylvania Dutch diphthong), 21
Aurand, A. Monroe, Jr., 268–271, 299,
424n55
Aylmer, ON, 316

Baer, Samuel A., 220
Bahn, Rachel, 158, 242, 413n48, 418n119
Barba, Preston A.: coauthorship of
Pennsylvania Dutch grammar, 276;
and Pennsylvania Dutch spelling, xv,
377n31; publication of discovered Har-
baugh verses, 409n32; and 'S Pennsyl-
fawnisch Deitsch Eck, 276, 285, 319, 326
Barnabetta (novel), 248, 267
Bausman, Benjamin, 195–197, 221
Baver, Conrad, 157–158
Beachy Amish, 331
Beam, C. Richard, xv, 100, 276, 326
Beamesderfer, Gilbert J., 263–264
because, borrowed into Pennsylvania
Dutch, 35–36
Bechtel, Catharine, 252
Bechtel, Ernest Waldo, 413n48
Bechtel murder case, 252
Beck, Jacob M., 196–197, 411n35
Beck Academy (Lititz, PA), 204
Becker, Christian, 18–20, 377n26

Beecher, Henry Ward, 241–242
Beethoven, Ludwig van, 3
Bender, Harold S., 307, 313–316
Bender, Ruth, 425n70, 430n37
Benner, Edwin M., 137
Benner, Enos, 137, 159–160, 186, 304. See
also Der Bauern Freund
Berks County, PA, 51, 64–65, 69, 239,
245, 404n3; 1864 election in, 208–209;
African American Pennsylvania Dutch
speakers in, 54–55; Amish Northkill
settlement in, 64, 67, 70; Berks County
Zeitung, 204; English spoken in, 47,
345; migration out of, 118, 321, 391n93;
Pennsylvania Dutch varieties spoken
in, 321, 330; Reading Adler, 122; Jacob
Renno from, 157–158; sectarians in,
301, 321, 382n14; shift to English in
churches, 422–423n34; source of first
documented Pennsylvania Dutch
text, 101; Tulpehocken region in, 64,
67, 123; use of Pennsylvania Dutch in
legal proceedings, 251; and Don Yoder,
358. See also Kutztown; Wollenweber,
Ludwig A.
Berks County Zeitung (newspaper), 204
Bethlehem, Northampton and Lehigh
Counties, PA, 94–95, 292
Birlinger, Anton, 200
Birmelin, John, xv–xvii, 283
Black English, 10–11, 417n94
Bolivia, 366
Boyer, Melville J., 426n81
Breitmann's Ballads (book), 292, 414n72
Brobst, S. K., 76, 411n35, 411n36, 412n43
Brunner, Frank R., 234–235
Büchner, Georg, 429n13
Budget, The (newspaper), 326
Buehler, Allan M., 431n56
Buffington, Albert F.: coauthorship of
Pennsylvania Dutch grammar, 276;
Der Nixnutz radio program, 425n72;
documentation of regional varia-

tion in Pennsylvania Dutch, 321; and Dutchified German, 104, 336, 388n80; and Pennsylvania Dutch spelling, xv, 377n31; PhD dissertation, 276, 318, 323, 425n72

Buffington-Barba-Beam system, xiv–xvii, 377n31

Bukovina, 388n78

bundling (bed courtship), 424n52

Burns, Robert, 192

Byler, Uria R., 341–342

calque (loan translation): from English into Pennsylvania Dutch, 30, 37, 40, 97, 100, 389n86; from Pennsylvania Dutch into English, 47. *See also* Pennsylvania Dutch language: contact with English

Canada: detention of Pennsylvania Dutch speaker during World War I in, 260; migration of Hutterites to, 366; migration to Indiana from, 430–431n44; migration from Pennsylvania to, 68, 71, 253, 300, 321; Old Colony Mennonites in, 366; Old Order Mennonite life in, 431n56; Pennsylvania Dutch speakers in, 15, 50, 69, 237, 301, 326; Pennsylvania Dutch variety spoken in, 377n32, 383n17, 431n52; use of American Sign Language in, 53

case (Nominative, Accusative, Dative, Genitive): in English, 378n35; in Pennsylvania Dutch, 23–25, 322–324, 347, 352, 376n24, 431n46, 431n47, 431n52; in Pennsylvania High German, 130, 134, 308

Cather, Willa, 215

Charity School movement, 76–77, 82, 84

child-directed speech, 348–349

Christian Scientists, 357

Christian Union (periodical), 241–242

Christmas holiday, in Pennsylvania, 417n110

ch-sounds, 36–37

church people (*Kirchenleute*). *See* nonsectarians

Cist, Carl, 131

Clay, Henry, 400n55

compounding, nominal and adjectival in Pennsylvania Dutch, 37

Cookeville, TN, 316

"Country and Town" (*Busch un Schtettel*; poem), 201–202

covert prestige, 12, 118

"Crab Complains about the World, A" (*Ein Krittler klagt über die Welt*; poem), 175–176

Croll, Philip C., 241

Cushman, Joshua, 420n20

"Das Alt Schulhaus an der Krick" (poem), 135, 192, 193–195; compared to "Die Muttersprache," 333; nostalgic quality, 201–202; original compared with *Harfe* version, 197–199; and other writings by Harbaugh on school days, 410–411n34; popularity, 199–200, 409n31; reprinted and reworked by Edward H. Rauch, 212, 214–215; supplementary verses, 409–410n32

Das Christliche Volks-Blatt (The Christian people's paper; newspaper), 303–308

Das Neue ABC- und Buchstabir-Buch zum Gebrauch für Deutsche Volksschulen in Pennsylvanien und anderen Staaten (Pennsylvania German primer), 137

Dauphin County, PA, 65, 404n3; use of Pennsylvania Dutch in, 252, 295

Declaration of Independence, 130–134

Deitschlenner (nineteenth-century German Americans): attitudes toward language, 307; attitudes toward religion, 361–364; and *Deutschtum*, 11, 121; differences with Pennsylvania Dutch, 3–9, 59, 119–121, 171–174, 363–364; and German-American press, 168, 247; shift from German to English, 121; use

Deitschlenner (cont.)
of term today, 374n4. *See also* Wollen-
weber, Ludwig A.
Democratic party (Jacksonian): and
Der Bauern Freund, 160, 168, 174–175,
400n54; and Edward H. Rauch, 204,
208–210, 216–217; and William H.
Sowden, 250; strength of in Pennsyl-
vania Dutch Country, 239, 259; and
Ludwig A. Wollenweber, 182, 185
Democratic-Republican party (Jefferso-
nian), 107, 112, 115–117, 146–148
Denglish (*Denglisch*): compared with
Dutch Dialect, 215, 414n71, 414n72;
in Europe, 40, 379n56; used to mimic
Pennsylvania Dutch, 96, 102, 240
"De Olta un Neia Tzeita" (The old and
new times; speech), 277–279, 284
Der Bauern Freund (newspaper), 150,
159–177, 186, 400n54
Der Bauernstand (poetic broadside),
74–75, 86
Der Deutsche Kirchenfreund (The Ger-
man church-friend; periodical), 191
Der Deutsche Pionier (periodical),
246–247
"Der Honsworsht" (The clown; poem),
288–291
Der Lange(e) Verborgene Freund (The
long lost friend; book), 122
Der Morgenstern (Morning star; newspa-
per), 182
Der Nixnutz (radio program), 425n72
Der Religiöse Botschafter (The religious
messenger; newspaper), 303
Der Wahre Amerikaner (The true Ameri-
can; newspaper), 102–108, 111–117,
132–134, 143–149
"Desecration of the German Language,
The" (*Die Schändung der deutschen
Sprache*; poem), 7–8
Detweiler, Henry C., 285–286
Deutschtum (Germanness), 2–3, 11, 121

dialect letters, Pennsylvania Dutch, 143,
185–186, 207–208, 221
dialects: in American literature, 215; and
covert prestige, 12, 284–285; distinguished from languages, 9–12, 375n10,
375n15; European German dialects, 9,
13–15, 23, 25, 171, 376n19, 433n80; eye
dialect, 43, 112–115, 169, 170, 217, 244;
Henry Harbaugh's views on, 193; language vs. dialect status of Pennsylvania
Dutch, 9–12; North American English
dialects, 9, 48–49, 377n29, 395n30
Die Botschaft (newspaper), 326
Die Inschurens Bisness (The insurance
business; play), 291
"Die Muttersprache" (The mother tongue;
poem), 331–333
"Die Wedderberichte" (The weather re-
ports; speech), 285–288
diglossia, 11–12, 60, 152, 375n12. See also
Mudderschprooch/Muttersprache
Di Heilich Shrift (Pennsylvania Dutch
Bible translation), 326–328
Dillinger, John E., 261–262
Donner, William W., 288
Dubbs, A. J. G., 411n35
Dubbs, Joseph Henry, 199
Dunkers (Dunkards, Church of the
Brethren), 67, 299. *See also* sectarians
Dunlap, John, 130
Dutch, use of term in English, 2, 59,
373–374n3
Dutch Dialect, 215–216, 292, 414n71,
414n72, 425n73
Dutchified English (Pennsylvania Dutch
English), 40–49; 1868 poem mocking,
41–42; addressed in Horne's *Pennsylva-
nia German Manual*, 226–228; clarified
by Alfred L. Shoemaker, 274–275; com-
pared with Dutch Dialect, 215; ele-
ments from nonstandard English, 43,
49, 395n30; equated with Pennsylvania
Dutch, 247–248; lexical transfer from

Pennsylvania Dutch, 47; phonological transfer from Pennsylvania Dutch, 43, 45–47, 227, 395n30; representations in popular literature, 48–49; and sectarians, 49, 344–347; and Swartzentruber Amish, 380n71; syntactic transfer from Pennsylvania Dutch, 47–48; in writings of A. Monroe Aurand, Jr., 269–271; in writings of Phebe Earle Gibbons, 243–245, 419n10; in writings of Helen R. Martin, 248, 266–268

Dutchified German: as antecedent of language of Pennsylvania Dutch dialect letters, 207–208; compared with Pennsylvania High German, 130, 336, 389n86; in *Der Bauern Freund*, 160–161, 167, 168, 169; in early Pennsylvania newspapers, 104–108, 111–112, 143–148, 150; early use in church, 79; functions of, 118, 144–145, 175, 181; in spirituals, 283, 388n80

Dutch language. *See* Netherlandic language

Easter holiday, in Pennsylvania, 417n110
Ebonics, 10–11, 417n94
education: Charity School movement, 76–77, 82, 84; traditional Pennsylvania Dutch views on, 81–84, 109, 155, 218–219. *See also* schools
Eichhoff, Jürgen, 433n97
Ellis, Alexander J., 206–207
English language: African American Vernacular English, 10–11, 417n94; case merger in, 378n35; early German American attitudes toward, 127–130, 150–155; history compared with Pennsylvania Dutch, 206; knowledge and use of, by sectarians, 49, 341–352, 380n71, 380n73, 433n89; lexical borrowing into, 2, 29, 281, 373–374n3; movement to recognize officially in United States, 357, 433n1; North American dialects, 9, 48–49, 377n29, 395n30;

Pennsylvania Dutch language in contact with, 7–8, 28–49, 60–62, 96–101, 343–352; Pennsylvania English, 18–20, 49; Pennsylvania Mountain English, 57–59; spoken by nonsectarians, 344–346, 433n89; use in early Pennsylvania schools, 135–141. *See also* Dutchified English

"En Tremp" (A tramp; poem), 4–6
Ermentrout, John S., 220
Erstwhile Susan (play), 247–248, 267
ethnolects, 10–11
Evangelical (Reformed) Synod, shift from German to English, 434–435n14
eye dialect, 43, 112–115, 169, 170, 217, 244

fakelore, 423n54
falling question intonation, 46–47, 419n10
Fancy Dutch. *See* nonsectarians
farmer's almanacs, 122
Father Abraham (newspapers), 208–210
Federalist party, 107, 115–117, 146–148, 169
fence words in Pennsylvania Dutch, 97–100
Ferdinand I, Emperor of Austria, 238
Ferhoodled English. *See* Dutchified English
fersommling movement, 281–288
fer . . . zu construction, 47–48
Fisher, Henry Lee: defense of Pennsylvania Dutch, 60–62; and founding of Pennsylvania German Society, 277; and Henry Harbaugh, 190, 200; recollections of school days, 135–141, 151, 394n27; verbal abilities, 395n31, 395n32
Flaten, Nils, 387n72
Florida, 51, 238, 354
Fogleman, Aaron Spencer, 50, 65, 67
folk astronomy, 122
Francke Foundations, 123
Franklin, Benjamin: linguistic treatise, 395n30; views on German immigrants to colonial Pennsylvania, 76–77, 85, 88

Franklin College (Franklin and
    Marshall College): founding of, 109;
    and Henry Harbaugh, 412n44; and
    Pennsylvania Dutch Folklore Center,
    271, 319, 358
Franklin County, PA, 135, 188
Frantz, John B., 85
Franz Joseph I, Emperor of Austria, 239
Freistadt, WI, 434–435n14
French language: affected use of, 249,
    272; and Henry Harbaugh, 408n27; as
    heritage language in United States, 52,
    378n42; influence on English, 29, 34,
    40, 245, 375n15; influence on German,
    394n26; putative influence on Penn-
    sylvania Dutch, 253–254, 259; source of
    Vendu, 400n58
Frey, J. William: "Amish 'Triple-Talk' "
    article, 323, 336, 343–346, 352; descrip-
    tion of Dutchified English, 45–46; early
    Pennsylvania Dutch letter discovered
    by, 155–157; and Pennsylvania Dutch
    Folklore Center, 271, 275–276, 295, 297,
    319; PhD dissertation, 275–276, 318–321,
    424n63, 425n72, 430n40; report of
    Pennsylvania Dutch–speaking parrot,
    381n86; *That* Amazing *Pennsylvania
    Dutch Language* pamphlet, 271–274
Fries's Rebellion, 81, 385n40
Frisian language, 379n55
Fröhlich Palz, Gott erhalts (book), 222,
    415n84
Fuller, Timothy, 249
future tense, in Pennsylvania Dutch, 39.
    See also tense/aspect

Gaelic language, 53
Gay Dutch. *See* nonsectarians
Gehman, Ernest G., 427n93
*Gemälde aus dem Pennsylvanischen
    Volksleben* (Sketches of domestic life in
    Pennsylvania; book), 158, 182–188, 242
Gemeinnützige Philadelphische Corre-

spondenz (Commonly useful Phila-
    delphia correspondence; newspaper),
    88–92
gender and language use, 396n35
General Conference Mennonite Church,
    429n14
"German in This Country, The" (*Der
    hiesige Deutsche*; poem), 148–149
German language: Alemannic dialects,
    191–192, 246, 408–409n28, 430–431n44;
    in American Midwest, 52, 76, 363,
    434–435n14; English influence on, 40,
    96, 240, 379n56, 414n72; European
    dialects (High vs. Low), 9, 13–15, 23, 25,
    171, 376n19, 433n80; European standard
    variety (High German / *Hochdeutsch*),
    7, 11, 13, 134, 375n13, 376n19, 386n52,
    386n63; lexical borrowing into, 33–34,
    167; myth regarding official status in
    United States, 120, 127–129, 357; Pala-
    tine dialects, 13–18, 360; as publishing
    medium in early America, 74; as spo-
    ken by God, 82, 287, 427n93; as subject
    in modern sectarian schools, 337; Swa-
    bian dialects, 171, 196, 246, 402n65; in
    Switzerland, 11; and Union of the Ger-
    man Press of Pennsylvania, 195–197,
    207, 223; word order, 379n55. See also
    Deitschlenner; Dutchified German; Lu-
    therans; Pennsylvania Dutch language;
    Pennsylvania High German
*German or English (Deutsch oder
    Englisch*; pamphlet), 153–155
German Reformed. *See* nonsectarians
German Society of Philadelphia (Ger-
    man Society of Pennsylvania), 88, 95,
    123–127
Germantown, PA, 63, 128, 303, 381n1,
    393n17
Gibbons, Phebe Earle, 242–247, 319
Gilbert, Russell Wieder, 284–285
Gimmeldingen, Palatinate, Germany,
    17–18, 23

Goethe, Johann Wolfgang von, 3, 121, 247, 385n39

"Goose letter," 112–115, 143

Gordon, Irving, 248–249

Greek language (Classical), 40, 116, 281, 370, 420n20

Grimler, Heinrich Augustus and Hannah, 388n81

Grimler brothers, Henry and Benjamin, 104

groundhog: and Grundsow Lodges, 281, 285–287; significance in Pennsylvania Dutch culture, 426n81

Grumbine, Ezra, 288, 291

Grundsow (Groundhog) Lodges, 281, 285–287

Guardian (periodical), 41, 190, 192; as outlet for poems by Henry Harbaugh, 193, 196, 197, 199, 205, 254, 412n44

Guengerich, S. D., 308–309, 430n44

Gustav III, King of Sweden, 90

"Gypsies." *See* Romani people; She-kener

Hahnemann, Samuel, 385n39

Haldeman, Samuel Stehman, 413n59; *Pennsylvania Dutch* treatise, 28, 206–207, 212, 318; and Schöpf's "jumping stallion" sentence, 387n72, 387n73

Hamlet (play), 212–214

"Hannickel Wahrheit," 111, 208

Harbaugh, Henry: ancestry, 407n21; and Rachel Bahn, 413n48; "Country and Town," 201–202; decline of Pennsylvania Dutch during lifetime, 254, 320; early life, 135, 188–189, 394n27; and Henry Lee Fisher, 190, 200; and Phebe Earle Gibbons, 244, 419n10; *Harbaugh's Harfe*, 195–199, 221, 223; and Johann Peter Hebel, 192–193, 199, 200, 235; "Heemweh," 192, 409n31, 428n6; knowledge of German, 204–205, 308, 408n24; "The New Kind of Gentlefolk," 201–202; praise for, 222, 279; use of

Pennsylvania Dutch in public, 412n44; writings of, 189–202, 210, 232, 284, 301. *See also* "Das Alt Schulhaus an der Krick"; *Guardian*

Harbaugh's Harfe (book), 195–199, 221, 223

Haredi Jews, 53, 367–369

Harrisburger Morgenröthe (Dawn; newspaper), 131–132

Harrison, William Henry, 204

Haugen, Einar, 386n52

Hebel, Johann Peter, 192–193, 246, 408–409n28

Hebrew language, 116, 367, 370, 412n44

"Heemweh" (Homesickness; poem), 192, 409n31, 428n6

Helffrich, Johannes, 81, 385n39

Helffrich, John Heinrich, 385n39

Helffrich, William A., 80–81, 135, 361–362

Helmuth, Justus H. C.: advocacy of German language, 152–153, 155, 394n22; and founding of German-Latin school in Philadelphia, 88; and myth regarding German as official language of United States, 127–130; professorship at University of Pennsylvania, 95

Henry, Patrick, 87

Herr, Hans, 63–64

Hershberger, Henry D., 326

hex signs, 423n50

Hiester, Daniel, 127, 128

High German, 7, 11, 13, 134, 375n13, 376n19, 386n52, 386n63. *See also* Pennsylvania High German

H.M.S. Pinafore (comic opera), 291–294

Hochdeitsch (High German). *See* Pennsylvania High German

Hochdeutsch (High German), 7, 11, 13, 134, 375n13, 376n19, 386n52, 386n63

Hoffmansleit (Hoffmanites, United Christians), 46

Hohman, John George, 122

Hoover, Amos B., 311–312

Horne, Abraham Reeser: as authority on Pennsylvania Dutch, 250; criticism and defense of, 221–223, 233–235; descriptions of early Pennsylvania schools, 79–80; early life, 218; *Pennsylvania German Manual*, 218, 220–224; preference for *Pennsylvania German*, 223, 277; views on language pedagogy for Pennsylvania Dutch youth, 219–221, 224–232

Horning Mennonites, 331

Horst, Isaac R., 431n56

Hostetler, John A., 274

Houck, Henry, 250, 421n24

Huffines, Marion Lois, 344–345

Humboldt, Alexander von, 246

humility (*Demut*) vs. pride (*Hochmut*), in Old Order society, 325–326, 332–333

Hutter, Jakob, 366

Hutterite German language (*Hutterisch*), 53, 367–369, 435n23

Hutterites, 53, 366–369

Idaho, 51

immigration to America: of European Anabaptists between 1815 and 1860, 391n2, 430–431n44; of European German speakers before 1760, 13, 50, 63–68, 77–78; of European German speakers after 1760, 3, 6, 72, 76, 119–121, 171–172, 363, 391–392n3; of non–English speakers generally, 28–29, 52, 376–377n25

Indiana: German American settlement in, 120; and Godlove S. Orth, 239; Pennsylvania Dutch migration to, 180, 382n16; sectarian communities in, 69, 301, 321; Swiss and Alsatian Amish in, 376n22, 391n2, 430–431n44

infinitival complementation, 47–48

inflection: absent in speech of African American German speakers, 162, 163; of borrowed verbs in Pennsylvania Dutch, 38, 98

Iowa: European Anabaptist migration to in nineteenth century, 391n2, 430–431n44; German American settlement in, 120; and S. D. Guengerich, 308; Pennsylvania Dutch variety spoken in, 425n70, 429–430n37

Irish language, 53

Irish Travelers, 53

Jackson, Andrew, 160, 169, 259, 400n55. *See also* Democratic party (Jacksonian)

Jehovah's Witnesses, 357

Jews: Haredi Jews, 53, 367–369; migration and language, 367–369

Joseph II, Holy Roman Emperor, 90

"jumping stallion" sentence, 98, 100, 126, 215, 387n72, 387n73

Keck, David S., 232

Keiser, Steven Hartman, 365

Keller, Eli, 4–6

Kemp, Alvin F., 281

Keystone State Normal School (Kutztown, PA), 218, 219, 234

Kipper, Heinrich, 388n78

Kishacoquillas ("Big") Valley, Mifflin County, PA, 382n14

Klees, Fredric, 54, 72

Klopstock, Friedrich Gottlieb, 223

Kloss, Heinz, 405n10

Knauss, James Owen, 101

Kneule, Albrecht, 400n54

Kneule, Henry A., 400n54

Koch, James A., 426n81

Kollmorgen, Walter, 72–73

Kraybill, Donald B., 315, 424n67

Krefeld, Germany, 63

Kreider, Mary C., 46, 47–48

Kremer, George, 249, 420n20

Kriebel, Howard W., 241

Kuhl, Marcus, 88–92, 95, 121, 394n22

Kunze, John Christopher, 88, 95–96, 123, 125–126, 130

Kurrent German script, 157–158

Kutztown, Lehigh County, PA: centennial monument in, 220; Keystone State Normal School in, 218, 219, 234; Pennsylvania Dutch Folk Festival in, 295. *See also* Horne, Abraham Reeser

Labov, William, 12, 396n35

Lahn, Jacob, 108

Lancaster County, PA, 51, 63–64, 65, 127–128, 301, 404n3; Amish affiliation, 69–71, 382n14, 404n4; "Amish 'Triple-Talk'" article, 319–320, 343–344; and Gilbert J. Beamesderfer, 263; English spoken by Amish in, 345–347, 352; and Phebe Earle Gibbons, 242; and Samuel Stehman Haldeman, 206; and Helen R. Martin, 248, 266–267; Pennsylvania Dutch varieties spoken in, 36, 70–71, 313, 321–325, 379n52, 382n15, 431n58, 433n81; and "Pit Schwefflebrenner," 210; and Edward H. Rauch, 204, 210; and "Stoffel Ehrlich," 102, 108, 143; use of German in during World War I, 255, 422n34; and Ludwig A. Wollenweber, 182

language acquisition, 386n57

"Language Barrier, The" (essay), 316–318

language endangerment, 52, 355, 381n81

Latin language, 370; English words derived from, 2, 29, 40, 245, 281, 373–374n3; and Henry Harbaugh, 408n27, 412n44; on Kutztown centennial monument, 220; Simon Snyder's lack of knowledge of, 116; use in Congress, 249, 420n20

Learned, Marion Dexter, 318, 425n72

Leasa, K. Varden, 427n93

Lebanon County, PA, 51, 65, 245, 301, 404n3; African American Pennsylvania Dutch speakers in, 54–55; *Hoffmansleit* in, 46; and Henry Houck, 250; and Martha Leidig, 156–157; and Hugh Lindsay, 288; and Godlove S. Orth, 239;

Pennsylvania Dutch variety spoken in, 251–252; Tulpehocken region in, 64, 67, 123; use of German in, during World War I, 255, 422–423n34

Lehigh County, PA, 51, 65, 301, 312–313, 404n3; and William A. Helffrich, 80; 301, 361–362; and Abraham Reeser Horne, 277; Pennsylvania Dutch varieties spoken in, 319, 321–322, 327, 433n81; and Edward H. Rauch, 202; report of harassment of Pennsylvania Dutch in during World War I, 254–255; schools in, 80; and Alfred L. Shoemaker, 319; and William H. Sowden, 249–250, 420–421n23; use of German in during World War I, 422–423n34; and Ludwig A. Wollenweber, 183; and Don Yoder, 358. *See also* Allentown; Kutztown

Leidig, Martha, 155–157

Leisenring, Edward D., 221–223, 411n35

Leland, Charles Godfrey, 215

letz ('wrong'; Pennsylvania Dutch word), 83, 84, 168–169, 312

lexical borrowing, 29–30, 373n1; from English into German, 40; from English into Pennsylvania Dutch, 6–7, 29–38, 96–101, 196–199, 231, 271–272, 348–352, 378n44, 400n58, 416n88; from English into Pennsylvania High German, 132, 389n86; into English, 2, 29, 281, 373–374n3; Pennsylvania Dutch in contact with English, 7–8, 28–49, 60–62, 96–101, 343–352; Pennsylvania Dutch into Dutchified/Pennsylvania English, 47, 130, 270, 347–352, 373n1; Swadesh lists, 34–35, 378–379n49. *See also* Denglish

Lincoln, Abraham, 208–209, 216, 269

Lindsay, Hugh, 288–291

loan shift, 30, 40, 97, 104, 360, 378n43; and Pennsylvania Dutch language in contact with English, 7–8, 28–49, 60–62, 96–101, 343–352. *See also* calque; lexical borrowing

Lochemes, Michael J., 414–415n72

Lochman, George, 88–92, 95, 121, 394n22

Locke, David Ross, 216–217

Löher, Franz von, 120–121, 128–129, 182, 238

Longswamp United Church of Christ, 434n8

love, verbal expressions of among sectarians and European Germans, 432n64

Lutheran Church–Missouri Synod, 363; shift from German to English, 434–435n14

Lutherans: contact with Prussian Mennonites, 365–366; and maintenance of German, 73, 76, 82, 176–177, 434–435n14; and Henry Melchior Muhlenberg, 123, 392n11; Old, 434–435n14; and St. Michael's and Zion Church, Philadelphia, 127–128, 152, 394n22, 434n10. See also Helmuth, Justus H. C.; Lutheran Church–Missouri Synod; nonsectarians

Luther German Bible: and history of standard German, 224, 376n19; prestige of, 287; use by sectarians, 313, 315, 326, 328–329, 338

Luxembourgish language, 10

MacMaster, Richard, 65–68

Maier, Emanuel, 367

Maine, 51, 420n20

Mandarin Chinese language, 52

Mannheim, Germany, and Palatine dialect of German language, 13–18, 360. See also Palatinate region of Germany

"Marrying outside the Faith" (Vom naus Heira; newspaper article), 304–305

Martin, Helen Reimensnyder, 248, 266–268, 319, 423n47

Mauch Chunk (Jim Thorpe), PA, 204

Mays, George, 82–84, 288–291

McKean, Thomas, 107, 112, 113, 115, 117, 147, 390n91

"Meik Fuchs" (Lochemes), 414n72

Mencken, H. L., 28, 387n72

Mennonite Church: Eastern District Conference, 303; Franconia Conference, 303, 312–313; and General Conference Mennonite Church, 429n14

Mennonite Low German language (Plautdietsch), 53, 338–340, 366, 369

Mennonites: in Canada, 366, 431n56; Conservative, 345; division between progressives and Old Orders, 311–312; in early Pennsylvania, 67–68; European, 63–64; Horning, 331; Mennonite Church, 345; Old Colony, 338–341, 365–366; Old Order, 11, 24, 50, 71, 72. See also Mennonite Church; sectarians

Mercersburg (PA) Seminary, 189

Metternich, Klemens von, 238

Mexico, 338–341, 366

Mifflin County, PA, 301; Kishacoquillas ("Big") Valley in, 382n14

Miller, Heinrich, 131

Miller, Lewis, 408n26, 413n48

Moelleken, Wolfgang W., 431n49, 433n97

Moravia, 366

Moravians, 67, 94–95, 191, 386n63

Mormons, 357

Mosheim Society, von, 394n22

Moss, Alfred Charles, 292, 427n101

"Mournful Song of Oppressed Freedom, The" (Das Trauer Lied der unterdrückten Freyheit; poem), 86–87

Mozart, Wolfgang Amadeus, 3

Mudderschprooch/Muttersprache (mother tongue): and childhood, 234; compared with linguistic concept of first language (L1), 386n52; criticism of maintenance of, 313–316; "Die Muttersprache," 331–333; maintenance of and spiritual health, 75, 82, 84–85, 92, 152, 307, 313, 347–348, 353, 359; and mame-loshn, 367; and Old Colony Mennonites, 341; as synonym for ancestral heritage language, 27, 30, 90–93, 153–154, 313–314, 335

Muhlenberg, Frederick Augustus Conrad, 123, 152, 394n22; 1784 parody of Pennsylvania Dutch, 88–92, 95–97, 102, 105–106; 1794 remarks on language to German Society in Philadelphia, 123–127; and myth regarding German as an official language of the United States, 120, 127–129, 357

Muhlenberg, Henry A., 218–219, 238–241, 249, 419n1

Muhlenberg, Henry Melchior, 123, 392n11

Muhlenberg, Margaret Henrietta, 123

Muhlenberg College, 199, 218, 256, 276, 285, 411n35, 423n39

Nadler, Karl Gottfried, 222, 415n84

Native American languages, 52, 357, 380n80

Netherlandic language: ancestral language of Old Colony Mennonites, 338, 365, 435n22; distinct from Pennsylvania Dutch, 2; relationship to Afrikaans, 375n10; and *Vendu*, 400n58; word order, 379n55

Neue Philadelphische Correspondenz (newspaper), 122–123

Neue Unpartheyische Lancäster Zeitung (newspaper), 143

Neue Unpartheyische Readinger Zeitung (New independent Reading newspaper), 101–102

Nevin, John W., 412n44

New-England Primer, 137

Newhard, Elwood L., 292

New Holland, Lancaster County, PA, 107, 373n2

New Jersey, 279

"New Kind of Gentlefolk, The" (*Die neue Sart Gentleleut*; poem), 201–202

"New Year's Present, A" (*Ein Neujahrs-Geschenk*; poem), 150–152

New York City: English spoken in, 10; meeting place of Pit Schwefflebrenner and Petroleum V. Nasby, 216–217; proximity to Dutch Country, 268

New York State: Amish settlements in, 69, 361; and Michael J. Lochemes, 414n72; New Netherland settlement in, 422n31; Conrad Weiser, 382n3

Nickel Mines school shooting, 429n35

Nolt, Steven, 85–86

nonconformity, 312

nonsectarians, 50, 65; conservative faith and agrarian culture of, 72–76, 150–155, 167–168, 175–177, 359; differences with *Deitschlenner*, 171–174, 245–247, 363–364; economic prosperity of, in early nineteenth century, 121–122; and education, 76–85, 218–221; English spoken by, 344–346, 433n89; fersommling movement, 281–288; geographic separation from sectarians, 70, 301–302; holidays celebrated by, 232, 417n110; hybrid culture of, 357–360; immigration of European German speakers to America before 1760, 13, 50, 63–68, 77–78; loss of Pennsylvania Dutch, 49, 50–53, 141–142, 179–180, 200–201, 320, 382n16; migration out of Pennsylvania, 70–71, 361, 364, 382n16; moral valuation of maintenance of German/Pennsylvania Dutch, 150–155; opposition to temperance, 241–242; patriotism, 148–149, 397n40; and peasant republicanism, 85–86, 92, 118, 359; political leanings, 85–88, 160–162, 208–210, 216–217; population size, 380n78; relations with sectarians in eighteenth and early nineteenth centuries, 65–69, 299–300, 429n13; suspicion of city-dwellers/gentlefolk, 73–74, 77–78, 145–146, 150–155, 160–162, 170–174, 185–186, 201, 230; unionism, 361–362; use of Pennsylvania High German, 122–123, 142, 155–158,

nonsectarians *(cont.)*
164–168, 319; varieties of Pennsylvania
Dutch spoken by, 32–34, 321–322, 327,
433n81. *See also* Dutchified English;
groundhog; Lutherans; patriotism;
Pennsylvania Dutch language; Penn-
sylvania High German; superstitions
Nordwestliche Post (Northwestern Post;
newspaper), 20–22, 77–78, 143
Northampton County, PA, 65, 150, 199,
280, 313, 377n26, 378n47
Northkill Amish settlement, 64, 67, 70
Northumberland Republicaner (newspa-
per), 143
Norwegian language, 10, 18, 387n72
Notz, Friedrich W. A., 411n35

Oberholtzer, John H., 303–308, 326, 364;
likely acquaintance with Enos Benner,
428n11
"Oh Du Grundsow" (Oh, you groundhog; poem), 285–286
Ohio: European Anabaptist migration to, 391n2, 430–431n44; German
American settlement in, 120; and
Henry Harbaugh, 188; loss of Pennsylvania Dutch in, 382n16; Pennsylvania
Dutch–German dialogs set in, 172–174;
Pennsylvania Dutch migration to, 70,
155–156, 157, 180, 237, 300; Pennsylvania
Dutch personal correspondence from,
156–158; Pennsylvania Dutch varieties
spoken in, 326–328; sectarian communities in, 69, 118, 301, 321, 361, 382n14;
and Swartzentruber Amish, 324; Wadsworth Mennonite School, 306
"Old and New Fashion" (*Alte und Neue
Mode*; poem), 176–177
Old Colony Mennonites, 338–341,
365–366
Old Colony Mennonite Support program,
338–341

Old Order Amish, 50–51, 65–67, 315,
380n72, 380n75, 382n13, 404n4
Old Order Mennonites, 11, 24, 50, 71, 72
Ontario. *See* Canada
Orth, Godlove S., 239–241
outen the light, 49

Page, Eugene R., 44–47
Page, Patti, 248
Palatinate (*Pfalz*) region of Germany:
and Henry Harbaugh, 407n21; and
Edward D. Leisenring, 222; location
in German-speaking Europe, 339; and
Michael J. Lochemes, 414–415n72;
migration (Anabaptist) from, in nineteenth century, 391n2; migration from,
in eighteenth century, 13–14, 63, 274,
299, 312; relations between sectarians
and nonsectarians in, 300; and
Ludwig A. Wollenweber, 181
Palatine German (*Pfälzisch*), Pennsylvania Dutch language compared with,
15–18, 360
Paraguay, 366
Patch, Sam, 238
patriotism: of early nonsectarian Pennsylvania Dutch, 85–88, 92; at fersommlinge, 283; questioned during World
War I, 253–260; and sectarians, 397n40,
428n8; as theme in Pennsylvania High
German poetry, 148
peasant republicanism, 85–86, 92, 118,
359. *See also* patriotism
Pennsilfaanisch Deitsch / *Pennsylvania
Dutch* / *Pennsylvania German*, as names
for Pennsylvania Dutch language, 1–9,
205–206, 277
Pennsylvania Dutch and Other Essays
(book), 242–247
Pennsylvania Dutch culture, hybrid character of, 358–359
Pennsylvania Dutch Days, 295–296

Pennsylvania Dutch English. *See* Dutch-ified English

Pennsylvania Dutch Folk Festival (Kutztown Folk Festival), 295

Pennsylvania Dutch Folklore Center, 271–274, 295, 319

Pennsylvania Dutch Hand-Book (book), 210–214

Pennsylvania Dutch language: compared with Palatine German, 15–18, 360; compared with standard German, 23–27; contact with English, 7–8, 28–49, 60–62, 96–101, 343–352; earliest attested example in print, 101–102; in early nineteenth century, 20–23; in early Pennsylvania newspapers, 143–148; emergence in eighteenth century, 63–64, 68–71; language vs. dialect status, 9–12; maintenance/loss of, 50–53, 121–122, 179–180; morphology, 23, 37–38; mutual intelligibility of sectarian and nonsectarian varieties, 68, 70, 71; names for, 1–9, 205–206, 277; numbers of speakers, 50, 404n3; and Pennsylvania Dutch–speaking African Americans, 54–56; Pennsylvania Mountain English, 57–59; as "portable language," 360–361, 364–365; regional differences, 36, 321–322; semantics, 40; She-kener, 56–57; sounds, 16–17, 21, 36–37, 45–46; spelling, xiv–xvii, 377n31; use in politics and legal system, 249–252; vocabulary, 22–23, 29–36, 47. *See also* Dutchified English; lexical borrowing; nonsectarians; sectarians; *and particular linguistic features*

Pennsylvania Dutch Literary Society, 280–281

Pennsylvania Dutchman (nineteenth-century periodical), 202, 205–206, 211, 220–221

Pennsylvania Dutchman (twentieth-century newspaper), 271

Pennsylvania Dutch writers, profile of, 200–201, 302

Pennsylvania English, 18–20, 49; Pennsylvania Mountain English, 57–59; "The Pensilwan'yah Inglish," 41–43, 48. *See also* Dutchified English

Pennsylvania-German Dialect: Stories and Poems (pamphlet), 269

Pennsylvania German Folklore Society, 298, 425n79

Pennsylvania German language. *See* Pennsylvania Dutch language

Pennsylvania German Manual (book), 218, 220–224

Pennsylvania German Society, 277–280

Pennsylvania High German, 11–12, 19; difference from European standard German, 130–135, 389n86; in early Pennsylvania schools, 78–79, 135–141; linguistic and orthographic features, 130, 164–168, 174; maintenance among Pennsylvania Dutch, 129, 134–135; and modern sectarians, 333–337; in newspapers, 122–123; shift away from in nonsectarian churches, 422–423n34. *See also* Dutchified German

Pennsylvania Mountain English, 57–59

Pennsylvanischer Staatsbote (newspaper), 131

Pennypacker, Samuel W., 421n24

"Pensilwan'yah Inglish, The" (poem), 41–43, 48

Penzl, Herbert, 319–320, 346–347

Peretz, I. L., 368

Pestalozzi, Johann Heinrich, 225–226

"Petroleum V. Nasby," 216–217

Philadelphia, PA, 63, 81, 88, 122, 263; anglicization of, 71, 122–123, 127–128, 362; German Society of Philadelphia, 88, 95, 123–127; Grundsow Lodge in, 285–287; as port of entry for immigrants, 13, 64; use of German in, 88–92, 95, 118, 121,

Philadelphia, PA *(cont.)*
122–131, 152–153, 384n22; and Ludwig A.
Wollenweber, 181–184, 223, 406n13
Pinckney, Charles C., 146
"Pit Schwefflebrenner," 210, 216–217
Plain people. *See* Amish; Mennonites:
Old Order; sectarians
Plattdeutsch: etymology, 433n80; and
Mennonite Low German language, 53,
338–340, 366, 369
Plautdietsch language, 53, 338–340,
366, 369
Pledge of Allegiance (*Versprechnis zum
Flag*), 283
politics. *See* nonsectarians: political lean-
ings; patriotism; peasant republican-
ism; *and particular parties*
Portuguese language, 52
Post, Rudolf, 402n65
powwowing, 122
preterite tense, in Pennsylvania High
German, 308
progressive aspect, 39. *See also* tense/
aspect

*Quaint Idioms and Expressions of the
Pennsylvania Germans* (pamphlet),
269–271
Quakers, 63, 71, 242, 299, 358, 417n110

/r/: in Pennsylvania Dutch, 21, 36,
324–325, 379n52; in Pennsylvania High
German, 336–337
Radical Pietists. *See* sectarians
Radical Republicans, 204, 208, 210, 216,
420–421n23
Raith, Joachim, 345
Randolph, John, 420n20
Rattermann, Heinrich A., 246
Rauch, Edward H.: biography, 204; "De
Olta un Neia Tzeita," 277–279, 284;
dialect letters, 216–217; and Dutch
Dialect, 214–216; and Alexander J. Ellis,

206–207; *Father Abraham* newspapers,
208–210; and Samuel Stehman Haldeman, 206–207; obituary in *New York
Times*, 202–203; *Pennsylvania Dutch
Hand-Book*, 210–214; *Pennsylvania
Dutchman* (periodical), 202, 205–206,
211, 220–221; and Pennsylvania Ger-
man Society, 276–279; "Pit Schweffle-
brenner," 210, 216–217; preference for
Pennsylvania Dutch, 204–206; transla-
tions, 212–214, 292; writings, 208–212
Reading Adler (newspaper), 122, 129, 142,
159, 196
Reed, Carroll E., 318, 321, 425n72
Reformed Church Messenger (periodical),
205
Reichard, Harry Hess, 199–200, 285–288,
426n87
Reichard, Ida Ruch, 426n87
Renno, Jacob, 157–158
Reschly, Steven, 365
Rip Van Winkle (play), 292
Ritner, Joseph, 220
Robacker, Earl F., 122, 181, 400n51, 404n2,
414n72
Rogers, Will, 288
Romani language, 53
Romani people, 53–54, 56–57. *See also*
She-kener
Rondthaler, Emanuel, Sr., 191
Roosevelt, Theodore, 240
Root, Elihu, 240
Rosenberger, Homer Tope, 254–255
Ross, James, 107, 115–117
Runyeon, Mildred, 159
Rupp, Israel Daniel, 392n11
Russ, William A., Jr., 420n20
Russian Empire, 53, 366
Russian language, 52
Russian Mennonites, 338–341, 365–366

Sau(e)r, Christopher, 126, 393n17
Schaeffer, Nathan C., 188, 412n44

Schaff, Philip, 191–192
Schiller, Friedrich, 3, 121, 247
Schlabach, Theron, 299–300
schools: Charity School movement,
    76–77, 82, 84; in contemporary sectar-
    ian communities, 337–338, 343, 432n76;
    in early Pennsylvania, 68–69, 76–85,
    135–141, 220–221, 384n36; Old Colony
    Mennonite, 338–341; Pennsylvania
    Dutch resistance to public administra-
    tion of, 81–84; uffsaage in, 79, 135. See
    also education
Schöpf, Johann David: description of
    Pennsylvania Dutch people and lan-
    guage, 27, 30, 40, 92–102; "jumping
    stallion" sentence quoted by, 98, 100,
    126, 215, 387n72, 387n73; and Freder-
    ick A. Muhlenberg, 125–126
Schwartz, Berthold, 398n44
Schwenkfelders, 67. See also sectarians
sectarians: avoidance of profanity / idle
    speech, 329–330; conservative faith
    and agrarian culture of, 72–74, 359,
    362; contact with German POWs dur-
    ing World War II, 264–265; dynamic
    social character, 72, 357–360; in early
    Pennsylvania, 67–68, 77; and educa-
    tion, 76–85; ethnicity, 368; European
    origins and immigration to America,
    50, 65–67, 300–301; geographic dis-
    tribution across North America, 50,
    69–71; knowledge and use of English,
    49, 341–352, 380n71, 380n73, 433n89;
    knowledge and use of Pennsylvania
    Dutch, 325–330, 431n55; knowledge and
    use of Pennsylvania High German, 142,
    153, 307–310, 331–341; lack of involve-
    ment in nonsectarian Pennsylvania
    Dutch culture and literature, 298, 301–
    303, 428n8; language maintenance/shift
    patterns, 51–53, 179–180, 302–303, 310–
    318, 320, 355–359, 364, 429n23; Moravi-
    ans, 67, 94–95, 191, 386n63; in popular

and tourist literature, 244, 246–247,
    248, 268, 274–275, 298–299, 423n47;
    population size and growth, 50–51,
    180, 361; relations with nonsectarians
    in America, 67–69, 299–301, 429n13;
    relations with nonsectarians in Europe,
    300–301; relations with Old Colony
    Mennonites, 338–341; scholarly study
    of verbal behavior of, 275–276, 319–320,
    425n70, 429–430n37; Schwenk-
    felders, 67; sociolinguistic similarity to
    other minority language communities,
    53, 365–369; varieties of Pennsylva-
    nia Dutch spoken by, 24–26, 31–34,
    68, 70–71, 320–325, 347–352, 376n24,
    380n74. See also Amish; immigration
    to America; Mennonites
sect people (Sektenleute). See sectarians
Seifert, Lester W. J., 318, 321, 425n72
semilingualism, 93–94, 96
She-kener (ethnic Romani Pennsylvania
    Dutch speakers), 56–57
Shelta language, 53
Shimmell, L. S., 82
Shoemaker, Alfred L.: documentation of
    early Pennsylvania Dutch, 143; mystery
    surrounding later life of, 424n60; and
    Pennsylvania Dutch Folklore Center,
    271, 274–276, 295; PhD dissertation,
    319–320
Shryock, Richard H., 3
Shunk, Francis R., 220
"Sim Schmalzgsicht," 258
Singer, Isaac Bashevis, 368
Snyder, Simon, 112–117, 147, 249, 377n26,
    391n93
Snyder County, PA, 281, 391n93
Somerset County, PA: Amish in, 70, 301,
    382n14; European Anabaptist migra-
    tion to, 391n2, 430–431n44; and S. D.
    Guengerich, 308; importance in history
    of midwestern Pennsylvania Dutch, 70,
    118, 321–322, 430–431n44

Sowden, William H., 249–250, 420–421n23

"Spanglish", 29

Spanish language, 29, 52, 116, 272, 329; and Old Colony Mennonites, 339, 341

"Speak German!" (*Sprich deutsch!*; article), 307

'S Pennsylfawnisch Deitsch Eck (The Pennsylvania German corner; newspaper column), 276, 285, 326

Stahr, J. S., 244, 419n13

Steiner, Melchior, 95, 131–132

Stevens, Thaddeus, 204

Stiemer, Anton, 108

Stine, Clyde, 76, 232

St. Michael's and Zion Church, Philadelphia, 127–128, 152, 394n22, 434n10

"Stoffel" (Bukovina German poem), 388n78

"Stoffel Ehrlich," 102–112, 114, 143–145, 208, 210, 305, 388n78

Stoll, Elmo, 316–318

Stoltzfus, Amos J., 264–265, 345–346, 428n6

Stoltzfus, Lillian, 431n58

Struble, George R., 43–46

Stump, Adam, 370–372

superstitions: in tourist literature, 268; traditional Pennsylvania Dutch, 109–110, 122

Swadesh lists, 34–35, 378–379n49

Swartzentruber Amish, 324, 352, 380n71, 380n73, 384n36, 432n76

Swedish language, 10, 18

Swiss Amish, 376n22, 391n2, 430–431n44

Swiss Volhynian German, 435n22

Swope, Pierce E., 255, 428n105

tense/aspect, 25–26, 38–40

terminal devoicing (*Auslautverhärtung*), 46

Texas German, 391–392n3

That Amazing *Pennsylvania Dutch Language* (pamphlet), 271–274

"Tight Pants and Standup Collars Do Not Make the Man" (*Teite Hosen un Ständups mache der Mann net*; dialect letter), 186

Tillie: A Mennonite Maid (novel), 266–267

tourism, 268–275

Tourist Dutch. *See* Dutchified English

Trexler, Benjamin F., 411n35

Troxell, William S. "Pumpernickle Bill," 426n81

/ts/, in Pennsylvania Dutch, 37

Tulpehocken region, Lebanon and Berks Counties, PA, 64, 67, 123

Twain, Mark, 215, 288

Tyrol, 366, 368

uffsaage (recitation), 79, 135

umlauted vowels, pronunciation of, 395–396n34

Unabhängiger Republikaner (newspaper), 143

union churches, 361–362

Union of the German Press of Pennsylvania (*Verein der Deutschen Presse von Pennsylvanien*), 195–197, 207, 223

University of Illinois at Urbana-Champaign, 319

Van Buren, Martin, 204

Vella Laysa (Let's read; Pennsylvania Dutch Bible stories), 326–328

Vendu ('auction'; Pennsylvania Dutch word), 400n58

verb clusters, 378n37

verb-second rule, 38, 340

Verein der Deutschen Presse von Pennsylvanien (Union of the German Press of Pennsylvania), 195–197, 207, 223

Virginia: migration of Pennsylvania

Dutch to, 71, 361; Pennsylvania Dutch spoken in, 237, 383n18; petition from German speakers to Congress, 127; suspicion directed toward Pennsylvania Dutch speakers during World War I, 260

Vorderpfalz (Eastern Palatinate). *See* Palatinate region of Germany

Wadsworth (OH) Mennonite School, 306

"Wagoner's Song, The" (*Das Fuhrman's Lied*), 408n26

Waterloo County, ON, 68, 71, 253, 300, 321; Pennsylvania Dutch variety spoken in, 377n32, 383n17, 431n52

Weber, Edwin Gehman, 413n48

wedding poems, 186–188

Weiser, Charles W., 257–258

Weiser, Conrad, 64, 67, 123, 382n3

Weissenburg Academy, 81

Weitzel, Louisa, 382–383n16

Weitzmann, Carl Borromäus, 246

Welt-Bote (newspaper), 142, 221

Wenger, J. C., 312–313

Wesselhöft, Wilhelm (William), 385n39

West Virginia, Pennsylvania Dutch spoken in, 383n18

White, Joseph M., 418–419n1

"Wie Soll Mer Schpelle?" (How should one spell?; poem), xv–xvii

wine-whine merger, 227–228

Wisconsin, German in, 382–383n16, 391–392n3

Wittke, Carl, 255, 422n28

Wokeck, Marianne, 13, 50, 64

Wolf, George, 220

Wollenweber, Ludwig A., 158, 181–188, 238; biography, 404n7; *Gemälde aus dem Pennsylvanischen Volksleben*, 158, 182–188, 242; knowledge of Pennsylvania Dutch, 405n10; religious faith, 406n13

Wood, Ralph Charles, 327, 362

word order: in Germanic languages, 379n55; in Pennsylvania Dutch, 26–27, 35–36, 38

World War I, use of Pennsylvania Dutch during, 252–263

World War II, use of Pennsylvania Dutch during, 263–265

"Wu is mai schwarzer Gaul?" (Where is my black horse; early text), 20–23, 29–30

Yiddish language, 28, 53, 367–368, 379n55

Yoder, Don, 2, 271, 275, 295, 319, 358

Yoder, Joseph W., 428n1

York County, PA, 65, 128, 263, 404n3; English spoken in, 45; and Henry Lee Fisher, 137–138; and J. William Frey, 45, 276, 320; and Lewis Miller, 408n27; Pennsylvania Dutch variety spoken in, 321

Ziegler, Charles C., 425n79

Zimmerman, Thomas C., 279–280

YOUNG CENTER BOOKS IN ANABAPTIST & PIETIST STUDIES

James A. Cates, *Serving the Amish: A Cultural Guide for Professionals*

D. Rose Elder, *Why the Amish Sing: Songs of Solidarity and Identity*

Brian Froese, *California Mennonites*

Charles E. Hurst and David L. McConnell, *An Amish Paradox: Diversity and Change in the World's Largest Amish Community*

Rod Janzen and Max Stanton, *The Hutterites in North America*

Karen M. Johnson-Weiner, *Train Up a Child: Old Order Amish and Mennonite Schools*

Peter J. Klassen, *Mennonites in Early Modern Poland and Prussia*

James O. Lehman and Steven M. Nolt, *Mennonites, Amish, and the American Civil War*

Mark L. Louden, *Pennsylvania Dutch: The Story of an American Language*

Steven M. Nolt and Thomas J. Meyers, *Plain Diversity: Amish Cultures and Identities*

Douglas H. Shantz, *A New Introduction to German Pietism: Protestant Renewal at the Dawn of Modern Europe*

Tobin Miller Shearer, *Daily Demonstrators: The Civil Rights Movement in Mennonite Homes and Sanctuaries*

Janneken Smucker, *Amish Quilts: Crafting an American Icon*

Richard A. Stevick, *Growing Up Amish: The Rumspringa Years* (second edition)

Duane C. S. Stoltzfus, *Pacifists in Chains: The Persecution of Hutterites during the Great War*

Susan L. Trollinger, *Selling the Amish: The Tourism of Nostalgia*

Diane Zimmerman Umble and David L. Weaver-Zercher, eds., *The Amish and the Media*

Valerie Weaver-Zercher, *Thrill of the Chaste: The Allure of Amish Romance Novels*